T0329029

THE NATIONAL INSTITUTE OF
ECONOMIC AND SOCIAL RESEARCH

Economic and Social Studies

XIII

RETAIL TRADING IN BRITAIN

1850-1950

RETAIL TRADING IN BRITAIN

1850-1950

A study of trends in retailing with special reference to the development of Co-operative, multiple shop and department store methods of trading

BY

JAMES B. JEFFERYS

CAMBRIDGE
AT THE UNIVERSITY PRESS
1954

CAMBRIDGE UNIVERSITY PRESS
Cambridge, New York, Melbourne, Madrid, Cape Town,
Singapore, São Paulo, Delhi, Tokyo, Mexico City

Cambridge University Press
The Edinburgh Building, Cambridge CB2 8RU, UK

Published in the United States of America by Cambridge University Press, New York

www.cambridge.org
Information on this title: www.cambridge.org/9781107602731

© Cambridge University Press 1954

First published 1954
First paperback edition 2011

A catalogue record for this publication is available from the British Library

ISBN 978-1-107-60273-1 Paperback

CONTENTS

LIST OF TABLES

LIST OF CHARTS

LIST OF PLATES

PREFACE

The study by the British, a nation of shopkeepers, of the art of shop-keeping has been surprisingly neglected. American, German and Swedish economic literature, for example, is relatively rich in works, both general and specialized, on the development and problems of the retail trades; in Britain, however, apart from the well-cultivated consumer Co-operative sector, less than a dozen serious economic studies exist.

One factor in this neglect is undoubtedly the technical and physical difficulty of undertaking research in this field. There are the well-known problems of the very large number of units engaged, their small size, the high rate of turnover, the scarcity of tidy, well-kept records and until recently the absence of a Census of Distribution. An equally important factor is, however, the failure of those engaged in educational and research institutions, from schools to technical colleges and universities, to accord to the distributive trades the status, careful attention and study that is warranted by the importance of these trades in the social structure and economy as a whole. The false belief that distribution is a sterile, unproductive activity is still very deep rooted in Britain, and while the concept that the supply of goods and services to the consumer is the ultimate aim of economic activity is perhaps better established in the thinking of today than it was twenty-five or fifty years ago, it is still an uphill task to establish the essential corollary to such an approach, the concept of production and distribution as a single continuous process.

The National Institute of Economic and Social Research and its Distribution Advisory Committee (whose members are Mr Hugh Weeks (Chairman), Mr Paul Cadbury, Sir Henry Clay, Sir Geoffrey Heyworth, Professor Sir Arnold Plant, Mr W. B. Reddaway, Professor Austin Robinson, Sir George Schuster and Mr Richard Stone) have done much in the past eight years, by encouragement of research into distribution, to help redress the unbalance referred to above. This is the second study to be published by the Institute on distribution questions. The first volume was concerned with the problems of the methods and costs of distribution. This volume is intended as a contribution toward the study of the history and structure of the retail trades. And it is hoped that by showing that some of the physical and technical problems of research can be overcome, this study will stimulate others to make further explorations to fill the many obvious gaps.

It should perhaps be pointed out at the start that no attempt is made in this study to give a completely balanced picture of retail trading in Britain in the last hundred years. While the role of the small retailers is not entirely neglected, the emphasis throughout is on the development, problems and significance of large-scale retailing. This bias arises in part from the fact that large-scale retailing, that is co-operative, multiple shop and department store retailing, plays a more important role in Britain than in any other country, including the United States. But the small-scale retailers, though described by Marshall in 1890 as 'losing ground daily' to 'massive retailing' are still, over sixty years later, responsible for some 60% of the total retail turnover and more than 80% of the total number of retail establishments. The story of these small-scale retailers has still to be written. Further, when it comes to be written some satisfactory explanation will perhaps be possible of the striking difference in the economic history of retailing in Europe and the United States on the one hand and in Britain on the other. In the former countries the development of large-scale retailing has led to the emergence of organizational techniques such as retail buying groups and voluntary wholesale chains whereby the small-scale retailers combine with each other and with wholesalers to obtain some of the obvious economies of scale and specialization. In Britain, where large-scale retailing has made the greatest advances, such collective efforts by the small retailers are practically unknown.

A second important gap in this study is a discussion of the rôle of the shop assistant. As massive retailing grew in significance so did paid employment and with paid employment came the problems of industrial relations, for example questions of wages and working conditions, of labour cost in relation to turnover and margins, of trade union organization and collective bargaining, and of legislation affecting the retail trades from the Shop Hours Acts to Wages Councils. This omission is a deliberate one made necessary by considerations of time and space, and is not intended in any sense to represent a judgement on the importance of these questions.

The plan of the volume is straightforward. After three chapters which attempt to summarize the main features of the developments in retailing in Britain there follow detailed studies of the evolution in individual trades. A word of caution is perhaps needed, however, in regard to the statistical estimates made of the relative importance of different economic types of retailers. The methods of making the estimates are explained in an Appendix, but it cannot be stressed too often that the figures given in the various chapters are in the form of ranges and are estimates only, and that while they are probably sound enough to indicate general trends, the middle points of the ranges cannot and should not be used as precise figures to pin-point the exact picture in an individual year. The data on which the estimates are based are not yet sufficiently reliable to enable this to be done.

In conclusion I wish to take this opportunity of thanking the very many individuals and associations who have helped to make this study possible. In the first place, apart from the assistance from members of the Institute's Distribution Advisory Committee, in particular Mr Paul Cadbury, Sir Geoffrey Heyworth and Sir George Schuster, I wish to acknowledge a very heavy debt to business men, particularly to managers of multiple shop organizations. The size of this debt will be readily appreciated when it is recalled that information has been supplied in the course of this enquiry by over 800 firms and organizations. In many instances there was an extensive correspondence with the firms and in nearly 300 cases personal interviews were given. Further, a special word of thanks is due to those firms making available the illustrations used in this volume. This type of applied economic research cannot take place without the co-operation of business men and it is hoped that they will not feel that the considerable time and trouble they took to assist this enquiry has been wasted.

Secondly, I wish to thank Mr Owen S. Hiner, now at University College, Hull, for his help during a year of the research. Mr Hiner conducted a number of the interviews, was responsible for organizing the sample survey of the small multiple shop organizations and undertook a great part of the slow, but essential work of checking and collating information obtained from street directories and similar sources. In this regard his researches into data before 1914 were of particular value in making possible a relatively detailed analysis of the long-term trends.

Thirdly, I wish to thank my colleagues at the Institute: the Director and the Secretary, Mr W. A. B. Hopkin and Mrs F. S. Stone, for their ready help and encouragement at all times; Miss Margaret Rogers for her invaluable assistance in preparing the manuscript and care in seeing the book through the press; and Miss Dorothy Walters and Mr Deryck Rowe for their willingness to discuss the problems of retailing and of the book at all times and for the provision of essential data and many helpful suggestions. Lastly but by no means least my sincere thanks are due to Miss Pamela Wood who throughout the enquiry with loyalty and efficiency fulfilled her task of maintaining order in the midst of chaos and who typed and re-typed with care and accuracy the innumerable letters, drafts, redrafts, revisions and final chapters that are the inevitable accompaniment of such an investigation.

J. B. J.

NATIONAL INSTITUTE OF ECONOMIC
AND SOCIAL RESEARCH

April 1954

CHAPTER I

THE TRANSFORMATION OF THE DISTRIBUTIVE TRADES, 1850–1914

I. THE DISTRIBUTIVE TRADES IN THE MIDDLE OF THE NINETEENTH CENTURY

By the middle of the nineteenth century the first phase of the Industrial Revolution in Britain was complete. Steam power and iron had transformed the face of the country and had revolutionized the thinking of its people. Factory chimneys, blast furnaces and pit winding gear had become familiar sights; the railway network was spreading rapidly; and nearly one-half of the population was living in towns. At the same time outworn shibboleths and doctrines were passing. Free Trade was a triumphant reality and old views of the relationships between masters and men and between citizens and the state were being challenged. The course for further expansion, for growth and prosperity, was set fair. But Britain was not yet an 'industry state'. More people were still employed in agriculture than in any other single occupation. Many trades and industries were more familiar with handicraft methods and outworking than with power-driven machines and factories. The national market had not yet been fully opened up by the railways and, until the success of the steamship, the sailing ships placed limits on the development of world trade.

The wholesale and retail trades in Britain in the middle of the nineteenth century were examples of those trades that still bore the marks of the old system rather than of the new. The Industrial Revolution and the rapid rate of urban growth in the first half of the nineteenth century had increased the pressure for reorganization of these trades, but by the middle of the century the modifications in structure and method had been relatively slight. Not until the second half of the century did this pressure, combined with the effects of further developments in the character of the economy as a whole, lead to major changes in the methods and fabric of the distributive trades.

The methods of distribution

In the first half of the nineteenth century the people of Britain purchased their supplies of finished consumer goods in four main ways. Firstly there were the retail units proper, such as the grocers, the hosiers, the mercers of various descriptions, the drapers, the haberdashers, the chandlers, the oil and colourmen and the village general dealers. These retailers bought their goods from manufacturers, producers, wholesalers and other intermediaries and sold them from fixed shops in the towns and villages. Secondly there was the group of producer/retailers, the skilled tradesmen who made, produced or grew their wares as well as selling them. The leading examples of this class were the boot and shoe makers, the tailors, the blacksmiths and tinkers, the cabinet-makers, the basket-makers, the butchers and the dairy farmers. Thirdly there were the markets, usually weekly but sometimes daily, where the farmers and growers displayed their butter, cheese, eggs, vegetables and fruit, and, less important, the fairs where all types of dealers, producers, wholesalers and importers put up a wide range of goods for sale. In the newer industrial towns the crowded market-halls had begun to fulfil the same functions as the market-places and fairs of the country towns. Finally, supplementing these sources in all seasons and in all areas were the itinerant tradesmen and travelling salesmen answering to many different names such as pedlars, chapmen, packmen, bagmen, and 'Scotch drapers'.

The retailers proper and the producer/retailers were for the most part craftsmen, apprenticed to the trade they served. Almost without exception they were working for themselves, controlling only one business or owning only one shop. The family tradition of son succeeding father was dominant, and the 'living-in' system for apprentices, very often relatives of the shopkeeper, was accepted as natural and usual in the medium and large-sized towns. This background of training and apprenticeship was fundamental to the art of retailing. Upon the retailer's skill depended success in the selection and purchase of goods in large quantities from merchants, wholesalers and importers, and there were few trades in which the retailer was not called upon to undertake some processing of the goods before sale to the consumer. In the grocery trade, for example, the blending of tea, the mixing of herbs and spices, the curing and cutting of bacon, the cleaning and washing of dried fruits, the cutting and millgrinding of sugar, and the roasting and grinding of coffee were essential functions of the retailer, apart entirely from the tasks of weighing out and bagging. In their turn, the farmers selling in the markets and the salesmen on the roads had to be equally experienced and knowledgeable as to the quality, uses and value of the goods they offered for sale.

Supplies of goods to the retailers passed through many different types of channels in the different trades, and the length of the chain between producer and consumer varied between commodities and between town and country. In the case of the important proportion of finished consumer goods sold by the producer/retailers and by the farmers in the markets, no intermediaries were needed, though the raw materials and semi-finished products supplied to the producer/retailers often passed through the hands of many jobbers, merchants and wholesalers. In the case of finished consumer goods in the textile, grocery and coal trades, to take three examples, the chain from the producer at home or overseas to the consumer was a long one. The goods tended to move forward slowly in a series of short stages, changing hands at each stage. In the larger towns, and in London in particular, very few manufactured or imported goods reached the consumer without passing through the hands of at least two intermediaries. Many different types of inter-mediaries—agents, jobbers, factors, wholesalers, dead meat salesmen, bummarrees in the fish markets, cheesemongers, butter factors and so on—played a part, and a profitable part, inside and outside the central wholesale markets in equating supply and demand.

The retail market and retailing techniques

The buying and selling techniques and practices of the different types of retailers naturally varied between trades and between the towns and the countryside. The general pattern, however, and in fact the whole character of the distributive trades at this date, were strongly influenced by the emphasis on retailing as a skilled trade on the one hand and by the nature of consumer demand on the other. As mentioned above, Britain in the middle of the nineteenth century was not yet a fully industrial society. The changes of the previous hundred years had ended the practice of the family unit growing and making an important pro-portion of the essential goods it required, but dependence of the whole population on the market for the supplies of necessities was not yet complete. Further, the low standard of living of the great majority of the people, of the village labourers, hand workers and outworkers as well as of a large section of the new factory operatives herded in the new towns, meant that the effective market demand for very many goods was limited. The living conditions characteristic of these classes, a poor and monotonous diet, shoddy or home-made clothing with a life pro-longed by endless darning and mending, and a few sticks of home-made furniture along with the basic pots and pans, did not offer great scope to the retail trades. At the same time, however, the economy was expanding and with it the numbers and the demand of the well-to-do classes. This rising demand was encouraging the production and marketing of a wider range and a greater variety of consumer goods.

It is possible, therefore, to make a broad and somewhat rough distinc-tion between those retailers catering chiefly though not exclusively for the limited demand of the working classes of the towns and of the countryside and those retailers catering more exclusively for the well-to-do. In the former category come the markets and the market-halls, the fairs and the pedlars and travelling salesmen; in the latter category fall most, though by no means all, of the craftsmen producer/retailers and the fixed-shop retailers of the towns.[1]

The farmers, dealers, pedlars and others selling in the markets and on the road depended, of course, on open display and vociferous advertisement of their wares to attract custom. The selling methods of the fixed-shop retailers and the producer/retailers were very different. Window display was practically unknown outside some of the shops in the larger towns. Symbols of the trade or a few articles showing the type of shop were often placed in the windows, but the use of bottle glass in the windows frequently obscured even these. Drapery establishments in towns such as London were beginning to make a proud display of their finery, and 'window shopping' in certain areas had just begun to appeal, but in the great majority of instances the retailer relied upon his reputation and skill to attract his custom rather than on any bright or elaborate display. Open advertisement or 'puffery' was frowned upon by all established tradesmen.[2]

The purchases made by all classes of consumer of the goods that were not immediately perishable tended to be of large quantities. The practice of home cooking, baking and clothes making, the existence of large families and the lack of leisure for frequent shopping expeditions encouraged this tendency. Stones, half butts or pipes, hogsheads, chests and rolls were the measures frequently demanded rather than pounds, gallons or yards. The retailers were expected to stock sufficient quantities to meet such orders and to be of sufficient substance to provide the long credit that was inevitably requested.

The quality of the goods sold by the different types of retailers varied tremendously. The standards of quality were individual to each retailer, since the retailer played an important role in the preparation and processing of the goods for sale, and accusations of adulteration and light weight were common. The complaints were the most frequent in the grocery, milk and tobacco trades, and there can be little doubt that in working-class areas and in 'truck' shops where the consumers had little

---

[1] Cf. J. Aubrey Rees, *The Grocery Trade*, vol. II, London, 1910, p. 198. 'The grocer had been up to 1846 at any rate...minister of luxuries to the rich.' The year refers to the introduction of Free Trade.

[2] Cf. Lord Macaulay in the *Edinburgh Review*, April 1830. 'A butcher of the higher class disdains to ticket his meat. A mercer of the higher class would be ashamed to hang up papers in his window inviting the passers-by to look at the stock of a bankrupt, all of the first quality, and going for half the value. We expect some reserve, some decent pride in our hatter and our bootmaker.' (From 'Mr Robert Montgomery's Poems'.)

knowledge of the goods and few alternative sources of supply the practice of adulteration was widespread.[1]

Finally, common to practically all methods of retailing was the method of haggling, higgling or chaffering as to the price between the retailer or seller and the customer. In some trades, for example drapery and haberdashery, this practice was taken to greater lengths than in others, but very few retailers ever clearly and openly marked the prices of their goods or expected the customer to pay promptly and without question the price first demanded. Each transaction was individual, slow but no doubt in the end amicable.

The transformation of the distributive trades

This picture of the distributive trades in Britain in the middle of the nineteenth century differs in a number of ways from the glimpses of the wholesale and retail structure given by writers such as Daniel Defoe in the early part of the eighteenth century.[2] The changes in agriculture transforming the peasant into the village labourer, the growth of towns, the increase in the volume of manufactured goods and the improvements in the methods of transport had resulted in a decline of family and of local self-sufficiency and in a decline in the role of fairs; they had led to a corresponding increase in the importance of marketing and particularly of fixed-shop retailing. Further, with the widening of the gap in some trades between producer and consumer the relative importance of the wholesaler and of other intermediaries increased. But these changes and developments in the distributive structure and techniques between the middle eighteenth and middle nineteenth centuries though widespread would appear to be mainly ones of degree, of modification and of shift of emphasis rather than of transformation and re-organization. The basic structure and character of the distributive trades, the small scale of the units engaged in the trade, the emphasis on skill and experience in retailing, the higgling as to price, and the important role played by open markets, had not been changed fundamentally. The methods and techniques used had been adapted to meet the new demands brought about by the Industrial Revolution, but the distributive system as a whole still bore the marks of a pre-industrial economy.

In contrast to this relative stability or near-stability in distributive organization and method up to the middle of the nineteenth century,

---

[1] *The Lancet* carried on a courageous campaign in the middle of the century, exposing the extent and character of adulteration practised by the retail trade.

[2] The chief writings of Defoe, who had himself been a shopkeeper, describing wholesale and retail trading are: *A Tour through Great Britain*, 1724–26, and *The Complete English Tradesman*, vol. I, 1725 and vol. II, 1727.

the following half-century or so, particularly the period 1875–1914, witnessed a transformation of the distributive trades comparable in many ways to the revolutionary changes that had taken place in the industrial structure of the country in the previous century. In these years new techniques of selling, new methods of wholesale and retail organization, new trades, new types of consumer goods and new forms of retailing units began to emerge, at first alongside the older-established traditional methods and then in place of them. The branding of goods, their advertisement by the producers, and the determination of the retail selling prices under systems of resale price maintenance were introduced widely in some trades. Flamboyant window displays and advertisement by retailers and the use of clearly marked prices were replacing the older customs of reticence and higgling. Finally these years saw the triumph of the fixed shop as the dominant form of retail trading, and the emergence on a significant scale of large-scale distributive organizations—the department store, the Co-operative Society and the multiple shop firm. These units employed hundreds and thousands of workers, in a sector of the economy hitherto the untouched preserve of the small-scale independent master employing at the most a handful.[1]

This revolution in the distributive trades, if it can be called that, was the product of two main forces. On the one hand the distributive trades were compelled to adapt themselves to the shifts and changes in the economic and social structure of the country. On the other hand the distributive trades possessed their own dynamic, and the methods and techniques evolved in their turn hastened or delayed changes in the organization of production. These factors were interacting but for convenience of treatment a brief account will first be given of the main economic and social changes that had a direct bearing on the distributive trades, followed by a discussion of the main changes taking place in the distributive trades in these years.

2. THE CHANGES IN THE ECONOMIC AND SOCIAL BACKGROUND

There were two main features of the development of the British economy between the middle of the nineteenth century and the First World War. These trends were interconnected. Firstly, within Britain, the victory of machine power was completed and Britain emerged as a fully indus-

---

[1] Relatively little attention has been paid by historians to this series of related developments in the distributive trades which stand out in such marked contrast to the stability of these trades in previous centuries. The remark by J. E. Thorold Rogers in the late 'eighties on one aspect of this revolution is of interest: 'The epoch of shops is comparatively recent...we are now further removed from the experiences of my youth in these matters than our fathers were from the age of Elizabeth and the Stuarts.' *The Industrial and Commercial History of England*, sixth edition, 1909, p. 386. This volume consists of lectures delivered in 1888–89.

trialized society. Secondly, Britain became dominant in and dependent upon the world market and extended her direct financial and economic interests to all parts of the globe. The effects of these developments on Britain's economic and social structure are well known. The basic industries of the country, coal, iron and steel, textiles, engineering and shipbuilding, developed practically continuously. At the same time manufacturing and large-scale production techniques spread to nearly all corners of the economy, transforming most of the secondary industries that had remained little removed from the handicraft stage at the completion of the first phase of the Industrial Revolution. This growth of industry and the constant technological changes taking place, which required greater and greater amounts of fixed capital, gave rise to large-scale production units, to giant firms and to amalgamations and combinations between enterprises. The introduction and growing use of the limited company form of business ownership facilitated the increase in size and in its turn increased the importance of financial control and direction of both home and overseas investment. The 'small master' economy of the early part of the nineteenth century was passing. Finally, these were the years of the export of capital and of the export of finished industrial and consumer goods in exchange for cheap foodstuffs and raw materials as the whole world was opened up for trade and the resources of new areas were developed. The steamship revolutionized ideas of distance, and freight rates fell. The consequent fall in prices and the shift in demand towards cheap, imported foodstuffs dealt a near death-blow to British agriculture.

The economic and social changes and the distributive trades

These changes and their consequences all influenced the development of the distributive trades in these years. Some, however, had a more immediate impact than others and attention will be focused briefly on the aspects of these changes which would appear to have had the greatest bearing on the developments in the organization and method of the distributive trades.

Firstly, the emergence of a fully industrialized society in the second half of the nineteenth century was accompanied by a great expansion and consolidation of working-class demand. The industrial working classes, living in towns, dependent entirely upon wages, developing their trade union organization and collective bargaining strength and able, with certain exceptions in some trades, to secure regular employment and draw regular pay packets, provided a concentrated and consistent demand for consumer goods. This growing demand enabled the distributive trades to expand and permitted the development of large-scale distributive organizations. Two of the forms of large-scale distribution that arose in these years, the Co-operative Societies and the multiple shop retailers, were rooted in and developed with this mass demand of the industrial working classes. Secondly, the development of large-scale industry, of impersonal investment at home and over-seas, of Britain as the centre of world trade, and of imperial connexions, led to a rapid growth of the middle classes. This class was composed not of the small masters and farmers who formed the core of the middle class of the early nineteenth century but rather of the investors, rentiers, clerks, agents, professional workers, managers and office workers and the many civil servants and functionaries who were an inevitable by-product of an industrial and imperial trading economy. The middle class living in towns and, with improvement in transport, moving out to the first of the outer rings of suburbs, represented another new type of demand and purchasing power not fully catered for by the older methods of distribution. Department stores and the higher class multiple shop organizations are two examples of new forms of distribution that were developed to meet this demand.

Thirdly, the decline of British agriculture and the import of cheap, standardized foodstuffs from abroad, particularly of provisions, bacon, eggs, cheese, butter, tea and meat, presented the wholesale and retail food trades of the country with problems that could be and were only overcome by the construction of entirely new channels of distribution. The weekly markets with their sale of locally produced foodstuffs, and the skilled grocers and butchers with their traditional range of products, were unfitted and often unwilling to deal with this flood of cheap food. Fourthly, the spread of manufacturing and mass production techniques to practically all industries led to what may be called a delayed industrial revolution in many consumer goods industries. The boot and shoe industry, the food manufacturing industry and the men's clothing industry may be instanced as three examples of trades that were practically transformed in these years from near-handicraft, small-scale production to factory mass production industries. The goods produced by these large-scale factory methods carried traditional names and served traditional purposes, but to the distributive trades they were virtually new products requiring new methods of sale and new types of outlet. Further, the use of these new production methods in place of the older producer/retailer system led to the production of goods in anticipation of demand rather than in response to orders and increased both the gap and the number of intermediaries between the producer and the ultimate consumer.

Finally—the outcome of the changes outlined above and in particular of the increase in productivity and the fall in prices—there was a rapid increase in the real income per head of the population, at least up to the turn of the century. This increase in real income provided a buoyant demand for the goods handled by the distributive trades and created an economic atmosphere conducive to experiment.[1]

Illustrative of the rise in real income are the figures of the increased consumption per head of foodstuffs in these years. Examples of this increase are: the consumption of tea per head of the population rose from 2·7 lb. in 1860 to 6·1 lb. in 1900. The consumption of sugar rose from 34·1 lb. in 1860 to 87·1 lb. in 1900. The consumption of meat, bacon and ham rose from 101·4 lb. per head in 1870 to 130·6 lb. per head in 1896 and, less rapidly, the consumption of tobacco rose from 1·7 lb. in 1870 to 2·1 lb. in 1900. After the turn of the century the slowing down in the rate of increase in real income per head, and the rise in prices after 1909, changed the economic climate, but the new methods of distribution had already proved themselves by this date and subsequent developments lay in a forward rather than in a backward direction.

This sketch of the main economic and social changes in Britain in the years between the middle of the nineteenth century and the start of the First World War provides a background in which the characteristics and features of the distributive revolution taking place in these years can be more closely delineated. The outline given above of the methods and structure of the distributive trades in the middle of the nineteenth century is taken as the starting point and the developments taking place up to 1914 will be discussed under three headings; first the method of distribution; second the structure and organization of the retail trades; and third the retailing and selling techniques.

3. THE SHIFTS IN THE CHANNELS OF DISTRIBUTION

The different methods or channels of distribution existing in 1914 were broadly the same as those existing in the middle of the nineteenth century, but important shifts took place between these dates in the relative importance of the different methods. Statistical measurement of this change is not possible but the main features are clear.

The producer/retailer

There was, first, a consistent decrease in the relative importance of the producer/retailer. There were several reasons for this decline. The

[1] A. R. Prest, 'National Income of the United Kingdom, 1870–1946', *Economic Journal*, vol. LVIII, no. 229, March 1948. The index of real income per head at 1900 prices (1900 = 100) rose as follows: 57·7 in 1870; 63·2 in 1880; 89·4 in 1890; 100 in 1900; 102·0 in 1910; and 104·9 in 1914. The only years before 1900 when the real income per head fell more than two points were 1891 and 1892. The figure for the year 1890 is therefore a peak, and the average, 1888–92, was 85·9.

spread of factory and mass production techniques to many consumer goods industries provided the consumer, particularly the working-class consumer, with a greater variety of cheaper goods than did the handicraft producer/retailer. This growth of manufacturing was encouraged by the widening demand of the working classes for goods other than food as their real income rose and by the bigger orders which were beginning to be placed by large-scale retailers. Other factors were the continuous growth in the size of towns, which made direct contact between say the dairy farmers and the consumers increasingly difficult, and the substitution of imported foodstuffs for home-grown produce.

Alongside this development a contrary trend can also be observed, that of the emergence of the large-scale producer/retailer. In some trades, for example footwear, the manufacturers in order to secure guaranteed and reliable outlets for their products opened retail branches in different parts of the country. Similarly some multiple shop retailing organizations extended their interests backwards to the manufacturing of some of the products that they handled. Further, the retail Co-operative Societies established the two Co-operative Wholesale Societies —the English and the Scottish—which from the 'seventies onwards began to develop the factory production of a wide range of goods sold by the Retail Societies. Many of the trades in which the large-scale producer/retailers were beginning to emerge were those in which the small-scale producer/retailer had previously been prominent, for example footwear, men's clothing, and sugar confectionery. The large-scale producer/retailers, however, were producing standardized goods and catering for a mass demand in contrast to the essentially individual characteristics of both the production and demand of the small-scale producer/retailer economy.

The wholesaler

The second change in the channels of distribution in these years was an increase in the relative importance of the wholesaler as an intermediary between the manufacturer or producer and the retailer. The development was not, however, straightforward. On the one hand there is evidence to show that with the improvement and extension of systems of inland transport and communication there was a speeding up of the lengthy stage-by-stage distribution of many commodities that had existed in the first half of the nineteenth century. The number of separate links in the chain was reduced and in some instances wholesalers were by-passed altogether. On the other hand many of the developments mentioned above, such as the concentration of production in factories, the growth of towns and the switch to imported food-stuffs, with the corresponding decline in the importance of the locally supplied weekly markets as the main source of fresh produce, tended to increase the part played by intermediaries.[1]

In most trades up to the turn of the century at least, any widening of the gap in time and space between the producer and the retailer tended to result in the intervention of an intermediary, and the widening of this gap was one of the main characteristics of the economic development in these years.

Other factors that operated to strengthen the role of the wholesaler, though not necessarily to lead to an increase in the number of links in any given distributive chain, were the growing specialization of function as between wholesaling and retailing and the disappearance in most trades of the combined wholesale/retail houses, the increase in the number of retail outlets and the widening variety of different types and brands of goods stocked by the retailers, and the growing assumption by customers that retailers should stock goods from all parts of the country and overseas. In some trades a further factor of importance was the transference of certain pre-distributive processes, such as bacon curing and tea blending, from the retailer to the wholesaler, who could perform the operations on a larger and more economical scale. All these developments tended to lead the retailer to place increased reliance on the wholesaler and to expect greater service from him.

Selling direct to the retailer

The third development in the channels of distribution was a change in the character of the sales by producers or manufacturers direct to the retailers. In the middle of the nineteenth century the producer who sold direct to a retailer did so on a local scale. Very often he was a producer/retailer who had outgrown the selling capacity of his own retail outlet and looked for other outlets in adjacent areas or towns. In the following years, up to the First World War, while this type of sale by producers to local or regional outlets continued, the significant developments were the beginnings of national marketing direct to retailers by large-scale producers, and of bulk purchasing by large-scale retailing organizations direct from the manufacturers.

An important factor in the development of sales by manufacturers direct to retailers was the growth of the practice in some trades of the

[1] Cf. J. H. Clapham, *An Economic History of Modern Britain*, vol. II, Cambridge University Press, 1932, pp. 302 ff. Professor Clapham would appear to over-stress the trend towards the elimination of intermediaries between producer and consumer if the whole field of retail trading is taken into account. He does, however, point out that 'as one door was shut in the middleman's face another often opened on his left hand'.

branding and advertising of products by the producers. The growing complexity of the production of consumer goods, the increased amounts of capital laid out in machinery and buildings, and the greater volume of output, meant that the larger-scale producers could not afford, while planning their production, to leave the distribution of their goods unplanned and dependent upon the whims and fancies of wholesalers, retailers and consumers. To deal with this problem the larger firms began to make the marketing of their goods a specialized function, and sales managers were appointed with staff to direct and organize the work.[1]

The branding of the products and the advertisement of the brand was a method of building goodwill among consumers; the practice of selling directly to retailers, using salesmen and a network of depots, was a method of ensuring that the retailers regularly stocked the goods on which so much had been spent by way of factory equipment and advertisement. In the case of speciality products, particularly those of the light metal industries, the appointment of retailers as exclusive agents was another method used to ensure distribution. Competition amongst the manufacturers of branded products and, in the early twentieth century, the rapidly increasing number of different brands of the same type of article, had the effect of redoubling the attempts of manufacturers to ensure a regular outlet for their goods by by-passing the wholesaler and selling direct to the retailer.

The importance of this direct selling to the retailer in the years before 1914 must not be exaggerated. Only the largest of the manufacturers found it worth while to employ an army of salesmen and to arrange for direct delivery to the individual retailers. Further, in practically no case did the manufacturers who adopted such methods sell the whole of their output in this manner. The smaller orders were invariably left for wholesalers to fulfil. Nevertheless, by the First World War the concept of marketing consumer goods on a national scale, which was unheard of in the middle of the nineteenth century, had become a common discussion point at meetings of sales managers, and by-passing the wholesaler was becoming a growing practice in certain trades.

The growth of the different forms of large-scale retailing, the Co-operative Societies, the department stores and the multiple shop organizations, similarly had the effect of limiting the role of the wholesaler. The evolution of these types of retailer is discussed in some detail below, and all that need be pointed out in regard to the shifts in the channels of distribution is that purchase in bulk direct from manu-

[1] Illustrative of this development was the foundation in 1911 of the Incorporated Sales Managers' Association.

facturer or producer was a fundamental principle of the buying methods of such organizations. Only for certain marginal purchases did the large-scale retailers have recourse to wholesalers.[1]

The variations between trades

This account of the shifts in the relative importance of the different channels of distribution is somewhat over-simplified. The incidence of the changes in the methods of distribution, for example, varied in each consumer good trade, and generalizations relating to all trades together can be misleading. The producer/retailer method of distribution in the milk trade, for example, while declining in importance in these years, continued to be of great significance right up to the First World War. In the footwear trade, by contrast, this method had been almost completely superseded as early as 1900. Again, at no time in the furniture trade did wholesalers ever play an effective role, whereas there was little or no shift in their considerable importance in the textile trades. Finally, developments such as advertising, branding, national marketing direct to retailers, and large-scale retailing, remained virtually unknown in some trades such as fruit and vegetables, while the emergence of these methods and techniques was one of the outstanding features of the development of other trades such as the footwear trade, the chemists' goods trade and the tobacco goods trade. These variations on and exceptions to the general rule should be borne in mind in the consideration of this outline of the trends as a whole.

The use in this discussion of the words 'producers', 'wholesalers' and 'retailers' may also be misleading. It will be obvious that while the functions performed in relation to distribution by manufacturers or producers, by wholesalers and by retailers can be readily defined in general terms, the actual role played, the actual functions performed by the different units, vary from trade to trade. In other words the division of the whole economic function of distribution between the three main types of unit is not the same in all trades. The manufacturer who advertises and brands his product plays a different role in the chain of distribution to that of the farmer selling his produce to a commission buyer or a wholesaler in the nearest wholesale market. Similarly a retailer who has to undertake a considerable amount of processing of the goods before selling them performs a different function to that of the retailer selling pre-packaged advertised goods.

[1] Retail Co-operative Societies of course purchased an important proportion of their supplies from the Co-operative Wholesale Societies. These Wholesale Societies, however, played an entirely different role in relation to the Retail Societies from that played by the private wholesaler in relation to the private retailer. The Co-operative Wholesale Societies sold only to Co-operative Retail Societies and in fact were formed by and owned by the Retail Societies.

Changes also took place in the functions performed by producers, wholesalers and retailers over time. Very generally, and with much variation between individual trades, it may be suggested that throughout this period there was a tendency for distributive functions to be taken away from the retailer and shifted to the wholesaler and the manufacturer. In particular, in the middle of the nineteenth century it was the clear and undisputed function of the retailer in most trades to hold large stocks of goods, to undertake any necessary processing, grading and sorting, to provide the customer with information as to the type and qualities of the goods available, to determine the price that should be charged, and to perform all the final selling processes of weighing out, cutting to length, boxing, wrapping or bagging. By 1914, however, in a number of the consumer goods trades the wholesalers or even the manufacturers rather than the retailers were holding the bulk of the stocks; the wholesalers and the manufacturers rather than the retailers were undertaking the grading and sorting and the boxing and packing of the goods ready for final sales, and the manufacturers, in many instances, were taking over the task of informing consumers of the type and quality of the goods available and of the retail price. The effect of this shift in function on the activities and techniques of the retailers is discussed later in this chapter. All that need be added is that an opposite trend was to be seen in the emergence of large-scale retailers. These retailers undertook some of the functions hitherto performed by wholesalers and in some instances by manufacturers, as well as those of retailing. Both these developments were of course the outcome of the general tendency in these years towards the growth of scale in the unit of operation and of the production and distribution of standardized products.

4. CHANGES IN THE STRUCTURE AND ORGANIZATION OF RETAILING

No reliable figures are available to show the changes in the number of shops or in the numbers employed in retail or wholesale distribution in Britain before 1914. The figures of the number of shop properties in existence that are given in various sources are without exception the by-products of inquiries for other purposes and cannot be used directly. Similarly the changing definitions used in the various Censuses of Population render of little value comparisons over time of the numbers of persons returned as shopkeepers or shop assistants. The provisional conclusion that can be reached, based in part on such figures as are available and in part on contemporary evidence of various descriptions, is that in these years there was an increase in the number of fixed shops and that this number almost certainly increased at a rate faster than the rate of increase in population.[1] Further, as fixed shops meant specialization in retailing there may also have been an increase in the number of full-time shopkeepers and shop assistants at a rate faster than the increase of the population.[2]

The factors bringing about this suggested increase in the number of fixed shops at a rate faster than the increase in the population in these years and the considerable rise in the relative importance of fixed-shop retailing as against other methods of distribution have been mentioned above and need only be summarized briefly. The main forces operating were the growth of urbanization, the decline in many trades of the producer/retailer and the specialization of his retailing function, the pressure by manufacturers and consumers for more consistent and accessible retail outlets than those provided by fairs, pedlars and

[1] The *Report of the Commissioners of H.M. Inland Revenue* from 1867–1868 to 1915–1916 gives figures of the number of residential shops of a value of £20 or over assessed under the Inhabited House Duty. The number of such shops (hotels, public-houses, coffee-houses, etc., are excluded) in Great Britain at ten-yearly intervals between 1870 and 1910 and the number per 10,000 of the population are as follows:

Average of three years	Number of residential shops assessed		Number of residential shops per 10,000 population	
	Great Britain	England and Wales	Great Britain	England and Wales
1869–1872	177,000	n.a.	68	n.a.
1879–1882	230,000	224,000	77	86
1889–1892	249,000	244,000	76	84
1899–1902	293,000	287,000	79	88
1909–1911	310,000	304,000	76	84

The difficulties of interpretation of these figures, apart from the doubts about the completeness of the assessments and the revisions in assessments taking place at different times, are firstly that the producer/retailer, the tailor, bootmaker, etc., may have been classed as a workshop in some areas and a residential shop in others; secondly that no estimates are available to show the increase or decrease over time in the number of residential shops below the £20 limit; thirdly, the assessments exclude 'lock-up' shops, which undoubtedly increased in numbers in these years. The 1911 Census of Population showed the total number of shop properties in England and Wales to be 607,300, of which 172,000 or 28% were shops not used as dwellings. It may be argued, therefore, that while the number of residential shops, including those of below £20 in value and those above, per head of the population may have remained the same in those years or even with the rise in the value of money and therefore in the comprehensiveness of the assessment figures have actually decreased slightly, the increase in the number of 'lock-up', non-residential shops which represented a new concept of retailing certainly offset any slight decline in the number of residential shops per head of the population and almost certainly meant that there was an increase in the total number of shops [residential under £20, residential over £20, and shops not used as dwellings] at a rate faster than the increase in the population.

[2] This second conclusion is less firm, for the evidence suggests that some of the functions hitherto performed by retailers were transferred to wholesalers and manufacturers, leaving the retailers free to concentrate on selling. This may have meant a greater volume of sales per shopkeeper and shop assistant.

markets, and the shift away from home-grown foodstuffs purchased direct from farmers to the purchase of imported supplies which were sold by fixed-shop retailers.[1]

The second major change in the structure and organization of the retail trades was the emergence of various forms of large-scale retailing organizations, of Co-operative Societies, department stores and multiple shop retailers.[2] Data for this aspect of the change in the distributive structure are much fuller than are available for the shifts in the channels of distribution or the changes in the number of shops. Much of the detail of this development is set out in later chapters and a brief account only will be given here of the rise of the different types of large-scale retailer in the years up to 1914.

5. THE CO-OPERATIVE SOCIETIES

The story of the Co-operative movement from the early beginnings in the middle of the nineteenth century up to 1914 is one of an almost continuous increase in membership and retail turnover. This is a well-known story and is adequately substantiated, particularly after 1880, with a wealth of figures and statistics.[3] The membership of the Co-operative Retail Societies was in the region of 100,000 in 1863, and retail turnover was some £2,500,000. By 1881 the membership numbered 547,000 and total retail sales were over £15 millions. Ten years later both these figures had been doubled and at the turn of the century the membership was 1,707,000 and retail turnover some £50 millions. The rise continued to 1914 when the membership was 3,053,000 and retail turnover some £88 millions. In the thirty-five years between 1881 and 1914 the membership, drawn almost exclusively from the working classes, had increased nearly six times and retail turnover at constant prices just over five times. The number of separate Societies in existence increased rapidly from some 400 in 1862 to 1,043 in 1882,

---

[1] Cf. Thorold Rogers, *The Industrial and Commercial History of England*, p. 386, speaking in 1888–1889: 'The epoch of shops is comparatively recent' and 'the habit of buying everything at shops and nothing from the producer is peculiar to this country where the marketing by private families is practically obsolete'. Also (p. 385) 'Half a century or a little more ago the consumer was brought into contact with the producer, in a manner which modern experience or habit has no conception of. I speak from personal memory.'

[2] See Appendix D for the definitions used of the different types of retailer.

[3] The books dealing with the growth of the Co-operative movement are now very numerous. The most informative, apart from the official year books of the movement, are Sidney and Beatrice Webb, *The Consumers' Co-operative Movement*, London, 1921; A. M. Carr-Saunders, P. Sargant Florence and Robert Peers, *Consumers' Co-operation in Great Britain*, London, 1938; G. D. H. Cole, *A Century of Co-operation*, Manchester Co-operative Union Ltd., 1945; and J. A. Hough, *Co-operative Retailing 1914–1945*, London, International Co-operative Alliance, 1949. Further detail on the growth of Co-operative trading is given in the chapter on the grocery and provisions trade, p. 157, and the figures of membership and sales are given in Appendix B.

a period of expansion in new areas, and then more slowly to a peak in 1903 of 1,455. Each of the Societies was autonomous, with its own Board of Management, but they were associated with one another through the Co-operative Union and by the links with the two Co-operative Wholesale Societies. After 1903 the actual number of separate Societies declined slightly as amalgamation between them took place.

Throughout these years the movement had a marked bias towards the industrial North of England and Scotland. In 1914, for example, the Societies in the North East, the North West and the Northern Counties of England and in Scotland represented some two-thirds of the total membership and were responsible for nearly three-quarters of the total retail trade undertaken by the movement in that year.

The retail trade and the trading methods of the different Societies followed the same general pattern in almost all areas. Little or no change from the original practices of the Rochdale Pioneers in the middle of the century was introduced. The Retail Societies aimed at providing their members with the necessities of life, charged at current market prices, and—a matter of principle—cash had to be paid for the goods, no credit being allowed. Any surpluses that might accrue were to be distributed to members as a dividend on purchases. The Societies usually started with groceries and provisions as their main group of articles for sale and then added a wider range of foodstuffs such as bread, meat and tobacco. The next stage would vary between areas but most expanding Societies then added drapery and boots followed by other goods such as furniture and household utensils. Food remained, however, the dominant item in Co-operative retailing and, while exact figures are not available, it would appear that some four-fifths of total Co-operative retail sales in the years before the First World War were represented by the sale of food.

The most important development in Co-operative trading methods in the second half of the nineteenth century was the foundation and growth of the Co-operative Wholesale Societies. The English Co-operative Wholesale Society was founded in 1863 and the Scottish Co-operative Wholesale Society in 1868. Both these Societies undertook processing and production of goods for sale by Retail Societies and both purchased goods in large quantities from private manufacturers, producers and importers and resold them to the Retail Societies. The Co-operative Wholesale Society established a purchasing depot for butter in Ireland as early as 1866 and in 1876 went overseas and opened a depot in New York. Depots in Rouen in 1879, in Copenhagen in 1881, and in Hamburg in 1884, followed. In 1873 the Co-operative Wholesale Society opened its first factory at Crumpsall. This factory produced biscuits, sweets and currant bread and was followed in the same year by a boot factory at Leicester. In 1875 the first soap factory was opened in Durham. The subsequent progress of the Wholesale Societies on both the purchasing and production sides was continuous and the Retail Societies gradually increased the proportion of their total purchases that were made from the Wholesale Societies. Most of the Retail Societies had only a handful of branches. They were in fact similar to a small multiple shop organization, but centralization of their purchases through the Wholesale Societies gave them the advantages of large-scale buying.

The relative importance of Co-operative reailing

The Co-operative Societies were the first of the large-scale retailers to develop in importance in the second half of the nineteenth century and they were the subject, as were the other forms of large-scale retailing later, of attacks by the smaller, established traders.[1] No reliable estimates are available as to national retail sales before 1900. Therefore, while the retail sales of Co-operative Societies are known, no direct evidence exists as to the seriousness of the threat to the private traders represented by the Societies. Estimates can be made, however, of the share of the Co-operative Societies in the national retail trade as a whole and by four broad classes of commodity between 1900 and 1920. These estimates are presented in Table 1. Taking the estimate given in this table for 1900 in conjunction with the membership and turnover figures of the Co-operative Societies for the earlier decades, it would appear very doubtful if the total sales of Co-operative Societies at the beginning of the third quarter of the nineteenth century exceeded 2–3 % of total sales. The proportion of Co-operative sales to total sales at that date would, however, have been greater in some areas, for example in the North of England.

The individual trades in which the share of the Co-operative Societies was over 10 % of the total trade in 1900 were groceries and provisions, in which the share is estimated at 14–16 %, and household stores, 9–11 %. In 1915 there were still only two trades in which the share of Co-operative Societies was over 10 %—groceries and provisions, 17–19 %, and household stores, 11–13 %.

6. THE DEPARTMENT STORES

The development of the department store method of retailing is particularly difficult to trace and record, as on the one hand few writers or store owners are agreed on the definition of a department store, and on

---

[1] For example, in the late 'sixties and 'seventies *The Grocer*, the trade paper of the independent retailers, attempted to organize a boycott among retailers of all wholesalers and manufacturers who supplied goods to the Co-operative Retail Societies. P. Redfern, *The Story of the C.W.S.*, Manchester, Co-operative Wholesale Society Ltd., 1913, pp. 42–3.

Table 1. *Estimated share of the Co-operative Societies in the total retail sales by main commodity groups, 1900–20**

Commodity group	Proportion of total retail sales undertaken by Co-operative Societies				
	1900 %	1905 %	1910 %	1915 %	1920 %
Food and household stores	7·5–9·5	8·0–10·0	9·0–11·0	10·5–12·0	11·0–12·5
Confectionery, reading and writing materials and tobacco goods	1·0–2·0	1·0– 2·0	1·0– 2·5	1·5– 2·5	1·5– 2·5
Clothing and footwear	4·0–5·0	4·5– 5·5	4·5– 6·0	5·0– 6·0	5·0– 6·5
Other goods	1·0–2·5	1·5– 3·0	1·5– 3·0	2·0– 3·5	2·0– 3·5
All commodities	6·0–7·0	6·0– 7·5	7·0– 8·0	7·5– 9·0	7·5– 9·0

* See Table 10, p. 45, for the estimates of the value of retail sales of the different groups of commodities.

See Chapter IV and Appendix A for a discussion of the basis of these estimates, their reliability and the meaning of the ranges, and for the complete definitions of the different categories of goods included in the different commodity groups. Briefly, it should be noted that the estimates relate to the retail sales of finished consumer goods only, the sales of services being excluded. Further, the retail sales of some consumer goods are also omitted, the most important categories being alcoholic beverages, coal, and motor cars and motor car accessories.

See Appendix B for figures of total retail sales by Co-operative Societies.

The main items included in the commodity groups distinguished are as follows:

Food and household stores: All foodstuffs and household stores such as matches, soaps, polishes and cleaning materials.

Confectionery, reading and writing materials and tobacco goods: Sugar and chocolate confectionery, newspapers, books and magazines, stationery and tobacco, cigarettes and snuff.

Clothing and footwear: All men's, boys', women's, girls' and children's clothing, footwear and dress piece goods.

Other goods: Chemists' goods, bicycles, radio and electrical goods, sewing machines, perambulators, musical instruments, jewellery, clocks and watches, sports goods, toys and games, fancy goods and leather goods, furniture and furnishings, pottery, glass, hardware and ironmongery.

the other hand it is a story not of a movement or of the spread of a standardized technique but of the progress of a large number of individual shops located in different towns throughout the country. In a later chapter dealing with developments in the women's and girls' wear trade an attempt has been made to capture some of the detail of this story: here only an outline is given of the main phases in department store growth up to 1914.

In the middle of the nineteenth century it is fairly certain that no department store as defined in the modern sense existed in Great Britain. There were, however, at this date some medium-sized drapers, such as Shoolbred of London and J. & W. Campbell of Glasgow, who were extending their range of goods beyond the narrow limits of drapery.

In the next twenty-five years the department store proper emerged. The majority of these were fairly old-established firms, such as Shoolbred, Ponting Brothers and Marshall & Snelgrove, of London, and Anderson's Royal Polytechnic, of Glasgow, which had grown from drapery and clothing shops and had added departments selling different types of goods. Others were more recent foundations such as Whiteley's, the Civil Service Supply Association and the Army and Navy Co-operative Society, all of London. These firms had extended the number and range of their departments very quickly.

In the last decades of the nineteenth and in the early twentieth century the vigorous advertisement campaigns and attractive trading methods of the leading stores led to a rapid rise in the popularity of this form of retailing both among shoppers in the large towns and among investors. Existing stores enlarged their buildings and the range of goods and services provided, and other retailers, taking advantage of the eagerness of sections of the public to invest, converted their businesses into limited companies and started buying adjacent property and re-building their stores. The Victorian and Edwardian phase of growth was completed when Gordon Selfridge started building his mammoth store in Oxford Street in 1909. This was a store, planned to the last detail, that matched and in some respects surpassed in attractiveness and size the established giants, Whiteley's and Harrods.

As department store trading methods spread so there was a change in policy. The main type of goods sold by department stores remained women's and children's wear and piece goods and the wide selection and range of such goods offered by the stores was one of their main attractions. The price policy of the stores, however, was changed. In the late 'sixties, the 'seventies and the 'eighties the stores placed great stress on the low prices at which their goods were sold. 'Store prices' were synonymous with keen competitive prices and, as with Co-operative trading, the established traders criticized strongly the department store practices. Many of the stores were known as 'price-cutters' and 'under-cutters'. Gradually, towards the end of the century and particularly in the decade before 1914, the stores changed their tactics and the criticism died away. As the department stores grew in size they began to place the major stress on the attractiveness and amenities of shopping in a large store, the freedom given to customers to inspect and choose and the wide range of services available to all. Special lines were advertised at low prices from time to time, but the main sales emphasis had moved almost imperceptibly from price appeal to selection, amenity, comfort and service appeal.

Relative importance of department store trading

As no comprehensive data on the number of department stores in existence at different points of time in the nineteenth and twentieth centuries exist, any estimates of the relative importance of this form of trading in the national retail trade as a whole must be very tentative. Using the partial data that are available an attempt to measure the growth has been made for the years 1900–20 in Table 2.

Table 2. *Estimated share of department stores in the total retail sales by main commodity groups, 1900–20**

Commodity group	Proportion of total retail sales undertaken by department stores				
	1900 %	1905 %	1910 %	1915 %	1920 %
Clothing and footwear	5·5–7·0	6·5–8·0	8·0–9·0	9·5–11·0	9·0–11·0
Other goods	1·5–2·5	2·0–3·0	3·0–4·0	4·5– 6·0	5·5– 7·5
All commodities	1·0–2·0	1·0–2·5	1·5–3·0	2·0– 3·0	3·0– 4·0

* For the basis of the estimates and definitions used see Appendix A and also footnote to Table 1. The sales by department stores of food and tobacco, confectionery, and reading and writing material are not shown separately as their sales of these goods were very small. Such sales are, however, included in the estimates of sales of all commodities.

In individual trades, the department stores in 1900 are estimated to have undertaken just under 10 % of the total sales of women's and children's wear. By 1915 their share of this trade is estimated to have risen to 14–16 % of total sales.

7. THE MULTIPLE SHOP RETAILERS

The growth of multiple shop retailing in Britain in the second half of the nineteenth and first half of the twentieth centuries has been the main subject of this inquiry. The statistical and descriptive material relating to the development of this form of retailing in individual consumer goods trades is set out in later chapters. Here only an outline of the main features of the emergence and growth of this form of retailing in all trades as a whole in these years will be given.

The first multiple shop retailers and the increase in numbers of branches

Multiple shop retailing in Britain in its modern form can be traced back to the eighteen-fifties when the newsagent firms of W. H. Smith & Son and J. Menzies of Scotland, and the Singer Manufacturing Company, first began to build up their chains of bookstalls and retail shops. It

was not until the eighteen-seventies, however, that multiple shop retailing emerged in the main consumer goods trades. The oil and
colourmen's trade, the grocery trade and the footwear trades were the
first to witness this development, and the earliest firms included George
Mence Smith of London in the first-named trade, Walton Hassell &
Port, also of London, in the second trade, and R. & J. Dick of Scotland,
George Handyside of Newcastle, E. H. Rabbits and Pocock Brothers of
London, and George Oliver and G. & W. Morton of the Midlands in
the footwear trade. Altogether records have been traced of some 29
multiple shop organizations controlling 10 or more branches in existence in 1875, and these firms controlled in all close upon 1,000 branches,
including the multiple railway bookstalls and sewing machine shops.

Table 3. *Estimates of the total number of multiple shop firms
and branches in the United Kingdom, 1875–1920**

Year	10 or more branches		25 or more branches	
	Number of		Number of	
	Firms	Branches	Firms	Branches
1875	29	978	10	725
1880	48	1,564	15	1,093
1885	88	2,787	25	1,926
1890	135	4,671	47	3,468
1895	201	7,807	73	6,017
1900	257	11,645	94	9,256
1905	322	15,242	118	12,386
1910	395	19,852	149	16,462
1915	433	22,755	168	18,985
1920	471	24,713	180	20,602

* The basis of these estimates and the element of understatement contained in them is
discussed in Chapter IV and in Appendix A.

The main trades are shown in Table 4, but it should be stated that multiple shop retailing
organizations in the catering, beer, wines and spirits, motor cycle and car, laundering and
dry cleaning and service trades are omitted.

The records of firms that have gone out of existence, or have amalgamated with other
firms have been included as well as those of firms still existing in 1920.

In determining the number of organizations in existence, subsidiary companies or firms
are not counted separately even though they may trade under their own names. Only the
parent firms are counted, as financial control rather than trading practice is the criterion
used.

The subsequent story is one of a continuous increase in the number of
multiple shop firms and in the number of multiple shop branches in
existence. Estimates of the total number of firms and branches in
existence between 1875 and 1920 are given in Table 3 and in Table 4
a breakdown by trades of multiple shop branches is shown. In both
tables there is known to be an underestimate of the total number of

branches in existence. This underestimate is very slight in the case of firms with 25 or more branches but is probably over 25 % in the case of the 10–24 size group.

Table 4. *Estimates of the number of multiple shop branches in each of the main consumer goods trades, 1880–1920**

Trade	1880	1885	1890	1895	1900	1905	1910	1915	1920
Grocery and provisions	277	688	1,265	2,239	3,444	4,429	5,870	7,130	7,880
Meat	10	200	564	1,253	2,058	2,982	3,828	3,675	3,207
Bread and flour confectionery	—	—	10	33	105	261	451	628	850
Milk	—	22	41	53	101	203	324	401	750
Fish	—	—	—	—	12	34	59	92	425
Fruit and vegetables	—	—	—	—	21	49	84	142	120
Total: Food	287	910	1,880	3,578	5,741	7,958	10,616	12,068	13,232
Tobacco	—	10	27	80	210	372	502	567	644
Sugar confectionery and ice cream	—	—	—	24	83	163	308	496	565
Newspapers, magazines, books and stationery	410	490	595	700	865	892	1,159	1,229	1,299
Total: Tobacco/confectionery/reading and writing material	410	500	622	804	1,158	1,427	1,969	2,292	2,508
Men's and boys' wear	44	119	211	349	570	854	1,085	1,259	1,426
Women's and girls' wear	—	20	77	153	245	342	472	543	589
Footwear	500	757	1,231	1,967	2,589	2,962	3,544	3,879	3,942
Total: Clothing	544	896	1,519	2,469	3,404	4,158	5,101	5,681	5,957
Chemists' goods	—	28	62	178	410	543	700	941	1,044
Furniture and furnishings	—	—	—	12	54	82	128	162	196
Speciality goods	190	240	300	365	440	512	656	850	923
Household goods	133	201	264	362	359	397	404	350	384
Jewellery, leather goods, toys and fancy goods	—	12	24	39	57	110	148	164	169
Total: Other goods	323	481	650	956	1,320	1,644	2,036	2,467	2,716
Variety chain stores	—	—	—	—	22	55	130	247	300
ALL MULTIPLE SHOP BRANCHES	1,564	2,787	4,671	7,807	11,645	15,242	19,852	22,755	24,713

* The basis of the estimates is discussed in Appendix A. The classification by trades of the multiple shop branches is the same as that used in the later chapters dealing with individual trades and broadly is according to turnover. That is, a dairy multiple shop organization may sell provisions but will be classed in the milk trade if milk represents more than half of the total turnover. Multiple shop caterers are not included in food multiple organizations. Speciality goods include bicycles, sewing machines, perambulators, musical instruments, electrical goods and radios. Household goods include hardware and ironmongery, paint and wallpaper, brushes and brooms, pottery and glass and general domestic stores.

The figures in Table 3 can be used to illustrate the rate of growth of multiple shop trading as shown by the increase in the number of branches in existence between different dates. The use of the numbers of branches has many limitations, as there were variations in the size of branches between trades and over time. However, the rate of net increase in the number of branches does give a general indication of multiple shop activity at different dates and this analysis is undertaken in Table 5. This table shows the net increase and the rate of net increase in the number of branches in operation in different periods between 1876 and 1920. The rate of net increase is shown as a percentage increase in the numbers in each period and the absolute increase in the number of branches in each period is also shown as an average yearly net increase.

Table 5. *Rate of net increase in the number of branches of multiple shop firms in the United Kingdom, 1876–1920*

Year	Branches of firms with 10 or more branches			Branches of firms with 25 or more branches		
	Net increase in the number of branches	Percentage net increase	Average yearly net increase in numbers	Net increase in the number of branches	Percentage net increase	Average yearly net increase in numbers
1876–1880	586	60	117	368	51	74
1881–1885	1,223	78	245	833	76	167
1886–1890	1,884	68	377	1,542	80	308
1891–1895	3,136	67	627	2,549	74	510
1896–1900	3,838	49	768	3,239	54	648
1901–1905	3,597	31	719	3,130	34	626
1906–1910	4,610	30	922	4,076	33	815
1911–1915	2,903	15	580	2,523	15	505
1916–1920	1,958	9	392	1,617	9	323

Two main phases of multiple shop development

The figures given in these tables suggest that there were two main phases in multiple shop development up to the First World War. The first phase, extending from the early 'seventies to the middle 'nineties, was a period when multiple shop retailing was practically confined to the footwear, grocery and provisions, meat and household stores trades, apart from the special cases of railway bookstalls and sewing machine shops. The organizations in the footwear trade were the first off the mark and the number of footwear multiple shop branches was greater than that in the grocery trade up to 1890. In this year also there had emerged the first firms—apart from the newspaper and sewing machine retailers—to have over 100 branches each. These firms were the International Tea Company and the Home and Colonial Tea Company, Eastmans the butchers and the footwear retailers, Freeman Hardy and Willis, Stead & Simpson and George Oliver.

The second phase of development between the 'nineties and the First World War was marked by the rapid and continuous spread of the multiple shop form of retailing in the trades in which it had already gained a foothold, particularly in the grocery, meat and footwear trades. At the same time these techniques were extended successfully to a number of other trades. In the men's outfitting and tailoring trade, Joseph Hepworth of Leeds led the way in the late nineteenth century and other large firms appeared in the early twentieth century, such as Bradleys of Chester, G. A. Dunn & Company of London, Foster Brothers Clothing Company of the Midlands, the Cash Clothing Company of Leicester, and Stewarts 'the King Tailors' of Middlesbrough. In the women's wear trade, Fleming, Reid & Company (Scotch Wool & Hosiery Stores), selling knitting wools and similar goods, were the pioneers and this firm had over 200 branches by 1910. In the chemists' goods trade Jesse Boot had shown in the 'eighties and 'nineties that multiple shop methods could be applied in this skilled and individual trade and the expansion of his company from the turn of the century was rapid. The 50 branches of 1895 had increased to 150 by 1900 and to nearly 400 in 1910. Other firms in this trade, Taylors Drug Company, Day's Southern Drug Company, and Timothy White were also growing in these years.

In the newspaper and book trade W. H. Smith & Son from 1905 onwards opened newsagents' and bookshops as well as railway bookstalls, and had some 200 bookshops by 1914. Salmon & Gluckstein of London in the tobacco trade had opened over 100 branches by 1900 after a few years' trading, and Finlay & Co. of Newcastle increased the number of their branches in the same trade from about 50 in 1900 to over 200 by 1910. Finally Maynards Ltd., confectioners, grew steadily from the late 'nineties and had over 100 branches in 1910 and Marks & Spencer Ltd. had over 100 'Penny Bazaars' by 1914.

The growth of individual firms

Not only was there a spread of multiple shop techniques to a number of new trades but also the two decades before 1914 saw the emergence of giant firms possessing a national or near-national distributive network. By 1914 there were some 16 firms with over 200 branches each in existence and 7 with over 500 branches each. The largest, apart from W. H. Smith & Son and the Singer Sewing Machine Company, were the meat firms, Eastmans and James Nelson & Sons, with over 1,000 branches each, the Home and Colonial Tea Company, the Maypole Dairy Company, Lipton Ltd. and the Boots Pure Drug Company with over 500 branches each, while Freeman Hardy and Willis in the footwear trade had nearly 500 branches. In a few cases this growth in size was the result of amalgamation but in most instances in these years the firms had opened new branches.

The factors influencing the growth in size as measured by the number of branches and the rate of growth were, of course, in a large part individual to each firm.[1] Opportunities for expansion also varied between trades. In all trades and in most circumstances, however, an increase in the number of branches was a relatively simple affair once the principles of multiple shop organization had been mastered, as the same methods used in existing units were applied to the additional units. Capital for such expansion in the case of most of the firms operating on a local or regional scale with up to say 50 branches came out of retained profits.[2] The reinvestment of profits in this way was attractive and simple for the multiple shop retailer, who merely multiplied his units, in contrast to the manufacturing concern, which had to create new products or new openings for existing products before retained earnings could be usefully reinvested. But expansion from a local or regional market to a national market proved more difficult to accomplish entirely out of retained earnings. Additional depots and a larger transport organization were essential, and half-hearted expansion into a wider market, for example the use of existing depots for more widely dispersed branches, was disastrous. In these years, from the 'nineties onwards, therefore, the larger firms began to be converted into public limited liability companies and raised capital for further expansion on the public market. The largest firms by 1914 were practically all public companies, though in many instances, for example in the footwear and grocery trades, the additional capital raised on the market was required as much for the development and extension of manufacturing operations as for retailing operations.

There was no very marked geographical bias in the growth of multiple shop retailing in these years such as the bias towards the North of England and Scotland that appeared in the Co-operative movement and towards London in department store trading. Similarly, by the decade before the First World War the multiple shop organizations and branches were spread rather more evenly among all consumer

---

[1] It is reported that John Shillingford the grocer had 14 children and opened a new branch to mark each event. (*House Magazine*, International Tea Company's Stores Ltd., 1951.)

[2] The period of growth from 5 to say 35 branches was, however, a difficult one for many firms. With a relatively small number of branches the firms were unable to secure many buying economies, as they often had to purchase from wholesalers. To increase their sales they had to reduce prices and work on a lower profit. Such firms, however, rarely had shareholders to placate.

goods trades than were either the Co-operative Societies with their emphasis on foodstuffs or the department stores with their emphasis on clothing, particularly women's and children's clothing. By 1914 there was practically no important consumer good trade in which multiple shop retailers were totally absent. Just over 72 % of the total retail sales of these organizations are estimated to have been represented by the sale of foodstuffs (as against over 83 % of the total retail sales in the case of Co-operative Societies), 15 % of the total was represented by clothing (as against over 67 % of total retail sales in the case of department stores), 8 % was represented by other goods, and 5 % by confectionery, reading and writing material and tobacco goods.

The techniques of multiple shop retailing

In methods of trading, the multiple shop organizations concentrated to a much greater extent than was the case with either Co-operative or department store trade on economies of scale in buying, economies of specialization in administration and economies of standardization in selling. The particular techniques evolved and the advantages gained varied of course between firms and between trades. In the grocery and provisions and the meat trades, for example, bulk purchasing of imported foodstuffs on a scale undreamed of by the traditional retailer and the rapid distribution of these goods to a wide network of branches were the chief characteristics of the multiple shop methods. In the footwear and men's clothing trade, on the other hand, the main features of multiple shop techniques were the development of close links with manufacturers, and in many instances the integration of manufacture and distribution, to control the volume and variety of the goods sold in the retail branches, and the introduction of strict and standardized stock control systems in each of the branches. But whatever the circumstances of the particular trade, the outstanding contrast between the techniques used by multiple shop firms and those hitherto used in the distributive trades was the application of mass, standardized techniques to the problems of buying and selling in place of the essentially personal and individualistic approach of the one-shop, small-scale retailers.

Other features of multiple shop trading methods in these years were low prices, cash transactions and vigorous advertising. Until well after the turn of the century the multiple shop branch units in most trades made little or no attempt to provide comforts or amenities for their customers. Only the barest essentials by way of shop fittings were installed, but every effort was made to advertise in spectacular and noisy ways the goods for sale and the low prices at which they were being offered. With branches situated for the most part in working-class

districts, the multiple shop retailers developed a system of mass distribution with the minimum of frills to parallel the growth of large-scale
production and the bulked imports of standardized goods. As a reflection
of this policy, the largest and leading firms offered only a very limited
and narrow range of goods for sale; they were essentially specialists.

Relative importance of multiple shop trading

Estimates of the relative importance of multiple shop retailing in the
total national retail trade in the years 1900 to 1920 are presented in
Table 6. No estimates can be made relating to the years before 1900
as data on national retail sales do not exist, but the figures in Table 6
combined with the information on the number of multiple shop branches
in existence in earlier years suggest that the share of multiple shop
retailers in total retail trade before say 1885 was negligible.

Table 6. *Estimated share of multiple shop firms in the total*
retail sales by main commodity groups, 1900–20*

Commodity group	Proportion of total retail sales undertaken by multiple shop firms				
	1900 %	1905 %	1910 %	1915 %	1920 %
Food and household stores	3·5–4·5	4·0–7·0	6·5–9·0	8·0–10·5	8·5–11·0
Confectionery, reading and writing materials and tobacco goods	1·5–3·0	2·0–3·5	2·5–4·0	3·0– 4·5	3·5– 5·0
Clothing and footwear	3·5–5·5	4·5–6·5	6·0–8·0	6·0– 8·0	7·0–10·0
Other goods	2·0–3·5	3·0–5·0	3·5–5·0	4·5– 6·0	5·0– 6·5
All commodities	3·0–4·5	4·5–5·5	6·0–7·5	7·0– 8·5	7·0–10·0

* See Appendix A and Chapter IV for a discussion of the basis of these estimates. It should
be stressed that the estimates relating to turnover are not strictly comparable with the
estimates of the number of multiple shop branches given in Table 3. The categories of goods
making up the different commodity groups are noted in Table 1.

In 1900 only in the footwear and speciality goods trades was the
share of multiple shop organizations higher than 10 % of total trade.
In footwear the multiple shop proportion is estimated at 19–21 % of
the total trade, and in the bicycles and sewing machines trade at
9–11 %. In 1915 the share of multiple shop organizations was higher
than 10 % in the following trades: footwear, 32–34 %; chemists' goods,
13–15 %; bicycles, sewing machines, electrical goods, 12–14 %; groceries
and provisions, 12–14 %; and meat, 9–11 %.

8. THE IMPORTANCE OF LARGE-SCALE RETAILING AND THE FACTORS INFLUENCING ITS GROWTH

Using the material included in Tables 1, 2 and 6, Table 7 presents estimates for the years 1900–1920 of the shares of each of the large-scale retailers in the total national trade and, by difference, the share of other retailers.

Table 7. *Estimated shares of the different economic types of retailer in the total retail trade, 1900–20**

Type of retail organization	Proportions of total sales undertaken by different types of retailer				
	1900 %	1905 %	1910 %	1915 %	1920 %
Co-operative Societies	6·0– 7·0	6·0– 7·5	7·0– 8·0	7·5– 9·0	7·5– 9·0
Department stores	1·0– 2·0	1·0– 2·5	1·5– 3·0	2·0– 3·0	3·0– 4·0
Multiple shop retailers	3·0– 4·5	4·5– 5·5	6·0– 7·5	7·0– 8·5	7·0–10·0
Other retailers (by difference)	86·5–90·0	84·5–88·5	81·5–85·5	79·5–83·5	77·0–82·5

* The 'other retailers' group, as it is residual, includes all other types of retailing organizations including small-scale producer/retailers.

The share of large-scale retailers, that is Co-operative Societies, department stores and multiple shop organizations, in the total retail trade at the beginning of the third quarter of the nineteenth century cannot, for the reasons given above, be estimated directly, but, using the partial data that exist, it would appear extremely unlikely that these types of retailer were responsible for more than 2–3 % of the total trade at that date. The relative importance of large-scale retailing in national retail trade between 1875 and 1914 would therefore appear to have increased from about 2–3 % to some 17–21 %.

The decline in the share of the small-scale retailers (or the rise in the relative importance of large-scale retailing) varied of course as between the different consumer goods trades. The variations in trend as between the four main commodity groups distinguished above are presented in Table 8.

Table 8 brings out clearly the significant role that the large-scale retailers already played in the food and clothing trades by 1900. The relative importance of the different types of large-scale retailers in the individual consumer goods trades that make up the commodity groups is discussed in later chapters, but for 1900 and 1915 the trades in which large-scale retailing was most important were as follows. In 1900, taking the middle point of the range given in Table 8 below, large-scale retailers undertook some 11·7 % of total retail trade. The individual trades in which the share of large-scale retailers was higher than the average in this year were: the footwear trade in which, taking the middle point of the range, the large-scale retailers undertook 28 % of total sales; the grocery and provisions trade, 20·5 %; the women's wear trade, 15·5 %; and the household stores trade, 13 %. In 1915 the trades in which the share of the large-scale retailers was higher than the average were the footwear trade, 44 %; the grocery and provisions trade, 31 %; the women's wear trade, 23 %; and the household stores trade, 20 %.

Table 8. *Estimated share of large-scale retailers in the total retail sales by main commodity groups, 1900–20**

Commodity group	Proportion of total retail sales undertaken by large-scale retailers				
	1900 %	1905 %	1910 %	1915 %	1920 %
Food and household stores	11·5–13·5	13·5–16·0	17·0–19·0	19·5–22·0	20·0–24·0
Confectionery, reading and writing material and tobacco goods	3·0– 4·5	4·0– 5·0	4·5– 5·5	5·0– 6·0	6·0– 7·0
Clothing and footwear	14·0–16·0	17·0–18·5	20·0–21·5	21·0–24·5	23·0–25·5
Other goods	6·0– 7·5	8·0– 9·5	9·0–11·0	12·0–14·0	14·0–16·0
All commodities	11·0–12·5	13·0–14·5	15·5–17·5	17·0–20·0	19·0–21·5

* The sales of department stores are included in the sales of large-scale retailers in each of the commodity groups.

Factors influencing the growth of large-scale retailing

A number of factors combined to assist and encourage the growth of large-scale retailing in the last half of the nineteenth and early part of the twentieth centuries. Here the discussion will be focused on three aspects of this growth: first, the general economic advantages of large-scale retailing; secondly, the factors influencing the emergence of the different forms of large-scale retailing; and thirdly, some suggestions, based on British experience, as to the essential prerequisites for such a development.

The economic advantages of size in retailing can be said to arise out of the monopolistic or monopsonistic position of the large-scale unit and out of the economies gained through the scale of operations.[1] The

[1] The literature on this subject is extensive but no attempt will be made here to pursue the finer and more theoretical issues involved. This account of the economies of large-scale

monopolistic and monopsonistic advantages of size may take the form of charging higher retail prices for the goods and of purchasing the goods at lower prices, that is securing lower invoice costs. A strong buyer in the market can influence the pricing decisions of the producers and this is seen in various forms, for example the existence of special arrangements between producer and buyer for quantity discounts and so on. The advantages arising out of economies of scale may take the form of lower operating costs expressed as a percentage of net sales, defined as total retail sales less invoice costs. There are two aspects of lower operating costs in relation to size. Firstly, the scale of operations may allow for considerable specialization in function such as specialization in buying, in selling, in administration, in advertising and display and in staff training. Secondly, the scale of operations may be accompanied by an increase in the rate of stock turn since the need to increase the stocks held is not proportionate to the increase in the sales undertaken.

All the different types of large-scale retailers in Britain secured these advantages in one degree or another. There is little evidence however to show that a monopolistic policy of charging higher prices was adopted or was possible at least over any significant period. Rather the contrary, in that the early period of growth of large-scale retailing was distinguished by a low-price policy.[1] But while these advantages were present in all cases of growth in size, the actual form of the different large-scale retailing organization that was evolved in different trades depended on other factors.

The department store and the multiple shop development

Two main paths of expansion from small-scale retailing to large-scale retailing in Britain in these years can be distinguished. On the one hand the retailer wishing to increase and to enlarge his turnover and

retailing follows closely the interesting discussion by R. Bellamy in the *Bulletin of the Oxford University Institute of Statistics*, vol. 8, 1946: August, 'The Changing Pattern of Retail Distribution'; October, 'Size and Success in Retail Distribution'; November, 'Private and Social Cost in Retail Distribution'. See Appendix C for a summary discussion of the economic advantages of multiple shop retailing.

[1] Most of the large-scale retailing organizations, however, at one stage or another were assisted in their growth by other types of quasi-monopolistic advantages in relation to their competitors. The department stores, for example, by reason of size and siting, had marked advantages over the small-scale competitor, particularly in relation to the range and variety of women's clothing stocked; and the multiple shop firms in the footwear, provisions and meat trades were faced with little direct competition in their early period of growth from small-scale retailers, owing to the reluctance of the skilled boot and shoe maker to handle factory-made footwear and of the skilled grocer and butcher to handle imported provisions and frozen and chilled meat. In the case of the Co-operative movement the method of trading itself, that is democratic control by the working-class members and savings through the payment of a dividend on purchases at stated intervals, gave the Societies an important advantage over their commercial competitors, particularly in the years before 1914 when the appeal of democratic working-class control of trading organizations was strong.

profit could attempt to increase his sales by stocking a wider range of products for existing customers and by attracting other customers from over a larger geographical area. Alternatively the retailer could increase his total turnover by opening in new areas additional shops or branches selling the same type of goods. The first policy was that followed by the drapers, mercers, furnishers and some food retailers who expanded the range of goods sold and grew into department stores. To a less marked extent the Co-operative Societies adopted the same policies in their central premises. The second policy was that followed by the retailers who developed into multiple shop organizations and, again to a less marked extent, by Co-operative Retail Societies when they opened branch units.

In trades such as food, confectionery, tobacco goods, newspapers and chemists' goods, the consideration of convenience, that is of physical proximity to the home or to the normal journeys of the consumer, was of major importance in sales, as the goods of these trades were purchased frequently. There was therefore a limit to the number of additional customers that a retailer wishing to expand could expect to attract to make purchases in his shop. The method of multiplying the number of retailing units rather than increasing the size of the existing one was therefore the course usually adopted. On the other hand, in trades such as clothing and furniture and furnishings the physical proximity of the retailing unit to the home of the consumer was less important than the range and quality of goods stocked. The retailer could therefore increase his turnover by offering a wider range of products and adding to the number of different departments within the shop, thus intensifying his total sales to existing customers and attracting new customers from over a wider area.

The actual development of large-scale retailing in Britain was also influenced by the operation of other factors. The rising working-class demand, for example in the second half of the nineteenth century, for both food and goods other than food was still limited to a fairly short list of essentials. The demand was characterized not by a desire for variety, for selection and for range of commodities but by an acceptance of standardization and an emphasis on cheapness and reliability. Further, the leisure and opportunity to travel distances to make even the occasional purchases of goods other than food existed for the working classes to only a limited extent. The large-scale retailing organizations that emerged to meet this type of demand were therefore those which practised to the greatest extent economies in buying and in selling techniques, those that used standardized methods and sold standardized goods, those that took the shops to the consumer rather than expected the consumer to come to the shops, and those that directly or indirectly emphasized price appeal. The multiple shop and Co-operative forms of large-scale retailing fulfilled these requirements.

The successful introduction of such methods of retailing was influenced also by the production conditions in individual trades. Unless and until the production conditions in a given trade enabled this type of large-scale retailer to achieve buying and selling economies and to introduce standardization and stock control, these retailers had few advantages over the small-scale retailer. The development of factory production of consumer goods in place of handicraft methods and the importing of foodstuffs in bulk in these years gave the large-scale retailers their opportunity in many trades. But in other trades, for example the greengrocery trade or the women's wear trade, the retention of small-scale production methods curtailed the expansion of these forms of large-scale retailing.

The rising middle-class demand for consumer goods in late Victorian and Edwardian Britain was, by contrast, of an almost opposite character to that of the rising working-class demand. While price was important, choice and individuality were of equal if not greater importance, and, in addition, the problem of time and opportunity for shopping was far less pressing. The forms of large-scale retailing that developed to cater for this demand therefore were not necessarily those that secured considerable economies in large-scale purchasing of standardized articles. Rather were they those that placed the greater emphasis on specialization of the merchandising function, on specialization in buying, selling, display design and advertisement. And they were those that by providing a range, a selection and a distinctiveness that could not be matched by other retailers were successful in attracting customers from afar. Most of these characteristics were developed by the department store form of large-scale retailing and this form was not dependent in the same way as the multiple shop organizations on the existence of factory production or of bulked imports. The advantages lay rather in the development of specialization in buying, so that supplies from a number of small producers could be co-ordinated to meet demand, and specialization in selling, so that the particular type of demand of the middle classes in this period was fully catered for in all respects.

The main economic advantages of the multiple shop form of large-scale retailing in these years may be said to have arisen from economies of scale in buying, with all that that involved by way of the existence of bulk or factory production and the by-passing of the wholesaler, and from economies of specialization of function within the organization. Specialization was assisted by the adoption of standardized methods of selling a limited range of standardized goods. This form of large-scale retailing developed most rapidly in the convenience goods trades. The main economic advantages of the department store form of large-scale retailing arose to some extent from economies in buying but mainly from economies of specialization of function in the form of expert buying from a number of varied sources and skilled selling of a wide range of goods under one roof. This form of large-scale retailing emerged in sections of the shopping goods trades. The economic advantages of the Co-operative Societies were in a large part similar to those of the multiple shop organizations, and Co-operative retailing developed in the same types of trades. Some of the larger Societies adopted in their central premises the department store techniques of specialization. In addition, however, the Co-operative Societies had the unique advantages of working-class democratic control and of payment of a dividend on purchases. All three types of large-scale retailer would appear to have secured an increase in the rate of stock turn and therefore a reduction in operating expenses as a result of increase in size.

The prerequisites for the development of large-scale retailing

There remains the question, Why did large-scale retailing develop in these particular years, and at particular times in individual trades? Part of the answer to this question has been implied in the above discussion and many of the details are given in later chapters dealing with individual trades. All that is required here is a brief restatement of the main forces at work.

In the first place large-scale retailing methods were dependent upon the existence of a large, steady and consistent demand. In particular the Co-operative and the multiple shop forms of retailing were dependent upon the existence of a relatively homogeneous working class bringing with it a large, effective demand for the necessities of life and a demand behaviour that was roughly similar in all urban parts of the country.[1] The department store form of retailing was dependent in its

---

[1] The position of the Co-operative movement in relation to the existence of working-class demand differed slightly from that of the multiple shop form of large-scale retailing. The multiple shop firms in their selling policies stressed low prices and the offer of goods hitherto outside the reach of the working classes. Weak or inconsistent demand in any area would be combated by intensification of advertising and salesmanship. The Co-operative movement, on the other hand, did not attract by charging low prices directly and was not particularly forward in introducing new products in the working-class market. Its appeal lay rather in the dividend, in 'honest trading', and in the political doctrine of consumer control. The growth and expansion of the Co-operative movement in these years therefore tended to be confined to the strongly homogeneous working-class areas of the North of England and Scotland, and its progress was slow in the heterogeneous and shifting working-class areas of the Midlands and London. The multiple shop retailers, however, did not depend on the existence of loyalty and foresight among their customers and were able by salesmanship to expand both in the difficult and unstable markets of the Midlands and the South and in the more stable markets of the North.

turn on the existence of a strong middle-class demand, particularly for goods other than food. Both types of demand emerged in the second half of the nineteenth century. In the second place the large-scale retailing methods of the multiple shop organizations demanded the large-scale production of the goods distributed or their import in large quantities. Again, not until the second half of the nineteenth century did these conditions exist in most consumer goods trades. The Co-operative Societies were influenced in their development by the same factor, though not in such a marked degree. Large-scale production of consumer goods cannot, however, be described as an essential prerequisite to the growth of department stores, though it assisted the development of this form of retailing.

A third factor of importance in these years was the increase in the volume of goods entering directly into retail trading and the changed character of many of the goods. Some of the goods, for example factory-made footwear and clothing, patent medicines, margarine, eating chocolate and cigarettes were virtually new consumer goods. Other goods, such as imported butter, bacon, eggs and meat, were not new goods but their source of supply had changed. These new goods and the new sources of supply of other goods, which entailed bulk handling in a few importing centres rather than small-scale purchases throughout the country, demanded new methods of distribution. The traditional types of retailing units, the producer/retailer, the skilled tradesmen such as the grocer and the butcher, and the markets and pedlars, were unable and unfitted to handle these new goods, and the large-scale retailers with considerable vigour seized the opportunity of filling the gap. An important need was met by these new types of organization, handsome profits were made and fortunes were built almost overnight. The Co-operative Societies started paying dividends of 4s. and 5s. in the £ and many founders of department stores and multiple shop firms became public figures, active in Parliament, in Society, and in the world of sport.

These may be suggested as the main reasons for the development of large-scale retailing in Britain in the half-century or so before 1914. The many other factors operating, ranging from the general buoyancy of demand through most of these years to legal changes such as the introduction of limited liability enabling the large-scale retailers to obtain the capital for expansion, affected the rate and some of the characteristics of the growth of large-scale retailing, but their influence was secondary to that of the factors discussed above.

9. THE CHANGES IN THE TECHNIQUES OF RETAILING

The changes in the economic and social background, the shifts in the channels of distribution and the developments occurring in the structure and organization of the retail trades in the years between the middle of the nineteenth century and the First World War gave rise to, and were accompanied by, radical changes in the character and techniques of retailing. Two main types of change may be noted: firstly those taking place in the character of shopkeeping itself, and secondly those taking place in the techniques of selling.

The retail shopkeepers

The developments in the character of shopkeeping took several forms. For example there was a decline in the importance of skill in retailing and of apprenticeship.[1]   Some decay occurred in the family tradition of business, and new types of shopkeeper appeared who possessed entirely different qualifications to those of the older types of retailer.[2] Further, the combined shop and dwelling-house wherein lived the shop assistants as well as the owner and his family began to be replaced by the 'lock-up' shop. Retailing was becoming an occupation with starting and finishing times permitting a separate existence for the retailer away from the shop, instead of a life's work that was never completed. Finally, with the growth of large-scale retailing a new and impersonal 'race of managers' was appearing alongside the highly personal and individual shopkeepers.

These trends were by no means complete by 1914.   Many trades remained highly skilled and the family tradition was by no means dead.   Further, while contemporaries seemed overwhelmed by the growth of large-scale retailing[3] the tables presented above suggest that individual small-scale retailing was the most important business form in all trades in 1914 and that in some trades large-scale retailing had hardly made a start.   But the significant change in these years was that

---

[1] Cf. *The Times*, 18 August 1902. In a discussion of the grocery trade it was suggested that the last fifty years had converted 'the old fashioned grocer who required to know many things about the "art and mystery" of his trade into a vendor of packet goods so that a large proportion of the grocer's work of the present day could be accomplished almost equally well by an automatic machine delivering a packet of goods in exchange for a coin'.

[2] Cf. W. B. Robertson (editor) *Encyclopaedia of Retail Trading*, vol. i, London, 1911, p. 13. 'It is a remarkable sign of modern commercial life that knowledge of a shopkeeping trade is not nowadays considered nearly so necessary as purely commercial ability.'

[3] The literature on retailing in the pre-1914 years is full of references to the decline of the small man and contains most gloomy prognostications as to his future; for example the observation of two active trade unionists, Joseph Hallsworth and Rhys J. Davies, *The Working Life of Shop Assistants*, Manchester, 1910, p. 3, 'The small trader is more and more being relegated to the back streets, there to eke out a living as best he can on a poor class of trade.'

a breach in the old methods and traditions of shopkeeping had occurred and attention was being paid to the direction and control of the new trends rather than to the possibility of putting back the clock.

The selling techniques

The developments in the techniques of selling took the form of transforming the fixed shops from units that existed solely to fulfil customers' wants to units designed and planned to attract customers and create wants. Gone for the most part was the decent pride that Lord Macaulay had expected of retailers in their relations with their customers, and in its place, assisted by technical innovations such as plate glass and gas lighting, every possible device was being used to startle and attract passers-by.[1] In practically all trades and among nearly all types of retailers emphasis had begun to be placed on window display, on salesmanship and on advertisement. Some traders used only the windows, some displayed their wares from poles hung on rails outside the shops, and some used open-fronted structures where all or nearly all the goods were placed on direct view to the public, but all retailers ticketed their goods with the most catching phrases. Many of the vigorous selling methods hitherto used only in the markets were being adopted by the fixed-shop retailers, and advertisement of goods both by the retailers and the manufacturers was becoming an accepted practice. The late Victorian period was an era of retail advertisement by the distribution of handbills, the employment of sandwichmen and in some trades the use of 'hookers-in' or pavement salesmen who helped passers-by to make up their minds.

The most important change in the technique of selling was however the acceptance of clear and open pricing of the goods on sale as the standard commercial practice.[2] Haggling as to price still occurred in sections of the different trades, and the practice of auctioneering to clear stock at the end of the week was common in some of the perishable food trades, for example butchery, but a policy of clearly-marked fixed prices was being adopted by the majority of retailers in all trades and this trend was accepted, even welcomed, by the consumers.

The growth of the system of open pricing, which meant that consumers were influenced in their decisions as to where to buy by known

[1] As early as 1874 John Ruskin attributed, in part, the failure of his tea shop to his refusal to use such methods. He wrote 'the result of this experiment (the tea shop) has been my ascertaining that the poor only like to buy their tea where it is brilliantly lit and eloquently ticketed'. Ruskin added 'I resolutely refuse to compete with my neighbouring tradesmen either in gas or rhetoric.' Quoted in J. A. Rees, *The Grocery Trade*, vol. ii, p. 244.

[2] Cf. R. K. Philp, *Handybook of Shopkeeping*, 1892, p. 14. 'In Edinburgh, as in London, higgling is now gone out of date in all respectable establishments and so it is in Glasgow. Formerly no one could enter a haberdasher's shop in the cities without spending half-an-hour or so in higgling with the shopkeeper.'

price differentials, led in the last quarter of the nineteenth century to a period of severe price competition between retailers. This price competition, intensified by the general trend of falling prices, encouraged in its turn competition in salesmanship and advertisement. Further, the quality of the goods offered, which had hitherto rested largely on the reputation of the retailers, became a subject of vigorous assertion. In those trades where factory production of consumer goods was growing the manufacturers were, however, in a better position than the retailers to guarantee quality, and through branding and advertisement the producers themselves entered the fray, attempting to convince consumers that their particular brand provided the best value for the money. In this background of fierce price competition between retailers, of competition between the growing large-scale retailers and the small-scale retailers, and of the increasing concern of the larger manufacturers with the organization of stable marketing for their products and with the maintenance of a reputation among consumers for quality and consistency, the practice of resale price maintenance began to be introduced in some trades. Apart from the book trade with its somewhat special circumstances, the chemists' goods and tobacco goods trades were among the first to witness this development. The most vociferous pressure for the introduction of such a system came from the retailers, but the manufacturers and wholesalers would not appear to have been unduly reluctant to make its operation feasible.[1] In relation to the techniques of retail selling the development of this practice meant that one more function of the retailer, a function hitherto considered an essential part of retailing—that of price determination—was being taken away from the retailer and passed to the manufacturer.

10. CONCLUSION

The emergence of Britain as a fully industrialized state and as an imperial economy brought about the revolution in the distribution trades between the middle of the nineteenth century and 1914. New types and characteristics of demand, new methods of production, new sources of supply and new kinds of consumer goods allied with the rapid development of the system of transport in Britain and throughout the world made inevitable radical changes in the distribution trades. The methods, the forms, the techniques and the traditions of the distributive framework of the middle of the nineteenth century were totally unsuited to effect the marriage of the new demand for, and the supply of, the new products. The distributive framework existing was

[1] For a discussion of the origins of this movement see B. S. Yamey, 'The Origins of Resale Price Maintenance: A Study of Three Branches of Retail Trade', *Economic Journal*, vol. LXII, no. 247, September 1952.

basically a pre-industrial framework that had been modified and adjusted to meet the changing needs of a growing industrial economy, but the main structure had not been reorganized. Modifications and adjustments to the structure continued to be made in the decades following the middle of the nineteenth century, but the changes brought about by these gradual methods were too limited in their nature and too slow in their effect to match the growing tempo and problems of industrialization. The traditional channels of distribution could only cater for a part of the demand; the growing volume of goods spilled over into fresh channels, the new demands began to be supplied in novel ways, and radical shifts took place in the traditional divisions of distributive functions between manufacturer or producer, wholesaler and retailer. Similarly the retail structure was transformed; decaying and moribund institutions such as fairs and markets disappeared or completely changed their character and purpose; craftsmanship retailing began to be replaced by commercialized retailing; entirely new large-scale retailing organizations were fashioned; and the practices and techniques of retail salesmanship were revolutionized.

The actual extent to which the 'new' practices and methods had displaced the 'old' by the decade before the First World War is difficult to measure. Contemporaries in their speeches and writings inevitably tended to stress the importance of the new, though their unwritten memories present a somewhat different picture. Certainly many of the older types of institution and traditional techniques were maintained, and flourished, without making important concessions to the newer and more fashionable ideas. In most instances, however, the older types of wholesaler and retailer, much as they regretted dispensing with time-honoured methods, tended to follow and imitate their apparently successful rivals in the highly competitive struggle to maintain and increase their share of a given market. Particularly would this appear to have been the case in the decade or so before the First World War when, while the consumer good market was still growing with the increase in population, the slowing down in the rate of increase in real income per head had brought the different methods and concepts of trading into much more direct conflict than had taken place in the period of general expansion in the last quarter of the nineteenth century.

The revolution in the distributive trades was therefore far from complete by 1914. Some of the characteristics of this revolution were, in fact, still confined to small sections of a few trades. The main structural and organizational changes engendered by the new types of demand and the new types of goods had, however, been set in train, and the question outstanding was not would they be successful, but how rapidly would they spread to all sections of the distributive trade.

CHAPTER II

THE DISTRIBUTIVE TRADES, 1914–1939: THE SUCCESS OF LARGE-SCALE RETAILING

In many respects the changes taking place in the methods, structure and techniques of the distributive trades in Britain in the years from the First World War to 1939 were nearly as spectacular as and certainly more widespread than those observed in the half-century or so before 1914. The origins of these changes can, however, in practically all instances be traced back to the years before the First World War. The pre-1914 trends were modified and refined in many respects in the inter-war years but there was a continuity in the main features and characteristics of the development. The economic and social climate of Britain in the inter-war years was, however, markedly different to that of the years before 1914. This changed climate naturally affected the evolution of the distributive trades and had an important bearing on many of the modifications of the pre-1914 trends that were introduced.

I. THE ECONOMIC AND SOCIAL CHANGES AND THE DISTRIBUTIVE TRADES

The fundamental and far-reaching changes that took place in the British economy in the inter-war years are familiar ground. The period of expansion founded on the growth of basic industries, on the export of capital, and on the extension of overseas interests had come to an end. Instead of steady, if uneasy, expansion, the decades of the inter-war years were a period of painful and faltering adjustment to new world conditions, and of markedly uneven development in different industries and sectors of the economy. The decline in the basic and former export industries, transforming areas that had hitherto been centres of prosperity into depressed areas, was only partly offset by the progress in other areas of more resilient and youthful industries such as light and electrical engineering and of sheltered trades such as public service, transport and many consumer goods trades. The average proportion of the working population that was unemployed was over three times that of the pre-1914 decades and the number of insured workers who were unemployed rose to nearly three millions in the depth of the 1930–34 slump. In economic thought and policy, laissez-faire and emphasis on the importance of free and unfettered competition and of Free Trade was replaced by the acceptance of the need for governmental intervention in many spheres of economic and social life, by the growth of combination and amalgamation between firms, by the emergence of trade associations controlling prices and limiting output, and by introduction of quotas, tariffs and preference schemes.

The continued movement of the terms of trade in Britain's favour, the possession of considerable overseas investments, and the rising productivity of newer and still expanding industries, however, enabled the population of Britain as a whole to enjoy some increase in real income per head, though with fluctuations, between 1920 and 1938.[1] But the existence of heavy unemployment in certain trades and certain areas and the cyclical pattern of development meant that this increase in real income per head was not continuous and was not spread evenly over all classes of people or between all areas of the country.

Changes in the character of consumer goods and in the demand for those goods

In the inter-war years there was a continued growth of large-scale manufacturing of consumer goods and in most trades the producer/retailer virtually disappeared. Features of the growth of large-scale production were an increase in the range, variety, quality and standards of the goods produced by these methods, and the practice of integration in one establishment of all the various productive and predistributive processes involved in making the article, from the treatment of the raw materials to the final wrapping or boxing of the goods ready for retail sale to the consumer.

A second development was the extended use of standards and the identification of goods by brands. Both imported and home-grown foodstuffs for example began to be marked, graded and identified by standards, and the practice of branding by manufacturers spread in a large number of trades. A third development on the supply side was the appearance of a number of entirely new consumer goods such as electrical equipment and appliances of various kinds, the products of the rising radio and motor industries, new textiles such as artificial silk, and a wide range of chemists' goods and toilet articles.

The character of the demand for consumer goods also altered in a number of important ways. The slowing down in the rate of increase of the population, for example, and the decrease in the size of families coupled with the trend towards smaller houses and households,

---

[1] According to the estimates made by A. R. Prest, the pattern of the change in real income per head in these years was as follows. From a 1919–20 post-war peak real income per head dropped in the post-war depression to the 1903–4 level. There followed a fairly steady climb back to just above the 1919 level in 1929. Real income fell again in the slump, but from 1935 to 1938 there was a continuous and rapid rise. (A. R. Prest, *Economic Journal*, vol. LVIII, no. 229, 1948.)

influenced the home activities of and the type of purchases made by the housewife. There was a decrease in the volume of goods made, cooked and baked in the home, and in the place of infrequent bulk purchases of semi-processed or partly finished goods the housewife began to make regular and frequent purchases in small quantities of goods that were ready for consumption. The kitchens, larders and pantries of the newer houses of the inter-war years were stocked with tins, containers and packets weighing ounces and pounds rather than with sacks, bags and drums weighing stones and hundredweights.

A second shift in demand was brought about by what may be called the growing homogeneity of social behaviour of different classes and groups. The spread of education, the rising circulations of national newspapers and magazines and of the advertisements that were an essential part of these papers, the universal attraction of the cinema and the radio and the development of an easy, cheap and rapid internal transport network, all played their part in narrowing the gaps in behaviour between different groups. The growth of this homogeneity could be seen in such developments as the similarities in the dress of different classes, the repercussions of fashion changes among practically all sections of the people and the gradual disappearance of wide varia-tions in the type of goods demanded in different parts of the country and by different sections of the community. Shipyard workers and miners of the North and North-East, for example, began to wear at week-ends suits similar to those worn by London clerks and shop assistants, working-class girls in the cotton towns began to follow with interest and applica-tion the fashion changes in high society, and housewives in South Wales began to buy the same brand of breakfast cereals as housewives in Carlisle or Glasgow. This growth of homogeneity in social behaviour clearly widened the possibilities of national marketing by manufacturers and of the use of similar selling policies and techniques by large-scale retailers in different parts of the country.

At the same time, however, this merging and overlaying of the divisions in behaviour and demand between classes, groups and areas did not have the effect in any way of confining demand to fewer types of goods. In fact the inter-war years were a period of remarkable flowering and almost exotic growth of different types and brands of similar goods that were marketed. Further, in these years not only did fashion changes take place at a bewildering speed, but an element of 'style', and therefore of changes in style, spread to some consumer goods, such as men's clothing, which had hitherto been practically outside the scope of short-term changes. This great increase in the variety of pro-ducts was partly the outcome of improved methods and techniques of production and of a rise in the standard of living, but would appear to have resulted chiefly from the intensification of competition between producers and between retailers in a market that was not consistently buoyant and in which the appeal of something new, something novel, was effective in the short run.

Reference has been made to the growth in the second half of the nineteenth and the opening decades of the twentieth century, of a consistent working-class demand for consumer goods. In the inter-war years, while the basis of the demand remained in that there was, of course, no return to family self-sufficiency, the existence of widespread unemployment and the unevenness in the prosperity of different industries and trades and of different towns and areas of the country tended to reduce the consistency of the demand. This had the effect, contrary to that of the growth of homogeneity in social behaviour discussed above, of requiring increased flexibility on the part of the distributive trades to meet the varying conditions.

The existence of a significant middle-class demand in the decade before 1914 was also noted above. In the inter-war years the numbers of the so-called middle classes increased rapidly with the growth of tertiary industries and occupations, but at the same time stratification within this class began to appear . A realistic assessment of middle-class demand involved reference to both a lower-middle-class and an upper-middle-class and sometimes even to a middle-middle-class. These groups with different income levels and slightly different patterns of social behaviour again required of the distributive trades increasing flexibility of approach.

Changes in the pattern of consumers' expenditure

These changes in buying habits and in the composition of the different demand markets were accompanied by shifts in the pattern of consumers' expenditure. It is not possible to show the shifts in the expenditure pattern of the different income groups, but some material is available on working-class expenditure and on the retail expenditure of all consumers.

There have been two working-class household budgetary inquiries: one was made by the Board of Trade in 1904 and used later as the basis of the 1914 Cost of Living Index, and the other was made by the Ministry of Labour in 1937–38 and used later on as the basis of the 1947 Interim Index of Retail Prices. A broad indication of the shift in the pattern of working-class expenditure is given in Table 9 by a comparison of the 'weights' used for the different items in 1914 and in 1947.

The weights used for the different items in the 1914 Cost of Living Index cannot, however, be satisfactorily compared with those of 1947 to show the detailed shifts in the working-class pattern of expenditure,

Table 9. *Comparison of the 1914 Cost of Living Index with the Interim Index of Retail Prices 1947**

Group	Weight in 1914 Index	Weight in 1947 Index
Food	60	35
Rent and rates	16	9
Clothing	12	9
Fuel and light	8	7
Other items in 1914 Index	4	16
Total: Items covered by 1914 Index	100	76
Items not covered by 1914 Index	—	24
Total	—	100

* This table is based on the explanatory note appearing in the Ministry of Labour and National Service *Interim Index of Retail Prices*, 1947, p. 4.

as many items such as alcoholic drinks, medicines, furniture and floor coverings and fruit and vegetables, on which the working class spent at least a small proportion of their income, are not included in the 1914 figures. The weights given in Table 9 undoubtedly overstate the proportion of total working-class household expenditure on food in 1914.

The information on the expenditure by all types of consumers is more detailed, and estimates showing the changes in the pattern of total retail expenditure between 1900 and 1950 are presented in Table 10. These estimates relate to the retail expenditure by private domestic consumers on finished goods only and exclude expenditure on services of all kinds.

The figures presented in Table 10 are estimates only and are subject to error. Too great stress must not be placed, therefore, upon the short-term fluctuations shown, but the long-term trends indicated are probably sound. These trends suggest that there was a decline in the proportion of total retail expenditure of all private domestic consumers represented by expenditure on food between 1900 and 1938, particularly in the years 1920–38; and that there was an increase in the proportion spent on confectionery, reading and writing materials and tobacco goods and on the other goods group which includes items such as furniture and furnishings, chemists' goods, and pottery, glass, hardware and ironmongery. The proportion of total consumer expenditure represented by the purchases of clothing did not change greatly in these years. In individual consumer goods trades the relative importance of the grocery and provisions trade fell markedly between 1900 and 1938, and the trades showing the greatest proportional rises were those of bicycles and electrical goods, tobacco and cigarettes, confectionery and ice cream, chemists' goods, furniture and furnishings and jewellery, sports goods, toys and fancy goods. The estimates for the year 1950, it will be appreciated, reflect the unusual conditions existing in that year, such as the shortages of supplies, for example meat, and the heavy taxation of other goods, for example tobacco and cigarettes. These shifts in the pattern of consumer demand for goods bought through retail channels, in particular the shift away from food to goods other than food, had a direct influence on the structure and development of the distributive trades as a whole and on the problems and relative rates of progress of individual trades.[1]

Table 10. *Estimated total retail sales by main commodity groups, 1900–50**

Commodity group		1900	1905	1910	1915	1920	1925	1930	1935	1938	1950
Food	Sales £m.	441	477	515	669	1,451	1,137	1,078	981	1,072	2,141
Proportion of total sales	%	58·8	58·7	57·7	58·6	50·7	52·9	49·8	46·6	46·6	40·3
Confectionery, reading and writing material and tobacco goods	Sales £m.	57	68	78	116	265	242	277	295	332	1,121
Proportion of total sales	%	7·6	8·4	8·8	10·2	9·3	11·3	12·8	14·0	14·4	21·1
Clothing	Sales £m.	144	148	168	184	705	395	410	396	446	1,005
Proportion of total sales	%	19·2	18·2	18·8	16·1	24·6	18·4	19·0	18·8	19·4	18·9
Other goods	Sales £m.	108	120	131	173	442	373	398	435	452	1,045
Proportion of total sales	%	14·4	14·7	14·7	15·1	15·4	17·4	18·4	20·6	19·6	19·7
Total retail sales		750	813	892	1,142	2,863	2,147	2,163	2,107	2,302	5,312

* See Appendix A for the basis of the estimates and for estimates of the retail sales of the individual commodities comprising the main commodity groups. The estimates relate to total sales of the various goods including sales of trades excluded from this inquiry such as on- and off-licences, caterers, hairdressers. The estimates are at current market prices including indirect taxation. Retail sales in Southern Ireland are excluded throughout.

Other economic and social changes influencing the distributive trades

Many other economic and social developments in these years had a direct impact on the organization of the distributive trades. For example, the uneven growth of the population and of urbanization in different areas directly influenced the structure of the distributive trades. Whereas in the second half of the nineteenth century the areas

[1] For a discussion of the interaction of the income and price factors influencing this shift in demand see Richard Stone, assisted by D. A. Rowe and by W. J. Corlett, Renée Hurstfield and Muriel Potter, *The Measurement of Consumers' Expenditure and Behaviour in the United Kingdom, 1920–1938*, Cambridge University Press, 1953 (no. 1 in the series *Studies in the National Income and Expenditure of the United Kingdom* issued under the auspices of the National Institute of Economic and Social Research and the Department of Applied Economics of the University of Cambridge).

of greatest population growth and urbanization were the basic industrial areas, that is Lancashire, the West Riding, Tyneside, Clydeside, South Wales and London, in the inter-war years the Midlands and the South were the areas showing the greatest increase. These two areas, which contained some 44 % of the total population in 1921, accounted for some 88 % of the total increase in the population between 1921 and 1938. Further, it was in these areas that the towns and conurbations grew most rapidly and where the spread of new housing estates was most marked. A feature of the growth of towns in all areas in these years was the relative depopulation of the inner centres and the rapid growth of the suburbs. These shifts in the location of the population both in the towns and in the country as a whole influenced the physical location of the retail distributive trades and presented the firms which had grown and expanded in earlier years in the older areas with difficult problems of adjustment.

The widespread use of the petrol engine for both business and personal purposes similarly had an important effect on the location of shops and the type of service that manufacturers, wholesalers and retailers could provide for their customers. In retailing there was a considerable extension of the possibilities both of attracting customers from over a wider area and of following the customer to his home. In manufacturing and wholesaling the selling areas were greatly increased. Hitherto the area of operations had tended to be limited by the distance a horse and van could cover in a day and return to the stables at night. The return journey to the garage still had to be made but the motor van had at least trebled the radius of operations.

Finally the existence of continuous and heavy unemployment throughout the inter-war years influenced the distributive trades in many ways. Two may be mentioned. To those who wished to earn a living but were unable to find anyone to employ them, retailing, 'owning a shop', 'working for oneself', offered a nearly irresistible attraction, particularly if there were still some savings in the bank or a loan that could be negotiated. Again the failure of industry to provide employment and training in a trade drove hundreds of thousands of young and adult persons towards the still largely unmechanized distributive trades. Any job was better than none even if it was clearly a 'blind alley' one giving no training and providing no prospects, and the distributive trades welcomed the additional manpower.

This sketch of some of the economic and social developments in Britain in the inter-war years provides a background in which the changes taking place in the distributive trades can be discussed.

2. THE SHIFTS IN THE CHANNELS OF DISTRIBUTION

Two of the three general trends discussed above in relation to the shifts in the channels of distribution in the pre-1914 years were continued in the inter-war years. The small-scale producer/retailer continued to lose ground. Only in a very few trades such as milk and bread was the method still of any significance by 1938. The importance of the sales by producers direct to retailers continued to increase. This trend was assisted by the further development of large-scale production in the consumer goods trades, by the competition among these producers to induce retailers to stock their brands, and by the ubiquitous motor van. By the middle 'thirties sales direct to the retailers had become a favourite remedy of many sales managers when the orders placed by wholesalers were tending to fall or were failing to increase at the rate anticipated. The logic of the argument was that the wholesaler stocks a large number of different articles of the same type and has no interest in pushing the sales of one make or brand rather than another. Direct contact with and service to the retailer on the other hand would, it was argued, persuade the latter of the advantages of stocking and selling this particular make or brand. Sales by manufacturers direct to the retailers were also encouraged from the buying end by the continued growth of large-scale retailing organizations.

The shift, if any took place, in the relative importance of the third channel, the sales made by producers through wholesalers and then to retailers, is more difficult to determine. There were variations between trades and between sections of individual trades. In some instances the decline in the importance of the producer/retailer method of distribution, for example in the fruit and vegetables trade and in sections of the made-up women's wear trade, was accompanied by a relative increase in the role of the wholesaler. Again, in those trades where the number of retail outlets increased rapidly, for example the confectionery, tobacco goods and proprietary medicines trades, the wholesaler in many instances increased his relative importance. Only the local wholesalers found it worth while to take and fulfil the very small orders of many of those retailers and to provide the long credit demanded by most of them. Moreover, the general spread through all sections of the retail trade of hand-to-mouth buying that was characteristic of these years tended to bolster up the position of the wholesaler, as he was usually closer to hand than the producer and could supply the retailers' requirements at short notice.

On the other hand, as suggested above, manufacturers in some trades where the goods were branded began to by-pass the wholesaler in order to ensure that the retailers stocked their goods. In other trades manufacturers became dissatisfied with the wholesalers' short-sighted ordering methods, which handicapped their efforts to secure continuity in production, and this led them to deal direct with the retailers.[1] And in yet other trades the growth of large-scale retailing undoubtedly led to a relative decline in the importance of wholesaling. On balance it would appear that the wholesaler lost ground in the inter-war years but that the decline in his relative importance, taking the whole range of consumer goods trades into consideration, was not very great.

Two further developments in the channels of distribution may be noted. The first, of relatively minor importance, was the use by manufacturers of mail order and club trading as a method of distribution of their products. The second, a further development of this principle, was the practice of sales by manufacturers direct to the consumers by the use of the door-to-door technique. The most notable example of the latter development took place in the new electrical equipment trade, and it also existed in the book, brush and household stores trades. In these instances the producers in their desire to develop their sales were by-passing all the intermediaries and using direct salesmanship on the consumer.

For the year 1938 some estimates are available as to the relative importance of the different channels of distribution. In this year, of a total retail expenditure on consumer goods estimated at just over £2,650 millions approximately 4 % by value was estimated to have been sold by producer/retailers and by producers using mail order or other direct means; approximately 43 % was estimated to have passed through one or more wholesaler or intermediary (excluding the Co-operative Wholesale Societies) on the way from producer or importer to the retailer; and approximately 53 % passed directly from producer or importer to the retailer, including that proportion passing through the Co-operative Wholesale Societies.[2]

Mention was made above of the need, when interpreting the shifts in the relative importance of the different channels of distribution, to bear in mind the parallel changes that might be taking place in the functions performed by the different links in the distributive chain.

[1] Cf. Wholesale Textile Association, *Third and Final Report issued by the Post-War Reconstruction Committee*, 1946, p. 38. Reviewing the pre-1938 methods the report states, 'The methods adopted by many wholesale departmental buyers in purchasing their requirements have contributed in a high degree to the tendency on the part of manufacturers to seek outlets for their productions other than through the wholesale distributing trade'.

[2] James B. Jefferys, *The Distribution of Consumer Goods*, National Institute of Economic and Social Research, Economic and Social Studies IX, Cambridge University Press, 1949, p. 152. The estimates are only approximate and the middle point of ranges has been taken. The difference between the estimate of total consumers' expenditure in 1938 given here and that given on p. 45 of this volume is accounted for by the exclusion from the latter figure of many groups of goods such as coal, motor cars and alcoholic beverages.

These shifts of function were of two types. Firstly, a change in the method of distribution of a particular commodity almost invariably brought with it a change in the functions performed by the different units. For example, with the by-passing of the wholesaler the wholesaler's functions of holding stock, breaking bulk and giving credit and delivery to retailers were not eliminated but were taken over by either the producer or the retailer, depending on the particular circumstances. The second shift of function occurred when there was no change in the channels of distribution but shifts in function took place between the different units, for example the manufacturer taking over some of the functions hitherto performed by the wholesaler or retailer. It is this second type of shift that is being discussed here.

In the inter-war years the pre-1914 trend of a transference of function from the retailer to the wholesaler and to the producer undoubtedly continued. In addition, some of the wholesaler's functions were also transferred to the producer. The first main reason for this trend was the economies that could be secured by undertaking in one place and on a large scale many of the operations hitherto performed on a very small scale by scattered industrial units. Standardization in taste in some commodities assisted this development. A second factor was the growing concern of manufacturers with the marketing of their goods. This led them to plan their sales and, as far as possible, to leave nothing to chance and to make the wholesalers' and the retailers' selling tasks simple and automatic. The wide extension of advertising by producers and of the practice of resale price maintenance in these years is an illustration of this trend. Even in the case of large-scale retailing units there was a development of the system of producers making split deliveries to individual branches of the multiple shop firms instead of continuing the pre-1914 practice of delivery in bulk to the multiple shop warehouses.

3. THE CHANGES IN THE STRUCTURE AND CHARACTERISTICS OF RETAILING

There are no reliable data available as to the number of retail shops in Britain in the inter-war years, and therefore no final conclusions are possible regarding the trend in the numbers in existence or in the number per head of the population.[1] It is known, however, that the

---

[1] The 1921 *Census of Population* gives 614,579 as the number of shop premises in existence in England and Wales, of which 150,828 were classified as not containing dwellings. Inns and public houses were classed as shops in this Census, but undivided private houses used partly for trading purposes were not classed as shops unless the non-domestic portion consisted of at least three rooms or represented more than one quarter of the whole premises. These

numbers of persons employed in the distributive trades between 1920 and 1938 increased at a rate faster than the increase in the population and faster than the increase in numbers employed in all trades in these years.[1] This increase in the total numbers employed in the distributive trades at a rate faster than the increase in the total population could imply that for the country as a whole the rate of increase in the number of shops was also faster. This conclusion is however rather doubtful. These were years of the continued growth of large-scale retailing and the retailing units of such organizations were larger, that is had a higher number of employees per shop, than the average retailing unit. Again these were years when an increase took place in the services rendered to customers by retailers, and these services, while requiring additional manpower, did not necessarily lead to additional numbers of shops per head of the population. Finally the shift of the population towards the South of England probably resulted in a trend towards slightly fewer but rather larger shops per unit of the population.[2] Whatever the conclusion as to the rate of increase in the number of shops in those years,

definitions prevent comparison with the 1911 *Census of Population* and no return of shop properties was made in the 1931 Census.

An analysis made by P. Ford of the number of shops listed in directories in twelve 'typical' towns in 1901 and 1931 showed that the number of shops per head of the population had declined very slightly between these two dates. While not claiming that this inquiry was conclusive, Professor Ford suggested '. . . if its results can be regarded as representative, that statements asserting or implying that there has been a relative increase in the number of shops cannot yet be regarded as proven'. 'Excessive Competition in the Retail Trades. Changes in the Numbers of Shops, 1901–1931', *Economic Journal*, vol. XLV, no. 179, September 1935.

[1] Agatha L. Chapman, *Wages and Salaries in the United Kingdom, 1920–1938*, Cambridge University Press, 1952 (no. 5 in the series *Studies in the National Income and Expenditure of the United Kingdom*), pp. 19–20 and 146–51. The figures at five-yearly intervals are as follows:

Year	Numbers employed in the distributive trades (thousands)	Numbers employed in the distributive trades as percentage of all employment %
1920	1,773·2	10·0
1925	1,714·2	10·7
1930	2,083·6	12·6
1935	2,313·6	13·2
1938	2,438·2	12·9

These estimates relate to wholesale and retail trade but exclude unemployed, employers working on own account, and those employed by manufacturers on selling. The number of persons working on own account in 1931 was 458,400 excluding Northern Ireland. The population of the United Kingdom rose from 43·7 millions in 1920 to 47·5 millions in 1938.

[2] There is some direct evidence in the grocery trade, for example (see pp. 167–8), that the shops in the South of England had more customers per shop than those in the North and in Scotland, and also that the large-scale retailers had more customers per shop than the independent retailers.

however, there is no doubt about the increase in the relative importance in terms of employment of the distributive trades. This may be suggested as a reflection of both the increase in the volume of consumer goods entering into retail distribution and the rise in the extent and standards of the distributive services provided in these years.

Convenience shopping and main street shopping

In the physical organization of retailing there would appear to have been two contrasting developments. On the one hand the consumer was surrounded by an increasingly finer net of distributive services. The practice of the consumer in these years of buying essential goods in smaller quantities and of making purchases more frequently, and the addition to the range of goods considered to be essential, led to a stress on shops and selling points being conveniently situated near to the consumer. There was also a wide extension of the practice of delivering some of these goods to the consumer's doorstep. In trades such as foodstuffs, tobacco and cigarettes, confectionery, and newspapers, the shop just round the corner or just down the street and the delivery van or travelling shop fulfilled many of the needs of the consumers. On the other hand the consumers began to be increasingly attracted away from local shops and over longer distances to make their purchases of other types of goods. The shift in the pattern of consumers' expenditure away from food towards other goods, and the general increase in these years in the importance of fashion, style, choice and selection and therefore of window display and window shopping, led to a parallel stress on bigger, brighter and better laid-out shops in main street sites. Shops sited in the busiest streets of the towns attracted consumers. Such shops gave the consumer an opportunity to make comparisons, to see what was new, and to make a choice with relative ease; such shops also gave the retailer the opportunity to display his goods to a greater number of people. The improvement in public transport and the greater distances travelled to and from work in the inter-war years widened the possibilities of, and encouraged the move towards, main street siting.

These two trends, one in the direction of 'corner shop' retailing and of following the consumer, if necessary, to his home, and the other towards attracting the consumer away from his home to closely-packed main street shopping areas, had operated before the First World War. But in the inter-war years the change in consumer shopping habits, the existence of surplus labour, the tendency towards the replacement of price competition between retailers by competition in service, and the wide spread of style and fashion consciousness, all combined to bring about a great extension of the physical services undertaken by retailers and of the main street siting of shops in long unbroken avenues. Further, particularly in the case of the main street shops, there was a remarkable advance in the standards of design and appearance. Window display, assisted by electric lighting and shop-front design, became a profession and not just a spare-time occupation and—an even more radical change —the cleanliness, layout and fittings of the interior of the shop became as important a factor in attracting customers as the outward display.

Changes in the techniques of retailing

Accompanying and assisting these changes in the physical organization of retailing were what may be called changes in the characteristics and techniques of retailing. Again these changes were for the most part a continuation and extension of tendencies noted in the years before 1914. First the need for technical skill in the retailing trades continued to decline. Women began to be employed in large numbers in many trades and the practices of apprenticeship and 'living-in' were becoming unusual. The factors bringing about this decline in demand for skill, such as the growth of large-scale manufacture leading to the transference of pre-distributive processes from the retailer to the producer, the use of mechanical aids in the shop, the sale of packaged finished goods, and so on, have been discussed above. All that need be added is that as the incidence of these changes was uneven between trades so was the relative decline in skill. The technical knowledge and skill required of the butcher, for example, did not decline in the same way as that required of, say, the tobacconist. Again some of the newer trades developing in these years, for example the electrical goods trades, required in selling and in after-sales service a high level of technical knowledge. But viewing the retail trades as a whole there can be little doubt as to the main trend. The parallel growth of the need for increased commercial skill as distinct from technical skill and for business knowledge on the part of the retailer, if not on the part of his assistant, should not however be overlooked.

A second development was the increase in overlapping between trades. Again this was not a new phenomenon. At no time had every retailer stuck to his last, and some, for example the village general dealer who had flourished for generations, had no last to stick to. He sold the products of half-a-dozen different trades. In the inter-war years, however, many additional breaches were made in what could be called the accepted dividing lines between trades, and in a number of trades the relative importance of the specialist retailer decreased. This development was assisted by the decline in the need for technical skill in the handling and selling of some goods, by the pressure of manufacturers and wholesalers in certain trades to increase the total number of outlets for their products, and by the hopes of retailers that in adding new lines to the range of goods sold they would maintain and increase their turnover. For example, the number of outlets for commodities such as confectionery, tobacco goods and proprietary medicines rose very rapidly in these years.[1] The specialists in these trades lost ground, though many reacted by widening their own range of goods and selling toys, fancy goods, stationery, books and so on. In other trades, such as hardware, electrical goods and books, a similar though less marked increase took place in the total number of outlets, and a new type of retailer, the variety chain store, appeared which was essentially based on selling the products of a number of different trades. The 'penny bazaar' of the pre-1914 years had of course adopted the same methods, but the variety chain stores far exceeded the bazaars in significance.

The trend towards overlapping between trades, or 'poaching' as it was called, did not pass without protest.[2] The complaint of the specialist retailer against the non-specialist 'poacher' was that the non-specialist did not perform the essential functions of a retailer in relation to the consumer. The non-specialist did not hold large stocks or provide a full range to meet every demand, but rather stocked only a few fast-moving lines, leaving the specialist to stock the slow-moving and usually less profitable lines. Such practices it was argued would, unless halted, lead to the disappearance of the specialist through bankruptcy and would discourage skill in retailing. In reply the non-specialists argued that if the public purchased goods from them then it was sufficient proof that they were supplying a need, and further that there appeared to be no logical reason why existing, established traders should have the right to determine whether and what type of competition should be permitted in their trade.

The spread of resale price maintenance

Finally the spread of the practice of resale price maintenance in the inter-war years both encouraged some of these developments in the character of retailing and also provided one more contrast between the retailing methods of the pre-1914 era and those of the inter-war years. Resale price maintenance, in both its individual and collective forms, had developed in some consumer goods trades at the end of the nineteenth century, but the proportion of total consumers' expenditure

---

[1] The number of tobacco licences issued rose from 352,000 in 1911 to 530,400 in 1939 (see p. 269). The number of outlets for confectionery is estimated to have increased from approximately 100,000 before 1914 to 250,000–300,000 in 1938. The number of makers and vendors paying medicine stamp duty rose from 46,000 in 1920 to 164,000 in 1938 (see p. 383).

[2] Many retail trade associations, for example in the chemists' trade, the hardware trade and the newspaper trade, attempted to stem the tide by securing the agreement of manufacturers to supply only bona fide retailers.

represented by resale price maintained goods in 1900 is provisionally estimated at not more than 3 %. By the end of the inter-war years, in 1938, the proportion is suggested as nearer 30 % of the total consumers' expenditure.[1] This important increase in the extent of the practice was accompanied by a growth in the numbers and representativeness of trade associations in the distributive trades. These associations were often directly or indirectly concerned both with the agreements as to the prices and margins involved in any system of resale price maintenance and with the enforcement of the agreed practices. The retailer was replacing the links with his fellow-retailers that had hitherto been based on an affinity of skill and craftsmanship with links based on an affinity of business and commercial interest.

The arguments as to the advantages and disadvantages of resale price maintenance do not call for elaboration here. But the consequences of the extension of the practice on the structure and character of the retailing trades may be outlined briefly. The spread of this practice, accompanied as it inevitably was by the use of branding and advertising by manufacturers, forced the retailers in many trades, as they could not compete in price, into competition with each other in the provision of services to the consumer. The character of this service competition ranged from the opening of shops close to the consumer or the delivery of goods to his home, to the provision of more comfortable shopping conditions or of a wider range and selection of stock. Such services were not of course peculiar or individual to the trades where resale price maintenance was the general rule: as suggested above a feature of retailing in all trades in the inter-war years was the provision of additional distributive services of various kinds. The existence of a significant measure of resale price maintenance in a given trade did however tend to confine the competitive energy of retailers to the provision of services.

A second consequence of the spread of resale price maintenance was the encouragement of overlapping between trades. Again this trend was a general one and certainly was not restricted to the trades where resale price maintenance was usual nor brought about solely by this practice, but the existence of fixed margins tended to encourage retailers to stock goods of trades other than their own. To give one example, grocers were encouraged to stock the price-maintained goods of the chemists, as, for a number of reasons, the fixed margins in the chemists' goods trades were usually higher than the normal margins in the grocery trade. The existence of fixed margins also made it possible for manufacturers, if they so wished, to increase the number of outlets for their goods. Lastly, as mentioned above, the spread of resale price maintenance meant that one more of the retailer's functions, namely

[1] *Report of the Committee on Resale Price Maintenance*, Cmd. 7696, 1949, p. 1, para. 5.

price determination to meet the needs of his particular market, was being transferred to the producer. This had the effect of reducing to some extent the skill required to undertake retailing, thus making entry to the trade easier.

There were a number of other consequences of the spread of resale price maintenance. For example, the problems of marketing for manufacturers became better-defined and therefore more susceptible of solution, the flow of goods became smoother and the market for them more stable, and the quality and standard of the products could be more readily guaranteed. The effects of these and other such developments on the character and structure of retail trading in these years were however more indirect than those discussed above.

4. THE DEVELOPMENT OF LARGE-SCALE RETAILING:
THE CO-OPERATIVE SOCIETIES

The membership of the Co-operative Societies rose from just over 3 millions in 1914 to 4·5 millions in 1920 and at the end of the First World War, in 1919, 10·7 million persons were registered with the Co-operative Societies for sugar, or 25-26 % of the resident population. The membership continued to rise in the inter-war years, reaching 6·5 millions in 1938 and 8·5 millions in 1939. In 1940, at the beginning of rationing in the Second World War, some 13·5 million persons were registered with the Co-operative Societies for sugar, or just over 28 % of the resident population. Only in the slump year of 1922 did the membership decrease and this decrease may in part have been due to the 'cleaning-up' of the membership returns by the various Societies.[1] There is no doubt, however, that the economic depression of the early 'twenties was a difficult period for the Co-operative Societies, and not until after 1925 did the movement fully regain its forward momentum.

This increase in the membership of the Co-operative Movement from about one in ten of the population in 1920 to about one in five of the population in 1939 is however a little misleading. There is reason to believe that the figures in the latter years were inflated by the inclusion of a large number of non-purchasing members. Also a direct comparison of the inter-war figures with the pre-1914 figures is made difficult owing to the growing practice of more than one person in a household becoming a member.[2] This factor and the fluctuations in the retail prices also make it difficult to compare sales per member. The Cost of Living Index can,

---

[1] See Appendix B for details of Co-operative membership and sales.

[2] In 1938 it was suggested that 'the trading membership of the Co-operative Movement is at least 1,000,000 less than the total membership figure' for the above reasons. *Report of the Economic Survey of the Services provided by Retail Co-operative Societies*, Manchester, Co-operative Union, Ltd., 1938.

however, be used to convert the turnover figures into terms of constant prices, with 1914 = 100. On this basis the retail sales per member fall from an average of £28 per head in 1914 to about £20 per head in 1920. From 1920 to 1939, while the membership nearly doubled, the average sales per head at constant prices would appear to have remained practically stable at around £20.[1]

The increase in the membership in these years was accompanied by a number of other developments in the character of Co-operative trading. One of the most important was the extension of Co-operative trading to areas that before 1914 had been known as 'Co-operative deserts', in particular the spread of the movement in the Midlands and in the South of England. These two areas in 1911 contained 49 % of the population of the United Kingdom (excluding Southern Ireland) but the Societies in these areas were responsible for only 23 % of the total Co-operative retail trade. By 1939 these areas contained 52 % of the total population and the Societies in these areas were responsible for 44 % of the total Co-operative retail trade.

A second feature of the Co-operative development was a growth in the scale of operations. This took many forms. Both the productive and buying activities of the Co-operative Wholesale Societies were increased. Large-scale factories were established and large contracts were placed with manufacturers and overseas producers for the purchase of goods and for imports of foodstuffs. Further, many societies joined together to form Federations which undertook certain processing and retailing activities on behalf of all the member Societies. For example, Federal Societies were established to undertake bread-baking and laundering on a scale beyond the potential of the individual Societies forming a part of the Federation. A third illustration of the growth in the size and scale of operations was the decrease in the number of individual Societies owing to amalgamations and mergers, and a growth in the relative importance of the largest Societies. In 1900 for example, the twenty-four largest Societies contained some 25 % of the total membership. In 1939 the twenty-four largest societies contained some 37 % of the total membership.

This increase in the scale of operations within the Co-operative movement gave greater scope for the introduction of centralized, standardized techniques of operation, and brought with it additional advantages of economies of scale. On the retail side for example there was an increase in the number of standard branch units operated by individual Societies, and multiple shop techniques of controlling the activities of these branches were introduced. No reliable figures are available as to the number of Co-operative shops in existence at the

[1] J. A. Hough, *Co-operative Retailing*, p. 163.

beginning of the inter-war years, but in 1937–38 some 1,100 Societies traded in approximately 24,000 shops.[1]

The proportion of total Co-operative turnover represented by different classes of consumer goods, did not change greatly in these years. Certainly the changes in the pattern were not as marked as those shown in working-class expenditure and in total consumers' retail expenditure. There would appear to have been a slight trend in Co-operative sales towards commodities other than food, but from 1930 to 1939, when relatively reliable figures are available to show the break-down of sales by departments, food was still responsible for a steady 74–76 % of total sales compared with an estimated four-fifths before 1914.

Within the food group, however, an increase had taken place in the relative importance of the sale of bread, milk and, to some extent, meat, and there had been a decline in the relative importance of the sale of groceries and provisions. In the group of goods other than food the sale of chemists' goods had risen the most rapidly, though chemists' goods remained of minor significance in total sales. There would also appear to have been a slight increase in the relative importance of the sale of the miscellaneous household goods group, including furniture and furnishings, hardware, electrical goods, and bicycles.

There were two main trends in the character of Co-operative retail sales in these years. On the one hand efforts were made by a number of Societies, in response to members' requests and assisted by the steadily growing range of Co-operative production, to widen the range and increase the volume of the sales of goods other than food. On the other hand the Societies, particularly the larger ones, developed with skill and efficiency large-scale methods of distributing staple, standardized commodities such as bread and milk. The successes in the latter direction offset to a large extent in the division of total sales the efforts to increase the proportion of sales represented by goods other than food.

In pricing and dividend policies no changes of importance took place in these years. While the membership was by no means unanimous throughout these years as to the correctness of the policy of charging market prices and of concentrating on the payment of the highest dividend possible, no breakaway from this general policy took place.[2] The rising Societies in the Midlands and the South paid, on the average, lower dividends than those paid by the older-established Societies of

---

[1] In 1919 the number of Co-operative branches holding permits for the sale of butter was 5,500. In 1937–38 the number of Co-operative grocery branches was 9,400 (see p. 159).

[2] The General Co-operative Survey Committee appointed in 1914 and presenting a final report in 1919 recommended a dividend rate not exceeding 2s. in the £ and welcomed experiments in the direction of abolishing dividends altogether, adopting instead a policy of low prices. No consistent attempt was made to follow out these recommendations.

the North of England and of Scotland; nevertheless all Societies followed the policy of payment of a dividend rather than a policy of low prices.

Relative importance of Co-operative retailing

Estimates of the importance of Co-operative retailing in relation to the national retail trade in the years 1920 to 1950 are presented in Table 11. The estimates given above for the years 1900 and 1910 are also included in order to indicate the longer-term trends. Table 11 brings out clearly the difficulties encountered by the Co-operative Movement in the years of the post-war depression, and the slow progress made until the rapid expansion in the Midlands and the South and the increasing share in trades such as bread and milk led to recovery in the 'thirties.

Table 11. *Estimated share of the Co-operative Societies in the total retail sales by main commodity groups, 1900–50**

Commodity group	Proportion of total retail sales undertaken by Co-operative Societies							
	1900 %	1910 %	1920 %	1925 %	1930 %	1935 %	1939 %	1950 %
Food and household stores	7·5–9·5	9·0–11·0	11·0–12·5	10·5–12·0	12·5–14·0	13·0–16·0	15·0–18·0	16·5–18·0
Confectionery, reading and writing materials and tobacco goods	1·0–2·0	1·0– 2·5	1·5– 2·5	2·0– 3·0	2·5– 4·0	3·0– 5·0	3·5– 5·5	5·0– 6·5
Clothing and footwear	4·0–5·0	4·5– 6·0	5·0– 6·5	5·5– 7·0	6·5– 8·0	6·5– 8·0	6·5– 8·5	8·0– 9·5
Other goods	1·5–2·5	1·5– 3·0	2·0– 3·5	2·0– 3·0	2·0– 3·5	2·0– 3·5	3·0– 4·0	4·0– 5·0
All commodities	6·0–7·0	7·0– 8·0	7·5– 9·0	7·5– 8·5	8·5–10·0	8·5–10·5	10·0–11·5	10·0–12·0

* See Appendix A for a discussion of the basis of the estimates and Table 1 above for the trades included in the broad commodity groups.

The individual trades in which the share of the Co-operative Societies was over 10 % of the total trade in 1920 were grocery and provisions, where the share was estimated at 18–20%, and household stores, 12–14%. In 1938 the Co-operative share of the grocery and provisions trade was estimated to have risen to 22–24 % and the share in the household store trade to 15–17%. In addition the Co-operative Societies in this year are estimated to have undertaken 25–27 % of the national retail milk trade, 15–17 % of the bread trade and 9–11 % of the meat trade.

5. THE DEPARTMENT STORES

The development of department store retailing in the inter-war years is, for the reasons discussed above, far less well documented than that of Co-operative and multiple shop trading. Only a very general account of the main features of the type of trading in these years can therefore be given.

The number of fully functioning department stores in Britain continued to increase in the inter-war years. Very tentative estimates suggest that the rise was from 175–225 stores in 1914 to about 475–525 in 1938. The increase in the number of stores was not however accompanied by any tendency for the size of the stores themselves to grow. The giant stores of the immediate pre-1914 years were not surpassed in any significant degree in the inter-war years either in the numbers of different departments or in size. Considerable improvements and refinements were made, however, in most existing stores in layout, in the use of space, in display, in the use of mechanical devices such as lifts and escalators, and in the provision of amenities for customers. The important development in these years was the trend away from establishing more and more stores cheek by jowl in the central shopping districts of the very large cities and the extension of department store trading to many of the medium-sized provincial towns and to the shopping centres of suburban districts of the larger towns. The stores emerging in these areas were usually smaller than those of the central districts and in a number of instances they catered for a lower price market. As in the pre-1914 years some of the new department stores were entirely new retailing units, but the majority were fairly old-established firms that had extended their trading operations.

These developments in the form and location of department stores did not lead to major changes in the methods of trading. Department stores continued to stand out from the retailers in their use of the whole of a building for trading purposes and not merely the section fronting on the road. The wide range of goods stocked, the effective display of these goods and, particularly in the inter-war years, the freedom of customers to inspect without obligation to buy, remained major attractions of the department stores. Similarly the provision of amenities, ranging from rest-rooms to restaurants, to make shopping pleasant and enjoyable, and the convenience to the consumer of buying a number of different types of goods under one roof, remained features of this form of retailing. To attract people to the stores and to make known these advantages, most department stores had a higher advertising expenditure in relation to turnover than any other type of retailer.[1]

---

[1] The average advertising expenditure of a group of about 100 department stores in the years 1931–38 was about 2·55 % of total sales. This estimate excludes display. Arnold Plant

An important change did take place, however, in the application of these general principles. Whereas in the years before 1914 the progress of a store was dependent to a large extent on the ability, foresight and 'hunches' of the founder and managing director, in the inter-war years policy decisions were more frequently the result of the application of scientific business principles by a team of experts. In this respect the department stores were probably ahead of any other form of retailing. The use of scientific methods and the exchange of ideas and information between stores did not in any way diminish the important characteristic of the individuality of each store. Financial integration between stores took place on an important scale in these years, and four groups emerged, Debenhams Ltd., United Drapery Stores Ltd., Great Northern & Southern Stores Ltd., and the John Lewis Partnership, that in all controlled some 200 stores. This development was not, however, accompanied by centralized direction of the individual stores. Buying on behalf of all the stores in the group was rare, as was standardization in selling and pricing policies. If anything, there was a rather greater diversity in trading policies of individual department stores in the inter-war years than had existed in the pre-1914 period, in spite of the growth of financial inter-connexion. This resulted from the efforts of different stores to cater for different price markets and from the wide differences in their size and location.

Relative importance of department store trading

Some indication of the part played by department stores in relation to total retail trade between 1900 and 1950 is given in Table 12. These estimates suggest that there was a steady increase in the relative importance of this form of trading, though the rate of increase would appear to have slowed down slightly in the inter-war years.

The emphasis in the sales by department stores on women's and children's wear and drapery was maintained, though with the expansion in the inter-war years of the retail market for furniture and furnishings and for household appliances there was a relative increase in the importance of this type of sale in the total turnover of the stores. The particular trades in which the share of department stores is estimated to have been more than 10% of the national retail sales in 1920 were, women's and girls' wear, 14–16%, and furniture and furnishings, 9–11%. In 1939 the share of department stores is estimated to have risen to 19–23% of the total sales of women's and girls' wear, and 16–19 % of the sales of furniture and furnishings. And in this year the department stores were responsible for some 11–14 % of the total sales of hardware, ironmongery, pottery and glass.

Table 12. *Estimated share of department stores in the total retail sales by main commodity groups, 1900–50**

Commodity group	Proportion of total retail sales undertaken by department stores							
	1900 %	1910 %	1920 %	1925 %	1930 %	1935 %	1939 %	1950 %
Clothing and footwear	5·5–7·0	8·0–9·0	9·0–11·0	11·0–13·0	12·0–14·0	13·0–14·5	13·0–15·5	13·0–15·5
Other goods	1·5–2·5	3·0–4·0	5·5– 7·5	7·0– 8·5	9·0–10·5	9·5–11·0	10·0–12·0	11·0–12·5
All commodities	1·0–2·0	1·5–3·0	3·0– 4·0	3·0– 4·0	3·5– 5·0	4·0– 5·5	4·5– 5·5	4·5– 6·0

* See Appendix A for a discussion of the basis of the estimates and Table 1 for the individual trades included in the commodity groups. The estimates of the share of department stores in the sale of all commodities include the small sales by the stores of food, tobacco, confectionery, books and stationery.

6. THE MULTIPLE SHOP RETAILERS

The development of multiple shop retailing is discussed in detail in the later chapters dealing with individual trades. The account given here will, therefore, be limited to an outline of the progress of this form of retailing as a whole and to a discussion of the main characteristics of multiple shop trading in the inter-war years.

Estimates of the total number of multiple shop firms and of the total

Table 13. *Estimates of the total number of multiple shop firms and branches in the United Kingdom, 1900–50**

Year	10 or more branches		25 or more branches	
	Number of		Number of	
	Firms	Branches	Firms	Branches
1900	257	11,645	94	9,256
1910	395	19,852	149	16,462
1920	471	24,713	180	20,602
1925	552	29,628	201	24,558
1930	633	35,894	258	30,594
1935	668	40,087	276	34,534
1939	680	44,487	303	39,013
1950	638	44,800	296	39,858

* See Table 3 above for notes on the construction of this table. There is undoubtedly an underestimate of the number of branches in the 10–24 size group.

number of branches controlled by them between 1920 and 1950 are presented in Table 13. The figures for 1900 and 1910 are also included to show the trend in numbers in the first half of the twentieth century. The numbers of branches can be further analysed by main trade groups and this breakdown is presented in Table 14.

Table 14. *Estimates of the number of multiple shop branches in each of the main consumer goods trades, 1900–50**

Trade	1900	1910	1920	1925	1930	1935	1939	1950
Grocery and provisions	3,444	5,870	7,880	9,477	11,761	12,328	13,118	13,663
Meat	2,058	3,828	3,207	3,209	3,243	3,361	3,592	3,775
Bread and flour confectionery	105	451	850	1,117	1,398	1,823	2,134	2,193
Milk	101	324	750	1,040	1,298	1,497	1,655	1,637
Fish	12	59	425	419	456	462	466	507
Fruit and vegetables	21	84	120	171	309	464	581	662
Total: Food	5,741	10,616	13,232	15,433	18,465	19,935	21,546	22,437
Tobacco	210	502	644	748	985	1,340	1,652	1,856
Sugar confectionery and ice cream	83	308	565	780	1,051	1,225	1,427	1,409
Newspapers, magazines, books and stationery	865	1,159	1,299	1,337	1,428	1,548	1,617	1,669
Total: Tobacco/confectionery/reading and writing material	1,158	1,969	2,508	2,865	3,464	4,113	4,696	4,934
Men's and boys' wear	570	1,085	1,426	2,075	2,684	2,894	3,233	3,068
Women's and girls' wear	245	472	589	725	946	1,169	1,412	1,539
Footwear	2,589	3,544	3,942	4,364	4,767	4,849	5,169	5,210
Total: Clothing	3,404	5,101	5,957	7,164	8,397	8,912	9,814	9,817
Chemists' goods	410	700	1,044	1,393	1,741	2,280	2,462	2,508
Furniture and furnishings	54	128	196	299	431	558	688	836
Speciality goods	440	656	923	1,159	1,439	1,708	2,125	1,412
Household goods	359	404	384	604	872	1,202	1,554	1,244
Jewellery, leather goods, toys and fancy goods	57	148	169	311	418	398	400	411
Total: Other goods	1,320	2,036	2,716	3,766	4,901	6,146	7,229	6,411
Variety chain stores	22	130	300	400	667	981	1,202	1,201
ALL MULTIPLE SHOP BRANCHES	11,645	19,852	24,713	29,628	35,894	40,087	44,487	44,800

* See Table 4 above for details of the construction of this table.

Finally the figures in Table 13 can be used to show the rate of net increase in the number of branches in existence between different periods. As suggested above the use of numbers of branches as an index of growth is not wholly satisfactory, but the changes in the number of branches trading give a general indication of the trend of multiple shop activity. The net increase in the number of multiple shop branches and the rate of net increase in different years between 1920 and 1950 is shown in Table 15.

Table 15. *Rate of net increase in the number of branches of multiple shop firms in the United Kingdom, 1921–50**

Year	Branches of firms with 10 or more branches			Branches of firms with 25 or more branches		
	Net increase in the number of branches	Percentage net increase	Average yearly net increase in numbers	Net increase in the number of branches	Percentage net increase	Average yearly net increase in numbers
1921–1925	4,915	20	983	3,956	19	791
1926–1930	6,266	21	1,253	6,036	25	1,207
1931–1935	4,193	12	839	3,940	13	788
1936–1939	4,400	11	1,100	4,479	13	1,120
1940–1950	313	1	28	845	2	77

* The rise in the importance of variety chain store trading in the inter-war years makes statistics of the net increase in the number of branches less valuable as a guide to multiple shop activity as a whole than in the pre-1914 years. The variety chain stores in these years increased in numbers and in size of branch. By 1938 the average employment per variety chain store branch was over seven times the average of all other branches of multiple shop organizations.

This rapid increase in the number of multiple shop branches in existence was accompanied by several shifts in the organization and trading emphasis of the multiple shop firms. The most important of these changes were the growth of large firms through amalgamations, the spread of multiple shop retailing to a number of new trades, a shift in the trading policies of multiple shop retailers towards different types of market, the development of integration of production and distribution and the emergence of a new type of multiple shop retailing organization, the variety chain store.

The increase in the size of multiple shop firms: amalgamations and mergers

In the period of the inter-war years and down to 1950 the number of branches in existence increased more rapidly than the number of multiple shop organizations. The main reason for this was not a decrease in the number of new multiple shop firms coming into existence, but an increase in the number of mergers and amalgamations. Amalgamations took place between small and medium-sized firms, but the outstanding feature was the amalgamations between very large firms. Practically all the firms in the grocery and meat trades that had grown rapidly in the years before 1914 were involved in amalgamations in the inter-war years. In the meat trade the leading firms joined together in 1923 to form the Union Cold Storage group, which had over 2,000 branches. In the grocery trade most of the leading firms and some smaller ones amalgamated between 1924 and 1931 to form the Home and Colonial group, with over 3,000 branches, and some of the other large firms merged between 1927 and 1934 in the International Tea group, which had over 1,000 branches in 1938. Other amalgamations took place in the chemists' trade in 1934 leading to the Timothy Whites and Taylors group, in the footwear trade in 1927 resulting in the Freeman Hardy and Willis group, and in the dairy trade in 1915–1921 leading to the United Dairies group. In 1939 there were 12 firms with over 500 branches each, and of these 5 had over 1,000 branches each. Only Boots Pure Drug Company and W. H. Smith & Son of the very large firms had grown mainly by opening new branches; the increase in the size of the other firms was chiefly the outcome of amalgamations.

To complete the story it should be added that amalgamations continued in the Second World War and in the post-war years. Three further large groups emerged with over 500 branches each—the Allied Bakeries group in the bread trade, the Moores group in the grocery trade and the Great Universal Stores group in the furniture and women's clothing trades.

The relative importance of the large multiple shop firms to other multiple shop firms in same trade varied. In the meat, chemists' goods, newspaper and books, fish and milk trades, for example, the development of multiple shop retailing is practically the story of the development of one or two firms. In the men's clothing, footwear, hardware, women's clothing, sugar confectionery and bread trades, on the other hand, there were a large number of competing multiple shop firms in different size groups. The size distribution of all multiple shop firms between 1880 and 1950 is given in Table 16. The figures in this table suggest that while there was a growth in the average size of multiple shop organizations, the emergence of very large firms by direct growth or amalgamation had not significantly altered the balance of the size distribution. Between 1900 and 1910, taking the figures of the branches of firms with 25 or more branches each, the proportion of the total controlled by firms with 200 or more branches each averaged some 52 %. In the years 1935–50 the corresponding average had risen only slightly to 55 %.[1] There had, however, been a shift by the end of the period within the 200 branches or more group towards the 1,000 branches or more group.

Table 16. *Estimates of the total number of multiple shop firms and branches by size groups, 1880–1950**

Year	10–24 branches		25–49 branches		50–99 branches		100–199 branches	
	Number of		Number of		Number of		Number of	
	Firms	Branches	Firms	Branches	Firms	Branches	Firms	Branches
1880	33	471	11	407	2	121	1	190
1890	88	1,203	27	775	12	806	4	477
1900	163	2,389	46	1,464	25	1,676	12	1,588
1910	246	3,390	78	2,698	35	2,409	20	2,808
1920	291	4,111	88	2,999	43	3,030	28	3,631
1930	375	5,300	117	3,810	74	4,887	44	6,204
1939	377	5,474	136	4,540	85	5,808	47	7,382
1950	342	4,942	128	4,290	77	5,211	51	7,284

Year	200–499 branches		500–999 branches		1000 or more branches	
	Number of		Number of		Number of	
	Firms	Branches	Firms	Branches	Firms	Branches
1880	1	375	—	—	—	—
1890	3	860	1	550	—	—
1900	8	2,308	3	2,220	—	—
1910	10	3,449	4	2,658	2	2,440
1920	12	3,906	8	5,876	1	1,160
1930	14	4,482	6	4,626	3	6,585
1939	23	6,483	7	5,184	5	9,616
1950	26	7,027	9	6,351	5	9,695

* The figures in this table do not correspond exactly with the totals of the figures given in later chapters in respect of individual trades. In this table a firm with subsidiaries in a number of different trades is only counted once and the number of branches controlled by subsidiary firms is added to the number controlled by the parent firm. There is undoubtedly an under-estimate throughout these years of the number of branches in the 10–24 size group. See discussion in Chapter IV and in Appendix A.

The exact reasons for the amalgamations and mergers in the inter-war years are difficult to state with certainty. There were in most instances advantages to be gained from amalgamation by way of increased specialization of management, economies in buying and in transport, and the elimination of redundant units. To firms wishing to

[1] Stability in the relative importance of the very large firms is shown also by the figures relating to the 5 largest multiple shop firms. In 1920 the 5 largest firms controlled some 23–24% of the total number of branches in existence. The proportion controlled by the 5 largest was practically unchanged in 1930, 1938 and 1950.

expand rapidly the acquisition of another concern which had good shopping sites was a more attractive proposition than the much slower process of acquiring sites one by one. In the case of some of the very large amalgamations, however, opinions were divided as to the actual advantages in terms of organization that were obtained. The Home and Colonial group, for example, after experimenting with close central control and direction of the trading organization and policies of the merging companies, reverted back to a fair measure of autonomy for each company. In addition to the purely economic and organizational questions, financial considerations also played a part in many mergers. In some instances the financial gains obtained from buying up a rival company which had met with difficulties were as important as the trading advantages that might accrue from such a merger.

The spread of multiple shop retailing in different trades

The continued growth of both old-established and new multiple shop firms in the trades in which this form of retailing had been prominent before 1914, for example the grocery and provisions, footwear, chemists' goods, newspaper and book and sewing machine trades, stands out clearly in Table 14. The exception to this was the meat trade where relatively little expansion took place. At the same time there was a considerable growth of multiple shop retailing in other trades. In the milk and fish trades, for example, there arose at the end of the First World War, almost overnight, two very large multiple shop firms, the United Dairies Ltd., and Mac Fisheries Ltd. The Express Dairy Company Ltd. also grew rapidly. An equally important but slower expansion took place in the bakery trade. Leading firms were George Lunt & Sons, A. B. Hemmings Ltd., and, at the end of the inter-war years, Allied Bakeries Ltd.

In the clothing trades also multiple shop retailing spread rapidly. On the men's clothing side there emerged large wholesale bespoke tailoring firms controlling a wide network of retail outlets, firms such as Montague Burton Ltd. and Prices, Tailors, Ltd. On the women's clothing side, multiple shop firms in the outfitting trade increased in numbers and in the 'thirties this form of retailing was developed in the women's outerwear trade. The groups known as Morrisons Associated Companies Ltd., Willsons (London & Provinces) Ltd., and Barnett-Hutton Ltd. were three of the larger firms emerging. Many, if not all, of the problems of handling style and fashion goods on a large scale were being successfully overcome. Other trades in which multiple shop methods of trading made significant progress in these years were the furniture and furnishings trade (the leading firms being Jays & Campbells Ltd. and the British and Colonial Furniture Company Ltd.), the new electrical and radio trades (J. & F. Stone, and Max Stone Ltd.), the jewellery trade (H. Samuel Ltd. and James Walker, Goldsmith and Silversmith Ltd.), and the wallpaper and paint and pottery and glass trades (Wallpaper Stores Ltd.).

Some indication of the widening of the scope of multiple shop retailing in these years is given by a comparison of the breakdown by main trade groups of the estimates of total retail sales of multiple shop organizations in 1915 and 1939. In 1915 just over 72 % of total sales is estimated to have been represented by the sale of food (mainly groceries and provisions and meat), the sale of clothing (mainly footwear) represented about 15 %, and the remainder was split between the confectionery, reading and writing materials and tobacco goods group, 5 %, and the miscellaneous other goods group, 8 %. In 1939 the sales of foodstuffs had fallen to about 45 % of total multiple shop sales, the sales of clothing had risen to 26 %, and the sales of other goods had risen to 21 %.

Changes in multiple shop trading policies

Accompanying this spread of multiple shop retailing to practically all important sectors of the consumer goods trades and the shift of emphasis away from the food trades, some important changes in retailing policies were introduced. Reviewing multiple shop retailing as a whole, the inter-war years may be said to have witnessed the transition from a system of trading characterized by emphasis on price appeal and by the mass distribution to the working class, with a minimum of frills and cost, of a relatively small range of essential goods, to a system of trading that catered in many different ways for the varied demands both in relation to goods and to services of wide sections of the community. This transition was marked by the appearance of service appeal alongside price appeal, by a greater stress on the outward attractiveness, layout and siting of the branches, by a trend away from specialization in a limited number of products, and by the emergence of a number of different types of multiple shop organizations appealing to different sections of the market.

This transition can be illustrated in many ways. The most important outward signs were in the branch shops themselves. Here there was a general trend towards larger, brighter and cleaner shops, containing more elaborate fittings, and the main street siting of these shops. In the case of non-food goods a main street site was an absolute necessity, but increasingly in the food trades the multiple shop branches were shifted from small premises in the back streets to larger shops in the main streets. Further, many organizations were no longer satisfied with taking over existing premises and adapting them, but rebuilt the property to fit their needs.

The prices charged by most multiple shop retailers remained low, though the gap between the prices charged by multiple shop retailers and those charged by other retailers would appear to have narrowed in these years compared with the gap in the pre-1914 era. In addition to the attraction of low prices, however, the multiple shops now began to provide a vastly improved standard of service and a wider range and choice of goods. The range of goods and number of lines in a particular trade carried by multiple shop retailers did not in most instances equal those carried by the independent retailer or the department store. Few multiple shop firms however continued the pre-1914 practice of limiting their products to, say, six types of provisions, or to a dozen styles of boots. In the footwear trade, in fact, some multiple shop firms were by the 'thirties offering a range of fittings and styles far surpassing that offered by any other type of retailer. Finally, alongside the 'cash and carry' approach of the earlier type of multiple shop retailer, firms were springing up that emphasized home delivery of goods, weekly orders, and free credit to customers. Words such as 'cash' and 'low price' were being eliminated from the titles of firms and from their advertisements, and in their place were being substituted words and phrases such as 'high class', 'family', and 'retailers of taste'.

The integration of production and distribution

The control of manufacturing facilities by multiple shop retailers, or the integration of production and distribution, was an important feature of the development of this form of retailing in some trades. The rapid rise in the inter-war years in multiple shop trading in the men's outerwear trade, in the bread and flour confectionery trade and in the wallpaper and paint trade was directly linked with the existence of integration. The control of pasteurization and bottling plant similarly assisted the rise of multiple shop retailing in the milk trade. Further, integration continued to be of importance for firms in the grocery trade, the footwear trade and the chemists' goods trade. On the other hand the rise of multiple shop retailing in the women's wear trade, the furniture trade, the bicycle and electrical goods trade and the household goods trade owed little or nothing to integration. The particular reasons for the development of integration in individual trades are discussed in later chapters but generally a measure of integration developed in those trades where the commodities were relatively standardized and where significant economies of scale in production were obtained.

In the inter-war years, however, while the overall importance of integration in relation to the total trade of multiple shop retailers may have increased slightly, owing mainly to integration in the men's outer-wear and bread trades, there was no marked trend in this direction. The increased complexity of the production of some goods, the control of the production by a few firms and the large amounts of capital required to enter the field placed limits on the growth of integration. Further, even where the firms did possess manufacturing facilities there was the problem of manufacturers' branding and advertising. The con-sumer no longer asked, for example, for plum jam or marmalade or for a pair of shoes sized 4½, but for some particular brand, and the retailer's 'own brand' was not always considered an adequate substitute. While some goods, for example men's suits and bread, became more standardized in the inter-war years and integration could develop, differentiation in product was the characteristic of other trades, such as footwear, grocery and chemists' goods, and there was some decline in the importance of integration.

Many of these developments, that is larger firms, bigger branches, more expensive sites and fittings, and integration, meant an increased demand for fixed capital. Self-financing or financing out of profits was no longer adequate if a firm wished to expand rapidly and to keep pace with its competitors in the type of branches opened. In the inter-war years and in the years following 1945, a large number of multiple shop firms became public limited liability companies and raised capital for expansion on the open market. By 1950 some 75–80% of the total number of branches of firms with 25 or more branches each were con-trolled by public companies. The era of private financing, at least for the medium-and large-sized firms, had passed.

The rise of variety chain stores

The fourth important development in multiple shop retailing in these years was the emergence of variety chain store trading, a development that in some ways cut across the trends that have just been discussed. This form of trading in Britain started in the 'nineties with the Penny Bazaars that Michael Marks established in the North of England, and the first British branch of F. W. Woolworth & Company Ltd., a firm that already had some 600 branches in the United States, was opened in Liverpool in 1909. It was, however, in the inter-war years that this form of multiple shop retailing grew most rapidly, and from an esti-mated 300 variety chain store branches in 1920 the number had risen to some 1,200 in 1939. This increase in numbers does not fully indicate the significance of the rise, as at the same time the size of the average variety chain store branch also grew rapidly, particularly after 1930. In relation to the total sales undertaken by multiple shop retailing organizations, the share of the variety chain store type of firm is estimated to have risen from negligible proportions in 1920 (well under 3 %) to nearly 20 % by 1938.

The firms that were mainly responsible for this striking growth are well known. F. W. Woolworth & Company Ltd., Marks & Spencer Ltd., the British Home Stores Ltd., and Littlewoods Ltd. were the leading firms, but in addition there have been a number of smaller regional firms at different times that adopted broadly the same trading principles. Variety chain store organizations followed the multiple shop pattern of development in that as they expanded they opened identical types of units in different areas, though there were a number of significant differences of emphasis in the trading policies pursued by variety chain stores as compared with those of most other types of multiple shop firms.

There were three main features of variety chain store trading. The sales policy was based on the open display of a wide variety of goods covering many trades in large premises utilizing the whole ground floor space of the building and sometimes the basement or first floor, and not merely the part adjoining the street. Customers were invited to walk round, select and buy, but were never under any obligation or the slightest pressure to make a purchase. The approach of the variety chain store to the customer was not the traditional retailing theme of 'What would you like? We will see if we can get it.' but 'This is what we have. We hope you will buy it.' The second feature was the charging of clearly-marked low prices, a function of the economies of bulk buying of individual lines and of low operating costs. Distributive service was reduced to a minimum, the customer practically serving himself, and the technique of display and selling adopted gave the variety stores a considerable advantage over most of their competitors in that un-skilled and therefore low paid labour was employed in the shops. The third feature of variety chain store trading paralleled more closely that of other multiple shop retailers, namely the establishment of close links with and the making of bulk purchases from producers. The distinctive feature of variety chain store buying was the tremendous range of goods bought and the very large number of separate producers who supplied the goods to any one variety chain store organization.

Individual variety chain store organizations, while following these general principles, gave a particular emphasis to certain aspects. F. W. Woolworth & Company Ltd., for example, displayed a very wide range of commodities, all of which had a very low unit value. Marks & Spencer Ltd., on the other hand, carried a smaller range of goods, allocating well over half their counter-space to low-priced articles of clothing, but planned in much greater detail than did other organizations the production, design and style of the goods to be sold.

Assistance and advice to their suppliers, even to the extent of helping the firms mechanize, lay out and extend their factories and the purchase of the raw and semi-finished materials used by their suppliers were features of the trading policy of this firm.

Whatever the particular emphasis in policy adopted, however, the variety chain store method of retailing fulfilled an important shopping need of the consumers. The success of this form of retailing was not dependent to any great extent upon the development of large-scale production of the particular goods sold, as was the case with the multiple shop firm specializing in a particular trade: it was more the outcome of the application of large-scale retailing techniques to the distribution of a wide range of physically small, low-priced, near-essential goods. The variety chain store combined many of the department store selling and merchandising techniques with the specialist multiple shop buying and organizational techniques. And this new method of distribution was applied to commodities and to a market that had hitherto been the practically undisturbed province of the small-scale retailer, the draper, the outfitter, the ironmonger, the confectioner and the general shop.

The rapid growth in importance of these organizations, which sold goods only on a cash and carry basis, which never advertised, which never or rarely sold branded and manufacturer-advertised goods, and which never pressed a customer to buy, was in somewhat ironic contrast to the great emphasis that was being increasingly placed in all other sectors of distribution on salesmanship, on advertising, on branding and on greater service to the consumer. The distinctive contribution of the variety chain stores to the distributive trades was their perfection of a new technique of merchandising and selling. If the pioneer multiple shop firms in the footwear, grocery and meat trades at the end of the nineteenth century could be said to have taken the lead by selling 'new' goods in new ways, the variety chain stores in the inter-war years showed how to sell 'old' goods in new ways. And as the consumer had been attracted by the inexpensive mass distribution methods of the early specialist multiple shop firms, so he was attracted by the simple selling techniques of the variety chain stores.

The relative importance of multiple shop trading

Estimates of the share in total retail trade undertaken by multiple shop organizations, including variety chain stores, between 1920 and 1950 are presented in Table 17. The estimates given above for the years 1900 and 1910 are also included in this table to give an indication of the long-term trend.

Table 17. *Estimated share of multiple shop firms in the total retail sales by main commodity groups, 1900–50**

Commodity group	Proportion of total retail sales undertaken by multiple shop firms							
	1900 %	1910 %	1920 %	1925 %	1930 %	1935 %	1939 %	1950 %
Food and household stores	3·5–4·5	6·5–9·0	8·5–11·0	10·5–12·0	12·5–14·0	14·0–16·0	16·5–18·0	17·5–19·0
Confectionery, reading and writing materials, and tobacco goods	1·5–3·0	2·5–4·0	3·5– 5·0	4·5– 5·5	6·0– 7·0	7·5– 9·5	9·5–11·5	9·0–11·0
Clothing and footwear	3·5–5·5	6·0–8·0	7·0–10·0	11·5–14·0	15·0–17·0	18·5–21·0	24·0–27·0	27·0–30·5
Other goods	2·0–3·5	3·5–5·0	5·0– 6·5	8·0–10·0	12·5–15·0	16·5–19·0	21·0–24·0	23·0–27·0
All commodities	3·0–4·5	6·0–7·5	7·0–10·0	9·5–11·5	12·0–14·0	14·0–17·0	18·0–19·5	18·0–20·5

* See Chapter IV and Appendix A for a discussion of the basis of the estimates. These estimates of turnover of multiple shop firms are not strictly comparable with the estimates of the total number of multiple shop branches given in Table 13. Table 1 shows the individual commodities included in the main commodity groups.

The individual trades in which the share of multiple shop retailers in 1920 is estimated to have been more than 10 % of the total national trade were footwear, 31–35 %; chemists' goods, 14–17 %; grocery and provisions, 13–16 %; bicycles, sewing machines and electrical goods, 13–15 %. In 1939 the individual trades in which the share of multiple shop retailers is estimated to have been more than 15 % of the total national trade were: footwear, 44–49 %; chemists' goods, 33–37 %; men's clothing, 29–31 %; pottery, glassware and ironmongery, 24–26 %; grocery and provisions, 22–25 %; jewellery, toys, sports goods and fancy goods, 21–23 %; milk, 20–23 %; bicycles, sewing machines, radio and electrical goods, 19–21 %; women's and girls' wear, 16–18 %; household stores, 15–18 %; bread and flour confectionery, 15–18 %; newspapers, magazines, stationery and books, 15–17 %; and furniture and furnishings, 15–17 %.

7. THE IMPORTANCE OF LARGE-SCALE RETAILING

The information given in Tables 11, 12 and 17 above may now be combined to show for the years 1900–50 the share undertaken by each of the different types of large-scale retailer in the national retail trade and the share, by difference, of all other types of retailers. These

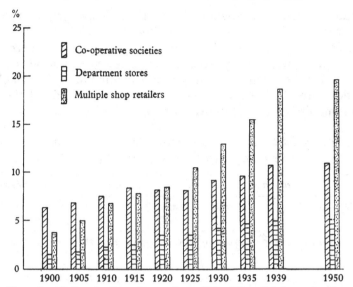

Chart I. All Commodities: Proportions of Total Retail Sales undertaken
by Different Economic Types of Large-scale Retailer, 1900–50

Table 18. *Estimated shares of the different economic types of retailer in
the total retail trade, 1900–50*

Type of organization	Proportion of total retail sales undertaken by the different types of retailers							
	1900 %	1910 %	1920 %	1925 %	1930 %	1935 %	1939 %	1950 %
Co-operative Societies	6·0– 7·0	7·0– 8·0	7·5– 9·0	7·5– 8·5	8·5–10·0	8·5–10·5	10·0–11·5	10·0–12·0
Department stores	1·0– 2·0	1·5– 3·0	3·0– 4·0	3·0– 4·0	3·5– 5·0	4·0– 5·5	4·5– 5·5	4·5– 6·0
Multiple shop retailers	3·0– 4·5	6·0– 7·5	7·0–10·0	9·5–11·5	12·0–14·0	14·0–17·0	18·0–19·5	18·0–20·5
Other retailers (by difference)	86·5–90·0	81·5–85·5	77·0–82·5	76·0–80·0	71·0–76·0	67·0–73·5	63·5–67·5	61·5–67·5

estimates are presented in Table 18, and Chart I shows the shares of
each of the large-scale retailers in the total trade in different years
from 1900 to 1950.

Above it was suggested that the share of large-scale retailers in the
national trade at the beginning of the third quarter of the nineteenth
century was, at most, of the order of 2–3%. By 1900 the share of

large-scale retailers had grown to some 11–12 %, by 1925 to 21–24 %, and by 1950 to about 34–38 %. Except for the years 1939–50 the rate of expansion would appear to have been fairly continuous. There were, however, variations in the relative importance of large-scale retailing organizations as between different groups of commodities, and Table 19 shows the share of large-scale retailers in the retail trade of the four main commodity groups in the years 1900–50.

Table 19. *Estimated share of large-scale retailers in the total retail sales by main commodity groups, 1900–50**

Commodity group	Proportion of total retail sales undertaken by large-scale retailers							
	1900 %	1910 %	1920 %	1925 %	1930 %	1935 %	1939 %	1950 %
Food and household stores	11·5–13·5	17·0–19·0	20·0–24·0	21·0–25·0	25·0–28·5	28·5–32·0	32·5–36·0	33·5–38·5
Confectionery, reading and writing materials and tobacco goods	3·0– 4·5	4·5– 5·5	6·0– 7·0	7·0– 8·5	9·0–10·5	12·0–14·0	14·5–16·5	15·0–17·5
Clothing and footwear	14·0–16·0	20·0–21·5	23·0–25·5	29·5–32·0	34·0–38·5	39·0–43·0	45·0–50·0	50·0–54·0
Other goods	6·0– 7·5	9·0–11·0	14·0–16·0	18·0–20·5	25·0–27·5	29·0–33·0	35·0–39·0	39·0–43·5
All commodities	11·0–12·5	15·5–17·5	19·0–21·5	21·0–23·5	24·5–28·0	28·0–32·0	33·0–36·0	34·0–38·0

* The changes in the pattern of consumers' retail expenditure in these years, in particular the increase in the relative importance of the confectionery, reading and writing materials and tobacco goods group from 7·6 % of total retail sales in 1900 to 14·4 % in 1938 and 21·1 % in 1950, influenced the rate of increase of the share of total retail sales undertaken by large-scale retailers.

Some detail may be added in respect of large-scale retailing in individual consumer goods trades. Table 19 suggests—taking the middle point of the range—that in 1920 the large-scale retailers were responsible for about 20 % of the national retail sales. The individual trades in which the share of large-scale retailers was estimated to have been greater than the average in that year were: the footwear trade in which, taking the middle point of the range, the large-scale retailers were responsible for some 44 % of the total trade; the grocery and provisions trades, 34 %; the women's wear trade, 23 %; and the household stores trade, 22 %. In 1939 Table 19 suggests that large-scale retailers were responsible for some 34–35 % of the total trade. The individual trades in which the share of the large-scale retailer was higher than this average

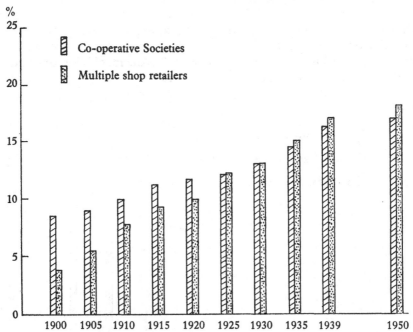

Chart II. Food and Household Stores: Proportions of Total Retail Sales undertaken by Different Economic Types of Large-scale Retailer, 1900–50

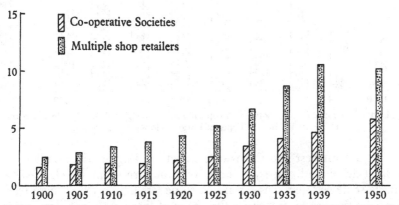

Chart III. Chocolate and Sugar Confectionery, Tobacco, Reading and Writing Materials: Proportions of Total Retail Sales undertaken by Different Economic Types of Large-scale Retailer, 1900–50

were: the footwear trade in which the share of large-scale retailers, taking the middle point of the range, was estimated at 61 %; the women's wear trade, 47 %; the grocery and provisions trade, 47 %; the dairy trade, 47 %; the chemists' goods trade, 42 %; the pottery and glass, hardware and ironmongery trade, 42 %; the men's clothing trade, 42 %; and the furniture and furnishings trade, 39 %.

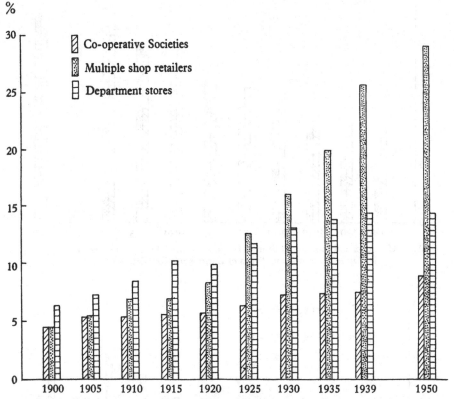

Chart IV. Clothing and Footwear: Proportions of Total Retail Sales undertaken by Different Economic Types of Large-scale Retailer, 1900–50

Of equal interest are the trades in which large-scale retailing was the least developed. In 1939 there were four trades in which the share of large-scale retailers was estimated to be less than 15 %. These trades were: the fish trade, in which the share of large-scale retailers, taking the middle point of the range, was some 13 %; the tobacco goods trade, 14 %; and the fruit and vegetables trade, 10 %.

Finally, the data given in a number of tables above can be re-arranged to enable comparisons to be made more readily between the different rates of growth of the different types of large-scale retailing organization

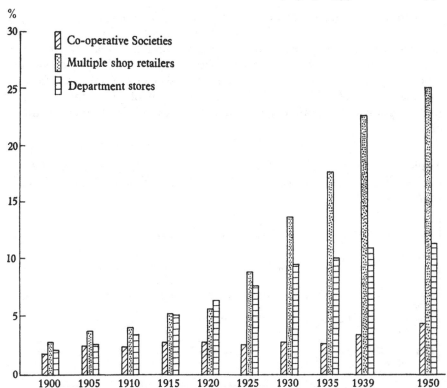

Chart V. Other Goods (Chemists' Goods, Furniture and Furnishings, Electrical Goods, Bicycles, Hardware, Ironmongery, Pottery, Glass, Jewellery, Leather Goods, Toys, Sports Goods, Fancy Goods): Proportions of Total Retail Sales undertaken by Different Economic Types of Large-scale Retailer, 1900–50

Table 20. *Estimated shares of the different economic types of retailer in the total retail sales of food and household stores, 1900–50**

Type of organization	Proportion of total retail sales undertaken by the different types of retailer					
	1900 %	1910 %	1920 %	1930 %	1939 %	1950 %
Co-operative Societies	7·5– 9·5	9·0–11·0	11·0–12·5	12·5–14·0	15·0–18·0	16·5–18·0
Multiple shop retailers	3·5– 4·5	6·5– 9·0	8·5–11·0	12·5–14·0	16·5–18·0	17·5–19·0
Other retailers (by differ-ence)	86·0–89·0	80·0–84·5	76·5–80·5	72·0–75·0	64·0–68·5	63·0–66·0

* Department store sales of these goods represented a very small proportion of total retail sales. They are therefore included in the 'other retailers' group.

in each of the main commodity groups. Tables 20, 21, 22 and 23 show in relation to food and household stores, confectionery, reading and writing material and tobacco, clothing and footwear and other goods, the relative rates of progress between 1900 and 1950 of each of the large-scale retailers. This progress is also shown in chart form in Charts II, III, IV and V. For convenience of presentation, the middle point of the range given in the tables has been used in the charts.

Table 21. *Estimated shares of the different economic types of retailer in the total retail sales of confectionery, reading and writing materials and tobacco goods, 1900–50**

Type of organization	Proportion of total retail sales undertaken by the different types of retailer					
	1900 %	1910 %	1920 %	1930 %	1939 %	1950 %
Co-operative Societies	1·0– 2·0	1·0– 2·5	1·5– 2·5	2·0– 4·0	3·5– 5·5	5·0– 6·5
Multiple shop retailers	1·5– 3·0	2·5– 4·0	3·5– 5·0	6·0– 7·0	9·5–11·5	9·0–11·0
Other retailers (by difference)	95·0–97·5	93·5–96·5	92·5–95·0	89·0–92·0	83·0–87·0	82·5–86·0

* Department store sales of these goods represented a very small proportion of total retail sales. They are therefore included in the 'other retailers' group.

Table 22. *Estimated shares of the different economic types of retailer in the total retail sales of clothing and footwear, 1900–50*

Type of organization	Proportion of total retail sales undertaken by the different types of retailer					
	1900 %	1910 %	1920 %	1930 %	1939 %	1950 %
Co-operative Societies	4·0– 5·0	4·5– 6·0	5·0– 6·5	6·5– 8·0	6·5– 8·5	8·0– 9·5
Department stores	5·5– 7·0	8·0– 9·0	9·0–11·0	12·0–14·0	13·0–15·5	13·0–15·5
Multiple shop retailers	3·5– 5·5	6·0– 8·0	7·0–10·0	15·0–17·0	24·0–27·0	27·0–30·5
Other retailers (by difference)	82·5–87·0	77·0–81·5	72·5–79·0	61·0–66·5	49·0–56·5	44·5–52·0

Table 23. *Estimated shares of the different economic types of retailer in the total retail sales of other goods, 1900–50*

Type of organization	Proportion of total retail sales undertaken by the different types of retailer					
	1900 %	1910 %	1920 %	1930 %	1939 %	1950 %
Co-operative Societies	1·5– 2·5	1·5– 3·0	2·0–3·5	2·0– 3·5	3·0– 4·0	4·0– 5·0
Department stores	1·5– 2·5	3·0– 4·0	5·5– 7·5	9·0–10·5	10·0–12·0	11·0–12·5
Multiple shop retailers	2·0– 3·5	3·5– 5·0	5·0– 6·5	12·5–15·0	21·0–24·0	23·0–27·0
Other retailers (by difference)	91·5–95·0	88·0–92·0	82·5–87·5	71·0–76·5	60·0–66·0	55·5–62·0

Rates of growth of different types of large-scale retailer

The rate of increase of the share of multiple shop retailers in the total retail trade was faster than that of both the Co-operative Societies and the department stores. The relative importance of multiple shop retailing in the total trade was less than that of Co-operative Societies in the years up to 1920, but in that year these two types of large-scale retailing organizations were of roughly equal importance. The Co-operative movement ran into difficulties in the post-war slump and by 1925 the multiple shop form of retailing was of greater relative importance. The faster rate of increase of multiple shop trading was maintained up to 1950. The share of department stores throughout these years was less than that of either of the other two types of large-scale retailer.

In the food and household stores group, the multiple shop retailers from 1900 to the middle of the inter-war years increased their share of the total trade more rapidly than did the Co-operative Societies, but after 1930 the rise in the relative importance of the two types of retailing organizations was approximately parallel, with multiple shop retailing rising a little more rapidly. In the confectionery, reading and writing materials and tobacco goods group, no type of large-scale retailer held a significant share of the total trade. The progress of multiple shop retailing was, however, rather faster than that of other types, particularly in the inter-war years. This progress, it should be added, was due as much to the growth of variety chain store trading as to the development of specialist multiple shop retailing in these trades. In both the clothing and the other goods groups, the outstanding development was the very rapid rise in the relative importance of multiple shop retailing in the inter-war years. In both groups the multiple shops caught up with and passed the department stores and left the Co-operative Societies far behind.

The rise in the importance of multiple shop retailing in the total national retail trade in the inter-war years was due largely to the successful extension of this form of trading to goods other than food. The Co-operative Societies increased their share of the national food trade, but with food representing a smaller proportion of total consumers' retail expenditure and the failure of the Co-operative Societies to make substantial headway in the trades other than food, the rate of progress of Co-operative Societies in retail trade as a whole was slower than that of the multiple shop organizations. The rate of progress of department stores in both the clothing and the other goods trades was roughly the same, and in both trades there was a slight decline in the rate of increase in the inter-war years.

8. FACTORS INFLUENCING THE GROWTH OF LARGE-SCALE RETAILING

The general reasons for the growth of large-scale retailing and the advantages and economies secured by such methods were discussed above in relation to the developments in the distributive trades in the years up to the First World War. In the inter-war years the same factors continued to operate. The basic prerequisites for the development of scale in retailing, that is the existence of large-scale production or the possibility of bulk purchases of imported goods and the existence of a consistent and relatively homogeneous demand for the products, continued to obtain in the consumer goods trades, where large-scale retailing organizations were already established by 1914. These conditions also began to emerge in new sectors and in new trades. In particular there was a spread of these conditions to many trades concerned with goods other than food, and contemporaneously there was a shift in consumers' retail expenditure away from food to other goods. Further, with experience and scientific training in managerial skills the techniques of large-scale retailing became more effective, and this assisted the development of this form of retailing in trades, in areas and in markets where the circumstances were not overwhelmingly favourable. The general advantages and techniques of scale in retailing remained largely unchanged in the inter-war years but there were some shifts of emphasis between the particular advantages of scale. These shifts can be noted briefly.

The buying advantages of the large-scale retailers

There would appear to have been some reduction in the buying economies secured by large-scale retailers in these years compared with the years before 1914. This suggestion applies to large-scale retailing as a whole and not necessarily to all individual firms or to particular types of retailer which may have improved their buying techniques. It is difficult to support this suggestion with statistical data, but there is some evidence of a strengthening of the position of manufacturers and producers vis-à-vis the large-scale retailers, in spite of the growth in size of many of the latter. The growth of large-scale production, the use by manufacturers of branding and advertising to build up goodwill for their products, and the trend towards combination between manufacturers gave them greater bargaining power. Similarly, in home agriculture the formation of Marketing Boards strengthened the position of the farmers. The development of grading and marking and the use of standards, particularly in the imported foodstuffs trades, also reduced some of the advantages that large-scale retailers had previously obtained through the employment of specialist buyers who knew the market thoroughly. Large and small retailers were placed on equal terms in their knowledge and recognition of quality and standards. The lower terms for bulk purchases of all kinds of goods still existed, but the days of fantastic purchasing coups, which characterized the trading of some of the earlier large-scale retailers, appeared to have passed. The only exceptions occurred in the depth of the depression when the unloading of stocks by manufacturers and the sale of job lots gave many large-scale buyers special opportunities and advantages.

At the same time, however, the parallel spread of homogeneity in consumer behaviour and taste and the growing importance of style and fashion in many trades gave the large-scale retailers new buying advantages. The gains from the first are obvious. Small markets were merged to form larger markets and the large-scale retailers operating in the larger markets could expand, place larger orders and secure lower prices. In style and fashion goods the employment by large-scale retailers of expert buyers and the specialization of the various elements making up the buying function, such as estimating demand and gauging changes in consumer taste, gave these firms an advantage over the smaller-scale retailer. The large-scale retailer was often able to anticipate demand, to place large orders and to have the goods on the hangers or the shelves before the small-scale retailer had even seen a sample of the new style in the wholesalers' showrooms. Naturally the risks taken by the large-scale retailers in this type of trade were greater than those taken by the small-scale retailers, but the gains were also much greater.

The advantages in sales organization

On the selling and retailing side there was also a change in the type of advantages secured by scale. The smaller economies obtained by bulk buying, the spread of resale price maintenance, and the rising operating costs meant that the large-scale retailers in the inter-war years no longer had a significant selling-price advantage over the small-scale retailers. On the other hand, the growing stress placed on siting, on size of shop, on window display and interior layout and on service to the consumer as weapons in the struggle to gain a larger share of the market operated in many instances to the advantage of the large-scale retailers. In the siting of shops, the large-scale retailers had the financial strength and the expert knowledge of real estate to enable them to out-bid and out-manoeuvre their smaller competitors. Options would be offered and leases and renewals of leases granted to firms with share capitals running into millions where they would be refused to a smaller-sized unit. Again the large-scale retailers were able to employ specialists on their window display and shop layout problems. They could buy their equipment in bulk more cheaply, and sometimes established a separate shop-fitting department within the firm. Further, in so far as the more elaborate shop exteriors and interiors meant an increase in the ratio of fixed investment to total investment, this presented fewer difficulties to the public limited company than to the small retailer who had invested his life's savings in a shop.

The demand for variety and selection of goods that developed in some trades and the demand for service that developed in others similarly did not handicap the large-scale retailer. In many instances and trades the reverse was true. A half, if not more, of the secret of handling successfully a fair selection and range of goods in a given trade was skilled buying and control over the rate of stock turn in the shop. If stock figures were obtained that revealed regularly and accurately what goods, what sizes and what lines were moving and what were not, rapid decisions could be made in relation to ordering, pricing, mark-downs, display and so on. Without such a system the buying, stocking and pricing policies tended to stagger from shortages of lines to mountains of 'cold pig', from exorbitant prices to ridiculous panic sales. The large-scale retailers with their emphasis—almost a fetish in some instances—on stock records were better able to master these problems than the small retailer who had difficulty in finding time to take stock, let alone interpret the figures recorded. The standardization in sizes and the simplification of ranges of colours and shapes that took place in these years in many trades, and which arose from the development of mass-production methods based on a close knowledge of the common essentials in demand, assisted both the large and small retailer in their stock-holding problems. The large retailer in addition was in a better position to gauge the trends as a whole and act with speed to keep up the rate of stock turn and to eliminate the slow-moving stocks.

In the organization of services to the consumer, particularly of standardized services such as bread or milk delivery, large-scale operation again brought advantages. The small-scale retailer however who planned an intensive service covering a very limited area was not always behind the larger-scale retailer, who was often faced with the problem of providing a less intensive service over a much larger area.

These particular advantages and shifts in emphasis were superimposed upon the general advantages of scale in retailing that were discussed in the previous chapter. The incidence of both the general and particular advantages, however, varied between the different types of large-scale retailer and the advantages and problems of each type of large-scale retailer will be discussed in turn.

9. THE PROGRESS AND PROBLEMS OF THE CO-OPERATIVE SOCIETIES

The Co-operative Societies continued to advance in the inter-war years in the food trades but made relatively little headway in other trades. Apart from the politico-economic appeal of Co-operative trading arising from the democratic system of control and the payment of a dividend, the advance in the food trades would appear to have been largely due to two factors: firstly the spread of the Co-operative movement to the Midlands and the South of England, with the development of a stable homogeneous working-class market in these areas; and secondly the changes in the methods of production and distribution of bread and milk in these years which permitted and encouraged the use of large-scale methods. The Co-operative Societies were among the first to exploit the possibilities of scale in the production, processing and distribution of these staple lines. The fact that these goods were not advertised or branded by private manufacturers to any significant extent was an advantage to the Societies, and their position as the main distributor of groceries and provisions to a large number of households assisted their development as the main distributor of bread and milk to the same households.

The obverse of this development in the food trades should also be emphasized, as it has an important bearing on the nature of Co-operative progress in these years and on the future possibilities and scope of this form of trading. Co-operative development before 1914 had been based mainly on the distribution of groceries and provisions to the working classes of the North of England and of Scotland. The limit of Co-operative penetration of these markets had not been reached by 1914, and some increase in Co-operative trading in these goods and in these areas, particularly in Scotland, took place in the inter-war years. But if in these inter-war years there had been no new areas into which the Co-operative movement could expand, and if there had been no changes in production and distribution conditions making large-scale methods applicable to additional foodstuffs, the overall rate of progress of Co-operative trading would have been negligible.[1]

There were a number of reasons for the relative failure of the Co-operative Societies to make significant headway in the particular trades, such as groceries and provisions, and in the particular areas, such as the North of England, in which they were already well established by the beginning of the First World War. Four of the reasons can be mentioned briefly. First, the Co-operative appeal tended to be limited to the working classes and no attempt was made by individual Societies to vary this appeal and attract customers in other sectional markets by the provision of additional services or higher quality goods or goods at lower prices. The Co-operative appeal was standardized, and while the limit of this appeal may not have been reached it was becoming evident that such a limit existed. Secondly, the practice of housewives in the inter-war years of making smaller and more frequent purchases of essential goods tended to put the Co-operative Societies at a disadvantage. The Societies had always pursued a policy of opening a small number of large branches rather than a large number of small branches located in every shopping area however minor. To some extent this policy was being reversed in the inter-war years. The number of Co-operative stores or branches in given areas increased; many Societies put travelling shops on the road, and goods such as bread and milk were delivered to the home. But in very many areas a large number of potential purchasers at the Societies' branches were lost, as housewives were not prepared to walk a long distance or use the public transport system to buy small quantities of essential goods. Thirdly, the grocery trade in the inter-war years was highly competitive both in relation to retailing and to branding and advertising by manufacturers. The retail Co-operative Societies had a bias towards the less well-known products of the Co-operative Wholesale Societies and away from the private-manufacturer-advertised brands, and this fact tended to tell against the Societies in this competitive market. Finally the areas of the North of

---

[1] In the grocery and provisions trade the share of the Co-operative Societies in the national trade is estimated to have risen from some 18–20% in 1920 to 22–24% in 1938. This includes the increase in the share of the trade in the Midlands and South in these years. The Co-operative share of the national trade in bread and milk in the same period is estimated to have risen from 6–9% in 1920 to 19–21% in 1938.

England and Scotland where the Co-operative movement was strongest were, of course, areas that suffered particularly in the inter-war years from unemployment, shifts of population and inconsistent demand.

Co-operative trading in goods other than food

In the trades other than food, while the production and demand conditions in these years permitted and encouraged the development of scale in retailing, for example in the men's wear trade, in sections of the women's wear trade, in the electrical goods trade and in the chemists' goods trade, the progress of Co-operative Societies was slow. The main reason for this slowness was inherent in the whole character of Co-operative trading. Each Retail Society had a monopoly of Co-operative trading within its boundaries. Any expansion of Co-operative trading had to be decided upon and undertaken by the existing Society. And when such an expansion was undertaken the new types or lines of goods were sold alongside the existing lines. The constitution and traditions of the movement prevented the emergence of a Society specializing in the sale of, say, footwear or men's clothing with selling points all over the country. The approach to the sale of new ranges of goods by Co-operative Societies was therefore the village general store or department store approach rather than the specialized multiple shop approach. Additional lines were stocked if the members demanded them, but national specialization in the buying and selling of the goods in separate trades was out of the question, and specialization within a Society was slow to develop and confined to the very large Societies. In some small Societies the grocery buyer bought the drapery goods as well as the grocery goods, and even in the medium-sized Societies there would often be only two buyers, one for food and one for 'dry goods'.

In the years before 1914 the general store approach to the sale of goods other than food did not appear to be a serious handicap to the Societies. The working-class demand for these goods was a stable one, the call for variety and style was at a minimum, and the competitors of the Societies in the working class market sold the same type of products as the Co-operative stores. In the inter-war years, however, there were radical changes in both the character and the retailing methods of these trades. On the one hand there was the stress on fashion, style, variety and novelty, and on the other hand the emphasis on main-street shopping and display of these goods. The retailers making the greatest progress in the sale of these goods in the inter-war years, that is the multiple shop firms and the department stores, succeeded in large part because of their specialization of the buying, selling and administrative functions connected with the sale of these goods, their heavy outlay on shops, sites and display, and the flexibility of these organizations in catering for different price and quality markets. Only by adopting a number, if not all, of these practices could the Co-operative Societies have hoped to increase significantly their share in these trades, but the adoption of such techniques would have involved a fundamental change in Co-operative structure and trading policies and in the organization of Co-operative production.[1]

Some changes were made in the organization of Co-operative production in the 'thirties, but the Wholesale Societies still had to deal with hundreds of different buyers each with their separate problems. Some Management Committees encouraged the development of a measure of specialization within their Societies in certain dry goods trades, but the obstacles were many. Further, the slowness of the movement in introducing hire-purchase schemes owing to the traditional opposition to credit, the hesitation shown by most Management Committees in paying the high salaries demanded by experts in the various trades, the timidity of many Societies in regard to heavy capital investment in main-street sites, and the possession by other Societies of old and badly-sited central premises, were additional handicaps. Therefore while the Co-operative Societies achieved some increase in their sales of goods other than food, and while their share of the national trade in these goods also rose owing to the increase in membership, the methods of organization and the trading policies of the Societies limited the economies and advantages of scale that could be obtained.

10. THE PROGRESS AND PROBLEMS OF THE DEPARTMENT STORES

The progress made by department stores in the clothing and in the miscellaneous other goods trades in the inter-war years was due mainly to three factors. Firstly, this method of retailing was well suited to meet the growing demand for variety, selection and choice and the spread of fashion consciousness. The shift in the pattern of consumers' retail expenditure away from foodstuffs similarly assisted the department stores, in that they had already an important standing and reputation in the trades other than food. A second factor was the extension of this form of retailing to new areas and new price markets. Thirdly, department stores through their method of operation secured many of the advantages and economies which, as suggested above, arose out of

---

[1] A problem facing the Co-operative movement in respect of some of these trades, for example bicycles, electrical goods, books and stationery and chemists' goods, was the practice of resale price maintenance. In some instances the private manufacturers and traders regarded the payment of a dividend on purchases as an infringement of resale price maintenance and the Co-operative Societies either did not handle the goods or were unable to pay a dividend on their sale.

expert merchandising and specialization of function in the trades other than food. This advantage was particularly marked in the inter-war years as department stores increasingly introduced scientific methods of management and control.

On the other hand the progress of department stores was by no means uninterrupted, and at the outbreak of the Second World War many problems were confronting the leaders of this form of retailing. Some of the stores were having difficulty in increasing or even in some cases in maintaining their turnover. For many the limits to physical size and to the number of different departments had been reached. Further, stores long established in central districts of the large towns were finding it increasingly difficult and costly to attract customers. The middle classes upon whose custom the large stores depended had been the first to move to the outer suburbs of the towns, and central shopping expeditions were made less frequently. The rise of suburban department stores was in part the answer, though this did not help the central stores. The department store form of trading involved heavy capital outlay on a particular site, and individual stores were unable to adapt themselves to long-term shifts in consumer living or shopping habits.

A much more serious question facing department stores was the rise of multiple shop retailing in many of the trades in which the stores had specialized. The department store method of trading, as suggested above, did not depend on the existence of large-scale methods of production; its success lay rather in the co-ordination of supplies from a large number of producers and provision of a much wider selection and range of goods, and more attractive shopping conditions, than could be offered by competitors. In the inter-war years the development of large-scale production and the improvements in retailing techniques and organization permitted and encouraged the rise of multiple shop organizations in trades, for example women's clothing, that had hitherto been a particular province of department stores. These multiple shop firms could offer in well-sited, attractive shops a selection and variety of goods nearly as wide as that offered by the stores. The purchasing power of the multiple shop organizations in a given line or group of goods was very much greater than that of the single department within a department store. The merchandising techniques employed began to equal and sometimes surpass those of department stores. Finally, the multiple shop branch was a far more flexible unit, far more adaptable to changes in consumer shopping or living habits, than the department store. The unique attraction of buying a large number of different products under one roof remained to the department store, but the uniqueness of many of the other advantages was passing.

Up to the Second World War the threat to department stores of competition from multiple shop retailing must be described as potential rather than actual. The multiple shop retailers in the men's clothing trade, the women's clothing trade and the furniture and pottery trades, for example, traded for the most part in a lower price market than that of department stores. Further, in the fashion trades the objection felt by many women to wearing mass-produced articles that might be worn the same or the next day by their neighbours had not yet been overcome. The successful growth of multiple shop retailing was, however, setting a limit to a possible low-price appeal by department stores. It was beginning to affect directly the progress of the smaller suburban and provincial department stores, which did not have in the same measure the superior attractions of the shopping amenities that were possessed by the larger central stores. Even in these central stores, however, the practice, just starting in the 'thirties, of leasing specialist departments within the store, for example for footwear, cosmetics, jewellery and woollen goods, to multiple shop organizations was an indication of the advantages of the specialist retailer.

II. THE PROGRESS AND PROBLEMS OF THE MULTIPLE SHOP RETAILERS

Many of the factors leading to the rapid development of multiple shop retailing in all types of trades in the inter-war years have been touched upon above.[1] The most important factors suggested were firstly the continued growth of large-scale production methods in consumer goods trades which made possible the use of large-scale distribution methods, secondly the trend towards homogeneity of demand as between different areas of the country and between different classes, thirdly the widening of the appeal of multiple shop retailers so that this type of retailing was effective in a number of different markets instead of being concentrated as in the pre-1914 period on the working-class market, and fourthly the improvement and refinement in multiple shop trading techniques. This improvement made possible both the successful application of multiple shop methods to trades in which variety, fashion and style were the important characteristics rather than standardization, and also led to the emergence of a new form of multiple shop retailing organization, the variety chain store. The multiple shop method of large-scale retailing in addition possessed three further advantages that were of particular importance in the inter-war years. These three were the possession of financial resources, opportunity to specialize managerial and technical functions, and flexibility of operation.

---

[1] A summary of the economic advantages of multiple shop retailing is given in Appendix C.

The trend in the inter-war years toward main-street shopping sites with large and costly shop premises gave the multiple shop retailers a great advantage over the small-scale retailer in that the former were able to raise the capital for the development of such sites with much greater ease. Similarly the trend towards hire-purchase trading in a number of commodities such as furniture and electrical goods assisted the financially stronger multiple shop organizations. The advantage arising out of specialization of managerial functions had of course existed from the early beginnings of multiple shop retailing, but in the inter-war years the important gains secured were on the selling side of the organizations rather than on the buying side. Whereas before 1914 the main emphasis had been placed on large-scale and expert buying, in the inter-war years the emphasis was more on the expert planning and standardization of methods of property acquisition and branch siting, of shop layout, fittings and decoration, of window display and lighting, of stock holding and stock control, of transport, delivery and the flow of goods, and of price, staffing and promotion policies. One example out of many of the advantages that flowed from increased specialization of function was the granting of credit to customers by some firms. This practice was made possible by vastly improved methods of staff control in the branches.

The flexibility of multiple shop retailing methods, which was particularly marked in comparison with the organization of Co-operative trading, operated in two ways. In the first place the multiple shop organizations measured and judged the performance of the individual branches solely by their profitability. If certain lines did not sell or if the branch was not making the minimum rate of profit, then the goods could be shifted to other branches where they were selling well or the branch itself could be closed with a view to re-opening in a different area or on a different site. The multiple shop organizations were not under pressure, as were Co-operative Societies, to stock lines because members at meetings insisted they should be stocked, or to carry on a branch at a loss because the Management Committee was reluctant to leave members in an area without a branch of the Society. Further, if an opportunity to open a new branch presented itself, this could be taken without reference to boundary lines or any factors other than the economic advantages of such a development. In the second place, as multiple shop trading was not a movement but a technique applied by a large number of independent firms, the decisions as to the form of application and as to the time and method of application of these techniques were individual decisions of separate, competitive business units. This fact gave the multiple shop form of retailing a flexibility unapproached by the Co-operative movement and led to great diversity of practice in regard to areas served, the location of branches, the price market catered for, the type and range of goods sold and the services provided to the consumer. In the inter-war years in Britain, when the demand for consumer goods was uneven in different parts of the country and uneven and stratified within classes, this flexibility and adaptability of multiple shop retailing was an important factor in its growth.

The many advantages of multiple shop retailing did not, of course, result in a consistently rapid rise in its importance in all trades, nor were all multiple shop firms consistently prosperous. In some trades very little progress was made, for example in fruit and vegetables; in others there was a falling-off in the rate of progress from the late 'twenties onwards, for example in the grocery and provisions trade. Further, there would appear to have been some slowing down in the rate of progress of the specialist multiple shop retailers. The increase in the share of the trade undertaken by multiple shop retailers of all descriptions between 1930 and 1938 was due in large part to the rapid rise in importance of the variety chain store form of retailing and not to a significant rise in the importance of the specialist type of organization.

The fortunes of individual multiple shop organizations within the same trade also varied. Apart from questions of efficiency and ability, some of the firms which had grown to importance in the years before 1914 found it particularly difficult and costly to adapt their trading methods and organization to the new techniques of retailing, and to the shifts in the location and shopping habits of the population. Entirely new firms which built up an organization based on the new retailing methods and on the new areas were often the more successful.

A more general problem facing both new and old multiple shop organizations was arising towards the end of the inter-war years: that of the physical limits of main-street siting. A multiple shop retailer in the 'twenties wishing to acquire a main-street site was usually able to purchase one from an independent retailer who was induced to sell out or who wished to retire. By the late 'thirties there were very few good main street sites that were not already occupied by other multiple shop retailers, department stores, or Co-operative Societies, and these organizations were most unlikely to give up their sites. Town planning controls and the layout of the newer housing estates were also limiting the number of shop sites in the main shopping districts, and for many multiple shop firms in the late 'thirties the desire to expand was not being matched with the physical opportunity to do so. In the case of individual firms this deadlock was resolved by amalgamation with another multiple organization, but such amalgamations did not solve the problem for multiple shop retailing as a whole.

12. THE SMALL-SCALE OR INDEPENDENT RETAILERS

The small-scale retailer, almost by definition, could not compete with the large-scale retailer in economies of buying, in specialization of function, in heavy outlay on large shops in main-street sites, or in the many other advantages discussed above of the large-scale organization. The small-scale retailer, however, had a number of different advantages. In the first place, as a business unit he was far more flexible than the retailing units of the large-scale organizations. The multiple shop firm or the Co-operative Society had, for example, a minimum size and turnover below which a branch could not be operated. These firms had fixed expenses such as the rental, the branch manager's salary, the cost of decoration, fixtures and layout of the shop, and the share in the total overhead charges of the whole organization which determined the bottom limit of turnover per branch or store. The independent retailer, on the other hand, had, almost literally, no limit or minimum size at all. From the parlour shop based on the part-time services of the wife or opened to eke out an old age pension, to the street barrow and to the lock-up shop employing assistants, all sizes of independent retailers existed and were able to operate in areas and sections of markets closed to larger-scale retailers as uneconomic. The trend in the inter-war years in the food and other trades away from relatively infrequent purchases of bulk goods to frequent purchases of very small quantities of goods had tended to accentuate the importance of the location of the shop in relation to the customers and to break up some of the older larger markets into a number of smaller ones. The small-scale retailer with no minimum limit as to size or turnover could enter and serve these very small markets. The gradual shifts in the population had the same effect in that in the areas where the population was slowly declining or was slowly rising the marginal shopkeepers, the last to leave and the first to enter, were the small-scale retailers.

A second advantage the small-scale retailer had over the large-scale unit in a number of trades was the variety of different goods stocked. Overlapping between trades, as mentioned above, was a feature of certain sections of the retail market in the inter-war years, and the small retailers located in the very small shopping areas and in side streets were rarely specialists. As this overlapping between trades was most marked in the case of commodities that were resale price maintained, the consumer lost nothing in price by purchasing at the mixed shop close at hand rather than visiting the specialist in the main street, and gained something in convenience. The large-scale retailers from the very nature of their trading methods could not compete with the small mixed retailer in the range of different goods stocked. Department stores and variety chain stores both stocked a wide range of goods but were located in major shopping areas.

Another, though less tangible and possibly less certain, advantage of the small-scale retailer was the quality of personal service and skill he could give his customers in contrast to the so-called impersonal service of the branch manager or assistant of the large-scale undertaking. The importance of this factor varied between trades and classes. Some customers preferred the impersonal efficiency of the branch shop to the friendliness of the private shopkeeper who often knew details of the health and wealth of the whole family. Others found the private shop-keeper far more accommodating in allowing credit, or they welcomed the show of a little extra individual attention. The staff of the large-scale retailers were, of course, far from automatons and the gap in the quality of service provided between the individual small-scale retailer and the branch or department of the large-scale retailer has perhaps been rather exaggerated. There would appear to be little doubt, how-ever, that in those trades which remained highly skilled, such as butchery, the personal qualities of the owner had a significant influence on trade.

In addition to these specific advantages of the small-scale retailer there were other factors operating. In some trades, for example, the conditions of production were such that there were few, if any, signi-ficant economies to be gained by retailing on a large scale. The fish and fruit and vegetables trades were cases in point. In other trades, such as sections of the women's wear and millinery trades, the objection to standardization on the demand side made the customers prefer the small shop that was different and whose goods, they hoped, were unique.

Equally important, the widening in the range of goods that con-sumers regarded as essential, and the development of advertising and branding attendant on the growth of large-scale methods of production in many trades, both operated in favour of the small-scale retailer. In addition to basic foodstuffs the typical consumer began in the inter-war years to regard other commodities such as tobacco and cigarettes, sugar and chocolate confectionery, newspapers and magazines and even proprietary medicines as essential goods. The estimates given in Table 10 above show a very significant rise in the inter-war years in the propor-tion of the total retail expenditure of consumers represented by the sale of these types of commodities, and the outstanding feature of their retail sale was that they were purchased frequently, in small quantities and in shops located conveniently to the home or in relation to the journey to and from work. While the large-scale retailers made some progress in the sale of these goods, the character of the demand for them gave great advantages to the flexible small-scale retailer.

Branding and resale price maintenance and the small scale retailer

The widespread development in many trades of manufacturer-branding, advertising and resale price maintenance would similarly appear to have had the effect of redressing the balance, in part at any rate, in favour of the small-scale retailer. The large-scale retailing organizations preferred wherever possible to sell their 'own brands' or at least goods that were not advertised by manufacturers. These firms were concerned with building up goodwill among customers as retailers who sold good quality products at low or reasonable prices. Freedom in buying, stocking and pricing policies was considered an important factor in establishing such a reputation. The alternative of handling only manufacturer-advertised products and retailing them at prices fixed by the manufacturers tended to make the large-scale retailers indistinguishable from other retailers. Further, the economies gained through large-scale buying of advertised products in some instances were not as great as those obtained through buying non-advertised products. In trades where practically all the products were manufacturer-advertised or price-maintained, for example tobacco goods or sections of the electrical and bicycle goods trades, the large-scale retailers had no alternative but to sell the same goods at the same prices as competing retailers. The large-scale retailers in these trades had therefore to develop other distinctive characteristics to build a reputation, such as securing the best shopping sites, offering a wider selection of goods, or providing better services such as more favourable hire-purchase terms. But in those trades where there was some possibility of selling substitutes for nationally advertised products the large-scale retailers pursued this policy.

The small-scale retailers, on the other hand, tended to prefer the manufacturer-advertised and price-maintained lines. With such commodities a large part of the task of selling, that of building up goodwill among customers, had already been undertaken for them by the manufacturers, and the fixed prices meant a guaranteed gross margin. In so far, therefore, as the manufacturers were successful in securing a demand for their products, and in so far as the small-scale rather than the large-scale retailer stocked and sold the articles, the development of manufacturer branding, advertising and price fixing tended to operate to the advantage of the small-scale retailer. Too much stress should not, however, be placed on this factor by itself, for the small-scale retailer did not have the whole field of advertised goods to himself. If the consumer asked for certain brands, the large-scale retailer would stock and sell them however much he might have preferred to sell other lines.

13. CONCLUSION

The suggestion was made at the beginning of this chapter that the developments in the distributive trades in the inter-war years were, for the most part, a continuation and fulfilment in somewhat different economic circumstances of the new trends that had emerged in the half-century before 1914. The detail given above of the developments in the method, structure, techniques and organization of the distributive trades in the inter-war years tends to confirm this generalization. For example, two of the major developments taking place in these years were undoubtedly the continuation of pre-1914 trends. The first of these was the increasing concern of manufacturers in many trades, particularly the large-scale manufacturers, with the distribution of their products. This concern took many forms, ranging from the use of salesmen, branding and advertising to direct control over parts of the distributive process by sales direct to retailers and the insistence on resale price maintenance. The second development was the continued growth in the relative importance of large-scale retailing organizations and the spread of these techniques to practically all trades and all areas. Other developments in the inter-war years may similarly be traced back to the pre-1914 period, such as the transfer of distributive functions from the retailer to the wholesaler or manufacturer, the stress on display and open pricing and the emphasis on main-street siting of shops.

The growth in services in the distributive trades

There was, however, one important feature of the development of the distributive trades in the inter-war years that was less clearly linked with the trends in the earlier years. This was the growth in the volume, variety and proliferation of services provided by the distributive trades to the consumer. Reference has been made to this development in the above discussion, but some examples may illustrate more clearly the contrast with the pre-1914 practices.

Starting with the first links in the distributive chain, manufacturers and wholesalers had begun to provide far more elaborate services to the retailers than those provided in the decades before 1914. For example, deliveries to retailers became more frequent, being made weekly instead of fortnightly or monthly, and sometimes, in the larger towns, daily instead of weekly; small orders by retailers were more readily accepted and fulfilled and single deliveries of very small quantities were undertaken; credit facilities were extended and the most ingenious purchasing terms were devised to attract every possible type of retailer and every possible type of order; personal visits to the retailer by the travellers of wholesalers and manufacturers became an accepted part of the machinery of selling, and the retailer was inundated from every quarter with 'information' as to what goods were available; finally, many manufacturers provided advertising material and dummies for the retailer's window display, and some even provided the services of expert window dressers.

The retailer in his turn had extended greatly his services to the consumer. Shops were better sited, more elaborately fitted and decorated, cleaner and more hygienic; the display methods were infinitely more attractive; many of the articles themselves were wrapped, boxed and packed with skill and artistry, and the range of goods stocked by retailers within given lines tended to be increased so as to give the consumer wider choice and selection; small orders and purchases were welcomed and encouraged and extensive delivery and sales services to the home, weekly, twice weekly, daily and sometimes twice a day, were undertaken; extensive use of credit and hire-purchase schemes made it easier for the customer to buy, and all types of sales-promotion activities from advertisement to the employment of door-to-door salesmen made the consumer fully aware of the character and quality of the goods available.

The distributive trades in the inter-war years continued to perform their basic function of making available the right type and quantities of goods to the consumer at the right place, time and price, but the detail of the performance had been greatly elaborated. Leaving on one side the question as to the need for some of the particular types of elaboration and the quality and value to the consumer of others, the main reasons for this marked stress on service in the distributive trades in the inter-war years would appear to be as follows. Firstly, the rise in the standard of living, albeit uneven over time and as between sections of the people, brought changes in consumer behaviour, taste and preference, and the distributive trades adapted themselves to these changes. Secondly, the continued development and improved techniques and standards of large-scale and mass-production methods leading to the output of a greater volume of improved quality goods at lower cost increased the magnitude of the task that had to be performed by the distributive trades. Not only had an increased volume of goods to be handled but, equally important, with the rise in the quality and standards of production the task of marrying the flow of mass-produced articles with the individual tastes, requirements and idiosyncrasies of each consumer was greatly increased. Inevitably there was an increase in the time, labour and outlay required to perform this task or at least give the appearance of so doing. In the third place the emphasis on services may be suggested as the outcome of competition between manufacturers, between wholesalers and between retailers. Competition had always existed, but the competition of the inter-war years took place in an economy that was haunted by a fear of over-production and in which consumer purchasing-power, while rising, was unstable and fluctuating. It took place in a market where prices were falling almost continuously and in a market which, owing to the geographical dispersion and the technical ignorance of the buyers, was particularly susceptible to service competition of all descriptions.

This growth in the volume and variety of the services provided by the distributive trades may therefore be seen primarily as the outcome of the changed productive, economic and social conditions of Britain in these years. The overall rise in the standard of living led inevitably to a demand by the consumers for increased services of many kinds. But this rise in the standard of living was uneven and manufacturers, wholesalers and retailers were faced with problems of maintaining and increasing sales. Low price appeal was possible in some markets but the general practice was competition in services rather than in price, as this method was effective in those markets where consumer demand was rising. The effect of this competition was to exaggerate the already existing trend, arising from the higher standard of living, in the direction of an increased volume of services.

Rigidity in the structure of the distributive trades

There remains one other aspect of the development in the distributive trades in the inter-war years to which brief reference must be made. An element of rigidity, a slowing down in the rate of development of new methods and new techniques of distribution, would appear to have been present in the closing years of the inter-war period—an element of rigidity that contrasted sharply with the fluidity of ideas, methods and structure in the decades before 1914. Some examples of this suggested rigidity may be given. Firstly, there had been a decline in price competition between retailers following the spread of resale price maintenance and the adoption by retailers of traditional and agreed markups. Secondly, there was a growing volume of support for proposals for the limitation of the channels of distribution and of the number and types of outlets. In a few trades some such limitation was practised through the use of devices such as exclusive dealing agreements, agencies and distance limits.

Finally and most important but difficult to describe and define, some rigidity would appear to have resulted from the parallel expansion of large-scale manufacturing on the one hand and of large-scale retailing on the other. The large-scale manufacturers were concerned with control over the marketing of their products; the large-scale retailers wished to have complete freedom in their buying, selling and pricing policies. In the inter-war years the trades in which large-scale retailing had developed most rapidly were those in which the production of the goods was still undertaken by a relatively large number of competing firms, for example women's clothing and furniture. They were trades in which the goods were imported or unbranded and unadvertised, for example milk, pottery and hardware and provisions, or were trades in which integration of production and distribution was practicable, for example bread and men's clothing. Large-scale retailing made relatively little headway in the trades where production was concentrated in the hands of a few firms or where the products were nationally advertised, branded and resale price maintained, for example tobacco and cigarettes, chocolate and sugar confectionery, certain grocery goods and electrical goods of various descriptions. While concentration of production and branding were not the only factors of significance in these trades, the appeal of large-scale retailing techniques and their economic advantages were far less in the case of the second group of trades than in the first. Similarly, producers had difficulty in controlling the marketing of their goods in trades that were dominated by large-scale retailing organizations. The limits of the development of large-scale retailing had not been reached by 1939 but the existence of large-scale manufacturers and the control of such manufacturers over the marketing of their goods would appear to have narrowed the possible fields of expansion.

The importance and significance of this element of rigidity should not perhaps be overstated. In some respects there was an increase in flexibility. For example, in spite of the factors mentioned above, the freedom of entry to retailing trades was, for a large number of reasons, much greater than in the years before the First World War, and the rate of entry and exit of small business units would appear almost certainly to have been much higher than in the earlier period. Nevertheless, viewing the structure and organization of the production and distribution of consumer goods as a whole there were important sectors where the small-scale unit had not the capital resources to engage in direct and effective competition with the large-scale unit, even if the techniques or market knowledge of the former were superior. The large-scale units, both manufacturers and retailers, had heavy and extensive investments in products and properties, in goodwill and reputation and in marketing methods and retail organization, and these investments tended to protect them from competition. At the same time, the size of these investments and the need to make them 'pay' consistently would appear to have encouraged these firms to pursue proved policies which would yield a minimum return on the investment rather than to try out new ideas. Modification and adjustment of techniques might take place, but only rarely were the larger firms forced or willing to adventure and experiment with new methods.

14. THE COST OF DISTRIBUTION

Finally, an important question to ask is, What has been the effect, if any, of the changes in the structure and organization of the distributive trades since the middle of the nineteenth century on the cost of distribution? Unfortunately, present information does not permit of even a partial statistical answer to the question; no data on costs of wholesaling and retailing in the nineteenth century exist that are sufficiently representative to mean anything. Some of the issues involved in the measurement of the cost of distribution over time and some suggestions as to the probable trends in different types of costs can, however, be outlined briefly.

The main problem of measurement of distribution cost over time is that of ensuring that exactly the same function or process is being measured at different points in time. The retailing 'costs' for example of retail bespoke tailoring in the nineteenth century cannot be compared with the wholesale and retail gross margins in the ready-made clothing trade in the twentieth century. Again, the gross margin of the grocer who did his own tea blending and sugar grinding cannot be compared with the margin of the grocer who sells packaged tea and sugar. And the cost of selling one pair of boots chosen by the consumer from a total range of two dozen different types and sizes cannot be compared with the cost of selling one pair of shoes chosen from a stock of hundreds of different types and ranges.

A more satisfactory way of looking at the question is to distinguish between the changes in the efficiency and cost of the physical processes of distribution on the one hand and the changes in the relationship between the distributive process as a whole and the productive process. In regard to the former there has undoubtedly been an increase in the efficiency, and a lowering of the cost, of distribution of a given quantity of goods. Lower transport costs per ton mile is an obvious example. Similarly in the warehouses and shops, better layout, the use of labour-saving devices for keeping stock records and accounts and the use of mechanical aids such as bacon slicers, automatic scales, crate openers and cash registers have increased productivity.

The effects of the changes in the relationships between the productive and the distributive processes are much more difficult to determine. The widening of the gap in space and time between the producer and the consumer has the effect of increasing distribution costs relative to production costs. The parallel transference of functions from the retailer to the manufacturer on the other hand has the effect of lowering distribution costs. Both the holding costs and the labour costs of the retailers tend to fall and the rate of stock turn tends to increase as the manufacturers take over and perform on a large scale the processing and pre-distributive operations, including weighing, bagging, and boxing, previously performed on a small scale by each retailer. Equally important, the use by manufacturers of branding and advertising, while adding to the cost of distribution, tended, through the concentration of demand, to reduce the selling problems of wholesalers and retailers and to increase their rate of stock turn.

But overshadowing the above trends is the longer-term trend in production cost. In these years in most trades, with increased scale of operations and mechanization, there was a fall in production costs even where additional processes were added. This fall in production costs was in practically all instances greater than the increase in the efficiency in the distributive processes discussed above. The result was an automatic rise in the relative cost of distribution. A simple example may be given. With more efficient production methods the cost of producing footwear tended to fall. The cost of retailing the cheaper boots and shoes, however, could not, without a complete change in selling techniques, be lowered, as each pair still had to be sold to customers individually. Distribution costs expressed as a proportion of the retail selling price tended therefore to rise.[1] In addition the consumer, with the rising standard of living, was demanding many types of new services. For example, the consumer wished to purchase some goods more frequently and in smaller quantities, and wished to have goods delivered to his home. The consumer welcomed more convenient selling points for the products. The consumer demanded greater variety and range of goods, demanded a choice of several styles, shades, sizes and fittings instead of a very limited number of each. And the consumer was attracted by the increased time and effort put into display and advertisement and the rise in the standard and siting of shops and equipment.

At any given time some forms or methods of distribution were more efficient and less costly than others current in the same trade. And by and large the more efficient and lower cost retailers tended to increase their share of the total trade. But viewing the developments in all consumer goods trades as a whole, the trend, particularly in the inter-war

---

[1] Data from three large multiple shop footwear firms suggest that the retail gross margin on the sale of footwear rose from an average of 20·5 % in 1920 to 23·0 % in 1930 and 24·2 % in 1938.

years, was away from simplification of the distributive process, away from mass distribution methods handing goods on to the consumer with a minimum of choice and service, and towards the more compli-cated and more elaborate forms of distribution including greater service to the consumer. This trend combined with the fall in production costs would appear almost certainly to have led to a relative increase in the cost of distribution over these years.

CHAPTER III

THE DISTRIBUTIVE TRADES IN THE SECOND WORLD WAR AND THE POST-WAR YEARS, 1939–1950: AND SUGGESTIONS AS TO FUTURE TRENDS

I. THE WAR AND POST-WAR YEARS

The distributive trades in the Second World War and post-war years were characterized by stability in methods and structure; by the maintenance of the *status quo* rather than by the emergence of new forces and new methods. This is not to say that no changes took place. The shortages of supplies, the controls direct and indirect over manpower, materials and capital, which existed in one degree or another throughout these years, affected the distributive trades in some respects more than any other sector of the economy. But the operation of these controls and the effects of the shortages resulted not in widespread reorganization or in the use of novel techniques but in the maintenance, practically intact, of the existing distributive framework, with fewer goods being distributed by fewer people.

The maintenance of the *status quo* was no accident, but the outcome of a deliberate and planned policy. The details of the various methods of control applied to the different trades at different times, ranging from the use of pre-war datum lines for allocations through distributive margin control to the insistence on licences to open and operate new shops, do not call for elaboration here. The principles upon which the policy of controls was based may, however, be stated briefly.

Government intervention in the working of the distributive trades was seen as a necessity and not a virtue. No attempt was made to reform, remodel or improve the main features of the system that had existed before the war. The overriding considerations of government policy were the maintenance of supplies to the consumers, the allocation of these supplies fairly, and, so far as was compatible with these aims, the reduction of the manpower employed in the distributive trades. These doctrines meant that the existing machinery was to be disturbed as little as possible for fear of inducing a breakdown in the flow of supplies, that new entrants to the trades were to be limited, and that changes and shifts in the methods and structure were to be discouraged. They also implied, as competitive bidding for scarce goods could not be allowed, that supplies to distributors should be determined on the basis of the number of customers and that margins should be fixed so that no exploitation of the public could take place and so that at the end of the emergency when controls could be lifted no sector or group would be either better off or worse off in relation to others than at the beginning. If necessity forced the curtailment of the activities of some distributive units or the merging of the activities of others, adequate safeguards were provided to ensure that when a return to free trading was possible such units should be the first to re-start operations. Even where direct government control did not operate or where the controls had been lifted, the shortage of supplies tended in the same way to maintain the existing relationships and the relative status of units and organizations. The fairest method and the method leading to least dispute was for producers to allocate scarce supplies evenly to their existing customers, and distributors had little hope of opening up new sources of supply of scarce goods.

Naturally no system of controls could succeed in eliminating all tendency towards change. Shifts in consumer habits, such as purchasing at shops close to hand during the years of heavy bombing rather than visiting shops further afield, and the destruction of shops by enemy action, for example, inevitably led to some changes from the pre-war pattern. But the pressure of government controls, the active part played by Trade Associations in fashioning these controls and sometimes in assisting in their enforcement, and the existence of a sellers' market in the post-war years which provided little inducement to develop or evolve new selling practices, combined to limit and contain the changes in the methods and structure of the distributive trades in these years.

The absence of change in distributive structure

Statistical data to illustrate this relative absence of significant change in the structure and organization of the distributive trades are not available for all aspects. Some examples can, however, be given of the absence of change in retail structure. There is no firm information about the change, if any, in the total number of retail shops between 1939 and 1950. While there is little doubt that the number declined in the war years as a result of rationing, shortages of goods and enemy action, it is not known whether the decrease had been made good by 1950.[1] Table 13 above, however, shows that the number of multiple shop branches increased only slightly. Between 1939 and 1950 there was an estimated increase of only 845, from 39,013 to 39,858, in the total number of branches of firms with 25 or more branches each. This compares with an increase of 8,439 in the years 1930 to 1939. The

---

[1] See Appendix E for a summary of the Census of Distribution figures of the number of shops in existence in 1950.

number of branches of Co-operative Societies increased by 1,140 between 1937–38 and 1946—from 23,954 to 25,094.[1] The increase in the number of department stores between 1939 and 1950 is thought to be less than 10.

The rationing statistics also show an absence of significant change between the early years of the war and 1950, though there were fluctuations in the war and immediate post-war years. The total number of shops holding registrations for meat, for example, was practically the same between 1942 and 1950. There were 45,489 retailers with meat registrations in 1942 and 45,022 in 1950. The decline in the number of grocery and provision dealers holding registrations was rather greater, from 157,800 in 1940 to 145,100 in 1951. The share of the total number of sugar registrations held by independent or small-scale retailers was however practically unchanged between the two dates—51·5 % in 1940 and 50·6 % in 1951. Finally, as shown in Table 19 above, the share of the large-scale retailers in the total retail trade of the country is estimated to have increased by only 1·5 % between 1939 and 1950, from about 34·5 % in 1939 to 36·0 % in 1950. This compares with an increase of 8·2 % between 1930 and 1939.[2]

The virtual disappearance of bankruptcy among firms engaged in wholesale and retail trading in these years was another reflection of the stability of the structure as a whole.[3] Price and margin control was in fact designed to avoid bankruptcies as far as possible in order to prevent a breakdown in supplies to the consumers. Further, the existence of price control combined with resale price maintenance meant that over large sections of consumer goods trades in these years there was no price competition between retailers. The price controls, it is true, fixed maximum prices only, but few retailers with limited supplies saw any advantages to be gained by selling below this maximum. Similarly controls over new building and investment curtailed the physical changes that could be made, though the shortage of supplies and manpower may have led to some reduction in the actual number of shops in existence.

The reduction in manpower

There were two developments however which, while they were the outcome of the policy described above, may have long-term effects on

[1] J. A. Hough, *Co-operative Retailing*, p. 169.

[2] The monthly figures of sales by different economic types of retailer published in the *Board of Trade Journal* since 1947 point to a rise in the sales of multiple shop retailers at a much faster rate than the increase in total retail sales between 1947 and 1950. This rapid increase, however, would appear in part to be a reflection of the efforts of multiple shop retailers to regain ground lost during the war owing to rationing, enemy action and the unwillingness of consumers to shop centrally.

[3] Bankruptcies of retail businesses in the trades other than food were 1,280 in 1938 and 161 in 1941. (*House of Commons Debates*, vol. 382, col. 220.)

the distributive trades. The first of these developments was the decrease in the manpower employed in the distributive trades which led to the disappearance of a number of the pre-1938 practices. The second was the emphasis placed by the government on reducing distribution costs and the practice of relying on costings to determine margins. This led to the abandonment in many trades of traditional mark-ups and margins.

There was a rapid decline in the numbers employed in the distributive trades from 1939 onwards, until in 1944, the lowest point reached, the numbers were some one-third fewer than in 1938. From 1945 onwards the trend was reversed and the numbers employed increased rapidly up to 1949, after which the rate of increase slowed down. Changes in classification prevent a direct comparison of the numbers employed in the pre- and post-war years, but there is little doubt that the employment in these trades in 1950 was below that of 1938, and certainly the distributive trades represented a smaller proportion of the total working population than in 1938.[1] At the same time there had been an increase in the proportion of women employed and a decrease in the proportion of juveniles.

This reduction in the manpower employed led to fewer services being provided for the consumer. Obvious examples are the curtailment of delivery of some goods, the reduction in the number of deliveries made, the employment of fewer assistants per customer and the development of self-service retailing units. The important consideration in relation to long-term trends was the indication that both the distributive trades and the consumers had begun to accept a situation in which less manpower was to be employed. The discussions and plans as to future developments were framed not in terms of a return to a period when manpower would be plentiful but in terms of methods and techniques of providing additional service to consumers without using additional manpower. The outlook differed markedly from that widely adopted in the inter-war years when the provision of extra services involving

[1] The Ministry of Labour 'old' series and 'new' series of employment cannot be compared directly, but the trend can be seen by placing the series side by side:

Year	Total working population	Total engaged in distribution	Proportion of total working population engaged in distribution %
1938 (a)	19,473,000	2,882,000	14·7
1948 (a)	20,274,000	2,354,000	11·5
1948 (b)	22,904,000	2,523,000	11·0
1950 (b)	23,327,000	2,643,000	11·3

(a) Old series.   (b) New series.

additional employment was considered as an answer to most problems of marketing. This change in outlook was in part a reflection of the difficulty of obtaining manpower. The raising of the school leaving age to 15 years, which reduced the supply of juvenile labour, was also of importance, as was the rise in wages cost relative to occupancy cost owing to the existence of many pre-1938 rent and lease agreements.

The shift from traditional mark-ups and margins to margins fixed by government control and based on costings encouraged the trend towards economy in the use of manpower. Price control, notably in the post-war years, led to a reduction in gross margins in many trades and made impossible a reversion to pre-1939 practices. Further, the reduction in gross margins in individual trades or in groups of commodities began to change many of the traditional relationships between trades. In some instances the reductions in margins meant that retailers who had sold the commodities as a side line no longer found it worth their while to stock the goods. In other instances the margins on the main groups of commodities had been so narrowed that specialist retailers felt compelled to add to the lines of goods sold to maintain their overall rate of profit. Trades such as confectionery, tobacco, bread and sections of the grocery and provisions trade were those most affected. Many of these forced shifts in the relative gross margins between different commodities will probably have permanent effects in that, even if price and margin controls are discontinued, it is most unlikely that any return to the earlier relationships will take place.

The effects of controls on the distributive trades

Apart from these two developments, however, and some others of a relatively minor character, the structure and organization of the distributive trades can best be described as 'frozen' during the war and immediate post-war years. Even in the early nineteen-fifties, when some of the controls had been lifted and some of the shortages ended, few new developments were to be observed. There can be no doubt that the controls, direct and indirect, over the distributive trades in these years achieved their main purpose. Goods in short supply were distributed consistently and equitably. Manpower and materials which might have been used in the distributive trades were otherwise employed, to the greater advantage of the nation as a whole. But the effects of these controls on the working and efficiency of the distributive trades were rarely the major consideration in determining policy, and some analysis of these effects is of value as an indication of the cost of securing these larger aims.

A distinction should perhaps be made between those controls that were the direct outcome of war conditions and shortages of supplies and those which were the outcome of attempts to plan the evolution of the economy as a whole. In the first category fall the *ad hoc* expedients such as rationing, limitation of entry to certain trades, and price and margin control. In the second category fall policies such as purchase tax, building licences and town planning schemes. A complete distinction between the two types of control is difficult to make in practice as the one clearly merges into the other, but in the following discussion the different origins or purposes of the controls will be kept in mind.

The main results of the controls, direct and indirect, over the distributive trades since 1940 may be suggested as the decline in competition in these trades, the relative absence of new entrants, and the strengthening of the position of existing or established firms. In those trades where shortages of goods and controls have persisted, the firms that were in the trades before the war were in a virtually monopolistic position. In the tobacco, confectionery, meat and milk trades and to a slightly smaller degree in the bread and grocery trades, the established wholesalers and retailers could hardly put a foot wrong and only the completely incompetent firms, once evacuation and bombing had been weathered, were likely to fail. Consumers it is true could change their retailer and to some extent the retailer could change his wholesaler, but shortages and price and margin control limited the advantage of such changes. In any event the entry of new firms, otherwise than by buying up existing firms at inflated prices, was practically out of the question. The magnitude of this problem may be seen from the fact that the trades listed above represented over one-half of total consumers' retail expenditure in 1950.

In other trades, when direct controls ended and supplies increased in the post-war years, competition played a slightly more important role in influencing developments. Here again however new entrants to the trades were limited in numbers owing partly to the difficulty of obtaining supplies of certain goods and partly to the difficulty of obtaining premises. Except in new housing areas and bombed areas, the building of new shops and warehouses was restricted. Only two new department stores, for example, were built in the whole of the United Kingdom between 1939 and 1951. New entrants could only come into a trade by taking over from existing and, for the most part, very prosperous retailers. The prices asked for the premises and the business were often completely uneconomic for a newcomer who had to build up his custom.

Similarly, existing retailers who wished to expand faced problems of high rentals and inflated property prices. Many firms preferred to postpone expansion rather than to pay a rent for a shop that was three or four times the pre-1938 rent already being paid for a similar-sized shop in the same town. Re-equipment and modernization of the whole-sale and retail premises presented the same type of difficulty in that the cost of modernization was many times that of the pre-war cost. The newly-equipped shop would however have to compete with one that had been modernized in, say, 1938. If the differential in efficiency and operating costs between the recently modernized shop and the older shops was clear and attractive to the consumer, the higher costs of installation or re-building would have been met by higher turnover. The existence of price controls and of resale price maintenance however limited the possibility of such an appeal, and the attraction to the con-sumer of existing retailing units that were close at hand out-weighed in many trades the attractions of shops further afield that were using the new techniques. Only in one or two trades, such as footwear, women's clothing and to a minor extent grocery and provisions, were a few firms showing that capital outlay and new methods could bring an increased volume of turnover.

The high initial cost of entry, expansion and innovation relative to existing costs is a well-known problem in productive industry. The risks associated with extending plant or introducing a new product can to some extent be calculated and measured, and the capital organization of industry is geared to take such risks. The distributive trades on the other hand were facing this problem for practically the first time in the years after 1945, and in these trades far less had been done to measure and calculate the risks of innovation. A feature of the distributive trades hitherto had been the ease of entry to the trade and the relatively small amounts of capital required to do business. To the general rigidity in the distributive trades introduced by controls there was added there-fore rigidity due to lack of knowledge and under-capitalization.

Some of the existing firms had resources as a result of re-investment of profits, or were able to raise funds on the market, and for these firms the problem of expansion was not insurmountable. In the post-war years many mergers took place between companies, particularly multiple shop firms. These firms found it easier to acquire a number of long-term leaseholds by taking over an existing multiple shop organization than by attempting to buy particular shops one by one. The growth in size of these larger firms did not however necessarily mean that re-equipment, experiment and innovation would follow. The majority of firms, both large and small, secure on their flanks by the obstacles to new entrants and able to maintain their turnover in a full employment economy, preferred, after making some adjustments for shortage of manpower, to follow existing practices and principles rather than to lead, and were content to delay reorganization as long as possible.

In the case of those commodities coming under direct governmental price control, an attempt was made to prevent this trend towards what may be called the ossification of the distributive trades from resulting in higher costs of distribution. The fixing of maximum margins based on examination of the costs of existing retailers and wholesalers is not however a policy aimed at improving efficiency in the distributive trades or at encouraging new methods and techniques. And viewing the economy as a whole there is some danger that the continuous improvements in production methods and techniques leading to lower real costs of production may in fact be more than offset by the use of the out-of-date methods, practices, equipment and buildings of the distributive trades.

The ending of shortages, of rationing and of price and margin control will undoubtedly lead to some return to competition in these trades. The exact moment in different trades to lift such controls is of course determined by the wider consideration of the advantages to the economy as a whole. In making such a decision however it is important that the effects of existing methods of control over the distributive trades and the possibility of using alternative systems of control that may not be subject to the same drawbacks should be taken fully into account. Moreover any easy assumption that the mere existence of a free market in the distributive trades would automatically lead to improvements in methods, techniques and organization and to an end of ossification is hardly justified on the basis of past experience. In the first place existing firms will have a cost advantage over newcomers for a very long time to come, apart from their dominant position in the trade resulting from over a decade of near-monopoly. In the second place the distributive trades, particularly retail trading, are a classic example of imperfect rather than of perfect competition. Competition in an imperfect market does not necessarily lead to the elimination of the economically inefficient firm, as such firms are protected from direct competition by many factors such as distance, the lack of special knowledge on the part of the consumer, and the minimum size of operating units. The twelve years of stability in the distributive trades have almost certainly increased the imperfections of the market rather than reduced them.

A policy of *laissez-faire* in the distributive trades, of freeing all goods from controls, may therefore be only slightly more effective in encouraging new developments than the system of controls in the past decade. There would however be a direct saving in the manpower employed to direct the controls. In regard to longer-term policies, and the problems of planning the uses of the national resources as a whole, attention has already been drawn to the danger of treating the distributive trades as a residual element, a sector of the economy for which a policy can be devised once the allocation of resources to the other sectors has been settled. Efficiency in the distributive trades is as essential as efficiency in productive industry. Of equal importance is the need to develop and devise yardsticks and standards which will enable differentiation to be made between sections and individual units in the distributive trades. Allocation of supplies, sites or capital on the basis of fair shares to all may be the simplest method. In certain fields this policy has much to commend it. But such a policy in the sectors of the economy where some firms and some methods are known to be superior to others tends to hold back and limit rather than to encourage efficiency.

2. FUTURE TRENDS IN THE DISTRIBUTIVE TRADES

The scope for developments in the distributive trades in the future and the general direction of such developments will clearly be dependent upon the character of the economic framework within which these trades will operate in the future. This framework will be influenced by a number of factors. The size of the national income, the rate of increase of this income, the division of the income between different purposes, for example final consumption and investment, and the distribution of the income between classes is one factor. The rate of increase in the population, the age composition of the population and the total man and woman power available is another factor. Technical developments such as improvements in transport, an increase in the number of private motor cars and progress in preserving perishable goods will also directly influence the distributive trades, as will changes in social habits, for example in the size of families, in the size and frequency of purchase of certain goods and in the importance and incidence of fashion. Finally central and local government policies in relation to the use of resources, town planning, opening hours of shops, standards of hygiene and so on will in part determine the nature of such changes in the distributive trades as take place.

Speculation as to the possible character of economic setting in which the distributive trades will operate in the future would be a lengthy process and need not be undertaken here. There is, however, a case for glancing briefly at what would appear to be the most likely organizational and technical developments in the distributive trades in the future and relating these possible developments to the present problems facing large- and small-scale distributors.

As far as it is possible to distinguish future trends, there would appear to be little doubt that the use of large-scale methods of production of consumer goods will continue and be extended, and that manufacturers and producers will play an increasingly active part in the marketing of their products. Further, the flow of goods will almost certainly become more even, with gluts and fluctuations in supplies being avoided by the use of improved methods of storage such as freezing and of fuller data on consumer demand. The practice of manufacturers or producers taking over more and more tasks from retailers will be continued and may extend to tasks at present undertaken by consumers. For example, grading, identification, specification and information for the consumer will probably become the producer's function in practically all trades, and even such processes as cleaning, peeling, preparing or cooking at present undertaken by the consumer will in many instances be transferred to the producer. An important feature of this development will be greater progress in the direction of standardization and simplification of the design of goods and of their shapes and sizes, based on extensive knowledge of the needs and requirements of the great majority of the consumers. Such a trend will reduce considerably the costly and time-consuming tasks at present performed by the retail trades of measuring, fitting, adjusting and special ordering for each individual consumer.

The general effect of these developments will be to make the distributive process as such for a wide range of goods one of organization only, or, to use an American term, an engineering operation. The major problem will be that of devising ways and means of matching the demands and needs of millions of consumers with the controlled flow of commodities, without limiting in any serious way the personal choice of each consumer. In relation to standardized, staple goods that are needed at regular and frequent intervals by practically every household, the solution will probably lie in the direction of planned and intensive services to the home. The actual form taken by these services will, of course, depend at any given time on the relative cost of different factors such as manpower, vehicles, petrol and so on, but there can be little doubt that the mechanization and organization of these services will eventually lead to the supply of these basic commodities as smoothly, regularly and economically as the supply of other necessities such as water, gas or electricity. In relation to the less standardized goods, the goods purchased individually by consumers, the solution is likely to lie in the direction of very much larger shops in shopping centres, many of the shops selling goods of more than one trade. In these shops the retailing techniques will be those of open display of the different types of goods available and of self-selection, self-service or semi-self-service by the consumer. Given considerable improvements in standardization and simplification in size and quality the consumer need consult only himself as to style and taste.

These developments, it will be appreciated, would mean that the role of the retailer—if the term is still used—in guiding and advising the consumer will become less and less important. The need for technical skill and knowledge on the part of the retailer in relation to particular products will decline, and the boundaries between trades will be determined by considerations of the character of consumer demand and of consumer convenience rather than by traditional divisions. The functions of the retailer will become essentially those of providing an opportunity for consumers to make their selection and choice, and of engineering the flow of goods from the producer to the consumer. These developments suggest further that the consumer, without the guidance of the retailer, will not only have personal preferences but should also possess the knowledge and ability to make a correct choice and should be protected against fraud. At present information enabling the consumer to make a choice is provided by the manufacturers in many instances by way of branding and advertising. With the growth of large-scale production methods and the increasing concern of manufacturers with the marketing of their products this type of informational service will no doubt increase in importance. It may well be, however, that in the future the consumer will demand fuller and more impartial information than that provided by competitive branding and advertising. This may be secured through the development of systems such as national standards of performance and quality, consumers' advice bureaux, and the publication of results of tests made by independent bodies.

Given larger shops, shops selling a wider range of goods, open display to enable selection to be made, and adequate consumer knowledge, two types of organizational problems remain. First there are the problems of merchandising so that the goods stocked and displayed keep abreast of changes in consumer taste, of matching the consumer's selection of style and shade with his or her requirements in size, and of planning delivery to the consumer of the selection of goods made. These are straightforward problems of organization, though their solution will demand a large measure of expert specialization. Secondly there are the problems of maintaining the demand of consumers over time so that full use is made of the capacity of retail establishments. As consumers are human this problem will never be solved as completely as is possible in, say, a factory where the maintenance of a flow of raw materials presents few problems. But the use of open display and of one form or another of self-service will make possible greater utilization of the manpower employed in distribution in that the tasks can be planned without direct reference to the shopping whims of consumers. In addition, however, it is probable that other efforts will be made to solve the problem of the flow of customers by such devices as greater flexibility in the opening and closing hours of shops, increased use of automatic machinery and direct encouragement of off-peak shopping.

These suggestions as to possible trends in the organization of the distributive trades relate to developments in urban densely populated districts and, further, are hardly practicable in all sections of the consumer goods trades. Only when consumer demand is relatively concentrated both geographically and within certain ranges of goods can an engineering approach to distribution be adopted. In the small towns and rural areas, for example, the changes in methods are likely to be relatively small but, as in the past, developments in distributive methods in urban areas will probably spread in a modified form to the rural areas. The attraction of the larger shops in the towns for purchases of goods such as clothing and household goods will no doubt be maintained even though the spread of advertising and branding of such goods may assist the local shops. The supply of essential goods in rural areas is likely to become more organized through the use of travelling self-service shops and regular home deliveries. In respect of the range and type of goods demanded the specialist retailer providing skilled counter service will continue, both in the town and in the country, to play an important role. While the assumption is made that in the future the consumer will be more knowledgeable and better informed as to the exact type and quality of goods he or she requires, these conditions will apply only to the medium- and lower-priced goods purchased fairly regularly. For purchases made occasionally, for the purchase of goods requiring after-sales service, and for the purchase of high-priced articles, for example special types of tools, motor-cars, and certain types of electrical equipment, furniture and expensive clothing, the range of goods stocked and the knowledge and service of the specialist retailer will be essential.

If the above suggestions are accepted as indicating the probable lines of evolution in the distributive trades in the future, questions may be asked as to whether such evolution will be rapid or slow, whether it will be straightforward or involve painful adjustments. More specifically, questions may be asked as to whether the present short-term trends in the distributive trades point in this direction, and if not, what will be the main problems of adjustment.

In relation to the short-term trends mention was made above of the element of rigidity that was appearing in the structure, organization and techniques of the distributive trades in the years immediately preceding the Second World War. The circumstances of the war and post-war years strengthened this tendency. The exception in the pre-war years was the development of the new form of trading, the variety chain store, and in the war and post-war years the economies secured in the use of man-power, the move away from traditional margins, and the few experiments with self-service units. Certainly the express limitations on the development of new methods, techniques and policies brought about by controls and shortages tend to make very difficult any clear assessment of the type of changes that might result if these limitations disappeared. Some doubts may, however, be expressed as to whether widespread experimentation and new thinking in the distributive trades would necessarily follow the relaxation of controls.

There would appear to be two main problems arising from the present trends in the distributive trades which will need to be resolved if the evolution towards the kind of system outlined above is to be fairly rapid and relatively smooth. The first of these relates to the policies of manufacturers: the second to the present methods and structure of large-scale retailing.

Producers and the future trends in distribution

Reference has been made to the growing concern of manufacturers with the marketing of their products in the past fifty years or so. The continued growth of large-scale production methods will tend to increase this interest. In the past, however, the practices arising out of this concern, such as sales by manufacturers direct to retailers, advertising and branding, and resale price maintenance, have not in most cases encouraged the development of new forms and techniques distribution but rather the reverse. In the inter-war years, in those trades where the manufacturers' concern with marketing was greatest there was a tendency towards the maintenance of the existing framework of distribution, towards marketing through the small-scale retailer and towards increasing the number of outlets for the products. This is not to say that many advantages were not obtained as a result of these methods. As suggested above, there were considerable improvements in standards and qualities of goods, the exact character of consumer demand was estimated more scientifically, and the concentration of demand on certain lines increased wholesale and retail stock turn and reduced holding costs. Manufacturers were not, however, alone in their introduction of these improvements. The advantages and the rapid rise in importance of variety chain stores was directly related to the use of these methods of determination of demand, standardization and simplification. But whereas the variety chain stores were concerned with the reduction of the cost both of manufacture and of distribution and with the low price of their goods, the producers of branded advertised goods were concerned mainly with differentiating their product from similar products and with sales promotion. These efforts at sales promotion, including a very large number of outlets, extensive advertising and free gifts and coupons, and even door-to-door salesmen, increased rather than decreased the complexity and cost of distribution and often offset the advantages gained by way of more standardized production methods.

Shortages of goods, price controls, shifts in traditional mark-ups and margins and the existence of a sellers' market in many commodities have brought about some changes in policy, but if the future sees an increase in the control exerted by manufacturers over the marketing of their goods and the spread of this policy to new trades such as furniture and textiles will not the results be somewhat similar to those of the inter-war years? There would appear to be a need for manufacturers to examine closely their selling policies; and, while continuing to be concerned with the marketing of their products, to give encouragement in every way possible to the distribution of the goods through the most efficient and inexpensive channels and forms of retailing. Preoccupation with the total volume of sales must not be allowed to over-shadow the problem of the cost of sales, including the wholesalers' and retailers' margins. Such an approach would almost certainly mean some modification of resale price maintenance policies and of the relationship between the large-scale producers and the large-scale retailers. Examples of possible changes in selling policies are an adjustment of selling terms and the granting of permission for variations in the resale prices to those firms and organizations that can handle larger quantities at lower costs. Too often with present selling schedules and volume rebates the large buyer helps to subsidize the very small buyer either as a matter of manufacturers' sales policy or as a result of insufficiently detailed costings of individual accounts. But the producers aiming at the national market are often reluctant to make changes in their selling methods which would lead them to become dependent on a few large contracts. The danger of this is real, as is also the difficulty of one producer on his own making changes in his selling policies which might lead to his exclusion from the national market through the activities of competitors following traditional practices. The solution to neither problem is simple.

Retail organizations and the future trends in distribution

While it is possible, therefore, that manufacturers' marketing policies will undergo some change, the shifts in policy will be significant only if developments in the retailing structure make them essential. Further, the suggested developments in the distributive methods mentioned above all involve an increase in the scale and size of retailing operations. Questions may be asked therefore as to whether the present forms of large-scale retailing will continue to increase in importance, whether new forms of large-scale retailing will emerge, and whether the large-scale retailers will take the lead in introducing and developing new techniques of distribution and new relationships with manufacturers. The answers to all these questions would appear to be 'yes', but the 'yes' is conditional upon many adjustments being made in existing policies and practices. The problems of the chief types of large-scale retailers may be considered in turn.

In the case of department store trading, present trends suggest a slowing down in the rate of progress. The central stores are fighting a difficult battle against the geographical dispersion of their customers and against rising overhead costs. The suburban and smaller provincial stores are threatened with severe competition from specialist multiple shop retailers and have not yet achieved an accepted and distinctive position in the distributive frame-work such as that occupied in the first twenty-five years of the century by the older types of store. The department store method of trading is, however, well suited to mass distribution techniques combined with a fair measure of self-service. While there may always be a place for the individual, central store with a particular tradition of service and amenities, the future of the suburban and provincial department stores would appear to lie in a different direction. What would appear to be needed are specially built stores based on the principle of maximum display coupled, as far as practicable, with self-selection and perhaps semi-self-service. The type of goods stocked and the price ranges would differ from those of the variety chain stores, but many of the merchandising techniques of the latter would need to be adopted. And the development of small chains of provincial and suburban stores that cater for similar types of markets in different areas would enable the stores to compete on more equal terms with the specialist multiple shop firms.

The Co-operative Societies face different problems of expansion and adjustment. With no geographical 'Co-operative deserts' into which they can expand, the Societies will have to turn to intensifying their sales in the areas already covered and to branching out towards new sections of the market. In the mass distribution of essential goods such as foodstuffs the Societies are in a good position to lead the way with new forms and techniques. Already many Societies are prominent in opening self-service units in the grocery and provisions trade, and the Co-operative organization of the distribution of bread and milk is ahead of most. Again, as the trend is likely to be towards larger shops selling a wide range of foodstuffs the Co-operative Societies are well placed. The maintenance of this lead and the development of new techniques may, however, force the Societies to reconsider their traditional dividend policy and their buying preference for products of the Wholesale

Societies. If a wider market is to be gained the appeal will have to stress efficiency and up-to-date methods of selling the goods the consumer demands, and not only the payment of dividends which in any event may be so small as to offer little attraction.

In relation to the trades other than food the central premises of many Co-operative Societies offer scope for large, attractive, well laid out semi-self-service stores. There are few signs, however, that this side of Co-operative trading will develop. The problems are clear enough. Specialization, employment of experts, prior claim to main-street sites, sales appeal directed to the public in general and not merely to members, and retail control over the wholesale production programmes are a few of the essential prerequisites, but the chances of these policies being adopted seem remote. Continued growth of the very large Societies which can afford to develop a measure of specialization will help to some extent, but what is needed is an entirely new approach by the Co-operative movement to the trades other than food.

Multiple shop retailing

The multiple shop form of retailing, because it comprises many different competing firms, would appear to be the most enterprising and the most likely to take the lead in developing the new methods and techniques mentioned above. Some difficulties will, however, have to be overcome. One of the most important of these is the problem of securing larger premises and selling a wider range of goods. In the foodstuffs trades, for example, any trend towards combination self-service stores, that is stores selling meat and vegetables and perhaps fish and poultry, as well as groceries and provisions, involves the abandonment of traditional frontage widths and the combination of many separate trades. Similar problems arise in the trades other than food. While some moves in these directions have been made by individual firms in the past, progress in the future is likely to be slow. A multiple shop firm in the butchery trade, for example, is unlikely to amalgamate with a multiple shop firm in the grocery and provisions trade, and even if this did happen the butchery and grocery premises would rarely be located next door to each other to enable a new combination store to be built. Again, two footwear firms which had branches in the same towns might amalgamate, but this would not lead necessarily to one larger shop in place of two separate branches. As pointed out above, the properties on either side of existing multiple shop branches are in most areas owned by other large-scale retailing organizations who are most unlikely to sell or move out. The bias in the past of multiple shop organizations towards specialization in trade, the tradition of 18 ft. and 24 ft. frontages in the main streets of most towns, and the occupation of practically all these sites by large-scale retailers, will tend to slow down the development of larger selling units handling a wider range of goods. In new housing estates, provided the local authorities do not insist on allocating shops according to traditional patterns, some development may take place, but with a slowly rising or stable population new building is not likely to be extensive. In older areas, while individual firms may succeed in increasing the size of their unit and the range of trade undertaken, it is difficult to envisage a general movement in this direction unless some arrangements for the exchange of shop properties are possible.

A second problem of the future development of multiple shop retailing and of other forms of large-scale trading is that of the relationship with the large-scale producers. A policy adopted by some multiple shop firms has been towards the integration of production and distribution units. In the past, however, this was rarely a complete solution. In order to give variety to the retail stock, firms found that some purchases had to be made from outside sources. In the future, with a trend towards shops selling a wider range of goods, the significance of integration is likely to be less. The solution to the problem will lie perhaps, as emphasis on display for selection and self-service develops, in the acceptance of a new division of functions between the large-scale producer and the large-scale distributor; the producer will take the responsibility of designing, planning, ascertaining demand and promoting the sale of the product, while the retailer takes the responsibility of displaying and pricing the product for the consumer to purchase if he wishes. The aim is a partnership of equals each respecting the other's function, rather than the domination of one by the other.

A final problem facing all types of large-scale retailers is that of raising the large amounts of capital required to finance such developments. There is a double problem here. First, the existing large-scale retailers already have extensive investments in property, equipment and good will. Secondly, practically all the developments envisaged involve additions to property or the erection of new buildings, and require increased amounts of fixed capital and the acquisition of property in shopping areas where the values are already inflated. Many of the existing assets are not easily realizable or adaptable to the newer methods of organization, and it is most unlikely that the additional outlay required can be met out of profits, at any rate in the initial stages. What will be needed if the new methods are to be developed fairly rapidly is much greater investment in the distributive trades than has been the case in the past. The practice in the United States of real estate companies, insurance companies and financial trusts building large shops and leasing them to retailers may be worth exploring in

Britain.[1] But whether any particular priority can be given to investment in the distributive trades as against other forms of investment will depend on the economic position of the country as a whole and on the assessment of the relative importance of improvements in distributive techniques.

3. CONCLUSION: THE DISTRIBUTIVE TRADES, 1850–1950, AND THE FUTURE

The war and the immediate post-war years have been described as a period in which the developments in the structure and techniques of the distributive trades were few. In the future, however, these years may also be seen as marking the end of one phase of the history of the distributive trades and the beginning of another.

The distinctive feature of the past hundred years in the distributive trades has been the consistent growth in the significance of large-scale distribution. This growth has accompanied and has influenced the development of scale in production and importing. Large-scale retailing has led to some measure of integration between factory production and distribution, to the placing of large orders for specific types of standardized goods with manufacturers and producers, and to direct purchases in bulk from overseas producers. These practices have had the effect of reducing the number of separate links in the distributive chain, of enabling economies in production to be secured by the concentration of demand on a limited number of lines of goods and, in so far as large-scale retailers must place forward orders, of helping to stabilize manufacturing and production conditions and prices.

The growth of scale in distribution and the effects of this growth on productive organization and conditions varied between trades and between commodities. Distribution and production developments in the footwear trade for example in these years were in marked contrast to those in the fruit and vegetables trade. Further, in some instances, for example in the chocolate and sugar confectionery and tobacco goods trades, the growth of scale in production was not accompanied by any significant growth of scale in retailing organization. Contrariwise, the growth of scale in retailing in other instances, as for example in the women's wear trade and in the case of the department store form of large-scale retailing, was not accompanied by any significant changes in the size of productive units or in their methods of organization.

After allowances have been made for these exceptions, however, and the existence of unevenness and of differing rates of development between

---

[1] *Retailing*, Productivity Team Report, Anglo-American Council on Productivity, London and New York, 1952, p. 4. This report gives an admirable summary of the main features of retailing in the United States.

different trades has been accepted, the pattern of development appears to have been that of a parallel extension of the use of large-scale methods of organization in both production and distribution in the past hundred years. In most instances the new methods and techniques of producers and the rise of a mass demand for the goods made possible the development of scale in distribution. In a few instances the growth of scale in retailing and the consequent consolidation and concentration of demand, as in the case of variety chain stores and the wholesale bespoke tailors, made possible the introduction of large-scale methods and economies of scale on the manufacturing side.

There are no signs, whatever may be the specific problems in particular trades or the problems facing particular types of producers and distributors, that this trend towards large-scale production and distribution of consumer goods has reached a limit. In fact, given full employment, a continued rise in the standard of living, and a policy of redistribution of incomes by fiscal or other measures, there will probably be an increase in the volume of demand for many types of goods that are now semi-luxuries. Such an increase in demand will make possible the standardization and large-scale production and distribution of such goods. The existence of conditions favourable to the further development of scale can, however, only indicate the main direction of the probable trend. The detail of the pattern and the rate of progress in the future, as in the past, will be influenced by a host of other factors.

Taking as given the consistent growth in the importance of large-scale retailing, two main phases in the evolution of the distributive trades since the middle of the nineteenth century have been discussed in the foregoing chapters. The first was characterized by the wealth of new ideas and new methods that emerged in the last quarter of the nineteenth century and opening decade of the twentieth. The growth of large-scale production methods in many consumer goods trades, the large-scale imports of cheap foodstuffs, and the growing consistency of consumer demand combined to make possible and to make necessary division of labour and specialization on an important scale in the distributive process. There appeared alongside the small-scale, costly, leisurely and skilled methods of the one-shop retailer the impersonal, speedy and cheaper methods of the large-scale retailer. There followed radical changes in trading techniques and policies, and in the conception of the role of the retailer in the distributive process.

The second phase, the inter-war years, was characterized not so much by the development of new methods and forms of organization, with the exception of the variety chain store, as by the extended development of the trends of the pre-1914 era. Many of these trends were, however, modified. The slowing down in the rate of expansion of the economy and the unevenness of what expansion did take place were factors modifying the trends. The considerable improvements in the range, scale and techniques of the manufacture of consumer goods and the increasing concern, evidenced in the growth of sales promotion, branding, advertising and resale price maintenance, of the larger manufacturers with the marketing of their products were other factors. There followed a tendency to shift the emphasis in distributive method away from stress on price, on inexpensiveness and on crude mass distribution techniques towards stress on quality and standards, on display and siting, on choice and variety and on service to the consumer. Further, the trends in the distributive structure as a whole began to be influenced as much by the marketing policies of the large-scale producers as by the initiative of the units engaged in distribution alone.

It remains to be seen whether a third phase in the evolution of the distributive trades is about to begin. In such a phase large-scale retailing will continue to expand, not merely because of the inability of newcomers to enter the field or of existing small-scale retailers to compete in buying sites or in advertising, but as a result of the speeding-up and simplification of the distributive process through the further combination of the experience and advantages of large-scale methods of distribution with the knowledge and techniques of large-scale production. In such a phase the problems of consumer taste, preference, whims and habits will no longer be seen as intractable, and emphasis will not be placed on the need for elaboration of distributive organizations to cater for diversity. But instead it will be a phase in which, in respect of a wide sector of demand, the problem of matching in time and place the flow of goods with the needs of the consumer and his right to select individually will be seen as reducible to a number of relatively simple principles that call for close co-ordination and co-operation between producer and distributor.

PLATES

ILLUSTRATING THE CHANGES IN
SHOP FRONTS AND SHOP LAYOUT
1850–1950

PLATE I

(a) Lipton Ltd., Ilfracombe, c. 1904

(b) Lipton Ltd., Queensway, London, 1952

PLATE II

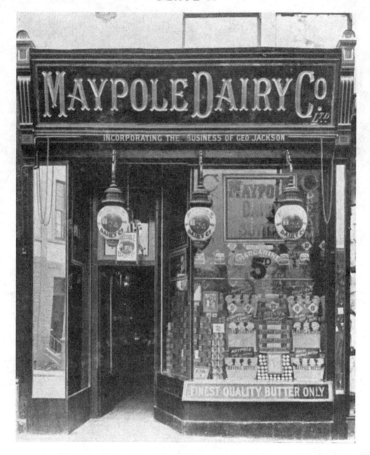

Maypole Dairy Company, Bristol, 1901

PLATE III

Home and Colonial Stores, Catford, London, *c.* 1905

PLATE IV

(*a*) Maypole Dairy Company, St Paul's Cray, 1952

(*b*) Home and Colonial Stores, Poplar, London, 1952

PLATE V

(a) Home and Colonial Stores, Catford, London, c. 1905

(b) Home and Colonial Stores, Poplar, London, 1952

PLATE VI

(*a*) International Stores, East Street, Chichester, *c.* 1888

(*b*) International Stores, Leatherhead, 1952

PLATE VII

(*a*) London Co-operative Society, Stratford, *c.* 1910

(*b*) London Co-operative Society, Shepherd's Bush, London, 1952

PLATE VIII

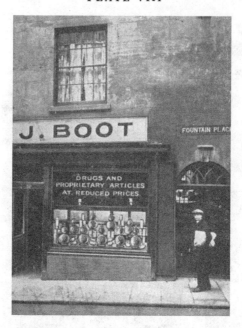

(a) Boots the Chemists. Jesse Boot's first shop in
Goosegate, Nottingham, opened 1877

(b) Boots the Chemists, Piccadilly Circus, London, 1952

PLATE IX

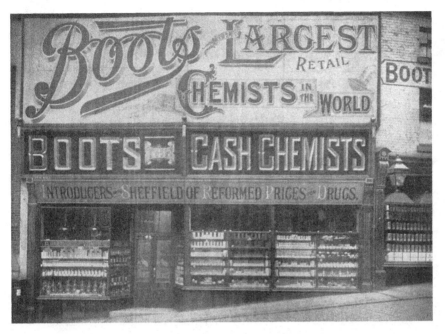

(a) Boots the Chemists, Sheffield, 1896

(b) Boots the Chemists, Swansea, 1952

PLATE X

(a) George Oliver, Worcester, c. 1890

(b) George Oliver, Portsmouth, 1952

PLATE XI

(a) Upsons Ltd. (Dolcis), Dartford, c. 1910

(b) Dolcis, Portsmouth, 1952

PLATE XII

(*a*) George Mence Smith, Maidstone, *c.* 1875

(*b*) George Mence Smith, Edgware, 1952

PLATE XIII

(*a*) Marks & Spencer, Ltd., Southampton, *c.* 1910

(*b*) Marks & Spencer, Ltd., Southampton, 1952

CHAPTER IV

THE DEVELOPMENT OF LARGE-SCALE RETAILING IN DIFFERENT TRADES, 1850–1950: METHOD OF PRESENTATION OF THE DATA

The following fourteen chapters discuss the chief developments in the retail organization and structure of the main consumer goods trades in the United Kingdom from the middle of the nineteenth to the middle of the twentieth century.

The trade-by-trade approach has been adopted as that most suited to the handling of the data, but as the dividing lines between trades are somewhat flexible at any given time, and certainly over time, the trade approach has been combined with the commodity approach. The grocery and provisions trade for example can be clearly recognized as a separate trade, but groceries and provisions were sold by retailers in other trades, for example by caterers. Also the grocery and provisions retailers sold some goods of other trades, for example tobacco and cigarettes, chocolate and sugar confectionery. The discussion of the grocery and provisions trade, as in the case of other trades, has however been confined to grocery and provisions and to the retailers whose main trade was in these goods. The role of the other types of retailers who also sold these goods is discussed only briefly. Similarly the sale by grocers of goods other than groceries and provisions is discussed in the chapters dealing with the other commodity trades, for example the tobacco and the household stores trades.

In some instances two or more trades are discussed in one chapter, for example the fruit and vegetables trade and the fish trade. In other instances a number of different commodities are discussed in the same chapter where there was a fair measure of affinity in the retailing methods and organization, for example bicycles, perambulators, electrical goods, radios and sewing machines. While the distribution of each of these commodities could be classed as a separate trade and some discussion of the retailing characteristics of each is given, individual treatment in separate chapters would have been an unnecessarily lengthy process.

The layout of the chapter on each trade follows the same general pattern. After an outline of the main changes in the conditions of production and in the character of consumer demand for the goods in the hundred years up to the middle of the twentieth century, a descriptive and where possible a statistical account is given of the development of the different economic types of retailer. In this account attention is focused on the development of large-scale retailing, and the growth of multiple shop retailing is discussed in particular detail. Many of the names of the first multiple shop firms are given, but it will be appreciated that the references to the dates when these firms first traded from a number of different branches do not refer to the dates of foundation of the firms themselves. The majority were established for many years before extending their activities on multiple shop lines. In the discussion of developments in the later years reference by name is made only to the largest firms.

There follows an assessment of the relative importance of the different economic types of retailer at different dates between 1900 and 1950 as measured by their shares in the total retail sales of the commodities making up the trade. These estimates are made on a commodity basis, that is they relate to the total retail sales of the commodity or group of commodities in question irrespective of whether the sales are undertaken by specialists in the particular trade or by retailers engaged in other trades. Similarly the estimates of the shares of the different economic types of retailer in the total trade of a given commodity or commodity group relate to the sales by each type of retailer of that commodity or group only, though they also include the estimates of sales of the commodity in question by non-specialist retailers of the appropriate type. For example, in the estimates of the total shares of the grocery and provisions trade undertaken by multiple shop retailers the sale by multiple shop grocery and provision dealers of tobacco or bread is excluded but the sale of groceries and provisions by multiple shop dairymen is included. This analysis of the shares of the different economic types of retailer is followed by an examination of the factors influencing the growth of each type. Finally, on the basis of past trends some suggestions are made as to possible future developments in the trade.

The treatment given to individual trades in these chapters has been influenced by the relative importance of large-scale retailing in the particular trades rather than by the importance of the trade in the retail structure of the country at any given time. Similarly, as this study is mainly concerned with the development of large-scale retailing the progress and problems of this type of retailer and in particular of the multiple shop retailer receive an emphasis in the individual chapter that is out of proportion to the actual share of this type of retailer in the trade as a whole.

The sources of the data used in these chapters and the basis of the estimates of consumers' expenditure and of the relative shares of the different types of retailer are discussed fully in Appendix A. There is no need to repeat that discussion here, but some brief reference must be made to the reliability of the data. The estimates of the number of multiple shop organizations and of the number of branches controlled by them in different years are known to be understated. While the figures include the details of firms that have gone out of existence or have amalgamated with other firms, there were a large number of instances where information was available on the number of branches possessed by a firm in one particular year but nothing was known as to its early history or, in some cases, its subsequent fate. The records of such firms have been excluded. A second source of understatement is undoubtedly the failure to trace the existence of some multiple shop firms altogether. In both instances, however, it appeared that the firms that were un-traced or whose history was not known were small multiple shop organizations, that is with less than 25 branches each. This is confirmed by the results of the Census of Distribution for 1950. Taking all trades together, the estimates made in this study of the number of multiple shop branches in existence in 1950 that were controlled by firms with more than 25 branches each were 97 % of the returns made in the Census of Distribution for the same class of firm and group of trades. The estimates made in this study of the number of branches in the 10–24 size group were however only 50 % of the Census returns.

As the same methods and techniques of estimation of the number of multiple shop branches in existence were used for the whole of the period 1850–1950, it is probable that the understatement in the estimates for each of the different years was also of the same order. No attempt has been made in this study to adjust the estimates of the number of multiple shop organizations and branches in existence in the light of the Census returns, but in most tables the figures relating to firms with 10 or more branches and those relating to firms with 25 or more branches are given separately.

In a number of the chapters tables have been constructed to show the rate of net increase in the number of multiple shop branches and the average yearly net increase in the number. In a few trades an attempt has also been made to show the relative importance of the largest multiple shop firms as shown by the proportion of the total number of branches in existence in different years that were controlled by these firms. In the interpretation of both of these types of tables, the under-statement in the number of multiple shop branches in the 10–24 branches size group and, of greater importance, the variations in the size of branches of multiple shop firms must be borne in mind. While in the majority of trades the variation in the size and turnover of branches of different firms was not very great, in some trades a firm with, say, 100 large branches has a total turnover equal to that of another firm with 350 small branches. The tables relating to the numbers and the increase in the numbers of multiple shop branches give a fair indication of the trend of development, but too much must not be read into the smaller fluctuations shown.

The estimates of the total turnover of multiple shop firms and therefore of their share of the total retail sales in different trades are for a number of reasons rather less reliable than the estimates of the number of branches in existence at various dates. The turnover estimates are based on information supplied by individual firms and from other sources. But the estimates have been increased or 'plussed up' in proportion to the understatement of the number of multiple shop branches in existence in different years as discussed above. The degree of understatement shown by the 1950 Census of Distribution returns to be present in the 1950 estimates of this inquiry is assumed, in the absence of other information, to have been of the same order in different size-groups and in different trades throughout the period 1900–50. It should be emphasized therefore that the estimates of turnover of multiple shop firms and the estimates of the number of branches of multiple shop firms presented in the study are not strictly comparable. The turnover estimates relate to the estimated total number of multiple shop branches in existence in various years and not to the number of branches given in various tables throughout this study, a number that is known to be understated. The methods of calculation of the turnover figures are discussed in Appendix A.

In this way an attempt has been made to place the estimates of the turnover of multiple shop organizations on a comparable basis with those of Co-operative Societies and department stores, as the estimates of both these types of large-scale retailer relate to total sales of all Societies or stores. The estimates of the sales of Co-operative Societies are, however, much more reliable than those either of multiple shop organizations or of department stores. The estimates of the share of the total trade in particular commodities undertaken by 'other retailers' are arrived at by difference and are not calculated separately.

The estimates of the total retail sales in different years and of the retail sales of different commodities are based on the work relating to total consumers' expenditure during the period 1900–38 undertaken by A. R. Prest and Richard Stone.[1] The adjustments made to these figures in order to construct a series for total retail sales are discussed in Appendix A. All that needs to be stressed here is that the figures

[1] A. R. Prest, assisted by A. A. Adams, *Consumers' Expenditure in the United Kingdom, 1900–1919*, Cambridge University Press, 1954 (no. 3 in the series Studies in the National Income and Expenditure of the United Kingdom issued under the joint auspices of the National Institute of Economic and Social Research and the Department of Applied Economics of the University of Cambridge), and Richard Stone, *Consumers' Expenditure, 1920–1938*.

given of retail sales of consumer goods can only be regarded as estimates subject to a margin of error.

As the figures of the total retail sales of different commodities and of the sales of these commodities by the different types of large-scale retailer are only estimates depending on a number of assumptions, ranges rather than single figures have been used in the various tables to show the estimated share of the different types of retailer in the total trade. These ranges are intended to convey a sense of the relative accuracy of the estimates. They do not mean more, however, than that on the basis of all existing data and by careful checking and cross-checking where possible it would appear that the actual figure falls somewhere within the range stated.

CHAPTER V

THE GROCERY AND PROVISIONS TRADE

The trade in the middle of the nineteenth century

In the middle of the nineteenth century the retail grocery and provisions trade was a combination of many different types of retailers. In the centre was the grocer dealing in the traditional groceries ranging from sugar to spices and from tea to cocoa and coffee, and he was flanked on the one side by the open markets where the farmers themselves offered their eggs, butter, cheese and bacon for sale, and on the other side by many different types of fixed-shop retailers. Among the latter were the old-established cheesemonger, the rapidly rising provision dealer, butter factor and bacon factor, the specialist tea dealer, the ubiquitous oil and colourman and drysalter, the tallow-chandler and the Italian warehouseman. The cheesemonger, with a history nearly as long as that of the grocer himself, was confined to the larger towns and represented a dying trade. The provision dealer, on the other hand, while as yet also found only in the larger towns, was slowly building for himself an accepted place in the retail framework as a more reliable and less troublesome alternative to the weekly markets.

The oil and colourman originally dealt chiefly in colours and paints and the oils for mixing them, but had widened his interests to sell a variety of household stores in the fullest sense of the word. His stock would include, as main lines, soap and candles, starch, matches, firewood, brushes, baskets and brooms, petroleum, lamps, linseed and other oils, beeswax and vegetable wax, colours, gums and resins, and would often extend to some groceries such as sauces, pickles and jams, to chemicals and drugs such as soda, Glauber's salts, quack pills and poor man's plaster, and to a miscellaneous mixture of commodities including hardware, ironmongery, china, lamp-black, size, ochre, chalk, sand, vitriol, brickdust, and gunpowder and shot. The Italian warehouseman, as the name implies, developed originally as a specialist in imported goods, especially edible oils. He was the retailer of olive oil, nut oil and salad oils and carried stocks of commodities such as condensed milk, macaroni and vermicelli, honey, jams, sauces and condiments, pickles, vinegar, preserved salmon, anchovies, sardines and polonies. The larger towns could support at least one representative of each of these different sections of the trade, though in the very small towns and rural areas one type of dealer, usually the grocer, could meet the main demands, supplemented by pedlars, markets and fairs.

The men of the trade, especially the grocers, were skilled craftsmen, part manufacturers as well as retailers. Food product manufacture was in its infancy and it was the grocer who, for example, chopped or ground by hand the cones of sugar into loaf or fine sugar according to the customers' wishes, who ground and mixed the variety of spices and who selected and blended the teas. Skill, experience and patience were the chief requisites for a retailer in this trade, and the only effective entry was by formal or informal apprenticeship. Success depended on word of mouth reputation stemming from the confidence of customers rather than on salesmanship, showmanship or price.

The shops themselves, with their dimly-lit interiors, their mixture of by no means unattractive smells, their rows of sombre jars and japanned canisters, their corners crowded with tea chests, barrels and drums, and with every imaginable object hung on hooks from the rafters, were attractive enough to the young as a centre of mystery, but hardly displayed goods to the best advantage. In fact, in spite of the cluttered-up character of the shop most of the goods for sale were kept out of sight in tall containers or brass-knobbed drawers, as the general smells and dust of the shop would have rendered them inedible in a matter of days. But the customers knew what they wanted, or if they were uncertain the expert knowledge of the grocer could solve the problem without any need for an elaborate window or shelf display.

The customers of the specialist grocer and the Italian warehouseman were, in large part, drawn from the well-to-do classes. The working classes made many purchases from the grocer, but the heavy duties on articles such as tea and sugar limited the volume of such sales, and for provisions the working-class housewife preferred to go to the weekly markets or market-halls of the industrial towns where prices were more competitive. The type of articles proudly stocked by many of the specialist grocers, such as orange and lemon peel, coffee, preserved turtles and tongues, muscatels, and nuts of all descriptions were certainly luxuries only for the rich. In some contrast the oil and colourman, with his ha'porth of this and his ha'porth of that, was concerned mainly with the working-class market in the towns.

Developments in the trade to the First World War

In the second half of the nineteenth century and continuing into the beginning of the new century, a series of radical developments and changes in the conditions of demand and supply of the goods interacted to transform this picture of the grocery and provisions trade. On the demand side, the steadily increasing numbers of the urban working classes who were obtaining regular employment and drawing regular pay packets was combined with a fall, from the 'seventies onwards, in the prices of foodstuffs to lead to a great increase in effective demand. And these years saw a rapid and practically continuous rise in real income per head of the whole population up to the turn of the century. On the supply side many factors brought about the great increase in the volume of foodstuffs available and the fall in their price. The reform and reduction, with the opening of the era of Free Trade, of the customs and excise duties on everyday commodities such as tea and sugar had already begun to lead to a rapid increase in consumption per head of those commodities in the 'fifties and 'sixties. Sugar consumption per head, for example, rose from 24·8 lb. in 1850 to 47·2 lb. in 1870 and tea consumption rose from 1·8 lb. per head in 1850 to 3·8 lb. per head in 1870.

The opening up of agricultural producing areas throughout the world to buyers from Britain and the great advantages the industrial countries began to enjoy in exporting dear manufactured goods in exchange for cheap foodstuffs were more important factors in bringing about the great increase in the volume of foodstuffs available. The railroad and the steamship began to open up continents and to revolutionize ideas of distance. Journeys that had taken months were reduced to weeks and journeys taking weeks to days. The produce of the world's agricultural areas could be brought to Britain's doorstep and the development of refrigeration made world trade in foodstuffs a reality. Lower freight charges meant lower prices, and the primary producing countries, as they saw the mass demand for their products growing, began developing bulk production methods in place of the small-scale production of luxuries, thus lowering costs further.

The statistics to illustrate the impact of these changes on the consumption of food in Britain are legion. Full details need not be given here but Table 24 illustrates for a group of imported grocery and provisions goods the steep increase in consumption per head per year in the second half of the nineteenth century.

Finally, the type of commodities sold by the grocery and provisions trade underwent a change with the development of food manufacture on a significant scale in the last quarter of the nineteenth century. Cheap sugar encouraged the manufacture of jams, jellies and confectionery, and in many other instances, for example tea blending and sugar and coffee grinding, the processing hitherto performed by the skilled grocer was beginning to be replaced by factory operations. At the same time new types of food products were appearing on the market. Margarine, for which the British patent was taken out in 1867, was probably the most outstanding example. In addition, however, at the turn of the century meat extracts, relishes, pickles, ketchup, sauces and canned milk, fruit, fish and meats were finding their way in considerable quantities to the grocer's shelves and counters. And these goods, in contrast to the preparations of the grocers in the middle of the century, were in a large number of instances ready-packed by the manufacturer and advertised by him under a brand name.

Table 24. *Quantities of imported foodstuffs retained for home consumption per head of total population of the United Kingdom, 1869–1911**

Commodity	Unit	1869–70–71 average	1889–90–91 average	1909–10–11 average
Tea	lb.	3·8	5·2	6·4
Sugar	lb.	45·5	76·8	87·4
Bacon and ham	lb.	2·7	13·1	13·1
Margarine	lb.	—	3·5	2·4
Butter	lb.	4·4	5·8	10·3
Cheese	lb.	3·8	5·9	5·8
Currants and raisins	lb.	4·2	4·5	4·8
Eggs	numbers	13·7	32·3	48·6

* These averages are taken from figures given in the *Statistical Abstract for the United Kingdom*, Command Paper, annual.

These radical changes in the volume and character of the goods and in the type of demand led to widespread developments in the organization and structure of the grocery and provisions trade in the second half of the nineteenth century and the early decades of the twentieth. The growth of fixed-shop retailing of these goods and the emergence of a new class of retailers may be suggested as the two most important changes. The need for increased numbers of fixed shops in the trade arose directly from the great volume of imported provisions entering Britain in these years. These goods could not of course be sold in markets in the same way as home-grown produce. The emergence of new types of retailers in the trade had more complex origins. Some of the existing skilled grocery retailers and home-produced-provision dealers and factors began to handle the imported produce, but reluctance to move far away from traditional lines of goods was marked. Up to the turn of the century many of the imported products were of low quality and were badly packed and shipped, and many grocers would not handle sub-standard goods. The grocers moreover often had not the facilities for or the experience of handling large quantities of perishable imported goods. Finally the traditional grocers were attuned to the medium- and higher-class markets in outlook, location and pricing policies and were not well placed for retailing the imported goods to the working-class market. The flood of imported provisions, therefore, called into existence a new race of fixed-shop retailers who were eagerly concerned to fill the gap left by the traditional types of retailers and to distribute the new types of goods to the working classes in the towns as rapidly and in as great a volume as possible. Many of these new types of retailers, for example the Co-operative Societies, already sold some of the goods, and had begun adapting their organizations to the new types of goods. Others, for example the majority of the multiple shop organizations that emerged, were new to the trade, and these new types of retailers without strong traditions behind them were able to break new ground in buying and selling policies and techniques.

The growth of food manufacture began to have equally important, though less dramatic, effects on the character of the trade. No new class of retailers was needed to handle these products but the hitherto unchallenged position of the skilled grocer began to be undermined. Specialized skill, training and experience were hardly necessary in the handling of the factory-made products and the advantage the skilled grocer had in respect of catering individually for the tastes and needs of his customers was no longer so all-important. Further, some of the new types of retailers who had entered the trade on the imported provisions side were beginning at the turn of the century to add to their range of goods by selling some manufactured food products, thus competing directly with the traditional grocer.

Both the development of food manufacture and the growth in the volume of imported provisions brought about changes in the divisions of the trade and in the techniques of retailing. Some of the older types of retailers, such as the Italian warehouseman, the specialist tea dealer and the cheesemonger virtually disappeared. The oil and colourmen moved away somewhat from the grocery trade and specialized rather in paints, hardware and ironmongery. Within the grocery and provisions trade proper the calling into existence of a new race of retailers to handle the vast quantities of imported provisions had the result, up to the turn of the century at least, of maintaining a broad division in the trade between the grocer and the provision dealer. The increase in the volume of manufactured food products on the one hand and the improvements in the qualities and the standards of grading and marking of imported produce on the other, which were being developed from the 'nineties onwards, however, made this division less clear. In the opening decades of the twentieth century the combined grocery and provisions dealer was appearing in important numbers. The traditional type of skilled grocer was being forced, or was becoming more willing, to handle imported produce and, equally important, the shifts in British agriculture towards dairy farming from the 'eighties onwards enabled this type of grocer to buy larger quantities of the higher-quality home-grown produce. The gap between the two sides of the trade had not, however, completely disappeared by 1914.

In retail techniques an important change in sales methods took place in the half-century up to 1914. Certainly in sections of the medium- and in the high-class end of the trade the skilled grocer continued to rely almost entirely upon his reputation and upon the quality of the service offered to the customer rather than on price appeal, advertisement or display. But in the lower-price trade and in sections of the medium-price trade emphasis on the display of the products and on clearly-marked low prices had become universal. Consumers were offered a minimum choice of goods at very low prices with next to no service or frills and with a maximum of advertisement. In many ways it could be said that the selling techniques of the open markets had been transferred to fixed-shop retailing, with the difference that open fixed pricing had taken the place of the higgling of the market place, and advertisement, both by the retailers and by the manufacturers of the food products, had made the din of rival claims even greater.

By 1914, therefore, the grocery and provisions trade from being a purveyor of luxuries to the rich had been transformed into a trade catering vigorously for all classes. There were still many different price markets and many different methods of organization and retailing techniques in use, but the gap between the old and the new methods at the beginning of the First World War was rather narrower than it had been in, say, the 'eighties and 'nineties. Factors bringing about this narrowing of the gap have been mentioned above, such as improved qualities and standards of imported goods and the growth of food manufacture, but in addition the rise in the prices of foodstuffs at the turn of the century and again in the five years before 1914, and the decline in the rate of increase in consumption per head of imported foodstuffs which is shown in part in Table 24, made the grocery and provisions trade highly competitive in the two decades preceding the First World War. Under the stress of this competition all types of retailers examined closely the methods of their rivals and made many adjustments to their previous methods and practices. The older types of retailers learnt something from the new and the newer types of retailers started widening their appeal to markets that had hitherto been the exclusive province of the older forms of retailing.

The trade in the inter-war years

In the inter-war years, while there was no dramatic change in the nature of the grocery and provisions trade equivalent to that brought about by the vast imports of provisions in the second half of the nineteenth century, there were a number of important shifts in the character of the trade and many of the developments that had begun to influence the trade in the decades before 1914 came to fruition. One important change in the general climate of the trade was that it was no longer expanding at a rate faster than the increase in the population. In the inter-war years there was a decline in the proportion of total retail expenditure by consumers represented by expenditure on foodstuffs, and within the foodstuffs group there was a decline in the proportion of total expenditure represented by expenditure on groceries and provisions.[1]

Another development that had important repercussions on distributive methods was the trend in these years towards the purchase by consumers of goods in smaller quantities. Smaller families, smaller houses, and a decline in the practice of home baking and home cooking led to the demand for smaller and more frequent purchases of essential goods in the place of the bulk purchases of the nineteenth century. These factors also led to the demand for ready-to-eat, ready-to-serve products that would cut down the time spent in preparing meals in the home. More frequent purchases of smaller quantities increased the work of the retailer in selling a given volume of goods, and the demand for processed packaged goods stimulated further the development of food manufacture.

The growth of food manufacture was an outstanding feature of the grocery and provisions trade in the inter-war years. As suggested above, the development dates back to before 1900, but in the inter-war years there was a marked increase in the size of the factories and in the range of different goods manufactured or processed before reaching the retailer. Inextricably joined with large-scale food manufacture was the growth of packaging, of branding, of advertising and of resale price maintenance in the grocery trade. In some ways the spread of food manufacturing in these years brought about nearly as many changes in the grocery side of the trade as the imports of cheap produce had effected on the provisions side of the trade in the second half of the nineteenth century.

Viewing the period as a whole the main contrasts with the trade of the pre-1914 era may be suggested as a decrease in the importance of the specialist type of retailer who handled only a few lines of goods, and a corresponding increase in the multiplicity of different lines carried by individual wholesalers and retailers. Secondly a further decline took place in the standard of skill and technical knowledge required of the retailer, and there was a further transfer of retailing functions to wholesalers and manufacturers. Thirdly there was an increase in the volume and the quality of services provided throughout the trade.

The specialist retailer handling only a few lines of provisions or groceries did not disappear in the inter-war years, and many firms maintained their reputation as specialists. The pressure however both

[1] See Appendix A, Table 85.

from the manufacturers, with their desire to increase the number of outlets for their products, and from the consumers, who wished to make small purchases of a large range of groceries and provisions from one shop rather than visit several different specialists, was consistently in the direction of diversification. Further, the retailer in a highly competitive market faced with stable or falling demand was also tempted to try and maintain or increase his turnover by widening the range of goods stocked. There still remained a distinction between those retailers who stocked a large number of lines, for example different cuts of bacon or different types of jam, within a given range of goods, and those retailers who stocked fewer lines of each type of good but a wider total range, that is everything that could possibly be sold in a grocer's, ranging from flour and cakes to brooms and proprietary medicines; but in both instances the trend in the inter-war years was towards a widening rather than a narrowing of the range.

The relative decline in the technical skill required of the retailer was a direct consequence of the growing importance of large-scale manufacturing and of packaging, of the transfer of food processing operations to the wholesaler and producer and of the introduction of mechanical labour-saving devices in the shops. At the same time, however, while the demands on the retailer as a tradesman were declining, those on his ability as a business man were growing. Knowledge of accounts, ability to keep them as a guide to policy, ingenuity and patience in maintaining stock records and in making the endless calculations and decisions as to the relative advantages of particular offers of manufacturers and wholesalers, became as necessary for the achievement of success as knowledge of blends of tea, of qualities of bacon and of the uses of herbs and spices, and as important as shrewdness in anticipating consumer needs and tastes.

In addition to these demands for greater business skill, the changed conditions of the trade in the inter-war years also called for the provision of greater services. In the nineteenth century the distributive services provided to the consumers were those of expert advice and knowledge, expert buying and expert selling. In the twentieth century, with the manufacturers, producers and importers taking over many of these functions and with the growth of standards and guarantees as to quality and consistency of the goods, the services provided became more physical and financial in their character. Retailers were assisted in their stocking and selling problems by more frequent deliveries, by delivery of small quantities, by longer credit and by advice as to window display. Consumers were assisted in making their choice of goods by advertisements, by extensive window and shelf display and by the widening of the range of goods stocked. And they were assisted in their shopping by larger and better laid-out premises, by improvements in the cleanliness and hygiene of the shops, by the sale of goods in smaller quantities attractively wrapped and packaged, by delivery of goods to the home and by the provision of credit.

In retailing techniques, therefore, many changes took place. The trend was in the direction of larger shops; and in many areas a double-fronted shop, with groceries displayed in one window and served from one counter and provisions displayed in the other window and served from a second counter, became a necessity. The open display of goods inside the shop, particularly of packaged goods, to remind the customers of the names they had read in the newspapers and seen on the hoardings, and the many elaborate fittings, cabinets and show-cases that were introduced, similarly required larger premises and better layout if confusion and congestion were to be avoided. More service was required in the shops. Instead of seven-pound jars, two-, one- and half-pound jars were sold; in place of half a stone of flour, three-pound bags were demanded, and instead of the weighing out of bulk quantities of oatmeal, the customer was served with two packets of breakfast cereals. Finally delivery of the purchases made, or sales from travelling shops, became common in certain working-class and most middle-class areas, and were no longer practices confined to the upper end of the trade.

One further consequence of the growth of food manufacturing was the development of competition from outside the grocery and provisions trade proper. Packaged goods could be sold as easily by non-grocery shops as by grocery shops, and the greengrocer, the butcher, the dairyman, the domestic stores dealers and the variety chain stores all began to add some groceries to their existing lines. The dairymen went further in certain areas and on their 'second' deliveries, or 'pudding' rounds, provided the housewife on her doorstep with a wide range of provisions and some groceries along with the milk. At the same time, as suggested above, the grocer himself was encouraged by the development of packaged goods in other trades to stock a wider range of goods. Whereas he might have had doubts about handling tobacco mixtures in jars and sweets and toffees that had to be broken up, weighed and bagged, he had no hesitation in adding ready-packaged cigarettes and wrapped bars of chocolate and sweets to the lines of goods he stocked.

This account of the changes in the practices of the grocery and provisions trade in the inter-war years has been somewhat simplified to highlight the main developments. The changes discussed did not penetrate to all sections of the trade or to all types of retailers. The provisions trade, for example, had remained comparatively free of branding and resale price maintenance and, with the exception of margarine, of manufactured food products. Again, many specialist retailers carrying but few lines remained in the trade, as did some of the old-fashioned type of grocers with their canisters, drawers, sacks and jars. Finally, the small grocer-cum-general-dealer was to be found in the villages and in tiny shops on the corner of back streets and in the side streets of most large towns. But dealers trading in fair-sized shops and surrounded by marble counters, shelving and glass show-cases stacked with half-a-dozen makes of breakfast cereals, a dozen types of jams, packages of various choices of biscuits, varieties of sugar and blends of tea, and literally hundreds of samples of branded condiments, sauces, pickles, spread, food beverages, gravy mixtures, essences and powders, were representative of the bulk of the trade in the 'twenties and 'thirties, as was the very full service they were prepared to provide for their customers.

The trade in the Second World War and post-war years

The unusual supply and demand conditions during the Second World War and in the immediate post-war years led to a number of further changes in the structure and organization of the grocery and provisions trade. Most of these changes proved, or will probably prove, to be of a temporary character only, and they do not call for discussion here. The few developments which would appear to be of a more permanent nature may, however, be noted. The first was the trend away from the specialist retailer. Under rationing the consumers preferred to register with dealers who carried a full range of groceries and provisions rather than with specialists, in the hope of being able to purchase from the former some of the non-rationed goods that were in short supply. This weakened the position of the specialist retailers who may have sold only a limited range of provisions. Many of these specialists were able to make a fundamental change in their trading policies by stocking a full range of groceries and provisions, but this was not a solution open to all. Other specialists, owing to the smallness of their shops, to shortages of supplies and to the lack of pre-war contracts with suppliers, had to close down. It would appear very unlikely that even with the ending of all rationing a return to the specialist grocery and provisions retailer of the old type will take place.

The shortage of manpower, particularly of men and boys, during these years led to other changes in the trade which may be permanent. First there was a big increase in the numbers of women employed, particularly on the retailing side, and secondly, in the hope of reducing the manpower required or of utilizing it more efficiently, many firms and organizations experimented with self-service grocery and provisions units. These self-service shops operated under difficulties in that rationed goods could not be served under full self-service conditions and building restrictions and shortages of materials limited the extent to which the premises could be completely equipped and designed to suit the needs of this form of retailing. Nevertheless, the initial success of these shops would suggest that the importance of this form of retailing will increase in the future rather than decline.

Finally, under government price and margin control the trend in both the war and post-war years has been towards a lowering of gross margins in the grocery and provisions trade. Whether margins will remain at these lower levels if and when price control is lifted must be a matter of conjecture. The existence of relatively small margins in a period of rising prices and rising costs has, however, certainly forced most firms in the trade to reconsider very carefully their methods and techniques of retailing. In particular economies in delivery and service have been made that may quite probably be of a permanent character.

Broadly, however, the years of the Second World War and the immediate post-war years were a period of standstill in the grocery and provisions trade. The shortages of goods and of manpower and the control by the government of prices and margins, entry to the trade, and materials and building licences, combined to limit new developments, to discourage diversity in trading policy, and to lead to an important measure of uniformity in practice between different types of wholesalers and retailers.

This account of the main developments in the character of the grocery and provisions trade since the middle of the nineteenth century provides a background against which the developments in the retail structure of the trade, and in particular the growth of large-scale retailing, in these years can be examined in closer detail. The growth and characteristics of multiple shop retailing in this trade will be analysed in some detail first, and a briefer discussion of the development of Co-operative trading will follow.

The first multiple shop firms and the growth of this form of retailing

The first firm to have more than 10 retail branches in the grocery and provisions trade was, according to existing records, Walton, Hassell & Port, of London. This firm had some 30 branches in 1870 and more than 40 branches in 1875, though its business at that time was more inclined towards the oil and colour and Italian warehouseman trade than to the grocery trade proper. The first firms to operate on a multiple branch scale in the grocery and tea trade were James Pegram of Liverpool, George Carter of London, Thomas Lewis of North Wales and two specialist tea companies, the London and Newcastle Tea Company of the North-East coast and the Star Tea Company of London and elsewhere. These 5 firms had between 10 and 20 branches each in 1875, and in all the 6 multiple firms known to have been in existence in the trade in that year controlled 108 branches.

Five years later there were 14 firms operating more than 10 branches each, and this number included the well-known firms of Leverett & Frye of London, Abraham Altham of Burnley, Burgon & Company and the Globe Tea Company of Manchester, the International Tea Company of London and elsewhere, and Thomas Lipton of Glasgow. These 14 firms operated 277 branches in 1880. Walton, Hassell & Port was still the largest firm, with nearly 50 branches. The London and Newcastle Tea Company was the second largest, with between 40 and 50 branches, and in the third place was the rapidly rising firm of Thomas Lipton. Of these 14 firms, 11 were in existence in 1950, though only 4 of them were still trading as independent units. Seven had become subsidiaries of other firms.

From 1880 onwards the increase in the number of multiple shop firms and in the number of branches controlled by these firms was rapid, and the estimates of the numbers in existence in different years between 1875 and 1950 are presented in Table 25. Altogether the records of some 260 firms have been included in this table, of which 145 were still in existence in 1950. Amalgamation accounted for 72 of the 115 firms that were no longer trading separately in 1950 and the remainder would

Table 25. *Estimates of the number of multiple shop firms and branches in the grocery and provisions trade, 1875–1950*

Year	10–24 branches		25–49 branches		50–99 branches		100 or more branches		Totals			
									10 or more branches		25 or more branches	
	Number of		Number of		Number of		Number of		Number of		Number of	
	Firms	Branches	Firms	Branches	Firms	Branches	Firms	Branches	Firms	Branches	Firms	Branches
1875	5	64	1	44	—	—	—	—	6	108	1	44
1880	12	183	2	94	—	—	—	—	14	277	2	94
1885	23	302	5	166	3	220	—	—	31	688	8	386
1890	32	470	9	278	3	200	2	317	46	1,265	14	795
1895	46	638	17	545	6	404	3	652	72	2,239	26	1,601
1900	49	755	16	504	8	522	7	1,663	80	3,444	31	2,689
1905	58	859	21	711	10	704	7	2,155	96	4,429	38	3,570
1910	70	1,033	21	741	12	820	11	3,276	114	5,870	44	4,837
1915	72	1,088	27	924	14	1,051	12	4,067	125	7,130	53	6,042
1920	80	1,161	31	1,016	10	664	17	5,039	138	7,880	58	6,719
1925	78	1,250	27	906	16	996	19	6,325	140	9,477	62	8,227
1930	84	1,297	33	1,036	29	1,753	21	7,675	167	11,761	83	10,464
1935	77	1,181	35	1,176	24	1,662	19	8,309	155	12,328	78	11,147
1939	68	1,056	39	1,275	24	1,589	26	9,198	157	13,118	89	12,062
1950	54	822	40	1,351	22	1,415	29	10,075	145	13,663	91	12,841

appear to have gone out of existence or to have ceased trading as multiple shop firms.

A minor difficulty which arose in the classification of firms in this trade was the somewhat indistinct division in the earlier years between grocers and oil and colourmen. The distinction between the two trades was much clearer by 1920 and the character of the firm at that date, if it was still in existence, has been used to decide the classification in the earlier years. For example, if an oil and colourman of the 'eighties had developed substantial grocery sales by 1920, the firm has been classed as a grocer throughout.

The figures given in Table 25 can be used to show the rate of growth of multiple shop retailing as indicated by the rate of increase in the number of branches in existence between different periods. The use of the numbers of branches in existence to indicate rate of growth is not satisfactory, as the average size of branches changed over time and the branches of different firms differed in size. The net increase in the number of branches in different years does, however, give a general indication of the progress of this form of retailing, and in Table 26 an attempt is made to show the net increase and the rate of net increase in five-yearly periods (except for the Second World War) between 1880 and 1950. The rate of net increase is shown as a percentage increase in the numbers as between two dates, and the absolute net increase in the number of branches is also shown as an average yearly net increase.

Table 26. *Rate of net increase in the number of branches of multiple shop firms in the grocery and provisions trade, 1881–1950*

Year	Branches of firms with 10 or more branches			Branches of firms with 25 or more branches		
	Net increase in number of branches	Percentage net increase	Average yearly net increase in numbers	Net increase in number of branches	Percentage net increase	Average yearly net increase in numbers
1881–1885	411	148	82	292	311	58
1886–1890	577	84	115	409	106	82
1891–1895	974	77	195	806	101	161
1896–1900	1,205	54	241	1,088	68	218
1901–1905	985	29	197	881	33	176
1906–1910	1,441	33	288	1,267	35	253
1911–1915	1,260	21	252	1,205	25	241
1916–1920	750	10	150	677	11	135
1921–1925	1,597	20	319	1,508	22	301
1926–1930	2,294	24	459	2,237	27	447
1931–1935	557	5	111	683	6	137
1936–1939	790	6	197	915	8	229
1940–1950	545	4	49	779	6	71

The fluctuations in the growth in the numbers of multiple shop branches appear clearly in Table 26. Steady growth from 1875 led to an early peak being reached in the years 1896–1900. This was followed by a slight decrease in the opening of branches after the turn of the century. But in the ten years from 1905 to the First World War the net gain in new branches averaged some 270 a year, or over 5 per week. The First World War halted development but in the 'twenties there was a spectacular increase in the number of branches, the absolute net increase in the number being of the order of 8 per week throughout these years. The depression of 1929–33 brought about an abrupt change. Some firms managed to expand in these years, but the majority did not add significantly to the numbers of their branches and a few firms had to close down some of their branch shops. The four years preceding the Second World War saw the rate of increase in the number of branches pick up again, but the high level of the earlier periods of expansion, 1896–1900, 1906–15 and 1921–30 was not reached. During the Second World War the number of branch shops in existence actually fell, owing to shifts of population, shortages and enemy action. In the post-war years, however, many branches were reopened or rebuilt and by 1950 there had been a slight increase in numbers over the pre-war figure.

The figures presented in Tables 25 and 26, however, give only a very general picture of the growth and the fluctuations in the growth of multiple shop retailing in the grocery and provisions trade in these years. Certain aspects and characteristics of this growth and some of the reasons for the success of multiple shop retailing in this trade need to be examined in closer detail, for example the developments in the size of firms and the growth of different types of firms, the sources of finance and the changes in the retailing methods and techniques.

The growth of different types of multiple shop firms

A striking feature of multiple shop development in the trade was the rapid growth of some very large firms that catered for the national market. Leading the way in the period of expansion up to 1914 was the International Tea Company, which had nearly 100 branches in 1885 and over 200 branches in 1890. The Home and Colonial Stores had also passed the 200 branches mark by 1895 after a short existence of ten years, and at the turn of the century this firm had over 400 branches. In addition to these two firms, three others passed the 200 branches mark by 1900—Thomas Lipton, the Maypole Dairy Company, and the Star Tea Company with which were associated Ridgways and James Pegram & Company. By 1910 these 5 firms each controlled more than 300 branches and by 1920 these 5, together with the Meadow Dairy Company, with which was associated Pearks Dairies, each controlled more than 400 branches. In the case of the Star Tea-Ridgways-Pegram group and the Meadow-Pearks group, amalgamation was in part responsible for the rapid increase in the size of the firms. But the other 4 firms had expanded by direct opening of additional branches, the number of mergers with smaller firms being of little significance.

The years 1920–50 saw a further growth in the size of the very large firms, with the significant difference, however, that this growth in size was due far more to amalgamations and mergers with other firms than to the opening of new branches. Further, as a result of amalgamations the actual number of giant firms decreased. In 1950 there were 3 organizations with over 600 branches each, one of which controlled more than 3,000 branches and another more than 1,000. Of the 6 large firms mentioned above that had over 400 branches each in 1920, 4, the Home and Colonial Stores Ltd., Lipton Ltd., the Maypole Dairy Company, Ltd., and the Meadow Dairy Company, Ltd., had combined, along with a number of smaller firms, to form the Home and Colonial group, though the individual companies continued to use separate trading names. The other two, the International Tea Company's Stores Ltd. and the Star Tea-Ridgways-Pegram group, again with a number of slightly smaller firms, had combined to form the International Tea group. These mergers and acquisitions took place chiefly in the years 1923 to 1933. The third large firm, Moores Stores Ltd., was the outcome of the merger of a number of medium- and small-sized firms, mainly in the five years or so before the Second World War and in the post-war years. In all some 40 separate firms were acquired in these thirty years by the 3 largest companies in existence in 1950. Some of these amalgamations were, however, financial in character rather than commercial. That is, while financial control of one firm by another existed, the trading and commercial practice of the subsidiary firm remained, for a number of reasons, independent of the controlling firm.

The rise of these very large firms with a national coverage of branches was paralleled by an equally vigorous growth of smaller firms that had a local or regional coverage, so that while a gap in the size between the national firms and the local and regional firms developed, there was only a slight increase in the relative importance of the largest firms. The gap in the size between the very large firms and the small and medium-sized firms in the period 1900–50 is shown in Table 27, which gives a breakdown of the size-groups of firms in greater detail than that given in Table 25.

Table 27 suggests that after 1900 there was no real halfway house in size between a local or regional multiple shop organization with 25–200 branches and a national organization with over 400 branches.

The table also shows that the proportion of the total number of branches controlled by local or regional multiple shop firms and those controlled by national multiple shop firms remained relatively steady in these years. There is a slight shift in time towards the right in this table, that is towards the larger size-groups, but the firms with 25–199 branches which controlled 50% of the total number of branches in 1910 and 51% in 1930 still controlled 44% of the total in 1950. Local and regional organizations had not lagged in any marked degree behind the national organizations.

Table 27. *Multiple shop firms in the grocery and provisions trade analysed by size of firm, 1900–50*

Year	Total number of branches controlled by firms with 25 or more branches	Proportions of total number of branches controlled by firms in different size-groups					
		25–99 branches %	100–199 branches %	200–299 branches %	300–399 branches %	400–599 branches %	600 or more branches %
1900	2,689	38	9	38	—	15	—
1910	4,837	33	17	—	14	36	—
1920	6,719	25	20	—	—	28	27
1930	10,464	27	24	—	3	5	41
1939	12,062	24	20	11	3	—	42
1950	12,841	21	23	9	3	—	44

This parallel growth of the very large and of the smaller firms is also seen if the changes in the relative importance of the largest firms are examined. This analysis is made in Table 28.

Table 28 confirms the impression that there was no significant change in these years in the relative importance of the leading group of largest firms, though within the group a marked increase took place after 1920 in the relative importance of the 2 largest firms. This increase was largely the result of the mergers discussed above between some of the largest firms and not so much of the opening of new branches by the largest firms at a rate faster than the increase in the total number of multiple shop branches.

The relative stability throughout these years of the proportion of the total number of branches represented by firms with less than 200 branches each meant that there was a continuous increase in the number of such local and regional firms. In this size-group, therefore, some of the firms at any given point of time had about reached the limit of their expansion, while others were just entering the field or growing rapidly. The firms tended to grow up to the 100–200 branch size and then remain fairly static in numbers, though the organization of the

Table 28. *Relative importance of the largest multiple shop firms in the grocery and provisions trade, 1900–50*

Year	Total branches of firms with 10 or more branches			Total branches of firms with 25 or more branches		
	Proportion controlled by			Proportion controlled by		
	The largest firm %	The 2 largest firms %	The 5 largest firms %	The largest firm %	The 2 largest firms %	The 5 largest firms %
1900	12	20	42	15	26	53
1910	11	22	42	13	27	50
1920	12	23	42	14	27	49
1930	27	36	45	31	40	51
1939	28	38	45	30	41	49
1950	26	37	46	28	39	49

firm might itself be improved. In a few cases, after reaching a peak the number of branches declined or the firm was amalgamated with another firm. The continuous entry of the new firms in the 1920–50 period does not appear clearly in Table 25, as, while new multiple shop firms began to grow, older firms amalgamated or merged with other firms and some went out of existence, so that the total number of multiple shop organizations remained fairly stable. In practice, however, a feature of the inter-war years was the rise of a number of new firms trading on a local and regional basis and growing to 100–200 branches each. Firms such as Green's Stores (Ilford) Ltd., Worthington's Cash Stores Ltd., Tesco Stores Ltd., Thomas & Evans Ltd., Wrenson's Stores Ltd., and Thompson's Red Stamp Stores are examples of this type of growth. Many of these were not new firms at the time of the First World War, in fact some had been in existence a great number of years, but they possessed relatively few branches in 1914 and grew rapidly in the inter-war years. Taking the growth in the number of multiple shop branches as a whole between 1920 and 1950, nearly one-half of the estimated net increase of 5,783 in the number of branches in existence was due to the expansion of some 37 firms which either were not in existence in 1920 or had under 50 branches each at that date.

There is some danger of attempting to read too much into the figures relating to the number of branches and the rate of increase in the number of branches controlled by individual firms, as there were marked variations in the sizes of branches, and also the closing down by firms of their branches in some areas and their replacement by new branches in other areas, which may have strengthened the economic and trading practice of the firm, would not be reflected in the total number of branches in existence as between two dates. Nevertheless, the broad conclusions that can be drawn from this discussion appear to be soundly enough based. These conclusions may be restated as, firstly, that conditions were favourable in the grocery and provisions trade for the rapid growth of a few giant firms which distributed a limited range of standardized goods; these firms grew in size in the early years through the opening of additional branches and in the later years through amalgamations with other firms. Secondly, the large firms did not dominate the opportunities for expansion, and while the growth in size of many firms tended to slow down after the 150–200 branches mark had been passed, new firms which traded on a local or regional scale were emerging continuously.

The finance of the firms

As was the case in other trades, the multiple shop firms in the grocery and provisions trade relied almost exclusively for the capital for their formation and expansion in the period up to the last decade of the nineteenth century on private sources and on reinvestment of profits. In the seven years 1894 to 1900, however, a minor revolution in financing occurred. By the latter year 15 of the 80 multiple shop firms in existence had become public companies and these 15 controlled some 45 % of the total number of branches in existence. Included among these 15 were the 4 largest firms, the International Tea Company's Stores Ltd., the Home and Colonial Stores Ltd., Lipton Ltd., and the Maypole Dairy Company, Ltd., each of which had 200 or more branches at the time of their flotation as public companies. This particular burst in company formation was in part due to the fact that some firms in these years had reached the crossroads of regional limits or national expansion, and if the policy of national expansion was to be adopted new sources of finance were required for consolidation and growth. The conversions in these years were also influenced by the general home investment fever in the air. The spectacular growth of multiple shop trading had caught the imagination of the investing public and every inducement was offered by company promoters to the proprietors of successful businesses to convert their firms into public companies. Not only this, but many public companies were launched to create entirely new multiple shop organizations, that is without taking over existing firms. Very few of these new projects, however, got beyond the stage of the issue of a prospectus.[1] The successful public companies were conversions of going concerns.

---

[1] An example of the optimism of some of the new companies is seen in the *Prospectus* of the Imperial Co-operative Stores Ltd. of 1897. Part of the Prospectus read: 'The system of trading by means of numerous branch establishments supplied from producing centres, or

Multiple shop retailing organizations in the next half-century from 1900 to 1950 continued to be financed partly by appeals to public sources and partly by reinvestment of profits by the firms themselves. In 1920 some 53 % of the total number of branches were controlled by public companies and in 1950 some 63 %. All the giant firms were public companies and they raised additional capital on the market when it was needed for expansion. There were two more bursts of new company formation after 1918, one between 1931 and 1935 and one between 1946 and 1949. Ten firms in this trade became public companies in the first period and most of them were concerns that had developed rapidly and successfully since 1920 and had reached a stage where further expansion was possible but falling prices had made it difficult to finance such expansion out of profits. Nine firms became public companies in the second period 1946–49. These again were firms that had grown rapidly in the inter-war years but, faced with the very steep rise in costs in the post-war period, needed outside capital to continue expansion. In all, some 34 of the 145 in existence in 1950 were public companies.

After the Second World War public financing would appear to have become necessary for all firms that had achieved or aspired to a national coverage, that wished to amalgamate with other firms, or that had reached a medium size after a period of rapid growth and wished to go on expanding. But the private company methods of finance were still adequate in most instances for the firms that had less than 100 branches each.

The retailing methods of the multiple shop firms

The increase in the number of branches, the developments in the size of firms and the changes in the methods of finance tell only a part of the story of the growth of multiple shop retailing in the trade. To complete the story some details of the trading characteristics and retailing techniques must be given.

The early multiple shop firms were of two main types. On the one hand there were the firms, some of which had originally been oil and colourmen, that sold a fair range of groceries though usually with an emphasis on the sale of standardized groceries such as sugar and tea. These firms were the first type of multiple shop retailers in the field. They were usually local or regional in coverage, though one or two of them grew to be very large. For convenience in the subsequent discussion these firms will be referred to as the 'grocery' type of multiple shop organization. On the other hand there were the multiple shop

first hand from the importers, minimizes the cost to such an extent that a company such as this can supply consumers on their own doors, with goods of a high quality and yet at such a price as to leave a handsome return for shareholders.' The company went into voluntary liquidation in September 1897.

firms that specialized in the sale of a very limited range of tea and provisions, usually three or four lines, or six at the outside. These will be referred to as the 'provision' type of organization. Most of these firms started rather later than the grocery type of multiple firm, but grew very rapidly, and a number of them became very large. The International Tea Company and Hunters the Teamen were examples of the grocery type of firm in the years before 1914, while the Home and Colonial Stores, Lipton's and the Maypole Dairy Company were examples of the latter type. The very rapid growth in the number of multiple shop branches from the middle 'eighties up to 1914 was due in large part to the growth of the provision type of firm.

The branch shops of the grocery type of firm were usually larger than those of the provision type of firm and the possession of larger shops stocking a much wider range of commodities was one of the reasons why the grocery type of firm grew rather more slowly than the provision type. Another factor influencing rate of growth was that the provision type of firm had a much clearer field for expansion, the main competition coming from other multiple shop firms rather than from established retailers.

Both types of firms supplemented their large-scale purchases direct from importers, producers or manufacturers by undertaking food processing and manufacturing wherever possible. Most of the large firms dealing in tea, for example, had their own blending warehouses and aimed at placing contracts with the growers. A few, for example Lipton Ltd., owned plantations. Again, some of the large firms dealing in butter and margarine, for example the Maypole Dairy Company Ltd., had their own creameries and margarine factories, and the grocery type firm began in the early decades of the twentieth century to manufacture a number of the products, such as preserves, self-raising flour, sauces, pickles and cooked meats, that were sold in their shops.[1] This growth of integration was in a sense a continuation of the earlier practice of the traditional grocer. In the case of the specialist provision firms, concentrating on the retailing of three or four articles, the proportion of the sales represented by goods manufactured, produced or processed by the firm might rise as high as 50 %, but in the grocery type firm selling a much wider range of goods the proportion would rarely rise above 15–20 %.

The shops, the selling methods, the salesmen and the customers of the multiple shop organizations in the early years contrasted strongly with

---

[1] Integration was considered of great importance by some firms. The International Tea Company for example in 1895 attributed its success not only to the opening of new branches but to the fact that the firm had 'undertaken within recent years the successful manufacture of many of the commodities for which they have an assured retail and wholesale outlet by which means additional profits have been made'. *Prospectus*, May 1895.

those of the traditional grocer. The typical multiple shop branch unit on the provisions side of the trade was not so much a shop as a simple structure for distributing a limited number of articles to the public in the minimum of time and space. Physically, the unit was small, with one counter as practically the only fitting, and the main display of the goods was in the open shop fronts and hanging from rails outside the shop. Most of the trade was undertaken in the evenings, the shops being open until 10 or 11 p.m. and often to midnight on Saturdays, and the hissing fish-tail gas jets or oil lamps lit up the heaped piles of eggs, the mountains of butter and margarine, the bacon, sugar and tea that customers were invited to purchase. The staff numbered two or three and the 'outside man' in his white serving coat would be shouting the price, value and quality of the goods, enticing and attending to customers and handing or throwing purchases or money back to the counter for weighing, wrapping or putting in the till. Retailing methods in the grocery type of multiple shop and in branches in the smaller and country towns were less flamboyant, but the principle was essentially the same, namely rapid and large-scale distribution.

Standardization in all essentials, in the bold fascia and nameplate across the shop-front, in fittings, in commodities and even in the serving coats or aprons or sometimes the straw hats of the assistants, was usual in the case of the larger firms. Trading was strictly for cash, and to make all customers aware of this many of the firms included the term 'cash grocers' in their name. Delivery to the home was rarely demanded or provided. Inducements to shop, such as overweight butter or margarine, 'bonus' tea or sugar were usual, and in the industrial North dividends on purchases in the form of cash, stamps or free gifts in order to compete with the dividend paid by Co-operative Societies, were an accepted part of sales policy. The publicity of the branches themselves was supplemented by ingenious and startling advertising campaigns run by the firms centrally to draw attention to the value and cheapness of the goods sold. Such campaigns ranged from posters, leaflets, handbills and free gifts, to elephants pulling outsize cheeses through the streets and processions of men dressed as coolies carrying chests of tea.

The brightness, busyness, shouting and advertising of the multiple shop retailers contrasted with the practices and traditional methods of the private grocer. A further difference lay in the extent to which the multiple organizations developed division of labour and aimed at sending goods to their branches pre-weighed and pre-packed ready for sale. The time taken to perform the various operations of blending, mixing, cutting, grinding and measuring, a part and parcel of the craft of the private grocer, would have slowed down sales and reduced turnover. The multiple shop organizations therefore tended to concentrate their sales on goods which did not require this preparation, such as pre-blended and pre-packed tea and goods in tins and jars, thus eliminating, for example, the blending and bagging of tea and the cumbersome and sticky process of serving syrup and jams out of barrels and vast pots. As food manufacturing increased, so the multiple organizations could increase their range of pre-packed goods.

The customers of these early multiple shop retailers were drawn almost exclusively from the working classes. Their shops, with few exceptions, were located in industrial towns and in working-class areas of larger towns, and, while many were in main streets, side streets also served their purpose. The goods sold, and the price policy and the advertising of the firms, were directed to groups who were not in a position to make comparisons between the courtesy of the traditional grocer and the noisy brusqueness of the new 'company' shops as they were called. The mass distribution methods certainly lacked refinement, and consumer choice and service was kept to an absolute minimum. But thanks to these organizations and to other representatives of the new race of retailers, commodities such as butter, eggs, tea, bacon, ceased to be special luxuries on the working-class table and could be and were purchased by the working classes easily, cheaply and regularly.

After the turn of the century some small but significant changes in retailing methods began to be made by existing multiple shop firms or to be introduced by new firms. The growth of food manufacture, the improved standards in quality, grading and marking of imported produce and the greater experience and larger capital resources of many multiple shop firms were the main factors bringing about the changes. The rising volume of factory-made products enabled the grocery type of multiple shop firms to start competing with the traditional grocer on his own ground. The introduction of standards of imported goods meant the end of the first flood of goods when practically anything, good or bad, could be sold to an eager public. Buying now became a more routine occupation based on known grades, with skill being shown in price and quantity quotations rather than in guesses and judgement as to quality. These changes took place against the background of stable or rising prices of foodstuffs, in contrast to the practically continuous fall in prices since the last quarter of the nineteenth century, and of a slowing down in the rate of increase in consumption per head.

The days of easy growth of multiple shop retailing had come to an end, competition between multiple shops themselves and with other retailers became severe, and if progress was to be continued new techniques were necessary and new markets had to be entered. Shops began to be improved in layout, larger shops were acquired to sell the larger stocks and ranges of goods, and additional fittings, for example display cases, the bacon slicer and the cash register, began to be installed. On the provisions side marble slabs and tiled floors began to replace the deal or mahogany counters and the sawdust, and some firms began to display goods behind windows instead of leaving them open to the dirt and dust from the streets. Some of the newer grocery type multiple shop firms no longer emphasized 'cash' in their names but used the phrase 'family grocers', with all that that implied by way of provision of a wide range of high-quality goods, of credit and of delivery, and of the type of customers sought. Some of the newer provision type of multiple shop firms aimed at overcoming the prejudices of the middle classes regarding 'foreign' butter, bacon, cheese and eggs and, equally significant, began to make large-scale purchases of home-grown produce.

Before 1914 these new trends were in their infancy. All the multiple organizations with a national coverage, with the exception of the International Tea Company Ltd., were specialists distributing a limited range of products in bulk through a very large number of outlets and at an absolute minimum of cost and service. To give an example, just before the First World War over three-quarters of the trade of the 800 odd branches of the Maypole Dairy Company Ltd. was in margarine. Nevertheless the smaller local and regional firms which had been increasing in importance alongside the giants, firms such as John Sainsbury and David Greig of London, Coopers of Liverpool, Burgons and John Williams of Manchester and Willsons of Newcastle were developing successfully some of the newer techniques of multiple shop retailing.

Changes in multiple shop retailing methods after the First World War

In the three decades following the First World War further adjustments and alterations in multiple shop trading techniques and methods of organization had to be made to keep abreast with the changes in the character of the trade and in the nature of consumer demand. Most of the changes are not measurable statistically, but a description of the most important developments should convey a broad impression of the main shifts that took place.

The first major development was that the term 'multiple shop grocery and provision dealer' ceased to be synonymous in the public mind with the small specialist shop dealing in a limited range of provisions and catering mainly for the working classes. Certainly, until 1939 at least, these specialist shops played an important part in multiple shop retailing as a whole, but they came to be outnumbered by a wide variety of different types of multiple shop retailers, all of whom carried larger ranges of goods and catered for wider sections of the community. At the end of the First World War about 40 % of the multiple shops could be classed as specialists, defined as shops having three-quarters or more of their turnover in six lines; by 1939 not more than 25 % of the shops fell in this category. This decline, however, was uneven.

Up to the early 1930's there was no significant decline in the importance of this type of firm. The number of branches of specialist multiple shop retailers appears in fact to have increased between 1920 and 1930, but the economic depression of the early 'thirties weakened the position of these firms and led to closures of branches and changes in trading policies. The rationing system introduced in the Second World War, as mentioned above, undermined the position of this type of retailer still further, and by 1950 not more than 10 % of the total number of multiple shop branches in the trade could be described as specialists.

Apart from the internal financial problems which troubled some of the larger specialist firms in the late 'twenties, the uneven purchasing power of the working classes in the depression years was one of the main factors leading to a slowing down in the rate of increase of, and later to an actual fall in, the number of specialist shops. The prices of the goods sold by these shops, that is, mainly imported provisions, tea and margarine, fell in the depression years, but this fall was not accompanied by any significant increase in the sales of the goods. But while turnover declined, overheads and fixed costs hardly fell at all. The multiple shop branches selling a wide range of groceries were not faced with quite so serious a problem. The prices of their goods did not fall as rapidly, and they offered in their shops a wide and attractive range of goods which could be and were purchased as the price of other necessities fell. This was one factor telling against the specialist multiple shop firm in the depression years. Others were the growth of economic nationalism leading to import restrictions, the setting up of agricultural Marketing Boards, which improved the bargaining position of the farmer and producers, and, a factor of very great importance in the case of the older and larger specialist firms, the shifts in the location of the population of the United Kingdom which were proceeding throughout the inter-war years.

The difficulties faced by such firms are well illustrated by the following extract from the 29th Annual Report of the Meadow Dairy Company, Ltd., 1935.

Quite apart from the handicaps imposed on us as retailers by the continued curtailment of the spending power of so many of our customers, and the interference caused to our business by quotas and restrictions of various kinds, we have also, as proprietors of multiple shops, to contend with the changes in shopping districts which have been gradually taking place during recent years but which have latterly been much more marked, by reason of the movement of such a large proportion of the population to the new housing areas which have been developed as a result of the Government's plans for housing extensions and slum clearance. Many of the old market thoroughfares have entirely altered in character and the population which supported them is no longer there, whilst on the new estates the houses are spread out over so wide an area that it is often difficult to open a shop in a position which will command a trade sufficient to make it profitable.

This company closed 49 shops in 1935 and opened 24 new branches in the same period, principally in the new housing areas. Such a readjustment was typical of those attempted by most of the larger and older firms in the 'thirties, though the process was by no means painless. The small or nil dividends paid by these companies in these years reflect among other things the disadvantages of an early start in the field, of the possession of freehold properties in older areas which were no longer valuable trading sites, and of attempting, somewhat later than their competitors, to obtain suitable sites in developing areas. Moreover, this adjustment had to be made in a period when turnover was obstinately refusing to rise. Another readjustment made by some of the specialist firms in the years before 1938 and by most of them, owing to the system of rationing, in the Second World War, was that of adding to the range of goods sold. The smallness of some of the older branches placed physical limits on the extent of this reorganization, but additional lines such as jams and marmalade, canned goods and biscuits were introduced, and most of the newer branches that these firms opened were planned from the start to carry a wider range of goods.

A third type of adjustment made by the larger specialist firms, which was mainly financial in character and did not affect the character of the branches, was that of acquiring smaller and growing multiple shop firms whose trading and business was complementary to, rather than competitive with, the parent firms. In particular towns this type of acquisition delayed, for a time at any rate, the need to consider changing the character of the specialist branch shops of the parent company. Very broadly it can be said that the mergers between and acquisitions of other firms by the specialist companies in the years before 1930 had been mainly of like businesses, while from 1930 onwards the acquisitions were those of contrasting businesses.

The second main development in the character of multiple shop retailing in this trade was the obverse of the foregoing trend, that is, a great widening of the range of different types of multiple shop firms and of the range of goods stocked. Whereas before 1914 it was possible to refer to provision types and grocery types of multiple shop retailer, in the inter-war years, except for the specialist discussed above, no single classification would cover more than a fraction of the other types of firms. Each of the regional and local organizations developed characteristics that suited and fitted their particular market, and, within each firm, branches in different localities in the same town or region often adopted slightly varying trading policies. Some of the multiple shop firms were at the top end of the trade, giving extensive credit, receiving a part of their business by telephone, and providing full delivery, while others opened small, standardized but attractive shops in main thoroughfares and on the new housing estates, and traded for cash. Again some firms concentrated on developing a general grocery and provisions business in county and market towns, often taking over existing businesses and using the old trading names, while others developed groups of small shops in small local shopping areas of older industrial towns.

The variety of development makes generalizations regarding changes in the character of multiple shop retailing as a whole particularly difficult, but there is little doubt that multiple shop firms in the inter-war years were no longer solely concerned with the working-class market and that a marked improvement took place in the layout, lighting and fittings of the branches, in their size, and in the design and dressing of the windows. The physical and aesthetic appeal of the retail unit as a pleasant place in which to shop, a consideration which before 1914 had in most instances been secondary to the policy of low prices, tended in the inter-war years to be of equal, if not of greater, importance than the price policy. Particularly was this development encouraged as the scope for significant differences in price between shops in the grocery and provisions trade narrowed in these years. The multiple shop organizations aiming at the middle-class market reached a very high standard of shop layout, display and cleanliness, and these firms played a leading part in introducing new methods and techniques in their shops.

These changes were accompanied by changes in methods of sales promotion. As the gas-lit open-front shop was replaced by the shop with plate-glass windows and lit by electricity, so advertising methods changed. If parades through the streets to draw attention to the goods and prices of multiple shop retailers were typical of the go-ahead firms of the pre-1914 era, the use of well-produced catalogues and of polite letters to householders, followed up by canvassing for orders backed by a wide range of goods and full delivery service, was perhaps more typical of the expanding firms of the late 'twenties and 'thirties.

There is equally little doubt that, taking a general view of the trend in multiple shop retailing in this trade, there was an increase both in the range of goods stocked and in the variety of goods offered within the range. The private dealer in most instances still tended to carry a wider range of goods than the multiple shop branch, though the difference in this respect was not so great as in the pre-1914 period. But in regard to variety or the number of lines within a given range the multiple shop branch very frequently offered the greater choice. The main distinction between the goods stocked by these two types of retailer, however, lay in the extent to which the private dealer stocked branded, advertised and price maintained lines while the multiple shop branch carried fewer national brands and more of their 'own' brands, that is brands of goods individual to the particular multiple shop organization. Food manufacture by multiple shop retailing firms, which made 'own' brands possible, had begun before 1914. The inter-war years saw a big increase in this practice, and nearly all the firms with 100 or more branches each by the Second World War undertook some food manufacture or processing. In addition multiple shop firms often had agreements with manufacturers for the exclusive supply of particular brands of goods which they themselves did not manufacture. In one sense the positions of the multiple shop firm and the private grocer had been reversed in that in these years it was the multiple shop firms which undertook food manufacture and processing while the private grocer tended more and more to sell the ready manufactured branded and standardized products.

The growth of the food manufacturing industry itself in these years and the obvious advantages that accrued to multiple shop organizations by the extension of their operations to manufacture were two factors influencing this growth of integration. But a third factor considered of equal importance was the wish of multiple shop firms to avoid, as far as possible, the dangers that might arise from dependence on manu-facturers for the supply of advertised and branded products sold to the multiple shop firms under the same conditions as those agreed to by the small-scale retailer. Integration of production and distribution was, however, limited in this trade owing to the wide variety of goods and lines carried by the retail branch. In fact many multiple shop retailers were finding that there were diseconomies in attempting to manufacture too many lines, and they began to limit the range of their productive activities to a few basic and staple lines. In 1939 the proportion of the total sales of the larger multiple shop firms represented by goods of their own manufacture was rarely more than one-quarter and usually 10–15%. Inevitably, therefore, except for the firms concentrating on the provisions side of the trade, the multiple shop retailers sold some goods that were manufacturer branded and nationally advertised products.

The location of multiple shop branches

A final aspect of the changes in the methods of organization and retailing techniques of multiple shop firms was the shifts in the location of the branches which took place in response to the movement of the population and as a result of the changed trading policies of the firms. Reliable figures before 1919 are not available, but it is possible to use the figures relating to the permits for the sale of government-controlled butter in 1919 and the permits for the sale of sugar in 1949 to indicate the broad changes in the location of multiple shop branches as between the two dates and also in the number of multiple shops per head of the population in different areas. These comparisons are presented in Table 29. Both sets of figures have limitations. In the case of the 1919 figures not all multiple shop organizations in the grocery and provisions trade applied for permits to sell government butter and not all multiple shop organizations applied for permits centrally as multiple shop firms. The term multiple shop organization in 1919 relates to organizations with 6 or more branches. The 1949 figures are subject to similar limitations in that not all multiple shop branches sold sugar or registered as multiple shop firms, though the coverage of multiple shop organizations is certainly very much more complete in the 1949 figures than in the 1919 figures. The definition of a multiple firm in 1949 relates to firms with 10 or more branches.

As figures at the two dates are not strictly comparable too much stress cannot be placed on small changes shown in Table 29, but the broad trends would appear to be soundly based. The shifts in the proportion of the total number of branches located in different regions do not appear to have been very great, and those shifts that did occur corresponded on the whole with the movement in the population. The exceptions to this would appear to be the Northumberland and Durham region and the Welsh region. In these regions there was an increase in the proportion of the total number of branches between the two dates, but a decrease in the proportion of the total population represented by these regions. This relatively rapid increase in the number of multiple shop branches in these areas is confirmed by the figures relating to the number of branches per 10,000 of the population at the two dates. In both areas the increase in the number of multiple shops per 10,000 of the population was much greater than the average increase for the whole country.

Table 29 also suggests that in both 1919 and 1949 branches of multiple shop organizations were thicker on the ground in the North of England and in Scotland than in the rest of the country with the exception of London, that is there were more branches per 10,000 of

Table 29. *Regional distribution of branches of multiple shop firms, and the number of branches per 10,000 of the population, in the grocery and provisions trade in 1919 and in 1949**

Region	Proportion of total number of multiple shop branches in different regions		Number of multiple shop branches per 10,000 of the population in different regions	
	1919 %	1949 %	1919 number	1949 number
Scotland	10·3	9·1	1·5	2·7
Northumberland and Durham	6·5	7·4	2·1	5·0
Yorkshire	11·0	10·4	1·9	3·5
Lancashire, Cheshire, Westmorland and Cumberland	18·3	14·1	2·1	3·2
North Midlands	4·8	4·9	1·2	2·2
Midlands	6·7	7·6	1·4	2·7
South Midlands	4·5	4·3	1·7	2·4
Eastern Counties	2·1	1·8	1·1	1·8
London and Home Counties	28·0	31·0	2·0	3·9
South West	3·7	3·7	1·1	2·0
Wales	4·1	5·7	1·1	3·4
Great Britain	100·0	100·0	1·7	3·2

* The figures for 1919 are adapted from those given by S. Bushell, 'The Relative Importance of Co-operative and Other Retail Traders', *Economica*, vol. 1, no. 1, January 1921. In 1919 each shop in the country which sold government butter had to obtain a permit from the Ministry of Food and its customers had to register. The permits for branches of multiple shop organizations were applied for under one name, hence it is known how many branches were owned by each firm and where they were situated. The figures for 1949 are adapted from those of sugar registrations provided by the Ministry of Food. The 1919 figures relate to 7,062 multiple shop branches and the 1949 figures to 15,406 branches. The inclusion in the 1919 figures of multiple shop firms with 6–9 branches does not seriously affect the comparison with the 1949 figures, as there were only 254 such branches and these 254 branches supplied only 1·5% of the total number of customers registered with multiple shop firms.

A comparison of the number of branches of multiple shop firms holding registrations for butter in 1919 with the number of grocery and provisions branches listed in this inquiry is made in Appendix A.

The constitution of the various regions distinguished is as follows:

The North Midland region consists of Lincolnshire, Nottinghamshire, Derbyshire, Leicestershire, Northamptonshire and Rutland.

The Midlands region consists of Staffordshire, Shropshire, Warwickshire, Worcestershire and Herefordshire.

The South Midlands region consists of Buckinghamshire, Oxfordshire, Berkshire, Wiltshire, Hampshire and the Isle of Wight.

The Eastern Counties region consists of Norfolk, Cambridgeshire, Bedfordshire, Suffolk and Huntingdonshire.

The London and Home Counties region consists of London, Essex, Hertfordshire, Middlesex, Kent, Surrey and Sussex.

The South West region consists of Gloucestershire, Somerset, Devonshire, Cornwall and Dorset.

the population in these areas. This was, however, mainly a reflection of the smaller size of the typical units in the Northern areas than of those in the South. This difference is illustrated in Table 30, which shows the regional distribution of the total number of multiple shop branches and of the total number of customers registered with multiple shop firms for butter and sugar in 1919 and 1949, and also the average number of registrations per multiple shop branch in the different regions.

Table 30. *Branches and registered customers of multiple shop retailers by regions, for butter in 1919 and for sugar in 1949*

Region	1919—Government butter			1949—Sugar		
	Distribution by regions of the total number of multiple shops		Average number of registrations per multiple shop branch	Distribution by regions of the total number of multiple shops		Average number of registrations per multiple shop branch
	Branches %	Registrations %		Branches %	Registrations %	
Scotland	10·3	7·6	920	9·1	8·1	585
Northern	40·6	34·4	1,040	36·8	28·6	511
Midland	6·7	7·7	1,410	7·6	9·0	775
London, East and South East	30·1	38·5	1,579	32·8	40·6	812
South and South West	8·2	8·5	1,258	8·0	9·0	735
Wales	4·1	3·5	1,023	5·7	4·7	536
Great Britain	100·0	100·0	1,228	100·0	100·0	658

The regions used are as follows:

The Northern region consists of Northumberland, Durham, Yorkshire, Lancashire, Cheshire, Westmorland, Cumberland, Lincolnshire, Nottinghamshire, Derbyshire, Leicestershire, Northamptonshire and Rutland.

The Midland region consists of Herefordshire, Shropshire, Staffordshire, Warwickshire and Worcestershire.

The London, East and South East region consists of Bedfordshire, Cambridgeshire, Essex, Hertfordshire, Huntingdonshire, Norfolk, Suffolk, London, Middlesex, Surrey, Kent and Sussex.

The South and South West region consists of Berkshire, Buckinghamshire, Dorset, Hampshire, Oxfordshire, Somerset, Gloucestershire, Wiltshire, Devonshire and Cornwall.

The use of averages conceals significant variations between different multiple shop organizations. There were organizations with small branches and a small number of registered customers per branch in, say, the London region, and firms with large branches existed in the North of England, but the broad difference between the two areas is clear enough. In 1919 some 51 % of the total number of branches of multiple shop firms were in the North of England and Scotland, but only 42 % of the total number of multiple shop customers were registered with these branches. The Midlands and the London areas, on the other hand, contained 37 % of the branches but these branches catered for 45 % of the registered customers. In 1949 the contrast still existed, 46 % of the branches being in the North of England and Scotland, with 37 % of the registrations, while 40 % of the branches were in the Midlands and London regions and served 50 % of the registered customers.

The reduction by about one-half of the average number of registered customers per multiple shop branch over the whole country between 1919 and 1949 was in no way related to a change in the size of branches. The larger number of customers per branch in 1919 was a reflection of the important role played by the specialist multiple shop provision firms at this date. The 5 national organizations, in fact, with 2,790 branches, served 62 % of the total number of customers registered with multiple shop firms, and the average number of customers per branch was 1,957. The remaining 4,272 branches of multiple shop firms had an average of only 774 registered customers per branch. Customers tended to register for butter with the specialist firms because of their reputation, but the registered customers went elsewhere for their purchases of other provisions and groceries. In 1949, on the other hand, the customers registering at a branch for sugar purchased a fairly high proportion of their other groceries and provisions at the same shop. As discussed above, the trend in the size of multiple shop branches in the inter-war years was one of an increase in size, the reverse of the impression given in Table 30.

The main features of multiple shop development in the grocery and provisions trade from the last quarter of the nineteenth century to 1950 may now be summarized. In terms of numbers of branches in existence the story is one of a rapid and continuous increase since the 'eighties with the exception of the two war periods. The outstanding feature of the period of growth up to the First World War was the emergence of a few giant firms that opened hundreds of standardized branches throughout the country, selling a limited range of groceries and imported provisions and catering mainly for the expanding working-class market. These giants led the way, though the smaller firms were not far behind in introducing new methods and techniques of retailing to the trade. Vigorous salesmanship backed by low prices and advertisement was the keynote, and refinements in retailing were kept to a minimum. As food manufacturing developed so did multiple shop trading on the grocery side of the trade and in the decades before the First World War many firms were widening the range of the goods sold and their appeal to different price markets. The inter-war years were years both

THE GROCERY AND PROVISIONS TRADE 157

of expansion and re-orientation of multiple shop trading. The giant firms, now publicly financed, continued to grow, mainly by amalgamation, and a large number of new, smaller organizations arose. Many firms remained specialists with a reputation for good quality and low prices in a narrow range of goods, but the main trend, in keeping with changes in consumer habit and taste, was towards improving the standards and siting of the multiple shop branches, increasing the range of goods stocked, and catering for the family trade and middle-class trade and not only the working-class cash trade. Practically all the larger firms undertook some food manufacture or processing as well as retailing, though the increasing variety of goods sold limited the significance of integration. Regionally multiple shop trading had always had a bias towards the Midlands and the South, particularly London, but the distribution of the branches, mainly in industrial towns and market towns, was fairly even in the inter-war years throughout the country and adjustments, some painful, had to be made by some of the older firms to match the movements of the population. The shortages and controls of the Second World War brought the progress of multiple shop trading to a halt and saw the end, probably for ever, of the specialist multiple shop retailer concentrating on four or six commodities. In the post-war years, however, considerable recovery was made and most firms had regained their pre-war positions, in numbers of branches at least, and a few firms had expanded considerably beyond this level.

The Co-operative Societies

The Co-operative Societies were the first distributive organizations to develop large-scale methods of retailing in the United Kingdom. The story of the movement is one of consistent growth since the Rochdale Pioneers opened their first shop in 1844, and as the movement grew, as the number of Societies increased and the membership rose, so the Co-operative Societies led the way in open pricing of their goods, in emphasis on standards and quality, and in cash trading at fair prices. As the bias of Co-operative trading has always been towards foodstuffs, particularly groceries and provisions, the Co-operative Societies were the first organizations to introduce large-scale buying and selling methods in this trade.

By 1880 there were already about half-a-million members of over 900 Co-operative Societies, and the retail trade of these Societies in groceries and provisions was more than £10 millions. By contrast, in this year there were only a handful of department stores in existence and the total number of branches of multiple shop retailers selling groceries and provisions was under 300. Twenty years later the membership had risen to some 1,700,000 and the total retail trade in groceries and provisions to over £30 millions. And while the multiple shop movement had grown rapidly in these two decades the Co-operative Societies were still by far the most important large-scale retailers.

In the last quarter of the nineteenth century the Co-operative Societies played a prominent part in the distribution of the rapidly increasing volume of imported provisions, and the two Wholesale Societies were among the first organizations to develop the large-scale purchasing of provisions and manufacture of food products. By the turn of the century the Wholesale Societies were placing direct con- tracts with overseas producers; in 1902 they went further and owned their first tea plantations; they were chartering ships to bring produce to Britain; and they were manufacturing in more than half-a-dozen factories a wide range of groceries, including biscuits, preserves, pickles, flour, cocoa, lard and soap, which were sold by the Retail Societies.

The membership of the Societies was drawn almost exclusively from the working classes, and the Societies themselves and their shops were found in the industrial districts of the North of England and of Scotland. The Societies did not follow the aggressive advertising and pricing policies of the multiple shop retailers in the grocery and provisions trade, nor did they specialize in imported provisions to the same extent. The aim of the Co-operative Societies was rather to provide their members with a full range of essential groceries and provisions of good quality at the prevailing market prices, and to pay back to the members through the dividend any trading surplus that might be made. And the dividends in these years before 1914 were high, sometimes reaching 5s. and 6s. in the pound. The attraction of the dividend on purchases, the reputation for honest trading and the loyalty of the working-class members to the democratic ideals of consumers' co-operation, together with the growing efficiency of the Societies, were more important in the success of Co-operative retailing than the practice of the Societies in relation to the siting of shops, display, advertising or price.

Co-operative trading after 1918

By 1919 the four million membership mark had been passed and in this year 10·7 million consumers were registered with Co-operative Societies for sugar and 8·7 million for butter out of a resident population of 41·7 millions. The Societies undertook a higher proportion of the total trade in these standardized products than in the total trade of all groceries and provisions, but these registration figures indicate the significant role the Co-operative movement was playing at this date. In the case of the sales of butter some regional details are available showing that 30% of the population of the North of England and Scotland were registered with Co-operative Societies in 1919. These figures can also be used to illustrate the regional bias of the movement in that 70 % of the total butter registrations held by Co-operative Societies were in these two northern areas.

In the decades following the First World War the Co-operative movement, after a set-back in the depression of 1922–24, was able to record a fairly continuous increase in membership and in the sale of groceries and provisions. Membership rose from 4·1 millions in 1919 to 8·5 millions in 1939. The increase in the number of Co-operative branches selling groceries and provisions is more difficult to determine, but in 1919 5,500 shop permits for the sale of government butter were issued to Co-operative branches, in 1937–38 the Co-operative Union estimate of the number of Co-operative branches selling groceries and provisions was 9,400, and in 1940 9,500 Co-operative branches received permits for the sale of rationed sugar. As not all Co-operative branches sold government butter in 1919 the figure of 5,500 shops in that year is probably a slight underestimate of the total. The increase of 55–60 % in the number of Co-operative branches between 1919 and 1940 may be compared with the increase of 65–70 % in the number of grocery and provisions multiple shop branches in approximately the same period. The growth in membership and in the sales of groceries and provisions was not accompanied by any fundamental changes in the basic principles of Co-operative trading, but there were a number of developments in the methods and areas of trading.

Changes in the character of the retail shops and branches of the Societies followed the general trend in the trade in the direction of stocking and selling a wider range of groceries and provisions, of displaying the goods more attractively and of improving the layout and fittings of the interiors of the shops. The Co-operative Societies had always possessed rather larger shops than those of their competitors, and the new shops opened in the inter-war years were similarly larger. Further, the Co-operative Societies began to provide more services to members, delivery to the home was undertaken and in some areas 'travelling' shops were introduced widely. Broadly, however, with the exception of the newer shops in areas where the Co-operative movement was expanding in these years, such as the Midlands and the South of England, the Co-operative grocery and provisions shops did not keep pace in standards of layout, fittings, display and attractiveness with the leading multiple shop grocers and private traders. The Co-operative Societies followed only slowly the move towards prominent main-street siting of their branches; the premises built in side streets and in main streets that had been by-passed with shifts in the population were considered quite adequate by many Societies. Further, the widening of the range of lines of groceries and provisions sold was only a partial success.

The Societies developed a large trade in the basic standardized groceries and provisions such as sugar, butter, margarine, bacon, cheese and cooking fats, but the sales of other goods such as biscuits, canned goods and fancy groceries were less satisfactory.

The Wholesale Societies continued to expand their large-scale buying and productive activities. Additional tea estates were acquired in India and Ceylon, bacon factories were built in Denmark, farming was undertaken in the United Kingdom and overseas purchasing depots were established in Canada, Australia, South America, New Zealand and Africa. The number of food factories increased and manufacturing was extended to practically all major lines of groceries. But once again these developments were not perhaps as smooth and successful as was hoped. On the one hand the Wholesale Societies were at a disadvantage compared with the manufacturing and buying departments of a large multiple shop organization in that, whereas the central buying department of a multiple shop firm had complete control over the trading activities of the retail branches, the Co-operative Wholesale Societies could only treat with the Retail Societies as equals. The Retail Societies were free to buy what they liked and to charge what prices they liked. In the case of standardized commodities such as butter, bacon and tea the relationships between the Retail Societies and the Wholesale Societies presented few problems. In the case of less standardized grocery goods, however, the Wholesale Societies were never sure of a guaranteed market. On the other hand, the productive activities of the Wholesale Societies were being faced with increasing competition from the branded and advertised food products of private manufacturers. The members of Retail Societies were influenced by the advertising campaigns of private manufacturers and in some cases by the higher quality of the goods themselves, and demands for these branded advertised commodities increased. The Wholesale Societies attempted to counteract this trend by developing their own branding and advertising campaigns, but reluctance in the earlier years to 'waste money on advertising' meant that the Wholesale Societies got away to a late start in a field where an early start was vital. Further, Retail Societies, anxious to maintain and increase their turnover, were not always active in countering private manufacturer advertising by salesmanship of the products of the Wholesale Societies.

The major change in the spheres of trading of the Co-operative movement in the years after the First World War was the growth of the movement in the Midlands and the South of England. Some detail of this development has been given above and will be discussed later in this chapter during the examination of the regional shifts in all types of large-scale retailing. All that need be added here is that this expansion of Co-operative trading in the Midlands and the South of England applied to the trade in groceries and provisions as well as in other goods. Further, many of the improvements in the standards of Co-operative retailing of these goods and in the range of services offered to consumers in these years took place in the developing regions. The bias of the movement towards the North of England and Scotland remained, however, and of the total sugar registrations held by Co-operative Societies in 1949 some 60 % were in the North of England and in Scotland.

In the Second World War and post-war years the development of Co-operative trading was uneven. In the war years, with bombing and the movement of the population, there was a trend away from large-scale retailing and in favour of the more conveniently located smaller shops, and the Societies' trade decreased. In the post-war years, however, they recovered the lost ground and, to take one yardstick, the number of customers registering with the Societies for sugar, which had totalled 13·6 millions in 1940 and had fallen to 10·7 millions in 1941, had passed the 1940 peak by the end of 1950. At this date some 28 % of the total sugar registrations in the country were held by Co-operative Societies. There were, however, other problems facing the Societies. One was the limits placed on the activities of the Wholesale Societies by Ministry of Food control of many imports. A second and more serious development was the fall in the dividend on purchases. Throughout the inter-war years the dividends of practically all Societies had been lower than those of the pre-1914 era. But increase in prices and costs and the controls by the Ministry of Food over margins in the war and post-war years reduced further the trading surplus of Retail Societies. This surplus stood at 9·87 % of retail sales in 1938 and had fallen to 7·1 % in 1950. This 1950 figure can be compared with trading surpluses of 13·8 % of retail sales in 1900, 13·4 % in 1910, 8·75 % in 1920 and 10·18 % in 1930.

The reduction of nearly 30 % in rate of surplus had not led, as shown above, by 1950 to any decline in membership or in sales, but as dividend on purchases had always played such an important part in the trade of the Co-operative movement in groceries and provisions the rapid fall in the average rate of dividend in the post-war years from 1s. 9d. in 1945 to 1s. 3¼d. in 1950 was posing serious problems as to the future of Co-operative trading policies.

One last development in methods of Co-operative retailing in groceries and provisions was the lead taken by many Co-operative Societies in the establishment of self-service units. By 1950 over 600 of such units were in full or partial operation. The fact that the branches of Co-operative Societies were larger than the average multiple shop branch in the grocery and provisions trade and very much larger than those of the private trader assisted this development of Co-operative self-service units. The Societies establishing such units were for the most part trading in the Midlands and the South rather than in the North of England and Scotland.[1] Experience of these units had been too short to permit final judgement as to their future place in Co-operative trading, but the experiments to 1950 have been regarded by the Societies as highly successful.

The main features of Co-operative trading in groceries and provisions in the hundred years between 1850 and 1950 may be summarized. Co-operative retailing was the first type of large-scale retailing to emerge in this trade. It was founded on a policy of honest trading and the payment of a dividend on purchases and its main field of advance was among the working classes. The marked rise in the real purchasing power of these classes enabled the movement to grow rapidly in the last quarter of the nineteenth century, and the parallel development of large-scale buying and food manufacture by the Wholesale Societies assisted this expansion. In the twentieth century, particularly in the inter-war years, the Co-operative movement was faced with more severe competition from other types of retailers, and the growth of branding and advertising of grocery goods by private manufacturers limited to some extent the appeal of Co-operative food products. Membership and the sales of groceries and provisions continued to rise, however, after a set-back in 1922–3, throughout the inter-war years. The number of branches increased rapidly and an important factor in this continued progress was the expansion of Co-operative trading in the Midlands and the South of England. The standards of Co-operative retailing improved in these years, as did standards throughout the grocery and provisions trade, and the basis of the Co-operative membership was widened slightly to include sections of the middle classes.[2] The Second World War, with controls, shortages, and movement of the population led to a slight decline in Co-operative trading, but by 1950 the lost ground had been regained. Price and margin control had, however, led to a serious reduction in Co-operative dividends.

[1] Of the 607 self-service units in operation at the end of 1950 some 60 % were in the Midlands, South and South West of England and Wales. These areas had converted about 12–15 % of their grocery and provisions shops to self-service, while in the Northern Counties and Scotland only 2–3 % had been so converted.

[2] A survey undertaken by the Co-operative Wholesale Society Market Research Department in 1944 made estimates of the proportions of the different occupational groups in the country that were members of Co-operative Societies. The results suggested that 25 % of the professional classes, salaried executives, etc., were in membership, and 37 % of the salaried clerical workers. These figures compared with 67 % of the miners and 53 % of the heavy industrial and transport workers, etc. *A Consumers' Democracy*, Manchester, Co-operative Wholesale Society Ltd., 1951, p. 120.

Shares of the different economic types of retailer in the total trade

Estimates of the shares of the different economic types of retailers in the total retail trade in groceries and provisions between 1900 and 1950 are presented in Table 31. The estimates relate to the sales of groceries and provisions only. The retail sales by grocers and provision dealers of goods other than groceries, for example wines and spirits and tobacco and cigarettes, are excluded from the estimates. The sales of groceries and provisions by firms engaged primarily in other trades, for example dairymen, are, however, included in the estimates of sales according to the classification by economic types of these non-grocery retailers.

Table 31. *Estimated shares of the different economic types of retailer in the total retail sales of groceries and provisions, 1900–50**

Year	Proportion of total sales undertaken by		
	Co-operative Societies %	Multiple shop retailers %	Other retailers (by difference) %
1900	14·0–16·0	4·0– 7·0	77·0–82·0
1905	15·0–17·0	6·0– 9·0	74·0–79·0
1910	16·0–18·0	9·0–12·0	70·0–75·0
1915	17·0–19·0	12·0–14·0	67·0–71·0
1920	18·0–20·5	13·0–16·0	63·5–69·0
1925	17·0–20·0	16·0–18·0	62·0–67·0
1930	19·0–21·0	18·0–20·0	59·0–63·0
1935	20·0–22·0	20·0–22·5	57·5–60·0
1939	22·0–24·0	22·0–25·0	51·0–56·0
1950	21·0–23·0	23·0–25·0	52·0–56·0

* For a discussion of the basis of these estimates see Appendix A. The 'other retailer' category is a residual group and therefore includes the sales of groceries and provisions by department stores and the sales by producer/retailers, e.g. the sale of butter by farmers, as well as the sales by small-scale grocers and provision dealers.

The trends shown in Table 31 are sufficiently clear to obviate the need for elaboration. The general pattern is that the share of the multiple shop retailers rose more rapidly than the increase in the share of Co-operative Societies until the middle of the inter-war years and that from these years onwards the rate of increase of the two types was roughly parallel.

Regional comparisons of the trade of the different types of retailer

Some detail can, however, usefully be added for the thirty years following the First World War as to the regional shifts in the importance of the different economic types of retailer. Reference has been made to the pattern of regional growth in the above discussion of two types of large-scale retailer, but here a comparative analysis of the regional importance of all types of retailers can be attempted.

Estimates of the shares by regions of the different types of retailers in the total trade in groceries and provisions are not available for individual years, but the outlines of the regional shifts can be seen fairly clearly when use is made of the figures relating to butter registrations in 1919 and sugar registrations in 1949. The 1919 figures overstate considerably the relative importance of large-scale retailing in the grocery and provisions trade as a whole, the share of the multiple shop retailers being greatly inflated. Adjustments can, however, be made so that the incidence of overstatement is not greater in one region than another, thus permitting regional comparisons.[1] Similarly, the proportions of the total sugar registrations held by the different types of retailers in 1949 are not fully representative of the trade in all groceries and provisions, but again this fact would not appear to invalidate regional comparisons in that year.[2]

The registrations for butter held by the different economic types of retailer in 1919 expressed as a proportion of the total resident population by regions in that year, and registrations for sugar held by the different economic types of retailer in 1949 expressed as a proportion of the total sugar registrations by regions, are shown in Table 32.

[1] In 1919 150,000 permits were issued to shops for the sale of government butter, and multiple shop retailers (that is firms with 6 or more branches) took 7,062 permits for their branches, the Co-operative Societies took 5,500 permits and the remainder, approximately 137,000, were taken out by small-scale retailers. To purchase the butter customers had to register with retailers, but as some consumers made their own butter, or purchased only home-produced butter, the number of registered customers was only 90 % of the total resident population of Great Britain in that year of 41,760,000. The incidence of non-registration for imported butter was not even throughout the country, being higher in rural areas such as the South West of England and North Wales than in urban areas such as London. Further, the consumers who did not register for imported butter purchased their home-produced butter from small-scale retailers or producer/retailers rather than from large-scale retailers. In order to avoid regional distortion of the share of large-scale retailers in the total trade in butter, the number of butter registrations with such retailers are expressed therefore as a percentage of the total resident population in each region rather than as a percentage of the total imported butter registrations in each region.

This regional adjustment does not, however, offset the main bias of the butter registration figures towards the large-scale retailers. Both multiple shop retailers and Co-operative Societies tended to specialize in imported provisions to a greater extent than the small-scale retailer, and customers would register for butter at the shops of large-scale retailers but make purchases of other groceries and provisions from small-scale retailers. Further, multiple shop retailers tended to specialize in imported provisions to a much greater extent than Co-operative Societies. Therefore the overstatement contained in the proportion of the total resident population registered with multiple shop retailers for butter in the consideration of the total trade in all groceries and provisions is very much greater than in the case of Co-operative Societies.

[2] As the number of customers registered for sugar with different retailers in each region in 1949 coincides closely with the estimates of the resident population in each region, the registrations held by each type of retailer can be presented as a proportion of the total registrations.

Table 32. *Registrations for butter in 1919 and for sugar in 1949 held by different economic types of retailer, by regions**

Region	1919 Proportion of total resident population buying butter from			1949 Proportion of total sugar registrations held by		
	Co-operative Societies %	Multiple shop retailers %	Other retailers %	Co-operative Societies %	Multiple shop retailers %	Other retailers %
Scotland	27·4	13·6	59·0	44·5	16·7	38·8
Northern	31·2	19·6	49·2	35·1	17·7	47·2
Midland	16·8	19·7	63·5	24·5	21·4	54·0
London, East and South-East	8·8	29·4	61·8	17·5	31·0	51·5
South and South-West	15·0	17·0	68·0	21·4	17·7	60·9
Wales	16·7	11·6	71·7	20·3	19·2	60·5
Great Britain	20·9	20·8	58·3	27·8	21·8	50·4

* The composition of the different regions is given above, p. 155.
The total resident population in 1919 was 41,760,000. The total number of registrations for sugar in July 1949 was 46,305,000.
The number of consumers registered for butter with Co-operative Societies in 1919 was 8,730,000. The total number registered with multiple shop retailers was 8,690,000. The number purchasing butter from other retailers in each region is arrived at by deducting the sum of the customers registered with large-scale retailers from the total resident population in each region. The other retailers group therefore includes producer/retailers and consumers making their own butter.
The number of consumers registered with Co-operative Societies for sugar in 1949 was 12,871,000. The number registered with multiple shop retailers (firms with 10 or more branches) was 10,112,000. The figures relating to the 1919 registrations are based on those given by S. Bushell, *Economica*, vol. 1, no. 1, January 1921.

The figures in Table 32 show clearly the importance of the Co-operative Societies in the North of England and in Scotland in 1919 and their relative weakness in London, the Eastern Counties and the South East. If the analysis is extended to areas within the broad regions given, 45 % of the 2,160,000 resident population of Northumberland and Durham in 1919 were registered with Co-operative Societies but only 5 % of the 4,466,000 resident population of London were so registered. The multiple shop retailers, on the other hand, were strongest in the London, East and South East region and weakest in Wales and Scotland. Some 34 % of the population of London in 1919 were registered with multiple shop retailers for butter, but only 12 % of the 2,103,000 resident population of South Wales. Large-scale retailing, that is Co-operative and multiple shop trading together, was most prominent in the Northern region and in Scotland and least important in the Midlands and Wales.

In 1949 the overall pattern of the relative importance of Co-operative and multiple shop trading as between different regions had not changed greatly. The Co-operative Societies were still strongest in the North of England and in Scotland and the multiple shop retailers strongest in London, the Eastern Counties and the South East, but progress had been made in different areas. The Co-operative Societies would appear to have advanced most rapidly in Scotland, and in the London area where they now held 17 % of total registrations, and least rapidly in the Northern region. Multiple shop traders would appear to have advanced most rapidly in Wales, where they now held 19 % of total registrations, and in Scotland, and least rapidly in the Northern region and in the South and South West. Large-scale retailing was still most prominent in 1949 in Scotland and the Northern Counties and least important in Wales and the South and South West.

The changes in the regional activity of the different types of retailer can also be examined by reference to the proportion of the total registrations held by each type in the different regions in 1919 and 1949. This analysis is made in Table 33, and the regional distribution of the resident population in 1919 and of the sugar buying population in 1949 is given alongside to indicate the changes in the proportion of the total population as between regions.

The regional contrasts between Co-operative and multiple shop retailing appear clearly in this table. In 1919 nearly 70 % of the total registrations held by the Co-operative Societies were in the North of

Table 33. *Regional distribution of registered customers of different economic types of retailer in 1919 and in 1949*

Region	1919 Distribution by regions of			1949 Distribution by regions of		
	Resident population %	Co-operative butter registrations %	Multiple shop butter registrations %	Sugar buying population %	Co-operative sugar registrations %	Multiple shop sugar registrations %
Scotland	11·7	15·3	7·6	10·5	16·9	8·1
Northern	36·6	54·5	34·4	35·3	44·7	28·6
Midland	8·2	6·5	7·7	9·1	8·0	9·0
London, East and South-East	27·2	11·4	38·5	28·7	18·0	40·6
South and South-West	10·1	7·3	8·3	11·0	8·5	9·0
Wales	6·2	5·0	3·5	5·4	3·9	4·7
Great Britain	100·0	100·0	100·0	100·0	100·0	100·0

England and Scotland, an area containing some 48 % of the population. Only 42 % of the multiple shop registrations were in these two areas at this date. In the Midlands, the London and the Home Counties areas, comprising 35 % of the population, the Co-operative Societies had 18 % of their registered customers in 1919 while the multiple shop retailers had 46 %. In 1949 just over 61 % of the Co-operative registrations were in the North of England and Scotland, comprising 46 % of the population, and the proportion in the Midlands, London and the Home Counties, comprising 38 % of the population, had risen to 26 %. The multiple shop proportions had shifted to 37 % in the North and Scotland and nearly 50 % in the Midlands, London and the Home Counties.

Both types of retailers had changed the pattern of their regional distribution with the shifts in the population between 1919 and 1949. New multiple shop organizations had come into existence and grown in new areas and Co-operative Societies had increased their membership at different rates in different areas. The change in the pattern of Co-operative activity had been greater than the change in multiple shop activity, and Co-operative trading was more evenly spread in relation to the distribution of the population in 1949 than it had been in 1919. Multiple shop retailing had been more widely distributed in 1919 than Co-operative trading, and the adjustments made in the subsequent thirty years were fewer. Both types of retailers had, however, maintained their original biases. In 1949 for every consumer in the North of England and Scotland registered with a multiple shop retailer there were more than two registered with Co-operative Societies. In London and the Home Counties, by contrast, for every consumer registered with the Co-operative Societies there were nearly two registered with multiple shop retailers.

A final comparison between the different economic types of retailers and between the structure of the trade in different regions may be made in respect of the number of customers per branch. In 1919 there are no regional figures available, except those given above for multiple shop firms, but the average number of customers registered for butter per shop over the whole country was as follows: Co-operative Society branches, 1,585 customers; multiple shop branches, 1,225 customers; other retailers, 146 customers. The number of customers per multiple shop branch is not representative of the number of customers regularly purchasing a wide range of groceries and provisions from such branches, owing to the specialization of multiple shop branches in the sale of provisions. To a much less extent the number of customers per Co-operative branch is also inflated. For 1949 both national and regional figures of the number of customers registered for sugar with different economic types of retailers are available and these are presented in Table 34.

Table 34 suggests that in 1949, as in 1919, the Co-operative Societies had the largest number of registered customers per shop and that in 1949 there is a close similarity in the regional size pattern of the different economic types of retailer. In all three cases the number of registered customers per shop is highest in the London and Home Counties area and in all three cases the number of registrations per shop increases as one moves down the map from the Northern region to London. The only significant exception to the general pattern is the high number of registrations per Co-operative branch in Scotland, the region where the Co-operative Societies had the highest proportion of total registrations.

Table 34. *Average number of registrations for sugar per shop of the different economic types of retailer by regions in 1949*

| Region | Average number of sugar registrations per shop | | | |
	Co-operative Societies	Multiple shop retailers	Other retailers	All retailers
Scotland	1,440	585	201	324
Northern	1,030	511	161	276
Midlands	1,340	755	166	271
London, East and South East	1,740	812	296	456
South and South West	1,300	735	215	309
Wales	940	536	171	246
Great Britain	1,210	656	201	324

The reasons for the development of large-scale retailing: multiple shop trading

Many of the basic economic advantages of large-scale retailing have been discussed in earlier chapters. Some of the reasons for the growth of large-scale retailing in the grocery and provisions trade have been mentioned in this chapter in the course of the outlining of the development of multiple shop and Co-operative retailing. No attempt will be made to cover the whole of this ground again, but a summary of the main factors operating in each case may be given.

Multiple shop retailing emerged in the grocery and provisions trade as soon as the supply of and effective demand for a number of standardized commodities had become sufficiently great in volume and consistent in character to make possible economies of large-scale buying and selling. These conditions were developing in the second half of the nineteenth century with the growth in the numbers of the regular wage earning classes, the flood of imported provisions entering Britain, the beginnings of large-scale food manufacture and the fall in the prices of foodstuffs. The rapid growth and success of the multiple shop retailers in this trade was due, apart from the basic advantages of large-scale operation, to two main factors. First the methods of trading they introduced were novel and were particularly suited to the task of distributing the cheap imported foodstuffs to the working classes. Important features of these methods were the multiplication as rapidly as possible of the number of selling points, thus bringing the goods practically to the door steps of potential customers, the insistence on open pricing and on low prices, the adoption of a vigorous advertising and sales policy, the skill shown in buying as a result of specialization in a period when standards and quality were a matter of guess-work, and the elimination of all the traditional distributive practices such as credit, delivery, and heavy stockholding, that might add to the cost of distribution. Secondly the multiple shop retailers were a part of the new race of retailers that had been called into existence through the inability and unsuitability of many of the established grocers and pro-vision dealers to handle the new types of goods and cater for the new types of demand. The rapidity of advance of multiple shop retailing was in part a reflection of the relative absence of direct competition in the section of the market in which they traded.

By the first decades of the twentieth century and markedly in the inter-war years, many of these original advantages of the early multiple shop retailers began to pass. Most of the methods and techniques mentioned above were no longer peculiar to multiple shop retailers. But as some advantages passed others were secured. The greater capital resources of multiple shop retailers, obtained both from the market and from the reinvestment of the profits of many shops and not just one shop, were used to extend the operations of the firms backwards to food manu-facture and to improve the siting of their branches and the layout of their shops. The integration of production and distribution proved very successful in some cases as the branches provided a guaranteed outlet for the products and enabled the factories to operate on long runs. Thus the integrated firms could add low production cost goods to their existing large-scale buying economies. The development of food manu-facture also enabled the multiple shop retailers, with their mass distribu-tive methods, to widen considerably the range of goods that could be sold and to invade a section of the market that had hitherto been the province of the skilled grocer/tradesman.

The possession of capital resources to buy the best sites, to enlarge the size and improve the layout and fittings of the branches, and to provide better services, was of great importance in the inter-war years when the emphasis of competition in the trade began to shift slightly from price to service. Further, many multiple shop firms began to move into the higher-priced markets in which attractive, well-sited shops and the provision of credit and home delivery were essential. These developments were beginning by 1950 to bring about a reversal of the position that had existed fifty years earlier. In 1900 it was the private skilled grocer who led the way in the range of goods sold, in the quality of the products and in the standard of service provided to the consumer, while the multiple shop retailer cut to a minimum both the range of goods stocked and the service offered. By the middle of the twentieth century it was the multiple shop retailers who in many instances possessed the most hygienic and attractive shops, who could offer for selection the greatest number of lines within a given range, who sold the freshest stock and who provided the most efficient service. The small-scale retailer was often restricted to small shops and out-of-date premises in side streets. Division of labour in management permitting the employment of experts not only in buying and selling but also in real estate, shop layout, window display and transport and, most important as the range of stock sold widened, the use of centralized methods of stock control in the individual branches were the main factors helping to bring about this change.

Factors influencing the development of Co-operative trading

As with the growth of multiple shop retailing, the beginnings and consistent growth of the Co-operative movement depended upon the existence of demand and supply conditions favourable to the development of scale in retailing. The Co-operative movement started some quarter of a century earlier than multiple shop retailing in the grocery and provisions trade partly because the founders of Co-operation were pursuing an ideal and not merely profit, and partly because the earliest Societies operated on a small scale and were content to grow slowly. In the 'fifties and 'sixties of the nineteenth century the Retail Co-operative Societies attracted customers and members because of their reputation for honest trading. The Co-operative store was practically the first store in the working-class districts of the North of England where the working-class housewife knew she would not be sold adulterated goods, would not be enticed to run up more credit than she could afford, and would be told clearly the prices of the different articles. Further, it was the first store run by working men—in many instances the shop was only open in the evenings when the management committee came straight from work to serve in the store; and it was the first store that paid the profits made back to the customers.

The Co-operative movement never lost its reputation for honest trading, but with the growing real purchasing power of the working classes and with an increased volume of foodstuffs becoming available the rapid growth of the movement from the 'sixties onwards was the outcome not only of the ideals and trading practices of the Societies but also of the advantages of larger-scale organization. The Co-operative Societies in which the members held shares had greater capital resources than most small-scale retailers and could expand more rapidly. The establishment in the 'sixties of the Wholesale Societies meant that centralized large-scale buying began to be added to the advantages of scale in retailing. And in the last quarter of the nineteenth century the growing productive activities of the Wholesale Societies gave the movement further advantages of integration.

In the first half of the twentieth century these advantages of Co-operative trading continued to exist and to be developed. The system whereby members invested in share capital proved adequate for expansion and growth at least up to the Second World War. The Wholesale Societies greatly extended their large-scale purchasing and productive activities and many of the larger Retail Societies also developed food manufacturing. Marked improvements made possible by greater experience and training were introduced in the management technique of both wholesaling and retailing. In addition to these advantages the growth of Co-operative trading was also assisted by the extension of the movement to the developing industrial areas of the Midlands and the South, areas that because of their shifting population and absence of basic industries had been Co-operative 'deserts' before the First World War.

But these economic advantages of scale developed by the Co-operative Societies would not have led to a rapid development of this form of trading without the attractions of the dividend on purchases, the reputation for honest trading and the democratic system of control. These features enabled the Societies to secure a measure of loyalty and interest on the part of their customers unapproached by any other form of retailing. And this loyalty and the ideals of the movement led in turn to other advantages. One of these was the ability to attract members from over a wide area, thus enabling the Societies to trade from larger shops and to secure the attendant economies. A second was the existence of good labour relations with their staffs, the payment of higher wages than those paid in most sections of the distributive trades, and the attraction of a higher quality of staff.

The small-scale retailer

This account of the developments in the grocery and provisions trade would not be complete without a brief glance at the progress and position of the small-scale retailer. The evidence, both statistical and descriptive, of the activities of these retailers is, however, extremely fragmentary and therefore the suggestions made as to developments must be very tentative.

In the second half of the nineteenth century the great expansion of the grocery and provisions trade resulting from the increased quantities of foodstuffs available, the growth in fixed-shop retailing as against sales in markets, and the development of food manufacture in place of processing and preparation of food in the home, undoubtedly led to a rapid growth in the numbers and prosperity of small-scale retailers as well as to the parallel growth of multiple shop and Co-operative trading. By the closing decades of the century, however, the competition between the older small-scale types of retailer and the new large-scale types of retailer in certain areas of the country, particularly the North, was becoming very fierce. For the first time the cry that the private trader was being extinguished was raised. At the turn of the century *The Times* commented, 'The individual or "single" shop grocer as his fellow traders term him, is indeed between the upper and nether millstone; and the process of attrition is proceeding at such a rate that in many districts he will soon have almost disappeared.'[1] A somewhat alarmist forecast, but the slowing down in the rate of increase of demand for groceries and provisions in the years up to the First World War and the rise in retail prices after 1909 increased the competitive nature of the trade and the fears of extinction of the private trader mounted rather than lessened.

The estimates presented in Table 31 above suggest that at the time of the First World War at least these fears were somewhat exaggerated, though the analysis of imported butter registrations in 1919 show that in the counties of Northumberland and Durham some 65% of the resident population were registered with the large-scale retailers and in Yorkshire and Lancashire about 55% were so registered. In individual towns and districts of towns the eclipse of the small-scale retailer will have been even more complete.

In the inter-war years the small-scale grocer and provision dealer continued to lose ground to the large-scale retailers. In some ways this loss of ground was more conspicuous in these years than in the period before 1914, partly because of the physical disappearance of the small-scale retailer from the main shopping streets and areas and his replace-

[1] *The Times*, 18 August 1902.

ment by the branches of large-scale retailers, and partly because of the slowing down in the rate of increase of the sales per head of groceries and provisions. The noteworthy feature of the trade in these years is, however, not the disappearance of the private grocer but his resilience. Many of the reasons for this resilience have been discussed above in an earlier chapter. For example, the small-scale grocer was much more flexible in size, turnover and location than the multiple shop branch or Co-operative store. He moved into areas where other types of retailer could not exist and, equally important, could stay on in areas where population and turnover were declining. Again the greater stress being placed by the housewife in these years on convenience shopping gave the ubiquitous small one-man shop a new lease of life. He was the shop round the corner for the busy working woman. Similarly demands for extra service, whether for small quantities at a time or for credit or delivery, could be met more readily by one man trusting his judgement—though often with serious consequences—and working very long hours, than by a manager who had to work within the letter of company or Society trading policies. In a trade where labour costs represented a high proportion of total costs the willingness of the one-man retailer to work without reference to trade union rules and regulations regarding wages rates and hours of work also strengthened his competitive position.

The most important reason, however, for the survival of the small-scale grocer would appear to be the growth of the practice of branding and resale price maintenance in this trade. No evidence exists to show the rate of increase in the extent of those practices, but a careful estimate for the year 1938 suggests that over one-third of the total sales of groceries and provisions by independent retailers were resale price maintained.[1] If the goods that were branded but which were not rigidly price maintained were included, the proportion would have been much higher. An outcome of the growth of resale price maintenance was the improvement in the competitive position of the small and independent retailer vis-à-vis the large-scale trading units. This came about in several ways.

The decline in the amount of technical skill required in the trade which followed the general introduction of packaged and branded goods made entry to the trade easier, and thus increased the size and location

[1] J. D. Kuipers, *Resale Price Maintenance in Great Britain*, Wageningen, N. V. Drukkerij 'Vada', 1950, p. 221. The estimates suggest that in the case of independent retailers resale price maintained merchandise amounted to 36% of the industrial working class grocery trade, 37% of the agricultural working class trade and 33·5% of the medium class trade. In the case of the combined multiple shop and Co-operative group the proportions of resale price maintained merchandise sold was 13% in the industrial working class trade, 13% in the agricultural working class trade and 11% in the medium class trade.

flexibility of the independent retailer. The extensive advertising of many of these products by the manufacturers and the reluctance of Co-operative Societies and multiple shop organizations to handle nationally advertised goods assisted the independent retailer. The advertised and branded goods were purchased from the independent retailer by the consumers irrespective of the fact that the multiple shop branch or Co-operative store might be providing similar, but not identical, products at a lower price or with a dividend and in more attractive surroundings. The policy adopted by a number of the larger manufacturers to secure the greatest possible number of outlets for their products meant that the margins fixed for the goods tended to be such as allowed the highest cost retailers at least a small margin of profit. While the proportion of price maintained goods was not sufficiently large and the margins allowed not sufficiently great to ensure that all retailers would in practice make a profit on their total turnover, nevertheless the use of resale price maintenance introduced an element of stability into the trade. The development of branding and resale price maintenance also tended to lessen to some extent the differences in the type of goods and lines stocked and in the prices charged as between one small-scale retailer and another, and, in so far as multiple shop firms and Co-operative Societies handled nationally branded goods, as between the small-scale and the large-scale retailer. Differentiation between shops came to be related as much to the range and quality of the services provided as to the type and price of the goods sold. The small-scale retailer was moreover in a strong competitive position in relation to the provision of some of these services, for example in the location of his shops close to the home and in the personal and individual attention paid to his customers.

Finally, the spread of packaging, branding and resale price maintenance to a number of trades and not only groceries and provisions enabled small-scale grocers and provision dealers to extend the range of goods sold outside the limits of the trade proper and also made it possible for small-scale retailers in other trades to extend their range of goods to include some packaged groceries. The effect of this development was to lead to an increase in the number of marginal retailers in the trade. Some indication of the number of such retailers is provided by the rationing statistics of the Second World War. In 1940 there were some 170,000 small-scale retailers with registered customers for the sale of sugar. In 1941 the Ministry of Food introduced the 25 minimum registrations rule and the number of small-scale retailers with registered customers had fallen to 133,000 by the end of 1941. The reduction in numbers was partly due to bombing and to closures due to shortages of manpower, but it is clear that a large number of retailers in the trade in the years immediately preceding the Second World War had only a very small turnover in groceries and provisions as such.

A broad indication of the regional shifts in the relative importance of the small-scale retailers between 1919 and 1949 was given in Table 32 above. In so far as comparisons can be made between the butter and sugar registration figures, the small-scale retailers would appear to have lost ground in these years most heavily in Scotland and least heavily in the Northern Counties and the South and South West. Without detail as to the changes in the number of shops of the different types of retailer in each region it is not possible to reach any clear conclusions as to the reasons for these variations in the regional rates of survival of the small-scale retailer. This is unfortunate as the contrast in the development between the Northern Counties and Scotland in these thirty years is most striking, particularly as it was in these two areas that large-scale retailing had made the greatest headway by the time of the First World War and the economic climate of these two areas in the inter-war years was roughly similar. An examination of Table 32 and of the more detailed figures available by smaller regions leaves little doubt, however, that there is a broad connexion between the growth of scale in retailing and urbanization and vice versa. The small-scale retailer was most prominent in the rural and semi-rural areas. In North Wales, North Scotland and the South West—Cornwall, Devonshire, Gloucestershire, Somerset and Wiltshire—the small-scale retailer was responsible for some 61–63 % of total sugar registrations in 1949, while in the urbanized counties of Northumberland and Durham and South East and West Scotland he was responsible for only 33–38 % and in London for only 48 % of the total.

The small-scale retailer lost ground continuously to large-scale retailers in the grocery and provisions trade; but the decline, at least to 1950, had not turned into a rout. The economic flexibility of the small-scale retailer, his ability to survive and flourish in the rural markets and the small local markets in urban areas which the less flexible large-scale retailers could not enter, his readiness to provide services of all types to his customers, and above all the support he received from food manufacturers as the main distributor of their products under resale price maintenance terms, enabled the small-scale retailer to slow down the rate of his decline.

Suggestions as to future trends in the trade

Any discussion of future trends in the grocery and provisions trade must of necessity be of a very tentative nature. The number of unknowns, particularly in relation to the supply of goods and government controls and policies is considerable. Some suggestions based on an interpretation of the past trends in the trade outlined above can, however, be put forward as at least a starting-point for discussion.

The main features of the grocery and provisions trade in the three decades from 1920 to 1950 were firstly the slowing down of the rate of expansion of the trade compared with the expansion in the last half of the nineteenth century, and secondly the rapid growth of food manufacturing, of packaging and of grading and marking. The proportion of total consumers' expenditure represented by retail purchases of groceries and provisions tended to fall in these years, while the proportion spent on some other foodstuffs, such as milk and fruit and vegetables, and on goods other than food, such as tobacco, tended to rise.[1] The growth of food manufacture is difficult to measure statistically, but by 1950 practically all the groceries sold by retailers arrived in a processed, packaged state ready for direct sale to the public, and an important proportion of the provisions arrived packaged or wrapped or were graded and marked to standards known to the consumer.

The effects on the distributive structure of these developments in the character of the trade were many. The most important of these was that the emphasis in the trade was shifted from distributing greater and greater quantities of goods and providing only a limited choice and service to consumers, to distributing goods for which consumers had expressed preferences and providing with those goods the services that appeared to meet the consumers' needs. At the risk of over-simplification it may be suggested that there was a shift from the supply of goods to the joint supply of goods and services, and under the heading of services came a number of developments such as cleaner, larger and better laid out shops, the provision of a wider choice of lines, sales in smaller quantities, delivery to the home, the provision of credit and so on. Two other significant changes in the organization of retailing that resulted from the changed character of the trade were the widening of the range of goods stocked by the grocer and provision dealer to include household stores, tobacco goods, sugar confectionery and even meat, and the increased proportion of the goods that were branded and advertised by manufacturers.

In these thirty years the greatest progress was made by those distributive firms and organizations that adjusted or developed their trading policies to meet the changed situation in the trade. The firms that were most sensitive to the changes in consumer tastes and habits, that improved the standards and attractiveness of their commodities and their shops and that were prepared to provide the widest range of goods and services were the firms that outdistanced their competitors in a market that was expanding only slowly. Conditions in the war and post-war

[1] See Appendix A, Table 85.

years modified the trends to some extent in that unemployment, the existence of which had been an important factor in the development of physical services in this trade in the inter-war years, virtually disappeared and consumer choice was limited by shortages and rationing.

What of the future? In regard to the character of the trade it may be suggested that the two broad trends distinguished above will be continued: first that no significant expansion in the trade as a whole will take place and that any general improvement in the standard of living is unlikely to lead to an increase in the share of total consumers' expenditure represented by food, though higher-priced and better goods may be bought; secondly, that the importance of large-scale food manufacture will increase and that the advertising, branding and packaging of practically all groceries and provisions will become universal. To take a minor example, there will clearly be no return to the pre-war practice of the retailer's cutting, shaping and weighing out of goods such as margarine and butter, and other goods such as cheese and bacon will similarly came to be sold ready packaged.

The effects of these developments on the structure and organization of the grocery and provisions trade in the future are difficult to forecast, but some suggestions can be made first as to the general changes in the character of retailing that appear the most likely to emerge, and secondly as to the possible shifts in the positions of the different economic types of retailer.

The changes in retailing are likely to be in the direction of the building of larger shops carrying a wider range of goods and designed in layout and in fittings to give the consumer a wide choice of goods and the convenience of purchasing a number of different types of goods in the same shop. The use of refrigerated display cabinets, deep-freeze units and cellophane or plastic sealed wrappings will become usual, and the combination store, that is the shop selling both groceries and provisions and meat, will grow rapidly in numbers. Given these trends and extended food manufacturing, there can be little doubt that in the densely populated districts these larger stores will be conducted completely or largely on self-service lines. At the same time, however, acceptance of orders by telephone, the provision of credit to customers and delivery to the home is unlikely to disappear and may be undertaken by the self-service units themselves. What does appear moderately certain is that counter service, as known in the inter-war years, will gradually disappear from the larger shops, first in the South of England and later in the North. In rural and semi-rural areas fully equipped travelling shops appear the most likely path of development, though undoubtedly the small general food shop will continue to play an important role in these areas for a considerable time to come.

If these suggestions as to the long-term trends in the organization of the trade are correct the question may be asked as to what will be the effect of these changes on the different economic types of retailer. The Co-operative Societies with their larger shops have already experimented with self-service units in this trade and are likely to continue to develop such units in the future. The Societies are, however, faced with a number of problems which must be overcome if Co-operative trading is to increase markedly its share of the national trade. One of these problems is that the retail developments envisaged above involve considerable capital expenditure on premises and require prominent siting. The present system of raising share capital from members may not be adequate to permit of the scale of investment that is necessary. Particularly is this true of some of the older and smaller Societies in the North of England, and it is these Societies that possess the most out-of-date and most badly sited premises. Further, without regrouping and amalgamation of many of these Societies progress will be slow. Another problem is that of the relationship of the productive activities of the Wholesale Societies with the selling campaigns of the Retail Societies. Initially the existence of close links between production and retailing should assist the Societies in the development of self-service in that the requirements of self-service in relation, for example, to the size of the package, its design and shape, and the unit of delivery to the shop can be met more readily than in the case of purchases from private manufacturers who supply a large number of different types of retailer. But as food manufacture and packaging grows and the advertisement and branding of the goods becomes widespread, the Retail Societies may find that serve-yourself retailing results in sales resistance to the lesser-known brands of the Wholesale Societies. A complete turn to nationally-advertised products would weaken the advantages of integration and of Co-operation, but the stocking of articles that consumers may regard only as the second best will not lead to popularity and a rapid increase in turnover. More advertising by Wholesale Societies is a part of the answer to this problem, but only a part.

Lastly the Co-operative Societies will face the problem of the payment of a dividend on purchases. If full employment is maintained and the standard of living rises, it may be asked whether a small dividend will remain an attraction to purchase foodstuffs at the Co-operative Society branches and, more important, whether the dividend will induce new members, particularly from middle-class households, to join the Societies. It may be true that with a higher standard of living the alternative of using the trading surplus to reduce prices of groceries and provisions will equally fail to attract large numbers of new members. There is, however, a third possibility that the trading surplus, instead of being paid out as a small dividend or used to lower prices slightly, could be used to enable the Co-operative Societies to lead the way throughout the country in modern and up-to-date trading methods. Such a policy would call for a radical change in Co-operative thinking and for much closer links between the individual Societies and between the Retail and the Wholesale Societies, as action and development would need to be co-ordinated. But there should not be any weakening of the basic principle of Co-operation, namely democratic consumer control, or the Co-operative movement will lose completely its unique features.

Many multiple shop organizations are better placed than any other types of retailer for developing the new methods of distribution outlined above. With large, well-sited shops and adequate capital resources, rapid advances in trading techniques appear to be mainly a question of opportunity. Further, the more standardized or simplified the process of retailing becomes, as it does under self-service, the greater are the advantages that can be secured by the large-scale organizations. Expert design and large-scale purchasing of the many shop fittings and the equipment needed in self-service units is an obvious example of this. Not all multiple shop organizations are, however, in the position described above. Many are beginning to suffer from the disadvantages of an early start in regard to the size of their premises and the location of their depots and branches. But an even more important problem, if branding becomes practically universal in the grocery and provisions trade, will be that of relations with the brand manufacturers. If price maintenance develops as it has done in the past along with branding, and the multiple shop retailers are forced by consumer demand to stock these brands, there will be little to distinguish the multiple shop retailer from the private retailer except perhaps the size of the premises, the range of goods sold, and the layout of the shop. These advantages alone may lead to an increase in the relative importance of multiple shop retailing, but certainly not so consistently or so rapidly as when the appeal of multiple shop retailing was new and dramatic and directed effectively at the consumers' pockets. Increased integration between production and distribution is a possibility, taking the form of mergers between existing food manufacturers and some of the larger multiple shop firms, but the increasing variety of manufactured foodstuffs places limits on the efficacy of this policy. It may well be that multiple shop retailers will be faced with the same type of problem in regard to the handling of nationally advertised products as that facing Co-operative Societies, without the democratic control and dividend appeals of the latter organizations.

The role of the small-scale retailers in the future is problematical.

On the one hand any trend towards larger-scale and more costly techniques of retailing will put him at a marked disadvantage vis-à-vis the large-scale retailer. Further, his advantages of physical and economic flexibility will become less important and less effective as the size and location of the population becomes more stable and planning controls over new building areas limit the numbers and types of shops. On the other hand, the continued growth of food manufacture and of the importance of branded and advertised products would appear certain to provide the small-scale retailer, who has been the major outlet for such products, with a buoyancy he might otherwise lack. Again, manufacturers in their concern with the marketing of their products may extend greatly the assistance they give to the small-scale retailer. Advice and assistance on bookkeeping and stock control may be added to the help already given in regard to window display and advertisement. Finally it is certain that, even if the large-scale retailers gain ground with bigger shops, self-service units, combination stores, 'super markets' and travelling shops, the physical structure of the grocery and provisions trade with its myriads of small shops in towns and villages throughout the country, and the conservative shopping habits of consumers, can be changed only slowly. For a long time to come the small-scale retailer will continue to play an important role in the distribution of groceries and provisions.

CHAPTER VI

THE MEAT TRADE

The retail meat trade of the United Kingdom in the middle of the nineteenth century was dominated by the skilled butcher who slaughtered as well as retailed meat. In practically all areas of the country, except in certain large towns, the butcher bought livestock on the hoof from local farmers or from livestock markets, slaughtered the animals in his slaughterhouse, dressed the carcase, disposed of the waste products, and cut up and sold the meat to his customers. In some instances the butcher himself owned a livestock farm or grazing grounds for the fattening of the cattle before slaughtering. Only in the large towns such as London and Manchester were there butchers who confined their activities to retailing and bought carcases from wholesale markets. A number of these town butchers had stalls and barrows rather than fixed shops and some of them specialized in particular lines, such as offal or the poorer quality cuts often purchased from other butchers who had no sale for them.

The butchers combining the three tasks of skilled buying of live animals, skilled slaughtering and skilled cutting had to be first-class tradesmen and were dependent for success on their training, experience and judgement. The butcher's shop and slaughterhouse played a prominent part in the retail network of any town or village, and as one butcher would often serve all sections of the community the differences in the tastes and pockets of his customers had to be matched by ability in buying his animals, in cutting and in pricing.

Changes in the trade up to 1914

By the beginning of the last quarter of the nineteenth century the continued growth of towns had increased to some extent the importance of the carcase meat markets as distinct from the livestock markets and more butchers were restricting their activities to retailing only, but the combination of slaughtering and retailing was by far the most usual practice. The trade was still overwhelmingly in home-killed meat and only a trickle of imported meat was reaching the butchers' shops. But in the following four decades up to the First World War the character of the meat trade of the United Kingdom was transformed by a vast increase in the supplies of imported meat.

The chief factors bringing about this transformation were the replacement of sailing ships by steamships, the development of refrigeration and refrigerator ships, and the low prices of imported compared with home-killed meat. The first consignment of chilled meat came from the United States in 1875 and this was followed in the next four years by consignments of frozen meat from South America, New Zealand and Australia. As both shipping and refrigeration techniques improved from 1880 onwards so the imports of frozen meat rose by leaps and bounds. To illustrate this change estimates of the consumption of meat per head of the population between 1870 and 1896 are presented in Table 35.

Table 35. *Consumption of meat including bacon and ham per head of the population of the United Kingdom, 1870–96**

Year	1870	1880	1890	1896
Consumption per head (lb.)	104·4	114·1	124·1	130·6
Imported meat as proportion of total consumption (%)	10	28	32	37

* This table is based on figures given by G. H. Wood, 'Some Statistics Relating to Working Class Progress since 1860', *Journal of the Royal Statistical Society*, December 1899. The proportion of imports to total consumption has been calculated directly from the figures given in the *Statistical Abstract for the United Kingdom*. Southern Ireland is included throughout.

The estimates of imported meat include the import of live animals (converted to a dead meat basis). If the imports of animals and of bacon and ham are excluded the consumption of imported beef, veal, mutton and lamb per head of the population was as follows: 1870, 1·1 lb.; 1880, 5·3 lb.; 1890, 12·8 lb.; 1896, 18·1 lb. These estimates combined with those given in Table 35 indicate the rapid expansion of the meat trade and particularly the great increase in the volume of imported meat in the last quarter of the nineteenth century.

This increased volume of imported meat called for radical changes in the retail structure and organization of the meat trade. Many of the skilled butchers would not handle the cheap and often, in the earlier years, poor quality imported meat, and new types of retailers concerned only with cutting and selling the imported meat entered the trade. Prominent among these new types of retailer were the first multiple shop firms in the meat trade. The rise of this form of retailing, the selling techniques adopted, and the impact of the new methods on the retail structure of the meat trade are discussed later in this chapter.

At the same time in the thirty or so years before the First World War other factors were bringing about some changes in the home-killed trade. The growth in the size of cities and towns encouraged the trade of intermediaries who bought livestock, arranged for slaughtering on a fairly large scale and sold carcase meat to the town butchers. The concentration of slaughtering that this involved was assisted in some measure by the increase in the number of larger public abattoirs, and at the same time the closer inspection and tighter system of licensing of abattoirs that was introduced in the Public Health Amendment Act of 1890 raised the standards of hygiene in the handling of meat. Differentiation in tastes and in incomes and improvements in transport giving individual areas a wider choice of types of home-killed meat also led to more specialization among butchers. The retailers began to cater for different price and taste markets, and in the larger towns the number of stalls and barrows increased, though many of these were open only on Fridays and Saturdays and sold the unwanted cuts from the shops in better-class areas. Up to 1914, however, the skilled butcher selecting and buying livestock on the hoof, slaughtering, and retailing remained the dominant figure in the home-killed trade and the developments mentioned above were of the nature of adjustments rather than of transformation such as occurred in these years in relation to the imported meat trade.

Table 36. *Consumption of meat per head of the population of the United Kingdom, 1900–50**

Year	1900	1905	1910	1914	1920	1925	1930	1935	1938	1950
Consumption per head (lb.)	96·9	96·4	95·5	94·9	94·1	100·0	96·2	99·5	98·1	82·8
Imported meat as proportion of total consumption (%)	36·0	39·0	39·5	41·0	42·5	45·5	47·4	46·0	48·5	45·4

* This table is based on data given in A. R. Prest and A. A. Adams, *Consumers' Expenditure, 1900–1919*, and Richard Stone, *Consumers' Expenditure, 1920–1938*. Beef, veal, mutton, lamb, pork and offal constitute meat. The estimates of the population include South and Northern Ireland to 1914 but only Northern Ireland 1920–1950.

A particular feature of the trend in the period up to the First World War was the stability or slight decline in consumption per head between 1900 and 1914. This stability is shown in the estimates presented in Table 36. The table shows the consumption of meat per head of the population between 1900 and 1950, but the figures are not directly comparable with those given in Table 35 above as the latter includes bacon and ham with other meat and different conversion factors of live animals were used.

The relative stability of consumption of meat per head after the turn of the century, particularly after 1905, was influenced by the rise in price of both home-killed and imported meat. The average price of imported meat in the years 1908–11 was 7 % higher than the average between 1900 and 1907, and in 1912–13 the price of imported beef and veal jumped 9 % over the 1908–11 price. The average price of home-killed meat rose more slowly. The price in 1908–11 was 2 % above the 1900–07 average price and the price in 1912–13 was 7 % above the 1908–11 average price. These years of rising prices and of stable or declining consumption were difficult ones for the retail meat trade.

The meat trade, 1918–1950

In the inter-war years the meat trade ceased to expand at a rate faster than the increase in the population. Consumption per head as shown in Table 36 rose from 1920 to 1925 but was practically stable between 1926 and 1938 with a slight fall in the depression years 1930 to 1933. The consumption per head of imported meat, however, continued to rise as prejudice against it declined and improvements were made in the freezing and chilling techniques and in the use of grading and trade marks. Chilled beef from South America was popular and there was a marked increase in the acceptance of and demand for the high quality frozen lamb from New Zealand and Australia. The rate of increase in the consumption per head of imported meat was not, however, as rapid as the increase in the decades before 1914.

The trends noted above in the home-killed meat trade before 1914 were continued in the inter-war years. Increased reliance was placed by retail butchers on the wholesalers and jobbers of the dead meat markets, and there was a growing practice of selling part carcases instead of whole carcases, thus enabling the retailer to specialize in certain cuts and types of meat. But the purchase of cattle on the hoof and slaughtering by the retail butcher remained a prominent feature of the home-killed trade. There were approximately 15,000–16,000 slaughter-houses in existence in Great Britain in the inter-war years, the majority of which were owned by small-scale butchers, though many were not used very frequently. In addition the butcher who had not the capital or the trade to permit ownership of a private slaughterhouse, or who could not get a licence to establish one, could use the municipal abattoirs. These were very much larger and more fully employed than the private slaughterhouses and there were some 270 in existence prior to the Second World War. These municipal slaughterhouses, which were used by wholesalers as well as by retailers, were responsible for about a quarter of the total slaughterings of home-killed meat.

The changes in the inter-war years in the retail shops themselves were mainly in the direction of greater hygiene and more elaborate fittings. A refrigerator became a necessity and a freezing room an asset. Marble tiling on walls and glazed tiles on the floors replaced the wood-work and the sawdust. The shop-fronts open to the street disappeared and the display of meat behind plate glass windows became practically universal. Glass screens and even air-conditioning were introduced into some shops, making a strong contrast with the atmosphere of the butcher's shop of the nineteenth century. These and other improvements in standards meant that the stalls in markets and the barrows selling the poorer quality meats virtually disappeared from the trade.

Another development was the provision of additional services to the consumer. Delivery to the home of the weekly joint and calling to collect orders had always been the practice in the upper end of the trade, but in the inter-war years it became a feature of other sections of the trade as well. The ease with which juvenile labour could be obtained in these years and its relative cheapness assisted this trend, and the butcher's boy became a familiar sight, not only to the cook or maid of the big house, but also to the suburban housewife. In salesmanship little new emerged in these years. Price tickets came into widespread use and the windows of the shops began to be designed and displayed to attract customers by showing the choice and prices available and not merely the quantity in the form of carcases or part carcases. The reduction of prices at the end of the week and at the end of the last day of the week became the accepted practice in the shops in the larger towns catering mainly for a cash trade. But the essence of salesmanship, both in respect of home-killed and imported meat, remained the skill of the butcher in cutting his carcases and sides and providing for his customers just the cut they wanted or that they had been persuaded they wanted. With the preferences of consumers for particular types and cuts of meat varying widely, and sometimes illogically, with every change in the weather, in the temperature and in the supply of substitute products, this task was far from simple and required training and experience.

The changes introduced into or forced upon the trade during the Second World War and during the period of rationing and shortages of supplies that followed the war need not be described in detail as their influence on the future developments in the trade in many instances would not appear to be of a permanent nature. Briefly the significant changes were firstly the taking over by the Ministry of Food, through the agency of the Meat Importers National Defence Association Ltd. and the eight Wholesale Meat Supply Associations, of the importing, wholesaling and distribution of all meat, whether home-killed or purchased from overseas. The retail structure remained intact, but the flow of meat to the retailers was controlled by the Ministry of Food. Secondly, as the Ministry took over the control of the wholesale distribution of home-killed meat, the slaughtering of meat was centralized, the number of slaughterhouses being reduced to 600–700, each operating on behalf of the Ministry. Thirdly, neither retailers nor consumers had any effective choice of the type of quality of meat sold or purchased, and the need to freeze instead of chill all imported beef led to a general decline in quality. Fourthly, there was a sharp decline in consumption per head; the amount of meat made available to individual butchers was limited by the number of their registered customers and similarly the amount of meat purchased by the consumer was determined by the cash value of the meat ration at any particular time. Lastly, the prices charged by the butchers and the net margins allowed to them were controlled throughout these years by the Ministry of Food, adjustments being made as costs and the value of the meat ration fluctuated.

The effects of these changes on the character of the retail meat trade were profound. The closing down of the majority of the slaughterhouses and the control of the remainder by the Ministry of Food meant an end, temporarily at least, of the traditional arrangement in the trade whereby one person or firm combined the three functions of selecting his live-stock and slaughtering and retailing the meat. The butchers' lack of choice as to type or quality of meat purchased meant that the taste and price preferences of individual customers could no longer be catered for effectively by the skill of the individual butchers, and the differentia-tion between particular shops began to be obscured. Shortages of man-power reduced service and delivery and made difficult the recruitment and training of skilled cutters. The system of rationing and the smallness of the ration itself had placed a premium on skill in cutting and demanded almost mathematical precision with the cleaver, though at the same time the ease with which the ration was sold reduced the average em-ployment per shop. On the other hand the butchers had, for the first time in their existence, a practically guaranteed market, their Friday and Saturday evening worries disappeared and the problems of income and price elasticities of demand for meat, if they were ever recognized as this, no longer had to be solved. The Ministry of Food, recognizing the danger of a breakdown in the wholesale and retail distribution of meat, took every care when fixing margins to ensure that the machine worked fairly smoothly. A measure of the success of this policy was the very small change in the number of registered butchers; between 1942 and 1950 the number decreased by only 1 %.

This sketch of the main developments in the meat trade in the hundred years 1850–1950 provides a background for the discussion of the develop-ment of the different economic types of retailer in the meat trade in these years. The development of multiple shop retailing will be discussed in detail first, and will be followed by briefer accounts of Co-operative trading and the role of the small-scale retailer.

The development of multiple shop retailing to 1914

The first firm in the United Kingdom to operate more than 10 retail butchers' shops would appear to have been John Bell & Sons of Glasgow and later of London. This firm, an old-established butcher's business dating back to 1827, began expanding rapidly in the early 1880's and had well over 100 shops by 1885. Three years later the firm became a limited company and in 1889 it amalgamated with T. C. and Joseph Eastman of New York to form Eastmans Ltd. The new company at this date controlled an American cattle and shipping business and nearly 350 retail shops and stalls in the United Kingdom. The second firm in the field was James Nelson and Sons Ltd. This company was one of the first firms to develop the River Plate meat trade and it started opening retail meat shops in the United Kingdom in the middle and late 'eighties. Other important firms in the early 'nineties were the River Plate Fresh Meat Company, Ltd., the London Central Meat Company, Ltd., and W. & R. Fletcher Ltd., which had taken over some shops from two earlier companies, the New Zealand Mutton Company Ltd., and the Direct Supply Meat Company Ltd. At the turn of the century the Argenta Meat Company Ltd. joined the leading firms. A number of smaller multiple shop firms were also established in these early years but the above 6 companies dwarfed all others by their size.

Estimates of the number of multiple shop organizations in existence and the number of shops or branches controlled by these organizations

Table 37. *Estimates of the number of multiple shop firms and branches in the meat trade, 1885–1950*

Year	10–24 branches		25–49 branches		50–99 branches		100 or more branches		Totals			
									10 or more branches		25 or more branches	
	Number of		Number of		Number of		Number of		Number of		Number of	
	Firms	Branches	Firms	Branches	Firms	Branches	Firms	Branches	Firms	Branches	Firms	Branches
1885	4	50	—	—	—	—	1	150	5	200	1	150
1890	4	61	2	78	1	65	1	360	8	564	4	503
1895	5	57	1	31	1	60	4	1,105	11	1,253	6	1,196
1900	6	71	2	67	—	—	5	1,920	13	2,058	7	1,987
1905	9	111	2	56	1	65	5	2,750	17	2 982	8	2,871
1910	13	144	4	139	—	—	6	3,545	23	3,828	10	3,684
1915	17	212	3	108	1	55	6	3,300	27	3,675	10	3,463
1920	20	245	4	159	1	98	5	2,705	30	3,207	10	2,962
1925	24	301	2	56	2	115	3	2,737	31	3,209	7	2,908
1930	27	336	2	67	3	190	2	2,650	34	3,243	7	2,907
1935	33	436	3	81	2	139	2	2,705	40	3,361	7	2,925
1939	39	538	6	186	2	143	2	2,725	49	3,592	10	3,054
1950	45	639	9	301	3	177	2	2,658	59	3,775	14	3,136

between 1885 and 1950 are presented in Table 37. The estimates in this table must be treated with some reserve as the information upon which they are based is somewhat unreliable. The records of the number of shops in this trade are difficult to check and the practice of the larger companies, particularly in the earlier years, of opening and closing branches frequently adds to the problems. Altogether the records of 83 separate firms have been used in the construction of this table, and of the 24 firms that do not appear as trading independently in 1950 13 had amalgamated with other firms and 11 would appear to have gone out of existence. The estimates relate to butchery firms and shops only. The branches of multiple shop grocery and provisions firms which sold meat have not been included in these figures.

The figures given in Table 37 can be used to illustrate the rate of growth of multiple shop retailing as shown by the rate of increase in the number of branches in existence between different periods. The use of numbers of branches in existence has some limitations but in this trade there was not a great variation in the size of branches of individual multiple shop firms at any given point of time, although the average size of branches changed over time. Table 38 shows the net increase and the rate of net increase in five-yearly periods (except for the period of the Second World War) between 1886 and 1950. The rate of net increase is shown as a percentage increase in the numbers as between two dates, and the absolute net increase in the number of branches is also shown as an average yearly net increase.

Table 38. *Rate of net increase in the number of branches of multiple shop firms in the meat trade, 1886–1950*

Year	Branches of firms with 10 or more branches			Branches of firms with 25 or more branches		
	Net increase in number of branches	Per-centage net increase	Average yearly net increase in numbers	Net increase in number of branches	Per-centage net increase	Average yearly net increase in numbers
1886–1890	364	182	73	353	235	71
1891–1895	689	122	138	693	138	139
1896–1900	805	64	161	791	66	158
1901–1905	924	45	185	884	44	177
1906–1910	846	28	169	813	28	163
1911–1915	−153	−4	−31	−221	−6	−44
1916–1920	−468	−13	−94	−501	−14	−100
1921–1925	2	—	—	−54	−2	−11
1926–1930	34	1	7	−1	—	—
1931–1935	118	4	24	18	1	3
1936–1939	231	7	58	129	4	32
1940–1950	183	5	16	82	3	7

A clear pattern of growth emerges from the figures given in Table 38. Between the late 'eighties and the end of the first decade of the twentieth century there was a rapid and consistent increase in the number of branches in existence, the net increase in the number of branches between 1896 and 1910 averaging over 3 branches per week. From 1910 to 1935 there was a dramatic change in the pattern. In the years immediately before and during the First World War the number of closures exceeded the number of new branches opened and only in the years immediately preceding the Second World War did the net increase rise to one shop a week.

This unusual pattern of multiple shop development in the meat trade arises in large part from the dominant role played by a few very large concerns. In fact the history of multiple shop retailing in this trade is practically the history of 7 large firms. Six of the firms were mentioned above and these 6 in the period up to 1920 controlled over 90 % of the multiple shop branches in existence. In 1923 the number of large firms was reduced to 2 by amalgamation, and these two firms, the Union Cold Storage Company Ltd. and the London Central Meat Company Ltd., controlled 70–85 % of the branches in existence between 1925 and 1950. The discussion of the development and characteristics of multiple shop retailing in the meat trade will therefore be largely a discussion of the practices and policies of these companies.

By 1900 2 of the firms, Eastmans Ltd. and James Nelson and Sons Ltd., had over 400 branches each, and 3 firms, the River Plate Fresh Meat Company Ltd., the London Central Meat Company Ltd., and W. & R. Fletcher Ltd., had 100 or more branches each. The sixth firm, the Argenta Meat Company Ltd., which took over shops in Lancashire run by Rushworth and Ward, was founded in 1899 and had reached more than 100 branches by 1910.[1]

These firms were concerned almost exclusively with the imported meat trade, and at least 4 of the 6 firms controlled refrigerator ships and overseas meat packing and storage plants. Eastmans Ltd. had interests in the United States until they disposed of them in 1900, and were employed mainly in the import and retailing of meat from America. James Nelson and Sons Ltd. and the River Plate Fresh Meat Company Ltd. were the first two British meat firms to operate plants on the River Plate in South America. W. & R. Fletcher Ltd. had interests in Australia and in South America besides extensive cold store plant in the United Kingdom, and the Argenta Meat Company Ltd. had direct arrangements with an American meat exporting firm operating in South America.

[1] The only other multiple shop firm of any size in the meat trade before 1920 was Daniel Higgin of Liverpool.

The main reason for the rapid development of the retailing activities of these firms from 1880 to 1910 was the need to find guaranteed outlets for the vast quantities of frozen and later chilled meat that were pouring into the United Kingdom. The skilled butcher showed little desire or willingness to handle it. This meant that the firms that did the packing, shipping and importing also had to undertake the retailing of the meat through a network of their own shops to ensure the necessary wide and rapid distribution. This was the impetus in the early part of the period which led firms like Eastmans, Nelsons and the River Plate Meat Company to develop extensive retailing activities. Later, retail firms in the United Kingdom which had found the handling of imported frozen and chilled meat in multiple shop outlets effective and profitable extended their interests overseas to the sources of supply.

The retailing units of these multiple shop organizations were primitive in the extreme. The majority of the shops were very small (employing only 2–3 persons), had an absolute minimum of fittings, and in some instances were not fixed shops at all but stalls or barrows in markets. More often than not they were located in side streets or just off the main streets rather than in the main streets themselves. The trade was entirely for cash, with no credit or delivery being provided. The quantity and quality of the supplies throughout these early years were uncertain from week to week, and no regular order or 'family' trade could be undertaken. The job of the managers and assistants of the shops was to sell for cash as fast as they could the consignments of the frozen and chilled meat from the central cold stores before they became unfit for human consumption. If the price tickets and salesmanship had not succeeded in attracting sufficient customers by Saturday evening, the prices charged fell lower and lower until even auctioneering of the meat was tried to finally empty the shop.

Naturally, the frozen and chilled meat did not suit all tastes and there were many prejudices to overcome. The multiple shop branches specializing in this trade were often called 'the foreign meat shops' and it was considered by some a social stigma to be seen entering or leaving such a place. But the meat was cheap, and as techniques of freezing and particularly of chilling improved so the quality rose, and the popularity of imported meat spread not only among the very poor but among wide sections of the working classes. A geographical bias in sales however remained. The main areas of consumption of imported meat were London, the Midlands and parts of Lancashire around Liverpool. The butchers and housewives of Yorkshire, the Northern Counties, the South West, Wales, and particularly Scotland refused to handle or buy imported meat except as a very last resort.

The geographical bias in taste, and the distribution of the main ports and cold storage facilities, tended to determine the location of the branches of the multiple shop organizations. There was a very high concentration of branches in London and in some of the towns of the Midlands and North West, but very few were established in Yorkshire or Scotland. And the branches themselves were located almost without exception in the industrial and working-class areas of the towns.

The continued and rapid rise in the number of branches of multiple shop organizations in the years 1900 to 1910, a period when the total consumption of meat per head of the population was no longer rising, was a reflection of the growing popularity of imported meat. The real wages of the working classes were falling slightly and the cheaper imported meat rose in favour. There is, however, also some evidence to suggest that the rate of increase in the number of branches ran somewhat ahead of demand and was the outcome of strenuous competition between the large rival packer-importers. These firms, it is true, did not sell the whole of their imports through their own shops. Some of them sold as much as half through the wholesale market at Smithfield, but the surest way of increasing their turnover appeared to be by multiplying their contacts with the consumer.

Between 1909 and 1914 the imported meat trade passed through a severe crisis brought about by rising prices. There was a sharp fall in demand, the companies stopped paying dividends, and practically all multiple shop retailers had to close down some of their branches.[1] The crisis also led to a 'war' in the South American trade between the British and American packer-exporters and to the first round of amalgamations between the giant British meat firms.

Amalgamations between multiple shop firms

The first amalgamation took place in 1911. Late in that year the cold storage, shipping and meat importing business of Union Cold Storage Company Ltd. took over the cold storage business of W. & R. Fletcher Ltd. Two years later discussions started between James Nelson and Sons Ltd. and the River Plate Fresh Meat Company Ltd. with a view to amalgamation. Early in 1914 the plans were complete and the directors, explaining that 'for some little time the competition in the importation of meat from the River Plate has been exceedingly difficult to work in such a manner as to leave a fair profit to those interested in it', suggested that 'the altered conditions would be best met by the amalgamation of their interests'. The fact that the two companies had

[1] J. J. Thompson, Chairman of Eastmans Ltd., in the Annual Report of the Company, 14 March 1914 said, 'The higher cost of meat has brought about the closing of a good many retail shops all over the country', and added, referring to the tendency to over-shop the trade, 'especially where they were too crowded to do any good even when meat was cheaper'.

operated on a friendly basis in the past was no argument against amalgamation, as it was pointed out that 'however friendly competition might be, it was still competition'.[1] Both the companies had been closing branches in the months before amalgamation and the formation of the new Company, the British and Argentine Meat Company, Ltd., led immediately to the weeding out of further redundant units.

At the outbreak of the First World War all the leading multiple shop retailers had fewer branches operating than two or three years earlier, though the largest and oldest of the firms had closed more than the smaller firms. The war, bringing with it the call-up of staff and shortage of meat supplies, led to further closures. At the same time many of the firms were realizing that the battle of introducing and gaining acceptance for imported meat had been won and that it was becoming no longer so necessary to multiply the number of retail outlets to bring the goods and the prices to the attention of all potential purchasers. Instead a policy of maintaining slightly fewer but larger shops, one large one having the turnover of two small ones, gave promise of reducing overheads and increasing profits, in spite of the rise in prices.

The years immediately following the First World War witnessed the second round of amalgamations, and control of the large multiple shop butchery firms that had dominated the multiple shop scene before 1914 passed to the Union Cold Storage Company in 1923. In that year direct control—a measure of indirect control had already been in existence— was obtained by the purchase by the Union Cold Storage Company Ltd. of all the ordinary shares of the British and Argentine Meat Company Ltd., Eastmans Ltd., W. & R. Fletcher Ltd., and the Argenta Meat Company Ltd. At the same time the shares in a number of other food, storage and importing companies were purchased though none of these undertook retailing. Only one of the multiple meat retailing companies that had been of any size in the pre-1914 period— the London Central Meat Company, Ltd.—continued an independent existence.

The Union Cold Storage Company Ltd., in a *Prospectus* issued in 1923, gave some idea of its size and activities in announcing that 'besides 51 cold stores and freezing works at home and abroad it [the Company] has one of the largest fleets of refrigerated vessels in the world as well as other transport facilities'. The acquisition of the retailing companies was explained in these terms: 'Having thus provided for the collection, preparation, carriage and storage of perishable food products, it is now intended to complete the organization by arranging for the distribution (both wholesale and retail) of the products of the Company in the best

[1] Edward Nelson, Managing Director, at the Extraordinary General Meeting of James Nelson and Sons Ltd., 7 April 1914.

and most economical manner. It is believed that this will add materially to the prosperity of the company'. The *Prospectus* concluded by claiming that the Company will now 'constitute by far the largest and most complete organization of its kind in the world'. Few would wish to contradict.

Lord Vestey and Sir Edmund Vestey added some further details on the activities of the Company when they gave evidence before the Royal Commission on Food Prices early in 1925. The total employment of the Union Cold Storage Company Ltd. and its subsidiaries was stated to be over 30,000 persons, and some 450,000 head of cattle were owned overseas. The Company was responsible for some 20 % of the total imports by the United Kingdom of chilled beef, and it controlled about one-third of the total cold storage capacity in Great Britain used for foodstuffs. Asked why the Company had extended their interests to the retail side of the meat trade, Lord Vestey replied:

'There is only one reason why we do it. The position is this. We have a very large business. We heard that one of these big shopping companies with many hundreds of shops had been to see the Americans and were going to sell out to one of these firms in Chicago. We thought, well now, that is going to be a very bad thing, not only for us but for the country: therefore we bought them.'[1]

The difficulties in which some of the large multiple retailers found themselves in the years following 1912 no doubt made many of the firms look round for external financial backing, both in Great Britain and overseas, but the real advantages of this purchase to the Union Cold Storage Company itself as outlined in the *Prospectus* cannot be overlooked. In fact Lord Vestey later in his evidence stressed the immense gains of guaranteed outlets for the Company's imports, pointing out that '...we can bring our goods and take a chance the other fellows cannot take, because we have an outlet for a very large proportion of it'.

Multiple shop retailing 1920–1950

The subsequent history up to 1938 of the retailing side of the Union Cold Storage Company is one of rationalization and consolidation, but little or no expansion. The branches continued to trade under the names of the separate companies before the amalgamation, and from time to time other small multiple firms were acquired. In all some fifteen different trading names were used. Any branches that were not paying their way were closed down, and slowly but consistently the standards and

---

[1] *Report of the Royal Commission on Food Prices*, 1925, vol. II, Minutes of Evidence, p. 225.

standing of the one-time 'foreign meat shops' were improved. Branches bought in a hurry by the old companies and branches located in side streets were shut, new properties were taken in main streets and their interiors were planned and fitted with the latest butchery equipment. Improvements in fittings and equipment did not, however, lead to very large shops. The typical branch in these years employed some 4 persons including the manager, though the emphasis on the lower-priced imported meat meant that the quantities of meat handled by a multiple shop branch were greater than those handled by the small-scale butcher for the same amount of cash turnover. The shifts in population in the inter-war years from the centre of towns to the suburbs and between different areas of the country involved the Company in some difficulties and required further re-location of the branches. At the same time efforts were made to end the heavy concentration of outlets in the London and Southern areas. One successful development took place in Scotland where, using a Scottish trading name, an important group of shops grew up in Glasgow and surrounding towns. The net result of this continuous rationalization and reorganization was to save some of the retailing subsidiaries from the bankruptcy to which they came perilously near after the over-optimistic growth in the pre-1914 years, to place the imported meat shops on a par in standards of hygiene, layout, site and appearance with any shop dealing in home-killed meat, and to balance the distribution of the branches through the country. In the course of these developments what expansion in trade occurred took the form of increased turnover per branch through the opening of larger and better-equipped shops and the weeding out of the smaller badly sited shops, rather than of an increase in the number of outlets as such.

The goods sold in the branches continued to be almost exclusively imported meat, though in certain areas some home-killed meat was also sold, and the customers were still, with some exceptions, drawn from the working class. Differences in income and taste that might appear in areas in which the individual branches were located were met by the supply of differing qualities of imported meat. Orders from the shops were usually handled centrally and the meat supplied from depots located in different parts of the country, but managers of the branches also bought part of their meat from the wholesale markets in their particular locality. Pricing policy was to a fair extent the responsibility of the branch manager, who received his bought-in supplies invoiced at the same price as that charged by the importing Company in the wholesale markets. In this way the manager was relatively free to meet local competition and the multiple shops were known for their low prices.

The progress, policy and method of organization of the other large multiple retailing firm, the London Central Meat Company Ltd., in these years, developed upon practically parallel lines to those followed by the Union Cold Storage Company, except that in this case a significant increase in the number of branches controlled also took place. The medium-sized multiple firms, that is those with between 25 and 100 branches each, all traded on a town or area basis. Here again, however, there is a distinction between the character of these organizations in the pre-1914 and immediate post-1920 period and in the years prior to the Second World War. In the earlier years these multiple shop firms developed in areas with easy access to cold stores and supplies of imported meat. In the case of the organizations that grew up later there was no such geographical limit, and the firms handled both home-killed and imported meat.

More important, however, than the growth of these medium-sized specialist butcher multiple organizations was the entry of some of the medium- to large-sized grocery and provision multiple firms into the butchery trade. This development, which dates from just prior to and immediately after the First World War, is not shown in the tables presented above, as firms with their main turnover in goods other than meat have been excluded. But the meat sales in these years of provision firms such as J. Sainsbury Ltd. were almost certainly greater than the sales of the few medium-sized butchery multiple organizations. These grocery and provisions firms usually handled both home-killed and imported meat, often buying the former on the hoof direct from the farmer and undertaking the slaughtering and dressing. In many instances they catered for a rather higher class of market than the specialist butchery multiple firms. The regular-order and family trade was attracted to these mixed firms which could supply and if requested deliver both the grocery and provisions and the meat. In the layout and size of their shops and in the choice of meat provided these firms competed directly with the small-scale butcher in the same type of trade.

Rationing and controls during the Second World War and in the post-war years affected the multiple shop organizations in the same general way as they did the small-scale and Co-operative butcher. Employment per shop was reduced, price and service competition virtually disappeared, and supplies of meat, manufactured meat products and canned goods were restricted. As the supply position of the latter type of goods eased somewhat in the post-war years many multiple shop branches increased their sales in this direction, but the general picture in these ten years was one of a complete lack of opportunities to expand, owing to the impossibility of differentiation in buying, pricing or trading policies. The growth of multiple shop organizations that did take place in these years was due almost entirely to the purchase and taking over either of the branches of small multiple shop butchery firms or of the shops of private retailers.

The Co-operative Societies

Co-operative retailing of meat dates back to the middle of the nineteenth century. The Rochdale Society had begun to sell meat along with groceries and provisions soon after its foundation and by 1850 the demand was sufficiently great to warrant the renting of a shop specially for the sale of meat.[1] This story was repeated in the case of most of the larger Societies in the second half of the nineteenth century. Once a strong trading position had been established in groceries and provisions, a ready-made market existed for the supply of meat. But the organization and character of the Co-operative meat trade, up to 1914 at least, differed fundamentally from that of the rising multiple shop retailers. The Co-operative Societies with their marked bias towards the North of England and Scotland dealt mainly in home-killed meat and only to a very limited extent in frozen and chilled imported meat. The growing Co-operative trade in meat was not based on the handling of new products in a new way but on supplying home-killed meat and paying a dividend on purchases in competition with the local skilled butcher. Further, there was practically no centralization of the trade and the methods of the individual Co-operative Society were practically identical with those of the small-scale butcher. The butchery manager of each Society bought the cattle on the hoof and most Societies dealing in meat undertook their own slaughtering in their own abattoirs. Some of the larger Societies with a number of branch butchery shops would supply these shops from a central slaughterhouse, but this practice developed only slowly. The exception was in Scotland where from the 'eighties onwards the Scottish Co-operative Wholesale Society purchased cattle centrally for a number of the Retail Societies on a commission basis, arranged for the import of cattle, particularly from Canada, and also undertook some slaughtering. Further, many of the Retail Societies in Scotland used municipal slaughterhouses in preference to buying or building their own.

Co-operative trading in meat in the fifty or so years up to 1914 certainly grew in volume with the increase in membership and the increase in the sales of other foodstuffs. But, with the exception of the trade in Scotland, Co-operative retailing of meat took the form of

---

[1] H. Holden and Percy Redfern, 'The Co-operative Societies', in *The Retail Meat Trade. A practical treatise by specialists in the meat trade*, London, 1928, vol. ii, p. 228.

providing a further service to the members who already bought their groceries and provisions from the Co-operative store. No significant economies of scale were introduced and the great increase in the imports of frozen and chilled meat had very little influence on Co-operative methods of trading.

In the inter-war years the extension of Co-operative trading in meat continued with the extension of the trade in groceries and provisions, and the sale of meat as well as of groceries and provisions by Retail Societies became practically universal. In 1923 some 77 % of the total membership belonged to Societies which had butchery departments. By 1937 some 96 % of the membership belonged to Societies with butchery departments.[1] The areas of the most rapid development of the Co-operative meat trade in the inter-war years would appear to have been in Scotland and in the expanding Co-operative regions of the Midlands and the South of England.

The Retail Societies, however, continued to show a marked bias towards home-killed meat. In 1934, for example, approximately 80 % by value of the Co-operative meat trade was represented by home-killed meat and only 20 % by imported meat. This compares with the estimated national proportions of approximately 60 % by value home-killed meat and 40 % imported meat. The reasons for the continued existence of this bias in the type of trade undertaken would appear to be mainly the continued preference of the consumers in the North of England and Scotland, where the Co-operative movement was strongest for home-killed meat. Tastes in the South of England were different and the Societies in these areas sold a higher proportion of imported meat.[2] Further, all the medium and large-sized Societies owned slaughter-houses, many built new ones in the inter-war years, and the meat from them was given priority in the retail shops. The butchery managers of Co-operative Societies were all skilled craftsmen and they took pride, perhaps excessive pride, in the quality of meat sold in their shops. Imported meat, with the possible exception of New Zealand lamb, was still regarded as being of somewhat inferior quality to home-killed meat, and only when the members could not afford home-killed meat were increased supplies of imported meat sold in the shops.

Another factor which had some influence on the type of trade undertaken by the Retail Societies and on the methods of Co-operative

[1] H. Holden and P. Redfern, op. cit. p. 229, and *Economic Survey of the Services provided by Retail Co-operative Societies*, Co-operative Union Ltd. 1938.

[2] Enquiries made in 1923–25 showed that five-sixths of London's meat was imported from abroad, while the proportion in Bristol and Birmingham was about two-thirds. The proportion in country districts was much lower and of 150 butchers asked to make returns in Scotland only 30 handled imported meat. *First Report of the Royal Commission on Food Prices*, paragraphs 189 and 221.

organization was the small part played by the Wholesale Societies. The imported meat trade, as discussed above in relation to multiple shop retailing, was a trade in which there were considerable economies of scale in relation to packing, shipping and importing. The Co-operative Wholesale Societies, however, had taken little part in the early develop-ment of the chilled and frozen meat trade and they were at a disadvantage when trying to enter it in the inter-war years once the strategic positions had already been occupied by powerful private traders. A break-through into this market was made by the Co-operative Wholesale Society when in 1936 direct arrangements were made for the Argentine meat trade, but this agreement had only just begun to operate at the outbreak of the Second World War.

In home-killed meat, the Scottish Co-operative Wholesale Society had gone further ahead and had consolidated its position as the main supplier of livestock and meat to the Retail Societies in Scotland. In England and Wales, on the other hand, the Co-operative Wholesale Society made only slow progress. In the Manchester and Lancashire area the Retail Societies relied on the Wholesale Society for some of their supplies of livestock and meat, and in the South the Societies relied on the Wholesale Society for supplies of imported meat, but most of the Retail Societies in these and in other areas had their own abattoirs and undertook their own buying and slaughtering.

Co-operative trading methods in meat, therefore, outside Scotland, were closer to those of the small-scale retailer than to those of the multiple shop retailer. This similarity extended to the bias towards home-killed meat and the pricing policies of the Retail Societies. The Societies rarely attempted to compete with the cheaper prices of the multiple shops selling imported meat, and in charging the market price for their goods they tended to follow the prices of independent butchers. Further, the Societies were never prominent in the price-cutting and auctioneering frenzies of Saturday nights. They preferred, and de-liberately fostered wherever possible, the regular-order and family trade rather than the casual buying attracted by price or by cuts. In this they were assisted by the link between the butchery department and the grocery and provisions department and the payment of a dividend on purchases.

During the Second World War and in the post-war years the butchery departments of the Co-operative Societies underwent the same trials, suffered the same types of disadvantages and enjoyed the same stability of demand as the other types of retailers in the trade. When consumer choice of meat was practically eliminated, however, the payment of a dividend on purchases was an attraction and the Societies increased the number of their customers registered for meat in these years. The

Societies also expanded their activities by the purchase of existing butchers' shops and the number of Co-operative butchery shops rose from some 5,000 in 1937 to 5,500 in 1950.

The small-scale retailer

Throughout the hundred years between 1850 and 1950 the small-scale, independent butcher remained the dominant figure in the trade, and the discussion at the beginning of this chapter of the changes in the character of the trade in these years is in effect, therefore, an account of the development of the small-scale butcher. This discussion need not be repeated but some detail can be added on particular aspects.

Stress was laid, in the discussion of developments up to 1914, on the role of the skilled butcher who selected and slaughtered his livestock besides retailing the meat to his customers. But in addition to this type of retailer, the small-scale butcher who purchased dead meat, both home-killed and imported, from wholesale markets was growing in importance, particularly in relation to overseas supplies. The rise of multiple shop retailing in the imported meat trade can be measured more readily than the development of small-scale retailing in imported meat, but there can be no doubt that the independent butchers of the towns played as great a role in supplying the working classes with cheap imported meat as did the multiple shop organizations. Some of these independent butchers selling imported meat were recruited from the ranks of the skilled butchers who had hitherto concentrated on home-killed meat, but the reluctance of the home-killed specialists to handle imported meat meant that the majority of these retailers were new men to the trade. In fact there was a clear division in the trade before 1914 between the butchers who undertook the whole process of buying, slaughtering and retailing and who sold only home-killed meat and the butchers who specialized in retailing the cheaper imported meat.

In the inter-war years, with the weakening in most areas of the country of the prejudice of the skilled butcher and of his customers against imported meat, the sharp division in the trade between the home-killed butcher and the imported meat butcher faded. Butchers handled both types of meat, though the typical small-scale butcher remained a specialist in home-killed rather than in imported meat. Further, in spite of the growth of the practice of purchasing carcases and part carcases from wholesalers, as much as a third of the home-killed meat trade in the years just before the Second World War was undertaken by independent butchers who purchased the livestock from farmers or at auctions, undertook the slaughtering of the animals in their own or in municipal slaughterhouses, and retailed the cuts to their customers. The small-scale butcher, with the increase in the importance of imported meat and the growth in the wholesale markets, had tended to specialize more and more on the retailing side of the trade, but integration from selection of the animals to selling the joints and cuts had by no means disappeared.

The controls and rationing introduced in the Second World War and their continuance in the post-war period had a marked effect on the independent butcher. The particular services that he had been able to render to the community through his skill and experience in selecting, slaughtering and cutting the meat, and through his close attention to the individual preferences and needs of his customers, practically ceased overnight. Selection, slaughtering, service, choice and weekly family orders had all gone. He became a purveyor of meat rather than a skilled master craftsman. In some respects the shortages of supplies and the rationing system increased the demands on the skill, ingenuity and patience of the butcher, but differentiation in service, selection or price between each economic type of retailer was practically nil.

The war brought about some reduction in the numbers of independent butchers owing to the decision of some firms to close down in the early years of the war and of other firms to give up the retailing of meat where their turnover in this commodity was not sufficiently great to make it worth while dealing with the complications of rationing. Also a number of independent butchers sold out to multiple shop retailers and Co-operative Societies in these years. But a feature of equal interest was the increase in the number of firms that controlled from 2 up to 9 retail branches.

These firms could be defined as small multiple shop organizations, but in the discussion in this inquiry they are classed as small-scale traders. There are no data available on the number of such firms in the years before 1939, but the rationing statistics of the Second World War and post-war years enable some estimates to be made. By making adjustments to the Ministry of Food figures and by using some of the data collected in the course of this inquiry the number of firms in the butchery trade with between 2 and 9 branches each in 1939 is estimated as 1,000–1,300 controlling 3,000–4,000 shops. In 1945 the number had risen to an estimated 2,000 organizations controlling about 6,000 shops, and in 1950 2,000–2,500 organizations controlling 6,000–7,000 shops. In 1950 the Ministry of Food rationing statistics suggest that some 15 % of the total number of butchers' shops came into this category of 'small multiple shop firms', while only 8–9 % of the total were branches of organizations with 10 or more shops.

Shares of the different economic types of retailer in the total trade

This discussion of the development of the different economic types of retailers in the meat trade can now be supplemented by estimates as to the share of the total meat trade undertaken by each type of retailer between 1900 and 1950. These estimates are presented in Table 39.

Table 39. *Estimated shares of the different economic types of retailer in the total retail sales of meat and meat products, 1900–50*

Year	Proportion of total sales undertaken by		
	Co-operative Societies %	Multiple shop retailers %	Other retailers (by difference) %
1900	3·0– 5·0	4·5– 7·0	88·0–92·5
1905	3·5– 6·0	7·0–10·0	84·0–89·5
1910	4·0– 6·0	10·5–13·0	81·0–85·5
1915	5·0– 8·0	9·0–11·5	80·5–86·0
1920	6·0– 8·5	8·0–10·5	81·5–86·0
1925	5·0– 8·0	8·0–10·0	82·0–87·0
1930	7·0– 9·0	8·5–11·0	80·0–84·5
1935	8·0–10·0	9·0–11·5	78·5–83·0
1939	9·0–11·0	11·0–13·0	76·0–80·0
1950	12·0–14·5	12·0–14·0	71·5–76·0

* For a discussion of the basis of these estimates see Appendix A. These estimates relate to the retail sale of all meat and meat products, e.g. sausages, but they exclude the sales by butchers of goods other than meat, such as bacon, eggs, ham and similar products that are sometimes sold by butchers. The sales by Co-operative Societies include the sales of meat and meat products undertaken by grocery departments as well as those undertaken by the butchery departments. The estimates of the sales of multiple shop retailers and of the small-scale retailers include the sales of meat and meat products by firms whose main sales may have been in other goods, such as grocery and provisions. An attempt has been made to exclude from the sales of all types of retailers the sales on wholesale or semi-wholesale terms to caterers. The firms with 2–9 branches each have been included with the 'other retailers' group.

Table 39 brings out clearly the main trends in the structure of the retail meat trade between 1900 and 1950. The share of the Co-operative Societies in the total trade rose slowly but rose continuously while the share of the multiple shop retailers after rising rapidly up to 1910 remained practically stationary or declined somewhat in the inter-war years until the middle and late 'thirties. The share of the small-scale retailers declined slowly from about 90% in 1900 to about 75% in 1950.

Factors influencing the development of multiple shop trading

The reasons for the emergence of multiple shop retailing in the meat trade in the last quarter of the nineteenth century are fairly clear. The great increase in these years in the volume of low-priced imported meat both demanded, and provided the opportunity for, the growth of new forms of retail organization to distribute these products to the working classes in the growing towns. The rapidity of the growth of multiple shop retailing was due not only to the fact that the leading giant firms were themselves the packers, the shippers and the importers, or at least had close links with the packers, but also to the fact that the retail trade as it existed in the last quarter of the nineteenth century was not readily adapted to handling bulk supplies of frozen and chilled meat that fluctuated in quantity, quality and price. On some counts the expansion of the multiple shop retailers was too rapid, their methods of opening new branches wherever possible too wasteful and the basis of their support among consumers insufficiently well rooted to stand any significant change in the economic climate. When such a change did occur in the years just prior to the First World War, when the rate of increase in consumption per head of imported meat started slowing down and prices started rising, the little empires began to crumble. But without the activity of the leading multiple shop firms in building almost overnight an entirely new type of retail organization and handling a new product successfully, other retailers would have been more reluctant to enter this trade and it is doubtful if frozen and chilled imported meat would have been made available to sections of the working classes of Great Britain in the twenty years before the First World War in such quantities and at such prices.

The First World War, however, represented an end of the rapid increase of multiple shop retailing in this trade. Since the Union Cold Storage Company controlled some two-thirds of the total number of multiple shop branches in existence in the years following 1923, this slow growth is in the main a reflection of the slow retail growth of this firm. The chief reason for this relative stability appeared to be the preoccupation of the Company with reorganization and improvement of the existing retail network rather than with expansion.

But this was only one factor. Two other suggestions can be made. Firstly the Company with its world-wide interests and its important role in the British meat importing trade was not dependent for maintaining and improving its financial position solely upon the success and expansion of its retailing organization. Provided the retail side was not a liability and that it continued to offer a guaranteed market for an important proportion of the meat imported by the Company, vigorous expansion was hardly called for.[1] Further, importing or wholesaling

---

[1] The share of the Union Cold Storage Company in the total imports by the United Kingdom of chilled meat from South America hardly changed at all in these years and remained at about 20%. See *Report of the Royal Commission on Food Prices*, 1925, vol. II, Minutes of Evidence, p. 218, and *Report of the Joint Committee of Enquiry into the Anglo-Argentine*

organizations which control retail outlets are always in a somewhat delicate position in relation to expansion of retailing activities vis-à-vis their independent retail customers. The second reason for the slow retail growth would appear to arise to some extent from the concentration on imported meat. This bias, in the opposite direction to that of the Co-operative Societies, limited the appeal of the multiple shops to certain classes of customer and held back general expansion. In many respects the Co-operative branches and multiple shops in the butchery trade were complementary rather than competitive. The relative decline in the rate of increase of the imports of meat in these years was also of some importance in narrowing the possibilities of a rapid expansion based principally on the sale of imported meat.

The main reason, however, why the number and the importance of multiple shop organizations in this trade grew so slowly in the inter-war years, compared with the pre-1914 increase, would appear to be that once the competing firms had practically all been merged into one company, that company was more concerned with the expansion of its interests in directions other than retailing. A further question must, however, be posed. If the Union Cold Storage Company preferred to consolidate rather than to expand its retailing organization, why did not other large multiple firms emerge in this trade in these years?

Three answers can be suggested to this question. In the first place, with regard to imported supplies, while there were some economies in buying in bulk in wholesale markets and arranging transport from the markets to a small number of shops, the advantages did not increase markedly with a much larger number of retail outlets unless some control over the actual importing and cold storage was possible at the same time. The strategic positions in these packing, importing and storage trades were, however, already occupied by very large firms and the possibilities of a new firm entering the trade and securing an important position were very limited. In the second place the advantages of scale in the home-killed trade were not very great. Centralized slaughtering yielded some economies, but there was a limit to them inasmuch as it cost more to transport cattle than dead meat and in any event the economies gained were not sufficiently great by themselves to provide a multiple shop butcher possessing a large number of shops with a clear advantage over the independent master butcher who undertook his own slaughtering.

The third reason why new large multiple shop retailing organizations did not develop in the meat trade—apart from the firms that undertook

<hr>

Meat Trade, Cmd. 5839, 1938, p. 20. Total imports of meat, however, increased in these years and the Company also increased its share of the imports of frozen mutton and lamb to about 17 % of the total imports of these goods by the United Kingdom.

the sale of meat alongside the sale of other goods such as provisions—lies in the nature of the trade itself. While the product in some respects was standard, the skill of the butcher in dressing and cutting and his business sense in pricing and anticipating demand were, in the years between the wars, with the improvements in qualities and the widening of consumer choice, key elements in the success or failure of an individual shop. These qualities and abilities, while assisted by good shop layouts and fittings, by large-scale buying and by centralized accounts, were essentially individual in their character. The standardized principles and techniques of multiple shop trading—and to some extent of Co-operative trading—could be used to set broad limits to the variations in these individual qualities and abilities but could never achieve control in detail or reproduce the same characteristics in every shop. In the case of imported meat the problems of cutting were slightly less severe than in the case of home-killed meat, but selling and pricing difficulties remained.

Apart from the policy of the Union Cold Storage Company itself, the slow growth of multiple shop retailing in the meat trade in the inter-war years may therefore be suggested as arising from three main factors. First the opportunities for achieving economies of scale by way of control over packing, shipping, importing and storage of imported meat were limited. Secondly, the advantages to be gained from centralizing the slaughtering and transport of home-killed meat were not very great and in any case the home-killed trade had to be combined with the imported meat trade if the shops were to provide a full selection for the consumer. Thirdly, while in the pre-1914 period the demand for cheap imported meat was both large and undiscriminating, thereby permitting the development of large-scale techniques, in the inter-war years quality and consumer choice became far more important and only slow progress was made by multiple shop retailers in catering for these variations in taste by the use of standardized techniques.

The progress of the Co-operative Societies

The general progress of the Co-operative Societies in the meat trade was due, as suggested above, to the attraction of the Co-operative method of trading, including the payment of a dividend on purchases, and to the existence of a relatively guaranteed market for Co-operative butchery in the form of households who already bought groceries and provisions from the Societies. In particular, the rise in the Co-operative share of the meat trade was assisted by the increase in the number of Societies establishing butchery departments and by the expansion of the Co-operative movement in the Midlands and South in the inter-war years. The existence of some economies of scale in the method of organization of the Co-operative meat trade, in the form of centralized purchases of livestock, large-scale slaughtering and bulk importing, also assisted the development of the Co-operative retail trade in meat. But as discussed above, except in Scotland and in the case of some of the larger Societies in the South of England, centralization had not proceeded very far and less use was made by the Retail Societies of the centralized activities of the Wholesale Societies in the meat trade than in the groceries and provisions trade. The bias in the Co-operative meat trade towards home-killed meat was in part a reflection of the tastes of the members, and the Societies achieved a reputation for selling good quality meat. At the same time, however, the concentration on the higher-quality, higher-priced meat was a limiting factor to Co-operative progress and led many members to purchase only a part of their requirements of meat from the Co-operative stores.

The resilience of the small-scale retailer

Little need be added on the role of the small-scale retailer. Some of the disadvantages of large-scale retailing and the difficulties of developing large-scale retailing in this trade are reflections of the continued advantages of small-scale retailing. In the years up to the First World War, it appeared that the economies of scale would lead to a considerable reduction in the part played in the trade by small-scale retailers. In the years following the First World War, however, while the small-scale retailer lost ground the decline in his importance was not rapid. This resilience of the small-scale retailer would appear to have been due to a number of factors. Among these were firstly the ability of the small-scale retailer to meet the demand of the housewife for variety in price, cuts and quality. Secondly there was an increasing demand for home delivery, particularly in the growing suburbs of the larger towns, and in the provision of this type of service the small-scale retailer practically had the field to himself. Thirdly, the small-scale retailing unit was economically more flexible than the branch of the large-scale unit and could be established in areas and markets where the initial turnover was insufficient to warrant the opening of a branch shop. Fourthly, the growing practice of jobbing and selling part carcases in the wholesale meat markets enabled the small-scale butcher to avoid unwanted cuts and compete with the larger-scale units. Lastly, no great economies of scale had appeared in the meat trade in relation to the size of the individual retail unit. The size, employment and turnover of the multiple shop branch, for example, was very similar to that of the shop of the small-scale retailer in the same section of the trade. Further, while improvements in the fittings and equipment of the butcher's shop took place in the inter-war years, hire-purchase systems for the most expensive items of equipment meant that the increase in fixed capital requirements did not place the small-scale retailer at a great disadvantage vis-à-vis the large-scale retailer possessing greater capital resources. The small-scale retailer, therefore, provided he ran his business efficiently and used his personal skill in catering for his customers, was able to compete on nearly equal terms with the retailing units of the large-scale firms.

There was, however, some increase in the scale of operations of the small-scale retailer. The figures given above show that between 1939 and 1950 at least there was a trend in the direction of very small multiple shop organizations, that is firms controlling 2 to 9 branches each. It would appear that some economies of scale existed in the very early stages of growth in size, both in relation to home-killed and to imported meat. Some immediate gains were made in purchasing, transport, delivery and overheads when a retailer controlled two, three or four shops instead of one, and a small slaughterhouse, in the pre-1938 period, servicing four or five shops in a group yielded equal advantages. As the shops of a small firm would be concentrated in one town there were further gains obtained by way of allocating different types and cuts of meat to branches in areas with differing tastes and customs and thus avoiding the excessive mark-downs of unsaleable cuts in individual shops. Not only were there these economies to be achieved but also, with a small group of shops, the founder of the business could continue to give personal attention to each of them, thus reducing the magnitude of, if not eliminating, the problem of remote control in a trade with marked individual characteristics.

Expansion of these very small multiple shop firms beyond a limit of 10 or 20 shops meant that personal attention to the shops could no longer be given, and in the inter-war years, as shown by the figures in the tables presented above, such expansion in the meat trade was unusual. Lord Vestey told the Royal Commission on Food Prices in 1925 that 'There is nothing to stop the man with 20 or 30 shops to-day gradually getting 2,000 or 3,000 shops, if he is such a fool'.[1] Whether the suggestion of the absence of obstacles was correct or not, the evidence certainly shows that the retail butchers were not foolish.

Suggestions as to future trends in the trade

Guesses as to the time in the future when the meat trade in the United Kingdom will return to conditions where free choice of quantity and quality by retailers and by consumers is possible, or as to future governmental policies in respect of slaughtering, importing and wholesaling, are of little value. But assuming that at some stage the retail trade at

---

[1] *Report of the Royal Commission on Food Prices*, vol. II, Minutes of Evidence, p. 225.

least will be free from shortages and direct government control, some suggestions may be made on the basis of past trends as to possible future developments.

The individual and skilled character of the retail side of the meat trade will undoubtedly continue to be the dominant characteristics of the trade for many years to come, but the significant development, provided meat becomes available in considerable quantities, will probably be in the direction of larger-scale processing of the meat for ready sale to consumers and towards standardization and simplification of retailing. The appearance of self-service in the meat trade, whereby the consumer serves himself from refrigerated display cabinets with pre-cut, wrapped and sealed joints, chops, offal and so on, such as has begun to be developed in the United States and Canada, is practically certain in the United Kingdom at some stage in the future. Such methods permit of greater division of labour in the process of preparing the meat for sale, and dressing and cutting becomes a specialized, continuous operation. At the same time there will no doubt be a number of other developments influencing the character of the trade, such as improvements in refrigeration techniques, the increased use of freezing units in the home, and even the sale of ready-cooked meat and meals.

In the retailing of meat the development of pre-processing and preparation of meat and of self-service will probably lead to the appearance of self-service combination stores, that is retail units selling meat and groceries and provisions. Any reduction in the monopoly of skill held by the individual butcher will result, as it has done in other trades, in the entry into the trade of other types of retailers, and to the housewife the attraction of a combined food store would undoubtedly be great. The spread of self-service methods in larger shops in the densely populated areas will probably be paralleled by more extensive delivery to the home in other areas and by the wider use of travelling shops. Such developments would not, however, run counter to the suggestions of a trend towards pre-cutting and packaging of meat. And if wrapping and packaging starts, branding and guarantees of quality will not be far behind.

With the above suggestions as a long-term perspective of the pattern of development in the meat trade, the problems of and possible trends in the structure of the trade may be examined. First, some expansion of Co-operative trading is most probable. Many of the weaknesses of lack of co-ordination and centralization in the organization of the Co-operative meat trade were being recognized by the Movement in the years immediately prior to 1939, and with the removal of controls and the end of shortages many of the plans made earlier will no doubt be put into operation to the advantage of the Retail Societies. Autonomy as to prices and policies of the individual Societies will no doubt remain, but any increase in the activities of the Wholesale Societies in the meat trade should lead to some further economies of scale being secured. The fact that in 1950 only about one-half of the households buying groceries and provisions from the Co-operative Societies purchased their meat from the same sources is an indication that there is considerable room for Co-operative expansion in this trade, provided the Retail Societies are able, in respect of the number of shops, the type of meat sold and the prices charged, to meet the demands of the members. In the longer term the Co-operative Societies, with their large premises frequently undertaking the sales of groceries and provisions as well as meat in the same shop or in adjoining shops, will be well placed to develop the self-service combination stores envisaged above, and this should further increase the share of the trade held by the Societies. It is true that many of these premises are not well located in main shopping areas and that the capital investment required to develop combination stores will be heavy, but these are problems that the Societies can overcome.

As regards the multiple shop organizations, it would appear doubtful whether these firms as at present constituted will advance at all rapidly. Historically the main impetus for the growth of this type of retailing came from the handling of a new product in a new way. Subsequently, while the firms improved their techniques and refined their methods of importing and retailing, they did not change the essential character of their business. And in the absence of new fields or areas of expansion and of new types of product, in the absence of a new impetus and the weakening of the strength of the old impetus, the advance of multiple shop retailing in this trade was slow. In the future, if the trends suggested above towards self-service and pre-cutting and packaging materialize, the organizations with capital resources, with good trading sites and with experience in large-scale methods will have advantages over their competitors. But the harvest is unlikely to be reaped by the specialist multiple shop butchery firms. The new techniques of retailing will call for fewer but larger shops rather than for numerous small ones, and each large shop will have to have a large turnover to cover the much higher overhead costs; and it is extremely doubtful whether the sale of meat alone will attract the additional customers to make a large specialist butchery shop practicable. Other goods will have to be stocked and sold if the customer is to consider her longer journey to the larger shop worth while; in other words the combination meat and grocery store rather than the large meat shop is most likely to be the next stage in development.

If this does come about, the specialist meat multiple organizations will probably be slower to pioneer and introduce this new form of retailing, since it would involve changing the character of their trade, than the grocery and provisions multiple shop firms. These retailers, who already handle meat in some instances and possess, or are planning, very much larger retailing units than those at present owned by the specialist butchery multiple shop organizations, will be better able to adapt themselves to the new methods of trading. The existing specialist multiple shop firms may develop travelling shops and home deliveries. Both of these developments would however involve a considerable change in trading policies, and in any event a wide range of foodstuffs, including meat, rather than meat alone will probably be sold by the travelling shops of the future or jointly delivered to the home.

The future of the independent skilled butcher is difficult to forecast. As discussed above, the small-scale retailer has had in the past a great number of advantages in this trade. These advantages, as seen in the skill of the proprietors, the location and flexibility of the small butchery shop in meeting different demands in different areas, and the close attention that could be paid by the small-scale butchers to the individual needs, tastes and preferences of their customers, will undoubtedly continue for some time in the future to assist the small-scale unit to hold the major share of the trade. But if the trends suggested above develop in the trade the advantages, in the urban areas at least, of the large-scale retailers with their greater capital resources, better sites and ability to specialize in management functions will increase and the small-scale retailer, unable to promote large combination self-service stores, will probably diminish in importance in the trade.

CHAPTER VII

THE BREAD AND FLOUR CONFECTIONERY TRADE

The trade in the nineteenth century

In the second half of the nineteenth century home bread baking by the housewife was a common feature in most areas of the United Kingdom, particularly in the North of England, but in the growing towns the baker, selling bread on retail terms, was increasing in importance. Practically all the these bakers were independent master bakers who prepared, baked and sold their bread on the same premises. Baking was a strenuous as well as a skilled job, and in the bakehouse, which was either at the rear of or under the shop, practically no mechanical devices were used, the entire preparation of the dough, including the heavy job of mixing, being done by hand. Some delivery and 'hawking' of bread from hand-carts was undertaken, but the major part of the sales in the towns was made over the counter by the baker or his wife. More than in any other trade at this date, marriage and a wife was an economic proposition for the baker. Division of labour between the husband who made the bread and the wife who sold it was usual.

Bread and wheat products such as flour, biscuits, bran and provender were the main lines offered for sale, only a very small amount of flour confectionery being made. The bakeries were located in relation to the convenience of the customers in the area they served rather than in shopping streets aiming at catching the custom of the passer-by. The type of service provided and relationship existing with the customers may be seen from the practice in some areas of housewives taking the dough they had mixed themselves to be baked in the ovens of the local baker.

Apart from the small-scale master baker, the number and activities of other economic types of retailer were small. Co-operative flour milling can be said to date back to the end of the eighteenth century, and in the nineteenth century a number of Co-operative mills were established, with varying degrees of success. In 1850 the Rochdale Corn Mill, linked closely with the pioneer Rochdale Retail Society, was started. The number and output of Co-operative mills increased in the second half of the nineteenth century, and with their expansion the Retail Societies established bakeries utilizing the Co-operative flour. Most of the bakeries, while larger than the typical independent unit, supplied shops of the local Societies only, and these would rarely be more than ten in number. An important exception to this was the United Co-operative Baking Society of the Clydeside, which was a central baking Society founded in 1869 by a number of separate Retail Societies. Slowly at first, but rapidly in the last decade of the nineteenth century, the output of this central Society increased, and by the turn of the century the majority of the larger Retail Societies of Scotland were receiving daily deliveries of bread from the central bakery. The wholesale turnover in bread, biscuits and flour confectionery of the United Co-operative Baking Society had reached nearly £320,000 in 1900 compared with £32,000 in 1880. This represented some 5–10 % of total sales of these goods in Scotland.

The only other large-scale baking and retailing organization in the third quarter of the nineteenth century was the Aerated Bread Company Ltd. of London, which was founded in 1862. This firm concentrated in its early stages on the production and sale of bread, but in the 'eighties and 'nineties the catering side of the business was developed. By 1885 the firm had more than 30 branches or depots and by the turn of the century about 100. These branches undertook retail sales of bread and flour confectionery, baked and made in central bakeries, and also of other goods such as tea, coffee, and milk. The receipts of the Company from the catering services were, however, more important than the sales 'over the counter'. A second firm with somewhat similar retailing methods that developed in the bread trade at the end of the century was J. Lyons & Company Ltd. The first branch of this firm was opened in 1894 and by 1900 some 40 branches were in operation.

This pattern of the bulk of the bread being baked at home or baked and sold to the public by the small-scale independent master baker, with only a small proportion being handled by the large-scale Co-operative bakeries and multiple shop retailers, changed quite radically between the turn of the century and 1950. While the trade itself expanded slowly, important developments took place in the techniques of production, in the number and character of the retail outlets, in the type of goods handled, and in the methods of selling.

Changes in the methods of production

The changes in the techniques of production took the form of the introduction of mechanical aids for the preparation, mixing and baking of bread. The first International Exhibition of Flour Mill Machinery in London in 1881 can be said to mark the beginning of mechanical baking in the United Kingdom, and in the last decade of the nineteenth century and the first decade of the twentieth invention followed invention. Engineering firms like Joseph Baker & Sons, A. M. Perkins & Sons, David Thompson and Lewis & Pointon led the way, and these years saw the introduction of aids and machines such as the flour hoist, the hand and mechanical flour sifter, steam pipe ovens such as the Draw-plate and Peel ovens, mechanical mixers, dough kneaders, and handling and moulding machines. The dough dividing machine, developed at the turn of the century, which cut the dough into pieces suitable for baking in the oven and of the correct weight for producing a loaf, was an important advance towards large-scale baking. The dough prover, a mechanical conveyor that carried the dough in a suitable atmosphere while it was proving or rising, enabled the bakers to control and raise the quality and standard of the bread produced by large-scale methods. Just before the First World War the first travelling oven was being marketed.

The spread of these new techniques was slow inasmuch as many independent master bakers did not have an output sufficient to warrant their use, but they made possible the development of large-scale or factory baking. Wholesale bakeries, as the large firms were called, supplying baked bread to a number of retailers or establishing central bakeries and selling through their own retail outlets, began to appear in the bread trade. In the inter-war years considerable strides were made in the improvement and perfection of these techniques, and with the widespread use of travelling ovens production line baking became common. With experience came marked improvements in the quality of the machine-made bread. To these developments were added further refinements such as the mechanical wrapping of bread introduced in the early nineteen-twenties and mechanical slicing and wrapping of bread introduced in the nineteen-thirties. Alongside the large-scale baking of bread came large-scale production of flour confectionery. Very few factory bakers confined themselves to production of bread and the technical changes in bread production were paralleled by developments in cake making, such as washing-machines for currants, sultanas and raisins, and various slicing and grinding machines and mills for peel and nuts. Some firms emerged which specialized entirely in the large-scale production of flour confectionery such as slab cake.

The firms adopting these large-scale methods of making bread and flour confectionery developed their sales in many different ways. Some wholesale bakers concentrated almost entirely on the production side and delivered the bread and flour confectionery to other retailers for resale to the public. Occasionally these other retailers would be bakers, but in most instances they would be retailers in other trades, such as grocers and dairymen. In the inter-war years when the development of wholesale baking was rapid, practically all the sales of bread produced by these wholesale firms were made through grocers, dairymen, cafés and general shops, apart from supplies on contracts to institutions, schools, hospitals and so on. The larger wholesale baking firms of this type producing hundreds of thousands of loaves a week would often deliver to their retail customers over a radius of anything from 50 to 100 miles of the factory.

Another type of wholesale baker also sold his output to other retailers but in addition sold direct to the public by retail round. This development was rare in the pre-1914 period, but in the inter-war years, as delivery to the home became general, particularly in the South of England, a number of wholesale bakers adopted this practice. Some, in fact, closed down their retail branches and concentrated entirely on retail rounds.

A third type of wholesale baker operated in connexion with a retail chain of cafés, teashops and restaurants. The A.B.C., J. Lyons & Company Ltd., and Carricks (Caterers) Ltd., are examples of this type of firm. In these instances, while retail sales of bread and flour confectionery were made, the wholesale baking business and the retail sales of bread were second in importance to the provision of a catering service.

The development of multiple shop retailing

The fourth type of wholesale baker sold his output largely through his own retail shops and by retail rounds, though some sales on wholesale terms to other retailers might also be undertaken. Firms of this description can be classed as multiple shop bakery organizations, and the following discussion will be confined to them. Apart from the A.B.C. and the Co-operative Societies, the first firms to develop a central bakery servicing a number of controlled retail outlets were, according to existing records, James Blackledge & Sons Ltd., founded in 1849, George Lunt & Sons Ltd. founded in 1850, and Richard Taylor & Sons Ltd. founded in 1850. All three firms were in Liverpool and all three had more than 10 branches each in the last decade of the nineteenth century. In the next fifteen years a large number of other bakers adopted similar production and distribution techniques and by 1914 there were some 8 firms in the trade with more than 25 branches each. The largest of these were the three firms mentioned above and the City Bakeries Ltd. and Kirkland & Sons of Glasgow, J. Miller Ltd. of London, and Benjamin Sykes & Sons Ltd. of Liverpool.

Estimates of the number of multiple shop organizations in the bakery trade and the number of branches controlled by them in different years between 1900 and 1950 are given in Table 40. An attempt has been made to include data on firms that have gone out of existence or have amalgamated with other firms, as well as those trading independently in 1950. Altogether data relating to 93 firms have been included in this table. Of the 31 firms no longer trading independently in 1950, 22 were merged with other firms and 9 appear to have gone out of existence or to have controlled less than 10 branches in 1950.

Table 40. *Estimates of the number of multiple shop firms and branches in the bread and flour confectionery trade, 1900–50*

Year	10–24 branches		25–49 branches		50–99 branches		100 or more branches		Totals			
									10 or more branches		25 or more branches	
	Number of		Number of		Number of		Number of		Number of		Number of	
	Firms	Branches	Firms	Branches	Firms	Branches	Firms	Branches	Firms	Branches	Firms	Branches
1900	8	105	—	—	—	—	—	—	8	105	—	—
1905	15	221	1	40	—	—	—	—	16	261	1	40
1910	14	194	6	187	1	70	—	—	21	451	7	257
1915	18	256	6	217	2	155	—	—	26	628	8	372
1920	24	339	8	280	3	231	—	—	35	850	11	511
1925	34	463	8	281	4	263	1	110	47	1,117	13	654
1930	41	560	13	436	5	302	1	100	60	1,398	19	838
1935	48	677	16	550	8	491	1	105	73	1,823	25	1,146
1939	44	667	15	518	7	438	3	511	69	2,134	25	1,467
1950	38	582	14	462	8	527	2	622	62	2,193	24	1,611

The multiple branch catering firms have been omitted from this table: the A.B.C., J. Lyons & Company Ltd., Cadena Cafés Ltd. and the Zeeta Company Ltd. may be cited as examples, and altogether some 7 multiple branch café and restaurant firms which sold bread and flour confectionery retail as an adjunct to their catering business have been excluded. These 7 firms had nearly 500 branches in 1950. If these firms had been included the number of organizations with 10 or more branches selling bread and flour confectionery and the number of branches controlled by them in different years would be as follows:

Year	Number of firms	Number of branches
1900	11	265
1910	25	782
1920	40	1237
1930	82	1820
1939	79	2390
1950	69	2659

The estimates given in Table 40 refer only to the fixed branch shops of the multiple shop organizations and take no account of the number of retail rounds undertaken by these firms. Delivery to the home by retail round was far more important in the South of England than in the North, and a big increase in this practice took place in the inter-war years. In 1950, for example, an analysis of the practice of 7 com-panies in the London area controlling 142 branches and operating 283 retail rounds showed that some 61 % of the total retail sales of bread took place on retail rounds. In the same year an analysis of 5 companies in Scotland and Liverpool controlling 193 shops and operating 38 retail rounds showed that only 18 % of total retail sales of bread took place on retail rounds.[1]

The estimates presented in Table 40 can be analysed to show the rate of growth of multiple shop retailing as shown by the number of branches existing in different years. This analysis is made in Table 41, which shows the net increase in the number of branches in existence, the rate of net increase and the average yearly net increase between different years. It must be emphasized, however, that as these figures relate to branches only and exclude retail rounds the trends shown give only a general indication of the pattern of growth.

Table 41. *Rate of net increase in the number of branches of multiple shop firms in the bread and flour confectionery trade, 1911–50*

Year	Branches of firms with 10 or more branches			Branches of firms with 25 or more branches		
	Net increase in number of branches	Per-centage net increase	Average yearly net increase in numbers	Net increase in number of branches	Per-centage net increase	Average yearly net increase in numbers
1911–1915	177	39	38	115	45	23
1916–1920	222	35	44	139	37	28
1921–1925	267	31	53	143	28	29
1926–1930	281	25	56	184	28	37
1931–1935	425	30	85	308	37	62
1936–1939	211	12	53	321	28	80
1940–1950	59	3	6	144	10	13

A feature of the growth of multiple shop retailing in this trade was the consistent rate of increase in the number of shops and the steady increase in the number of new firms coming into the trade. Between 1915 and 1925, for example, 21 new multiple shop organizations emerged, and between 1926 and 1935 26 new firms. Of equal interest was the relatively small size of the firms, at least up to the years just prior to the Second World War. In the bakery trade the multiple shop

[1] Sales on retail rounds were much less important in the case of flour confectionery. Of the retail sales of the 7 London firms mentioned above only 16 % of their sales of flour confec-tionery were made on retail rounds in 1950, the remainder being through the shops. In the case of the 5 Scottish and Liverpool firms only 3·5 % of the sales of flour confectionery was made on retail rounds.

organizations were local or regional in character, and while some firms reached the 50–90 branches size group this appeared to be the economic limit to the number of shops that could be developed in a given area. The formation of Allied Bakeries Ltd. in the middle 'thirties changed the statistical picture. This firm, between 1935 and 1950, amalgamated a number of local and regional firms, and whereas the largest multiple shop firms in the bakery trade in 1935 controlled only 9 % of the total number of multiple shop branches in existence belonging to firms with 25 or more branches each, in 1950 the largest firm, Allied Bakeries Ltd., controlled some 32 % of the total number of branches. The firms that became members of the Allied Bakeries group, however, continued to trade under their own names and to a large extent continued their previous trading practices, and no national network of retail shops supplied centrally had yet come into existence in the trade.

Features of multiple shop retailing

All the multiple shop firms in the bakery trade were producer/retailers and undertook the baking of practically all the bread and flour confectionery that was sold in their retail shops and by retail rounds. One or more central bakeries supplying the retail branches daily was the usual arrangement, though the case of some firms with more than 50 branches and with retail rounds scattered over a fairly wide area there might be as many as 5–10 medium-sized central bakeries. When bakers' shops were acquired by multiple shop firms it was usual to close down the bakery or to utilize it for special types of baking and supply the additional shop from an existing central unit. Apart from the improvements in the techniques of baking, no fundamental changes took place in the method of operating multiple shop bakery firms between 1910 and 1950, though the proportion of total production and sales represented by flour confectionery tended to increase. In the case, however, of the multiple shop firms taken over by Allied Bakeries Ltd. considerable rationalization in the number of branches, in their location and in the system of supply from central bakeries was introduced.

The type of shops operated by the multiple branch firms and the type of goods sold, however, changed in a number of ways in these years. Very generally, it may be said that the trend was for the shops of multiple bakers to move out of the side streets into the main shopping streets, and for the emphasis in the retail shop to shift from bread to flour confectionery. The move to main shopping streets was by no means universal. Many branches of multiple shop firms remained in side streets and minor shopping centres where they had been located in the early part of the century, but the freeing of the baker's shop from the necessity of additional space for baking made the move possible.

The growing emphasis on flour confectionery encouraged this trend inasmuch as only a very small proportion of flour confectionery was sold by retail round and the most effective way of selling such goods was by well-designed displays in busy shopping streets. This development proceeded so rapidly that by the end of the inter-war years some of the multiple shop bakers were selling, by value, more flour confectionery than bread, including the bread sold on retail rounds.

The reasons for the growing importance of flour confectionery sales by multiple shop firms are not difficult to discern. The consumption per head of flour confectionery rose faster than that of bread in the inter-war years.[1] Also, with the development of factory-produced bread, which was sold in all types of retail outlets and not only by bakers, the role of the baker as the only outlet selling a particular type of bread diminished slightly. The baker, however, was still the only retailer who could afford the space for an adequate display of flour confectionery, and the small loss of bread sales to other types of outlets was more than compensated for by the increased sales of the baker of flour confectionery. A further factor, particularly in the South of England, was the growth of the practice of selling bread on retail rounds, leaving the retail shop as such with little else to sell over the counter but flour confectionery.

Another change in the type of goods sold by the branches of multiple shop bakery firms was the introduction of packaged grocery goods. This development was not general, but tended to be confined to the North Western area of England and to Northern Ireland. The particular reasons for this development would appear to be the ease with which such lines could be added to the bread and flour confectionery lines, and the fact that as retail rounds were not usual in these areas the customers visited the baker's shop regularly for bread and could be persuaded without much difficulty to buy other goods as well. A third factor may possibly have been the need to maintain turnover, which began to fall as grocers started handling the factory-made bread.

[1] The consumption of bread and flour per head of the population in the inter-war years is estimated as follows:

Average of three years	Consumption per head of the population (lb.)	
	Bread	Flour confectionery
1920–1922	147·8	22·0
1925–1927	148·4	26·7
1930–1932	147·1	29·6
1936–1938	151·9	35·5

These estimates are based on data given in Richard Stone, *Consumers' Expenditure, 1920–1938*. In 1950 the estimated consumption per head was 175·1 lb. bread and 27·7 lb. flour confectionery.

The bread sold by the multiple shop bakers also changed. Mechanical wrapping in waxed paper and, later, slicing of bread were developed in the nineteen-twenties and nineteen-thirties, and this allowed for an element of branding. A reputation over a wide area for good bread became possible. In the North of England and in Scotland the proportion of wrapped bread sold by the multiple shop bakers was over 75 % of total sales in the years immediately prior to the Second World War. Customers liked the wrapped bread, and only the large-scale bakers could afford to instal the expensive mechanical wrapping machines.

The geographical bias in the activities of multiple shop bakery firms was very marked. As mentioned above, the first multiple shop firms developed at the turn of the century in the Liverpool area, and in 1920 nearly two-thirds of the total number of branches controlled by firms with 25 or more branches each were in this area. In the inter-war years the firms in the Liverpool area met with varying fortunes, and the total number of branches increased only slowly. Further, few new large firms developed in that area though some emerged in Manchester and the surrounding district. On the other hand, existing firms in the Midlands and the South grew rapidly and a number of new multiple shop organizations appeared in these areas. This led to a shift in the regional distribution of the branches of the multiple shop firms; in 1930 the proportion of the total number of shops represented by those in the Liverpool area had fallen to about 40–45 %, and in 1950 to about 30–35 %. The proportion of branches in the Midland and Southern areas, including London, on the other hand, had increased from about 20–25 % in 1920 to 40–45 % in 1950. In the same period the proportion of the total number of branches in Scotland—mainly Glasgow—rose from about 10 % in 1920 to 15 % in 1950. Taking the country as a whole, in 1920 75–80 % of the branches were in Scotland, the Northern Counties and Lancashire, the remainder being in the Midlands and the South. In 1930 the proportion was 65–70 % in the North of England and in Scotland, and in 1950 50–55 % in the North of England and Scotland. The branches of the multiple shop organizations both in the North and in the South were practically confined to the urban areas of the larger towns.

The reasons for the early development of multiple shop trading in the North of England, particularly in Liverpool, and for the high proportion of the total number of branches in the North are somewhat mixed. The greater importance of shop sales of bread in the North of England compared with the South, where retail rounds were the more usual method of sale, led to firms in the North opening branch shops when they wished to expand, while firms in the South would develop their retail rounds rather than increase the number of their shop branches. Of particular importance also in the case of the Liverpool development was the role that that port played in the import and milling of grain, especially in the years before 1920. With abundant and cheap supplies of flour on their doorstep the enterprising bakers had every incentive to increase the scale of their production and distribution. It would also appear that the millers were prepared to give long credit to the local firms. Another factor was the simple one of imitation. The success of one firm in developing a group of retail shops in a town or area led to others adopting the same methods, though this factor would only be of significance if the conditions for such development were favourable. These are by no means all the reasons for the early development of multiple shop trading in Liverpool and the North of England, but whatever the particular advantages had been, they were passing in the inter-war years. Central bakeries supplying a large number of shops and retail rounds were becoming as common in the London and Southern areas in the nineteen-thirties as they had been in the North of England and in Scotland ten or twenty years earlier.

The Co-operative bakery trade

The early development of Co-operative flour milling and centralized baking was mentioned above. With the improvements in large-scale baking techniques and the entry of the Co-operative Wholesale Societies into flour milling in the eighteen-nineties, Co-operative baking made rapid strides.[1] The United Baking Society of the Clydeside remained the largest unit, and this Society opened its own retail shops as well as selling to other Retail Societies. After the turn of the century, other Societies, for example the Royal Arsenal Co-operative Society of London, also adopted the latest methods of production. One of the obstacles to the erection of large-scale bakeries was the relatively small sales of bread and flour confectionery made by some of the individual Retail Societies. In the inter-war years this problem was overcome to some extent by the setting up of Federal Bakery Societies which baked and supplied bread to a number of Retail Societies. By 1935 there were some 16 of these Federal Bakery Societies.

The Co-operative Societies followed the national trend in relation to sales by retail round or sales in the shops, that is, delivery was more important in the case of the Societies in the Midlands and South, which were growing rapidly in the inter-war years, than in the case of the Societies in the North of England and Scotland. The sales made through

[1] The Dunston mill was opened by the Co-operative Wholesale Society in 1891, the Silvertown mill in 1900 and the Avonmouth mill in 1910. The Scottish Co-operative Wholesale Society started flour milling in 1894.

the shops were almost all undertaken by the general grocery and provisions departments. Very few Co-operative shops existed that sold only bread and flour confectionery. For this reason the sales by the Co-operative Retail Societies of flour confectionery, which required a measure of specialist handling and space for display, were, relatively, very much smaller than the sales of bread.

The small-scale retailer

There were two main types of small-scale retailer of bread and flour confectionery in these years. On the one hand there was the baker who baked and sold his own goods; on the other hand there was the general food retailer, usually dealing mainly in groceries and provisions or in milk products, who also sold bread and a little flour confectionery.

The methods and trade of the master baker changed in a number of ways between the turn of the century and 1950. The smallness of the bakehouses and the lack of capital resources were an obstacle to the adoption of all the improvements in baking technique and in the mechanical handling of the raw materials. But by the nineteen-twenties some of the heavy manual labour connected with baking had been dispensed with in the small bakehouses as well as in the large ones by the use of hoists and mechanical mixers and kneaders. Small-scale mechanization made possible the growth in the inter-war years of the firms with two, three, four or five shops supplied by one bakery, but the great majority of the master bakers remained producer/retailers baking and selling their own bread in a single shop.

The very small rise in the total demand for bread per head of the population, the rapid growth of large-scale or factory baking from the first decade of the twentieth century onwards, and the increasing sales of bread by non-bakers in the inter-war years, combined to confront the master baker with a problem of maintaining his turnover. For some period the superiority of the product of the small baker over the factory-made bread helped his competitive position, but improvements in the factory methods and particularly the introduction of wrapped and branded bread undermined this advantage. The small baker in the rural districts and small towns kept his position as the only source of bread supplies. But the ever-widening delivery by the factory bakers in semi-rural and urban areas began to threaten his monopoly, even though the factory bread might be twelve hours old by the time it reached the shops or the consumer's door-step. In the towns the master baker faced greater competition from the growing large-scale bakers, the wholesale bakers, the multiple shop firms and the Co-operative Societies. These bakers in their planned delivery organization and prominent retail shops could often give better service and offer a far greater range of goods than could the small-scale baker.

These factors led the master baker to attempt to widen the range of the goods sold. In the case of bakers with shops near or in main shopping areas greater attention was paid to the production, display and sales of flour confectionery, and sometimes of other cooked products such as pies. Other bakers, following the example of some of the multiple shop firms and in some respects retaliating for the grocers' practice of selling bread, started selling prepacked groceries. This development was more common in the North of England and to some extent in Scotland than in the South of England. The independent bakers away from the main streets or local shopping areas, however, had to continue to rely on the sale of bread through their shops or by retail round for their turnover, and a number of such firms in the inter-war years went out of business or merged with other firms.

The non-bakers, mainly grocers and dairymen, who began to undertake the sale of bread in the years immediately prior to the First World War and in the inter-war years were of both the independent and multiple shop types. The increase in the number of such outlets for bread was made possible by the larger-scale methods of bread production. The suppliers to these outlets were mainly the factory bakers, but the smaller bakers who produced more bread than could be sold in their own shops also sold to local grocers. The grocers and dairymen handling small quantities of bread did so for the convenience of their customers, and rarely would such sales represent a significant item of their turnover. Bread and flour confectionery were bulky goods in relation to their unit value, and the carrying of too large a stock would have reduced the display and sales of the main lines of these outlets. The sale by such retailers of bread, while not constituting a major channel of distribution, did, however, add to the number of those competing with the master bakers.

Price fixing and price wars in the bread trade

A reference must be made to the price-fixing practices of the bakers and the price 'wars' in the trade. Beginning in the decades before the First World War and continuing far more actively in the inter-war years, local associations of bakers attempted to fix the retail price of bread in their areas. Such prices fluctuated to some extent with the price of flour, and in the 'twenties and 'thirties the prices in different areas were related to the maximum prices laid down by the Food Council for the London area. The effectiveness of this price fixing in different areas of the country varied widely, as did the support given to such practices by the large-scale factory bakers, including the multiple shop bakers. The Co-operative Societies, while taking no direct part in the determination of the price schedules, sometimes followed them very closely, though in a few areas the Societies consistently sold below the agreed prices. Such price-fixing policies were adopted in an attempt to prevent undercutting of the bakers by the non-baker retailers and certainly gave the master baker a measure of protection in his struggle to keep pace with the improvements in production technique and the increase in the number of outlets. To enforce the price agreements when necessary, arrangements were made with some of the millers to refuse to supply flour to bakers who were regularly selling under the agreed prices, though here again the effectiveness of such measures varied.

Inevitably attempts to fix prices also led to so-called 'price wars', and in Liverpool and Glasgow, two areas where the local Associations of bakers were not very strong, price cutting developed in the 'twenties and 'thirties. The initiative in the 'war' might come from a multiple shop grocery organization using bread as a 'loss leader', or from a small-scale baker attempting to increase his wholesale and retail sales, but once one firm had started reducing the price of bread others competing in the same area found they had to follow suit. The lower prices meant lower turnover per unit, and the bakers sought ways of adding to turnover by increasing the number of outlets or widening the range of goods sold. Even when some general agreement on prices had been reached and was being followed, the competitive character of the bread trade, particularly in the two towns mentioned, led to other devices, such as the sale of 'sides' and 'ends' at lower prices, to attract customers and to increase turnover.

The results of price fixing and price wars in this trade are difficult to determine. On the whole it would appear that the maintenance of prices at a level that enabled the highest-cost baker to stay in existence tended to maintain small-scale baking to a greater extent than might otherwise have been the case. In the absence of price competition, greater stress would also appear to have been placed by the retailers on delivery, on the supply of other goods, on the quality of the product, and so on, in order to maintain or increase their sales. Again the price wars, when they did occur, would appear to have been carried to further lengths and in many ways were more wasteful of resources and effort than might have been the case if an element of price competition had been continuously present. Lastly, in those areas where the Co-operative Societies refused to follow the agreed prices an important increase took place in the sale of bread by such Societies, as for example in the South-Eastern area of London.

Shares of the different economic types of retailing in the total trade

An attempt can now be made to summarize the above discussion by presenting estimates of the proportions of the national sales of bread and flour confectionery that were undertaken by different economic types of retailer in different years, and to indicate briefly the main economic factors that would appear to have been responsible for the shifts that took place in these proportions. The estimates of the changing shares of the different economic types of retailer in the years 1900 to 1950 are presented in Table 42.

Table 42. *Estimated shares of the different economic types of retailer in the total retail sales of bread and flour confectionery, 1900–50**

| Year | Proportion of total sales undertaken by | | |
	Co-operative Societies %	Multiple shop retailers %	Other retailers (by difference) %
1900	3·5– 4·5	Under 1	95·0–96·0
1905	4·5– 6·0	About 1	93·0–94·5
1910	6·5– 7·5	1·5– 2·5	90·0–92·0
1915	7·0– 9·0	3·0– 4·5	86·5–90·0
1920	9·0–10·0	4·5– 5·5	84·5–86·5
1925	8·5– 9·5	7·0– 8·5	82·0–84·5
1930	11·0–13·0	9·0–11·0	76·0–80·0
1935	13·0–15·0	12·0–15·0	70·0–75·0
1939	15·0–17·0	16·0–17·5	65·5–69·0
1950	15·5–17·5	17·0–19·0	63·5–67·5

* For a discussion of the basis of these estimates see Appendix A. The estimates of total sales include all retail sales of bread and flour confectionery—the sales by retail rounds as well as the sales through retail shops. The sales of bread and flour confectionery by multiple shop grocers, dairies, caterers and variety chain stores have been included with the sales of multiple shop bakers, as have also the sales by wholesale bakers to consumers by retail round. The sales of these goods by small-scale grocers, dairymen, caterers and general shops have been included in the 'other retailers' group.

The broad trends in the retail structure of the trade appear clearly in this table. It is perhaps necessary to add that the share of the trade held by the small-scale master baker declined at a slightly faster rate than that shown for the 'other retailers' group in Table 42, and also the share of multiple shop wholesale bakers rose rather less rapidly than the share of all multiple shop retailers shown in this table. These differences in trend arise, in both instances, from the growth in the sales of these goods by non-bakery firms. Whereas in 1900 the sale of bread and flour confectionery was practically confined to bakers, in 1950 only about three-quarters of the total sales by 'other retailers' were sales by bakers and only about four-fifths of the sales by multiple shop retailers were sales by multiple shop wholesale bakers.

Many of the factors influencing the shifts in the share of the total trade undertaken by different economic types of retailers have been discussed above. Here a summary of the main factors will be given, along with some suggestions as to future trends in the trade.

The increase in the share of both Co-operative Societies and multiple shop retailers was primarily due to the advantages these organizations possessed over the small-scale retailer in regard to the use of large-scale methods of production. These methods reduced the wages cost per unit of output, enabled the firms to introduce popular refinements such as the wrapping and slicing of bread, and made it possible for the large-scale bakers to compete with the small-scale units in service to the customers. These advantages were present in the case of the sales of flour confectionery as well as of bread, though the economies of scale were slightly less marked in the former case. The multiple shop retailers developed their trade by the opening of attractive shops in main shopping areas and the provision of well laid out displays of flour confectionery and bread as well as by extensive delivery rounds to the consumer's home. The Co-operative Societies placed rather more emphasis on delivery and less on the acquisition of prominent shopping sites, but the Societies had the additional advantage of a practically guaranteed market for their goods. The expansion of Co-operative trading in bread followed on the heels of Co-operative trading in groceries and provisions. The members, who already purchased their groceries and provisions from a Co-operative Society and received a dividend on purchases, were persuaded relatively easily to purchase their bread from the same source once a bakery service was provided.

The master baker, in the early period at any rate, had a clear advantage over his competitors in relation to the quality of the bread baked. After the First World War, however, this advantage ceased to be general and only a few of the master bakers could claim a clear superiority of product over the factory bakers. In the inter-war years the master baker had a measure of price protection against undercutting by the large-scale bakers, and he possessed other advantages such as the greater services he could provide in the form of nearness to the consumer, the provision of fresher bread, and the sale of speciality bread and 'home-made' flour confectionery. For a while it seemed that the lower production costs of the large-scale bakers were offset by the higher distribution and transport costs incurred when delivering from a central point, and that the small-scale baker would survive in considerable strength.[1] But the policy of agreed retail prices and the use of motor vans would

[1] E.g. *First Report of the Royal Commission on Food Prices*, 1925, para. 59, p. 23.

appear to have enabled the large-scale bakers to compete on the consumer's doorstep with the local baker, and in the densely populated urban areas at least the costs of distribution and transport did not become prohibitive in relation to turnover.

Throughout the inter-war years, therefore, the master bakers were losing ground on the retail side, though many were increasing their wholesale sales to non-bakers; and the number of small-scale bakers diminished. The Second World War brought a temporary halt to growth of the large-scale bakers, but the advance continued in the post-war years. The master baker remained throughout these years practically without rivals in the rural areas and in some of the smaller towns, but it would appear to be mainly a matter of time before the large-scale factory bakers with their continued improvements in production technique and delivery organization threaten the supremacy of the master baker in these areas as well.

The importance of large-scale baking should not be exaggerated. About one-half of the bread and flour confectionery sold in 1950 was baked and sold by the independent master baker. But the economic and technical superiority of factory-made bread and flour confectionery seems to be established and the further advance of factory production at the expense of small-scale production following improvements in techniques of baking and preservation seems fairly certain. Such an advance will lead to a further growth in the importance of the large-scale retailing organizations, the multiple shop retailers, the wholesale bakers delivering direct to customers by retail rounds, and the Co-operative Societies. At the same time, however, there may be a further trend towards the sale of wrapped bread in grocery and provision shops and in general food shops which would have the effect of taking trade away from the bakery trade proper.

CHAPTER VIII

THE MILK TRADE

The trade in the nineteenth century and developments to 1914

The dairy trade of the United Kingdom in the second half of the nineteenth century was almost entirely in the hands of the producer/retailers, that is the farmers who sold milk to consumers direct from their own farms. In the rural areas the producer/retailers were the only source of supply and the towns also drew their supplies from farmers in the surrounding areas and from stall-fed cows kept in the towns. Only in the very large towns, such as London, had a distinction begun to appear between the producer, that is the farmer, and the retailer or dealer.[1] The latter bought milk from the farmers and resold to the public. But the wholesaling of milk, that is the intervention of an intermediary who bought from farmers and sold to retailers, was practically unkown until the end of the century.

As the urban districts grew in size and density, the supplies of milk were drawn from wider areas. The scope of the producer/retailer, who could not undertake retailing in towns above, say, twenty-five miles from his farms, became more limited, and the number of retailers or dealers who only retailed the milk increased rapidly. But a more important force in bringing about a change in the character of milk distribution was the great increase in the volume of cheap imported dairy produce from the continent of Europe in the last two decades of the nineteenth century and the first decade of the twentieth. Some details of this increase have been given above in the discussion of the grocery and provisions trade. Here all that need be said is that these imports undermined the position of the British farmer as a producer of dairy goods, such as butter and cheese, and led him to place increased emphasis on the sales of liquid milk for distant markets.[2]

Three main developments followed. In the first place, as a result of the increased production and rising real income, the consumption per head of liquid milk rose rapidly; secondly, wholesale dairies acting as intermediaries between the farmers in the producing areas and the retailers began to play an important role in the trade in the towns;

---

[1] Stall-fed cows played an important part in the London milk supply however up to the turn of the century. In 1865 there were 40,000 cows in London and in 1888 732 licensed cow sheds. (*The New Survey of London Life and Labour*, London, 1933, vol. v, pt. II, p. 66.)

[2] In 1878 44% of total production of milk was estimated as being sold as liquid milk; in 1890 the proportion rose to 54% and in 1907-8 to 69%. (Viscount Astor and B. Seebohm Rowntree, *British Agriculture*, 1938, p. 285.)

thirdly, improved methods of handling and transporting milk were developed.

Reliable figures for the increase in the consumption of milk prior to 1900 are difficult to obtain, but two estimates made for 1878 and 1890 suggest an increase of 34–35 % in milk consumption between the two dates as against an increase in the same years of 13–14 % in the population.[1] More reliable estimates of consumption are available for the years 1900 to 1950 and these are given in Table 43.

Table 43. *Consumption of milk per head of the population of the United Kingdom, 1900–50**

Average of three years	Estimated annual consumption per head (gallons)	Average of three years	Estimated annual consumption per head (gallons)
1900–2	14·5	1920–22	16·1
1905–7	16·1	1925–27	18·9
1910–12	16·3	1930–32	18·9
1915–17	13·3	1936–38	19·3
		1950	25·3

* The estimates up to 1920 relate to Great Britain and Ireland including Southern Ireland. The estimates from 1900 to 1938 are based on data given in A. R. Prest and A. A. Adams, *Consumers' Expenditure, 1900–1919*, and Richard Stone, *Consumers' Expenditure, 1920–1938*. The estimate for 1950 is based on Ministry of Food data.

The rise in the consumption of milk, in the thirty or so years up to 1914, led to changes in the distributive methods and structure. In the closing decade of the nineteenth century a number of milk wholesaling companies were formed, and of these the Wilts United Dairies Ltd. of Charles Maggs and Reginald Butler was to be one of the most important. At the same time in the London area itself the first multiple shop dairy firms were developing; the Express Dairy Company Ltd., the Belgravia Dairy Company Ltd., the Aylesbury Dairy Company Ltd., and the Friern Manor Dairy Farm Ltd. were among the earliest firms. In the first decade of the century another change was the beginning of delivery of milk by retailers to the homes of customers in the larger towns. Producer/retailers had usually delivered as they had no fixed shops, but the retailers with dairy shops in the towns had previously expected customers to collect their milk. As yet delivery was by no means universal, and an important proportion of the milk purchased was

[1] J. C. Morton, 'Dairy Farming', *Journal of the Royal Agricultural Society of England*, vol. xiv, 1878, and R. H. Rew, 'An Inquiry into the Statistics of the Production and Consumption of Milk and Milk Products in Great Britain', *Journal of the Royal Statistical Society*, 1892.

collected by customers from shops or depots, but in the growing suburbs of the larger towns the enterprising dairymen were going round with horse-drawn floats serving customers with measures from open cans. Bottling of the milk could hardly be said to have begun. Some London firms experimented in 1897–98 with glass bottles, but the increase in the retail price of milk that was necessary to cover the cost of bottling did not meet with a favourable response among consumers.

The increased sales of milk in the years before the First World War were undertaken by the small-scale retailer. In the rural areas and in the small towns the producer/retailer remained practically the only channel of milk distribution. In the larger towns the part played by the producer/retailer was not insignificant, and stall-fed cows were still a common feature, but this method was becoming second in importance to that of the retailer who obtained his supplies on contract direct from farms or who bought a part or all of his supplies from the wholesaler or at railway stations. Increasing demand meant increasing difficulties in regard to the fluctuations in supply, and the wholesalers could, in part, even out some of these fluctuations by obtaining the milk from different areas. Many of these wholesalers undertook direct retail sales of milk to consumers as well as sales to retailers. The Co-operative Societies up to 1914 took little or no part in milk distribution and the multiple shop firms, though fairly numerous in London, were usually quite small. Those with 10 or more branches controlled only some 200 branches in 1905 and just over 300 in 1910.

Changes in the trade, 1914–1950

Some important changes took place in the trade during the First World War and immediate post-war years. In contrast to the circumstances assisting the changes that began at the end of the nineteenth century, the war and post-war years were a period of shortage of supplies and of government price control. The outstanding development was the emergence of a very large multiple shop organization, the United Dairies Ltd., which was founded in 1915. This Company was a holding company amalgamating three of the leading wholesale companies—including the Wilts United Dairies Ltd.—in the South of England together with a company that manufactured dairy machinery and utensils. This amalgamation was followed two years later by the acquisition of a large number of retailing firms. Some of these firms were producer/retailers, but most of them were small multiple shop retailers, and by the beginning of 1920 the company controlled some 470 shops, almost all situated in the London area. The company also possessed farming, wholesaling and manufacturing interests. Apart from the foresight and energy of its founders, the main impetus given to this movement towards amalgamation was the curtailment of supplies of milk, leading to a wasteful scramble between the wholesalers and retailers for what supplies existed, the shortages of manpower, horses and materials due to the war, and the strong bargaining position that could be secured by such a whole-sale retail group vis-à-vis producers within the framework of government control of prices. The London market, dependent as it was on supplies from distant areas and on the intervention of wholesalers, favoured such a development and the increased retail margins allowed under the government price control system encouraged wholesale firms to extend their activities on the retailing side.

Apart from the increase in the size of firms there were a number of other developments in the structure of the dairy trade in the inter-war years and up to 1950. The growth in the size of towns and the increased consumption of milk, coupled with improvements in the techniques of handling, bulking and transporting milk, ended the dependence of towns on surrounding areas for their supplies of milk and turned practically the whole country into a single market for milk. This trend was particularly marked in the case of the supply of milk for London, a part of which began to be drawn from as far afield as North Wales and Scotland.[1] With the growth of a national market, the number of country depots for collecting supplies of milk increased. In the pre-1914 period the farmers producing for the market had sent supplies of milk direct to the retailers or to be sold at railway stations, and only occasionally were the supplies bulked in depots. In the inter-war years there was a growing practice, particularly in areas remote from large towns, of sending the milk to country depots to be bulked and brine-cooled and then transported to the towns by rail or road tanker or in churn lorries or wagons. The developments in the transport of milk, particularly of motor transport, in their turn encouraged the establishment of country depots. These depots or creameries also undertook in many instances the manufacture of milk products from the surplus milk. They were owned by the large private wholesaling companies, some of whom had retail branches, by Co-operative Societies, by manufacturers and, after 1933, by the English and Scottish Milk Marketing Boards.

A second major development in the trade was the increased attention paid to the supply of clean safe milk. In 1901 the fat and water content of milk was laid down under the Sale of Milk Regulations, but the first effective legislation regarding grading of safe milk was introduced in 1923 by the Milk (Special Designation) Order, under the Milk and Dairies (Amendment) Act of 1922. This Order specified the conditions that had to be fulfilled before milk could be classed in the three categories

[1] *New Survey of London Life and Labour*, loc. cit. The number of cows in London in 1929 was 1,087 and the number of licensed cowhouses in 1930 was 50.

of Certified, Grade A (Tuberculin Tested) and Grade A. Pasteurization of milk (long urged by the medical profession and dairy engineers) began to be undertaken by the larger firms which handled sufficient quantities of milk to make worth while the installation of the necessary expensive plant. Pasteurization or heat treatment also had advantages in that the milk could be kept longer, an important consideration as the distances between the farm and the consumer lengthened and the number of intermediate stops increased.

The small producer/retailer and the retailer buying relatively small quantities direct from the farmer turned only slowly to pasteurization, but the large wholesaling and wholesale/retailing organizations supplying the larger towns began to heat-treat in one way or another practically all their supplies. Accurate figures on the amount of milk pasteurized are not available for the inter-war years, but careful estimates suggest that some 25 % of all milk was pasteurized or heat-treated in 1930 and about 50 % in 1939. In the administrative county of London in 1939, 98 % of the milk was heat-treated in some way.[1] The efforts of the Government and of Milk Marketing Boards to encourage and increase the supply of safe milk were continued during the Second World War, and by 1947 some 71 % of the total liquid milk supplies of Great Britain were heat-treated.[2]

As pasteurization of milk spread, so did bottling. While convenience to the consumer and the saving of labour time on delivery were important factors leading to the introduction of bottling, it was also clear that time and money would be wasted if pasteurized milk were allowed to be re-contaminated by the use of open churns and cans, dippers and measures. The large wholesaling organizations were again in the lead in this development and the most usual practice in the town areas was to pasteurize and bottle on the same premises. Bottled milk with sealed caps had become general in the London area by the early 'thirties and common in all the large towns by 1939. By 1950 it could be said to be practically universal.

A third and from an economic point of view a most important change affecting the retail character of the trade in the inter-war years was the practice of collective price negotiations between distributors and farmers and the determination of fixed retail prices for milk. There were two phases in this development. The first was between 1922 and 1932 when the Permanent Joint Milk Committee representative of the National Farmers Union and the National Federation of Dairymen's Associations attempted by annual negotiations to fix the price of milk for farmers and for retailers. The Committee was formed after the sharp

[1] E. Arnold, *Pasteurisation of Milk*, second edition, 1942, pp. 77–8.
[2] Ministry of Food, *Report of the Committee on Milk Distribution*, 1948, p. 22.

fall in milk prices following the end of government price control in 1920 and the increased volume of milk production in 1921–22. The prices fixed by this Committee were followed only in a few towns—London being one—and by no means all distributors accepted the prices. The Co-operative Societies, for example, declined to take part in the discussions until 1929. But the largest wholesale and retailing organizations supported the Committee and even if the prices were not followed in every area they tended to be the guide used by non-participating firms when making contracts with farmers or in fixing retail prices.

The fall in world prices of dairy products from 1929 onwards placed this voluntary price-fixing scheme in jeopardy. Complaints of 'undercutting' were numerous and the fall in the selling price of milk for manufacturing led to what some described as chaos in the liquid milk market. Dairy farming was not the only home farming industry in these years to face the problem of over-production and a fall in prices and, as with many other foodstuffs, a Marketing Scheme was introduced to strengthen the position of the producers and to stabilize the wholesale and retail price of milk. The second phase of price control, far more complete than the first, dates from the setting up of the Milk Marketing Boards of England and of Scotland at the end of 1933. Control of milk prices by these Boards continued until the Second World War when the Ministry of Food took over many of the Boards' functions. During these years adherence to the prices fixed by the Boards and the Ministry was universal.

The development of multiple shop retailing

A picture of the development of multiple shop retailing as a whole in this trade is presented in Table 44. This table gives estimates of the number of firms in the dairy trade controlling 10 or more branches each and the number of branches controlled by them in different years from 1900 to 1950. Some difficulty of classification arises in this trade in so far as very few of the dairy firms sold only milk; in fact in the later years of the period the greater part of the turnover of the retail shops themselves was in goods other than milk. Further, with milk being sold increasingly on retail rounds, the number of shops possessed by a dairy firm was not an accurate reflection of its importance in the milk trade. These problems will be discussed later and in Table 44 the estimates relate to the number of retail branches in different years that were controlled by organizations which were primarily retailers of milk and dairy products. The decision as to whether the firm—whatever it may have called itself—should be classed as a dairy or as a grocery and provisions dealer has been made on the basis of the division of sales. Firms have been classed as dairies if more than one-half of their total turnover in the shops and by retail rounds—excluding café and restaurant sales if any—was represented by milk. Distributing depots controlled by large firms, which were not part of a shop and did not sell milk or other goods 'over the counter' have not been classed as shops.

Included in these estimates are data relating to firms that have gone out of existence or have amalgamated with other firms, as well as those relating to firms trading independently in 1950. Altogether information relating to 53 separate firms has been included in the table, and of the 30 no longer trading separately in 1950 23 have amalgamated with other concerns and 7 appear to have gone out of existence.

Table 44. *Estimates of the number of multiple shop firms and branches in the dairy trade, 1900–50*

Year	10–24 branches		25–49 branches		50–99 branches		100 or more branches		Totals			
									10 or more branches		25 or more branches	
	Number of		Number of		Number of		Number of		Number of		Number of	
	Firms	Branches	Firms	Branches	Firms	Branches	Firms	Branches	Firms	Branches	Firms	Branches
1900	8	101	—	—	—	—	—	—	8	101	—	—
1905	13	153	2	50	—	—	—	—	15	203	2	50
1910	15	184	5	140	—	—	—	—	20	324	5	140
1915	17	216	6	185	—	—	—	—	23	401	6	185
1920	13	174	3	106	—	—	1	470	17	750	4	576
1925	15	191	3	107	—	—	2	742	20	1,040	5	849
1930	15	193	2	67	1	88	2	950	20	1,298	5	1,105
1935	18	259	2	74	1	54	3	1,110	24	1,497	6	1,238
1939	21	280	4	124	2	127	3	1,124	30	1,655	9	1,375
1950	14	180	5	143	—	—	4	1,314	23	1,637	9	1,457

The pattern of the growth of the number of branches of multiple shop organizations in this trade is seen clearly in Table 44. After a rapid advance in the amalgamation period of 1916–20, the rate of increase declines to 1939. Between 1920 and 1929 the average net increase in the number of branches was approximately one per week. In the years 1930–39 the average net increase declined slightly to 1–2 branches per fortnight. In the Second World War and post-war years there were two trends not shown fully in this table. Firstly, some of the existing large firms closed a number of their branches. Secondly, amalgamations between a number of small organizations and the subsequent growth of the new company offset the decline in the number of branches of the older firms.

The importance of the large multiple shop organizations in this trade is apparent in the figures presented in Table 44. In 1920 the two largest firms controlled 68% of the total number of branches. In 1925 and

1930 this proportion rose to 73 %. In 1935 it declined to 67 % and in 1939 to 60 %. In the post-war period, although a number of branches of the two leading organizations had been closed, further amalgamations by these firms kept the proportion at about 60 %. In other words, the two leading firms, the United Dairies Ltd. and the Express Dairy Company Ltd., controlled about two-thirds of the total number of branches in the years 1920–50. In the last twelve years of the period considered, these two companies had been joined by two others which controlled over 100 branches each, the East Kilbride Dairy Company Ltd. and the Home Counties Dairy Company Ltd., and altogether these four companies controlled some nine-tenths of the total number of multiple dairy branches in 1950.

Trading methods of the multiple shop firms

The main features of the development of multiple shop firms in the inter-war years were the leading role they played, along with the Co-operative Societies and large wholesalers, in the development of a supply of clean and safe milk, the marked geographical bias in the location of the firms, and the extended services that they offered to the consumer. The part that the large wholesaling and retailing firms played in the introduction of pasteurization and bottling has already been mentioned. All that need be added is that the large-scale firms were the only ones with the capital resources and the through-put of milk to permit of the outlay necessary to set up country depots and pasteurization and bottling plants.

These techniques of handling and treating milk were essential when supplying a large town, and between 1920 and 1950 some four-fifths of the total number of branches of multiple shop organizations were in two densely populated areas, London and Central Scotland. About two-thirds to three-quarters of the branches were in the greater London area and the proportion in Central Scotland rose from 10 % in 1920–25 to 15–20 % in 1939–50. In sharp contrast, in towns such as Birmingham, Manchester, Liverpool and Sheffield there were very few branches of multiple shop firms. The absence of multiple shop retailing organizations in these towns does not imply the absence of large-scale wholesaling of milk. It was rather the case that the large-scale wholesalers in the London and Central Scottish areas had developed retailing through fixed shops as well as by retail rounds, whereas the wholesalers in the other large towns either sold to other retailers or distributed to the consumer by retail rounds.

The development of organizations with fixed branch shops in the milk trade in London and Central Scotland would appear to have been influenced by a number of factors. Among these were the particular economic conditions at the time of the formation of the United Dairies Ltd., the fact that the retail shops of these firms developed and maintained their position as outlets for grocery goods and provisions rather than as outlets for milk alone, and the continued practice in Scotland of many of the consumers of collecting their supplies of milk from the dairy. This made the possession of retail shops of some importance in increasing the sale of milk. Even in Scotland, however, the success of the milk side of the business was dependent more on the sales by retail rounds than on the sales in the shops themselves.

Features of the retailing methods of the multiple shop firms in the inter-war years were the sale of bottled, pasteurized milk, house-to-house delivery, which in the London area from the middle 'twenties up to 1940 took the form of two deliveries a day, and the sale, by some firms before 1930 and practically all firms after 1930, of some groceries, provisions and bread to their customers as well as milk. Such sales were in many instances made on retail rounds, on the second delivery, as well as from the fixed shops. In some areas the sales of grocery and provisions on the retail rounds were greater than the sales of these goods in the shops from which the round was operating.

During the Second World War and in the post-war years the introduction of rationing of groceries and provisions and the rationalization of milk distribution ended the second daily delivery and the sale of other goods alongside milk on retail rounds. These factors, combined with the great increase in the consumption of milk, meant that the proportion of total turnover of multiple shop firms represented by milk sales increased in those years.

The multiple shop firms in the dairy trade can therefore be said to have changed their character in some ways between the pre-1914 years and 1939, with some reversion to the older form taking place between 1939 and 1950. In the pre-1914 years the multiple shop dairymen who existed were primarily retailers of milk. They sold a few other dairy products, but the shops were the basis of their 'over the counter' sales of milk, and of their retail rounds. In the inter-war years the increased cost of handling, transporting and treating milk, the relative sluggishness of demand due in part to price and to unemployment, and the virtual absence of price competition, led these firms to attempt to maintain and increase their turnover by increased services to the consumer and by the sale of a wide range of goods other than milk. The extensive use of retail rounds in the London area turned the retail branches of the multiple shop firms into practically grocery and provision dealers only. Large-scale distribution of milk was undertaken almost independently of the fixed shops and the dairymen controlling such outlets had to utilize them either as cafés or tea rooms or as general grocers and provision dealers. Failure to do this successfully meant that the high costs of running the shop would be added to the cost of distributing the milk. In the Second World War and post-war years a large number of the branches were closed and those remaining open were linked more closely than they had been before with the retailing of milk.

The Co-operative Societies

The Co-operative Societies, as mentioned above, took little part in milk distribution in the years before 1914. But in the inter-war years when the introduction of new methods and techniques of handling and retailing milk widened the scope for large-scale organization, the Co-operative Societies began to play an increasingly important part in the trade. Apart from the sales of milk in the grocery and provisions departments by some of the Scottish Societies and the establishment of a few dairy shops in Liverpool and in Scotland, the Co-operative Societies from the start made most of their sales by retail rounds. The rounds were organized from distributing depots and no attempt was made by the Societies either to sell goods other than milk on these rounds or to undertake canvassing.

The Co-operative trade in milk developed very rapidly in the inter-war years and a number of factors combined to assist this development. The Societies, as with other large-scale firms in the trade, had the advantage of the possession of the capital resources to enable them to build and equip their dairies with the most up-to-date plant. Both the larger Retail Societies and the Co-operative Wholesale Society played a leading role in developing pasteurization, and the sale by the Societies of bottled, pasteurized milk at a time when many other retailers were still using churns and measures proved an attraction to the consumer. Another factor in the development of Co-operative sales of milk was the payment of a dividend. The Societies charged the same price as the private trader, and also paid a dividend on purchases. Finally, in some ways the market for Co-operative milk was ready-made, that is, families already purchasing their other foodstuffs from the Co-operative Societies were willing in most cases to purchase their milk also from the Societies. A large number of consumers, however, confined their purchases from the Societies to milk, as the Co-operative delivery of milk was widespread whereas the consumers might be some distance from the nearest Co-operative grocery shop.

As with the multiple shop retailers, the Co-operative Societies were most prominent in the milk trade in the densely populated areas. In rural areas many Societies did not handle milk, making no attempt to compete with the local dairy or the producer/retailer. The strength of the multiple shop firms in the London area and their practice of selling goods in addition to milk on the retail rounds limited to some extent the growth of the Co-operative milk trade in this region, but in other towns, in many of which multiple shop trading was practically non-existent, the Co-operative Societies were responsible for over 50% of the total milk trade. In Derby and Nottingham, for example, the Co-operative Societies undertook more than four-fifths of the total milk trade in 1950.

The small-scale retailer

There were three types of small-scale retailer handling milk in the years following the First World War. In the first place there was the producer/retailer; secondly, the dairyman who bought his supplies direct from farms and/or from wholesalers; thirdly, there was the non-dairy retailer, the grocer and provisions or general food dealer who sold small quantities of milk.

The importance of the producer/retailer as a retail channel of distribution of milk declined in these years. As towns grew larger and a higher proportion of the total population lived in towns, so the opportunities of the producer/retailer declined. Further, the introduction of pasteurization and bottling placed the small farmer at a disadvantage. At the turn of the century over one-half, probably as much as two-thirds, of the milk sold retail was sold by producer/retailers. Estimates of his importance in 1930 ranged from 30–50% of total sales, but the latter figure was considered too high. Just under one-third would probably be a more correct estimate. By 1938 the proportion had dropped to some 17–20% and by 1947 to 15–16%.[1] This decline did not, of course, mean that the producer/retailers went out of business. Practically all producer/retailers undertook wholesale sales of milk as well as retail sales and a decline in the latter market meant an increase in the former. The number of producer/retailers in earlier years is not known, but at the start of the Milk Marketing Board Scheme in 1934 some 66,000 were registered in England and Wales and just over 3,000 in Scotland. About 10% of this number, however, undertook more than half of the total sales of producer/retailers. By 1947 the number of registered producer/retailers in England and Wales had dropped to about 46,000 and in Scotland to just under 3,000. In the rural areas and the very small towns of under 5,000 inhabitants the producer/retailer, however, remained practically the only source of supply of milk.

[1] Ministry of Agriculture, *Report of the Reorganisation Commission for Milk*, Economic Series No. 38, 1933, p. 28. Also Ministry of Food, *Report of the Committee on Milk Distribution*, 1948, pp. 67–8.

The dairyman buying supplies direct from farmers, depots or town wholesalers, or supplementing his farm contract with supplies from wholesalers, similarly declined in importance in these years. The major problem facing the small dairyman was that of keeping pace with the technical improvements in milk handling and preparation. In the 'twenties, with a horse-drawn float and churns with a tap, the dairyman was the main source of supply of milk in the towns outside of London, but in the 'thirties the growing popularity of bottled, pasteurized milk as against 'raw' milk and the attractions of the services offered by the alternative suppliers led to increased competition. Some of the independent dairymen installed small pasteurization and bottling plants, and kept abreast of the larger organizations. Others relied on wholesalers for pasteurization and merely undertook the bottling, and still others bought their supplies pasteurized and bottled from wholesalers.

The absence of competition in price between the different types of retailers during most of the inter-war years was a factor in maintaining the position of the small-scale dairyman, or at least preventing a more rapid decline in his importance, but the increased competition in services which took place in these years meant a great deal of hard work for a relatively small return. As with most of the multiple shop firms in the trade the small-scale dairyman began selling groceries, provisions and bread as well as milk, and in any area where a rival firm started two deliveries a day the dairyman had to follow suit. Naturally attempts were made on the retail rounds to cultivate a given area round the dairy as intensively as possible, but the ideal of a compact round was rarely achieved. The typical picture of milk delivery in the larger towns in the 'thirties was three or four milkmen supplying one street, though in some instances ten or twelve were not unknown, and in few cases could a dairyman claim the custom of three-quarters or even half the households in one street.

The non-dairy retailer increased in importance to some extent in the inter-war years. The difficulties of handling churns and cans had kept down the number of such outlets in the 'twenties, but with the general introduction of the bottling of milk and, to a limited extent, of milk in paper cartons in the 'thirties, and later of sterilized milk in bottles, there was a marked increase in the preparedness of retailers to sell milk alongside other goods, usually groceries and provisions. The number of such selling points for milk is not known, but there were probably upwards of 50,000 in 1938, though the proportion of the total sales of milk undertaken by these outlets was small.

Shares of the different economic types of retailer in the total trade

The discussion of the development of the different economic types of
retailer can now be summarized by presenting estimates of the proportions of the total retail sales of milk undertaken by different types
of retailers between 1910 and 1950. These estimates are given in
Table 45.

Table 45. *Estimated shares of the different economic types of retailer in
the total retail sales of milk, 1910–50**

| Year | Proportion of total sales undertaken by | | |
	Co-operative Societies %	Multiple shop retailers %	Other retailers (by difference) %
1910	About 1	1·5– 2·5	96·5–97·5
1920	2·5– 3·5	6·0– 7·0	89·5–91·5
1925	5·5– 6·5	9·5–11·0	82·5–85·0
1930	13·0–15·0	13·0–16·0	69·0–74·0
1935	19·0–22·0	17·0–20·0	58·0–64·0
1939	24·0–28·0	20·0–23·5	48·5–56·0
1950	28·0–32·0	23·0–26·5	41·5–49·0

* For a discussion of the basis of these estimates see Appendix A. The total retail sales of
milk exclude the sales on wholesale terms to caterers and other institutions and the sale
of welfare milk and school milk. The sales by multiple shop retailers include the sales of
milk by multiple shop organizations other than dairies, for example multiple shop grocers,
and also the sales to consumers by retail rounds that were undertaken by wholesale dairymen
who had more than 10 retail rounds but no fixed shops. Included in the 'other retailers'
group are sales by producer/retailers and small-scale non-dairy retailers.

The rapid growth of large-scale retailing in this trade emerges clearly
from this table, and in particular the rapid growth of Co-operative
retailing of milk. The share of the trade held by multiple shop retailers
may, however, be somewhat understated. The importance of the trade
of the large wholesale firms which did not possess shops and sold direct
to the consumer by retail rounds was difficult to ascertain, as complete
information on the activities of such firms was not available. The estimates used, therefore, may have understated the role of this form of
large-scale retailing. Further, many of the larger multiple shop firms
were wholesalers as well as retailers and they sold milk not only through
their own retail outlets and retail rounds but also to small-scale independent dairymen and other retailers. The proportion of the total trade
in milk handled by multiple shop firms on both wholesale and retail
terms is therefore understated in Table 45.

In relation to the sales by other retailers it is possible to make some
broad estimates as to the shares of the different categories of these in

the different years. The share of the producer/retailer in the total trade is estimated to have fallen from 40–50 % in 1910 to 35–40 % in 1920, 28–32 % in 1930, 17–20 % in 1939 and 13–15 % in 1950. The share of non-dairy outlets is estimated to have risen from under 5 % in 1910–20 to about 5 % in 1930 and between 5–10 % in 1935–50. The share of independent dairymen other than producer/retailers, therefore, would appear to have fallen, by difference, from about 50 % of the total trade in 1910 to 35–40 % in 1930, and to just over one-quarter between 1939 and 1950.

The factors influencing the changes in the retail structure of the trade

Many of the reasons for the shifts in the relative importance of different types of retailer have been mentioned in the course of the above discussion. Here a brief summary of the main factors will be given along with some suggestions as to the possible future trends in the trade.

The decline in the importance of the producer/retailer was clearly the result of the growth of urbanization and the size of towns. Producer/retailers were also faced with the further problem of meeting the consumers' demand for pasteurized and bottled milk. The sales appeal of the phrase 'the firm with the farms' or 'straight from the cow' was beginning to weaken in the 'thirties, and while tubercle-free herds solved one problem few farmers could provide the bottle-filling and washing plants that consumers were beginning to expect.

The decline in the importance of the independent dairyman was similarly due in part to the difficulties of setting up pasteurization and bottling plants and their high cost of operation when the through-put was small. These retailers in the large towns were able if they wished to purchase supplies of milk pasteurized and/or bottled from wholesalers, and large retailers competing with them could not undercut in retail selling price. But this method of purchase left the independent dairyman a very small margin and his ability to compete in services with the large retailer was curtailed.

The growth of large-scale wholesaling and retailing by both Cooperative and multiple shop organizations was encouraged firstly by the increase in the size of towns and by the turning of the whole country into one market for liquid milk, which enabled the large organizations to secure economies in the scale of operations. Secondly, the trend towards pasteurization and bottling of milk gave the large-scale units further advantages in that they alone had the capital resources to install the expensive equipment. In turn, the sale of pasteurized, bottled milk by these firms increased the demand for their goods. Further, from 1933 onwards additional encouragement was given to the larger dealers by the methods of charging and allocating freight and transport costs of the Milk Marketing Board.[1] The existence of fixed retail prices for milk, however, meant that these advantages of scale were not reflected directly in the price charged for the milk by the large organizations except in so far as the dividend paid by the Co-operative Societies represented a reduction in price. To attract additional customers other methods were used. In the case of the multiple shop dairymen, efforts were concentrated on providing safer and cleaner milk and additional services such as more frequent deliveries and the sale of other goods. In the case of Co-operative Societies, while no extra services other than those of cleanliness, quality and efficiency were provided, an important impetus to increased sales came from the existence of a ready-made market. One of the reasons for the relatively slower development of multiple shop retailing as compared with Co-operative retailing would appear to have been the extensive wholesaling operations of the leading multiple shop firms. Expansion in this direction was an alternative to increasing the number of their retail rounds and retail branches. The Co-operative Societies, on the other hand, undertook no wholesaling of milk to private retailers.

Suggestions as to future trends in the trade

The milk trade was the subject of a special investigation by a Government Committee in 1948 which had the task of advising 'on any changes which are necessary to ensure that clean safe milk is delivered as efficiently and cheaply as possible'.[2] Many of the recommendations made by this Committee, while they have been discussed, have not yet been the subject of legislative action. At the same time suggestions regarding nationalization of the trade have been made and such action would, of course, completely transform the wholesale and retail framework of the trade. But if it can be assumed that the trade remains in private hands and that the organization of the trade will remain broadly in the form already existing under the Milk Marketing Boards, some tentative suggestions can be made as to possible trends in the future.

Legislation is already planned to ensure that in the fairly near future all milk sold retail will be pasteurized or will come from tubercle-free herds. Further, given a measure of full employment the consumption of milk per head of the population, which rose so rapidly from 1940 to 1950, would appear likely to be maintained. With increased pasteurization and bottling and a higher consumption per head, it is fairly certain that there will be a greater flow of milk through the wholesalers and retailers who possess medium and large-scale pasteurization and bottling

[1] Ministry of Agriculture, *Report of the Reorganisation Commission for Milk*, Economic Series No. 44, 1935, pp. 90–2.
[2] Ministry of Food, *Report of the Committee on Milk Distribution*, 1948.

plants, at the expense of the activities of producer/retailers and of sales by farmers direct to small retailers. There is, of course, a limit to the economies that can be secured by large-scale pasteurization and bottling. That is, the transport of bottled milk over long distances to the consumer is very much more costly than the transport of milk in bulk containers, and after a certain stage the economies of a large through-put in the pasteurization and bottling plants are outweighed by the increased cost of transport. Further, the home delivery of milk is an economic proposition to large-scale retailers only in urban areas. Delivery from a central depot in semi-rural and rural areas is a costly operation and hitherto has been left to the small-scale retailers. But while a limit to the economies of scale in pasteurization and bottling may have been reached in certain large towns such as London, given present technical conditions and the use of glass bottles, and while large-scale rural delivery would appear unlikely to develop, there are still many urban areas and towns where further economies of scale of operation can be secured.

The increase in the total consumption of milk in the twenty-five years between 1925 and 1950 led to some marked changes, as noted above, in the method of handling and transporting the milk between farmer and retailer. The most important development was the establishment of country depots which bulked and cooled the milk received from farmers before transporting it to the town depots. In 1938–39 some 25 % of the total liquid milk consumed in England and Wales passed through depots and in 1946–47 the proportion had risen to 40 %. Increased consumption of milk makes the greater use of country depots inevitable and in the future the trend towards pasteurization will probably further encourage the practice of bulking supplies in country depots to secure an even flow to the town depots. This in its turn will strengthen the importance of the large-scale wholesalers and retailers in the trade, except in so far as smaller-scale units install pasteurization and bottling plants and are able to secure even supplies direct from farmers.

The future trends in the methods of retailing and in the competitive positions of the different economic types of retailer are difficult to anticipate. Apart from the suggestions made above that in regard to the handling and treatment of milk the large-scale organizations are likely to increase in importance with the greater stress placed on pasteurization and the continuance of a high level of demand, the developments in the actual retailing of milk will be dependent on a number of other factors. The changes, if any, in the character of consumer demand for milk are one factor, the retail price policy is another.

In regard to consumer demand, one of the main reasons why milk, in spite of the developments in large-scale processing and bottling and consequent standardization, has remained a trade separate from other food trades has been the need for daily and early morning supplies to the home. Other foodstuffs, for example bread, may have been purchased daily but not necessarily in the early morning, while groceries and provisions need only be purchased weekly or bi-weekly. Apart from further changes in the quality and in the preservation of milk, the development of refrigeration in the home on a wide enough scale would remove the need for early morning deliveries and present the prospect of milk sales and deliveries being geared into the sale and delivery of other goods. This would end the position whereby the milk retailer has an unused capacity of delivery vans after 10 a.m. Such a development, however, while it would result in radical changes in the milk trade, would appear to be rather remote.

Guesses as to retail pricing policy in the milk trade in the future serve little purpose, but if some form of price fixing continues and the distribution rationalization schemes are ended competition between retailers will, with little doubt, once again take the form of emphasis on quality and service. With the stabilizing of the demand for milk around the level reached in 1948–50, and the ending of rationing and of short supplies of groceries and provisions, the second deliveries of milk and other foodstuffs are likely to return and spread. Continuance of short supplies of groceries and provisions but not of milk may, however, delay such developments. Even if retail price fixing as such is discontinued, however, the retail developments may not be very different. With the intermediate handling of milk passing more and more into the hands of large concerns and with the continuance of the Co-operative policy of following rather than initiating price changes, the retail prices charged by the larger retailers will probably vary but little and the smaller retailers, as they become increasingly dependent for their supplies of pasteurized milk on the larger firms, will have little scope to develop significant price competition. Further, the reductions in the price per pint of milk that can be made are so small that the attraction of additional customers by charging a farthing less per pint is unlikely to be very effective. Increased price competition at the wholesale pasteurization and bottling stages may, however, lead to some reductions in the general level of retail prices, though the current methods of retailing are the most costly part of the whole process of distributing milk.

Whether wholesale and retail price competition becomes a reality or no, some increase in the share of the retail trade undertaken by the multiple shop dairy firms and the Co-operative Societies seems certain. It is probable that for some years at least the former will advance by increasing the intensity of their retail rounds from depots rather than by adding to the number of their fixed shops as such. The progress of the Co-operative Societies in the milk trade would appear to depend in part on the progress of the movement in its grocery and provisions sales. If the share of the national trade held by the Co-operative Societies in these goods increases, the share in the milk trade is almost certain to rise. But the Co-operative Societies have in the past also attracted customers who did not purchase their other foodstuffs from the Societies, and a reliable, efficient delivery service based on well-equipped and up-to-date processing plants and vehicles may continue to attract such customers. Both the multiple shop retailers and the Co-operative Societies, however, are likely to find retailing as it is at present organized very costly in the less densely populated areas outside the towns, and in those areas the small-scale retailer is likely to be unchallenged for some time to come.

CHAPTER IX

THE FRUIT AND VEGETABLES AND FISH TRADES

The retail sale of fruit and vegetables and of fish has remained mainly in the hands of the independent, small-scale retailer throughout the years 1850 to 1950. The development of large-scale retailing of these goods has been conspicuously small. No general account of the trends in the production and retailing methods in these trades will therefore be attempted. But accepting the position that the bulk of the sales was undertaken by the small-scale retailer, such developments of large-scale retailing as did occur in these trades will be discussed briefly along with some suggestions as to the reasons for the relative absence of economies of scale in retailing in these trades.

The fruit and vegetables trade: multiple shop retailing

The earliest multiple shop retailers in the fruit and vegetables trade emerged about the turn of the century and by the First World War there were, according to existing records, some half-a-dozen multiple shop firms trading with about 150 branches in all. Far and away the largest of these firms was Waterworth Brothers of Liverpool which, prior to the splitting of the firm into three firms at the outbreak of the War, had close upon 100 branches.

The subsequent growth in the number of multiple shop organizations and in the number of branches controlled by them between 1920 and 1950 is shown in Table 46. This Table includes details of firms that have gone out of existence as well as those of firms still trading in 1950. Altogether the records of some 22 firms have been included.

The rate of increase of multiple shop firms as shown in Table 46 was fairly steady in the inter-war years, a slight peak being reached in the years 1931–35. This steadiness, however, conceals the meteoric rise of some firms which were launched in the late 'twenties as public companies 'to supply best quality garden produce direct from grower to consumer' through a large number of retail outlets, and which failed within a few years of their creation. The majority of the multiple firms, however, grew steadily rather than rapidly or dramatically. Two other features of multiple shop development in this trade may be noted. The first is that all the organizations were regional in character; there were no firms with a national coverage. Secondly, in the early years there was a marked bias in development towards Liverpool. In 1930, for example, more than half the branches of multiple shop organizations in existence were in this area. In the next twenty years, particularly in the years following the Second World War, the number of branches in the Greater London area increased rapidly. In 1950 some 70–80 % of all the multiple shop branches in existence in this trade were in these two areas, about 35–40 % being in the London area and the same proportion in the Liverpool area. The reasons for this concentration in these two areas would appear to be partly the density of population and partly the importance of these two towns as ports of landing for imported fruit and vegetables.

Table 46. *Estimates of the number of multiple shop firms and branches in the fruit and vegetables trade, 1920–50*

Year	10–24 branches		25–49 branches		50–99 branches		100 or more branches		Totals 10 or more branches	
	Number of		Number of		Number of		Number of		Number of	
	Firms	Branches	Firms	Branches	Firms	Branches	Firms	Branches	Firms	Branches
1920	5	70	2	50	—	—	—	—	7	120
1925	5	81	3	90	—	—	—	—	8	171
1930	6	67	6	192	1	50	—	—	13	309
1935	7	92	6	216	2	156	—	—	15	464
1939	8	107	1	27	4	221	2	226	15	581
1950	8	110	2	52	4	243	2	257	16	662

The differences between the trading policies and methods of organization of the multiple shop firms and those of the small-scale fruiterers and greengrocers were not very great. The multiple shop firms, however, in addition to making purchases from wholesalers in town markets also placed direct contracts with growers for some of their supplies, notably in the case of potatoes and root crops. A few of the firms had direct contracts with overseas growers or exporters. The greater buying power of the multiple shop firms was of importance in that these firms visited the wholesale markets daily, as against the twice or three times a week visits of the small-scale retailer, and the multiple shop firms were therefore able to despatch fresh stock daily to their branches. These branches, in some contrast to the shops of the small-scale retailers, were usually on main streets and busy sites. Some of the firms secured sites on railway and underground stations, and all the multiple shop retailers placed particular emphasis on having clean and attractive displays of produce clearly price-ticketed. The multiple shop firms were also able, owing to the location of their branches and their buying policies, to carry a wider range of some types of fruit, and many acquired a reputation for stocking special and luxury fruit.

In addition to the specialist multiple shop firms, variety chain stores also sold fruit in some quantities from the middle 'thirties onwards. For the most part the fruit sold by these firms was imported, supplies being secured by direct contracts with overseas producers. Such sales were increasing rapidly in the years just prior to the Second World War and continued in the post-war years, though the post-war limitations on overseas supplies reduced sales. Fruit and vegetables were also sold by a number of multiple shop grocery and provisions firms, either in separate shops or in a section of the grocery and provisions shop. Where separate fruit and vegetable shops were established the firms found it effective to locate these branches close to their grocery and provision branches, thus encouraging housewives, who tended to shop daily for fruit and vegetables, to pass the grocery branch each day.

Large-scale retailing in the fruit and vegetables trade

The Co-operative Societies undertook some sales of fruit and vegetables in the latter part of the nineteenth century, and in the inter-war years some specialist branches were established to sell these goods. The Societies did not, however, introduce any new methods of marketing. Supplies were usually obtained from local farmers or wholesale markets, the Co-operative Wholesale Societies playing a very minor role.

In 1920 the Co-operative Societies are estimated to have been responsible for some 2–3 % of the total sales of fruit and vegetables and the multiple shop retailers for about 1 %. In 1930 the proportions are estimated to have risen to 3–4 % and 2·5–3·5 % respectively. By 1950 the Co-operative share of the total trade is estimated to have risen slightly to 3·5–4·5 %, while the share of the multiple shop retailers rose more quickly to 5–7 %. Specialist multiple shop retailers were responsible for about one-half of the total sales made by multiple shop firms in 1950, the remainder being undertaken by variety chain stores and grocery and provisions multiple shop firms.

The fish trade: multiple shop retailing

The development of multiple shop trading in the fish trade is virtually the story of one firm—Mac Fisheries Ltd. Before 1914 there were a few multiple shop fishmongers in existence, but none of them had more than 30 branches each. With the foundation of Mac Fisheries Ltd. by Lord Leverhulme in the early part of 1919 the position was rapidly changed, and at the end of the year the firm had grown to over 200 retail branches. The numbers continued to rise in 1920 and at the end of the year the branches totalled over 370. This rapid increase in numbers sprang from the determination of Lord Leverhulme to build a national organization as quickly as possible, as being the only way to carry on a multiple fishmongers' business. The great majority of the branches opened had previously been independent fishmongers, the owners of which were often installed as managers of the new branches. Some four small multiple shop fishmongers with about 70 branches in all were also acquired by Mac Fisheries in 1919 and 1920. The subsequent development of multiple shop organizations in the fish trade is shown in Table 47.

Table 47. *Estimate of the number of multiple shop firms and branches in the fish trade, 1920–50*

Year	10–24 branches		25–49 branches		100 or more branches		Totals 10 or more branches	
	Number of		Number of		Number of		Number of	
	Firms	Branches	Firms	Branches	Firms	Branches	Firms	Branches
1920	4	52	—	—	1	373	5	435
1925	7	88	—	—	1	331	8	419
1930	7	92	—	—	1	364	8	456
1935	6	71	1	28	1	363	8	462
1939	5	62	1	28	1	376	7	466
1950	7	93	1	28	1	386	9	507

There is probably some understatement of the number of the smaller organizations that existed in the trade in various years, owing to the difficulty of tracing records, but even allowing for this the dominant position of Mac Fisheries Ltd. stands out clearly. The branches of this firm represented between 75–85 % of the total number of multiple shop branches in existence throughout these years. A second feature of the table is the relatively slow growth in the total number of branches of multiple shop fishmongers. The number in operation in 1950 was only some 70 more than the number in 1920, though in the case of Mac Fisheries Ltd. this slow growth conceals a certain measure of re-organization that took place in those years—viz. the closing down of unsuccessful branches and the opening of new branches in more advantageous areas and sites.

The organization of the multiple shop firms in this trade, while following broadly similar lines to the methods used in other trades, differed in some important respects. Central buying was undertaken on behalf of the branches through one wholesaling organization, and in the case of Mac Fisheries Ltd. some trawler fleets were also controlled, but central buying of all supplies for a firm with a large number of branches in different parts of the country was not possible. Branch managers were allowed to purchase directly from other wholesale firms, and on the average only about two-thirds of the fish sold in Mac Fisheries' retail branches was supplied through the firm's wholesaling depots, which were situated both on the coast and in inland towns. A second problem facing the multiple shop fishmonger was that the selling price of the fish in the retail branches could not be predetermined. Wholesale prices varied and the retail price had to be determined by each branch manager in relation to the quality of the goods, the service offered by the shop, the state of the market and the general level of fish prices at any given time. A considerable responsibility rested on the branch managers; and on their skill and experience, assisted by frequent visits from Head Office staff, largely depended the success of the multiple shop firm.

The size of the multiple shop branches varied but they were usually larger than those of the independent fishmonger. The average employment per branch in the 'thirties was 7–9 persons, though with shortage of manpower and other difficulties this had fallen in the post-war years to 6–7 per branch. The large size of the branch of the multiple shop fishmonger was due in part to the practice of securing sites on main or busy streets where the trade per shop was much greater than that of the smaller fishmonger's shop in the side street, and in part to a policy of carrying an important range of goods other than fish, particularly poultry, game and rabbits.

Large-scale retailing in the fish trade

In 1920 the Co-operative Societies are estimated to have undertaken about 1 % of the total retail sales of fish and the multiple shop organizations 5–6 %. In 1930 the proportions were Co-operative Societies 1·5–2·5 % and multiple shop firms 8–9 %. In 1938 Co-operative Societies are estimated to have undertaken some 2–3 % of total trade while the share of the multiple shop firms had risen to 9–11 %. By 1950 the share of the Co-operative Societies had not changed, but the share of the multiple shop retailers is estimated at 11–12 % of the total retail trade.

The slow development of large-scale retailing in the fruit and vegetable and fish trades

The reasons for the relatively slow development of large-scale retailing in the fruit and vegetables and fish trades are complex. Some of the factors may be suggested here. In the first place the geographically diverse character of the production of the goods, or landing of the fish, the small scale of the units engaged in production and fishing, and the unevenness of supplies both in respect of quantity and quality, combined to make essential, in one degree or another, reliance by the retailers on the wholesalers. The retailer, if his business was large enough, could make some direct contracts with growers or could buy at port auctions, or could place direct contracts overseas, but even with these methods of buying he could not dispense with the wholesaler. If there was delay in supplying the goods, or a failure of a particular crop or catch, the retailer had to turn to the wholesaler for alternative supplies. More important, no retailer could place a sufficient number of direct contracts or make enough direct purchases to cover the whole range of fruit and vegetables or all the different types of fish that the customer expected the fruiterer, greengrocer and fishmonger to stock.

A very large multiple shop organization might go a long way towards 'buying centrally' a substantial proportion of its supplies first-hand from the growers or at the ports, but the complete range of goods required in each branch could only be secured by additional and local purchases from wholesalers. Even in the case of the large firms the advantages of centralized buying were often outweighed by the difficulties of estimating at the purchasing centre the fluctuations in demand and supply of commodities that were extremely perishable. It follows that the need to purchase some supplies from wholesalers in the same way as the small-scale retailers reduced the competitive advantage of the multiple shop method of trading. It is true that the larger-scale retailers often cut out one stage in the wholesale chain of distribution, that is, they bought from the first wholesaler or port wholesaler and did not deal with the second wholesaler or the inland wholesaler, though frequently supplementary lines had to be purchased from the latter types of wholesaler. Only if a multiple shop firm in these trades developed its buying and wholesaling business on a completely national scale, with offices and depots in every growing area or port, and maintained an intricate system of main depots and sub-depots and an extensive transport network: in other words, only if it organized a service that completely paralleled the existing services provided by a great number of wholesale firms each undertaking different functions would it achieve the full buying economies of purchasing all goods direct from the source. When that point was reached, the costs of running such a giant buying organization would almost certainly offset the gains made in the first-hand price, unless the retail network was very large and was responsible for a substantial proportion of the total national sales.

A second factor, connected with the first, that has told against the development of centralized large-scale trading methods in fruit and vegetables and fish was the perishability of the products. Individual retailers close to supply areas had an advantage over others, and any method of organization that added in any way to the length of routing or the time taken in transit from the source of supply to the consumer was at a disadvantage. The usual techniques of large-scale retailing invariably involved a measure of central physical control of supplies in that goods passed through the central warehouse or local depot to individual branches rather than to the branch direct. In the case of small compact multiple shop organizations, however, this factor was less important.

A third factor making extremely difficult the application of large-scale retailing methods in these trades was the impossibility of maintaining close control at the retail branch level. While the management of a small multiple shop organization with less than 25 branches all situated close together in an urban area could exert some control over the prices charged in the branches, such prices tended to vary from day to day and in some instances had to vary at the end of the day from those charged at the beginning of the day. In any event there were continual variations between branch and branch in wastage, deterioration of goods, losses in weighing out, and so on. The larger the firms, the more scattered the branches and the more varied the range of products handled, the more the difficulties of control increased. Until the products themselves are completely graded and fully consistent in quality within grades, and by freezing or other methods can be kept in even supply without shortages or gluts on the market, no foolproof method of controlling centrally the detailed trading practices of individual branches can be devised.

In the fruit and vegetables trade and in the fish trade, therefore, the conditions of production and distribution which in other trades have made possible the growth of large-scale retailing did not exist, or existed only to a very limited extent. In other trades the advantages of scale operated in respect of buying, of the planned flow of supplies and of the central control of retailing operations. In the fruit and vegetables and fish trades significant economies of buying were limited to certain lines of goods or to certain organizations such as variety chain stores which confined their sales activity to a narrow range of goods. The planning of the flow of goods was restricted by the uncertainty of supplies, the great variety of sources of supply and the varying perishability of the goods. Lastly, central control of retail trading practice, other than within broad limits, was more or less out of the question. The partial advantages of large-scale trading did, however, allow some advance to be made and in particular the larger resources of the retailers using such methods enabled them to obtain good sites and use the most up-to-date methods of display and salesmanship in their shops. But by and large the position of the small-scale independent retailer was not seriously threatened.

Suggestions as to future trends in the fish and fruit and vegetables trades

Future trends in the retailing structure of both the fish and fruit and vegetables trades would appear to depend largely on technical developments and changes in consumer taste and buying habits. In the fish trade, for example, the freezing of fish is only resorted to at present when there is a glut of landings, in order to even out supplies, and frozen fish is far from popular with the consumers. Improvements in the techniques of freezing or chilling and an increase in the number of home refrigerators may well lead to a radical change in this outlook and to the acceptance of frozen fish as being the equal of fresh fish. In this event many of the problems facing the large-scale retailers in this trade will tend to diminish in importance and the superiority of their buying, organizational and selling methods will become more marked. A significant advance in the importance of large-scale retailing may then be expected in this trade. On the other hand, if little or no change takes place in consumer buying habits, if prejudice against frozen fish remains strong, there would appear to be no reason to expect any major shift in the structure of retailing in this trade in the foreseeable future.

In the case of fruit and vegetables similar questions may be posed. Any trend towards the increased sale of ready-packed and ready-cleaned vegetables and of quick-frozen perishable fruits, any increase in consumer demand for canned goods, for example for apples prepared ready for cooking in preference to fresh apples, and any growth of standardization and grading of qualities of fresh fruit and vegetables, will be to the advantage of the larger-scale retailers. The closer, in fact, the goods approach to factory-produced articles and the more the variable elements of quality, seasonability and fluctuations in supplies are eliminated, the greater will be the advantages of larger-scale buying, planning, control and selling. Further, inasmuch as such developments require a measure of integration of processing and distribution and additional retailing equipment and services, the larger-scale units have the greater capital resources to enable them to lead in the field. But again, without a marked trend in the direction of standardization and pre-processing there would appear to be no reason to expect a significant growth of large-scale retailing in this trade.

A problem which may face the larger-scale retailers in both the fish and fruit and vegetables trades can be mentioned. If developments in these trades are in the direction of freezing, pre-packaging and standardization, the commodities will no longer be particular to these trades.

As canned fish and fruit and vegetables are already sold mainly by retailers other than fishmongers and greengrocers, so a further section of the trade may be lost. Retailers of other foodstuffs, for example butchers and grocers and provision dealers, will undoubtedly add to the range of their products by including fish, fruit and vegetables if the present problems of smell, deterioration, waste and dirt, and weighing out disappear. Unless the advantage of specialization in the trade is reflected in a significant price differential, the 'convenience' sale of fish, fruit and vegetables alongside meat and groceries and provisions may restrict and undermine the development of the specialist retailers. Further, processing, pre-packaging and standardization carry with them the possibility of branding, and such a trend, with or without resale price maintenance, improves the competitive position of the smaller shop that is closer to the consumer.

CHAPTER X

THE CHOCOLATE AND SUGAR CONFECTIONERY TRADE

The chocolate and sugar confectionery trade, as was the case with the tobacco goods trade, was a continuously expanding trade through the second half of the nineteenth and first half of the twentieth century. Estimates of the increase in consumption per head do not tell the whole story as there were changes in the type and in the quality of the product over time. The estimates that are available, however, suggest that the increase in consumption per head was of the order of 45–50 % between 1900 and 1914 and 55–60 % between 1920 and 1938.[1] Only during the years of the two World Wars was there any significant decline in consumption, and this was due to the shortages of raw materials. In 1950 shortages and rationing still continued and the consumption per head was one-third below that of 1938.

Changes in the character of the trade

The main changes in the conditions of production and in the character of the product since the middle of the nineteenth century were the growth of the factory system of production and an increase in the relative importance of chocolate confectionery as against sugar confectionery. In the third quarter of the nineteenth century there were a number of very small 'factories', if they could be called that, making sweetmeats of various kinds, and the baker also produced some goods as a by-product of his flour confectionery trade. The few larger units that existed were primarily producers of cocoa and drinking chocolate, the output of eating chocolate being a side-line. In the last quarter of the nineteenth and opening decade of the twentieth century the position began to change rapidly with the development of mechanization in the chocolate factories, and some large production units began to emerge. In the inter-war years this trend towards an increase in size continued, and by the Second World War 6 firms were responsible for some 60 % of the total production of chocolate confectionery. On the sugar confectionery side some large producing units had appeared, but the feature of this section of the trade was the very small scale of the bulk of the units.

[1] These estimates are based on data given by A. R. Prest and A. A. Adams, *Consumers' Expenditure, 1900–1919*, and Richard Stone, *Consumers' Expenditure, 1920–1938*.

The trade up to the beginning of the fourth quarter of the nineteenth century was confined almost entirely to sugar confectionery. Sweet-meats, candied nuts and fruit, toffee, flavoured drops, boiled sweets and similar products bearing exotic names were the mainstay of the trade, and eating chocolate was a relatively rare luxury. In the following decades 'French', 'Mexican' and 'Dutch' eating chocolate began to be sold widely and chocolate drops became a familiar sight in every sweet shop. At the turn of the century, however, the output of moulded chocolate and chocolate confectionery represented only about one-third by weight of the total output of the trade. In the succeeding fifty years changed methods of production, the development of milk chocolate, and changed consumer taste led to a steady increase in the importance of chocolate confectionery, and by 1950 these goods repre-sented about half of the total trade in volume and just over 60 % by value.

This shift in the character of the goods produced was accompanied by a growth of packaging and branding. Eating chocolate of various descriptions was essentially a product that could be sold packaged, and with the growth in the scale of production the practice of packaging and branding began to spread to the sugar confectionery side also. At the same time there was a parallel development of national adver-tising by manufacturers and, a little later, of resale price maintenance. The uneven extension of the latter system is discussed later in this chapter, but by the Second World War some four-fifths of the total sales of chocolate confectionery and about one-half of the sales of sugar confectionery are estimated to have been branded and price-maintained.

The increased consumption of chocolate and sugar confectionery and the changes in the production conditions led to a series of developments in the retail structure of the trade. Precise details and evidence of these changes are not available, but a short account of the main features of the retail structure in the nineteenth century and some statistical data on the structure in the middle of the twentieth century provide a general indication of the pattern of the developments in retailing in these years.

In the second half of the nineteenth century some four main types of retail outlet can be distinguished. First there was the grocer's and general food shop which as the chief outlet for cocoa and drinking chocolate also became an important outlet for eating chocolate and for other manufactured sweets. Secondly, the baker in many areas made and sold sugar confectionery such as marzipan and fondants as well as flour confectionery. Thirdly, there were the 'sweetie' shops, the tuck shops and the confectioners proper. These retailers were of all types and catered for a wide range of different price markets. Some of these retailers possessed high-class establishments in fashionable shopping areas; others had tiny shops in the side streets of industrial towns. Some of the retailers made a number of their lines at the back of the shop and emphasized the 'home-made' character of their goods. Others confined their sale to the products purchased from the small manufacturing confectioners who were to be found in most towns.

Fourthly, supplementing these retailers, there were a large number of other outlets, for example the mixed businesses selling tobacco, news-

Table 48. *Analysis of the chocolate and sugar confectionery distributive trade, 1951**

Type of outlet	Outlets		Personal points deposited as equivalent rations	
	Number	%	Number millions	%
I. Grocers and general food retailers:				
(1) Independent retailers	101,600	44·8	11·7	25·2
(2) Multiple shop retailers	8,335	3·7	0·8	1·7
(3) Co-operative Societies	8,969	3·9	1·3	2·8
TOTAL	118,904	52·4	13·8	29·7
II. Confectioners and other retailers:				
(1) Independent retailers	102,644	45·2	27·1	58·3
(2) Multiple shop retailers	5,431	2·4	5·6	12·0
TOTAL	108,075	47·6	32·7	70·3
TOTAL—ALL OUTLETS	226,979	100·0	46·5	100·0

* This table is based on an analysis undertaken by the Cocoa, Chocolate and Confectionery Alliance, Ltd. of the Ministry of Food data on personal points rationing. The statistics relate to the United Kingdom and to the position in the eight weeks from 4 November to 29 December 1951. At the time of the inquiry the ration was 6½ oz. a week.

Grocers and general food retailers are defined as including all retail outlets with registrations for one or more of the following commodities: fats, bacon, eggs, cheese or sugar.

Multiple shop retailers are defined as firms, other than Co-operative Societies, having 10 or more branches.

papers and confectionery, the numerous general shops in the rural and semi-rural areas, the chemists, who often sold boiled sweets, and, an important outlet in some districts, the stalls in the markets and at the fairs. It is probable that the grocers and the bakers—and the more occasional stallholders in fairs—were the first to develop the retailing of chocolate and sugar confectionery, and later, with the growing popularity of the products and the growth of manufacture, the specialist and mixed shops began to play an important part in the trade. As manufacturing developed the specialist confectioners and the retailers in the mixed shops of the tobacconist/confectioner type started stocking a wider range of goods than the grocer or baker, and the relative importance, though not the number, of the later outlets declined.

The number of outlets for chocolate and sugar confectionery just prior to the Second World War was estimated at some 300,000, but a striking feature of the trade was the small sale of chocolate and sugar confectionery by the majority of such outlets. The system of rationing chocolate and sugar confectionery during the war and in the post-war years reduced the total number of outlets, as many retailers who had only a small sale of these goods ceased to stock them altogether. Even after this reduction in the total number of outlets an analysis of the personal points rationing figures relating to 1945 and to 1951 suggests that some 9 % of the total number of outlets—that is of 226,000 in 1945 and 227,000 in 1951—were responsible for some 50–51 % of the total sales. At the other end of the range some 55 % of the total number of outlets in 1951 were responsible for only some 12 % of the total sales.

The personal points rationing statistics make it possible to give a fairly detailed picture of the structure of the retail trade in chocolate and sugar confectionery in the middle of the twentieth century, and this analysis is presented in Table 48. This table shows the total number of outlets, and the total sales classified according to trade types and according to economic types of outlet.

A further analysis of the trades of the retailers selling chocolate and sugar confectionery in the post-war years suggests a division of the 225,000 outlets into the following categories:[1]

Specialist confectioners	10,000
Tobacconist/confectioners	29,000
Newsagent/confectioners	10,000
Grocers and provision dealers	60,000
Bakers and cafés	15,000
General shops	75,000
Other outlets, including cinemas, theatres, railway kiosks and caterers	26,000

The main features of the development of the chocolate and sugar confectionery trade in the second half of the nineteenth and first half of the twentieth century may therefore be suggested as the rapid increase in consumption per head of the population, the growth in size of manufacturing units, the development of packaging, national advertising, branding and resale price maintenance, and a rapid increase in the number of outlets for the goods. Against this background the development of the different economic types of retailer will be discussed.

[1] *Sweet Shop Success*, Cadbury Brothers Ltd., London, 1949, p. 18.

The progress of multiple shop retailing is examined in detail first, followed by a shorter discussion of the role of Co-operative Societies and the small-scale retailers.

The development of multiple shop retailing

The first firm specializing in the sale of confectionery to possess over 10 retail branches was, according to existing records, Maynards Ltd. of London. This was a family business which acquired a number of other confectioners' shops and formed a public company in 1896 with 51 branches. The next firms to operate more than 10 branches were Arthur Meeson of Lancashire, some of whose shops were under the name of Moakler, and Fullers Ltd. of London which developed by way of the flour confectionery trade and tea rooms. The ten years after 1900 saw the growth of some 7 other multiple shop confectionery firms, of which the most important were R. S. McColl Ltd., Birrells Ltd., and McMillan & Munro Ltd., all of Glasgow. The growth of the number of all multiple shop organizations and of the number of branches controlled by them in this trade between 1905 and 1950 is presented in Table 49.

Table 49. *Estimates of the number of multiple shop firms and branches in the chocolate and sugar confectionery trade, 1905–50*

Year	10–24 branches		25–49 branches		50–99 branches		100 or more branches		Totals			
									10 or more branches		25 or more branches	
	Number of		Number of		Number of		Number of		Number of		Number of	
	Firms	Branches	Firms	Branches	Firms	Branches	Firms	Branches	Firms	Branches	Firms	Branches
1905	3	47	1	25	1	91	—	—	5	163	2	116
1910	6	66	2	61	1	55	1	126	10	308	4	242
1915	9	122	4	148	1	65	1	161	15	496	6	374
1920	8	120	2	74	3	192	1	179	14	565	6	445
1925	12	150	1	30	5	371	1	229	19	780	7	630
1930	12	139	2	62	5	374	3	476	22	1,051	10	912
1935	14	173	1	40	3	220	4	792	22	1,225	8	1,052
1939	12	156	4	119	4	268	4	884	24	1,427	12	1,271
1950	10	133	2	66	6	408	4	802	22	1,409	12	1,276

The estimates of the number of firms and of the number of branches in existence in the various years include information on the firms that have gone out of existence as well as those still trading in 1950. Altogether data relating to 38 different firms have been included, and of the 16 firms that were no longer trading separately in 1950 6 had merged or amalgamated with existing firms and 10 appeared to have ceased trading.

The estimates given in Table 49 of the number of branches in existence in different years can be used to provide some indication of the rate of growth of multiple shop trading in different periods. There are disadvantages in using numbers of branches alone to show growth as the branch is a changing unit over time, but the changes in the number of branches give a general indication of the fluctuations in growth. Table 50 shows the net increase and the rate of net increase in the number of branches in operation at five-yearly intervals between 1906 and 1950. The rate of net increase is shown as a percentage increase in the numbers in each period and the absolute increase in the number of branches in each period is also shown as an average yearly net increase.

Table 50. *Rate of net increase in the number of branches of multiple shop firms in the chocolate and sugar confectionery trade, 1906–50*

Year	Branches of firms with 10 or more branches			Branches of firms with 25 or more branches		
	Net increase in number of branches	Percentage net increase	Average yearly net increase in numbers	Net increase in number of branches	Percentage net increase	Average yearly net increase in numbers
1906–1910	145	89	29	126	108	25
1911–1915	188	61	38	132	54	26
1916–1920	69	14	12	71	19	14
1921–1925	215	38	43	185	42	37
1926–1930	271	35	54	282	45	56
1931–1935	174	17	35	140	15	28
1936–1939	202	17	51	219	21	55
1940–1950	− 18	− 1	− 2	5	—	—

The pattern of growth shown in Table 50 is one of a fairly consistent increase in the number of branches with the exception of the two World War periods. The average net increase in the number of branches per year of the firms with 10 or more branches rose from an average of 34 branches a year in the ten years before 1915 to 49 a year, or an average net increase of nearly one branch a week, in the ten years 1920–1930. The rate falls slightly between 1931 and 1939 to 43 a year, but was showing signs of rising just before the outbreak of the Second World War. Between 1939 and 1950 the additions to the total number of multiple shop branches were virtually nil. With goods in short supply and rationing in force expansion was limited to the purchase of existing retailers. A few multiple shop firms expanded in this way, but other firms closed branches, so that on balance there was no net increase. The firms that closed some of their branches in these years were often able to transfer their quota to the remaining branches, and under rationing this resulted in increased turnover per branch with lower overhead costs.

The organization and trading methods of the multiple shop retailers

A feature of multiple shop retailing in the chocolate and sugar confectionery trade was the importance of integration of production and distribution. All but one of the first ten multiple shop firms in the trade were manufacturers as well as retailers. This is not to say that these firms necessarily started with a factory. Very often a small group oi shops was built up first before the firm extended to manufacture, but, whatever the precise stages of development, most of these firms when they had more than a dozen branches each also possessed facilities for manufacturing. In the inter-war years the need for larger-scale production units lessened the possibility of firms entering the trade as small producer/retailers and gradually building up a chain of retail outlets partly supplied by their own factory. New entrants to the trade tended to specialize in production or in distribution, and three of the largest multiple shop retailers that grew rapidly in the inter-war years were retailers only. The firms which had been integrated in the pre-1914 period, however, remained integrated, and a few new firms with a small number of branches developed on an integrated basis, particularly on the sugar confectionery side. In all in 1950 about two-thirds of the branches controlled by organizations with 25 or more branches each were owned by firms possessing manufacturing facilities.

The proportion of total sales by the integrated firms that was represented by goods of their own manufacture was rarely 100% except in a few instances before 1914. The retail branches had to provide a range of goods and choice for consumers, and this range could not be met from one factory. The growing popularity in the inter-war years of nationally advertised products also limited the scope for 'own brands', and by 1938, while there were variations between firms, the proportion of own manufacture to the total sales of chocolate and sugar confectionery of the integrated firms was of the order of 50%.

Apart from the particular production conditions on the sugar confectionery side of the trade and the strong producer/retailer tradition, there were a number of advantages of integration. Economies in production were secured, inasmuch as moderately long runs and planned quantities were possible with guaranteed outlets for the goods. The selling expenses of the manufacturing side, a large item in this trade, were at a minimum, and little or no advertising had to be undertaken as the retail shops themselves were the advertisement for the goods. Also the products could be manufactured to cater for local tastes more readily than did the nationally advertised goods. Some economies were also secured in relation to packing and packing materials—another important item in this trade. The integrated firms used standardized returnable containers and tins for their products which could be kept flowing back to the factory easily.[1]

The branch units of the multiple shop confectionery firms did not change greatly in size between the pre-1914 years and 1950. They were usually small, the average employment being a little over 2 per shop including the manager. The staff was female and the majority of the branches had a woman as manager. Many of the multiple shop retailers in the inter-war years began to stock cigarettes and tobacco and in some cases to sell ice cream, but the sales of these goods rarely represented more than 10–15 % of the turnover. In the Second World War and post-war years, with the shortages of chocolate and sugar confectionery and the lower gross margins allowed, there was a trend towards increasing the proportion of other goods sold in the branches.

The most important change in the shops themselves between the pre-1914 period and the Second World War was their increased attractiveness. The shift from side streets to main streets or from subsidiary shopping centres to main shopping centres was in part responsible for this development. Many of the larger multiple organizations, however, pursued a mixed policy of opening and maintaining a few large 'show' branches in main streets, leaving other branches in less important shopping centres. But in addition to the shifts in location the appearance of the shops changed. Well laid out shop fronts, elaborate window dressing and spotlessly clean and brightly lit interiors, often with glass showcases, tiled shelving and counters, replaced the somewhat gloomy and dusty shops of the earlier years with their limited window space crammed with goods and faded 'dummies', the wooden counter and fittings, the all-important pair of scales, the weights, the toffee hammer and the other implements, and the rows and rows of jars and tins. The change that took place in the shops was in fact a part of the change from serving and attracting children to serving and attracting both children and adults, including the male adult.

[1] The advantages of integration were not always clear-cut, particularly in the case of a firm entering the production side in the later years when nationally advertised and branded products played an important role in the market. For example, the Chairman of Meesons Ltd., which began manufacturing in 1933, in his annual report in 1939 stated, 'The policy of manufacturing the Company's own requirements which the Directors felt confident was most advantageous, has been proved by the experience of the last three years to be unsuccessful and to prejudice the retail trade. During the latter part of the year the Board decided to discontinue manufacturing and return to the previous successful policy of trading.'

The multiple shop branches were, of course, confined to the densely populated urban districts, and a notable feature in their location was the bias towards Glasgow and Scotland. In 1920 some 20% of the total number of multiple shop branches were in Scotland. By 1930 the proportion had risen to about 40% and it stayed around this figure up to 1950. The successful establishment of multiple shop branches in Scotland, while due partly to the energy and ability of the founders of the firms and to historical accident, was also due to the strong competitive position of the multiple shop firms in that area. Until the emergence of the multiple shop retailers, the confectionery trade was in the hands of ice cream parlours, greengrocery shops and other mixed outlets, and the multiple shop firms were among the first to establish clean, well-lit and well-stocked branches specializing in the sale of confectionery in the main shopping streets. The fact that the three leading retailing firms in Scotland were also manufacturers was also of some importance in this development.

The pricing policy of the multiple shop retailers and the 'price wars'

In price policy the multiple shop retailers tended to follow the practice of other retailers rather than to lead, and the firms emphasized the wide range of goods stocked rather than the low prices charged. Inevitably, however, some of the firms were involved in the 'price wars' in the trade in the inter-war years. Resale price maintenance was practised in this trade before 1914 in so far as a few of the larger manufacturers stated the retail price on some of their lines, but not until the depression of 1921–22 was price cutting an important issue in the trade. The relatively high gross margins in the chocolate and sugar confectionery trade encouraged retailers in other trades, for example grocery, to sell well-known lines under the stated price, and between 1921 and 1939 some price cutting took place, consistently or sporadically, in most towns in the United Kingdom. Up to 1927 the manufacturers continued to supply the firms selling under the fixed prices, but from that year down to the start of the Second World War when price cutting ceased with the introduction of rationing various methods were tried, and with increasing success, to limit the extent of price cutting.[1]

In the early stages the established multiple shop firms took no part in price cutting, but some of the retailers who adopted a low price policy were able, with the success of their first experiments, to build up a chain of shops. At least 5 multiple shop firms grew in this manner and, while 4 had at most 15 shops each, one grew to over 50 branches. With the rise of these newer organizations, some of the older-established multiple

[1] For a short account of the methods used see *Report of the Committee on Resale Price Maintenance*, Cmd. 7696, 1949, p. 59.

shop retailers started selling at competitive prices. Once one multiple shop organization in a particular area started selling nationally-known brands at low prices, others in the same area had to follow suit or face a loss of trade. Further, price cutting led some of the multiple shop firms into a race to maintain and increase their sales by opening additional branches. The results of the rapid expansion were not too happy for some of the firms. A few, after a rapid growth, had to close down, and went out of business altogether in the 'thirties. One large firm found that the trading sites acquired at the height of the 'war' were a liability once the first rush to buy had passed, and had to reduce the number of its outlets by half in the early 'thirties. Two other large firms that had grown rapidly in the late 'twenties and early 'thirties closed one-third of their branches at the beginning of the Second World War. The multiple shops however that had taken but little part in the price war in these years increased the number of their branches fairly steadily.

One important feature of the participation by multiple shop retailers in the price war was the establishment of branches in the main shopping streets. If prices were to be reduced then the best sites for selling at such prices were to be found in the main streets. The increased rate of stock turn and higher turnover of these shops more than compensated for the heavier overhead costs and enabled low prices to be charged, at least for a while. The attractiveness of the well-sited main street shops led to their retention by the multiple shop retailers even when the policy of low prices was abandoned.

The variety chain stores

In addition to the specialist multiple shop confectioners, the other multiple shop retailers which sold chocolate and sugar confectionery were multiple shop grocers and the variety chain stores. The multiple shop grocers in selling these goods were carrying on the tradition of the earlier grocers, and the increase in the importance of packaged, easily handled lines encouraged this development, as did the higher gross margin on the sale of confectionery as compared with the sale of groceries. These firms could not, however, handle a very wide range of confectionery and, as shown in Table 48, their importance in the trade was not very great. Variety chain stores, however, which had been practically non-existent before 1914, increased rapidly in numbers and importance in the inter-war years, and these stores became prominent as mass distributors of sugar and chocolate confectionery. By 1930 the sales of these goods by variety chain stores were approaching the total sales of specialist multiple shop retailers in the trade, and by 1938 the sales by variety chain stores were of greater significance than the sales of the specialist multiple shops. The range of lines that were sold by the variety chain stores was far narrower than that stocked by the specialist multiple shop organization and the range in price was smaller, but the methods of open display and low prices had considerable appeal. The introduction of rationing limited the further advance of the variety chain stores in this trade but their general position was maintained and with the abandonment of the price limit policy they stocked a wider range of goods.

The Co-operative Societies

The Co-operative Societies approached the chocolate and sugar confectionery trade in much the same way as did the multiple shop grocer. Co-operative retailing of confectionery dates back to the nineteenth century, and an increasing number of the grocery and provisions departments of the Societies sold sugar confectionery in the inter-war years as a convenience for their customers. By 1945 some four-fifths of the 10,500 grocery and provisions shops had selling points for these goods. Only 31 Co-operative specialist confectionery shops were, however, in existence in that year, and the total sales by the Co-operative Societies of chocolate and sugar confectionery were very small. The Societies sold both the products of private manufacturers as well as the products of the Co-operative Wholesale Societies.

The small-scale retailer

From the account given at the beginning of this chapter it is clear that far and away the most numerous and most important retailers in the chocolate and sugar confectionery trade throughout these years were the small-scale retailers. Direct evidence is not available, but it would appear that the share of the trade undertaken by the specialist small-scale confectioner decreased between 1900 and 1950 and possibly the numbers of such units also decreased to the estimated 9,000–10,000 in 1950. Further, whereas the specialist confectioner at the beginning of the century frequently made some of the sweets sold in the shop, this practice became unusual in the inter-war years. On the other hand, many of the specialist confectionery retailers had, with the increase in the total number of outlets for these goods, taken over wholesaling functions as well as retailing and were supplying a number of the retailers in their area with these goods.

If the number of the small-scale specialist retailers had decreased, there is no doubt that the number of small-scale mixed shops selling confectionery and other goods, usually tobacco goods or less frequently newspapers, stationery, fancy goods and toys, had increased. The continuously expanding demand in the twentieth century for confectionery, tobacco and newspapers, the packaged, branded and resale price maintained character of the goods and the seasonal fluctuations in demand for chocolate and sugar confectionery combined to encourage a rapid increase in the number of these types of mixed shops, and next to the specialist confectioner and variety chain store they became the most important outlet for confectionery.

A large number of the mixed shops, both of the 'general shop' type and the more limited confectioner/tobacconist type, were literally one-man or one-woman businesses, and their total turnover was often extremely small. In many instances the sales did not afford their proprietor a large enough net profit to constitute a full living, and the shops, which were often combined with living accommodation, were seen as providing the supplementary income rather than the main income. The full- or part-time earnings of the head of the family, or the old-age, retirement or widow's pension would often be supplemented in this way.

Shares of the different economic types of retailer in the total trade

This discussion of the development of the different economic types of retailer can be concluded by presenting estimates of the proportions of the total retail trade in chocolate and sugar confectionery undertaken by the different economic types of retailer between 1910 and 1950. These estimates are given in Table 51.

Table 51. *Estimated shares of the different economic types of retailer in the total retail sales of chocolate and sugar confectionery and ice cream, 1910–50**

Year	Proportion of total sales undertaken by		
	Co-operative Societies %	Multiple shop retailers %	Other retailers (by difference) %
1910	About 1	1·0– 2·0	97·0–98·0
1920	About 1	2·5– 3·5	95·5–96·5
1925	About 1	4·0– 5·0	94·0–95·0
1930	1·0–2·0	7·0– 8·0	90·0–92·0
1935	1·5–2·5	10·0–12·0	85·5–88·5
1939	1·5–3·0	13·0–15·0	82·0–85·5
1950	1·5–3·0	14·0–16·0	81·0–84·5

* For a discussion of the basis of these estimates see Appendix A. The sales of ice cream are included in the estimates of total sales.

Included in the sales of multiple shop retailers are the sales of variety chain stores and of multiple shop retailers in other trades, for example the grocery, newspaper and catering trades.

The 'other retailers' category is residual and includes the sales of small-scale retailers engaged in other trades and of cinemas, garages and theatres as well as those of small-scale specialist confectioners.

The main features of the trends shown in Table 51 are the small role of Co-operative trading, the rapid rise of multiple shop retailing in the inter-war years, and the dominant part played in the trade by the small-scale retailer. Many of the factors influencing these trends have been discussed above, and here a brief summary only will be given.

The minor part played by the Co-operative Societies in this trade arose directly from the absence of specialist selling points. The sale of chocolate and sugar confectionery was a side-line, as it was with the majority of the grocery and provisions multiple shop organizations, and the share of the confectionery trade held by the Co-operative Societies was about equal to that of the grocery and provisions multiple shop firms. The sales by Co-operative Societies expanded with the expansion in the trade, but not at a very much faster rate.

The slow development of specialist multiple shop retailing

Any discussion of the growth in the importance of multiple shop organizations in the confectionery trade must be divided into two. The development of the specialist multiple shop confectioners must be considered apart from the development of variety chain stores. In the former case the reasons for advance are fairly plain. These were the integration of production and distribution by the leading firms, the policy—and the financial resources to back the policy—of establishing clean and attractive shops in main shopping streets, and the general advantages accruing to all multiple shop organizations in the form of economies through bulk buying, the use of specialist services, and close stock control. But the advance was not very rapid in these years and, as pointed out above, it tended to be localized. In 1920 the share of specialist multiple shop confectioners is estimated to have been about 2 % of total sales and in 1950 about 4–6 % of total sales. An equally interesting question to ask is why the specialist multiple shop firms did not advance more rapidly.

The sales of chocolate and sugar confectionery increased continuously in these years, and as the market widened the goods tended to become 'convenience' goods, bought largely on impulse. The leading manufacturers recognized this trend by encouraging the distribution of their products through the greatest possible number of outlets. Faced with this type of demand the multiple shop organizations could not ensure that their branches were more 'convenient' to the consumer than all the other selling points for these goods, but had to attempt, by the range of goods stocked, and by their pricing, siting and service policies, to attract customers who might otherwise have made purchases at more 'convenient' outlets. In practice, as discussed above, the multiple firms increased the number of their outlets, but of greater importance were their efforts to gain additional customers. 'Own' brands catering for particular tastes, low prices, good sites, and a wide range of stock that was well displayed in well-designed shops helped in this. There were, however, clear limits to the efficacy of this type of attraction in a convenience goods trade where a significant proportion of the goods are nationally advertised and resale price maintained.

A second factor limiting the development of multiple shop retailing was the decline in the importance and possibility of integration of production and distribution in the inter-war years. In the pre-1914 period the scale of production and the extent of mechanization were both sufficiently small to allow firms with relatively little capital to develop both production and distribution. In the inter-war years the growth of scale in production, increased mechanization, and the considerable investment of the existing manufacturers in branding and advertising their products, made the emergence of new integrated firms a virtual impossibility except as a result of amalgamation. In this way the opportunities for new integrated multiple shop organizations in the trade were limited and the advance of firms that undertook retailing only was, for the reasons given above, very slow.

A more particular factor affecting the slow development of specialist multiple organizations was the 'price war'. Many of the multiple shop firms had attempted to advance both by attracting customers by lower prices and by increasing turnover through opening additional branches, but the combination of the economic depression and the pressure of manufacturers who discouraged price cutting of branded lines led to the economic weakening of some of the firms, to the closing of branches, and to the virtual ending of price competition in price maintained lines. On balance the multiple shop organizations had probably lost rather than gained ground at the end of the price war.

The great advantage of the variety chain stores over both the small-scale and the multiple shop retailer was their very high turnover per selling unit: the average turnover per store in chocolate and sugar confectionery was two to three times as high as that of the specialist confectioner. The variety chain stores had solved the problem which the multiple shop specialist confectioners had only partly been able to solve, that of attracting additional customers to a shop which was selling a convenience good that was available in all types of outlets. Low prices and fresh stocks were two reasons for the success of the variety chain store. But more important, the variety chain store by selling a wide range of goods as well as confectionery attracted far more customers to their branches than were attracted by the sale of chocolate and sugar confectionery alone. Few customers went to variety chain stores with the sole or main purpose of purchasing confectionery, but once they were in the store to purchase other goods the effective display of confectionery led to further 'convenient' purchases.

The relative strength of the small-scale independent retailer in this trade arose in the earlier years from the conditions and circumstances of production and in the later years, as production conditions changed, from the development of the product as a good bought on impulse and of the branding, advertising and resale price maintenance policies of the manufacturers. In the earlier years the producer/retailer, the grocer, the small sweet-shop and the general shop in the towns and villages were all small-scale retailers. In the later years the ease with which the products could be handled and sold, the relatively high gross margins, and the fixed prices again favoured the small-scale retailer. The specialist multiple shop retailers increased their share of the trade slightly and were able to attract customers with 'own' brands and by more attractive shops, but these advantages were offset by those of the small-scale retailer. Only when the variety chain stores began to show that a very large turnover in chocolate and sugar confectionery in a single unit was possible was the dominant position of the small-scale retailer in the trade to some extent undermined.

CHAPTER XI

THE TOBACCO TRADE

Changes in consumption and in the character of the trade

The tobacco trade throughout the years between the middle of the nineteenth and the middle of the twentieth century was an expanding trade. This expansion is illustrated by the figures of the consumption per head of tobacco goods in different years between 1870 and 1950 which are given in Table 52. The consumption per head rose steadily up to the First World War and then rapidly, though with fluctuations, up to 1950.

Table 52. *Consumption of tobacco goods per head of the population of the United Kingdom, 1870–1950**

Average of three years	Consumption per head of the population		Consumption per head of the population aged 15 years and over	
	lb.	Index	lb.	Index
1870–72	1·77	100	2·73	100
1880–82	1·83	103	2·87	105
1890–92	1·99	112	3·05	112
1900–02	2·19	124	3·24	119
1910–12	2·23	126	3·21	118
1920–22	3·20	181	4·12	151
1930–32	3·47	196	4·57	167
1936–38	4·06	229	5·12	188
1948–50	4·38	247	5·68	208

* This table is based on information given by A. R. Prest and A. A. Adams, *Consumers' Expenditure, 1900–1919*, and Richard Stone, *Consumers' Expenditure, 1920–1938*. The estimates up to 1910–12 include Southern Ireland. These estimates include the consumption of snuff and cigars as well as tobacco and cigarettes.

The increased consumption of tobacco per head of the population was accompanied by an increase in the proportion of total retail expenditure by consumers that was represented by the purchase of tobacco goods. In 1900, tobacco goods are estimated to have represented 3·5 % of consumers' total retail expenditure. In 1920 the proportion had risen to 4·2 %, in 1930 to 6·5 % and in 1938 to 7·7 %. By 1950 the proportion had risen to 14·6 % of total retail expenditure.[1] These estimates include duty and the duty on tobacco has always repre-

[1] For details of these estimates see Appendix A.

sented an important proportion of the retail price paid by the consumer. In the years 1870–1938, duty expressed as a percentage of retail value varied between 45 % and 53 %. In 1950 the rate of duty was some 80 % of retail value.

The increase in consumption and the increase in the proportion of total consumers' retail expenditure represented by tobacco goods were paralleled by an increase in the number of retail outlets for tobacco goods. An indication of the total number of outlets for tobacco and of the increase in the number of such outlets is gained from the figures of Tobacco Dealer's Licences that were issued. The number of licences issued in various years does not, of course, mean that all the outlets sold tobacco goods in appreciable quantities, but if a licence was obtained it is fairly certain that some tobacco was sold during the year by the holder of the licence. The number of dealer's licences issued, excluding occasional licences, in Great Britain in various years since 1871 is given in Table 53.

Table 53. *Number of Tobacco Dealer's Licences issued in Great Britain, 1871–1950**

Year ending 31 March	1871	1881	1891	1901	1911	1921	1931	1936	1939	1950
Number of licences issued (thousands)	257·5	266·5	270·4	311·4	352·5	365·2	486·9	540·3	530·4	408·8

* *Reports of the Commissioners of H.M. Customs and Excise*, Command Paper, annual.

The number of licences issued includes those taken out by wholesalers, and about 8,000 of these issued in the later years of this table would come into this category. The majority of the wholesalers, however, also carry on some retail trade in the same premises. In the 'twenties and 'thirties the number of licences issued include licences for automatic machines that were situated on unlicensed premises.

The trend in the number of tobacco licences was that of a slow increase up to 1890, but towards the end of the century there was a marked annual rise in numbers which continued until the First World War. During the war few new licences were taken out, but in the years between the wars there was a further rapid increase in the number of licences until a peak of over half-a-million was reached in 1936. The number of licences fell slightly to 1938 and during the Second World War, with the shortage of supplies, they fell rapidly until they became stabilized in the post-war years at about 400,000. The increase in the number of licences between 1921 and 1939 was, however, only some 45 % compared with an increase in total consumption of tobacco goods over the same period of 55 %.

On the manufacturing side a feature of the development of the trade was the concentration of production in the hands of a few large firms and the extensive use of manufacturer branding and advertising. Concentration on the manufacturing side of the industry dates back to the foundation of the Imperial Tobacco Company (of Great Britain and Ireland), Ltd. in 1901. The company was formed following the attempt of the American Tobacco Company of James B. Duke to own and control manufacturing and distributing units in Great Britain. The American firm took over one British manufacturing company but thirteen of the other leading manufacturers combined to form the Imperial Tobacco Company to defeat this threat to their interests in the British market. By vigorous trading and development methods the Imperial Tobacco Company prevented further accessions by the American firm and eventually an agreement between the two companies was signed recognizing the rights of the British firm in the British market and providing for co-operation between the British and American companies in the export field. The Imperial Tobacco Company was the dominant manufacturer in the United Kingdom market and was responsible for over one half of the total production in 1914. This proportion steadily increased and by 1938 the output of the firm represented some three-quarters of total production. The individual companies making up the Imperial Tobacco Company continued however to manufacture, advertise and trade as semi-autonomous units.

Branding had played a part in the tobacco trade from the very early days inasmuch as different mixtures and blends were given different names to assist the consumer to choose and differentiate easily. The retailers however in the second half of the nineteenth century played a more prominent part in most instances in the blending, naming and advertising of the goods than did the manufacturers. But from the late 'nineties and the turn of the century onwards there was a steadily growing trend, aided by the concentration of manufacturing and the changes in the form of the product, towards packaging, branding and resale price maintenance.

The changes in the product took the form firstly of a decline in the proportion of total sales represented by snuff and cigars. These two products represented about 5 % of total sales before 1914, but only just over 1 % in the inter-war years. Secondly there was a gradual replacement of retailer-blended and loose pipe tobaccos by packaged products. From being a mainstay of the trade in the nineteenth century, the proportion of non-manufacturer-branded loose tobacco sold is estimated to have fallen after the First World War to less than 20 % of sales, and to have fallen further to about 5 % of sales just before the Second World War. A third change in the product was the replacement of pipe tobacco by cigarettes as the main type of good sold. At the turn of the century less than 20 % of the sales of tobacco products was in the form of cigarettes. In the following ten years the proportion slightly more than doubled, and by 1920 some 54 % of total sales are estimated to have been represented by the sale of cigarettes. The increase continued and by 1938 approximately three-quarters of the total sales were in this form.

The spread of resale price maintenance in the tobacco trade dates from the turn of the century, but quantitative estimates of the proportion of total sales that carried a fixed price and that were sold by retailers at that fixed price are difficult to make for the years before 1914. To a large extent, as in the chemists' goods trade, the pressure for fixed prices on tobacco goods and for a reasonable gross margin would appear to have come from the retailers.[1] By themselves the retailers in association were ineffective, but the acceptance of the system by the powerful Imperial Tobacco Company in the first decade of the twentieth century helped to reduce and eventually brought to an end the price cutting and price wars that were a feature of the trade in the 'eighties and 'nineties. Price cutting was still practised after the first World War, and in the depression years 1931–33 there may have been some increase. With the inception however in 1933 of the registration scheme of the Tobacco Trade Association, which was founded in 1931 and was representative of manufacturers', wholesalers' and retailers' organizations, price cutting was effectively curbed, and by the Second World War it was negligible.

The development of packaging, branding and advertising and resale price maintenance made possible and encouraged the handling of tobacco goods by retailers engaged primarily in other trades. The retailer of these goods no longer needed special knowledge and experience regarding the different blends; the goods could be stocked and sold easily, and the process of weighing out and packaging had been eliminated in the case of cigarettes and in a wide range of pipe tobaccos. The rapid increase in the number of outlets between 1918 and 1939 took place in a period of great popularity of the packaged cigarette, of the decline and virtual disappearance of the demand for loose tobaccos, and of extensive advertising and branding.

[1] For a valuable discussion of the forces and events leading to the acceptance of resale price maintenance in this trade see B. S. Yamey, 'The Origins of Resale Price Maintenance: A Study of Three Branches of Retail Trade', *Economic Journal*, vol. LXII, no. 247, September 1952.

*Developments in the retail structure of the trade: the rise
of multiple shop retailing*

In the second half of the nineteenth century the great bulk of the
200,000–300,000 outlets for tobacco goods were not specialist tobacconists. But the specialist retailers who did exist undertook a fairly
significant proportion of the total trade. No fully reliable estimates
exist of such retailers,[1] but before manufacturer packaging, branding
and advertising became widespread the knowledge and the skill of the
specialist retailer was of importance to the consumer. Practically all
the retailers of these goods at the beginning of the third quarter of the
nineteenth century were small-scale independent retailers. The only
exceptions were the branches of Co-operative Societies, which in many
instances sold tobacco and snuff to their members.[2]

In the middle 'eighties, however, the first multiple shop retailer
specializing in the tobacco trade appeared in London, the firm of
Salmon & Gluckstein Ltd., and this firm was followed in the early
'nineties by J. H. Finlay & Company of Newcastle and W. H. Newman
Ltd. of the Midlands. These firms increased the number of their
branches rapidly, and two other companies, A. I. Jones & Company
Ltd. and Albert Baker & Company (1898) Ltd., both of London,
started opening branch shops in the late 'nineties. Altogether at the
time of the American 'invasion' of the British market there were,
according to existing records, some 5 firms in existence with over
10 branches each, controlling some 210 branches in all. Of these,
Salmon & Gluckstein was easily the largest at this date, with over
100 branches.

The subsequent increase in the number of multiple retailing organizations specializing in the tobacco trade and in the number of branches
controlled by them at different years between 1905 and 1950 are presented in Table 54. An attempt has been made to include in these
figures the details of firms which have gone out of existence as well as
those still in operation in 1950. Altogether the records of some 45 firms
have been used in the construction of this table, and of the 13 firms no
longer trading separately in 1950 8 amalgamated with other firms and

---

[1] A. E. Turner, *Tobacco from the Grower to the Smoker*, London, 1912 suggests that there might
be '40–50,000 retailers who depend solely upon the retailing of tobacco as their means to
livelihood'. This estimate appears on the high side. H. W. Macrosty, *The Trust Movement
in British Industry*, London, 1912, p. 231, suggests that there were '20,000 tobacconists in the
United Kingdom'.

[2] Tobacco and snuff represented some 8 % of the total turnover of the Rochdale Store in
1861 in groceries and provisions. (P. Redfern, *History of the C.W.S.*, 1913, p. 409.) The wider
range of goods sold by the Societies in later years reduced this proportion, but most Societies
sold tobacco in spite of the opposition of many members who were adherents of the Anti-
Narcotic League.

5 appear to have gone out of existence. Only multiple shop organizations whose main trade was in tobacco and associated goods have been included in these estimates, though in the case of some of the smaller firms doing a mixed business, for example tobacconist-confectioner or tobacconist-confectioner-newsagent, the classification presented difficulties and some understatement may have occurred. The numbers of branches relate to kiosks as well as shops. The fact that the turnover and, occasionally, the employment in outlets defined as kiosks was sometimes greater than that in shops makes the distinction of little value.

Table 54. *Estimates of the number of multiple shop firms and branches in the tobacco trade, 1905–50*

Year	10–24 branches		25–49 branches		50–99 branches		100 or more branches		Totals			
									10 or more branches		25 or more branches	
	Number of		Number of		Number of		Number of		Number of		Number of	
	Firms	Branches	Firms	Branches	Firms	Branches	Firms	Branches	Firms	Branches	Firms	Branches
1905	3	33	1	34	—	—	2	305	6	372	3	339
1910	5	55	1	40	—	—	2	407	8	502	3	447
1915	6	72	1	42	—	—	2	453	9	567	3	495
1920	10	148	1	45	—	—	2	451	13	644	3	496
1925	11	178	2	50	1	51	2	469	16	748	5	570
1930	13	175	4	127	1	52	2	631	20	985	7	810
1935	17	229	5	180	1	59	3	872	26	1,340	9	1,111
1939	17	256	7	261	1	76	3	1,059	28	1,652	11	1,396
1950	17	236	9	303	3	197	3	1,120	32	1,856	15	1,620

The figures given in Table 54 of the number of branches of multiple shop organizations in existence in different years can be analysed to show the rate of growth of this form of trading. Table 55 shows the net increase and the rate of net increase in the number of branches in operation at five-yearly intervals between 1900 and 1950. The rate of net increase in each period is shown as a percentage increase in the numbers in each period. The absolute net increase in the number of branches in each period is also shown as an average yearly net increase.

The main feature of Table 55 is the contrast between the consistent slowing down from 1900 to 1920 of the rate of net increase in the number of branches, together with the fall in the net increase in the number of branches on the one hand, and the increase in the tempo of activity in the inter-war years on the other. The main reason for the relatively slow increase in the number of branches of multiple shop organizations in the years before the First World War was the decision of the Imperial

Tobacco Company, which had acquired Salmon & Gluckstein in 1901, not to increase the number of branches controlled by the latter company. This decision was taken to convince the retailers during the period of the tobacco 'war' that the Company had no expansionist intentions, and not because multiple shop trading techniques had failed. The possibilities of these methods were in fact shown clearly by the expansion of Finlay & Company Ltd., which increased the number of its branches from some 50 in 1901–2 to over 200 by 1907 and to some 275 by 1914.

Table 55. *Rate of net increase in the number of branches of multiple shop firms in the tobacco trade, 1901–50*

Years	Branches of firms with 10 or more branches			Branches of firms with 25 or more branches		
	Net increase in number of branches	Percentage net increase	Average yearly net increase in numbers	Net increase in number of branches	Percentage net increase	Average yearly net increase in numbers
1901–1905	162	77	32	154	83	31
1906–1910	130	35	26	108	32	22
1911–1915	65	13	13	48	11	10
1916–1920	77	14	15	1	—	—
1921–1925	104	16	21	74	15	15
1926–1930	237	32	47	240	42	48
1930–1935	355	36	71	301	37	60
1936–1939	312	23	78	285	26	70
1940–1950	204	12	18	224	16	20

During the First World War multiple shop growth came to a halt, but in the post-war years, as it became clear that smoking was now a firmly established habit among all classes and that the purchase, when required and at the nearest shop, of packaged and branded goods had almost completely taken the place of choice and selection at a favourite tobacconist, the leading multiple organizations, with the exception of Salmon & Gluckstein for the reasons given above, increased the number of their outlets rapidly. At the same time the continued expansion of the trade and the apparent advantages and simplicity of multiple shop trading in branded packaged goods attracted new multiple organizations into the trade. One firm in 1929 told the public in its *Prospectus*:

'The excellent financial results from multiple shop trading and the economies effected thereby are outstanding features of modern commerce and probably no other trade presents such opportunities for the lucrative employment of capital as the tobacco trade.'[1]

[1] *Prospectus* of Alfred A. Drapkin (Tobacco) Ltd., July 1929.

Multiple shop retailing in the tobacco trade was not however quite so simple as might appear, and this particular firm was in voluntary liquidation in two years. Other firms however were more successful.

Prominent among the multiple shop organizations that built up a sound business in the inter-war years were firms that originally had been wholesalers and were in a good position to see the needs of the trade and the opportunities in different areas. In most instances these firms continued their wholesaling activities as well as controlling a small group of shops. There was less opposition in this trade than in most others to wholesalers supplying independent retailers as well as directly entering the retail trade. This position arose partly from the great multiplicity of outlets, which meant that one shop was rarely competing directly with another for a share of a limited market, and partly from the terms of sale offered by the leading manufacturers, which did not give the wholesaler as such any preferential treatment.

During the Second World War, with shortages of supplies and war damage, the number of multiple shop branches decreased. In the post-war years some of the newer firms continued their expansion and the older-established ones reopened closed branches, but the quota system of supplies to individual retail units virtually meant that only by purchasing existing tobacconists and so obtaining their quota could multiple shop organizations grow.

Trading methods of the multiple shop retailers

The shops and kiosks of the multiple branch firms were small. There were very few branches with as many as 4 employees and the average in the inter-war years was nearer 2 per branch. Up to the First World War employment was almost exclusively male, but in the 'twenties some of the multiple shop firms introduced women assistants. The packaging of the goods sold and the increase in the number of women smokers helped to make this transition possible. At first women were employed in kiosks rather than shops, but in the 'thirties many firms were employing them in the shops. The most dramatic change however occurred during the Second World War and in the post-war years. Not only were women employed in these years in much greater numbers than men but between one-third and one-half of the branches had women managers.

The siting of the shops was probably a more important factor in the eventual success of the shop in this trade than in any other. In the nineteenth and early twentieth centuries, when the skill and experience of the tobacconist himself attracted the customers, the question of the site of his shop was an important but not a dominating factor in trading policy. The development of packaging, branding and national advertising and the sale of cigarettes in place of loose tobacco transformed the trade into one where convenience of location in relation to the customer was practically the only consideration. The multiple shop organizations, therefore, if they were to be successful, paid as much, if not more, attention to the siting of their branches as to the fittings and equipment and to the buying and selling of the product. The larger firms had estate departments and were able to plan their development. Long-term contracts were concluded for sites in railway and underground stations, in cinema buildings and in other large retailing units, and sites were purchased in main shopping streets, by bus and tram stops and near crossings, and in the newly built shopping centres of housing estates. Economies were secured in some instances by buying or leasing well-sited properties that were too large for the sale of tobacco goods alone and letting a part of the building to other traders, particularly to hairdressers. Arrangements were made with multiple shop retailers in other trades for the renting of selling space in their buildings. The smaller multiple shop organizations could rarely develop in this planned fashion and their expansion came about mainly by purchasing existing shops, whose owner retired or continued as the manager of the branch. The branches of the multiple shop organizations were found only in the densely populated areas and there was a fairly definite tendency for them to be concentrated in the southern half of the country, especially in and around London.

There were two phases in the pricing policy of the multiple shop firms. The pricing policy of Salmon & Gluckstein in the years of their rapid expansion up to 1901 was that of low prices and goods were sold below the prices charged by other retailers. This firm manufactured as well as retailed at this date and was able to meet threats of withdrawal of supplies by increasing the output of its own brands. After the turn of the century, however, with the general spread of the system of resale price maintenance and of national branding and advertisement, the multiple shop retailers ceased to play any part in price cutting.

The methods of organization of the multiple shop tobacconists were similar to those employed by all multiple shop firms. The control of branches through head office or area office was close, and specialization of function at head office was usual. Orders from the branches were placed through head office and delivery to the branches made from central depots or, in the case of some larger firms, by the manufacturers direct to the branch itself. Specialists from the head office or the area office were usually responsible for window displays and window dressing and for branch stock taking. The branch manager had few other tasks beyond that of selling.

The small-scale tobacconists and the Co-operative Societies

The changes in the character of the trade from the late nineteenth century to 1950, the growth of multiple shop retail organizations with their well-sited shops, and the sale of tobacco goods by non-specialist retailers combined to limit the number and importance of specialist, independent tobacconists. Only those shops that commanded good sites and those selling a wide range of tobacco goods, often including their own blends and home-made cigarettes, could secure the turnover to specialize in the sales of tobacco goods. New firms coming into the trade in the 'twenties and 'thirties tended from the beginning to sell other goods as well as tobacco, and many of the specialists of the pre-1914 period widened the range of goods sold in the inter-war years. The number of independent specialists in 1950 was certainly not more than 10,000 and probably nearer 8,000,[1] or about 2 % of the total number of outlets for tobacco goods.

Some Co-operative Societies, as mentioned above, had sold tobacco goods through their grocery departments practically since foundation. Such goods were, however, the product of private manufacturers until 1898 when the Co-operative Wholesale Society opened its first tobacco factory. This factory made rapid progress in the first ten years and in 1910 the retail value of its output was approaching £1 million or 2–3 % of the total sales of tobacco goods. The growth of resale price maintenance in the tobacco trade in the first decade of the twentieth century raised the problem of the position of the dividend paid by Retail Societies on purchases by members of privately manufactured tobacco goods. The private manufacturers, however, did not object to the payment of a dividend and subsequently the popularity among the members of the nationally advertised brands of private manufacturers grew more rapidly than that of Co-operative brands. Co-operative manufacturing expanded but the share of Co-operative production in total national output of tobacco goods remained at practically the same figure between 1910 and 1950. The sales by Co-operative Societies of tobacco goods were practically all made through the grocery departments. In 1937 only some 260 separate Co-operative tobacconist shops were in existence but the total number of Co-operative 'sales points' of tobacco in that year, that is where tobacco goods were sold, was nearly 4,000. No important change took place during the Second World War and post-war years in the methods or importance of Co-operative retailing of tobacco goods, though the monetary value of such sales, owing to the very steep increase in taxation, rose dramatically

[1] The 1950 Census of Distribution gives the number of specialist tobacconists, excluding multiple shops and Co-operative branches, as 8,261.

in relation to the sales of other goods and some Societies ceased paying a dividend or the full dividend on the purchases of tobacco.

Shares of the different economic types of retailer in the total trade

This discussion of the changes in the retail structure of the tobacco goods trade may be concluded by presenting estimates of the proportions of the total retail trade undertaken by different economic types of retailer between 1910 and 1950. These estimates are presented in Table 56.

Table 56. *Estimated shares of the different economic types of retailer in the total retail sales of tobacco goods, 1910–50**

Year	Proportion of total sales undertaken by		
	Co-operative Societies %	Multiple shop retailers %	Other retailers (by difference) %
1910	3·0–4·0	2·0–3·5	92·5–95·0
1920	3·5–4·5	3·5–5·0	90·5–93·0
1925	4·0–5·0	4·0–5·0	90·0–92·0
1930	5·0–6·0	4·0–5·5	88·5–91·0
1935	6·0–7·5	5·0–6·5	86·0–89·0
1939	7·0–8·0	6·0–7·0	85·0–87·0
1950	7·0–8·5	7·0–8·0	83·5–86·0

* For a discussion of the basis of these estimates see Appendix A. The sales of smokers' requisites and accessories are included in these estimates as well as the sales of tobacco goods, but the sales of fancy goods and non-tobacco goods by tobacconists are excluded. The sales by multiple shop retailers include the sales by multiple shop organizations in other trades, such as multiple shop grocery and provisions firms and multiple shop off-licences and caterers, as well as the sales of multiple shop tobacconists. Chains of cinemas and 'tied' licensed houses are not, however, classed as multiple shop retailers and therefore the sales by such outlets are included with 'other retailers'. The 'other retailers' group is a residual category and includes all other types of retail outlet from the small-scale independent specialist tobacconist to canteens and automatic machines. The sales by department stores are included with the sales of 'other retailers'.

The estimates in this table suggest that the rise in the share of Co-operative Societies and of multiple shop retailers in the total trade was roughly parallel in these years. In the case of the sales of multiple shop retailers, however, the increase in the share of total sales was due rather more to the increased sales of these goods by multiple shop organizations in other trades than to the increased share of the total sales undertaken by the specialist multiple shop tobacconists. The share of the total sales undertaken by these firms would appear to have increased only slightly from some 2–3 % of total sales in 1920 to 3·5–4·5 % in 1950.

The increase in the share of the total trade held by the large-scale retailers, that is the Co-operative Societies and the multiple shop retailers, was therefore mainly a reflection of the growth of large-scale retailing in other trades in these years rather than a reflection of the advantages of large-scale retailing in the tobacco trade as such, although it is clear that the specialist multiple shop retailers increased their share of the dwindling section of the total trade undertaken by all specialists. It may be suggested, therefore, that while the techniques and methods of multiple shop retailing provided many economies and advantages in relation to the section of the trade undertaken by specialists, these advantages were less marked in relation to the trade as a whole.

The specialist multiple shop retailers possessed few advantages of bulk purchase, owing to the absence of quantity discounts in this trade. These firms did, however, possess the advantages of sufficient capital and high enough credit rating to obtain the best sites and to install attractive fittings, of specialization and the use of detailed stock control methods to ensure a range and freshness of stock which could be matched by few other retailers, and of economies in the utilization of manpower, including the employment of part-time labour. Against these, the small-scale specialist retailer had little to offer except the personal service and attention to customers' wishes that few branch managers of multiple organizations were able to match. In some cases the independent specialist could also offer particular brands and blends of tobacco goods.

The non-specialist small-scale retailer, on the other hand, while selling the same goods at the same prices, had the double advantage over the multiple shop specialist retailer of location near the consumer and of the sale of other goods. In semi-rural and rural districts practically the entire sale of tobacco goods was undertaken by the non-specialist small-scale retailer. In urban districts and towns there were in 1950 something of the order of 100–150 non-specialist outlets for tobacco goods to every specialist outlet. In a trade where practically all the goods were standard in form, quality and price and the purchases by customers were made frequently and in small quantities, the advantage of convenience was overwhelming. That is, the customer in his decision as to where to shop was influenced mainly by the location of the outlet. The fact that the non-specialist retailer sold other goods in addition to tobacco goods also made the non-specialist retailer attractive to the consumer, in that one visit to such a shop or outlet meant that two or more types of goods could be purchased at the same time. The stock held by these retailers may have compared unfavourably with the specialist in regard to range or freshness, but although some 2,000 different brands of tobacco goods are estimated to have existed in 1938 the main demand, for cigarettes at least, was concentrated on some dozen brands; this suggests that the majority of consumers found a limitation in range no serious disadvantage.

The developments in the retail structure of the tobacco trade in the past fifty years would suggest therefore that the advantages of the methods and techniques of multiple shop trading over other forms of retailing in a convenience goods trade where the products are mainly pre-packaged, branded, advertised and resale price maintained, and are purchased frequently and in small quantities, are very small. The specialist multiple shop organizations, lacking the possibility of passing on to the consumer in the form of lower prices the advantages of the superior trading methods, were able to make some advance vis-à-vis independent retailers specializing in the same type of goods but made little or no headway vis-à-vis other types of small-scale retailers. These retailers had the advantages of numbers and location to offset the advantages of the multiple firms and had little disadvantage in regard to buying and none in relation to the price charged to the consumer.

CHAPTER XII

THE NEWSPAPER, PERIODICAL AND MAGAZINE, STATIONERY AND BOOK TRADES

The newspaper, periodical and magazine trade, the stationery trade and the book trade each have distinct characteristics, and their retail structures in the past hundred years have evolved in different ways. There is a case, however, for their discussion together, inasmuch as the growth of all these trades in Britain from the second half of the nineteenth century was influenced directly by the spread of universal elementary education, and retailers concerned primarily with one of the trades frequently handled the goods of a second or all three trades. In regard to the development of large-scale retailing the case for joint treatment of the three trades is even stronger. The only form of large-scale retailing to develop to any significant extent in these trades was multiple shop retailing, and the largest multiple shop retailers practically from their foundation handled the goods of all three trades. In the discussion which follows therefore all three trades will be treated together. Attention will be focused mainly on the developments in the newspaper, periodical and magazine trade, as the retail sale of these goods represented about one-half of the consumers' expenditure on the goods of the three trades. Also large-scale retailing was of some significance in the newspaper, periodical and magazine trade but not in the stationery or book trades.

Changes in the character of the trades

Until the last decades of the nineteenth century these three trades measured in terms of circulation and sales of newspapers, books and stationery were of limited importance. The reading of newspapers and books was practically confined to the educated well-to-do classes, except for some badly-printed novelettes and single-page sheets of news, stories and songs, and the publishers, editors and authors made little attempt in their sales organizations, columns or pages to widen this appeal. Further, only the middle and upper classes had the literacy or leisure time for extensive letter-writing.

This position was changed radically in the newspaper trade in the closing decades of the nineteenth and opening decades of the twentieth century, when a revolution occurred both in the method of production and in the demand for newspapers, magazines and periodicals. This revolution was made possible by improvements in technical methods, in particular the introduction of linotype, and by the growth of literacy following the introduction of compulsory universal education. The founding of *Tit-Bits* in 1881 and *Answers* in 1888, followed by many similar publications of all types such as *Home Chat*, *Comic Cuts*, and *Boys' Friend*, launched the new era on the periodicals side. The founding of the *Daily Mail* in 1896, the *Daily Express* in 1900 and the *Daily Mirror* in 1903 marked the change on the newspaper side. In particular the success of the *Daily Mail*, 'a penny newspaper for a half-penny', was enormous. By the turn of the century its circulation had risen to the hitherto unheard-of figure of one million copies a day, and the circulation of similar papers began to rise rapidly. The Sunday newspaper *News of the World* had also reached a circulation of over one million by 1905. Statistics of the total circulation of all newspapers are not available for these early years, but between 1900 and 1913, a period when the retail price of newspapers was tending to fall slightly, consumers' expenditure increased by nearly 60%, and a similar increase took place in the expenditure on periodicals and magazines.

The task of selling newspapers, periodicals and magazines to millions instead of to thousands called for new methods and channels of retail distribution. The booksellers, the stationers and the small number of newsagents who had been the main retail outlets for newspapers in the early part of the nineteenth century were too limited in numbers and outlook to handle the newspapers for the many, and additional outlets were sought. In the early stages of expansion the newspaper proprietors had to organize in part their own retail network—this was particularly true of the rising Sunday newspapers—but the popular demand for the products of the new style of journalism and the parallel expansion in the confectionery and tobacco trades provided the long-term solution. Some tobacconists and, to a lesser extent, confectioners, particularly those with tea or coffee rooms, had sold the older type of newspaper. The new types of newspaper and periodical and magazine demanded the same kind of retail outlet as did the newer branded tobacco and cigarettes and the mass-produced chocolate and sugar confectionery, namely shops well placed in relation to the customers' homes and early morning journeys.

Further, the complementary character of these trades assisted the expansion of each. The sales of newspapers, magazines and periodicals alone did not provide a retailer in a fixed shop with sufficient turnover to enable him to earn a living, and the sale of these goods had to be supplemented by the sale of other goods. While some retailers sold stationery and books, the demand for these was limited. Packaged tobacco and cigarettes, on the other hand, were growing in popularity and required no skill or special knowledge in their handling, and the joint sale of newspapers and tobacco goods suited both the retailer and the public.

After an initial stage when all manner of means were used to distribute the new mass circulation newspapers—and in this phase the kiosks and newspaper stalls, the agents and the street vendors played an important role—the main retail outlets settled down as the newspaper stall and bookstall, the newsagent/confectioner and, most important of all, the newsagent/tobacconist.

The changes in the stationery and book trades were rather less dramatic. The production of and demand for these goods rose almost as fast as that of newspapers with the spread of literacy, and the old-established stationers and booksellers had to adapt themselves to the new types of demand. This process was not a simple one, as with the growth in demand and the production of cheap but well-printed books and inexpensive stationery many retailers in other trades, including news-agents, chemists, general shops and department stores started handling some of the goods. In many instances these retailers offered the goods to the public at lower prices than those charged by the specialists. In the book trade, the booksellers themselves attempted to outbid one another by offering increased discounts off the standard price to attract customers. Experience of this type of competition both within and from outside the trades led the established specialist retailers to attempt, in conjunction with the manufacturers, to limit price cutting and underselling in the trade even if the actual number of outlets for the goods could not be controlled.[1]

Developments in the inter-war years

In the inter-war years the sales of these goods continued to increase.[2] The circulation of newspapers rose by just over 20% in the years 1920–30 compared with an increase of 5% in the total population and just over 15% in the number of households in the same period. The rate of increase in circulation slowed down between 1930 and 1938 and limitation of newsprint during the Second World War led to a slight fall in circulations in 1940–42.[3] With smaller-sized newspapers, however, circulation began to rise again and with the increased supplies of newsprint at the end of the war a rapid increase in circulation took place.

[1] The Booksellers' Association was founded in 1896 and the Net Book Agreement came into force in 1900. The Stationers' Proprietary Articles Trade Association was established in 1905, its principal object being 'the prevention of the excessive underselling practised by certain Trades'.
[2] The proportion of total retail expenditure of consumers represented by the purchase of newspapers, magazines, periodicals, books and stationery rose from an estimated 1·9% in 1920 to 3·4% in 1938. See Appendix A.
[3] N. Kaldor and R. Silverman, *A Statistical Analysis of Advertising Expenditure and of the Revenue of the Press*, National Institute of Economic and Social Research, Economic and Social Studies VIII, Cambridge University Press, 1948, p. 84.

The leading national daily morning papers in 1930 had a circulation of 8,567,000 copies a day. The circulation had risen to 10,029,000 copies by 1937 and had jumped to 16,672,000 copies in 1950, an increase of some 160 % over 1930. The circulation of the leading London Sunday papers rose from 12,560,000 in 1930 to 13,307,000 in 1937 and then to 28,308,000 in 1950.[1] As these figures do not include the circulation of all newspapers the proportionate rise may be slightly exaggerated, but the number of newspapers taken per household would appear to have practically doubled between 1930 and 1950. Data on the increase in the circulation of periodicals and magazines are not available but there is little doubt that the same trend occurred.

The distributive framework for newspapers did not change greatly in the inter-war years. The Sunday newspapers continued to be distributed by special agents as well as by newspaper shops, as many of the latter were closed on Sundays. Street vendors of newspapers—there were some 13,000 listed in the 1931 Census of Population—remained an important channel of distribution for Sunday newspapers and for evening newspapers. The increase in the number of newsagents from some 40,000 in 1914 to 45,000 in 1938[2] and in the practice of delivery of the morning newspaper to the home[3] had reduced the number of street vendors handling morning papers. This reduction was however compensated for to some extent by an increase in the circulation of evening newspapers and in their number. Many of the provincial and local daily newspapers in these years gave up trying to compete with the national morning daily papers and came out as evening papers, and evening papers had a far greater sale through street vendors than through fixed shops.

A feature of the newsagent's trade which was not paralleled in other trades in these years was the development from 1925 onwards of a measure of control over the number of retail outlets for newspapers and periodicals exercised by the newspaper proprietors, the periodical publishers, the wholesalers and the retailers. The Trade Associations of these different interests were agreed not to supply daily morning newspapers to a new entrant to the trade unless it could be shown satisfactorily that a need existed which was not already covered by existing outlets.

Statistics of the increase in the number of books and in the volume of stationery sold in the years after the First World War are not available, but in money terms the consumers' expenditure on these goods would

[1] Marjorie Deane, 'United Kingdom Publishing Statistics', *Journal of the Royal Statistical Society*, vol. CXIV, 1951, part IV.

[2] Estimate made in the *Manchester Guardian Commercial*, 8 July 1938.

[3] Cf. the estimate in the P.E.P. *Report on the British Press*, London, 1938, p. 39, that some three-quarters of national morning daily papers were delivered to the home.

appear to have kept pace with the expenditure on newspapers, magazines and periodicals. Books were produced at various price levels to suit all pockets and there was a great improvement in the quality of production of some of the lower-priced books. In the stationery trade the inter-war years were a period of wide extension of the range of goods produced and purchased by the private consumer. On the retail side the efforts of the trade associations to stabilize the prices in the trade were relatively successful. In the book trade price-cutting virtually disappeared, though in the stationery trade, while branded lines were usually sold at fixed prices, the sale at low prices of unbranded goods or goods branded in the name of the retailer was common. The wide sale of these goods by non-specialist retailers that had developed before 1914 continued in the inter-war years, particularly in the case of low-priced and paper-covered books and common stationery requisites such as pens, paper, and ink.

The features of development common to all three trades in the last part of the nineteenth and first half of the twentieth centuries, therefore, were the expanding character of the trades, the existence of resale price maintenance, and the ease with which the goods could be handled by all types of retailers. The specialist bookseller and the specialist stationer had, however, with the range of goods carried and with their knowledge of the trade a particular role to play, but the sale of newspapers made no comparable demand of the retailer's skill and experience. This short account of the development of the trades provides a background in which the development of large-scale retailing can be considered.

The development of multiple shop retailing

As mentioned above, multiple shop retailing was the only form of large-scale retailing to grow to importance in these trades. The first multiple shop to emerge was W. H. Smith & Son and, as this firm opened a number of branches to sell newspapers and books in the middle of the nineteenth century, it can be said to be the first multiple shop organization in existence in the United Kingdom. This development, however, took place under very special conditions, as until after the turn of the century the branches of this firm were exclusively news-stands and bookstalls on railway stations and their operation was dependent upon the securing of a contract with the railway company concerned. The railway companies in their turn directly encouraged multiple branch development by preferring to place contracts with one firm relating to all their stations rather than to negotiate separate contracts with individual retailers for each station, though the latter type of contract was not unknown in the earlier years of railway development. The news-stands and bookstalls of the retailing firms that obtained contracts were therefore in a semi-monopolistic position. No rival shop could be established on the same station and therefore the development of this type of multiple shop retailing is not strictly comparable with its development in other trades; the increase in the number of 'multiple' news-stands was a function of the number of contracts obtained with railway companies, of the number of railway stations and of the number of passengers using the stations, and not only of the particular advantages of large-scale retailing.

W. H. Smith & Son, a firm founded as a small newspaper shop in London in the late eighteenth century, obtained their initial railway contracts in the years 1848 to 1853 and in the next half-century established some 800 news-stands and bookstalls, taking in practically all the important railway stations in Great Britain. This number represented the peak in the number of stalls controlled by W. H. Smith & Son, as in 1905 the contract for railway bookstalls on the Great Western Railway passed to Wyman & Sons Ltd. Wymans opened branches rapidly and by 1920 there were some 250 news-stands and bookstalls belonging to this company. A third firm, which started soon after W. H. Smith & Son, was John Menzies & Co. Ltd. of Edinburgh, which secured similar rights to open news-stands on many stations in Scotland, the first bookstall being opened in 1857. Altogether nearly 1,000 railway news-stands and bookstalls were operated by these three firms in 1920.

The character of these railway news-stands and bookstalls varied widely. Some were little more than temporary structures and kiosks open for short periods of the day and confining their sales to newspapers, while others, for example those at the main line termini, were permanent fixed shops, open all day and selling books in addition to newspapers, periodicals and magazines. In some instances cigarettes and confectionery were also sold.

In addition to the railway bookstalls, W. H. Smith & Son in the first decade of the twentieth century started to open newspaper and bookshops. The first shops of this description were opened in 1905, and the main reason for this development was the loss by W. H. Smith & Son of the G.W.R. bookstall contract. No less than 180 shops were opened by this firm in 1905 and a large number of these were established in the vicinity of railway stations, in direct competition with the railway bookstalls of Wymans. By 1914 the number of such shops had risen to 200. No other multiple shop organizations in the newspaper, book and stationery trades approached this number of ordinary branch units. The next largest was W. Straker Ltd. of London which had under 25 branches.

In the inter-war years the development of the multiple shop organizations in these trades was along two lines. On the one hand, while the number of main news-stands and bookstalls on the railway networks hardly increased, the service provided was intensified. On the other hand, the number of retail shops operated by multiple shop organizations in these trades rose appreciably.

There was little scope for further increase in the number of news-stands on railway stations after 1920, as the railway network was no longer expanding and the motor coach and bus reduced the traffic on some smaller lines. The main news-stands and bookstalls were, however, enlarged, all were housed in permanent buildings often fitting in with the general architecture of the stations, and in most instances the stands were open throughout the day, selling a wide range of books as well as newspapers and magazines. In addition there was a large increase in the number of sub-stalls, that is smaller stands or kiosks usually open during only a part of the day. The sub-stalls were placed on certain platforms of main line termini and junctions which already had one main stall, and they were also established on smaller stations. The range of goods sold by these sub-stalls was usually limited to newspapers and magazines.

The number of main stalls controlled by the leading multiple shop organizations in the years 1920 to 1950 was as follows:

Year	Number	Year	Number
1920	977	1935	1046
1925	965	1939	1082
1930	984	1950	997

The number of sub-stalls in existence in the same years is estimated as: 1925, 490; 1930, 550; 1935, 600; 1939, 725; 1950, 460.

Sub-stalls are not recorded as existing as such in the pre-1920 period, though the boys operating from the main stalls and selling newspapers from bags on the platforms performed the same function. Further, some of the stands classed as main stalls in the pre-1920 period would probably be better classed as sub-stalls to obtain complete comparability.

The growth in the number of non-railway branches of multiple shop organizations and in the number of branches of multiple shop firms specializing in the sale of books and stationery in the years 1920–50 is shown in Table 57. The majority of the branches shown in Table 57 were controlled by the firms operating railway bookstalls. The number of shops of this description controlled by W. H. Smith & Son rose from some 225 in 1920 to 300 in 1930 and 350 in 1938. The other multiple shop firms were specialist stationers or booksellers.

Table 57. *Estimates of the number of multiple shop firms and branches other than railway bookstalls in the newspaper, stationery and book trades, 1920–50**

Year	Number of firms with 10 or more branches	Number of branches controlled by these firms
1920	7	322
1925	8	372
1930	10	444
1935	11	502
1939	11	535
1950	17	672

* The number of railway bookstalls in existence at different dates is excluded from these figures. The classification of the firms that sold tobacco and cigarettes and sugar confectionery as well as newspapers has been according to turnover. If more than one-half of their turnover was in goods other than newspapers, periodicals, magazines, books and stationery they have been excluded from this table.

The branches of these multiple shop organizations were for the most part sited in main shopping streets and they were usually larger than the typical newsagent's and stationer's shop. The average number of staff per branch was approaching 10 in 1938 and the average conceals a wide difference between some organizations whose average employment would be not much more than 4 per branch and others with an average employment of over 10 per branch. The window dressing and the shop interior layouts were in marked contrast to the arrangements in the small-scale mixed tobacconist's and newsagent's shop. Particular stress was placed by the multiple shop retailers on the display of goods, and the majority of the branches that sold and delivered newspapers and magazines also sold books, stationery and fancy goods. Some of the shops also sold tobacco and sugar confectionery, and W. H. Smith & Son operated a lending library service at practically all of their branches. This was an effective way of encouraging customers to enter the shops and to see the displays of the varied goods. In 1950 the exchanges of books in these libraries numbered 25 million.

Other retailers in the trades

The Co-operative Societies and department stores took no part in the sale of newspapers, though both undertook some sales of books and stationery. The Co-operative sales of these goods were very small. Stationery departments however had been established in some of the earliest department stores and the larger stores continued this practice with some success. A few added a book department, but the stores never carried the range of stock that was to be found in the specialist booksellers. The remainder of the trade was in the hands of the small-scale, independent retailer, the newsagent, the newsagent/tobacconist, the stationer and the bookseller. The units for the most part were small, employing no assistants other than delivery boys. In the sale of newspapers, once a retailer was established in a given area with a home delivery round, his competitive position was strong. Sales of magazines and periodicals presented more difficulties than the sales of morning newspapers, as a smaller proportion were delivered to the home. The main problem faced was that of selecting the lines to stock out of the tremendous range available, and of determining the quantities to buy. On this side of the trade, sites in busy streets were an advantage but it did not follow that a newsagent successful in selling magazines and periodicals to passers-by in a main street had any advantage over the small retailer in the side street in regard to home delivery of newspapers and periodicals. Home delivery along with the sale of other goods such as tobacco and sugar confectionery was the sheet anchor of the small-scale newsagent.

Little need be added on the independent stationer and bookseller. In the former case the retailer frequently expanded his activities beyond the scope of one shop. In some instances he had a small printing works at the rear of his shop and undertook jobbing printing. In other instances he branched out and opened other stationer's shops in the same town or area. Stationery was a trade in which there were appreciable economies in buying and stockholding on a moderately small scale. Bookselling, in many respects more than any other trade, was a business in which the individual characteristics of the retailer were of key importance. This trade required a combination of a deep interest in books and a flair for business and, while larger-scale techniques could be used with advantage to control stock, to plan buying and to decide on mark-downs, these techniques could not reproduce the individuality of the small-scale, one-shop bookseller. Nevertheless this combination of virtues was not found too readily; the small-scale bookseller did not in many instances keep pace with the increased demand for books in the inter-war years, and some trade was lost to the outwardly more attractive multiple shops in the main streets.

Shares of different economic types of retailer in the total trade

This discussion of the development of the different economic types of retailers can be concluded by presenting estimates of the shares of the different types of retailer in the total trade in newspapers, books and stationery between 1910 and 1950. These estimates are presented in Table 58.

Table 58. *Estimated shares of the different economic types of retailer in the total retail sales of newspapers, magazines, periodicals, books and stationery, 1910–50**

Year	Proportion of total sales undertaken by	
	Multiple shop retailers %	Other retailers (by difference) %
1910	5·0– 6·0	94·0–95·0
1920	6·0– 7·0	93·0–94·0
1930	9·0–10·0	90·0–91·0
1939	15·0–17·0	83·0–85·0
1950	15·0–18·0	82·0–85·0

* For a discussion of the basis of these estimates see Appendix A. The sales by Co-operative Societies and by department stores are included in the sales by 'other retailers'. The sales by department stores are estimated at 1–2 % of total sales between 1930 and 1950.

Many of the factors influencing the trends in the structure of the trade that are shown in Table 58 have been referred to in the above discussion. Here a brief summary of the main factors operating will be given.

The multiple shop retailers clearly owed their early advance and important position in the newspaper trade to the system of contracts for bookstalls granted by the railway companies, supplemented by the economic advantages of centralized control over a number of basically similar trading units. In the case of the ordinary newsagent's, bookseller's and stationer's branches, the multiple shop organizations had the advantage of larger capital resources enabling them to open well-sited attractive shops in the main streets, and of considerable economies in the buying of commodities such as stationery and fancy goods. The ability to purchase 'own brand' or exclusive brand stationery is an example of this. Two other advantages of the multiple shop retailers were firstly the more specialized attention that could be paid to display and stock control in the branches, and secondly the fact that these firms could afford to attract the trained and skilled branch managers and staff who were essential to success on the bookselling and stationery side of the business.

The small-scale retailer, however, was by no means in a weak position in these trades. Most of the goods sold were resale price maintained, and the consumer, having no choice as to price, was concerned primarily with convenience, service and selection. In the newspaper trade the small-scale retailer could provide the service as effectively as the large-scale retailer, and the shops of the small-scale retailer were located more conveniently to the consumer than most of the branches of the large-scale retailer. Further, in newspapers, magazines and periodicals there were no significant economies of large-scale buying to be obtained, so that the small shop could compete directly with the larger organization though the latter firms usually undertook general wholesaling as well as retailing. In the stationery and bookselling trades, the advantages of scale were more marked both in respect of purchasing economies and in that large well-sited shops were essential. The very wide range of stock that had to be carried by specialists in both of these trades and the slow rate of stock turn of the goods, however, limited the appeal of these trades to the multiple shop retailers. The small-scale stationer and bookseller were the most important retailers of the goods and the multiple shop firms confined themselves for the most part to the sales of a more limited range of two or all three classes of goods rather than specialization in one.

CHAPTER XIII

THE CLOTHING TRADES

The clothing trade in Britain in the middle of the nineteenth century centred, both in respect of production and distribution, upon the bespoke tailor and dressmaker, and the draper, mercer and haberdasher. The bespoke tailor and dressmaker were the mainstay of the made-up trade, while the draper or mercer sold all manner of goods to the house-wife, who undertook the making up for herself and her family. In addition to these units there were the specialist retailers, the clothiers, hosiers, shirtmakers, hatters, milliners and glovers in the larger towns, selling mainly ready-made, though some bespoke, goods which had been 'manufactured' in workrooms at the back of the shop or by outworkers or home workers who sewed materials supplied by merchants. Finally, supplementing these outlets, there were the second-hand clothiers, some with fixed shops, some with only stalls or barrow, and the pedlars, who did a fair trade in nearly all the areas.

The bespoke tailors and dressmakers would work either on materials supplied by the customer or on material selected in the shop. All sewing was done by hand and the quality of the work and of the cloth would vary with the location of the shop and with the customer. In addition the itinerant tailor was still a common sight in some districts with his 'goose', sleeve board and other paraphernalia. He visited his customers in their houses, and cut and made up their garments on the spot.

Drapers, mercers and haberdashers had been a feature of the retail structure of the larger towns for more than two centuries. Many carried wide ranges of piece goods of all descriptions, while others specialized in particular goods such as silks or linens. In the smaller towns and rural areas the travelling draper or 'Scotch draper', rather than the shop draper, had been the main source of supply, and he appeared on market days and at fairs until, as demand increased in the early nineteenth century, fixed shops became possible.

The clothiers selling ready-made goods, mainly men's, were of all types. Some had little more than barrows or stalls in markets, while others had well-appointed fashionable hatter's and hosier's shops. The quality of the clothes, too, varied from the 'slop' clothing, rough ill-fitting garments, sold by some shops, to the elegant hats, hose and gloves sold by others. The majority of the ready-made clothiers in the middle of the century were, however, found in the industrial districts selling to the working classes, though in these areas, as elsewhere, the bespoke tailor was a prominent figure.

Changes in the methods of production

To this trade dominated by hand sewing and home work and small-scale retailing came the sewing machine. The Singer sewing machine, which was developed successfully following a series of inventions and experiments just after the middle of the century, was to transform the clothing trades in the next half-century. On the men's clothing side of the trade, that is the heavy clothing side, the developments were slow up to 1879. But with the perfection in this year of the oscillating shuttle which enabled the sewing machines to be run by power instead of by a treadle, the speeds were increased considerably and new production methods were practicable. Steam or gas engine motive power was available and the factory system of production in place of the out-working system became a possibility. With the power-driven sewing machine came the band-knife cutting through many thicknesses of cloth, and other special machines for operations such as button-holing and pressing. London, Leeds and Manchester were the leading centres of the new factory clothing industry, and advance was rapid. In Leeds, for example, there were only 7 or 8 clothing factories in 1881, while ten years later there were 54. Progress of factory production in London and Manchester was nearly as great. Certainly the older methods of production, the small workshop with half-a-dozen machines at the most where all operations were performed in the same crowded room, continued to exist in the trade until well into the new century, as did the practice of employing cutters to cut up the cloth which was then given out to makers-up who worked in their own homes. But the new and advancing practice in the trade in the last decades of the nineteenth and opening decades of the twentieth centuries was that of factory production.

On the light clothing side of the trade, women's wear for the most part, the arrival of the sewing machine produced somewhat different results. The position of the outworker was strengthened rather than weakened. With housewives making the majority of their own and their children's clothes, particularly under-garments, aprons and dresses, and also some of their men's clothes such as shirts and underclothes, the demand for finished goods had always been much smaller than that on the heavy clothing side of the industry. Demand increased only slowly and this factor, coupled with the ease with which light clothing products could be made up by domestic out-workers using the new sewing machines, delayed the introduction of factory mass production methods. Garments were cut in warehouses and shops and sent to women to make up in their homes on the new treadle sewing machines, and the light clothing factories that did exist were extremely small. Not until after the turn of the century did factories on this side of the trade appear in any significant numbers, and this development was hastened by the replacement of the gas engine by the electric motor.

The other trade playing a large part in the clothing industry was the hosiery and knitwear trade. Factory development started rather earlier in this industry than in the heavy and light clothing industries, and in 1871 the Factory Inspectors reported 129 factories in Great Britain employing 9,700 workers as against a total of 58 rather larger tailoring and clothing factories at the same date. The subsequent development in hosiery manufacture to the turn of the century saw the virtual disappearance of frame-work knitting and the domestic outworker system, and the concentration of production in factories. This change to factory production was more complete than in either the heavy or light clothing industries, owing to the clear superiority of the factory methods of production, though the largest hosiery factories did not reach the size or volume of output of the largest heavy clothing factories in the first decade of the twentieth century.

By the beginning of the twentieth century, therefore, the factory method of production had triumphed in the hosiery and knitwear trade, was rising rapidly in importance in the heavy clothing trade, but was still in its infancy in sections of the light clothing trade, where, while the new machines were being used, the factory method of organization was relatively undeveloped. The following half-century saw further changes both in the techniques of production and in the methods of organization in all sections of the industry. Very large units appeared in the heavy clothing trade, more expensive and complex machinery was installed, and the wholesale bespoke method of production took its place alongside the output of ready-made goods on the one hand and the retail bespoke products on the other. In the light clothing trade the factory system finally conquered, though the units remained for the most part small. There was a great increase in the variety of goods produced by factory methods. And finally new materials such as artificial silk brought about further changes in the methods of production and in the type of products.

Changes in demand

But equal in importance to these developments in production methods and techniques and in the materials used in the first half of the twentieth century were the changes in the nature of consumer demand. The proportion of total retail expenditure by consumers that was represented by clothing did not change greatly in these years,[1] but the changes in the type of goods purchased were very marked. In the case of both

---

[1] See Appendix A, Table 85.

the men's and the women's trade there was a shift from the purchase of piece goods for making up at home to the purchase of ready-made articles: the heavier goods of the Manchester market, the cottons, the calicos, the flannels and the shirtings, were replaced by purchases of blouses, mantles, dresses, shirts and underclothing. The growing homogeneity in social behaviour and taste as between different regions of the country and as between different classes led to a widening of the demand for types and styles of goods and to increased attention being paid to questions of dress. In the men's trade greater emphasis was placed in all price markets on the fit and style of the goods purchased. In the women's trade the outstanding feature was the growth of fashion consciousness and the radical changes in style and fashion that took place.

These changes in the methods of production in the clothing trades and in the nature of consumer demand were accompanied by changes in the distributive structure. Such changes can best be discussed in relation to the men's and women's clothing trades separately, and in this discussion some of the gaps in this very general sketch of the changes in the production and demand conditions of the trade can be filled. A distinction between the men's and women's clothing trades cuts, to some extent, across the production divisions in the trade inasmuch as women's outerwear is a part of the heavy clothing trade, men's underwear, hats, caps and ties are a part of the light clothing trade, and the hosiery and knitwear trade supplies both men's and women's clothing. In retail distribution, however, there is a clear distinction between the two sections of the trade, and this will be followed, a further sub-division being made, when necessary, between outer clothing and other types of clothing.

1. THE MEN'S AND BOYS' CLOTHING TRADE

The development of the wholesale clothing and factory hosiery trades in the last quarter of the nineteenth century brought about many changes in the structure of the retail trade in men's wear. Alongside the bespoke tailor, shirtmaker, hatter and hosier at one end of the trade and the general draper, clothier and fair salesman at the other, there began to appear specialist men's outfitting and clothing shops selling factory ready-made clothing. Many of these retailers had themselves been tailors who now sold both factory-made goods as well as bespoke goods, others were hosiers and clothiers who began to specialize in men's outfitting, and yet others were new to the trade. And among this growing number of specialist retailers were the first multiple shop organizations in the men's clothing trade.

The first multiple shop organizations

The first multiple shop firms to emerge in the men's clothing trade, according to existing records, were J. Crook and Sons of Manchester, Joseph Hepworth and Sons of Leeds, Hope Brothers of London, John Jamieson of Scotland, and S. Redmayne of Carlisle. All these firms had opened branch shops in the late 'seventies and most of them had many more than 10 branches by the middle 'eighties. Close on their heels came Egerton & Company Ltd., Ansells Ltd. of Leeds, Masters & Company of Cardiff, G. A. Dunn & Company, the hatters, of London, and Wm. Blackburn of Leeds. These firms in many cases controlled a small factory or workroom, and at some of their branches undertook ordinary bespoke tailoring, but ready-made, bought-out goods formed a significant proportion of their turnover. The branch shops were outfitters rather than tailors.

Between 1890 and 1900 the number of multiple shop retailers in the men's clothing trade increased rapidly, keeping pace with the spread of factory production. The leading firms at the turn of the century, in addition to those already mentioned, were Bradley of Chester, Foster Brothers Clothing Company of Birmingham, Grand Clothing Hall (Hart & Levy) of Leicester, and the Cash Clothing Company (Levy Brothers) of Leeds. Many of these firms, which had grown in size quickly in the last decade of the century, differed from some of the earlier multiple shop organizations in being retailers only, and in concentrating on ready-made outerwear as well as general outfitting. At the same time, some small retail bespoke multiple shop organizations had developed in the larger towns. Firms like George C. Dean of Birmingham, the West End Clothiers Company Ltd., and McCombie Brothers of London, possessed a number of branch shops. Altogether there were at least 22 multiple shop men's tailoring and outfitting firms in existence in 1900 with 10 or more branches each, and they controlled over 550 branches in all. The largest firms at this date were Joseph Hepworth & Sons Ltd (which had taken over Ansells Ltd.) with over 100 branches, G. A. Dunn & Company and Bradley of Chester with over 50 branches each, and the Cash Clothing Company Ltd., Joseph Crook & Company Ltd., Hope Brothers Ltd. and John Jamieson Ltd. with between 25 and 50 branches each.

The trading methods of these early multiple shop organizations in the outfitting and ready-made clothing trades were simple and direct. The shops or branches were for the most part small, though with the need to stock ready-mades the shops were slightly larger than those of the bespoke tailor, and from the start great emphasis was placed on salesmanship. Two features distinguished the ready-made clothing and outfitting shops of the 'eighties and 'nineties, whether they were multiple shop branches or independent units, from the clothing shops of the middle of the century. One of these was the vigorous display of the goods, and the other was the method of pricing the goods. In most of the shops, particularly those catering for the working-class trade, more stock was displayed outside the shop on rails and poles in the front and in the doorways than inside, and the windows, in so far as there were windows as many of the shops were open-fronted, were crammed with suits, overcoats, trousers, shirts and caps. The use of dummies requiring space for display was practically unknown. Then to this array of goods were added plainly marked price tickets on every article. This latter practice was a feature of the trading methods of the multiple shop retailers rather than of the independent retailers. Some firms also distributed leaflets advertising the bargains offered, and employed 'hookers-in', that is salesmen on the pavement outside the shop encouraging all who passed to inspect, admire and purchase.

These methods were in sharp contrast to the practice of the earlier tailors, drapers, hosiers, and hatters, who had minimized display, save for some rolls of cloth or an unchanging and discreet display of a few articles of clothing, and had rarely put any price ticket on an article either inside or outside the shop. The price charged, particularly in the case of the draper and bespoke tailor, had been a matter of sizing up the customer and bargaining. If any price was marked on the cloth it was in hieroglyphics that only the retailer could understand. Further, these retailers would usually grant credit. The early multiple shop organizations, by contrast, as many of their trading names implied, were catering mainly for the cash working-class trade, selling at low prices and offering no credit, and if the clothing sold was of indifferent quality and cut an important need was nevertheless fulfilled. Along with the branches of Co-operative Societies and the small-scale retail clothiers, the multiple shop outfitters and clothiers in the last quarter of the nineteenth century helped to distribute the growing quantities of factory-made clothes to the working classes and to replace the cotton corduroy, leather and moleskin suits, jackets and trousers of the mid-nineteenth century by woollens and worsteds.

The wholesale bespoke multiple shop tailors

In the opening decades of the twentieth century a second major development in the men's clothing trade took place.[1] This development was characterized not so much by changes in the technical methods of production as by changes in the organization of production and distribu-

[1] Some of the data for this development are drawn from an informative and interesting article by Sir Montague Burton in *Men's Wear*, 6 February 1932.

tion. The demand for men's outerwear, that is, for suits and overcoats, was increasing continuously, particularly among the working classes, and the steady improvements in factory methods were making possible the production of cheap and well-cut clothes. But the consumer was limited in his choice between taking a chance in respect of fit, cut and quality with ready-made factory clothing, or placing an order with the more expensive retail bespoke tailor. What was needed was the development of some method of organization that would bridge the gap between factory and consumer and provide low-priced well-cut clothing made to measure. Between 1900 and 1914 dozens of wholesale bespoke tailors, as they were termed, came into existence to bridge this gap.

Some of the earlier and smaller multiple shop firms mentioned above, such as Hope Brothers, had central workrooms where they made up the bespoke orders from retail branches, but not until the turn of the century did firms emerge that explored fully the technique of combining the individual measurement of the customer with the large-scale production of the goods. The rising wholesale bespoke tailors in many instances worked against orders from independent tailors and outfitters, but the most important development was the appearance of wholesale bespoke tailors who themselves controlled a chain of retail branches. The leading firms of this type in these years were Stewarts Clothiers Ltd., later known as 'Stewarts the King Tailors', with headquarters in Middlesbrough, the County Tailoring Company Ltd., of Leeds and London, the City Tailors Ltd., of London, trading as Lockwood and Bradley, Hipps Ltd. of Leeds, and Marshall & Wright of London and the provinces. By 1910 these firms had been joined by others such as Lupinsky and Brandon, the Donegal Tweed Company Ltd., the City Tailoring Company Ltd., Rego Clothiers Ltd., Carlish Ltd., Carton Ltd., and Walker's 30s. Tailors, a subsidiary of Montague Burton.

Some of the firms, for example Stewarts and Montague Burton, had originally been clothiers and outfitters selling ready-made goods before entering the wholesale bespoke trade. Others started as manufacturers and later acquired retail outlets, while yet others started their manufacturing and retailing activities simultaneously. Some practically confined themselves to wholesale bespoke tailoring, while others sold a fair proportion of ready-made goods as well as bespoke tailored articles, but the common feature of the rise of this group of firms in the first decades of the twentieth century was that they all combined manufacturing and retailing operations.

The methods of retailing and salesmanship of the wholesale bespoke multiple shop tailors were as different as they could be from the practice and methods of the traditional retail bespoke tailor. By and large, the multiple shop tailoring firms followed and improved upon the vigorous selling methods of the earlier multiple shop outfitters and clothiers. The greatest contrast with the retail bespoke tailor was in pricing practice. While the retail bespoke tailor would only state the price when the cloth had been chosen, the measurements made, the suit cut and made up and the alterations completed, the wholesale multiple shop tailor told the customers and the world by advertisement, by leaflet, and by window display, before any choice or measurement had been made, exactly how much the suit would cost. Many of the firms specialized at certain price levels, and boldly advertised one price and one price only for all made-to-measure suits bought at the branches. The two popular prices between 1900 and 1914 were the 20s. suit, which was sold by firms such as the County Tailoring Company Ltd., Hipps Ltd. and Stewarts Clothiers Ltd., and the 30s. suit, which was sold by firms such as Lupinsky and Brandon, Lockwood and Bradley, Rego Clothiers Ltd., and Montague Burton.

In window display and layout some break was made by the wholesale bespoke multiple shop tailors with the style of the earlier outfitters' and clothiers' shops. Inasmuch as a smaller selection of articles was sold, and the choice of cloth from the bunch books, measurement and fitting were an essential part of the sale, more attention was paid to the design and layout of the interior of the branch, and the window display became more specialized, emphasizing price and the cut and style of the suits by the use of dummies. Further, most of these shops had glass windows in place of the open-fronted shops of the earlier period, and the practice of displaying goods on rails outside the shops was less frequently adopted.

The shops and branches of both the multiple shop clothiers and outfitters and the wholesale multiple shop tailors were concentrated mainly in the working-class areas of the larger towns, an important number being in London in the earlier years, and they were almost always situated in busy shopping streets. The bold shop fronts and the display, pricing and lighting, coupled with the ingenious and enterprising advertisement of these firms, began a new era in salesmanship and shopping habits in the men's clothing trade. And, behind these new methods of retailing, which were rapidly imitated by the independent traders, was the growth of factory production in place of the workrooms and domestic outworkers. The setting up of a Trade Board for the Ready-made and Wholesale Bespoke Tailoring Trade in 1909 also marked the first stage in the removal of the stigma of 'sweating' from the clothing industry and placed all manufacturers on an equal competitive footing in regard to wages paid.

At the beginning of the First World War there were, according to existing records, some 40 multiple shop organizations in the men's clothing trade, controlling about 1,200 branches. The firms on the ready-made clothing and outfitting side of the trade, with their earlier start, were the most important type of multiple shop organization, but the wholesale multiple shop tailors had grown rapidly in the decade-and-a-half before the war. There were some 20 of these firms with more than 10 branches each engaged mainly in this trade in 1914. The greatest progress had been made by Stewarts the King Tailors, which had some 80 branches, and by Lockwood and Bradley, Hipps Ltd., the County Tailoring Company, Rego Clothiers Ltd., and Montague Burton.

The growth and rate of growth of multiple shop firms and branches

The statistical evidence on the rise and development of multiple shop retailing in the men's clothing trade is given in Table 59. Here estimates are presented of the number of multiple shop organizations in existence and the number of branches controlled by them between 1900 and 1950. The records of firms that have gone out of existence are included in this table as well as those of firms still trading in 1950. Altogether information relating to 80 firms has been included, and of the 37 firms that were no longer trading separately in 1950 some 12 had been amalgamated with existing firms and 25 firms had gone out of existence or had fewer than 10 branches each in 1950.

Table 59. *Estimates of the number of multiple shop firms and branches in the men's and boys' clothing trade, 1900–50*

Year	10–24 branches		25–49 branches		50–99 branches		100 or more branches		Totals			
									10 or more branches		25 or more branches	
	Number of		Number of		Number of		Number of		Number of		Number of	
	Firms	Branches	Firms	Branches	Firms	Branches	Firms	Branches	Firms	Branches	Firms	Branches
1900	15	194	4	127	2	123	1	126	22	570	7	376
1905	24	339	4	135	3	234	1	146	32	854	8	515
1910	27	385	5	143	4	287	2	270	38	1,085	11	700
1915	27	381	8	261	4	332	2	285	41	1,259	14	878
1920	29	424	8	270	5	357	3	375	45	1,426	16	1,002
1925	34	552	12	389	6	409	5	725	57	2,075	23	1,523
1930	27	437	18	635	6	396	7	1,216	58	2,684	31	2,247
1935	29	453	15	529	5	364	7	1,548	56	2,894	27	2,441
1939	21	326	13	432	7	511	8	1,964	49	3,233	28	2,907
1950	17	274	13	450	5	374	8	1,970	43	3,068	26	2,794

The figures given in Table 59 can be used to show the rate of growth of multiple shop trading as measured by the rate of increase in the number of branches in existence between different dates. This method is not a fully satisfactory one to use to indicate growth, as there were changes in the size of branches over time and also there were marked differences in the size of the branches on the outfitting side of the trade as compared with the wholesale bespoke tailoring side. However, the increases in the number of branches do give a broad indication of the rate of growth, and in Table 60 an attempt is made to show the absolute net increase and the rate of net increase in the number of branches in different years between 1900 and 1950. The rate of net increase is shown as a percentage increase in numbers as between two dates, and the absolute net increase in the number of branches is also shown as an average yearly net increase.

Table 60. *Rate of net increase in the number of branches of multiple shop firms in the men's and boys' clothing trade, 1896–1950*

Year	Branches of firms with 10 or more branches			Branches of firms with 25 or more branches		
	Net increase in number of branches	Percentage net increase	Average yearly net increase in numbers	Net increase in number of branches	Percentage net increase	Average yearly net increase in numbers
1896–1900	221	63	44	149	66	30
1901–1905	284	50	57	139	37	28
1906–1910	231	27	46	185	36	37
1911–1915	174	16	35	178	25	36
1916–1920	167	13	34	124	14	25
1921–1925	653	46	131	521	52	104
1926–1930	609	29	122	724	47	145
1931–1935	210	8	42	191	8	38
1936–1939	339	12	85	466	19	116
1940–1950	−165	−5	−15	−113	−4	−10

Tables 59 and 60 suggest that there was a rapid increase in the number of new multiple shop firms during the years 1900–05, and that the number of branches increased at the rate of approximately one additional shop a week in the fifteen years before the First World War. The immediate post-war years saw another large increase in the number of new multiple shop organizations in the trade, and between 1921 and 1930 the average rate of net increase in the number of branches in existence was of the order of 2–3 per week. After 1930 the number of firms in the trade decreased, owing to amalgamations and bankruptcies, and the average rate of net increase in the number of branches fell to less than 1 per week. Just before the Second World War, while the number of firms remained stationary or decreased slightly, the net increase in the number of branches rose to about 2 per week.

The Second World War led to an absolute decline in the number of branches in existence owing to closures arising from shortage of supplies and manpower and from enemy action. The firms with over 50 branches each in 1939, for example, had reduced the number of their trading branches by 1945 by some 9 %. In the post-war years expansion began again and branches were re-opened. Between 1946 and 1950 the increase in the number of branches controlled by the firms with more than 50 branches each was of the order of 4–5 %.

The developments in multiple shop retailing in this trade between 1918 and 1950 can most readily be discussed if a broad distinction is made between the men's and boy's outfitters and clothiers on the one hand and the wholesale multiple tailors on the other. The outfitters and clothiers are defined as firms selling ready-to-wear garments, suits, jackets, trousers, collars, ties, shirts, underclothing and so on, while the wholesale multiple shop tailors are defined as firms selling mainly made-to-measure men's and boys' outer clothing. A few firms fall on the border line between these definitions but, up to 1939 at least, the broad distinction was fairly clear.

The multiple shop outfitters and clothiers

In 1914 some two-thirds of the total number of multiple shop branches selling all types of men's and boys' wear were men's and boys' outfitters and clothiers. In the inter-war years the existing multiple shop firms selling these goods expanded and new firms came into the trade, but the rate of expansion of wholesale multiple shop tailors was very much more rapid than that of multiple shop outfitters and clothiers. Using the broad definitions discussed above, the number of branches of multiple shop clothiers and outfitters increased between 1920 and 1939 by some 66 %, while the number of branches of wholesale multiple shop tailors increased by some 240 %. The increase in the latter type of branch meant that the proportion of the total number of multiple shop branches in the men's and boys' clothing trade that could be described as primarily outfitters and clothiers fell from about two-thirds of the total in 1918 to one-half in 1939.

The development of the multiple shop outfitting and clothing firms was very diverse. In the pre-1914 period the majority of the firms had a marked bias towards the working-class trade and in the inter-war years many kept this bias. But alongside firms which claimed to be 'the cheapest clothiers in the world' others, such as Austin Reed Ltd., catered for a higher-class trade and provided a bespoke service alongside a wide range of other clothing. Similarly the physical size of the retail units began to vary widely between firm and firm. Some outfitters' shops, the majority, were small, rarely employing more than 3 or 4 assistants, but others were opened which employed as many as 10–20 assistants, and some contained separate departments for the sale of the different classes of goods. There were further variations between firms in the extent to which they undertook the manufacture of the goods sold in their branches. Some firms did not manufacture at all, and no firm attempted to produce the whole range of goods sold, but many firms in the inter-war years found it advantageous to undertake the manufacture of certain consistent selling lines such as shirts, collars, pyjamas and overalls. Very few of the firms that were primarily out-fitters, however, manufactured more than a quarter to a third of the goods sold in their branches.

While the development of individual multiple shop outfitters' organi-zations was therefore very diverse in the inter-war years, there were a number of characteristics which were common to practically all types of firm. First the open-fronted shop more or less disappeared, as did the use of poles and rails outside the shop and in the doorways for the display of goods. Shops with windows in busy shopping areas, though not necessarily main streets, and window displays carefully arranged to attract by style and variety rather than quantity, became the usual practice. The range of goods sold by the shops was widened considerably between the pre-1914 era and 1938. Greater variety in men's wear, with the growing demand for clothes to be worn during leisure time as well as for clothes for work and formal occasions, added new ranges to the shirts, ties, hosiery and lines of accessories stocked; and changes such as the replacement of the long-lived leather apron by the shorter-lived overalls, and the purchase of new boys' clothes instead of cutting down and making up at home, increased the sales and scope of the outfitters. A further feature common to most of the firms was a low price policy. As suggested above, not all firms catered for the market where such a policy was effective, but the largest multiple shop organizations, particularly those with branches in the Midlands, in the North of England and in Scotland, emphasized the low prices of the goods they sold.

A low price policy was made possible partly by the economies secured in undertaking some manufacturing, but mainly through the economies of bulk buying on behalf of all the branches and the fast rate of stock turn in each branch. The men's and boys' wear trade, while not in these years a fashion trade, was nevertheless subject to marked seasonal fluctuations in demand. The multiple shop firms by placing orders out of season could obtain much keener prices than those obtained by the independent retailer who bought just before the season started from a wholesaler who in turn had often been reluctant to place forward orders owing to doubts as to the decisions of the retailers. The multiple shop firms were also able to obtain exclusive lines from manufacturers by buying in large quantities.

A last feature common to all multiple shop outfitting firms was the policy of attempting to build a reputation for honest trading. In the clothing trades the customer was largely an amateur in buying but an expert in determining the value of a good in relation to price once the article had been bought and used. As practically none of the goods were branded by the manufacturers the retailer became identified with the article sold and in many instances branded the goods in his name. A customer dissatisfied with the quality of an article at the price paid therefore held the retailer responsible, and repeat orders and reputation were dependent on the quality of the goods sold. The small-scale retailer in the clothing and outfitting trade had, of course, the same problem, but the multiple shop outfitter, owing to his control of manufacturing facilities and to the placing of larger orders direct with individual manufacturers, was better able to maintain consistent control of the quality of the goods sold in relation to the price charged than was the small-scale retailer purchasing from wholesalers.

The progress of wholesale bespoke multiple shop tailors

The progress of the wholesale multiple shop tailors noted above in the period from the turn of the century to 1914 came to a halt during the First World War, but the end of the war witnessed an immediate revival of activity.[1] Firms that had only a handful of retail branches in the pre-1914 period started expanding rapidly, and over 15 new medium-sized wholesale multiple shop tailoring firms came into the trade. Stewarts the King Tailors were the first wholesale tailors to have over 100 branches in operation, and close on their heels came Montague Burton, which increased in size rapidly in the 'twenties and had nearly twice as many branches as Stewarts by 1925. Rego Clothiers Ltd., Brandons Ltd., Hipps Ltd., the Donegal Tweed Company Ltd., and Lockwood and Bradley were similarly increasing the number of their branches, and newer firms such as Prices, Tailors Ltd., John Bright Ltd. Kelletts Ltd., Vernon Heaton Ltd., Alexandre Ltd., Natco Ltd., M. & N. Horne Ltd., Russell Brothers, E. Mortimer Ltd., Packard (Tailors) Ltd., and Griffith Bros., which, before 1914, either had very few branches or did not exist, began to expand.

The 'twenties were years of intense competition in the men's wear trade, and the wholesale tailors to keep their factories fully employed opened more and more outlets for their goods. Shops of a sort were easy to acquire, and on the bespoke side little more was needed in the way of fittings than some rolls of cloth, some dummies for the windows

[1] The increase shown in Table 59 above in the number of branches between 1915 and 1920 arises almost entirely from expansion after 1918.

and a pattern 'bunch'. The rapid expansion of some of the firms was not, however, always carefully planned, and already by 1925 some firms had disappeared and others were in difficulties. Apart from the problems of organizing a wholesale bespoke business, the difficulties encountered by many of the firms were those of maintaining the quality of the goods and of the service that should go with the goods, of the disadvantage experienced by some of the London firms in competing with the lower cost Leeds firms and, in the background, the absence of any important fashion element in the men's outer clothing trade. This slowness of fashion change enabled customers to postpone new purchases when money was short. The wholesale bespoke technique attracted consumers inasmuch as it offered them either better fits than the ready-made clothiers or cheaper suits than the retail bespoke tailor, but total demand for outer clothing as such was not necessarily increased.

The depression years 1929–33 added to the problems of many of the firms, and there were further casualties. Altogether between 1920 and 1933 at least 25 firms in the wholesale multiple shop tailoring trade went out of existence, were acquired by other concerns, or shrank to fewer than 10 branches. There would appear to have been more failures of multiple shop organizations in this trade than in any other. By contrast, while many firms found the problems of organization too great and the demand for men's outerwear insufficiently elastic to permit of expansion, a few firms, having overcome the initial difficulties of keeping retail and manufacturing growth from getting out of line with each other, had developed rapidly. The best known of these successful firms were Montague Burton Ltd., Prices, Tailors Ltd., and Lockwood and Bradley Ltd. By 1935 Burtons had over 400 branches, Prices, which had acquired Stewarts the King Tailors in 1931, had over 250 branches, and Lockwood and Bradley, which had acquired Curzon Brothers and Maxims Ltd., had over 100 branches. By 1939, while Burtons and Prices had continued to expand to over 500 and over 300 branches respectively, Lockwood and Bradley had got into difficulties and had fallen out of the running. Their place with over 100 branches was, however, taken by Rego Clothiers Ltd., and a new firm starting in the early 'thirties, Town Tailors Ltd. (Weaver to Wearer).

In the inter-war years therefore there was in the wholesale men's outerwear trade an intital burst of multiple shop activity when a number of new firms joined the earlier firms and all expanded rapidly. These firms, with the exception of Stewarts, were of a relatively small size. This phase was followed by a period of difficulty for a number of the firms and their disappearance from the trade, while at the same time others were emerging from the ruck of small firms and developing very large organizations. In the third phase, the years just prior to the

Second World War, three or four new firms which had not been in existence in 1920 and only started developing in the middle and late 'twenties grew rapidly.

The importance of the large firms

The trend towards larger multiple shop organizations can be illustrated to some extent by an analysis of the total number of branches in existence in different years that were controlled by the largest multiple shop firms. Table 61 shows the changes in this proportion between 1910 and 1950 in respect of all types of multiple shop retailers in the men's and boys' wear trade.

Table 61. *Relative importance of the largest multiple shop firms in the men's and boys' clothing trade, 1910–50*

Year	Total branches of firms with 10 or more branches			Total branches of firms with 25 or more branches		
	Proportion controlled by			Proportion controlled by		
	The largest firm %	The 2 largest firms %	The 5 largest firms %	The largest firm %	The 2 largest firms %	The 5 largest firms %
1910	15	25	46	24	39	72
1920	12	19	39	17	27	55
1930	12	22	37	15	27	44
1939	18	29	49	20	33	55
1950	20	31	51	21	34	56

The shifts shown in this table in the proportion of the total number of branches controlled by the largest firms are not very significant, though there appears to have been a steady increase in the share of the 2 largest firms from 1920 onwards. In other words these firms were expanding at a faster rate than the increase in the total number of multiple shop branches. An analysis of the trend in the wholesale multiple shop tailoring section by itself cannot be made with precision, as the exact type of trade of some of the firms that went out of existence is difficult to determine, but an approximation of the trend is presented in Table 62.

This table shows a rapid increase in the relative importance of the two largest wholesale bespoke multiple shop firms from 1930 onwards. Further, while no data are available to show in relation to all the firms the changes in the size of branches in these years, it is known that the large firms that grew most rapidly in the late 'twenties and in the 'thirties were also the firms that opened and maintained the largest retailing units. This factor would tend to increase still further the relative importance of the two largest firms.

Table 62. *Relative importance of the largest multiple shop firms in the wholesale bespoke men's clothing trade, 1920–50*

Year	Proportion of total number of branches of firms with 10 or more branches controlled by		
	The largest firm %	The 2 largest firms %	The 5 largest firms %
1920	22	32	59
1930	24	33	55
1939	36	60	79
1950	39	63	85

The retailing methods and the multiple shop branches

The trading policies and characteristics of the wholesale multiple shop tailors are well known and do not require much elaboration. The sales by these organizations were practically confined to goods of their own manufacture and the only goods bought out would be special lines such as rainwear. Some ready-made garments were stocked, such as sports jackets and overcoats, but the bulk of the sales were in the form of made-to-measure or bespoke clothing.[1]

The pricing policy of most of the firms was to charge low prices, and the firms appealed to the working-class and lower middle-class markets. The various phrases used by the firms to describe their businesses illustrate this appeal, for example 'We clothe the man who cannot afford a suit', 'A suit should never cost a man as much as a week's money', and 'We supply the average wage-earner with a suit costing approximately a week's wage'. Prices were boldly and plainly marked, in many instances they were very widely advertised, and the majority of the firms traded on a cash basis. Some, however, operated on the check trading method and a few in the late 'twenties began to sell their suits on credit or hire purchase terms.

The branches of the wholesale multiple shop tailors were for the most part larger, and located in more prominent shopping sites, than those of the multiple shop outfitter and clothier. Well-designed display of the cloth, of the suits and of the attractions of the wholesale bespoke service in the busiest thoroughfares was an essential part of this form of trading. The two largest wholesale bespoke multiple shop firms in particular adopted a policy in the inter-war years of expanding only by way of sites in main shopping streets and of opening large, spacious and well

[1] In the 'thirties, for example, over 80% of Montague Burton's turnover was represented by bespoke sales.

fitted-out shops which in some cases had been specially designed and built. These shops were in marked contrast with the smallness and the side street situation of the typical retail bespoke tailor. Such a policy required expert guidance on real estate questions and considerable financial ingenuity to raise the capital to acquire the sites before the retail business had been undertaken to pay for them. Loans and mortgages figured prominently in the accounts of companies that developed in this way, and bankers became familiar figures on the Boards of Directors.

Not all firms managed to carry through such a bold policy success-fully. The problem of meeting the mortgages on shop property proved too great for some firms which from a technical tailoring point of view were soundly enough based, but the policy of large clean shops in main shopping streets paid handsome dividends to those firms which over-came the initial difficulties of obtaining a foothold. An interesting feature of the location of many of the branches of these firms was their proximity to one another—not only competing branches of different firms but also branches of the same firm. In this trade such a policy, which was in part design and in part necessity, inasmuch as the choice of main street sites by the 'thirties had become very limited, was not found to be detrimental to sales: if anything, the reverse. A group of men's tailoring shops fairly close together created a minor men's shopping centre, which attracted customers who in any event would look in all the shop windows of the different firms first before deciding to make a purchase.

The integration of production and distribution

The effective trading and pricing policies and the possession of well-sited, attractive outlets is, however, only a part of the story of the whole-sale multiple shop tailoring firms. Of equal importance was the organi-zation of the integration of production and distribution by these firms. The organizational problems have been well described by Sir Montague Burton who, after suggesting that 'the essence of successful multiple shop trading or mass distribution is that it should be automatic and consequently foolproof', added:

Made-to-measure tailoring is just the reverse from automatic—it is over-loaded with detail: the giving of a wrong cloth number, a wrong style number, a wrong figure description swiftly culminates in civil war on a small scale. Even if the order form reaches the factory safely and without a blemish, there are still many dangers lurking: the cloth is probably sold out, the cutter on a busy Monday may overlook one of the many instructions on a closely-written order form, a ticket pocket or a "hare" pocket (to which the customer attaches great importance) is overlooked, a tailor or a machinist may overlook an important item, a trouser button may be carelessly sewn on;

a garment may be despatched a day or two late. Any of the mishaps enumerated, which are only a few of many, is sufficient to nullify all the efforts to satisfy, resulting in the entire service being condemned and disqualified.[1]

While the suggestion of the entire service being condemned and disqualified owing to a carelessly sewn button may be an exaggeration, there is no dispute that in this trade the reputation of the firm was of vital importance to success. To encourage customers to return or the friends of customers to purchase, these firms had to establish a name for good quality at the price and for an efficient and accurate bespoke service. A firm might get first orders with badly-finished goods, careless fitting and cutting and late deliveries, but never repeat orders. Many of the multiple shop bespoke tailoring firms that went bankrupt were helped on their way by carelessness, inattention to detail and an ambition to expand before building the organization that could sustain the considerable administrative strain of wholesale bespoke tailoring.

The most difficult stage that the firms passed through in both this and other trades was that of middle growth. Problems such as those outlined above can be watched and controlled through the exertion of the personal energy of the leaders of the business when the firm is small, and by the introduction of elaborate checks, cross-checks and inspection devices when it is very large. The most troublesome period, as many firms in this trade found to their cost, was the intermediate stage where the energy and efforts of a few could not cover the whole of the problems and the turnover and size of the firms were not sufficient to allow the introduction of the whole range of checks and controls. The firms that passed through the intermediate stage with success tended to be those which supplemented the energy of the few at the earliest possible moment by simple and inexpensive organizational plans for work flow and checking.

A second problem of organization faced by the wholesale multiple tailors was that of matching orders from their branches with factory capacity throughout the year. There were two obvious dangers facing the firms. On the one hand, there was the risk of the factory 'leading' the shops, that is, in order to keep the manufacturing side fully employed the branches were regarded merely as outlets for the goods produced, whether the particular type of product suited all the shops or no. This danger arose mainly in the case of ready-made clothiers who possessed manufacturing facilities, but it also occurred with wholesale bespoke firms whose factories produced 'ready-made' goods in periods of slackness of bespoke orders. On the other hand, there was the danger of the

[1] *Men's Wear*, loc. cit.

shops 'leading' the factory, which led to unused factory capacity at certain periods of the year, and, at the rush periods, to the need to put work out, if possible, to other manufacturers to meet the orders from the branches. Unused capacity sent up overhead costs, and while standing men off was possible in periods of heavy unemployment, in the years of the Second World War and the post-war years such a policy was out of the question, as it would have led to the rapid disappearance of all the skilled men of the firm. Equally the putting out of work at rush periods was never satisfactory, as control over the quality of the workmanship was lost and in any case all tailoring firms had the same rush period. The balance between factory capacity and orders from branches was usually maintained by expanding factory capacity only when retail business fully warranted expansion, and by producing ready-to-wear goods in the off-peak periods, though reduction in employment in such periods was common in the inter-war years. In the post-war years the wholesale bespoke firms, to keep their manpower fully employed throughout the year, increased their production of ready-made clothing, and the growing popularity of these goods has to some extent reduced the magnitude of the problem.

The finance of the multiple shop firms

In the early period of growth before 1914 the multiple shop organizations in this trade, on both the outfitting and the tailoring sides, relied for their finance mainly on reinvestment of profits. The fixed capital requirements were not large, even for those undertaking manufacturing, as the factories were still comparatively small and the retail branches opened did not require extensive fitting and frequently were taken on leasehold. The majority of the firms by 1914 had become limited liability companies, but for the most part they were private companies and made no appeal for funds on the open market. While a few firms of necessity or from attraction had converted themselves into public limited companies in the general promoting spree of the late 'nineties, the public companies controlled only some 20 % of the total number of multiple shop branches in the men's wear trade in 1910.

In the inter-war years the situation changed radically. The apparent opportunities for general expansion of multiple shop retailing in this trade between 1920 and 1930, the development of large-scale factory production by the wholesale bespoke tailors, the increasing cost of fitting out shops, and the competition for good branch sites in main streets, led many firms to raise additional funds by the issue of shares on the market. Some of the smaller firms did this in the years 1920–25 and larger firms followed suit between 1926 and 1930. By the latter date practically one-half of all the branches of multiple shop firms were controlled by public companies. The process of conversion to public companies continued in the years up to the Second World War, though at a slower pace, and by 1939 the proportion of the total number of branches belonging to firms that were public companies was over 60 %. Moreover the public companies were the firms with the largest number of branches.

In the post-war years the high cost of developing factory production and of acquiring sites forced other firms to become public companies to raise the capital for maintaining their position in the trade and for expansion. By 1950 over 75 % of the total number of multiple shop branches were controlled by public companies.

The Co-operative Societies

Branches of Co-operative Societies in the eighteen-sixties and seventies had started selling a small range of men's clothing, and some of the earliest production units established by the Wholesale Societies were in this trade. The Scottish Co-operative Wholesale Society, for example, opened a factory to make shirts and some outer clothing in 1881, and the English Co-operative Wholesale Society in the late 'eighties had a factory first at Batley and then at Leeds which was producing men's ready-made clothing. Other factories making shirts and outfitters' goods were opened in the 'nineties, and in 1895 a bespoke tailoring factory was started at Broughton. At the turn of the century two more clothing factories came into operation in London and Newcastle. The factories established by the Wholesale Societies, like the majority of the factories in the clothing trade in these years, were small, but they won a reputation for good conditions for their employees in a trade that before the establishment of the Trade Board in 1909 was notorious for long hours, bad working conditions and low wages. The entire output of these factories was sold through the Co-operative Retail Societies, and many of the central stores of the Societies had separate clothing departments. In Scotland it was usual for one department, drapery, to sell both women's and men's clothing, though in England the larger Societies began to open separate departments for the two types of articles.

In the inter-war years Co-operative production of men's and boys' clothing of all descriptions increased. Existing factories were extended and two new ones were opened. The wholesale bespoke methods of the multiple shop tailors were paralleled to some extent, but the main bias of the productive units and of the Retail Societies was towards the sale of men's and boys' outfitting and ready-made clothing. While the total output of the Wholesale Societies continued to be purchased by the

Retail Societies, some purchases of men's and boys' wear would also be made from private manufacturers.

The goods sold by the Co-operative men's and boys' tailoring and outfitting shops had a fair reputation for quality but in style, cut and range they tended to lag behind the products of the wholesale multiple shop tailors. Further, in contrast to the emphasis the latter placed on display and advertising, the Co-operative shops or departments selling these goods were often badly laid out, they were frequently hidden at the back or side of a larger store instead of having main street sites and windows, and the quality of the service on the bespoke side was not high. The Retail Societies, in spite of the early start on the manufacturing side by the Wholesale Societies, had not been forward in developing the specialized sale of men's and boys' wear, and in 1937 there were only 730 Co-operative tailoring and outfitting shops or departments compared with some 3,000 multiple shop branches at that date. With the exception of the Southern Societies, particularly the London Societies, the sale of men's and boys' wear was secondary to drapery, and no sustained efforts were made to introduce sales-appeal in these goods. Most of the purchases were made by women, and the Societies tended to stock those goods that could be bought by women, such as outfitters' goods and boys' clothing, rather than to cater for men's tastes and needs.

Generally, it can be said that in this trade the Co-operative Societies did not keep pace in sales methods with other types of retailer. Certainly the character of the demand for men's clothing and outfitting was conservative, but many innovations were introduced into the trade in the inter-war years in respect of range of goods sold, cut, style and, particularly, methods of attracting customers. These innovations set the standard, and the organizations that were slow in imitating, following and improving on the successful methods of competitors could only advance slowly. Further, with the wholesale multiple shop tailors selling at low prices, the dividend appeal of the Co-operative Societies lost some of its effectiveness on the men's outer clothing side of the trade.

The department stores

The rise and development of department stores is discussed in the section of this chapter dealing with women's wear. So far as the men's and boys' outfitting and tailoring trade is concerned, the stores handled some of the goods practically from their foundation. At the turn of the century, for example, most of the stores in existence sold a range of outfitting and ready-to-wear boys' and men's outerwear, and in the inter-war years some of the stores added a bespoke service. The main differences, however, between the retailing of men's and boys' wear by department stores and by the specialist retailers lay in the stress, again practically from the earliest days, on those sections of the trade and on those articles which could be bought by women without fear of making a mistake. The overwhelming majority of the customers were women, and in their men's and boys' departments the department stores emphasized boys' wear, men's outfitting, particularly shirts, hosiery, underclothing and pyjamas, and some men's fashion and fancy goods such as ties, scarves and gloves.

In their sale of boys' wear the department stores provided a display and range of goods which gained them a reputation that few could match. Tailors and outfitters could not afford the space, or anticipate the turnover, to permit a special department for these goods, and as increased attention was paid both by the middle- and by the upper working-classes to the dressing of their children in the inter-war years the department stores increased their sales of these goods. Some stores, on their men's outfitting side, pursued a policy of low pricing in relation to quality. Certain lines, for example shirts and pyjamas, were widely advertised at low prices, and to some extent this policy took on the appearance of a 'loss-leader' technique. Women attracted to the store to buy bargains for their menfolk would rarely leave without visiting and almost certainly purchasing goods in other departments.

The sale of men's wear remained, however, second in importance to the sale of women's wear in department stores. No attempt was made in the period up to the Second World War to compete in the same market as the multiple shop retailers, and while some stores were attempting to develop greater specialization in this section of the trade by the institution of 'Men's Shops', the stores as a whole were not very successful in attracting men shoppers.

The small-scale outfitter and the retail bespoke tailor

The two main types of small-scale retailer in the men's and boys' wear clothing trade were the general outfitter and clothier and the retail bespoke tailor. The general outfitter group covered a wide range of different types and classes of shop, from the bespoke shirtmaker and the exclusive hatter and hosier at one end of the trade to the general clothes dealer selling ready-made cheap suits, working clothes and shirts at the other. As factory production of 'ready-mades' increased in the early twentieth century, and as the output of men's hosiery, shirts and undergarments rose, both the small-scale outfitter and the multiple shop outfitter increased in numbers. In the inter-war years the widening of the range and style of men's outfitting goods continued to give the small-scale retailer scope for advance, and with assistance from the wholesaler in the form of a wide selection of goods and of credit he continued to hold his own to some extent with the larger-scale retailers.

The widening of the range of goods stocked and the element of fashion that was being introduced into the men's outfitting trade, however, presented the small-scale retailer with the problem of a slowing down of the rate of stock turn and the piling up of out-of-date stock. The widening of the range of goods sold also lessened the control of the retailer over the quality of all the goods handled. Further, the small-scale retailer was at a disadvantage in many areas in so far as he was unable to compete with the large-scale retailer in the siting of his premises in the main street shopping districts. In a trade where display was becoming an important factor in sales this was a serious handicap.

The spread of factory methods of production of men's outerwear in the last quarter of the nineteenth and first half of the twentieth century inevitably meant a decline in the relative importance of the retail bespoke tailor in the trade. The growth of wholesale bespoke tailoring in the twentieth century and the improvement in the quality of the goods produced by these techniques had some bearing on the decline of the retail bespoke tailor, but to a large extent the wholesale bespoke firms catered for groups who had previously bought ready-made clothing. A more important factor in the decline of the retail bespoke tailor was the raising of the standard of the higher-class ready-made clothing and the growing emphasis in the inter-war years that was placed on less formal outerwear and clothes for leisure occasions.

There was, however, no comparison between the quality of the product of the retail bespoke tailor and that of the wholesale bespoke tailor or the ready-made factory goods, and the upper and top end of the trade remained firmly in the hands of the private retail bespoke tailor. At the time of the 1935 Census of Production the retail bespoke tailor is estimated to have represented 15–20 % of the total sales of men's outerwear expressed in terms of retail prices. Some other types of retail bespoke tailor had, however, lost ground heavily to the larger multiple shop wholesale tailors. These were the bespoke tailors who did not own a workroom but invited customers to select their cloth, took measurements, and passed on the orders to a wholesale bespoke factory. The superior service and lower prices of the multiple shop wholesale tailors limited the advance of this type of small-scale bespoke tailor.

Shares of the different economic types of retailer in the total trade

The discussion of the progress and problems of the different economic types of retailers in the men's and boys' wear trade may now be summarized by presenting estimates of the proportion of total sales undertaken by the different economic types of retailers in the years 1900–50. These estimates are given in Table 63.

Table 63. *Estimated shares of the different economic types of retailer in the total retail sales of men's and boys' wear, 1900–50**

Year	Proportion of total sales undertaken by			
	Co-operative Societies %	Department stores %	Multiple shop retailers %	Other retailers (by difference) %
1900	1·5–3·0	1·0–1·5	2·0– 3·5	92·0–95·5
1905	2·0–3·0	1·0–2·5	3·0– 4·0	90·5–94·0
1910	2·0–3·5	2·0–3·0	4·0– 5·0	88·5–92·0
1915	2·5–3·5	2·5–4·0	6·0– 7·5	85·0–89·0
1920	2·5–3·5	3·0–4·0	8·5–10·0	82·5–86·0
1925	2·5–4·0	4·0–5·0	15·0–17·0	74·0–78·5
1930	3·0–4·5	5·0–6·0	20·5–24·0	65·5–71·5
1935	3·5–4·5	5·5–6·5	23·5–27·0	62·0–67·5
1939	4·0–6·0	6·0–7·0	28·0–32·0	55·0–62·0
1950	5·0–7·0	6·5–7·5	30·0–34·0	51·5–58·5

* For a discussion of the basis of these estimates see Appendix A. The estimates of total sales of men's and boys' wear include the sale of articles such as braces, suspenders, handkerchiefs, ties, hats and proofed garments as well as of shirts, collars, underclothing, hosiery, outer clothing and overalls. The sales of both bespoke and ready-made goods are included. The sales of second-hand goods are excluded.

The trends shown in Table 63 are clear and do not require detailed elaboration. The growth in the shares of the Co-operative Societies and the department stores was slow and ran roughly parallel. The rise in the importance of multiple shop retailing, particularly after 1918, was very rapid, and the decline in the share of the small-scale retailer —his share in the total trade in 1900 was 90 % but in 1950 only about 50 %—was continuous. The share of the multiple shop retailing organizations in the total sales of men's and boys' outerwear was higher in 1950 than their share in the total sales of all men's and boys' clothing, and the increase in the share of multiple shop retailers on this side of the trade was more rapid in the years 1920–50 than on the outfitting side of the trade. Approximately 60–66 % of the total sales of multiple shop organizations were represented by goods from their own manufacturing establishments.

Factors influencing the growth of different types of retailer

The reasons for the significant growth of large-scale retailing in this trade and for the different rates of growth between 1900 and 1950 of the different economic types of retailers have been mentioned in the discussion above. Some purpose will be served, however, by reviewing briefly the main factors.

The growth of large-scale retailing was the outcome of the spread of large-scale production methods in a trade where the demand for the goods was relatively stable and the goods themselves were standardized and not subject to severe fluctuations in fashion, quality or price. The development of these large-scale methods was also assisted, in the inter-war years, by the growth in the homogeneity in social behaviour and taste as between different areas of the country and as between different classes. In the pre-1914 years, the style of the outerwear of the different classes in society tended to be determined by recognized occupational and regional standards or tastes. The men of the Tyneside, for example, dressed differently at work and on Sundays from the men of Lancashire, of South Wales or of London. The First World War had a marked effect on regional outlooks, and the increased leisure of the post-war years led to new demands. Gradually men's wear throughout the country began to be more standardized and more uniform, and the differences between the dress of different occupational groups, of different regions and of different classes began to diminish. Further, differences of age went into the melting-pot, and different generations of men began to wear the same general type of clothes. These changes in taste and custom meant that the market for both bespoke and ready-to-wear clothes became a national market. The large-scale retailers with a national coverage both took advantage of the growth of uniformity in demand and also in their turn, by display, advertisement and price policy, encouraged this uniformity.

In regard to the rates of growth of the different economic types of retailers, the increase in the share of the Co-operative Societies was due to expansion of manufacturing facilities, to the rise in the membership of the Societies, and to the widening sale of men's and boys' wear by the individual Retail Societies. Through the Wholesale Societies the Retail Societies possessed some of the advantages of large-scale buying and manufacturing, and in addition the dividend on purchases undoubtedly proved an inducement to the housewife to buy clothes for the family at the Co-operative store. The slowness of the growth of Co-operative trading in these goods would appear to result from the failure to specialize in production, buying and retailing of men's wear throughout the whole movement. Every Society acted on its own and the Wholesale Society had to deal with hundreds of different buyers each demanding different types of goods. Again, the Co-operative Societies concentrated on the sections of men's and boys' wear bought by women and did not directly appeal to men shoppers. Finally the Co-operative Societies lagged far behind other retailers in this trade in their methods of display and of attracting customers.

The share of department stores in the total trade increased with the increase in the number of department stores. Further, specialist displays and large stocks of certain types of goods such as boys' wear and men's accessories that could be readily purchased by women assisted department store sales. But the price market to which the department stores appealed was limited, the stores did not succeed in attracting male shoppers to any great extent, the buying economies secured by individual stores in their men's wear sections were small compared with those of the multiple shop retailers, and the stores possessed few or none of the advantages of integration of production and distribution.

The spectacular rise of the multiple shop retailers in the trade was the outcome of many factors. The multiple shop technique of trading was particularly well adapted in the early years to bridging the gap between the growing factory production on the one hand and the increasing working-class demand on the other. Large-scale buying coupled with a vigorous selling policy and an aggressive price policy led to the early success of these firms. But of greater importance was the later development of integration of production and distribution which enabled the multiple shop firms to guarantee quality at the price charged and to provide the working and middle classes with a well-cut bespoke suit at a low price. The character of demand in this trade and the methods of production were particularly favourable to the successful organization of integrated concerns operating on a national scale. Once the techniques of organization and control of multiple shop outfitting and multiple shop wholesale tailoring had been mastered, these organizations with their large capital resources led the way in standards of display, layout and siting of their retailing units and, in many respects, in the services provided to the customer. Working-class men's clothing, instead of being something that had to be sought at bargain prices in markets and jumbled clothing halls, became something to be displayed, arranged and made to appear attractive in shop windows and in the shops. And in the years just before the Second World War and in the post-war years some multiple shop firms were successfully extending these techniques to higher-priced markets.

Suggestions as to future trends in the trade

Suggestions as to the future trends in the trade can only be put forward tentatively. If assumptions can be made regarding adequate supplies of raw materials and the maintenance of purchasing power, the problems facing the trade as a whole in the future would appear to be firstly the change, if any, in the character of the demand for men's wear, and secondly the problem of the growing limitation of sites for main display shops.

The shortages of clothing and the rationing system of the Second World War extending to the post-war years carried further the trend of the previous twenty years in the direction of greater informality in men's outer clothing. The working suits of blue serge, or the black coat and striped trousers, depending on status, were supplemented and in some instances replaced by more informal dress, such as the lounge suit or the sports jacket and flannel trousers. The top hat and the bowler were replaced by the felt hat or no hat at all. The previously clear distinction between formal working attire and leisure attire began to be blurred. Similarly, the pre-war trend of greater variety of style and colour in men's outfitting continued in the post-war years. These trends are hardly likely to be reversed in the future, but along with them the fashion element in men's clothing may increase. That is to say that changes in generally accepted style may reduce the length of usable life of certain types of clothes, make the cuts of suits or overcoats or even shirts 'out of date' say in two or three years after purchase, and lead to more frequent replacement.

The development of high fashion in men's clothing, except in a fringe of the trade and for unimportant accessories such as ties, appears, however, to be somewhat unlikely in the foreseeable future. The suggestion of a continued increase in the informality of men's wear and in the variety of that wear may be more readily accepted. The consequences of such an increase in informality of dress for both work and leisure would appear to be a slightly shorter wearing life for each article of clothing, more frequent purchases, probably greater seasonal peaks, and an increased demand for ready-to-wear garments as against bespoke clothes. The effects of such a trend on the character of the trade would appear to be in the direction of greater stress on display in shop windows and by advertisement, a decline in the reliance of customers on one tailor or one outfitter and a greater tendency to 'shop around' before making a choice, increased purchasing by men instead of their leaving the buying of a wide range of men's wear to the womenfolk, a decline in the relative importance of wholesale and retail bespoke tailoring, and increased risks of stockholding on the part of the retailers resulting from greater variety.

Of the present types of retailer in the trade, the multiple shop organizations, in some ways, are in a position to gain most from such a trend as they possess the well-situated shops in the main streets, the window-dressing experts to ensure attractive displays and the stock control techniques to carry wide ranges. Any decline in the role of the woman as the purchaser of men's wear will affect adversely both the Co-operative stores and the department stores. On the other hand, the problems facing the multiple shop organizations that control manufacturing facilities will not be simple in their solution. A decline in the proportion of bespoke wear relative to ready-made articles, which has already occurred in the post-war years, would mean that some of the original appeal and economic advantages of the wholesale bespoke tailors would be weakened. The risk element in stocking ready-mades, with the inevitable 'sales' at the end of the season, would increase. Even if demand for bespoke wear is maintained—it would appear unlikely to increase—the wholesale bespoke tailors would be placing a considerable strain on their mass production methods if the consumer's demand for diversity and informality of dress is to be superimposed upon the existing problems of individual measurements and fittings. Further, some doubts may be expressed as to whether the firms which hitherto have taken a leading part in introducing standardization and uniformity in men's outer clothing would be able to lead the way in providing attractive diversity and informality. There is a slight parallel here with the footwear trade in that, except for standard ranges of footwear, no one firm with one team of designers and one factory can hope to provide all the ideas and the whole range of footwear required in a fully-stocked shop. The wholesale multiple shop tailors in the future may follow the practice of the integrated footwear firms by providing from their own factories the main 'bread and butter lines' in demand and adding to the range and variety of the goods sold by buying from other manufacturers.

This suggestion of increased diversity and informality in men's wear and of a growing demand for ready-to-wear clothing should not, however, be overstressed. Bespoke tailoring is certain to continue to play an important rôle in the trade. Wholesale bespoke tailoring is well established and the trading-up process to higher-priced markets of many of the multiple shop tailoring firms will almost certainly continue. The luxury of personal attention and fitting combined with the economies of factory tailoring has a strong appeal in relation to price and satisfaction. Some of the smaller wholesale bespoke multiple shop tailors may advance by catering exclusively for the medium and higher income groups and may also develop the technique of fittings and sales by representatives instead of relying exclusively on retail shops. The larger wholesale bespoke firms will probably continue to widen the range of the qualities of goods sold, buying out where necessary, and may develop special sections of their shops, or special shops, for the higher-class trade.

A second problem of the future facing the trade is that of acquiring sites in main shopping streets. This problem is of little consequence to the independent outfitter and retail bespoke tailor, but is a pressing one for the larger multiple shop organizations and to a lesser extent the Co-operative Societies. Multiple shop firms, as stressed above, have relied for their advance on salesmanship and display, on taking tailoring and outfitting from the side streets and placing them in the main shopping streets. The position, however, is rapidly being reached where there are no vacant sites in the main streets and, as most of the existing retailers in such streets have strong financial backing, there are unlikely to be any vacant sites in the future. Increased turnover in existing branches is possible, but the way is being closed to the emergence of new firms trading on these methods, and existing firms will have difficulty in continuing their pre-1938 rate of expansion, except at the expense of others. New shopping centres in re-built old towns, in new towns and on housing estates will provide some scope for expansion, but unless main street shopping centres overflow effectively into side streets this physical barrier to the advance of multiple shop firms and Co-operative stores may be serious. Some of the wholesale bespoke tailors, as suggested above, may overcome the problem by using representatives rather than fixed shops as their 'selling points', but this method can hardly be used by multiple shop outfitters and multiple tailors who rely on display and price to attract the working-class trade. Again some of the existing firms with main street shops will undoubtedly decline and will be willing to sell their properties to rising firms, but such a transfer will not increase the total number of main street sites in the trade.

What will be the effects of these trends and problems on the future structure of the trade? Clearly a definitive answer cannot be given, but on the basis of the past developments some suggestions may be made. There would appear to be no reason to expect the Co-operative Societies to expand very rapidly, if at all, in the men's and boys' wear trade. A further increase in membership may lead to increased sales, but unless there is a thoroughgoing reorganization of the whole approach to the integration of production and distribution of men's wear by the movement and unless the Societies are prepared by using specialists to take risks in the trade as variety and styling increase, the advance in the Co-operative share of the total trade will be small. Many of the original attractions of Co-operative trading, such as honest dealing and a high dividend on sales, no longer carry so much weight in face of the improvement in the standard of retailing of other firms and the greater attractiveness of the display and products of competitors. New methods will have to be developed if any progress is to be made. There are few signs at present that such a new approach is being seriously considered.

In the case of department stores, again there would appear to be little prospect of a significant advance. Certainly the stores would be in a position to offer considerable variety and numerous styles of men's wear, but the buying and pricing advantages of a single section in a department store as against the collective buying and pricing advantages of a multiple shop organization are already practically nil, and as some of the multiple shop retailers move into higher-priced, better quality markets in the future the advantages of department store trading vis-à-vis multiple shop trading in men's wear are likely to be even fewer. Some department stores may extend their high-class bespoke service, but, except for boys' wear, the store would appear to be likely to lose some ground to the multiple shop retailers.

The prospects of a further advance of multiple shop retailing in this trade at the rate evidenced in the past twenty-five years do not appear to be very great. This advance was effected to a large extent by the process of opening shops where the consumers could be attracted by displays, and by the successful employment of wholesale bespoke methods of production. But the possibilities of obtaining a number of additional sites that are suitable in respect of both situation and size would appear to be limited, and the demand for wholesale bespoke goods, if not actually declining in the future as the customer turns to ready-made goods, would appear unlikely to increase markedly. On the other hand, with any increase in variety and differentiation in men's clothing and the consequent emphasis on display, the existing multiple shop organizations are in a superior position to that of the independent retailer both in respect of sites and in respect of ability to control the wider range of stock, and some advance in the relative importance of these large-scale retailers would seem probable. Further, the multiple shop methods of trading may gain some ground at the expense of the small retail bespoke tailor as the trend of demand shifts slightly towards ready-made goods, and also at the expense of department stores. But the rate of advance of multiple shop retailing would appear almost certainly to be slower in the future than in past decades.

2. THE WOMEN'S AND GIRLS' CLOTHING TRADE

The slow development of factory or large-scale methods of production in the women's wear trade, the light clothing side of the industry, in the last quarter of the nineteenth and opening decades of the twentieth century, limited to some extent the changes made in these years in the structure of the retail trade. In contrast to the developments on the men's wear side of the trade the sales emphasis remained on goods and accessories for making up at home rather than on the sale of made-up or ready-made goods, and with the exception of the hosiery and knit-wear trade, where factory production was advancing, there was little or no trend towards standardization and simplification in the ranges of goods sold—if anything the reverse. In the retail organization of the women's wear trade, therefore, the character of demand encouraged general shops, which sold a very wide range of clothing goods, materials and accessories coming under the umbrella description of drapery, rather than specialist retailers. And with an increase in the consistency of demand for the goods making economies of scale possible the trend was in the direction of larger shops, that is department stores and to a lesser extent Co-operative stores, selling practically the whole range of goods required by the housewife, rather than towards multiple shop organization, of which a prerequisite was the production of and demand for relatively standardized goods. Further, with minor exceptions, the possibilities of large-scale integration of production and distribution were very limited.

In the years just prior to the First World War and in the inter-war years, a number of changes in the methods of organization of production and in the character of demand for women's wear combined to re-shape and transform the structure of this trade. Some of the trends of the earlier years were halted or reversed and new distributive forms emerged. A discussion of the developments of large-scale retailing in the women's wear trade in the hundred years from 1850 to 1950 can therefore be conveniently divided into two parts. First an account will be given of the main features of the trade up to 1914, and in this account particular emphasis will be placed on the rise and development of the most important form of large-scale retailing in these years, that is department stores. Secondly the period 1918–50 will be discussed, emphasis being given to the further progress of department stores and to the development of the other important form of large-scale retailing in this trade, that is multiple shop retailing.

The women's wear trade to 1914: the small-scale retailer

The methods of trading of the small-scale retailers of women's wear and drapery changed but little in the half-century before 1914. The general draper, with his main division between heavy drapery on the one hand and fancy goods on the other and purchasing the bulk of his supplies from wholesalers, remained the most familiar type of shop in the trade. In the larger towns the general draper was supplemented by specialists such as silk mercers, linen drapers, lace merchants, and at the top end of the trade by dressmakers and costumiers.

Towards the end of the nineteenth century and in the twentieth century there was some increase in this type of specialization. This was brought about by the growing demand for made-up goods, by the rise in the factory output of hosiery, knitted goods and made-up clothing in the decades before the First World War, and, in some areas, by the pressure of competition of the department stores. The drapers themselves began to concentrate their trade, in that the combination of wholesaling and retailing which was common in the middle of the nineteenth century disappeared and the firms specialized in one or the other. The number of shops specializing as hosiers, milliners, haberdashers, corsetières, modistes and mantle and gown shops began to increase in the medium- and large-sized towns, and with the growth of the middle classes in these areas the scope for bespoke dress and gown making grew. By and large, however, while specialization in types of shops had increased and the range of goods sold by the general drapers had widened with the inclusion of made-up goods, the main types of goods sold up to 1914 were piece goods and all the accessories for home clothes making, and the general draper was the main source of supply.

The Co-operative Societies

The sale of drapery by Retail Co-operative Societies was common at an early stage of their growth. Materials for the making of clothes and for home furnishing were the first need of the working-class housewife after food, and the Societies were pressed to supply that need. The Rochdale Pioneers Co-operative Society as early as 1847 is reported to have undertaken the sale of some drapery and in 1849 a decision was made to add the regular sale and display of plain drapery to the sale of groceries and provisions. Illustrative of the approach of the Co-operative Societies to the drapery trade in these years was the resolution of the Rochdale Society in 1849 on this subject, part of which read 'that they [the Society] should not provide a stock of fancy goods—"bobby-dazzlers"—to tempt working men's wives to indulge in unnecessary expense'.[1]

As the Co-operative movement grew in the last quarter of the nineteenth century and in the twentieth century, so the sales of drapery and women's wear increased, and this development was assisted by the centralized buying and productive activities of the Wholesale Societies. In 1874 the Co-operative Wholesale Society opened its first drapery warehouse, and in 1875 the Scottish Co-operative Wholesale Society followed suit. Travellers in drapery from the Wholesale Societies started visiting the Retail Societies, and additional show-rooms were opened at the end of the century in towns like Newcastle, London and Cardiff. In the early years the goods sold by the Wholesale Societies to the Retail Societies were purchased from private manufacturers, but in the 'nineties the Wholesale Societies started their own production of underwear, corsets, mantles and some piece goods. These were followed in the opening decade of the twentieth century by a new hosiery factory.

Most of the Retail Societies confined their sale of drapery to the

---

[1] P. Redfern, *The Story of the C.W.S.*, Manchester, 1913, p. 98.

central store, very little being sold by the smaller branches. Even in the central stores, while some Societies gave the drapery department adequate space for display many, partly for physical reasons and partly through lack of interest, hid the drapery and women's wear department away at the back of or over the grocery and provisions shop. The goods sold were for the most part dress materials and shirtings, mantles, underwear, corsets, aprons, pinafores and trimmings, and few Societies showed much boldness in the range of goods stocked. By the beginning of the twentieth century, while many Societies had gone beyond the range of plain drapery, the principle of not tempting the members with 'bobby dazzlers' continued to be followed. Up to the First World War at least the majority of the Retail Societies were content to supply their members with a relatively narrow range of women's wear and drapery, and only a handful of the Societies had attempted to develop their sales on department store lines.

The development of multiple shop retailing to 1914

The first multiple shop retailers in the women's and girls' wear trade appeared in the middle 'eighties, and by the middle 'nineties there were, according to existing records, some 5 firms operating more than 10 retail branches each. By far the largest of these was Fleming, Reid & Company Ltd., worsted spinners and hosiery manufacturers, of Greenock, who had opened their first retail branch in 1881. Growth was rapid and by 1890 they had over 50 retail branches and in 1895 over 75. At this date the firm, which specialized in the sale of knitting wools and hosiery, was the second largest multiple shop firm in the clothing trades as a whole, only Joseph Hepworth of Leeds, the men's outfitters, being larger. The other multiple shop firms in the women's wear trade were very small in comparison; among them were Dr Jaeger's Sanitary Woollen Company, which sold both men's and boys' wear, the Hosiery Manufacturing Company, the Nottingham Hosiery Company which also sold both men's and women's hosiery, the Provident Clothing and Supply Company, and Kendall & Company which sold umbrellas.

By 1900 there were 9 firms in existence with over 10 branches each and these 9 controlled in all 245 branches. By 1910 the number of firms had risen to 15 and the number of branches, including those of Kendall's, to 472. At this date Fleming, Reid's Scotch Wool and Hosiery Stores had over 200 branches, or more than two-thirds of the total number of women's wear multiple shop branches in existence if Kendall's is excluded. The next largest firm in 1910 was the Hosiery Manufacturing Company with about 40 branches. Among the small multiple shop firms that emerged just before the Second World War were some dealing in women's outer clothing and mantles, such as the London Drapery Stores, Goodson's Ltd., Style & Mantle Ltd. and Henry Dodgson Ltd. Most of the multiple shop firms, however, specialized in hosiery, underwear and knitted goods. Nearly four-fifths of the total number of branches of multiple shop organizations in the women's wear trade in the decade-and-a-half before 1914 were in fact engaged in the hosiery, knitwear and woollen goods side of the trade.

The largest of these firms were manufacturers as well as retailers and Fleming, Reid & Company undertook spinning and manufacturing as well as retailing. The growth of multiple shop retailing in hosiery was a reflection of the development of the factory system earlier in this industry than in other sections of the women's light clothing trade, the greater standardization of the product in hosiery and the rising demand for made-up hosiery products.[1] Integration of the production and distribution of the other types of goods sold in the women's wear trade, for example piece goods and accessories, was out of the question owing to the wide range of materials and qualities required, and there were no particular advantages in the multiple shop method of distribution of such goods. The branches of the multiple shop organizations in the pre-1914 years were for the most part very small. Further, as most of them were dependent on the products of one factory the range of goods stocked was not great. The prices charged were low, and the shops catered mainly for the working-class market.

The rise of the department stores

A brief account was given in an earlier chapter of the rise of department stores in Britain in the second half of the nineteenth century. Some detail can be added to that account here, but no attempt is made to tell the full story.[2] The rise and development of department stores are an important part of the history of retail trading in Britain and should one day receive the treatment they warrant, but here an outline of the main features of this form of trading in relation to the sales of women's and girls' wear must suffice.

At the outset of any discussion of department stores, problems of definition arise. The definition of a department store adopted in this

[1] Cf. Charles Booth, *Life and Labour of the People in London*, Second Series, Industry, 3, London, 1903, p. 80. 'The hosiery business is conducted on very different principles from those which govern the action and growth of drapers' establishments. Instead of increasing in size, adding shop to shop contiguously, and department to department, a hosier, if he enlarges his business, does so by taking another shop in a different district, and placing a manager in charge of it.'

[2] A part of the story is to be found in L. Neal, *Retailing and the Public*, London, 1932, and in the books and brochures on particular firms such as R. S. Lambert, *The Universal Provider, A Study of William Whiteley*, London, 1938, and *A Story of British Achievement, 1849–1949*, published by Harrods Ltd., 1950.

volume—a large retail store with 4 or more separate departments under one roof, each selling different classes of goods of which one is women's and children's wear—is fairly straightforward, but the application of the definition to conditions existing in the past is far from simple. Details of the past trading methods of individual stores that have subsequently gone out of existence or have lost their records are difficult to ascertain, and the exact dates when large shops moved from the category of, say, a large draper to that of a department store cannot be determined with accuracy in a number of instances. The account which follows, therefore, of the development of department store trading does not claim to give more than a general indication of the growth and characteristics of this form of retailing and, further, in the discussion of the earlier years of development a category of 'part department store' is introduced to suggest a large firm that had more than one retail department but would not appear to have reached the status of a full department store as defined above.

In the middle of the nineteenth century there would appear to have been no full department stores as defined above in existence in Great Britain, but some part department stores were already trading. Of these the most prominent was probably Shoolbred's which was founded in 1820, and there were a number of other large drapers that were increasing the range of the different types of goods sold. Among the latter may be mentioned George Hitchcock of the City of London, Swan & Edgar (founded in 1812), Dickins and Jones Ltd. (1803), Harvey's of Kensington (1820), Marshall & Snelgrove (1837), and Maple (1842), all of London, J. & W. Campbell (1817) and Anderson's Royal Polytechnic (1845) of Glasgow, and Duncan McLaren of Edinburgh.

Twenty-five years later in the 'seventies and 'eighties the first full department stores had appeared. These were of two types. First there were the firms, some mentioned above, which had been in existence for a quarter of a century or more and had gradually increased the range and number of departments operated, and secondly there were the firms which had grown very rapidly and within five years or so of foundation had planned and operated their sales on a departmental basis. Of the former type of firm the most prominent in the 'eighties were Shoolbred's, Ponting Brothers, Maple's, Harrods (founded in 1849) Marshall & Snelgrove, John Barker, Spencer, Turner and Boldero (1840), Debenhams (1778) and Anderson's Royal Polytechnic. Of the second type of firm the most prominent were William Whiteley's which was founded in 1863 and within four years had 10 separate departments, the Civil Service Supply Association Ltd. founded in 1866, and the Army and Navy Co-operative Society Ltd. founded in 1871. The two last-named organizations started business on a Co-operative basis and within a few years of foundation were supplying a wide range of foodstuffs, clothing and household goods to their customers. The difference between these firms and the ordinary type of Co-operative Society discussed above was that membership was originally limited to certain classes of person, in the former case Post Office employees and in the latter Army and Navy officers, and the trading profits of the firms were paid out in relation to shares held in the form of dividends.

In addition to these full department stores in the eighteen-seventies and eighties there were a large number of part department stores. Among these, in addition to the firms already mentioned, were firms such as Lewis's Ltd., Edwin Jones, John Lewis, Jays, Robinsons, Harvey Nicholls, Bentalls, Meekins, Tarns, Atkinsons, Owens, the West Kensington Stores and Gamages, all in London, Kendal Milne of Manchester, Browns of Chester, and Walter Wilson and Wylie & Lochhead in Scotland.

The success of the leading department stores, the publicity attaching to their success, and the willingness of the public to invest money in such undertakings, led to a spectacular increase in the number of full department stores in the last decade of the nineteenth century and the first decade of the twentieth. The great majority of the firms emerging as department stores in these years were of the first type mentioned above, namely old and well-established shops utilizing in a great number of cases additional capital, raised on the open market as public limited liability companies, to enlarge their physical size and the range of goods stocked. The list of firms developing in these years is too long to give in full, but Bon Marché Ltd., Bobby & Company Ltd., Plummer Roddis Ltd., Liberty & Company., McIlroy Ltd., Jones of Holloway, Robinson & Cleaver Ltd., Jones & Higgins Ltd., Gorringe Ltd., J. R. Robert's Stores Ltd. and T. R. Roberts Ltd. may be mentioned. In addition to the growth of stores in the large towns like London, Manchester and Glasgow, smaller units were arising in other provincial towns such as Southport, Cheltenham, Bath, Reading and Sheffield. To complete this phase of growth, Gordon Selfridge in 1909 started building his mammoth and fully-equipped modern department store in Oxford Street. In so far as quantitative estimates of numbers are possible there would appear to have been 150–200 full department stores in existence in Great Britain in 1910, of which about one-third were public limited liability companies. The total retail turnover of these stores in all types of goods is estimated at some £20 millions. This may be compared with a total retail turnover of Co-operative Societies in the same year of approximately £72 millions.

The trading methods of department stores

The methods of organization and the trading practices of these stores naturally varied widely between individual firms, but there were certain characteristics that were common to a great number of them. The common characteristics may be briefly discussed in order to present a general picture of the trading methods of the stores, though it should be borne in mind that there were many exceptions to these generalizations.

The majority of the department stores had a drapery background and developed their women's wear, drapery and furnishing departments first.[1] As these departments were successful, special departments within the women's wear trade were started, for example by the separation of outerwear from underwear, footwear from clothing, and ribbons, millinery and haberdashery from piece goods. Toilet and chemists' goods departments frequently followed. Further expansion took varied forms according to the location of the shop, the practice of near competitors and the interests of the founders. Some added furniture and hardware departments, others added separate departments for men's and boys' wear, and yet others introduced groceries and food. There appeared to be no limit to the number of separate departments that the stores would establish provided there was physical space for such growth, and a firm like William Whiteley's could claim thirty different departments at the turn of the century. Despite this increase in the number of departments, however, the stores continued to place women's and children's wear and drapery in the foreground and, taking together all stores in existence before 1914, these goods represented some two-thirds to three-quarters of their total turnover.

A trading characteristic of most of the stores, particularly in the formative years in the second half of the nineteenth century, was their emphasis on cheapness and open pricing. The multiple shop firms and the Co-operative stores had led the way in the working-class market in ending the traditional practice of chaffering, haggling or prigging between the sales assistant and the customer regarding the price of the article to be sold. The department stores were among the first retailers to limit this practice in the middle-class market. The example of some stores in using clear open pricing was rapidly followed by others and, with definite pricing, catalogues and advertisements became more effective and were more frequently used to attract customers.

The prices charged of course varied with the store and with the quality of the goods, but many of the stores in the 'seventies and

---

[1] A notable exception to this rule was Harrods. This firm started as a grocery and provisions dealer and widened its range via perfumes, patent medicines, stationery, fruit and vegetables and china before extending to women's wear and drapery.

'eighties had a reputation for cheapness and for selling at a penny off the price of a yard of ribbon or lace, or a few shillings off the price of a gown or cloak. In those instances where the prices charged could be directly measured against those of other retailers, for example groceries and provisions or chemists' goods and toilet preparations, the differences were sufficiently great for the cry of 'price cutting' to be raised against the stores. The small retailers, particularly in the London area, expressed themselves vehemently on the pricing policies of the 'giant emporia'.

By the opening decade of the twentieth century, however, while the policy of clearly pricing the goods had been maintained and extended, some of the earlier emphasis on low prices had disappeared. Firms which had been wavering in the 'seventies and 'eighties as to the class of market for which to cater had finally made up their minds that the growing middle classes of the larger towns were the customers most likely to be attracted by their wide range of goods. And by the beginning of the century the majority of the department stores could be said to be catering for the middle- and upper-class market where quality and service were more important than a reduction in price of the odd penny or the odd shilling. The rising overhead costs caused by the growing elaborateness of the buildings and of the services provided was a further factor discouraging a low price policy. A few of the stores, especially those in the provincial towns, appealed to a slightly lower price market than the stores in central shopping districts, but no stores could be said to be primarily concerned with the working-class market in the way that the early multiple shop organizations were.

The weakening of the attraction of low prices was, however, more than compensated for by the development of other features, in particular the wide range of goods stocked by the stores and the extensive services provided. Some firms claimed they would sell practically anything from a pin to an elephant, but more effective and important in the case of women's and children's wear was the reputation the stores acquired for having a wide selection and range in the lines stocked. In piece goods and dress materials, whether silks, cottons, muslins, woollens or lace, in clothing such as dresses, cloaks, and pinafores, and in haberdashery, ribbons, trimmings and fancy goods the department stores in their different sections carried a far wider range than ever would be stocked by an individual draper.

To this attraction of the range of goods stocked were added pleasant shopping conditions. Remarkable changes were made in the physical structure and size of the stores in the forty years before 1914, and all these changes were directed towards increasing the range of goods stocked, utilizing the whole of a given building for sales and not merely the ground floors adjoining the street, and providing additional amenities and services for the customers. Some idea of the growth in size of the stores can be obtained from the figures of employment. In the 'eighties Whiteley's was the largest store, with nearly 2,000 employees, but others were growing rapidly. For example, the number employed by Shoolbred's, John Barker, Spencer, Turner and Boldero, and Harrods was over 500 and approaching 1,000, and Debenhams, Marshall & Snelgrove and Jones of Holloway, to mention only a few, had some 500 employees each. These firms enlarged their premises, acquired leases of adjacent property, and built and rebuilt; and more and more attractive stores emerged. Lifts and moving staircases were installed to encourage and enable customers to visit the upper floors. Restaurants and tea rooms came to be a noted feature of most of the larger stores and added to the pleasantness of a shopping expedition, and even rest-rooms and writing-rooms were introduced by some of the largest stores. Each development meant an increase in employment, and by 1900 there were some dozen firms with 1,000 or more employees each. By the First World War the employment by the two giant stores, Harrods and Whiteley's, had risen to approximately 6,000 and 4,000 respectively. Not all these employees were engaged on retail selling. A half, and in some instances more, were employed on other activities, for example in maintenance sections, in workrooms, in the growing accounts departments, handling customers' credit orders, and in the transport section which arranged home delivery of the customers' purchases. As department stores grew in size and as the services provided to the customers developed, a large accounting department, kitchen staff and waitresses and a fleet of vans and drivers became as essential to their success as trained sales assistants.

Finally, to these advantages of a wide range of goods, of amenities, of services, and of the convenience of purchasing, in an era of home dressmaking, all requirements under one roof, Gordon Selfridge added the 'freedom of the stores'. In place of the implied obligation on all persons entering a retail establishment to make a purchase or at least give a reason for not making one, Gordon Selfridge in his new store allowed and encouraged shoppers to walk freely in, about and out of his store without being subject to the slightest pressure to make a purchase.

By 1914, therefore, in the space of some three or four decades, the department store method of trading had become well established in the women's wear trade in the largest towns of the United Kingdom and had overshadowed the growth of the other forms of large-scale retailing, the multiple shop and Co-operative Society, in this trade. The bulk of the trade still remained in the hands of the small-scale retailers, the drapers, the hosiers, the milliners and the haberdashers, but the outstanding development in the structure of the trade had been the rise of department stores.

The most important features of the department store method of trading were the provision of an additional range of goods to increase the volume of purchases of existing customers and the attraction of new customers from over a wider area. Achievement of the second aim was partly dependent on the existence of cheap and easy transport facilities, and as the horse-drawn and later motor-driven buses and trams appeared on the streets of the larger towns and the underground railway network in London spread—the first Underground Railway was opened in 1863—so the problem of distance was overcome. Once travelling had become relatively easy, the attractions of shopping in department stores that have been described above secured the additional customers. But the rise of this form of large-scale retailing was not so dependent as in the case of other forms on the existence of large-scale manufacture and the sale of standardized goods. The department stores in a great many instances cut out one link in the chain of distribution by buying directly from producers at home and overseas, but the stores bought as readily from small-scale units as from large-scale units and diversity and individuality in the products, rather than standardization, was encouraged. Finally the particular characteristics of the department stores that emerged in these years, that is the stress on amenities, on services and on choice and variety rather than on price, were influenced directly by the growth of the middle classes. The womenfolk of these classes had the leisure time for shopping in central districts and had the purchasing power to allow of discrimination as to quality and taste, and the department stores adapted their organizational and trading policies to meet this demand.

The changes in the trade, 1914–1950

Between 1914 and 1950 some major changes took place in the women's and girls' wear trade, changes which were to modify considerably the retail trade structure existing before 1914. Cause and effect in these changes are hard to distinguish, but three main developments can be delineated. First there was a marked increase in the importance and in the incidence of fashion in the trade. The most dramatic of these changes was the arrival of shorter skirts, and it is estimated that between 1913 and 1925 the material needed for a woman's complete outfit was reduced from over 20 yards to under 10 yards. But the spread of the fashion element was of significance not quite so much in regard to the rapidity or character of fashion changes themselves as in the wide range and scope of the repercussions of such changes of fashion as did occur. These were reflected not only in the growth of 'dress conscious-ness' among very wide sections of the female population, but also in the influence of fashion on underclothing, lingerie, corsets and stockings as well as outer clothing. Further, the increased attention to dress led to a multiplication of the number of styles of a given fashion, as women began to regard identical outer clothing with horror, and to an increase in the number of stock sizes, as matters such as good cut and fit received more emphasis.

The second major development was the shift in demand from piece goods for making up at home to ready-to-wear garments. This applied to both outerwear and underwear, and it was influenced by, and in its turn encouraged, the development of large-scale factory production of women's and girls' outerwear and light clothing of all descriptions. An illustration of the change in demand that took place is given by a com-parison of the figures in the first Cost of Living Index, based on working-class household budgets of 1904, with those of the 1937–38 working-class cost of living inquiry. The former Index gave a large allowance for piece goods, but very little for expenditure on women's and children's clothing and underclothing, the presumption being, apparently, that in 1904 working-class women made most of their own and their children's clothes. In the 1937–38 analysis of expenditure the allowance for piece goods was reduced by nearly 70 % and that for women's and children's clothing increased by nearly 1000 %.[1]

A third development in these years was the introduction of new materials. The rayon or artificial silk industry, which was in its infancy in the pre-1914 years, grew rapidly in the inter-war years, particularly after 1930. The women's hosiery industry was practically revolutionized by the production of artificial silk and rayon stockings in the late 'twenties and 'thirties, in place of the cotton and wool stockings of the early 'twenties and the pre-1914 era. Similarly the output of rayon underclothing trebled in the years 1930–35, whereas the output of the traditional woollen underclothing remained practically stationary between 1924 and 1935. Rayon was also used for outer clothing, such as blouses, and at the same time the wool industry began to produce lighter-weight fabrics for outer clothing. The varieties of cloth of all types that were available were immensely increased and a big expansion in the dyeing industry took place. One of the features of the introduction of the new materials was the tendency for price to fall as output increased in the years up to 1938. This in its turn stimulated demand and led to an increase in the demand for clothes and in the stocks of clothing held by women in their homes. During and after the Second World War yet

[1] This comparison is made in the Board of Trade *Working Party Report on Light Clothing*, 1947, p. 10.

another new fabric appeared, nylon, which began to lead to further changes in demand, but up to 1950 at least the supplies of this material were not sufficiently great and its price was too high to have a major influence on the trade.

This brief summary of the main changes in fashion and in consumer demand, in the methods of production and in the materials used in the women's wear trade in the three decades after the First World War, is far from complete. But while many gaps are left the account does provide a background in which the developments in the retail organization of the trade in these years can be discussed. Again, it is convenient to treat the different economic types of retailer separately, and after the main trends that emerged in the years 1918–50 have been outlined some estimates will be given of the relative importance and the shifts in importance of the different types of retailer in the total retail trade in women's and girls' wear in these years.

The small-scale retailer

The changes in the character of the trade in the years following the First World War influenced the small-scale retailer in many different ways. The decline in the demand for piece goods and for accessories for making clothes at home, coupled with the increased output of made-up goods, led to changes in the type of goods stocked by the drapers and also to an increase in the number of small-scale specialist retailers. These specialists, for example the dealers who concentrated on the sale of blouses and skirts, of lingerie, corsets and foundation garments, of gowns and dresses, and of knitting wools and baby clothes, were rarely found in the rural areas and country towns, but in the busier shopping districts of the larger towns they sometimes supplanted the traditional type of draper.

The small retail bespoke dressmaker, on the other hand, survived and may have increased in numbers. Capital requirements in this trade were small, little more being required than a cutting-out and making-up room, and sewing machines, which could be hired or purchased on an easy payments system. With such low overheads the small retail bespoke dressmaker or gown shop could compete with the larger-scale factory production and in many ways could more easily make adjustments to keep abreast of the changes in fashion.

A further factor affecting the position of the small-scale retailer was the growth of branding, particularly of hosiery. As against only one-fifth of the goods branded in 1914 it is estimated that some four-fifths of hosiery goods were branded at the end of the inter-war years.[1] Branding,

[1] *Studies in Industrial Organization*, edited by H. A. Silverman, London, 1946, p. 29.

combined with a measure of manufacturer-advertising, strengthened the position of the small-scale retailer in that the customer wishing to purchase a particular brand knew she could get exactly the same article at the local draper's or hosiery shop as in the department stores or multiple shop, and the local draper's was usually the more convenient shopping point.

The growth of branding, the increase in the output of factory-made women's clothing, and the more frequent purchases of clothing by women also had the effect of encouraging entry into the trade. In the same way as the idea of setting up a tobacconist/confectioner's shop proved attractive to many men, so the idea of setting up a small women's wear shop proved attractive to many women in the inter-war years. The detailed knowledge and experience required to run a dress, lingerie, blouse, or stocking shop in the inter-war years was far less than that required to run a draper's shop in the pre-1914 years. Credit and assistance from wholesalers in the early stages was easy to obtain, and the touch of personal service provided by such shops was attractive to customers. Such shops, known in the trade as 'Madam shops', were often very small with perhaps only one person serving, but the windows were usually well dressed and, more and more in this trade, display was becoming an important factor in success. This type of retailer was more prominent in the South of England than in the North, but was to be found in most suburbs of the larger towns.

An impetus of a different kind was given to certain small-scale retailers by the growth of club or check trading. This movement, which was more widespread in the North than in the South of England, flourished in the periods of heavy unemployment and for many families provided the only method of affording new clothes. Some multiple shop firms were prominent in this form of trading, for example the Provident Clothing and Supply Company Ltd., and other large firms, for example Great Universal Stores Ltd., operated the system by means of agents or collectors and mail order delivery rather than through fixed shops; but the majority of the retailers taking part in such schemes were small-scale retailers.

The high-class end of the trade, the couturiers and model houses, remained in the hands of the small-scale retailers. And in addition the bespoke private dressmaker, operating from a house rather than a shop, continued to make both outerwear and underwear for numbers of women.

The small-scale retailer certainly lost ground in the women's wear trade in these years to forms of large-scale retailing. As will be shown later the advance of multiple shop retailing from the 'thirties onwards was particularly rapid. The growing emphasis on display and fashion told against the small-scale retailer who did not possess the capital to establish main street shopping sites or to carry a wide range of stock. On the other hand the small-scale retailers showed ability to adapt their trading methods to changes in consumer demand and the individual nature of demand provided scope for the flexible small-scale unit.

The Co-operative Societies

The developments in the methods of Co-operative retailing in the women's wear trade between 1918 and 1950 were relatively few. The number of Co-operative outlets for these goods increased with the spread in the movement and the increase in membership. In 1937–38, for example, just over 2,000 Co-operative drapery shops were in existence and the proportion of the total membership represented by members in Societies having drapery departments was 97 %, a coverage second only to that of groceries and provisions. In other words, virtually all members of Co-operative Societies were able, if they so wished, to purchase women's and girls' wear and drapery from their local Society. Co-operative production of women's and children's wear increased with the general trend towards factory production of these goods, though the Retail Societies did not confine their sales of drapery and women's wear to goods produced within the movement. The Societies also, buying through the Wholesale Societies, sold the goods of private manufacturers.

The main characteristics of Co-operative retail trade in drapery and women's wear, however, remained little changed from those of the pre-1914 years. While practically all Retail Societies in the inter-war years sold drapery and women's wear, in the majority of instances the Co-operative drapery branches were not in commanding shopping sites. In the plans and layout of the retail shops, including the larger central stores, groceries and provisions tended to come first and drapery was left with second and sometimes third choice. There were some exceptions to this, and the department stores that were built by the larger Societies in these years gave full emphasis to drapery and women's wear, but the majority of the Societies only slowly grasped the importance of 'shopping' display in these goods. Similarly, in the range of goods stocked the Co-operative Societies remained conservative. The range was very much greater than in the pre-1914 years, and the Wholesale Societies by continuing their policy of opening large regional showrooms for the buyers from Retail Societies assisted in the widening of range. But the changes in fashion, in taste and in materials in the trade as a whole were equally great, and the Co-operative Societies tended in styling and fashion to lag behind the specialist shops, the multiple shop branches and the department stores. Cautiousness in buying was one factor leading to this lag, the suspicion of the 'bobby-dazzler' was not yet dead, and the lack of effective display space limited the scope of the buyers, but equally important was the inability or disinclination of many Societies to employ women's wear specialist buyers and to have their drapery and women's wear departments run by experts in this field. Until the late 'thirties graduation to positions of importance on the women's wear side was by way of the grocery departments in a number of Societies. A vicious circle was developing in that the turnover in women's wear and drapery of many Societies was too small to permit the employment of specialists, while without the employment of specialists there was little hope of turnover rising.

Similar problems faced the productive units of the Wholesale Societies in this field. Specialization of the factories in particular sections of the women's wear trade was late in developing. The policy in the pre-1914 years had been to establish general clothing factories and there was a tendency to add further lines of women's clothing to the range produced by existing factories rather than face the problems and risks of new specialized units. In the 'thirties, however, some changes were being made in this policy. The Co-operative factories also had the problem of serving a specialized market. While private manufacturers could produce for different price and income markets and follow a success in a higher-class market by mass production for a lower-class market, the appeal of the Retail Societies was to practically identical income groups throughout the country. This tended to limit the experiments and reduce the flexibility of the Co-operative factories.

The growing emphasis which was being placed by some Societies on the 'dry goods' trade in the 'thirties, and the development of a measure of specialization in buying, selling and display of the goods, were delayed in the Second World War by clothes rationing, shortage of manpower, and inability to build or undertake structural alterations. In the postwar years the threads were re-gathered and some Societies, notably the London Society, made significant progress in its sales of women's wear. By and large, however, the Co-operative drapery departments attracted only the confirmed Co-operator, the women who was satisfied with the quality of Co-operative goods, who was attracted by the dividend, and who wished to buy staple lines such as piece goods, blouses, stockings, skirts, underwear and nightwear. The system of mutuality trading, a form of credit trading, was of considerable importance particularly in the case of Societies in the Midlands and South of England in encouraging such purchases. But the members would often purchase articles in which the fashion element was of greater significance at other retail shops and stores. The Co-operative Retail Societies made no effort to cater for the high fashion trade and they had not succeeded by 1950 in penetrating very far into the middle fashion trade. The younger women seeking new styles and varieties of relatively low-priced jumpers, blouses, skirts and fancy lingerie rarely entered Co-operative stores.

The multiple shop retailers

A general picture of the development of multiple shop retailing in the women's wear trade is given by the estimates relating to the number of multiple shop organizations in existence in different years and the total number of branches controlled by these firms. These estimates are presented in Table 64 for the years 1910–50.

Groups of department stores under the control of one firm, and variety chain stores, are excluded from these estimates. An attempt has been made to include in this table details of firms which have gone out of existence or have amalgamated with other concerns, as well as of those trading independently in 1950. Altogether data relating to some 40 firms have been included in this table, and of the 12 firms which were no longer in existence in 1950 5 were amalgamated with other firms and the remaining 7 appear to have ceased trading.

Table 64. *Estimates of the number of multiple shop firms and branches in the women's and girls' wear trade, 1910–50*

Year	10–24 branches		25–49 branches		50–99 branches		100 or more branches		Totals			
									10 or more branches		25 or more branches	
	Number of		Number of		Number of		Number of		Number of		Number of	
	Firms	Branches	Firms	Branches	Firms	Branches	Firms	Branches	Firms	Branches	Firms	Branches
1910	12	170	1	39	1	53	1	210	15	472	3	302
1920	9	125	4	129	1	65	1	270	15	589	6	464
1925	13	168	4	118	2	130	1	309	20	725	7	557
1930	12	180	4	128	4	296	1	342	21	946	9	766
1935	10	136	8	273	5	389	1	371	24	1,169	14	1,033
1939	11	141	7	243	7	507	2	521	27	1,412	16	1,271
1950	14	202	3	109	7	488	4	740	28	1,539	14	1,337

The estimates in Table 64 can be used to give a general indication of the rate of growth of multiple shop trading as measured by the number of branches in existence in different years. This analysis is made in Table 65, which shows the net increase in the number of branches in existence in different years, the percentage rate of net increase, and the average yearly net increase in the number of branches at five-yearly intervals (except for the 1939–50 period). The use of the number of branches in existence is not an entirely satisfactory method of showing growth, as the size of branches varies over time. In this trade there was a marked increase in the average size of branches in the period 1930–50 arising from the growth of multiple shop firms specializing in the women's outerwear trade.

Table 65. *Rate of net increase in the number of branches of multiple shop firms in the women's and girls' wear trade, 1906–50*

Year	Branches of firms with 10 or more branches			Branches of firms with 25 or more branches		
	Net increase in number of branches	Percentage net increase	Average yearly net increase in numbers	Net increase in number of branches	Percentage net increase	Average yearly net increase in numbers
1906–1910	130	38	26	75	33	15
1911–1915	71	15	14	89	29	18
1916–1920	46	8	9	73	19	15
1921–1925	136	23	27	93	20	19
1926–1930	221	30	44	209	38	42
1931–1935	223	24	45	267	35	53
1936–1939	243	21	61	238	23	59
1940–1950	127	9	11	66	5	6

The pattern of growth suggested by the estimates in Table 65 is one of a steady increase in the years just before the First World War, when the net increase in the number of branches in existence averaged about one per fortnight. There was a sharp decline in activity in the war years, followed by a slow climb back to the pre-war rate of growth in 1921–25. From 1926 to the start of the Second World War the rate of increase was sustained and throughout these fourteen years there was an average net addition of one branch per week. The depression years would not appear to have had any marked influence on the rate of increase. During the Second World War, owing to shortages, clothes rationing and enemy action, many organizations had to close some of their branches. Some of these were re-opened in the post-war years, and other firms began to open new branches, so that by 1950 there was a slight increase in the number of branches in existence over the 1939 total.

The growth of multiple shop retailing in this trade was distinguished from the growth in a number of other trades by the rise of a number of medium-sized firms and a decrease in the proportion of the total number of branches controlled by the largest firms. In 1920, for example, the two largest firms controlled some 57 % of the total number of branches in existence, but by 1950 they controlled only 35 %. In other words, while the increase in the number of multiple shop firms engaged in the trade was not very great, the small and medium-sized firms increased their number of branches at a faster rate than the large-sized firms. Another feature was the relative absence of amalgamations or mergers between medium or large-sized firms. The amalgamations that did occur took the form of a larger firm acquiring a very small group of multiple shop branches.

The estimates presented in Tables 65 and 66 relate to all types of specialist multiple shop organizations in the women's wear trade. There was, however, an important difference between the rates of growth of the firms specializing in the hosiery and underwear trade and of those specializing in outerwear. In the decade before 1914 some four-fifths of the total number of multiple shop branches in existence were those of firms specializing on the hosiery and knitwear side of the trade. In the years 1920–50 a marked change took place. If shops specializing in the sale of blouses, jumpers, skirts and underwear are included with those selling hosiery, knitwear and woollen goods, the proportion of the total number of branches belonging to firms specializing on this side of the trade in 1920 was 65–70%, the number of branches that belonged to firms which specialized in outerwear, including dresses, jackets, suits, top-coats and furs, was 20–25%, and the remaining branches belonged to firms selling chiefly drapery goods, cotton goods and accessories such as umbrellas. By 1930 the proportions had changed so that 50–55% of the branches were selling hosiery and underwear and 30–35% outerwear of various descriptions. In 1939 the proportions were 48–52% hosiery and underwear and 35–40% outerwear, and in 1950 43–47% hosiery and underwear and 48–52% outerwear. Between 1930 and 1950 the increase in the number of branches of multiple shop organizations selling hosiery and underwear was of the order of 38%, while the increase in the number of branches selling outerwear was of the order of 150%. The development of multiple shop trading in the women's wear trade between 1920 and 1950 was therefore due in a large part to the successful introduction of this method of retailing into the women's outerwear trade. Nearly two-thirds of the total net additions to the number of multiple shop branches in these years was represented by branches selling outerwear.

There was, of course, some overlap between these two main types of firms in that some hosiery and underwear specialists sold a limited range of outerwear, for example dresses and skirts, and in the same way firms selling mainly outerwear also invariably sold some underwear. Between 1920 and 1950, in fact, the trend of the multiple shop firms was away from exclusive specialization in one type of goods such as stockings or dresses and towards a widening of the range of goods carried. But the broad distinction made above between the hosiery, knitwear and

22-2

underwear specialists on the one hand and the outer clothing specialists on the other remained fairly clear.

The leading multiple shop firms on the hosiery, knitted goods, woollen goods and underclothing side of the trade in these years were Fleming, Reid, which had nearly 400 branches in 1950, and Dorothy Perkins Ltd., Etam Ltd., and the Hosiery Manufacturing Company Ltd., which each had between 50 and 100 branches at this date. On the outerwear side of the trade the leading firms were Morrisons Associated Companies Ltd., the Swears and Wells group, and Willsons (London & Provinces) Ltd., each of which had 100 or more branches in 1950, and the Provident Clothing and Supply Company Ltd., Kendall Ltd., Barnett-Hutton Ltd., and Richard Shops Ltd., which had between 50 and 100 branches each.

As the type of goods sold differed, so to some extent did the structure and trading policies of the multiple shop organizations on the different sides of the trade. Most of the organizations specializing in the sale of hosiery and underwear in the 'twenties undertook some manufacturing as well as retailing. With the increase in the range of goods stocked by these shops, and as new materials—rayon and, later, nylon—appeared, the importance of integration decreased, but in 1950 about one-half of the goods sold by the older and larger firms on this side of the trade were products of their own factories. At the same time, however, a number of the newer and smaller firms which were emerging in the 'thirties and which specialized in selling a wide range of underwear, foundation garments and hosiery were retailers only.

The trading methods of the multiple shop retailers

The branches of these hosiery and underwear multiple shop firms were almost all situated in the main streets of towns or in main shopping districts of the suburbs of larger towns. This was particularly true of the newer multiple firms coming into the trade in the inter-war years, and these firms set a very high standard of window dressing, lighting, and clean, attractive shops. A prominent site and skilled display of the goods had become important factors in success. The size of the branches varied between firms and districts, but for the most part they were medium to small with employment per branch ranging between 4 and 9 persons. The firms for the most part emphasized cheapness in their pricing policies, small but frequent purchases were the aim, and they catered for the working-class and lower-middle-class markets. A few, however, built up a reputation in the higher-price market.

In the case of the multiple shop firms which specialized in the sale of outerwear, manufacturing, with the exception of the firms dealing mainly in furs and fur garments, was of only limited importance. While most of the firms possessed manufacturing facilities, the output of the factories represented only a small proportion, 10 % or at most 15 %, of total sales. The bulk of the goods sold were bought direct from manufacturers who produced special ranges and types of goods against the large orders placed by the multiple shop retailers. The goods sold by these retailers were mainly dresses, suits, jackets, top-coats, rainwear and skirts, and while minor alterations would be made the emphasis of the sale was on 'ready-to-wear'. The features of the trading methods of the organizations were the stress on window display and the up-to-date fashion of the goods sold. The shops were all on main street sites and were usually larger than those of the hosiery and underwear specialists, the average employment per branch being between 10 and 16 persons. Pricing policies varied, but the leading firms built their reputations on stocking an attractive selection of good-quality articles at a medium to low price.

Very few multiple shop retailing organizations developed in the drapery trade as such. While there were a number of firms with 2–5 branches each that sold mainly general drapery, only 2 firms specializing in these goods had more than 10 branches each. The variety of lines that the public expected the draper to stock was too great to allow of any important advantages being secured by multiple shop trading methods by way of bulk buying or rapid stock turn, and the control of stock in a large number of scattered branches would have been a tremendous problem. This side of the trade remained in the hands of the small-scale retailer, making his purchases from wholesalers, and of the department stores.

The relatively rapid increase in the number of multiple shop organizations and branches in the women's wear trade in the inter-war years, particularly after 1925, was due to the success of these units in taking advantage of the changes in production and demand conditions in the trade to develop new methods of retailing. The multiple shop organizations were among the first to offer consumers such goods as fully-fashioned stockings, rayon underclothing and a wide selection of low-priced and fashionable ready-to-wear outer clothing in stock sizes and not requiring fitting and alterations. The factors of importance on the underwear and hosiery side of the trade were the control of manufacturing facilities and, in the 'thirties, the ability of multiple shop firms—arising from economies in buying and careful attention to stock control—to offer a wide selection of fashionable and inexpensive underclothes, hosiery and knitwear displayed in an effective manner. On the outerwear side of the trade the particular achievement of the multiple shop firms was that of bringing well-cut and fashionable dresses, skirts, jackets and coats within the range of working-class and lower-middle-class incomes. Economies in buying were obtained by purchasing large quantities of goods in predetermined styles, ranges of colour and sizes direct from the manufacturers; and the employment of specialist buyers limited to some extent the risks involved in fashion changes. Further, variations in demand between different areas could be met by shifting stock between branches. Multiple shop retailers in the women's outer-wear trade were in fact the natural complement of the growth of standardized larger-scale production of these goods, and the multiple shop organizations had the advantage over the small-scale retailer who purchased through a wholesaler in that they had a clearer picture of the main types of demand in relation to size, were more sensitive to the changing pattern of consumer taste, and were in a much better position to translate these changes into new styles, colours, cuts and sizes through their close contact with suppliers.

The variety chain stores

Apart from the growth of specialist multiple shop organizations in the women's wear trade, the inter-war years also witnessed a spectacular rise of variety chain store trading in these goods. These firms, which had played no part in the trade in 1920 and a relatively minor role in 1930, became an important channel of distribution for goods such as under-wear, hosiery, dresses and some haberdashery items in the middle and late 'thirties; and after a period of stability during the Second World War their share of the trade increased still further in the years 1946-50. In a relatively short period of trading the variety chain stores had become, just before the Second World War, a more important outlet, measured by value of sales, for underwear and hosiery than the specialist women's wear multiple shop organizations, and in the post-war years the turnover of variety chain stores in outerwear, skirts, jackets, dresses and coats was beginning to approach that of the specialist multiple shop firms in this field.

The rapid increase in the importance of variety chain stores in this trade was influenced by the same general factors as those discussed above in relation to the specialist multiple shop firms. But to these factors were added, in the case of variety chain stores, the special advantages of their buying techniques and their low distribution costs. These two were combined to provide the public with good quality articles at very low prices. The buying techniques used involved close contact by the companies with the suppliers, arrangements for goods to be made to their own specifications, and the planning of their buying policy so as to keep their suppliers busy in out-of-season periods. An important factor in the buying and ordering policies was the consistent attempt, based on careful observations of demand, to narrow down the

number of different sizes and fittings, thus speeding up both the production process and the overall rate of stock turn in the branches. The
low distributive costs of these firms arose from the elimination of
practically all the usual services that were provided for customers in
this trade by way of fitting-rooms, alterations and personal attention,
so that the customer served herself. Further, a careful watch was kept
on the rate of stock turn and sales of different types of goods to ensure,
by immediate shifts and replacement of stock where necessary, a very
high rate of sales per square foot of selling space. While some other
multiple shop organizations in the women's wear trade followed slightly
similar policies in regard to buying and placing orders with suppliers
for stock styles and sizes, no other firms went to the same lengths as the
variety chain stores in planning production nearly to the last detail of
size, style and shade and in selling the articles on practically self-
service lines.

The success of these methods in some lines of goods led to other
articles being introduced, and between 1930 and 1950 not only had
the variety chain stores increased greatly the range of women's and
girls' clothing sold but also, without affecting materially the policy of
keeping to the low-price market, a considerable improvement in the
quality, cut and style of the goods sold had taken place. The limiting
factor in relation to the sale of fashion goods such as outer clothing was
the fear of almost all women of being found wearing a dress or coat
identical to that of their neighbour. This problem, of course, also faced
the multiple shop firms specializing in outerwear, though it was less
serious in their case as the sales of an identical style and colour by
a branch of the latter type of firm in a given area were very much fewer
than those made by a variety chain store branch. Nevertheless while
the problem, in theory at least, existed, tens of thousands of women
decided to take the risk.

The development of department store trading, 1914–1950

In many ways the First World War represented a watershed in the
history of department stores in the United Kingdom. The late Victorian
and Edwardian emphasis on continuous growth in size, in the range
of departments and in the number of services provided, for example,
was not carried over to the inter-war years to any significant extent.
Many firms, of course, increased in size and range, and many new
buildings were erected, but the pattern of what a department store
should be had been established in the pre-1914 years and there was no
fundamental change in the inter-war years in the outlines of this
pattern. To take size, for example, the 4,000–6,000 employees of
William Whiteley and Harrods in the pre-1914 years were not seriously

exceeded. In services, many refinements were introduced, but the basic services of a wide choice of goods and of different types of goods under one roof, of comfortable and pleasant shopping conditions, and in many instances of free credit and delivery services, were not surpassed. Similarly in trading practice and methods, while important strides were made in window dressing and display and interior layout, in techniques of control of stock, of manpower and of selling space, and in the organization of mark-downs and 'sales', no fundamental changes were made by the majority of the stores in regard to methods of buying, relationships with producers, or pricing policy.

There was extensive development in department store trading, even if, as suggested above, there was little intensive change. Whereas in 1914 department stores were well-established in the centres of large towns, and particularly in London, by the Second World War there had been a considerable increase in the number of department stores situated in the medium-sized provincial towns and in the suburbs of the larger towns. These newer department stores were relatively small in size, employment rarely climbing to over 500. In most instances they grew, as did the older stores, out of drapery or furnishing shops, though many were planned and built by firms as department stores without there being any previous trading tradition on the site. The development of provincial and suburban department stores was a reflection of the attractiveness of this method of trading, of the growth of urbanization, and of the increasing difficulties in a very large town of making frequent journeys to central shopping districts.

By 1950 the number of department stores in the United Kingdom, using the definition given above of firms with 4 or more separate departments, had risen to approximately 475–525. The number of stores in the provinces would appear to have increased rather more rapidly than the number of stores in the Greater London area, though in 1950 about one-fifth of the total number of stores, including some of the largest, were located in this area. Further, taking the country as a whole, the number of department stores in relation to population would appear to have been greater in London, the Midlands and the South than in the North and in Scotland.

A second development in the inter-war years was the diversification of the appeal of the department stores. Stress was laid above on the middle-class appeal of department stores in the pre-1914 years, and, while this was a slight over-simplification of the position, the statement reflected as a whole the trading policy of the largest and most important stores. In the inter-war years the growth of department stores in the provinces and in the suburbs of the larger towns led to a greater variety of appeal. A number of the stores established in the North of England, for example, catered for a very much lower price market than many of the stores in London and the South, though within each area individual stores pursued different policies. Further, some of the older-established stores changed their policies, a few catering exclusively for a very high-class market while others widened their appeal to the medium-low price market. A broad division of stores into the 'high-medium' class of trade and the 'medium-low' class of trade can be made and in 1950 the stores in respect of numbers and turnover would probably be divided about equally between the two categories.

A third feature of the development of department stores in the inter-war years was the number of amalgamations that took place between the firms, leading to the emergence of a few companies each controlling a great number of stores. The trend towards mergers or acquisitions of other stores had started before 1914. For example, John Barker acquired Ponting Brothers in 1907 and Harrods bought Dickins & Jones in 1914, and immediately after the war Debenhams acquired Marshall & Snelgrove and Harvey Nicholls. Harrods acquired Kendal Milne of Manchester in 1919 and Swan & Edgar in 1920 (the shares in this firm were resold in 1926), and John Barker bought Derry & Toms in the same year.

The major developments in the direction of grouping stores did not, however, occur until the late 'twenties and early 'thirties, and then it took two main forms. In some cases a company would acquire control of a number of separate department stores, primarily for financial reasons, and little or no change would be made in the trading or buying policies of the individual department stores thus acquired. In other cases a department store would acquire control of other stores in order to develop a 'multiple' department store organization, and practise an important measure of central control over buying and trading policies of the individual stores. The main developments in the 'twenties fell into the first category, and three main groups of department stores were formed. Firstly there was the Debenhams group, which had taken over a number of stores from the Drapery Trust in 1927, secondly there was the United Drapery Stores group founded in 1927, and thirdly the Selfridge Provincial Stores group that was started in 1926. The story of the varying fortunes of the groups in subsequent years does not concern us here and all that need be added to bring the story down to 1950 is that in 1940 the Selfridge Provincial Stores group, which numbered some 16 stores, passed to John Lewis Ltd., and that a fourth group of stores had been built up under the Great Northern and Southern Stores Ltd., which was founded in 1936. Altogether in 1950 these 4 major companies controlled some 200 department stores, or some two-fifths of the estimated total number of stores in existence.

The other type of amalgamation or growth is best exemplified by Lewis's Ltd., which, partly through building and partly through buying, developed a small chain of eight department stores in different parts of the country under a unified control. Buying for all the stores was centralized for a large number of lines, and the organization and trading policies of each of the stores were determined centrally. To some extent the Selfridge Provincial Stores group, and later the John Lewis group, adopted similar principles, though a major obstacle in these cases, not present in the case of Lewis's Ltd., was the wide variety of the type of stores acquired and the diversity in trading tradition, income group of customers, and physical size.

The direct effect of the financial amalgamations on the economic and trading policies of the stores concerned was, as suggested above, negligible. Only in the case of the second type of growth, of Lewis's Ltd. and one or two smaller groups where centralized buying and unified control was introduced, did a new departmental store technique emerge, a technique which attempted to combine the diverse shopping attractions of the department store with the economic and technical specialization of the multiple shop. The example of Lewis's Ltd. did not, however, attract many followers. Few would deny the economic advantages of employing such a technique, but many would argue, with a great wealth of detail, that the individual characteristics and reputation of department stores resulting from their long emphasis on service to the particular groups of consumers who patronized them makes essential a high degree of local and individual control over buying and trading practice.

A final feature of department store development which may be mentioned briefly was the practice of some stores of leasing departments to other retailers, usually multiple shop retailers. This had long been a practice in such things as the travel service or the sale of theatre tickets, but in the 'thirties and the years following 1945 it grew rapidly in traditional department store lines such as footwear, cosmetics and clothing. The firm leasing a section of the store usually paid a rental based on turnover. Many reasons are adduced for this practice, but the chief one was that the multiple shop organization, a specialist in the trade, could run certain types of section of the store more effectively than could the department store staff, and well-run individual departments attracted additional customers to the store as a whole. In 1950 the number of leased sections of department stores—apart from travel and theatre agencies, hairdressing and beauty salons and restaurants—was under 200, but even this small number may be a sign as to the future pattern of department store trading, a cloud no bigger than a man's hand.

During the Second World War the department stores, particularly the central department stores, suffered very heavily. Apart from the direct damage done by enemy action, the long working hours, blackout, curtailment of public transport and danger of air raids reduced perceptibly the willingness of the public to travel distances to shop, and department stores, built on the principle of attracting customers over a wide area, saw their turnover fall rapidly. In the post-war years much of the ground was regained, though the smaller suburban and provincial stores recovered and forged ahead more rapidly than did the central stores of the large towns. It remains to be seen whether the rise of the suburban stores, allied with the increasing traffic problems of travelling to and shopping in the centres of the largest towns, may not have begun to undermine the position of the central stores.

Department store trade in women's wear

Women's and girls' wear and drapery continued to be the most important single group of goods sold by department stores. The relative importance of this group in total sales had declined slightly since the pre-1914 period, owing to the increased range of consumer goods sold in other departments, but in the years just prior to the Second World War and in the post-war years women's and children's wear and drapery are estimated to have represented some 40–50% of total turnover of department stores. A shift had also taken place in the character of the goods sold in the women's wear departments. Whereas in the pre-1914 years dress piece goods and accessories for home dressmaking represented an important section of the trade, by 1950 women's ready-made outerwear represented far and away the largest single section, on the average about 40% of the total sales of women's and children's wear and drapery. In the majority of stores the millinery, gloves and haberdashery section would come next in importance, with about one-fifth of the total sales of the group, followed by dress materials. Some stores, of course, emphasized particular sections of women's wear and might have a different sales pattern, but the above order of importance would apply to a fairly large number of stores. The women's underwear, girls' and children's wear and women's stockings and socks sections completed the group.

In women's outerwear the department stores earned a high reputation for a wide selection of articles in the latest styles. The basis of this was laid by the employment by most of the larger stores of highly skilled, expert buyers, and no effort was spared to maintain a name for quality and fashion. The stock having been obtained, the initial attraction of the customer, apart from extensive advertising, was through window display. Department stores for the most part had an opportunity of window display unapproached by other retailers and, in contrast to the pre-1914 period when windows were regarded as of secondary importance, the stores took full advantage of this asset in the inter-war years. Fashion goods are essentially display goods, and the increasing interest in fashion on the part of all sections of the population made the windows of department stores a vital link in the chain of sales. To attractive external displays the stores added freedom to inspect without obligation to purchase. This practice, of great importance in fashion outerwear, was widely copied by all sections of the trade in the inter-war years, but only the department stores carried the range of goods and provided the physical space and amenities to enable this freedom to be fully enjoyed. Another attraction of women's outerwear in department stores was that long runs of particular styles, colours or patterns were avoided. A coat, suit or dress bought in a department store, though not unique, was only likely to be one of hundreds instead of one of thousands. Finally the emphasis on personal service, the provision of numerous well-appointed fitting-rooms, and the readiness to make any alterations necessary free of cost were other attractions of the department store method of retailing that few could equal.

Similar trading practices with varying emphasis according to the type of good sold were followed in the other women's wear sections of the department store, but special mention must be made of the piece goods and haberdashery sections. Although the significance of these sections in the total sales of department stores had declined since the pre-1914 years along with the general trend towards the purchase of ready-made clothes, the importance of department stores in the total trade of these goods had risen. Several factors operated here. First the draper had begun to specialize more in made-up goods. Secondly, with a decline in total demand, only shops that sold a wide range of such goods would attract customers. Thirdly, the heavy costs of holding a wide range of such articles could only be undertaken by retailers who provided other inducements to shop besides the sale of piece goods. Department stores therefore, which already before 1914 had gained a high reputation for their stock and range of piece goods and haberdashery, maintained and improved on this reputation with the disappearance of other retailers from the field or the narrowing of the range of stock carried by those remaining. By the beginning of the Second World War the stores were responsible for nearly one-half of the total national sales of dress piece goods.

The department stores therefore in relation to women's and girls' wear and drapery had maintained and developed in the years 1918–50 the same retailing practices as those adopted in the formative years before 1914. The bias of their sales had changed with shifts in demand

and changes in the methods of manufacture, but the main emphasis remained on the convenience and physical comfort of shopping for a wide range of goods under one roof, on the wide selection of goods offered, and in the wealth of services provided. There were some signs, however, towards the end of this period that while the department stores had few equals in the range carried of such goods as dress piece goods and haberdashery, some of the stores in the medium-low price market were beginning to find that the specialist multiple shop organizations could and did provide a rather wider selection of goods such as hosiery and underwear and an almost equally wide selection of outerwear. Further, the styling of the goods sold by some of these multiple shop outerwear specialists was beginning to equal that of the department stores, and the personal service to customers was not far behind.

Shares of the different economic types of retailer in the total trade

This discussion of the development of the different economic types of retailer in the women's wear trade may now be concluded by presenting estimates of the share of the total trade undertaken by each type of retailer in the years 1900–50. These estimates are given in Table 66.

The trends in the structure of the trade shown in this table are reasonably clear. The share of the Co-operative Societies in the total

Table 66. *Estimated shares of the different economic types of retailer in the total retail sales of women's and girls' wear, 1900–50**

Year	Proportion of total sales undertaken by			
	Co-operative Societies %	Department stores %	Multiple shop retailers %	Other retailers (by difference) %
1900	4·5– 6·0	9·0–10·0	Under 1	83·5–86·0
1905	5·5– 6·5	10·0–12·0	About 1	80·0–84·0
1910	5·5– 7·0	12·0–14·0	1·0– 2·0	77·0–81·5
1915	6·0– 7·0	14·0–16·0	1·0– 2·0	75·0–79·0
1920	6·0– 7·5	14·0–16·0	1·0– 2·0	74·5–79·0
1925	6·5– 8·0	16·0–20·0	3·0– 4·0	68·0–74·5
1930	8·0– 9·5	18·0–22·0	5·0– 6·0	62·5–69·0
1935	8·0– 9·5	19·0–23·0	9·0–10·0	57·5–64·0
1939	8·0– 9·0	19·0–23·0	16·0–18·0	50·0–57·0
1950	9·0–11·0	20·0–23·0	20·0–22·0	44·0–51·0

* For a discussion of the basis of these estimates see Appendix A. The estimates of total sales include all women's, girls' and children's wear and include piece goods, drapery, haberdashery and retail bespoke dressmaking as well as ready-made goods. The sales of these goods by variety chain stores are included with the sales of multiple shop organizations. The 'other retailers' group is a residual group and therefore includes the sales by mail order houses (other than the mail order sections of department stores) and the sales of private dressmakers.

trade rose very slowly. The department stores were by far the most important large-scale retailers in the trade at the turn of the century, and their increase in the share of the trade was rapid up to the middle 'twenties. From 1925 onwards, while there was a small increase in their share of the total trade, the rate of increase fell markedly. Multiple shop retailers did not play a significant role in the trade until the middle 'thirties, but since that date their expansion was very rapid. The expansion was due in a large part to the growth of variety chain store trading in these goods. The sales of such firms are estimated as representing over one-third of the total sales of multiple shop organizations in the women's wear trade in 1950.

Suggestions as to future trends in the trade

Future trends in the women's and girls' clothing trade depend on a very large number of factors, and no attempt will be made here to explore the various combinations of circumstances that may operate in the future. Some tentative suggestions can, however, be made on the basis of past trends as to the possible developments in the retail structure. First, however, the general assumptions must be made that there is unlikely to be any significant change in the general importance of fashion and style in women's wear, that there will be a continued trend towards larger-scale production, and that nylon and similar fabrics, including mixtures of nylon and wool or cotton, will be the basic materials of the future. The ultimate effects of widespread use of the long-wearing and easily laundered nylon and similar fabrics is difficult to foresee in detail. It would appear, however, that while changes in style and fashion will maintain and, with a higher standard of living, increase the demand for women's outerwear, the demand for underwear and the stocks of it held by women may actually become stabilized or decrease.

In relation to the retail structure there would appear to be no reason to anticipate an important or significant increase in the share of the total trade undertaken by the Co-operative Societies. The slow increase of the past three decades may continue, but a significant increase would involve a change of policy in regard to sites, to display, to the proportion of fashion goods stocked, to the employment of experts, and to the links between the Co-operative factories and the Retail Societies. Such a change of policy, on historical and present evidence, seems most unlikely to take place. At the same time it should be pointed out that some use of the techniques employed so successfully by the variety chain stores in the organization of their sales of women's clothing are not beyond the scope of the Co-operative Societies, given their present sites and trading policies, provided that co-ordination in sales effort and policies between the individual Retail Societies and the wholesale societies takes place.

The specialist multiple shop retailers and the variety chain stores would appear to be only on the threshold of their expansion. While the bulk production of standardized hosiery and knitted goods and their mass distribution by multiple shop retailers is of fairly long standing, only in the last two decades has it been shown possible to develop standardized techniques of production and distribution in regard to fashionable outerwear. Further, contrary to many expectations, the techniques have been successful and popular with the customers in respect of price, style and the type of service offered. With a continued improvement in the standardization of fittings and in the range of styles produced, there would appear to be every reason to expect multiple shop retailing in women's outerwear, allied with large-scale production, to widen its appeal and to increase in importance in the trade. The problem of sameness of dress will probably be overcome in the future by variations in trimmings, that is, buttons, belts, collars and cuffs and so on. In hosiery and underwear, on the other hand, the trend towards an increase in manufacturer branding may limit the rate of growth of multiple shop retailing.

A future increase in the importance of department store trading in women's and girls' wear is more doubtful. The position of these stores is firmly established, but a further increase in their share of the total market implies the tapping of some hitherto untouched market or the development of some method or technique of retailing women's wear which has a clear advantage over the growing multiple shop organizations of different types on the one hand or the small-scale retailer on the other. There would appear to be no signs of either development taking place in the foreseeable future. Few towns of any size are without department stores, and additions to the number of stores in a given town do not necessarily increase the total turnover of the stores. In trading methods the department stores are likely to progress further in the direction of styling together a group of associated women's wear, so that the customer buying a new dress or suit can see and buy matching accessories—hat, shoes, gloves, handbag, jewellery. This practice is attractive and beyond the scope of the specialist retailer, but no fundamental changes in the principles of department store retailing appear likely. Without such a change, without, for example, the development of 'chain' department stores, the competition of the specialist multiple shop organization in women's outerwear, with its considerable buying advantages over the medium- and small-sized department store, may well be severe in the future. Particularly will this be so as the multiple shop organizations spread to higher price markets. In many respects it would appear that the present department store technique of retailing has reached its limit of advance and that the future of the stores lies in a combination of the attraction and advantages of department store shopping with the price and specialist advantages of multiple shop organizations.

The obstacles to the development of a number of 'chains' of department stores, with each chain using centralized buying and trading methods, are probably too great to allow of a marked advance in this direction, though some increase of central buying for small groups of department stores would appear to be certain in the future. The emergence of a number of smaller provincial and suburban department stores may also make possible the establishment of voluntary buying organizations or of wholesale houses which buy in bulk on behalf of a group of independent stores. These methods would assist the department stores in their competition with multiple shop retailers. But the most important change in department store methods will probably be along the lines of leasing sections of the stores to specialist retailers who thereby either build up a chain of sections leased in stores or, if already multiple shop firms, add to the number of their outlets. Where this practice has already been adopted in individual stores and sections have been leased to woollen goods specialists, underwear and corset specialists and outer clothing specialists, the results have shown the superior attraction of the specialist firms. There may well be considerable extension of this practice in the future. If so, the department store would have new problems in regard to maintaining the cohesion and tradition of the store, but such a system would also offer advantages both to the department store in maintaining the general attraction of the store and to the multiple shop organization in solving the increasingly difficult problem of good locations.

In regard to the role of the small-scale independent retailer in the trade, while there can be no doubt that at the top end of the trade the bespoke dressmakers and model houses will maintain their position, the future of the small-scale specialist retailer and the general draper is less certain. Except in so far as branding by manufacturers increases, thus protecting to some extent the specialist retailer, these units will have to meet greater competition in the future from the growing multiple shop organizations. The drapers have steadily lost ground to the department store and the made-up clothing retailer in the past, and the widespread tendency of customers to visit and inspect the shops and stores of the larger towns will probably continue to tell against the general draper in the villages, the small towns and the suburbs. On the whole it would appear that, while the independent retailer in this trade is very resilient owing to the importance of the personal contact with the customer, the future lies in the advance of multiple shop retailing techniques, and directly or indirectly this will tend to take place at the expense of the position of the independent retailer.

CHAPTER XIV

THE FOOTWEAR TRADE

The footwear trade in the United Kingdom in the middle of the nineteenth century was a handicraft trade. The central figure in both production and distribution was the producer/retailer, that is the boot and shoe maker, the cordwainer and the clog maker. In some areas, for example in parts of Leicestershire and Staffordshire, division of labour in production had begun to develop, but the techniques were still at a handicraft stage with neither machines nor power being used, and the method of organization was that of outworking. The footwear that was not sold by the boot and shoe maker himself was distributed through retailers such as drapers, household goods dealers and leather merchants, and footwear was also sold in markets and at fairs. The specialist footwear retailer, that is the tradesman who did not make the footwear but specialized in its sale to the exclusion of other goods, was practically non-existent.

Changes in the trade, 1850–1914

Between the middle 'fifties and the 'seventies a series of inventions revolutionized the trade, leading to the replacement of the handicraft methods by the machine manufacture of boots and shoes. Blake's sole sewer, Crick's riveting process and the Goodyear welting machine were among the most important innovations, and these made possible first the semi-mechanization of the trade—a period when part of the manufacturing was done by machine and part by hand, and part of the process performed in a factory and part in workers' homes—then, with faster and more reliable machines and better organization, the development of fully mechanized factory production and, by the turn of the century, the virtual disappearance of outworking.[1]

These changes in the methods of production led to equally revolutionary changes in the system of distribution of footwear. In the early stages of part machine- and part handicraft-produced footwear the natural outlets for the goods were the cobblers or boot and shoe makers and the drapers and general clothing shops. Neither type of trader, however, proved able to handle the steadily increasing quantities of factory-made footwear coming on to the market. In the case of the

---

[1] Illustrative of the changes taking place in the trade in the 'sixties and 'seventies was the break-away of the new machine men from the old Amalgamated Society of Cordwainers to form the National Union of Operative Boot and Shoe Rivetters and Finishers (later the National Union of Boot and Shoe Operatives).

boot and shoe maker he was a craftsman rather than a retailer pure and simple. The early factory-made footwear was of poor quality and badly made, often not distinguishing between left and right, and the craftsman was reluctant to handle such products. He was willing to stock only the best of the factory products. The drapers and general clothiers sold the new factory-made goods but usually only in small quantities. The new methods of production began, therefore, to demand new forms and methods of distribution and the specialist footwear retailer began to appear in significant numbers in the trade. Some of these specialists were boot and shoe dealers who had given up their production activities, others were general clothing shops which had begun to specialize in the sale of footwear, but most of the growing number of specialists were new retailers in the trade who may have known little about the craft of making footwear but began to lead the way in the art of selling it. In this development of the specialist footwear retailer as the link between the factory and the consumer, multiple shop organizations played a leading part.

The main demand for the factory-made boots and shoes came from the working classes, and the new types of retailer concentrated on this market. The main goods sold were different types of black boots, mainly of the hob-nailed and elastic-sided varieties. Shoes had a vogue in the 'seventies and 'eighties but went out of favour until just prior to the First World War. Chrome-tanned leather boots and shoes similarly were not sold in significant numbers until the beginning of the twentieth century. For the most part the range of fittings of the factory-made footwear was very limited. There were no nationally accepted standards of fittings; each manufacturer had his own sizes. Lasts were made to a small number of sizes and the customer had to be content to buy the pair of boots that appeared the nearest fit to his feet and then 'break them in', no easy or painless operation with the stiff, badly-cut leather.

Refinements and improvements in the techniques of production and in the range of fittings were being introduced by some firms about the turn of the century. New types of American machinery were being used, and the market for factory-made footwear widened. Sections of the middle classes began buying factory-made boots and shoes for the first time. Up to the First World War, however, the upper-middle-class and better end of the trade was still mainly in the hands of the bespoke boot and shoe maker.

The trade in the inter-war years

Between the First World War and the middle of the twentieth century, while there were no major technical inventions to revolutionize the methods of production, the continuation of the refinements and improvements in techniques mentioned above and the development of new types of demand led to a transformation of the character of the footwear trade. Manufacturers improved the standards of fittings and the range and quality of their products and they began to find a market among the sections of the population which had hitherto relied entirely on bespoke goods. Throughout the inter-war years the bespoke trade was fighting a losing battle against manufacturers specializing in high quality machine-made products, and by the middle of the twentieth century this section of the trade had virtually ceased to be of importance. The boot and shoe makers had become footwear repairers only.

The introduction of shorter skirts for women at the end of the First World War led directly to an increase in the demand for women's footwear. In 1929 the output of women's and girls' leather footwear represented some 50 % by value of the total output. In 1935 the proportion had risen to 55 % in spite of the relatively greater fall in the price of women's footwear compared to men's, and in 1948 women's and girls' footwear represented some 58 % by value of the total output. Linked with the above trend, fashion became an important factor in footwear production and distribution. The growth of the fashion element is difficult to measure quantitatively but there is little doubt that from being of minor importance in the trade in the years before 1914 fashion had become a dominant factor—some say the dominant factor—in the women's footwear trade by the end of the inter-war period, and by 1950 had begun to have some influence in the men's trade. Finally, with the growing emphasis being placed on style and fashion, the branding of footwear became general. A few manufacturers in the better end of trade had started this practice before 1914, but in the inter-war years the branding of footwear accompanied by advertising spread to all but the lowest price sections of the trade.

These developments in production and demand naturally led to marked changes in the organization of the retail footwear trade in these years. The specialist footwear retailer became far and away the most important type of retail unit. If he had been called into existence in the nineteenth century through the inability and unwillingness of the craftsman retailer and the general clothing retailer to handle factory-made footwear on the scale required, in the inter-war years the specialist retailer carrying wide ranges of styles and fittings had become essential in the trade if the varied demands for goods of different qualities and for fashion goods were to be met. Further, the specialist retailer was no longer confined to the working-class market, but, with the decline in bespoke boot and shoe making, appeared in all types of markets. Finally, the task performed by the specialist retailer underwent some changes. The great increase in the variety, styles and sizes of footwear that had taken place meant that to the job of selling had been added the necessity of holding a wide range of stock to give the customer a wide choice and of providing adequate space and skilled service in fitting.

This short account of the main developments in the production and demand conditions in the footwear trade since the middle of the nineteenth century provides a background against which the progress of the different economic types of retailers in the trade may be traced and discussed. The main emphasis is given to a detailed examination of the growth and characteristics of multiple shop retailing in the footwear trade.

The development of multiple shop retailing

Apart from the special cases of the railway bookstall trade and the sewing machine trade, the footwear trade was the first in the United Kingdom to witness the development of multiple shop retailing on a significant scale. In this trade multiple shop retailing organizations were emerging in the 1860's, and by 1870 records exist of some 10 firms each of which had more than 10 branch shops. Together the 10 possessed some 175 branches in different parts of the United Kingdom. Their names and approximate areas of trading were as follows: E. H. Rabbits, Pocock Brothers and Pash & Sons with branches in London and the South; R. & J. Dick, A. & W. Paterson and John Gray with branches in Scotland—and Dick's also had a few branches in London; George Oliver with branches in the Midlands and South Wales; George Handyside with branches on the North-East Coast; Scales & Salter with branches in Leeds and Yorkshire, and G. & W. Morton with branches in the Midlands and the South-West.

Ten years later these firms had been joined by 11 other firms including Freeman Hardy and Willis, Thomas Lilley, Stead & Simpson, and Tyler Brothers, and the total number of branches in existence had been trebled. In all there were 21 firms with more than 10 branches each in 1880, and 9 of these were trading under their own names in 1950—A. & W. Paterson, George Oliver, Salter & Salter, G. & W. Morton, Freeman Hardy and Willis, Lilley & Skinner, Stead & Simpson, J. W. Lee, and John Tyler. Of the others, Rabbits & Sons and Pocock Brothers joined Freeman Hardy and Willis at the turn of the century, and R. & J. Dick and Scales and Son gave up retailing in the 1920's. The remainder went out of business.

The increase in the number of multiple shop organizations and the number of branches controlled by them was rapid after 1880. Table 67 shows the number of organizations and the number of branches in existence in different years from 1875 to 1950. Altogether the records of some 137 separate firms have been traced and are included in this table. Of this total, 69 firms were existing in 1950, 19 of the firms which had at one time traded separately had been merged with other firms, and 49 of the firms would appear to have gone out of existence as multiple shop retailers.

Table 67. *Estimates of the number of multiple shop firms and branches in the footwear trade, 1875–1950*

Year	10–24 branches		25–49 branches		50–99 branches		100 or more branches		Totals			
									10 or more branches		25 or more branches	
	Number of		Number of		Number of		Number of		Number of		Number of	
	Firms	Branches	Firms	Branches	Firms	Branches	Firms	Branches	Firms	Branches	Firms	Branches
1875	11	154	4	151	—	—	—	—	15	305	4	151
1880	13	186	6	193	2	121	—	—	21	500	8	314
1885	18	271	6	208	4	278	—	—	28	757	10	486
1890	26	331	12	280	4	250	3	370	45	1,231	19	900
1895	32	461	14	504	8	483	3	519	57	1,967	25	1,506
1900	32	522	17	579	10	685	5	803	64	2,589	32	2,067
1905	29	438	22	781	8	534	7	1,209	66	2,962	37	2,524
1910	31	470	20	759	10	717	9	1,598	70	3,544	39	3,074
1915	32	483	14	527	13	835	12	2,034	71	3,879	39	3,396
1920	34	493	15	546	12	803	12	2,100	73	3,942	39	3,449
1925	42	611	12	484	10	671	15	2,598	79	4,364	37	3,753
1930	40	588	17	581	10	753	14	2,845	81	4,767	41	4,179
1935	38	560	19	674	8	595	15	3,020	80	4,849	42	4,289
1939	34	498	18	649	9	645	16	3,377	77	5,169	43	4,671
1950	28	391	12	418	10	767	18	3,634	68	5,210	40	4,819

The figures given in Table 67 can be used to show the rate of growth of multiple shop retailing as indicated by the rate of the net increase in the number of branches in existence in different periods. The use of the numbers of branches in existence to indicate the rate of growth is not entirely satisfactory as the average size of the branch may change over time, but the estimates of the number of branches in existence at different dates give a general indication of multiple shop trading activity in different periods. Table 68 therefore shows the net increase and the rate of net increase in the number of branches in existence over the period 1880–1950. The rate of net increase is shown as a percentage increase in the numbers between two dates and the absolute net increase in the number of branches is also shown as an average yearly net increase.

The trends shown in Table 68 suggest an increase in the activity of firms in opening branch shops from the 'seventies until a peak is reached in the ten years up to the turn of the century. George Oliver, Freeman Hardy & Willis, and Stead & Simpson were three firms which expanded very rapidly in these years. The first years of the new century

Table 68. *Rate of net increase in the number of branches of multiple
shop firms in the footwear trade, 1881–1950*

Year	Branches of firms with 10 or more branches			Branches of firms with 25 or more branches		
	Net increase in number of branches	Percentage net increase	Average yearly net increase in numbers	Net increase in number of branches	Percentage net increase	Average yearly net increase in numbers
1881–1885	257	51	51	172	55	34
1886–1890	474	63	95	414	85	83
1891–1895	746	61	149	606	67	121
1896–1900	611	31	122	561	37	112
1901–1905	374	14	75	457	22	91
1906–1910	582	20	116	550	22	110
1911–1915	335	9	67	322	11	65
1916–1920	63	2	13	53	2	11
1921–1925	422	11	84	304	9	61
1926–1930	403	9	81	426	11	85
1931–1935	82	2	16	110	3	22
1936–1939	320	7	80	382	9	95
1940–1950	41	1	4	148	3	13

heard many complaints about too much competition in the footwear
trade, and this was reflected in a slight slowing down of activity. The
rate of increase picked up again after 1906, but in the First World War
the opening of new branches practically ceased. The inter-war years
were similarly characterized by fluctuations in activity. A considerable
burst of activity in the 'twenties came to an end in the 1929–33 depression, when a number of firms re-organized their structure and closed
branches. After 1935 the rate of increase picked up again but was
brought to a halt in the Second World War. In fact, during the war
there was an absolute decrease in the number of branches in operation,
the figure for 1945 being some 8–10 % below that of 1939. Most of the
branches that had been closed were, however, re-opened by 1950 and
the total number of multiple shop footwear branches had begun to
increase again.

These tables present a general picture of the growth and the rate of
growth of multiple shop retailing in the footwear trade. Some of the
aspects and characteristics of this growth and some of the reasons for
the success of multiple shop retailing can now be examined in closer
detail.

The development of different types of firms

There has been a consistent increase in the average size of multiple shop
firms. In 1880 the average number of branches per firm with 25 or
more branches each was 39. In 1900 the average had risen to 65 and

by 1920 to 88. In 1930 the average was 102 branches and in 1950 118 branches. Similarly there had been an increase in the proportion of the total numbers of branches controlled by firms with over 100 branches each. In 1900 the firms with 100 or more branches controlled some 31 % of the total number of multiple shop branches in existence. In 1920 the proportion had risen to 54 % and in 1950 to 70 %.

This increase in the size of the firms was a general characteristic and not the outcome of an exceptional increase in the size of the largest group of firms. This is shown in Table 69.

Table 69. *Relative importance of the largest multiple shop firms in the footwear trade, 1900–50*

Year	Total branches of firms with 10 or more branches			Total branches of firms with 25 or more branches		
	Proportion controlled by			Proportion controlled by		
	The largest firm %	The 2 largest firms %	The 5 largest firms %	The largest firm %	The 2 largest firms %	The 5 largest firms %
1900	11	18	31	14	23	39
1910	13	20	33	15	24	39
1920	12	18	32	14	21	36
1930	16	21	35	18	24	40
1939	17	22	35	18	25	39
1950	15	21	35	17	23	38

The proportion of the total number of branches controlled by the 5 largest firms is seen to be very constant in this period of fifty years when the total number of branches more than doubled from 2,588 to 5,210. There was, however, a fairly significant shift in the relative importance of the largest firm between 1920 and 1930, owing to the amalgamation of two large companies in 1928.[1] No marked trend towards concentration of branches in the hands of a small number of firms was, however, present.

These statistics of the increase in the number of branches in existence and of the average size of firms conceal however the differences in the rate of growth of individual firms. Broadly the evidence suggests that in the years up to the First World War practically all the firms were steadily growing in size by opening new branches. In the inter-war years, on the other hand, the rate of growth of the older-established firms, for example those which had over 100 branches each in 1920, was much slower than that of a number of newer firms, and the increase

---

[1] This amalgamation was, however, primarily a financial one. The companies remained separate trading organizations.

in the total number of multiple shop branches in existence was due largely to the expansion of these newer firms. Of the 18 firms with 100 or more branches in existence in 1950, some 11 (counting as one firm the two firms which had amalgamated in the middle of the period) had more than 100 branches each in 1920. These eleven firms controlled some 2,100 branches in 1920 and 2,400 branches in 1950, including 200 branches of smaller firms that had been acquired. Of the remaining 7 firms that had more than 100 branches in 1950, only 3 had been in existence in 1920 and they controlled some 200 branches. In 1950 these 7 controlled in all some 1,200 branches, including 150 branches of smaller firms that were acquired. In the case of the eleven older-established firms there had been a net increase of 100 branches, in the case of the seven newer firms a net increase of 850 branches, between 1920 and 1950.

The reasons for this variation in the rate of growth are difficult to determine in detail, as policy decisions of individual firms are made for a number of diverse reasons. Further, the use of the number of branches controlled by different firms can be misleading as no account is taken of the variations in size and turnover of the branches belonging to different firms. Some of the general factors that would appear to have operated may, however, be suggested. First there would appear to be some disadvantages attaching to an early start, particularly a start undertaken at the breakneck speed of some of the firms before 1914. The possession of freehold property of a type and in sites that could not be readily adapted to new trends in demand was one instance of this disadvantage. For example, many of the older firms had opened branches in small quiet country towns. Improvements in transport and the growth in size of the larger towns left many of these branches in backwaters. Secondly the depression in the basic industries in the inter-war years and the movement of the population hit the firms which had grown up before 1914 in the older industrial working-class areas. In the third place the slowing down in the rate of increase in the number of branches once the 100–150 branch mark has been passed may indicate the existence of an upper limit to the economic size of multiple shop organizations in the footwear trade. In part this is a problem of regional or national development. Many firms preferred not to face the risks, costs and problems of expanding to a national or near-national market which would require at least over 200 branches unless a very limited price or style market was being sought. In regard to the national market there again would appear to be an upper limit. In the past thirty years only one firm expanded beyond the 300 branch shops mark, while a number have been relatively stable with 200–300 branches.

Whether these limits to regional and national expansion will be passed or not in the future, the evidence of the development of multiple shop trading between 1910 and 1950 suggests that the advantages obtained by the large firms, regionally or nationally, have not so far been sufficiently great to enable them to dominate the new opportunities of expansion. Generally speaking the opportunities have been seized by newer firms rather than by existing large firms, though in the inter-war years owing to the widening of the market for factory-made footwear and the increase in the range of styles and of fashion the newer firms often expanded in a section of the market that was outside the scope of the older-established firms.

The finance of the multiple shop firms

Until the last decade of the nineteenth century the partnership and private limited liability company was the dominant form of business organization. Capital to increase the number of branches was found out of profits, and for working capital the firms relied on bank advances. At the turn of the century many factors were combining to change this picture. Some of the original founders of the older businesses were wishing to retire and there were not always younger members of the family willing and able to carry on. To many of the newer firms the finance of expansion out of profits seemed to be too slow a process to overcome the disadvantage of a late start. More important for the firms undertaking both production and retailing, self-finance was becoming a limiting factor. Finally the company promotion boom of the 'nineties made conversion to a public company easy, fashionable and, to the vendors and promotors at least, profitable. Between 1890 and 1900 7 multiple shop retailing organizations in the footwear trade became public companies, and these 7, with one other converted before these years, controlled in 1900 some 40% of the total number of branches in existence belonging to firms with more than 25 branches each. By 1920 another 4 firms had become public companies and these 12 controlled some 50% of the total number of branches. 9 of the 12 companies were manufacturers of footwear as well as retailers.

In the inter-war years a number of further conversions from private to public companies were made and there was a particular boom in public company flotation in the footwear trade in the years 1947–49 after the Second World War. By 1950 21 multiple shop firms in the footwear trade were public companies and these companies controlled 70% of the total number of branches belonging to firms with 25 or more branches each. Some 13 of the 18 firms with over 100 branches each in 1950 were public companies, and most of the public companies were manufacturers as well as retailers. The boom in public company formation in the years following the Second World War was due in part to founders wishing to retire and realize their assets and partly to the greatly increased costs of running the business. The post-war prices of stock, fittings, repairs and property made expansion or even re-equipment a task beyond the limited resources of a private firm. Financially the position had been reached where, save for a few firms that were exceptionally well-placed, any significant expansion of existing firms required an important measure of outside financing.

The use of the public company form in place of the partnership or small private company form brought about some changes in the directing personnel of the large firms. The changes in the footwear retailing trade were, however, less widespread than in many other trades, as there existed a very strong tradition of family succession and, even if capital was raised on the market, the sons or relatives succeeded fathers as directors. By 1950, however, there were signs that this tradition was weakening and managerial and administrative ability was being stressed as the first qualification for directing posts rather than close associations with the trade or the firm.

The integration of production and distribution

An important feature of multiple shop retailing in the footwear trade was the close link between production and distribution. From the beginnings of multiple shop retailing in the eighteen-seventies, integrated firms, that is firms with factories as well as retail outlets, have existed. No set pattern of development, however, emerges in their history. In some instances, in the period of growth before 1914 manufacturers developed the production and retailing sides of their business at the same time, as in the case of R. & J. Dick and Freeman Hardy and Willis. In other instances the manufacturing side was of some standing before retailing was developed on any significant scale. The reasons for branching out into retailing varied. The need to find additional outlets for the increased output of the factory consequent upon a growth in the scale of production was a factor in the case of a firm like Stead & Simpson. The limitation of the export sales was important in the case of a firm such as A. W. Flatau and, to a lesser extent, in the case of the Saxone Shoe Company. Again there are examples of manufacturers who developed a chain of retail shops and then ceased manufacturing in order to concentrate on retailing, as happened in the case of Thomas Lilley and George Oliver. And finally there were firms which built up a flourishing multiple retailing business and then added manu-facturing, as was the case with William Timpson and James Greenlees. The same mixed pattern is seen in the years 1914 to 1950. Of 8 inte-grated firms in 1950 which had either not been in existence in 1914 or not been integrated, 3 were originally retailers who acquired manufacturing establishments, 4 were originally manufacturers, and one firm started retailing and manufacturing at the same time.

Reviewing the period as a whole there can be said to have been a slight increase in the importance of integration of production and distribution. In 1900, for example, approximately 45 % of the total number of branches in existence controlled by firms with 25 or more branches belonged to firms that undertook both manufacturing and retailing. In 1920 the proportion had risen to some 50 % and in 1950 to nearly 65 %. The story is not, however, one of straightforward increase either in the number and importance of integrated firms or in the proportion of total footwear sold that was produced by integrated firms.

There is some evidence to show that the movement towards or away from the integration of production and distribution reflected the economic conditions in the trade. In the minor depression in the trade after the turn of the century, for example, one or two firms which had been integrated sold either their factory or their shops in order to specialize in manufacturing or in distribution. In the period before the First World War and noticeably in the 'twenties when the trade was expanding there was a marked growth of integration, many retailers acquiring factories and manufacturers acquiring chains of shops. In the depression years 1929–33 several retailers discontinued manufacturing and disposed of their factories and in 1939, although some new integrated firms had come into the field, the proportion of the total number of branches that were controlled by integrated firms was well below that of 1930 and only slightly higher than the proportion in 1920. Between 1939 and 1950, however, there was a marked increase in the numbers and importance of integrated firms. The shortages of supplies led many retailers to take over manufacturing units in order to guarantee supplies to their branches. At the same time some manufacturers who in the past had relied on independent retailers to sell their branded products felt their position threatened by the growth of multiple shop retailing and began to develop their own chain of retail outlets.

The proportion of the total retail sales by integrated firms that was represented by goods of their own manufacture varied widely over time and between firms. In the late nineteenth century and opening decades of the twentieth the usual practice was for integrated firms to sell mainly their own goods, provided of course the factory capacity was sufficiently great to supply the goods. In the inter-war years the practice and policy of integrated firms became more diversified and in 1950 in the case of one-third of the integrated firms the proportion of total sales represented by their own production was between 66 % and 90 %; in another third it was between 40 % and 66 %; and in the remaining third it ranged from 10 % to 40 %. This variation was in part due to differences in capacity of the factories in relation to the retail sales volume but, more important, the variation arose from the differences in the type of trade undertaken by the individual firms. For example, a firm in the low price range selling mainly non-fashion men's footwear would sell a higher proportion of goods of its own production than a firm in the middle price range that undertook a significant trade in women's fashion shoes. Taking the sales of all integrated firms in 1950 the proportion of the total represented by footwear of their own manufacture was 33–40 %. This proportion was less than it had been in 1920 and less than in 1900. The decline was a function of the widening of the range, the style and the type of footwear stocked and sold by multiple shop retailers over this period. No one manufacturing establishment could produce a complete range and no one designer or small group of designers could be expected to provide the variation in style and fashion that had become to be considered necessary in any well-stocked footwear shop.

The integration of large-scale production and distribution of footwear was therefore of considerable significance throughout these years, but its importance in relation to the total sales of footwear by multiple shop organizations would not appear to have changed greatly. The slight trend towards an increase in the proportion of the total number of branches that were controlled by integrated firms would appear to have been offset by the decline in the relative proportion of sales of the firms represented by goods of their own production. Diversity in types of footwear, the rapid growth of the women's fashion trade and the spread of multiple shop retailing to all price markets limited the importance of integration and proved wrong the forecasts made in the early 'twenties of the complete domination of the footwear trade by large integrated concerns.

The retailing methods of the multiple shop firms

This account of the main features of the growth of multiple shop retailing in the footwear trade may be concluded with a brief discussion of the trading characteristics and techniques of these firms. As suggested above, the main market for the factory-made boots and shoes was the working classes, and up to the First World War the majority of the multiple shop retailers concentrated on this market. There was no particular geographical bias in the location of the branches of the multiple shop firms; they were opened in market towns and country towns as well as in industrial and commercial towns. The only exception would appear to be parts of Lancashire where the practice of wearing clogs reduced to some extent the demand among the working classes for leather footwear. The branch shops of the multiple shop firms in these early years—in so far as they were called shops, warehouses being a term frequently used—were small and single-fronted, were fitted with only a counter and a long bench, and usually had a staff of two or at the most three, that is a manager, an assistant and a boy or girl. The hours worked were long, the shops being open until 11 p.m. on Saturdays, the best shopping day of the week. The boots arriving unboxed at the branches from the central warehouses were unsized, scratched and greasy and had to be prepared by the staff before sale. The wearing of aprons, sometimes white but usually black, was a necessity for the branch manager and his assistant, and to the general gloom and austerity of the shop interior there were added the dirt and odours of size, dubbin, blacking and cheap leather as well as those of gas flares and oil lamps.

The small and unattractive interiors of the branches did not, however, inhibit the multiple shop organizations in their selling policies. In marked contrast to the discreet approach of the bespoke boot and shoe maker and the general draper selling footwear, the multiple shop retailers adopted vigorous and aggressive methods of salesmanship. The first, and one of the most important, of the innovations was the use of plainly marked price tickets on all goods, and to allay fears of trickery notices were posted stating that the goods were sold at the 'Same Prices inside the Shop as Ticketed at the Doors and in the Windows'. This open pricing proved a great attraction in a trade hitherto dominated by the essentially indefinite pricing of the bespoke retailer. Secondly, instead of display being confined to symbols of the trade, the whole front and doorway of the branches were used to set out the wares. Footwear filled the windows in tremendous profusion and was hung on poles from rungs outside the shop fronts and in the doorways. Practically the entire stock could be inspected from the street. Thirdly, the multiple shop retailers used every method to advertise their bargains, low prices being a dominant note in their trading policies. Handbills, leaflets, sandwich-board parades, canvassers and spectacular advertisements were commonly used by these firms.

After the turn of the century the widening of the market for factory-made footwear and the improvements in fittings and quality called for advances in the design, layout, and siting of the branches of the multiple footwear retailers. Some of the newer firms coming into the trade began to acquire double-fronted shops which gave customers a better opportunity to inspect the goods, to compare style and leather and to be served in some comfort. Only a few multiple shop organizations were pursuing this policy by 1914. Many of the branch shops then in existence had hardly changed in appearance since the day they were first opened twenty-five or fifty years earlier. But in the section of the trade where up-grading was taking place, multiple shop retailers were playing a leading part.

In the inter-war years there were many developments in the methods and techniques of retailing used by multiple shop organizations. Improvements in the methods of production, in the standards of fittings and in the quality of the goods produced by machinery had enabled the multiple shop retailers to enter practically every section of the market. This factor diversified the trading practices of the multiple shop retailers and makes generalizations regarding retailing techniques difficult, as the practice of each firm was related to the market it served. Broadly, however, the major changes in multiple shop retailing methods in the inter-war years were as follows. A site in a main street or a shopping centre became a necessity, side-street retailing was no longer possible: the poles festooned with footwear outside the shops began to go and the windows, instead of looking like the cross-section of a warehouse, had to be planned and dressed to display as individually as possible the various types and styles of goods in stock. Inside the shop the apron had no place from necessity or tradition, and smartness, cleanliness and the provision of fittings in comfort became the first consideration. The physical size of the branch and the number of assistants per branch tended to increase, many of the newer multiple shop firms in particular securing very large premises and employing six to eight assistants per shop, more than double the employment in the typical multiple shop branch of the late nineteenth century.

These developments, and the increased demand for women's footwear and the growing fashion element that was appearing in all markets, made changes in shop management and the retail organization essential. The widening in the range of styles and of fittings, the emphasis on fashion, and the developments in the standards of window display and shop service, required a much greater measure of centralization and control by head office than had hitherto been practised. Instead of the branch manager being given a relatively free hand in regard to sales and sales promotion, stock holding and window display, the selling campaigns were centrally planned, stock was watched and controlled in the closest detail and experts were employed to plan, design and dress the windows and interiors. In the women's fashion trade in particular, while the prizes were high the risk of losses due to outmoded, unsold stocks was also very great. Only by elaborate checking, control, supervision and standardization of branch activities could these risks be limited. A final change in the specialist multiple shop retailing techniques in the inter-war years compared with those of before 1914 was the slight shift from emphasis on price to emphasis on service. In the earlier years the multiple shop footwear retailer had been distinguished from other retailers by the stress he placed on open pricing and on low prices. In the interwar years, while many multiple shop firms maintained this tradition, others stressed the superiority of the range of goods offered, of the variety of styles and of the conditions under which the customer could make his selection and choice.

In the years following the Second World War shortages of manpower and materials, as well as shortages, for a part of the period, of supplies, limited new developments in retailing. Nevertheless, in spite of these difficulties many of the footwear multiple shop firms were able to raise the retailing standards of their branches even higher. Full employment and a higher standard of living enabled the working classes to demand and buy better quality and better styled footwear, and most multiple shop firms reacted to this changed demand. At the same time other firms took the opportunity of post-war re-organization to upgrade their types of trade and to move into slightly higher price markets. The effect of both these trends was to bring about a marked improvement in the layout, design, lighting and display of many of the branch shops. With price controls in existence and the desire of the customer to buy the best, practically the whole selling emphasis was placed on the attractiveness of the shop and the goods offered for sale. In the larger towns the rise in the retailing standards of many of the branches of footwear multiple shop organizations was spectacular and these shops took the lead over all other types of retailers in the standards of layout and modern design: a far cry from the dimly-lit small branches, festooned with boots, of the late nineteenth century.

This account of the development of multiple shop retailers in the footwear trade would not, however, be complete without some reference to the growth of variety chain store trading in footwear. For the most part this trading was confined to rubber footwear or very low-priced leather footwear, but the techniques of retailing used contrasted markedly with the trend in the specialist trade in the direction of greater service. The sale of footwear in variety chain stores was practically on self-service lines.

Reasons for the growth of multiple shop retailing

The general advantages of the multiple shop form of trading and the economies secured in buying, selling and specialization of function have been outlined above. Here the discussion will be focused on the particular reasons for the growth of this form of retailing in the footwear trade and the particular advantages secured in this trade at different periods.

The early and rapid spread of the use of multiple shop techniques in the footwear trade was connected directly with the revolution in the methods of production that took place in the three or four decades after the middle of the nineteenth century. This revolution called into existence a new type of retailer, the specialist footwear retailer, and the multiple shop technique of retailing was suited to performing this type of distributive function. The beginnings of multiple shop footwear trading can therefore be said to be—in contrast to the postion in many other trades—practically simultaneous with the beginnings of the specialist retailing in the trade itself.

The job that had to be done was the rapid and mass distribution at very low cost of the new factory-made footwear throughout the country. With a limited number of fittings and styles, decisions as to what to buy could be made relatively easily and confidently by head office, and the approach of the multiple shop firms to sales was that of viewing purchases as an investment that had to be realized as speedily as possible, in other words achieving a high rate of stock turn. The use of standardized invoicing practices, retail pricing policies and elementary returns of stock enabled head office to direct the activities of the branches without a large supervising staff. To this advantage of simplicity of organization which enabled the firms to expand rapidly was added the fact that the goods being sold were new types of products and that there was therefore relatively little difficulty in overcoming traditional purchasing habits of consumers.

Multiple shop retailers were not, of course, the only units handling the factory-made footwear, but the rapid growth of this form of retailing and the encouragement their success gave to others to stock and sell the factory-made products played an important part in bringing the advantages of the cheaper factory-made article to the working classes. The development of the new manufacturing techniques would have been painfully slow if the distribution of the products had had to depend entirely on the hand-to-mouth buying and stockholding methods of the bespoke boot and shoe makers, the drapers, the clothiers and the leather goods dealers.

The early start of the multiple shop organizations was of course also assisted by the general economies these firms secured by way of large-scale buying and operating costs. Further, their low price and vigorous advertising policies were correctly attuned to the market situation of the period up to the turn of the century. In addition to these factors three other important advantages in the footwear trade of the multiple shop technique of trading may be noted. Firstly there were the advantages secured by some firms through the integration of production and distribution. The manufacturing units of the integrated concerns were able to concentrate on long runs of the lines in steady and stable demand and had no problem in disposing of the output. Similarly distribution of such lines to the retail branches could be planned and carried through with a minimum of cost. For the firms dealing in fashion goods, control over production meant a shortening of the time between the ideas on the drawing board and the new styles in the windows, and time was an important factor in success in this type of trade. At the same time, however, integration brought problems as well as advantages. Apart from the limits to the range of footwear that could be produced by one unit, there was a continual problem, more serious in the inter-war years with growing diversity of demand and more serious in times of depression than of prosperity, of keeping productive and distributive activities in line with each other. While in theory it was possible to plan and organize the production by reference to the demand in the retail branches, in practice productive policies were the less flexible and often the wish to keep the factory fully employed led to the piling up of unsaleable stock at the branches. On the other hand, a factory that was too dependent on the forward ordering of the retail branches found itself unable to develop long production runs.

A second advantage possessed by multiple shop retailers was that of financial strength enabling them both to purchase the best sites and to invest considerable sums in designing layout and rebuilding and in fittings and fixtures. An important aspect of this was specialized knowledge of the property market and economies in large-scale buying of fixtures and fittings or their manufacture within the concern itself. This advantage was perhaps of little importance before the turn of the century when the multiple shop branches were neither particularly well sited nor well designed, but in the inter-war and post-war years with the growth of main-street siting and emphasis in retailing on well laid out shops the advantage of the multiple shop firms over other types of retailers was considerable. The exceptions to this rule were some of the firms that had grown rapidly in the years before 1914 and which in the inter-war years found themselves with many properties that could not readily be re-designed or re-located to suit the new trends and were not easily realizable assets.

A third advantage of multiple shop retailers in the footwear trade related to control of stock. The gradual increase from the turn of the century onwards in the ranges of fittings and sizes and in the variety of styles and fashions presented all retailers with the problem of adding to the number of lines stocked while maintaining the rate of stock turn of the shop as a whole. Some multiple shop retailers did not attempt the task and continued to confine themselves to a relatively small range of footwear. Others, the majority, by the use of centralized stock control systems which became the intelligence unit of the firms were able to observe trends in sales, to spot problems of slow-moving stock, and to take the necessary action in regard to buying or selling policies long before the small-scale unit may have been aware that any shift in demand was taking place.

The most difficult problems of stock control arose at the fashion end of the trade. Again many multiple shop retailers tried to keep out of the trade as long as they were able, but others saw in the fashion trade the opportunity of developing to the full their advantages in relation to use of window display experts, main-street siting, up-to-date layout and decoration and advertising strength. Leadership in fashion in the women's section of the trade offered the same guarantee of a high turnover per branch in the inter-war years as leadership in low prices and good quality had offered in the men's section of the trade before the First World War. However, much was contained in the word leadership. Competition between multiple shop organizations for leadership in the fashion trade was severe, taking the form of emphasizing changes in fashion and the continuous development of new ideas and lines. Failure to maintain a leading position and to keep abreast of the changes in style resulted in serious losses. Certainly the multiple shop retailers had some advantages over the small-scale retailer in the handling of mark-downs made necessary by changes in fashion or bad buying. The head office of the multiple shop firm by the use of centralized stock control had an overall view of trends and could mark down far more decisively and dispassionately than could the single shop retailer. Again the multiple shop retailer could shift stock between branches according to the inevitable variations in the 'up-to-dateness' of demand in different areas. But many multiple shop firms, in spite of their advantages in handling the fashion trade, were becoming concerned towards the middle of the century as to whether the trade that they had done so much to promote had not become a monster destroying the balance of the industry and reducing its profitability.

The reasons for the growth of multiple shop retailing in the footwear trade and the particular advantages of this form of retailing in these years may be summarized as follows. In the initial stages, in the last three decades of the nineteenth century, the multiple shop form of retailing was well suited to handle the mass distribution of the new factory-made products. The use of vigorous selling methods and a low price policy, made possible by crude retailing techniques, low operating costs, large-scale buying and the integration of production and distribution, enabled the number of multiple shop branches to be increased rapidly. In the twentieth century the improvements in production techniques assisted this form of retailing to spread to practically all price markets and at the same time there was some change in the advantages secured by this form of retailing. In this period, particularly in the inter-war years, the ability to specialize the retailing functions and to employ experts in the different aspects of selling, from window display and shop layout to staff training, the possession of financial resources which enabled the best sites to be purchased, the use of centralized systems of stock control in a trade that was becoming rapidly diversified with style and fashion, and the stress placed by many of the firms on the comfort and service provided in their branches were factors as important, if not more important, in the advance of multiple shop retailing as the economies secured by large-scale buying and by the integration of production and distribution.

Co-operative and department store trading

The Co-operative Societies with their working-class membership took an active part in the distribution of the new factory-made footwear in the second half of the nineteenth century and also entered the production side of the trade. A few Societies had sold footwear alongside drapery goods in the 'sixties. In 1872 the Co-operative Wholesale Society opened a separate buying department for footwear and in 1873 the Society opened its first footwear factory. By 1914 footwear was being sold by practically all the Retail Societies, though the sales were usually made at their central premises, very few specialist footwear shops having been opened. Production had also been extended and the Co-operative Wholesale Societies controlled six factories, four in England and two in Scotland. No attempt was made, however, by the Wholesale or Retail Societies to specialize, advertise and press their sales of footwear in the manner of the multiple shop retailers in these years. The main appeal of the Retail Societies was to their members, who were attracted by the good-quality, well-made and long-lasting products and by the benefit of the dividend on sales.

In the years following the First World War Co-operative production and sales of footwear continued to increase with the increase in Co-operative membership. A number of changes were made in the methods of Co-operative production, leading to a greater degree of specialization. More attention was paid to styling, and on the retail side some separate shops or departments for the sale of footwear were established. The radical changes in the spirit and tempo of the retail footwear trade however between 1920 and 1950 were not reflected in Co-operative methods and techniques. While other retailers, led by multiple shop firms and department stores, were setting the pace with main street premises, extensive and attractive window displays and elaborate interiors, fixtures and fittings, and while both manufacturers and retailers were emphasizing style and fashion, the Co-operative Societies continued to treat footwear as something sold alongside drapery at

24-2

the central premises, rather than as a trade requiring specialized treatment and organization. Only a few Societies employed the experts in buying and selling who were essential if the Societies were to keep abreast of the new trends, and only a few Societies were prepared to give the footwear departments the prominent sites and positions and to encourage the adoption of modern methods of layout and design that were necessary if new customers were to be attracted. In all there were just over 1,000 Co-operative footwear shops in 1938. The approach of the Co-operative Societies with a few exceptions continued to be the provision of good-value footwear to members, coupled with the payment of a dividend, rather than the attraction of the public by window display, by the styling and fashion of their goods and by attractive shops.

Most department stores at the beginning of the twentieth century had footwear departments and the stores were prominent in the sale of the improved qualities and fittings of factory-made footwear that were coming on to the market in the first decades of the century. The department stores were concerned with the middle and upper price markets and in the inter-war years a well-designed and laid-out footwear department giving customers a wide choice of high quality footwear was considered essential in any store. More than in any other group of goods, however, the department stores were faced with direct competition from multiple shop retailers in their sale of footwear. Particularly was this so in the decades following the First World War when many of the multiple shop retailers successfully widened their appeal to the higher price markets. By the end of the inter-war years and in the years following the Second World War some of the multiple shop firms could be said to have surpassed the department stores in the middle and upper end of the footwear trade in the range of goods stocked, in styling and fashion and also in the attractiveness of the shops themselves. The specialist approach of the multiple shop retailers was proving superior to the single-department approach of the stores, and an indication of the problem facing the stores was the growing practice of leaving the footwear department of a store to a multiple shop retailer. By 1950 some 27 departments in different stores had been so leased.

Shares of the different economic types of retailer in the total trade

An attempt may now be made to show the relative importance of the different economic types of retailer in the total footwear trade between 1900 and 1950. These estimates are presented in Table 70.

The trends shown in Table 70 do not require elaboration, but the discussion of the development of the different economic types of retailers may be concluded by a glance at the position of the small-scale retailer.

Table 70. *Estimated shares of the different economic types of retailer in the total retail sales of footwear, 1900–50**

Year	Proportion of total sales undertaken by			
	Co-operative Societies %	Department stores %	Multiple shop retailers %	Other retailers (by difference) %
1900	5·0– 6·0	1·5–3·0	18·0–22·0	69·0–75·5
1905	6·0– 7·0	2·0–3·5	22·0–26·0	63·5–70·0
1910	6·0– 7·5	2·5–4·0	29·0–34·0	54·5–62·5
1915	7·0– 8·0	3·0–4·0	31·0–35·0	53·0–59·0
1920	7·0– 8·0	3·0–4·0	31·0–35·0	53·0–59·0
1925	7·5– 8·5	4·0–5·0	33·0–37·0	49·5–55·5
1930	7·5– 9·0	4·0–5·5	35·0–40·0	45·5–53·5
1935	8·0– 9·0	4·5–5·5	40·0–44·0	41·5–47·5
1939	8·0–10·0	4·5–6·0	44·0–49·0	35·0–43·5
1950	9·0–11·0	4·5–5·5	46·0–50·0	33·5–40·5

* For a discussion of the basis of these estimates see Appendix A. The estimated total sales of footwear and sales by different economic types of retailer include rubber footwear but exclude footwear repairs and the sale by footwear shops of goods other than footwear. The 'other retailers' group is a residual group and therefore includes all sales not covered in the other categories, including mail order sales and club trading.

Historically there have been three main types of small-scale retailer in the footwear trade: the producer/retailer, that is the boot and shoe maker, the general dealer who sold footwear and the small-scale specialist footwear retailer. The decline in the importance of the producer/retailer has been discussed above. The general dealer, usually a draper or clothier, selling footwear also declined steadily in importance throughout these years. A small, non-specialist retailer could not possibly stock the range of fittings and styles that were being demanded by customers following the improvements in manufacturing techniques. By 1950 only in rural areas were the general dealers of any significance with their small stock of working boots and shoes.

The small-scale specialist retailer passed through several phases of development. In the last quarter of the nineteenth century the numbers and importance of this type of retailer increased with the call for new outlets to distribute the factory-made footwear. There was a parallel expansion of multiple shop, Co-operative and small-scale specialist retailing in these years and a decline of the general dealer and the producer/retailer of footwear. From the first decades of the twentieth century, however, the continued success and widening appeal of the multiple shop technique of trading brought to a halt the progress of the small-scale retailer in the low- and medium-price trade. These types of retailers remained in the market but they became the marginal units. The small-scale retailer in the inter-war years could not afford the main street sites or imitate the display and service methods of the larger-scale retailers. Only in the very cheapest end of the trade and when the market was too small to warrant the establishment of a branch of the large-scale type of retailer, that is in the very small towns or small shopping areas of the larger towns, could the small-scale retailer survive.

At the same time, however, the loss by the small-scale retailer of a competitive position vis-à-vis the large-scale retailers in one respect was partly compensated for by two other developments. First the introduction of trade marks, branding, advertisement, and price maintenance by a number of manufacturers enabled the small-scale retailer to maintain some share of the medium-price market. Secondly the continued decline of bespoke shoe making at the upper end of the trade enabled the small-scale individual retailer to advance in this section by specialization in very high-class products. Both developments were assisted by the introduction of the in-stock system by manufacturers. Trade marks in the footwear trade began to appear in the first decades of the twentieth century following the considerable improvements in manufacturing technique and the production of higher grades of factory-made footwear. This higher-grade footwear was welcomed by many of the craftsmen producer/retailers and they began to shift from bespoke to specialist retailing. Further, some protection against the competition of the multiple shop retailers was being afforded by the parallel growth of manufacturer advertising and resale price maintenance.

The wholesalers assisted the small-scale retailers to keep abreast the trend towards diversification in styles and fittings in the inter-war years, but in the medium and upper end of the trade it was the in-stock system that proved of greatest benefit. This was a system whereby the retailer ordered and held only a very small stock of a particular line but was backed by a guarantee of immediate replacement when necessary from the manufacturer's warehouse. By this means the small-scale retailer was able to offer the consumer a wide range of styles and fittings, and in particular was able to develop the sale of the multi-fitting shoe, without locking up the whole of his capital in stock. The system also led to a decrease in fluctuations in employment on the manufacturing side, as production could be planned for stock-holding and was not dependent on orders all coming in a rush at the beginning of the season. Further, the close control over the sales position enabled manufacturers to gauge more accurately the exact nature of the consumer demand. By the middle of the century, however, the increasing concern of the manufacturers with the marketing of their branded goods had resulted in many of the independent retailers first becoming agents of the manufacturers and later coming under their direct financial control. Thus the firms were in effect branches of a multiple shop organization even though the earlier trading name was still used.

The first half of the twentieth century, therefore, witnessed a decline in the relative importance of the small-scale specialist footwear retailer in the trade as a whole. The developments in the techniques of production and marketing, however, meant that this decline was by no means as rapid as appeared probable at one stage, and the decline was uneven in different sections of the trade.

Suggestions as to future trends in the trade

The future trends in retailing in the footwear trade are of considerable interest if for no other reason than that this trade saw the earliest development of multiple shop retailing. Naturally a number of factors relating to the future are complete 'unknowns' and a detailed discussion of possible trends would be of no value. An attempt may be made, however, on the basis of past and present developments and problems of the different types of retailers, to make some suggestions as to possible future trends, couched in some instances in terms of questions rather than assertions.

As a background for the discussion, the assumption may be made that the future developments on the manufacturing side of the trade will be in the direction of greater emphasis on styling and perhaps on fashion in footwear and of improvements in fittings based on close study of consumer need. Such a study should reduce the number of different fittings rather than increase them. At the same time it can be assumed that there will be an increase in 'footwear consciousness' on the part of the consumer. It would appear most unlikely however that the proportion of total expenditure by consumers represented by expenditure on footwear will increase markedly.[1]

The future trends in department store and Co-operative trading in footwear would appear to be relatively easy to forecast. In the case of department stores there seems no reason for anticipating a rapid rise in the share held of the total trade; if anything, the reverse. The increased competition that the stores will face as a result of upgrading by some multiple shop retailers and an extension of the system of leasing departments in stores may reduce the share held by this type of retailer. In the case of the Co-operative Societies there may be some increase in

---

[1] The estimates of total retail expenditure by consumers given in Appendix A show that between 1900 and 1950 there was practically no change in the proportion of total expenditure in these years represented by purchase of footwear. Between 1938 and 1950 there has, however, with full employment, been an increase in the relative importance of the sales of children's footwear, and this position will probably be maintained.

their share of the total trade, but there are very few signs that any radical changes in the organization of the Co-operative footwear trade are envisaged which would enable the Societies to compete directly, using the same specialist techniques, with the multiple shop retailers.

The future of multiple shop retailing in the footwear trade is more problematical. While the general advantages of this form of retailing are clear enough, a number of problems are being faced which may set a limit to or at least hinder further significant expansion. One of these difficulties is that of obtaining sites. Main street siting has become an essential part of the footwear multiple shop method of trading. In the past, while there were still private traders in main streets, while there was an increasing and shifting population and new housing estates and shopping districts were being built, the expansion of multiple shop firms by purchasing existing properties and leasing new ones in new estates was practicable. But the number of private traders in main streets is now very small, the number interested in selling their shops even fewer, and both the rate of increase in the population and in the building of new estates is likely to be much lower in the future than in the years between the wars. Expansion might be possible if the multiple shop retailers extended their activities to the semi-urban areas and to the very small towns, but such an extension would entail a considerable change in the outlook of firms as to the minimum size and turnover of a profitable branch.

The alternative to more shops is bigger shops with a higher turnover per branch. There has undoubtedly been a trend since 1930 in the direction of the establishment of larger branches, that is branches with a larger number of employees, and since 1945 the preference for larger units has continued. Most multiple shop organizations would agree that there are at present rather too many footwear shops in the main streets of most towns, that the capacity of the existing shops is not fully utilized, and that one larger, better designed and laid out shop in the main street could undertake with ease and efficiency the trade now divided among three or four smaller shops. This element of 'overshopping' in the footwear trade has resulted from competition between multiple shop firms rather than competition between large-scale retailers and small-scale retailers.

But a trend towards larger shops or towards the replacement of two or three smaller branches by one larger, better designed one is unlikely to proceed smoothly. One problem is that of acquiring larger sites in main streets already saturated with large-scale retailers. Certainly there is the possibility of making greater use of existing premises by utilizing the basements and the first floors of buildings, but window display has always been extremely important in the fashion-conscious footwear trade. A second problem is the operation of competition between multiple shop firms. The decision to close a branch in one area and to attempt to attract the customer to a larger branch in an adjoining area is a difficult one to make when the branches of competitors remain in the former area. Competitive pressure in the past has led to both more and larger shops accompanied by an element of unused capacity rather than fewer but larger shops. No doubt firms will continue to make decisions to close down branches that are too small or uneconomic compared with newer larger ones that have been acquired, but the overall progress towards fewer but larger footwear multiple shop branches would appear likely to be very slow. Only if a series of agreements were to be made between two or three multiple shop firms in each of the separate price and geographical markets to pool their retailing resources and to trade jointly in a given area from one shop instead of say from three, would any rapid rationalization of the multiple shop footwear trade appear possible.

Even if larger branches are established, however, will such a development necessarily increase the share of the total trade held by the multiple shop retailer? For the last two decades a feature of the footwear trade has been competition not between the multiple shop retailer and the small-scale retailer but between rival multiple shop firms in each of the different price, quality, style and shopping markets. The small-scale retailers have tended to operate in different areas or have catered for a different section of the trade to that of the multiple shop retailers. Only the private traders who were agents for manufacturers or who specialized in branded footwear competed directly with multiple shop branches.

In the future the competition between multiple shop firms will undoubtedly continue. Those firms which possess the superior capital resources and managerial and administrative ability will no doubt acquire and build larger shops and offer a wider selection of goods to the consumer in more comfortable surroundings. Other firms will drop out of the race or will be acquired by the successful firms. But this process, while leading perhaps to some increase in the relative importance of the very large multiple shop firms, will not necessarily increase the share of multiple shop retailers in the total market. Only if the stronger multiple shop firms with their larger branches begin to attract customers away from the Co-operative Societies, the department stores, and the small-scale retailers will the share of multiple shop retailing increase. These other types of retailers are, however, protected to some extent by loyalty of customers, by shopping habits and, of considerable importance in the case of the small-scale one-shop retailers, by manufacturer branding, advertisement and resale price maintenance.

Viewing the trading methods and techniques of multiple shop organizations as a whole in 1950 there is no doubt that the merging of some firms with more progressive and go-ahead firms and the replacement of some of the older types of branches by those of a newer type will lead to the attraction of additional customers. The trading methods and the branches of a number of the older-established multiple shop firms are outdated and outmoded and have few, if any, advantages over other retailers. But in the longer run it may be asked whether the present policies of the leading multiple shop firms of purchasing larger shops with more elaborate interiors, of providing greater comfort and more complete fitting services, and of increasing overhead costs and the ratio of fixed investment are in fact the policies likely to lead to a further significant rise in the share of multiple shop retailers in the total trade. May not the answer lie rather in larger branch shops offering and displaying a wide variety of styles and fashions, including branded footwear, but operating on the basis of a measure of self-selection by the consumer? Such branches could utilize the advances in the direction of more simplified fittings, and might stress as vigorously as did the early multiple shop firms the price appeal of their goods. If these measures were adopted many of the advantages of the small-scale retailers in the manufacturer branded and advertised section of the market would disappear, and above all the multiple shop retailers would appear again as the method of retailing that represented a direct gain to the consumer. And it may be argued that if the specialist footwear multiple shop retailers do not develop their trading techniques along these lines a part of the market may be lost to other retailers trading in a wider range of goods and organized on variety chain store lines.

Finally, in regard to the future trends of the integration of production and distribution in the footwear trade, any further increase in the importance of integration would appear to be most unlikely. The need for the retailing side of the business to stock a variety of styles limits the possibilities of integration as discussed above, in most price markets. Further, if there is any tendency for the size of the multiple shop retailing firms to increase, for example by the doubling of the number of shops or the doubling of the size of shops at present controlled, this may encourage specialization on retailing only. On the other hand, it seems most probable that the association between multiple shop retailers and independent manufacturers will be much closer in the future and that a form of the in-stock system will assist the multiple shop retailers to widen even further the range of footwear stocked in their branches.

CHAPTER XV

THE CHEMISTS' AND DRUGGISTS' TRADE

The trade in the nineteenth century

The chemist and druggist stems from a number of different trades, and not until the end of the eighteenth century could the profession or trade of the chemist and druggist be said to be appearing as a distinct entity.[1] The recruits to this growing trade were drawn from the ranks of the apothecaries, the dispensers to physicians, and the manufacturing chemists and druggists, who extended their trade to include medicines generally, and from the ranks of the grocers, who for generations had sold drugs and medicines alongside spices and herbs and some of whom now began to specialize on the medicinal side. These early chemists and druggists reflected in their trade their diverse origins and their business included the sale of crude drugs and of chemicals, the dispensing of prescriptions, the prescribing of medicines, the sale of tea, spices, herbs and household requisites and often the sale of colours, paints and oils. As the apothecaries ceased their direct retailing activities so the business of the chemists and druggists grew, and in 1841 the Pharmaceutical Society of Great Britain was formed 'for the purpose of protecting the permanent interests and increasing the respectability of chemists and druggists'. The Society rapidly became representative of the whole trade. In 1843 it secured a Royal Charter and in the Pharmacy Acts of 1852 and 1868 the use of the titles of 'pharmaceutical chemist', of 'chemist and druggist', of 'chemist' and of 'druggist' was restricted to persons whose names were included, after examinations conducted by the Society, in the official register of the Society. Further, a Schedule of Poisons was attached to the 1868 Act and the sale of, and the keeping of open shop for the sale of, substances named therein was restricted to registered chemists and druggists and to pharmaceutical chemists.

At this date, therefore, while the sales of crude drugs, medicines proprietary and non-proprietary, herbs, chemicals and so on was by no means confined to the chemist and druggist—the grocer and the oil and colourman and even the bookseller sold some of these goods—the use of the title 'chemist and druggist' was confined to registered persons, as was the sale of substances listed in the Schedule of Poisons. The registra-

[1] The information in this section is based largely on an excellent account of the origins and history of the trade in *Report of the Committee of Enquiry*, Part 1, published by the Pharmaceutical Society of Great Britain, 1939, pp. 2 fol.

tion of chemists and druggists was an individual question and the trade was entirely in the hands of individual retailers.

The forty years between the Pharmacy Act of 1868 and the Poisons and Pharmacy Act of 1908 saw radical shifts in this pattern. Of considerable importance were the legal changes that were made. In the 'seventies some of the universal suppliers, the 'stores', which were growing in size and trade, notably in London, and which from their start were limited liability companies, began selling drugs and medicines. To attract customers they used the title 'chemist' for the part of their shop that dealt in drugs, and, if a qualified person was in charge, they also sold poisons. The Pharmaceutical Society held that this practice was contrary to the Act of 1868 and challenged one of the limited companies in the Courts. In 1880, however, the Society lost its appeal to the House of Lords when it was held that a limited liability company was not a person within the meaning of the Act and consequently in using the title 'Chemist and Druggist' no offence had been committed, provided the actual sale of poisons by the company was in the hands of a qualified person. This decision made possible the rise of the limited liability companies in the chemists' trade, though until the later Act of 1908 the Pharmaceutical Society discouraged the growth of companies and even tried to prevent qualified and registered chemists from taking employment with the companies. By the turn of the century, however, it had become clear that the company chemists were too well established to be defeated, and the Society concerned itself more with insisting that the companies themselves and the shops should be run by qualified persons than with attempting to put the companies out of the trade. Eventually the position was regularized in the 1908 Poisons and Pharmacy Act which provided that bodies corporate should be permitted to carry on the business of a chemist and druggist provided that the part of the business connected with poisons was under the control and management of a qualified superintendent. Further the titles used by registered persons could be used by companies provided that a qualified person was a member of the Board of Directors, and the Pharmacy Acts were made to apply to bodies corporate in the same way as they applied to individuals.

This Act thus removed any doubts as to the status of companies in the trade. At the same time the trade itself had been changing consequent upon developments in the methods of manufacturing, in the nature of the goods produced, and in the character of consumer demand. In the middle of the nineteenth century there was no sharp division between the manufacturing or, as the term is used in this trade, the wholesale chemist and druggist, and the retail chemist and druggist. The majority of wholesalers carried on businesses as retailers and all the retailers in their turn undertook some manufacture or preparation of drugs, chemicals and medicines. In the next half-century there was a growing trend towards specialization; the wholesale chemists giving up their retail activities and concentrating on large-scale production of chemicals, drugs and medicinal preparations, while the retail chemist restricted his own manufacturing and purchased a wide range of goods at a lower cost from the wholesale chemist. Particularly important was the growing efficiency in and the increased volume of the production of preparations and compounded medicines by the wholesale chemists and other manufacturers. Some production or preparation of crude drugs and galenicals by the retail chemist continued, but in the opening decades of the new century his purchases of packaged and branded medicines, drugs and other preparations were as important as his purchases of raw materials. The actual transition from own preparations to the branded goods of manufacturers often included an intermediate stage in which the wholesale chemist made up goods for the retailers but they were branded in the latter's name.

The sale of these packaged branded proprietary goods was by no means confined to the chemist and druggist. In fact in the early stages of their sale many of the bona fide chemists viewed these proprietary medicines as 'quack nostrums' which might find an outlet through the unqualified grocer or oil and colourman, or even bookseller, but had no place on the shelves of the chemist and druggist able to do both the prescribing and the dispensing of any preparation likely to be needed by his customers. Large-scale advertising accompanied the production of these packaged proprietary medicines, however, and the demand for them increased rapidly. Some of the chemists could stand aside but the majority found that failure to stock these products or to be able to offer near substitutes meant losing customers. In any event refusal to stock weakened the claim always made, though not always pressed, by the chemist and druggist to be the sole purveyor of medicines and drugs of all kinds.

The manufacturers of these branded and proprietary medicines were concerned chiefly with securing public goodwill and increasing sales, and to them advertising backed by a large number of outlets for the goods appeared to offer the greatest chance of success. It followed almost inevitably that the diversity of outlets and the ease with which the products could be handled led to their sale by non-chemists at prices and margins well below those traditionally charged and expected by the qualified chemist. These early proprietary medicines were among the first advertised packed and definitely-priced goods to come on to the market and they afforded a great attraction, both to retailers in other trades whose usual margins were lower than those in the chemists' and druggists' trade and to chemists and druggists who wished to employ the 'loss leader' principle of making customers believe that the low price of the proprietary lines was indicative of the low prices of the other goods sold.

The results of this 'price war' between chemists and other traders and between the chemists themselves are discussed later, but this 'war' was one more factor that helped to bring about a marked change in the character of the chemists' and druggists' trade between the middle of the nineteenth century and 1914. The growth of wholesale manufacturing of drugs and chemicals and the production of branded, packed proprietary medicines led to a decline in the role of the chemist as a producer/retailer who made and sold his own goods and prepared his own remedies. It also led to an increase in the sale of medicines by retailers outside the chemists' trade proper. And as demands on the chemist for skill in preparing his own remedies declined, the demands on him as a merchant and as a businessman able to control and watch the stock turn of the large number of lines he had to carry had increased. Finally the trade itself was no longer entirely in the hands of the small-scale independent chemist, but company shops had appeared in considerable numbers, and these businesses were run on entirely different lines to those of the traditional chemist.

The changes that took place in this half-century or so should not perhaps be exaggerated. The chemist of 1914 still practised a skilled trade, dispensing prescriptions and undertaking some preparation and packing of his own remedies, and the sale of medicines outside the chemists' trade was by no means entirely novel. But by the First World War there were signs that the whole character of the trade was shifting from that of a leisurely and skilled profession to one in which the economics, salesmanship, rival claims and bustle of the market place played a significant part.

The changes in the trade, 1914–1950

Between the First World War and 1950 the changes in the chemists' trade were ones of degree rather than of transformation. Little new legislation affecting the professional position of the chemist was introduced. The National Health Insurance Act, however, which provided that dispensing was to be performed only by, or under the direct supervision of, a pharmacist, and that the supply of medicines was permitted only through these persons and firms carrying on business under the Poisons and Pharmacy Act of 1908, secured for the pharmacist the whole of this sector of the trade at least. The volume of National Health dispensing grew steadily in the inter-war years and the operation of the National Health Act in the years following the Second World War brought a very great increase in the importance of this side of the chemists' business.

In other respects the trends noted above in the years before 1914 were continued in the trade. Large-scale production by wholesale chemists and manufacturers continued to increase, and with the use of more complex organic chemicals and biological products, which could only be prepared economically on a very large scale, the retail chemist practically ceased to undertake any manufacturing. The production and popularity of branded proprietary articles increased tremendously, as did the number of their retail outlets. The chemist and druggist remained the most important outlet for these products, but grocers, confectioners, tobacconists, licensed houses, hairdressers, general shops and variety chain stores, to mention a few, all carried some lines of these goods.[1]

The increase in the number of lines of branded goods sold by the chemist made further demands on his skill as a businessman in regard to ordering, stock-taking and controlling the rate of stock-turn. These demands were further increased by the trend in the inter-war years towards widening the range of goods stocked. The public began to expect the chemist to sell, alongside his medicines and dispensing service, a wide range of toilet preparations and toilet requisites, in particular cosmetics, sundries such as hot-water-bottles, hair brushes and lotions and sometimes even electrical apparatus and photographic goods of various sorts, and to provide services such as developing. The chemist in his turn was not unwilling to meet the demand of the public in this respect.

In one way the chemists' trade after 1914 differed from the trade at the turn of the century in that 'price wars' more or less ceased with the successful introduction of effective resale price maintenance of most of the proprietary medicines and of a fair range of toilet preparations and requisites. The first moves in this direction had been made before 1914, and in the years after the war price-cutting by non-chemist retailers was limited in extent and by chemists very rare indeed.

The chemist of 1950 had gone further along the road he was already travelling in 1914. He was protected in his sales of poisons and in his National Health dispensing by Acts of Parliament. With medical treatment becoming a right free to all irrespective of income, the latter part of his business was maintained and expanded. Particularly was this so in the years following the National Health Act of 1946 when dispensing rose from approximately 10–15 % of the chemists' turnover in the pre-1938 years to some 20–30 %.

---

[1] The number of makers and vendors in Great Britain paying medicine stamp duty rose from some 30,000 in 1895 to 40,000 in 1905. The numbers then rose slowly to 1920 when the figure stood at some 46,000. In the inter-war years the rise was very rapid, 56,000 in 1925, 100,000 in 1930 and 164,000 in 1938.

The developments of medical science in the decades following 1914 were paralleled by the raising of the standard of education and training required of the qualified chemist. The wider range and increased complexity and potency of the drugs and medicines prescribed by doctors called for a higher standard of knowledge on the part of the pharmacist to check the prescribing and the dosage, and the responsibility of the pharmacists had increased. For the rest of his business, the role of the chemist as a producer/retailer had practically disappeared, and the demands on his technical skill and training when selling the price-maintained proprietary medicines, toilet articles and non-chemists' goods such as stationery and photographic equipment which constituted the great bulk of his turnover were far less than the demands on his business and trading knowledge and acumen. And in this section of his trade, while the chemist was no longer faced with serious competition in price, he was being faced with increasing competition from a larger number of outlets, and many of these in terms of convenience to the consumers had an advantage over the chemist.

This brief account of the changes in the character of the chemists' trade in the years 1850–1950 and in the legislative framework within which these changes took place provides a background against which the developments in the retail structure of the trade can be discussed. The emergence of multiple shop trading and its evolution will be examined first and will be followed by a brief discussion of the chemists' shops in department stores and of those controlled by Co-operative Societies, as well as of the progress of the small-scale independent chemist.

The development of multiple shop retailing

Reference was made above to the success of the registered pharmacists in 1868 in securing statutory recognition of their sole right to handle poisons and to use the titles 'chemist' and 'druggist'. This victory did not, however, in any way prevent other unqualified or unregistered retailers from handling non-poisonous medicines and drugs, and the grocers and the oil and colourmen, to mention two trades, had regularly sold such goods. Further, the Pharmaceutical Society and the qualified pharmacists of the nineteenth century stressed the importance of individual qualifications and they did not envisage a registered chemist practising other than on his own account, after the same manner as the kindred profession, the doctors. It is no surprise, therefore, to find that the earliest multiple shop organizations in the chemists' and druggists' trade developed from outside the ranks of the registered chemists.

The first multiple shop organizations that sold drugs and medicines in most of their branches were probably the oil and colour multiple shop firms of the 1870's, for example G. Mence Smith of London. This type of firm, however, did not specialize in medicines and drugs, and their sale of such goods decreased as their interests centred more on hardware and household stores and groceries. The first multiple shop firm specializing in drugs was undoubtedly that of Jesse Boot of Nottingham, who, inheriting a small mixed herbalist and grocer's shop, boldly called himself a druggist in 1877 and a 'Cash Chemist' in 1880, and had formed a limited liability company with some 10 branches by 1883. The House of Lords decision of 1880 had opened the way for company chemists even if the directors, like Jesse Boot, were not qualified, and by 1890 there were 3 other firms in the trade with over 10 branches each. These were Taylors Drug Company Ltd. of Leeds and Yorkshire, W. T. Warhurst of Liverpool, and Timothy White of Portsmouth, the last two named being old-established firms—Timothy White, for example, having started as a ships' chandler and general store in 1848. The 'nineties saw a big increase in the number of multiple shop chemists' organizations, though by no means all of these survived to trade with more than 10 branches. Day's Southern Drug Company of Southampton, which dated back to 1874, was one firm to rise rapidly in the 'nineties, and Lewis & Burrows Ltd., with 11 branches, was founded in 1895. Other firms which emerged in these years were Magor Ltd. of Birmingham, Needhams Ltd. of Yorkshire, and H. B. Pare of Manchester. Day's Southern Drug Company was later merged with Day's Metropolitan Drug Company, which was taken over by Boots in 1901 to give the latter firm a strong foothold in the London area. Needhams Ltd. later merged with Squires Ltd. of Birmingham, which in 1929 changed its name to Taylors (Cash Chemists) Midland Ltd. and later became part of the Timothy Whites & Taylors group.

An outline of the development of multiple shop retailing in the trade from 1895 to 1950 is given in Table 71, which presents estimates of the number of firms in existence and the number of branches controlled by them in different years. An attempt has been made in the estimates given in Table 71 to include details of firms that have gone out of existence or have amalgamated with existing firms as well as data relating to firms operating in 1950. Altogether information relating to 49 firms has been included in this table, and of the 24 firms no longer trading separately in 1950 12 amalgamated with other firms and 12 appear to have gone out of existence or the numbers of branches trading fell below 10.

The estimates given in Table 71 can be used to show the rate of growth in the number of branches of multiple shop organizations in different periods. This analysis is attempted in Table 72, which shows the net increase and the rate of net increase in the number of branches

Table 71. *Estimates of the number of multiple shop firms and branches in the chemists' and druggists' trade, 1895–1950*

Year	10–24 branches		25–49 branches		50–99 branches		100 or more branches		Totals			
									10 or more branches		25 or more branches	
	Number of		Number of		Number of		Number of		Number of		Number of	
	Firms	Branches	Firms	Branches	Firms	Branches	Firms	Branches	Firms	Branches	Firms	Branches
1895	4	54	2	74	1	50	—	—	7	178	3	124
1900	8	131	1	30	1	68	1	181	11	410	3	279
1905	9	115	1	36	1	78	1	314	12	543	3	428
1910	8	101	2	61	2	144	1	394	13	700	5	599
1915	7	96	1	38	3	228	1	579	12	941	5	845
1920	10	149	1	36	3	241	1	618	15	1,044	5	895
1925	13	189	2	67	—	—	4	1,137	19	1,393	6	1,204
1930	16	204	3	98	—	—	3	1,439	22	1,741	6	1,537
1935	20	269	3	85	2	110	2	1,816	27	2,280	7	2,011
1939	22	316	5	155	1	58	2	1,933	30	2,462	8	2,146
1950	16	238	6	188	1	57	2	2,025	25	2,508	9	2,270

Table 72. *Rate of net increase in the number of branches of multiple shop firms in the chemists' and druggists' trade, 1901–50*

Year	Branches of firms with 10 or more branches			Branches of firms with 25 or more branches		
	Net increase in number of branches	Percentage net increase	Average yearly net increase in numbers	Net increase in number of branches	Percentage net increase	Average yearly net increase in numbers
1901–1905	133	32	27	149	53	30
1906–1910	157	30	31	171	40	34
1911–1915	241	34	48	246	41	49
1916–1920	103	11	21	50	6	10
1921–1925	349	33	70	309	34	62
1926–1930	348	25	70	333	28	67
1931–1935	539	31	108	474	31	95
1936–1939	182	8	45	135	7	34
1940–1950	46	2	4	124	6	11

in operation in different periods between 1901 and 1950. The rate of net increase is shown as a percentage increase in the numbers in each period and the absolute increase in the number of branches in each period is also shown as an average yearly net increase.

The main feature of the rate of growth in the number of multiple shop branches in this trade as indicated by Table 72 is the consistency shown. Except for the period of the First World War, the rate of increase in the five-yearly periods between 1900 and 1935 was between 25 % and 33 %. The peak periods of activity were the years following the passing of the 1908 Pharmacy Act and the years 1931–35. The slowing down in the rate of growth after 1935 was in part due to reorganization by one large firm following a series of amalgamations with other firms, and the Second World War brought about an actual decrease in the number of branches trading, the figure in 1945 being some 5 % below 1939. From 1946 onwards, however, many closed branches were re-opened, and by 1950 many new ones had been acquired, almost all purchases of existing chemists' shops.

The division of the firms by size-groups in Table 71 shows the importance throughout these years of the large firms with over 100 branches each. This is demonstrated more clearly in Table 73, which shows the proportion of the total number of branches in existence controlled by the largest firms.

Table 73. *Relative importance of the largest multiple shop firms in the chemists' and druggists' trade, 1900–50*

Year	Total branches of firms with 10 or more branches			Total branches of firms with 25 or more branches	
	Proportion controlled by			Proportion controlled by	
	The largest firm %	The 2 largest firms %	The 5 largest firms %	The largest firm %	The 2 largest firms %
1900	44	61	78	65	89
1910	56	69	86	66	80
1920	59	68	86	69	79
1925	53	64	85	61	75
1930	50	75	87	57	85
1935	47	79	86	54	90
1939	49	78	84	56	90
1950	51	81	86	56	89

The largest firm, Boots Pure Drug Company Ltd., is seen to have increased in size at approximately the same rate as the total increase in the number of branches in existence. Between 1900 and 1950 this firm controlled some 54–66 % of all the branches of firms with 25 branches or more. The increase in the proportion of the total number of branches controlled by the two largest firms from 1930 onwards was the result of a number of amalgamations and mergers between 1928 and 1934 which led to the emergence of a second large firm with a national coverage of branches—Timothy Whites & Taylors Ltd.

These two firms controlled some four-fifths of the total number of branches in existence belonging to firms with over 25 branches each, and to a large extent the history of the development of multiple shop retailing in the chemists' and druggists' trade is a story of the development of these two large firms and of the firms that amalgamated with them.

The trading policies and characteristics of multiple shop firms

Until the last decade of the nineteenth century, as suggested above most of the multiple shop firms came into the chemists' trade from the proprietary medicines and general drugs side rather than from the ranks of the chemists proper. Once the firms were established they widened their scope by the employment of qualified pharmacists. Jesse Boot, for example, engaged his first pharmacist in 1884 when the firm had just over 10 branches. The progress of these limited companies on the dispensing side was however slow, owing to the undertone of opposition from the Pharmaceutical Society and the lack of confidence on the part of the public. But the passing of the 1908 Poisons and Pharmacy Act removed remaining doubts, and practically all branches of multiple shop organizations at the end of the first decade of the twentieth century employed qualified pharmacists.[1]

The difference in the early years between the small-scale independent chemist and the multiple shop organization, however, extended further than the qualifications of the persons employed. There was also an important difference in the methods of trading. The multiple organizations from the start emphasized price appeal. Jesse Boot's first drug shop in Goose Gate, Nottingham, in 1877, carried the sign 'J. Boot, Drugs and Proprietary Articles at Reduced Prices', and this challenge set the tone of subsequent policy. The later multiple organizations in the 'nineties and at the turn of the century, particularly Taylors Drug Company Ltd., Day's Southern Drug Stores, Needhams and Squires of Birmingham, and Lewis & Burrows Ltd., followed the same trading practice.[2] As can be imagined, in a trade where price had seemed secondary to relief of pain or sickness, where skill in handling, making and mixing the drugs and in prescribing and dispensing the medicines seemed more important than salesmanship, where the retail gross

---

[1] Boots Pure Drug Company Ltd., for example, stated in a *Prospectus*, July 1911, that there were 550 fully qualified chemists employed by the Company, which then had 468 retail branches.

[2] When Lewis & Burrows Ltd. opened branches in the Pimlico area of London circulars were distributed announcing that the firm, 'the popular store chemists, have declared war against the extortionate prices charged by chemists in the district'. Quoted by B. S. Yamey, 'The Origin of Resale Price Maintenance: A Study of Three Branches of Retail Trade', *Economic Journal*, vol. LXII, no. 247, September 1952, p. 523n.

margin was traditional or almost hereditary, and where an element of state recognition suggested a professional status above the ordinary trader, such a direct price appeal, based on low margins and high turnover and backed by vigorous advertisement, caused many misgivings.

The multiple shop organizations were faced with strong opposition from existing retailers, and being to some extent handicapped in their entry into the prescribing side of the trade they broadened the range of non-medicinal goods handled at a very early date.[1] Further, when confronted with difficulties of obtaining supplies from wholesale chemists who disapproved of their pricing policy the multiple firms developed their own manufacturing. Jesse Boot opened his first factory in 1888 and other multiple shop organizations in the 'nineties and after the turn of the century followed suit, though in a less extensive fashion.

These developments, along with the popularity of the low pricing policy with the public, particularly among the working classes who were unable to afford a doctor except in serious emergency and were attracted by low cost remedies, enabled the multiple shop firms to outflank the opposition of the established chemists and druggists and to increase the number of their branches rapidly. The success of the multiple shop firms led many independent chemists to follow their example to the extent of stocking proprietary and branded medicines and some non-medicinal goods and selling them at low prices. The only chemists who could forswear imitation entirely were those at the higher end of the trade having a wealthy and loyal clientèle for their special products.

The success of the multiple shop trading policies and their imitation by others both within and without the confines of the chemists' trade proper was one of the factors leading to the severe price war of the 'nineties which continued into the opening years of the new century. Many of the independent retail chemists began losing heavily in the war, and if price cutting was allowed to proceed unchecked the virtual extinction of the specialist independent retailer appeared possible. Long used to association, the answer of the chemists was to combine, and in 1896, along with a handful of wholesalers and manufacturers, a group of retail chemists formed the Proprietary Articles Trade Association which was aimed at stopping the cutting of prices of proprietary articles. The founders stressed that all concerned in the chemists' trade tended to lose by price cutting, the manufacturers and the wholesalers as well as the retailers. One of the main arguments to manufacturers was that producers' sales suffered by allowing price

---

[1] Toilet preparations and requisites and surgical sundries were the most important lines of non-medical goods handled. Boots, however, in 1900 started selling stationery and operated a circulating library in some of their branches.

cutting to go unchecked, as retailers in order to gain a minimum livelihood were forced to practise 'substitution' whenever they could. That
is, the retailer offered the customer who had been attracted by manufacturers' advertisements to ask for a particular article an alternative
brand, or a brand of his own make, which carried a higher retail margin
than the cut-price brand, and used his privileged position to persuade
the customer to purchase the alternative. The brands that were sold
at low prices it was argued were driven out of the market, as the gross
margin had fallen so low that no retailer could afford to stock them.

The debates and conflicting theories put forward and the trials,
failures and successes of the resale price maintenance movement need
not be discussed here.[1] Suffice it to say that the movement was successful
among the independent chemists. Ten years after the foundation of the
P.A.T.A. more than one-third of all independent chemists, most of the
wholesale chemists and some 200 manufacturers had joined. In the
following ten years two or three multiple shop organizations joined the
Association while others, although not formally taking out membership,
agreed to adhere to fixed prices, and by 1914 resale price maintenance
was becoming the rule in the trade both in regard to chemists' goods
proper and to the widening range of toilet preparations and requisites
being sold.

The withdrawal by the Pharmaceutical Society, after the 1908 Act, of
opposition to multiple shop organizations describing themselves as
chemists and druggists and undertaking dispensing, and the practically
coincidental cessation by multiple shop firms of their direct price-cutting
activities, eased the strained relations in the trade. This was one of the
factors which led to the rapid advance of multiple shop firms in the
years just prior to the First World War. They were free from any legal
doubts as to their status, and opposition, overt at any rate, from the
professional organizations of the pharmacists had ceased. The change
in policy by multiple shop firms in regard to price cutting may have
been influenced by their clearly recognized status following the 1908
Act, but apart from the vigorous opposition their policies had aroused
the firms may also have found that price cutting, while efficacious in the
early stages of development, was neither necessary nor economically
sound once a strong position in the trade had been won.

In the inter-war years as the trade itself continued to expand so
did the multiple shop organizations. Practically all the fair-sized
firms increased their manufacturing activities and in many cases had
substitute products of their own manufacture to offer to customers
alongside the privately manufactured branded articles. This integration
of production and distribution was taking place at a time when the

[1] A short account is given by B. S. Yamey, loc. cit.

independent chemist, the earlier producer/retailer, was becoming more and more dependent upon bought-out proprietary lines. The increase in the volume of manufacturing by multiple shop retailing organizations did not, however, necessarily mean an increase in the proportion of goods sold that was represented by goods of their own manufacture. The continuous increase in the number of lines and the widening of the range of goods sold by the shops limited the possibilities in this direction, and the proportion of 'own specialities' to total sales of multiple shop organizations rarely exceeded one-third and was more usually between 15 and 25 %.

Integration by multiple shop firms had, however, existed prior to 1914. The new feature of the multiple shop development in the inter-war years was the shift of emphasis in their trading policies from price to service. This shift took many forms. In the first place, the passing of the 1908 Act left the path completely free to multiple shop firms to develop the dispensing side of their business by the employment of qualified chemists, and the multiple organizations took full advantage of the impetus to dispensing given by the National Insurance Act. To do this the multiple shop retailers had to 'up-grade' their branches, and in fact a transformation took place from a period when the customers had second thoughts about taking a prescription to a company shop that sold cut-rate drugs to a period when the reputation of some of the multiple shop organizations for the speed, reliability and efficiency of their prescribing was as high as any in the trade. In the case of Boots Pure Drug Company Ltd. alone the number of National Health prescriptions dispensed was over 5,000,000 in 1938, or three times the number in 1920, though the number of branches in existence in 1938 was less than double the number in 1920. By 1950 the number had risen to nearly 30,000,000. The dispensing of National Health prescriptions was never a particularly profitable line in a chemist's shop, but the provision of and reputation for such a service enhanced the standing of the shop, and dispensing brought potential customers into the shop—the goal of every retailer.

A second aspect of the development of service in the broadest sense was the increasing range of goods stocked by the multiple shop branches. All such branches in these years handled toilet and beauty preparations, toilet requisites and surgical goods and sundries in addition to drugs and medicines. A large number of them handled a further range, including photographic goods and sundries, fancy goods, household soaps and cleaners and stationery and books. This increased range of stock was laid out and displayed both in the windows and in the interiors of the shops in a way that attracted customers and encouraged them to purchase. The emphasis on display of goods, on encouragement of consumer inspection and choice, and on advertisement combined with trained service was a very far cry from the element of mystery—the bottles and jars, the awe-inspiring carboys of coloured water—of the chemist and druggist of the nineteenth century. The increase in dispensing and in the space required for display of the additional lines called for branches very much larger than those of the pre-1914 era, which had concentrated on selling a more limited range of low-priced medicines and drugs. Moreover, a wide range of stock made main street siting essential. These larger branches, most of which employed between 5 and 10 persons, provided with their brightly lit, clean and well laid out windows and interiors and their wide range of attractively displayed stock, apart entirely from the out-of-sight manufacturing and research activities, a particular quality of salesmanship and service which only some independent chemists could equal.

The variety chain stores

To complete the picture of multiple shop retailing in the chemists' trade a reference to the sales of chemists' goods and toilet articles by variety chain stores is necessary. In the inter-war years, particularly after 1930, as the number of branches of these organizations grew rapidly the stores represented an important outlet for certain lines. The trading policy of these firms was completely different from that of both the multiple shop chemist and the small-scale independent chemist. Instead of fixed prices and the provision of a maximum of service the variety chain stores emphasized low prices with practically no service, the consumer choosing and helping himself. The existence of the powerful Proprietary Articles Trade Association limited the number of lines which could be sold at prices under those charged by other retailers. Fixed-price lines were, however, sold alongside non-fixed-price lines and the attraction of the latter plus the general attraction of being able to see and choose a wide range of products under one roof tended to increase the sales by such branches of the former type of product even though the price gains of the consumer were nil. The variety chain stores in fact had combined the price appeal of the shops of the early multiple organizations with some of the display appeal of the shops of the later multiple organizations.

The Co-operative Societies

The Co-operative Societies, approaching the drug trade from the grocery and drysaltery angle, had practically since foundation always sold some chemists' goods to their members. The expansion in the trade in the last decades of the nineteenth century and the growing popularity of packaged branded proprietary lines led to some increase in the sales by the Co-operative Societies through the grocery departments, and in 1902 the Co-operative Wholesale Society established its own drug and drysaltery works producing proprietary medicines as well as crude drugs, polishes and other household requirements. The Societies sold some of the privately manufactured proprietary lines, but they had not played an important part in the 'price war' and fell in readily, at the turn of the century, with the campaign for general adherence to the retail prices fixed by many of the manufacturers. A dividend on purchases of these goods was, however, paid to members until in 1906 the Proprietary Articles Trade Association decided that this policy was equivalent to price cutting and therefore asked the Co-operative Societies to cease paying a dividend on proprietary brands. The Societies in many instances refused to do this and supplies from the manufacturers of proprietary goods were withheld. There followed an attempt by the Societies to develop the sales of lines produced by Wholesale Societies. This was successful in some goods of a relatively simple nature, such as cod liver oil, but the power of national advertising of complex proprietary lines, with recommendations from nurses, doctors and so on, was too strong for the Societies. A compromise was necessary and in the inter-war years the Co-operative Societies, in order to maintain some sale of drugs and medicines and toilet articles and requisites, had to come to an agreement with the Proprietary Articles Trade Association to sell the goods on the protected list at fixed prices without giving members a dividend on these purchases.

The sales by Co-operative Societies of drugs and sundries through a part of the grocery department continued, but with the development of the demand for medicines and toilet articles and the employment of qualified chemists for dispensing separate chemists' shops began to be established in the inter-war years. By 1937 there were some 420 such shops and the number increased rapidly in the following years, largely through the purchase of existing chemists' shops, until there were some 720 in 1946.

The department stores

Department stores, like Co-operative Societies, handled chemists' goods practically from their foundation, though unlike Co-operative stores they played a leading part in the late nineteenth century in selling drugs and proprietary medicines at reduced prices. The history of the handling of drugs and medicines by department stores was similar to that of the early multiple shop chemists in that they were under fire from the established chemists both for using the term 'chemist and druggist' and for selling at low prices. The developments after the turn of the century again followed a pattern similar to that of multiple shop retailing. When the legal doubts regarding the use of titles by the chemists' shops within department stores were removed by the 1908 Act, the department stores, partly as a result of a process of 'trading up', or catering for higher income groups, and partly as a result of the campaigns of the P.A.T.A., ceased price cutting to any serious extent. In the inter-war years the character of the trade of chemists' shops in department stores tended to change. While in some stores the employment of qualified chemists emphasized the all-round scope of the shops, in the majority the stress was increasingly placed on the sale of toilet preparations, toilet requisites and surgical goods and sundries. In the range of such goods and in the service accompanying their sale the department stores had a clear advantage over the independent chemist and some advantage over most branches of multiple shop organizations.

The small-scale retailer

References have been made in the above discussion to the activities and policies in these years of the independent chemists. They fought a losing battle in the attempt to keep companies and multiple shop firms out of the trade and failed to prevent the sale of drugs and medicines, mainly proprietary medicines, by a large number of retail outlets which had no connexion with the chemist's trade. On the other hand they were successful in keeping dispensing in the trade and, with the co-operation of manufacturers, in operating and enforcing the resale price maintenance of most branded medicines and drugs whether sold within the trade or outside. Further, many chemists were able to develop the sale of their 'own brand' goods, that is goods prepared by wholesale houses but branded in the name of the retailer. These successes and failures took place in the background of a continuously expanding trade, the main characteristic of which was the growth in the importance and sale of proprietary goods of all types—drugs, medicines, toilet preparations and requisites—at the expense of unbranded articles and packs made up by the chemist himself.

In meeting these changes the independent retailer tended to follow the example of other retailers, particularly multiple shop retailers, rather than to initiate new developments, and the process of adaptation was far from simple. The attempts to enlarge the range of goods sold and to keep pace with the ever-growing variety of brands of particular lines that were being produced and advertised led to problems of stock holding and stock control that demanded the highest commercial ability. The attempts to follow the leading shops in the trade in window design, layout and dressing and in elaborateness of interior display involved a scale of capital expenditure that not all chemists could meet without suffering financially. In particular the small-scale chemist had little chance of obtaining the sites or the size of shop that would allow of direct imitation of the much larger multiple shop branches, but even in the smaller shops the public had begun to expect the same type, if not the same range, of stock as that found in the larger shops.

However, the general buoyancy and expansion of the trade through-out these years, the flexibility and economic adaptability of the small-scale chemists, and above all the important personal relationship which continued to exist between the customer and the chemist, led to an increase rather than a decrease in his numbers. The number of such chemists rose from an estimated 8,000–9,000 in 1895 to 9,000–10,000 in 1914. In the inter-war years the rise was from just under 10,000 in 1920 to 12,000–13,000 in 1938. These estimates include the branches of firms controlling more than one shop and up to 10 shops.

The number of firms of this type, which could be called small multiple shop organizations, had grown fairly rapidly in the inter-war years, and their growth was encouraged by the practice of practically all manufacturers of branded proprietary medicines and toilet pre-parations of allowing attractive quantity discounts and rebates. Just prior to the Second World War it is estimated that there were over 1,300 such firms controlling over 3,500 branches, or about 20 % of the total number of chemists and druggists in existence at that date. Over 1,200 of the firms controlling about 3,000 branches had less than 5 branches each. These small groups of shops purchased goods in bulk, and one shop in the group would act as a 'warehouse' for the others, the goods being transferred when necessary.

One development in the trade that was sponsored largely by the small-scale independent chemist was the attempt started in the inter-war years, under the title of the Chemists' Friends Scheme, to persuade manufacturers to limit the sale of their proprietary articles to the qualified chemist and druggist. Under this scheme retailers agreed to give special prominence to the goods of manufacturers who would accept this limitation of outlets, and at the same time undertook not to give prominence to the goods of manufacturers who did not join the scheme. The effort to limit the number and importance of the non-chemist outlets was having some success in the years prior to the Second World War.

Shares of the different economic types of retailer in the total trade

An attempt can now be made to summarize the trends in the retail structure of the chemists' and druggists' trade discussed above by pre-senting estimates of the changes in the relative importance of different economic types of retailer between 1900 and 1950. These estimates are presented in Table 74.

Table 74. *Estimated shares of the different economic types of retailer in the
total retail sales of chemists' goods, 1900–50**

| Year | Proportion of total sales undertaken by | | | |
	Co-operative Societies %	Department stores %	Multiple shop retailers %	Other retailers (by difference) %
1900	Under 1	Under 1	6·5– 8·0	90·5–93·5
1905	Under 1	Under 1	8·0–10·0	88·5–91·5
1910	Under 1	About 1	10·0–12·0	86·0–89·0
1915	Under 1	1·0–3·0	13·0–14·5	82·0–85·5
1920	Under 1	2·0–3·0	14·5–16·5	80·0–83·0
1925	About 1	2·0–3·5	18·0–22·0	73·5–79·0
1930	1·5–2·5	2·0–3·5	24·0–28·0	66·0–72·5
1935	2·0–3·0	2·5–3·5	28·0–32·0	61·5–67·5
1939	3·0–4·5	2·5–4·0	33·0–37·0	54·5–61·5
1950	4·0–6·0	3·0–4·0	35·0–39·0	51·0–58·0

* For a discussion of the basis of these estimates see Appendix A. Included in chemists'
goods are all proprietary and non-proprietary medicines and drugs, toilet and beauty preparations and toilet requisites, surgical goods and sundries and photographic and optical goods.
National Health and private dispensing are also included. Goods and services such as
stationery, books, hardware, jewellery and lending libraries are excluded, as are other goods
sold in small quantities by chemists such as tobacco, spirits and confectionery. The table
relates to total sales of chemists' goods irrespective of the particular trade of the outlet;
similarly in the classification of sales by different economic types of retailers the sales, for
example, of all multiple shop organizations of these goods, that is multiple shop grocers and
variety chain stores as well as multiple shop chemists, are included in the sales of multiple
shop retailers, and the sales of all small-scale retailers whatever their trade are included
in the residual group of 'other retailers'.

The main feature of the development of large-scale retailing in the
chemists' goods trade as shown in this table is the rapid growth in the
importance of multiple shop retailing, the shares of department stores
and Co-operative Societies being very small. A major role in the
advance of multiple shop trading was played by one firm, the Boots
Pure Drug Company Ltd., which not only controlled more retail
branches than any other multiple shop organization throughout these
years but also had an average turnover per branch of 2 to 3 times the
average turnover of the branches of other multiple shop firms.

Factors influencing the rise of multiple shop retailing

Many of the reasons for the growth of multiple shop retailing in this
trade have been mentioned above in the discussion of the characteristics
and trading methods of these firms. Here all that need be attempted is
a brief summary of the main factors. In the opening phases of multiple
shop trading low prices combined with high turnover and low margins,
plus uninhibited advertising and salesmanship, were the most important

factors in assisting a rapid advance. The multiple shop organizations in these years were handling what were virtually entirely new types of products, that is proprietary medicines in place of chemist-prescribed and dispensed mixtures, at new kinds of prices and in a new and vigorous fashion. The appeal made and the methods used were sufficiently soundly based to withstand and defeat a not inconsiderable attack by the traditional interest in the trade. In the second phase of their existence, which extends roughly from the end of the first decade of the twentieth century to the end of the period being considered, the multiple shop firms maintained their advantages of bulk buying of drugs, chemicals and medicines and of specialization of function within the organizations, enabling each aspect of the business to be undertaken by an expert, whether it was printing and advertisement or buying, transport or branch stock control. To these were added the further advantages of integration of production and distribution and the possession of sufficient capital, both by raising capital on the market and by re-investment of profits, to extend their operations in the best sites by buying or building.[1]

These advantages of large-scale buying, specialization, integration with manufacturing and large capital assets had an important bearing on the success of the new trading policies developed by the leading multiple shop firms in this second phase. The appeal to the public was no longer made on the basis of 'drugs at cut prices' but rather on the basis of the attractive range of chemists' and non-chemists' goods stocked and the prominent and well designed and laid out shops in which this wide range of goods was sold. And to the range of goods displayed was added a reputation for speedy and efficient dispensing.

The position of the small-scale retailer

The size and turnover of the small-scale or independent chemist was less than half that of the typical branch of a multiple shop organization. The small-scale chemist had lost ground to the larger-scale retailers and had been driven out of the busiest shopping streets by the multiple shop firms. In the smaller shopping areas, however—the smaller towns, the market towns and the rural areas—the independent chemist still played the major role in the trade. The small-scale retailer could not compete with the multiple shop retailer in the purchase of main street sites or in stocking a wide range of non-chemists' goods in large attractive shops, but he possessed other advantages. The knowledge and standard of

---

[1] In the case of the Boots Pure Drug Company Ltd. re-investment of profits was the usual method. The Chairman reported that 'during the period 1930–39 we were able to build and equip our manufacturing laboratories at Beeston, and, in addition, open 360 retail branches, out of monies we had ploughed back into the business'. Chairman's report to Sixty-Fourth Annual Meeting, 17 July 1952.

education required of the individual chemist in relation to his dispensing activities were the same for the multiple shop branch as for the single chemist's shop. But the small-scale chemist had the economic advantage of flexibility in size and in turnover range which enabled him to exist and prosper in areas where demand was insufficient to support a multiple shop branch with its minimum staff of 3 or 4 and its heavy overhead charges. With resale price maintenance in general operation there was no incentive to the consumer to go further afield than the small local chemist's for purchases of immediate requirements. The small-scale retailer also had the advantage of being able to provide, often on the basis of years of service in a district, the personal attention to the needs of his customers that no manager of a multiple shop branch could match. This advantage was of great importance in the higher-class end of the trade but also existed in other sections of the trade. The chemist who knew the people in his district by name, who was willing to help his neighbours on questions outside the trade itself, and who lived over the shop and was available in times of emergency had a considerable appeal in a trade where, in spite of the advertising of so many of the products, the advice of the retailer was still regarded highly by the customers.

By 1950, therefore, the multiple shop organizations through their methods of organization and trading policies had secured most of the strategic positions in the trade, but the small-scale independent chemist, thanks to his flexibility and the provision of personal service, appeared to be equally strongly rooted in the smaller markets of the towns and the rural areas.

Suggestions as to future trends in the trade

Suggestions as to future trends in the chemists' trade can only be put forward very tentatively, as the course of government action on such issues as payment for National Health prescriptions and resale price maintenance is unknown. Assuming, however, that the general demand conditions in the trade will not undergo any radical change and that resale price maintenance in one form or another will continue to be of importance, a brief discussion of future trends in the trade can be attempted.

First it may be suggested that the present trend towards larger shops selling chemists' goods will continue and, an essential part of this trend, that the widening of the range of goods stocked by the chemists will also be maintained. Already in some towns shops that are ostensibly chemists' shops sell a tremendously wide range of goods, from pottery and jewellery to books, in addition to chemists' goods. In the future practically all fair-sized towns will probably have one or more of this type of very large chemist's shop. Secondly, sections of the chemists' trade are suited to the introduction of self-service shopping and this form of retailing will probably spread in this trade in the future. In the smaller units open display of the goods and semi-self-service will be the rule, but in the larger shops, except of course in regard to the sale of drugs and poisons, the full self-service principles will probably be operated. Thirdly, if self-service methods also develop in the grocery trade and in the variety chain stores, it is probable that there will be a marked trend towards setting aside a part of the self-service grocery unit for the sale of chemists' goods such as shampoos, dentifrice, shaving cream and razor blades and first aid items. Most of these products require no selling on the part of the retailer and are conveniently bought by the housewife when purchasing her groceries. The chemists' and druggists' shops in the future, therefore, while maintaining their particular status and character in regard to dispensing, may sell a very much more general range of goods than in the past. At the same time they may lose a proportion of their sales of traditional lines to other types of retailer. Further, in the larger units counter service may give place to self-service.

If the trade does develop along the lines envisaged above there can be little doubt that the large-scale retailers, particularly the multiple shop retailers, will increase their share of the total trade. Only the large-scale retailers have the resources to finance and organize such developments, and the larger shops will attract custom away from those selling a more limited range of goods. On the other hand, for a very long time to come, the role of the small-scale independent chemist in the smaller shopping areas and in rural areas is unlikely to diminish greatly. A reversal of the present practice in regard to resale price maintenance, however, may make it advantageous to the consumer to purchase his requirements at a lower price at the larger self-service unit rather than at the neighbourhood chemists' shop.

400

CHAPTER XVI

THE SEWING MACHINE, BICYCLE AND
PERAMBULATOR, AND RADIO AND
ELECTRICAL GOODS TRADES

The somewhat diverse trades of sewing machines, bicycles and perambulators, and radio and electrical goods are classed together for two main
reasons. In the first place the main products of these trades were new
goods, invented in the hundred years between the middle of the
nineteenth and twentieth centuries. The domestic sewing machine was
being sold generally by the third quarter of the nineteenth century,
but the widespread sale of bicycles and perambulators dates only from
the last decade of the nineteenth and first decade of the twentieth
century. The retail sale of radio and electrical goods was not common
until the inter-war years. It follows that the retail structure of all these
trades is of relatively recent growth. In the second place there is an
overlap in retailing between these trades. The boundaries between the
individual trades are extremely difficult to draw, and many retail
firms starting in one of the trades, for example bicycles, have moved
into another, for example radio. Further, while a number of retailers
specialized in the sale of one or other of the main groups of goods, an
almost equal number dealt in two or more of the groups. There is the
added complication that retailers specializing in other trades, for
example furniture, also sell goods such as radios and sewing machines,
and equally, firms specializing in one or more of these main groups, for
example perambulators, also sell goods of other trades, for example toys
and kitchen furniture.

The relatively short history of these trades, the fluid boundaries
between them, and the scattered and incomplete information on the
character of the retailing structure in the earlier years, prevent any
full account being given of the growth and changes in the methods of
organization of the retail trade. Equally difficult to make are generalizations of any value regarding the character of the trades. All that will
be attempted here, therefore, is to give a short account of the salient
features of the development of each of the trades and of the general
retail framework, and this is followed by a more detailed analysis of the
growth of multiple shop retailing in this group of trades as a whole.

The sewing machine trade

The sale of sewing machines to the general public dates back at least to 1856 when the Singer Manufacturing Company opened its first retail branch in Glasgow. The subsequent development of retailing in this trade right up to 1950 is that of the sale of machines through specialist shops maintained by the Singer Company on the one hand and of sales by a mixed group of retailers—ironmongers, cycle shops, clothing shops, department stores and Co-operative Societies—on the other. The bulk of the sales throughout this period were however made through the first channel. By 1938 over four-fifths of the total sales of sewing machines were undertaken by branches or sales depots controlled by manufacturers.

The Singer Sewing Machine Company Ltd. was one of the earliest multiple shop firms in existence in the United Kingdom, and from the first shop in 1856 the total number of branches had risen to over 160 by 1877 and to nearly 400 by 1900. By 1910 there were some 500 branches, and in 1920 over 600. This number was increased by 1938 to close on 900 branches. The only other firm of any size specializing in the sale of sewing machines was the Jones Sewing Machine Company Ltd. which was founded in 1859. By the turn of the century this firm had a small network of sales centres in the main towns of the United Kingdom and the number of branches rose steadily in the inter-war years until in 1938 some 90 branches were operating.

The other retailers sold imported machines or in many cases were accredited agents of the manufacturers in towns where the latter had no branch. Some of the larger retailers such as department stores and Co-operative Societies sold machines under their own brand names. An important feature of the trading methods of all types of retailers was the sale of the machines on hire-purchase terms. Hire-purchase and instalment or similar methods began to be adopted in the late nineteenth century and came into widespread use in the inter-war years, when some three-quarters of the sales were made on these terms.

The main reason for the development of a network of sales outlets controlled by the Singer Company was, in the earlier years, the difficulty of finding existing retailers who could finance the holding of stocks of a relatively expensive article, and who could sell the new and complicated product successfully. Almost from the start some after-sales service was a necessity, and the manufacturers found that the most effective way of providing this was by their own trained staff attached to branch shops or depots. In the twentieth century, while the familiarity of the housewife with the machines grew, so did the number of refinements and improvements, and the instructional service as well as the after-sales service that could be provided by trained representatives of the manufacturers continued to be important. At the same time there were clear advantages, once the sales outlets had been established, in maintaining the integration of production and distribution, in respect both of the efficiency of physical distribution and stockholding and of advertisement and the promotion of sales. Sewing machines had a long life and the consumer in times of financial difficulty put off replacement of old models. A large number of shops in fairly prominent sites was, however, a continuous advertisement of the name of the firm and of the up-to-date replacement models that had become available. Further, to overcome slumps in sales the trained retail staff attached to shops could be used as canvassers for sales on a commission basis. As with many other speciality goods in the inter-war years the 'selling' of the goods was almost as important as their production.

Between 1938 and 1950 the important development in the retailing structure of the trade was the marked reduction in the number of specialist outlets. By 1950 from a figure of nearly a thousand in 1938 the number of multiple shop branches had dropped to about 300. The main reasons for the decrease were the shortage of supplies during the war years, the emphasis on the export trade in the post-war years, and the existence of a sellers' market for the goods. The reduction in the number of shops took the form of closing the smaller branches and maintaining the larger and better-placed shops. In addition the range of goods sold by these shops was widened to include other domestic appliances such as electric irons, and services such as button covering and belt making began to be provided. In the post-war years it was found that for a speciality good like sewing machines consumers were quite prepared to travel some distance to inspect and buy, and shops or branches near their homes were not a necessity to maintain sales.

The bicycle and perambulator trade

Both the bicycle and the perambulator or baby-carriage date from the eighteen-seventies, but progress of the industry was slow and erratic until the development of the pneumatic tyre at the close of the 'eighties. By the middle 'nineties the popularity of the bicycle was established and there followed the bicycle boom, accompanied by much publicity and by the financial juggling of men like E. T. Hooley. As the excitement died down, after 1897 an inevitable recession in the trade followed, but from the turn of the century the industry started expanding steadily and regularly. A reliable bicycle at a low price was being produced— a hitherto unknown combination—and sales increased, particularly after the fall in the retail price from 1905 onwards.

The methods of distribution used in the early years were many and various. As the trade started with an emphasis on recreation the seasonality of sales was most marked and specialist retailers were a rarity. The manufacturers undertook some direct sales to the public, but the usual method of distribution was that of the appointment by the manufacturers of agents for the exclusive sale of their machines. The agents were liberally supplied with catalogues and leaflets and, where practicable, stocked a few cycles for advertisement purposes. The manufacturers with depots in different parts of the country fulfilled the orders passed on to them by their agents. These agents situated in every town in the country were drawn from all types of trades from the blacksmith to the general dealer, and a frequent comment was that every other shoe retailer and greengrocer was a cycle agent. Prominent among the agents in the early years were mechanics of various sorts who not only sold cycles but also undertook some assembly of machines and handled the inevitably heavy repairs that were necessary in the trade. These mechanics or handymen filled in the off-season in the cycle trade by sales of and repairs to a wide range of other goods, mainly new products, such as gramophones, typewriters, gas and electrical fittings, roller skates and sewing machines.

In addition to these small-scale retailers, department stores and some Co-operative Societies also sold bicycles and perambulators from an early date. Department stores added bicycles to their growing sports goods and hardware departments, and Retail Co-operative Societies started selling bicycles just after the turn of the century. By 1907–8, however, the Societies had run into difficulties with some of the manufacturers, who refused to supply the Co-operative Wholesale Society because the Retail Societies were paying dividends on sales to the members. The Wholesale Society attempted to meet the problem by assembling cycle parts themselves, but not until a Co-operative bicycle factory was built in 1920 were the sales by the Retail Societies of any significance.

The steady increase in the sales of bicycles and accessories for work as well as recreation purposes, and the use of bicycles by business houses, retail distributors and others in the years just prior to the First World War, saw the emergence of specialist shops undertaking their main turnover in these goods. The repairing element was still important and the agency system was maintained, but as the basic pattern of the bicycle became standardized, ending the danger of out-of-date stocks caused by an entirely new invention, and as demand for the new products became stable, retailers were encouraged to stock for direct sale. Among the earliest of the specialist retailers were the first multiple shop organizations in the trade. Currys of Leicester and later of London had a dozen or so shops by 1910 and the Halford Cycle Company Ltd. of Birmingham, which was founded in 1907, had over 30 branches in that year. On the perambulator side, where demand had been steadily increasing, W. J. Harris & Company Ltd. of London had some 20 branches by 1914.

In the inter-war years the bicycle trade continued to expand and with it there was an increase in the number of specialist retailers and a growth of multiple shop organizations. At the same time the importance in the trade of other types of retailer, particularly of department stores and Co-operative Societies, began to increase. A notable feature of the trade, dating back to the issuing of catalogues to the manufacturers' agents, was the fixing by manufacturers of the retail price of the goods. Only by the guarantee of a definite and clear margin could the manufacturers in the earlier years encourage the many different types of retailers to act as agents for the 'new-fangled' product. Once the system of resale price maintenance was established it was continued during the expansion of the inter-war years and spread to practically every accessory stocked by the cycle retailers. A second feature was the early introduction of the instalment system of selling. This developed in the trade in the years just before the First World War and remained a common practice throughout the inter-war years. The major boom of the inter-war years in the bicycle trade from 1931 to 1938 was assisted considerably by the hire-purchase method of trading.

While the number of specialist cycle dealers increased in the inter-war years these dealers also began to supplement their sales of bicycles and accessories by the sale of other new products coming on to the market, particularly of radio and electrical goods and motor car accessories. Electrical goods were especially welcomed as helping to offset the still seasonal character of the sales of bicycles.

The multiple shop retailers in the bicycle and bicycle accessory trade were for the most part retailers only. One or two controlled small firms which undertook some manufacturing, but the sales of such goods represented only a very small proportion of the total turnover of the branches. The majority of the branches of these firms were established in main-street sites, in contrast to the shops of the cycle repairer and independent cycle dealer, which were usually to be found in the less busy shopping streets. During the inter-war years, partly as a result of the acquisition of better sites and partly as a result of the increase in the range of goods sold, the average size of the multiple shop branches was increased. From 3–4 employees per branch in the nineteen-twenties the average number of assistants had risen to about 5–6 by 1950.

Two large multiple shop firms emerged in this trade. These were Halfords and Currys, which by 1925 had over 100 branches each and by 1938 over 200 branches each, spread widely over the country. No other firm specializing mainly in the sale of bicycles grew beyond the confines of one town or had more than 25 branches. There would appear to be no particular economic reason for this unusual size distribution of multiple shop firms, but, apart from the abilities and foresight of the founders, this development would appear to be linked with the early start of the two firms and the relative lack of opportunity for growth in the bicycle retailing trade as such by the middle 'thirties. Ambitious retailing firms in the inter-war period found that concentration on the rapidly rising electrical goods and radio trades offered more scope for expansion than the bicycle trade.

The advantages of the multiple shop retailers in the bicycle and perambulator trades were mainly related to their ability to obtain the best selling sites and to carry a very wide range of goods, particularly of accessories. The multiple shop organizations secured buying economies by placing large orders centrally on behalf of all their branches, but as most of the goods were resale price maintained they had no competitive selling price advantage over other retailers. The branches were, however, able to display their wide selection of goods attractively, and by close supervision of the branches and by the planning of the sale policies to maintain a good rate of stock turn. The multiple shop firms were also prominent in offering goods on hire-purchase terms, and possessed the financial resources to undertake this type of sale successfully.

The radio and electrical goods trade

Before the First World War, the only electrical goods retailed to the general public comprised a small range of electric lighting fittings and lamps. After the war, however, there was a tremendous increase in sales. The wiring of houses for electricity was one factor in this increase; the development of broadcasting and radio was a second. The combination of these factors meant that the retailing of electrical goods to the general public developed into a major trade in less than two decades. And throughout the inter-war years and in the years following the Second World War the trade was stimulated by the rapid rate of technical change, which added replacement demand, the discarding of obsolete models, to the general expansion demand.

The rapidity of the development of this trade meant that the retailers who in, say, 1938 could be described as specialists in electrical goods and radio had very diverse origins. In the years up to the middle 'thirties many amateur electrical and wireless enthusiasts turned professional by extending their part-time hobby into a full-time livelihood, selling and repairing electrical goods. Deficiencies of the product in the early years and lack of knowledge on the part of the general public provided a great opportunity for this type of expert retailer. In this way many of the retailers were entirely new firms that had grown up with the electrical industry. Others had started life as specialists in gas lighting supplies and had moved over to electrical goods as the latter became popular. Others had started as ironmongers, as furnishers, or as cycle dealers and repairers, and yet others as dealers in pianos, gramophones and musical instruments. The development of the trade as a whole was by no means purely in the direction of the specialist retailer and outlet. While the complex nature of some of the goods sold, for example radio and television sets, and the importance of the after-sales service and repair work connected with their sale demanded specialist retailers, other products of the trade, as familiarity of the general public with electrical equipment grew, could be and were sold by completely non-specialist and non-electrical retailers—for example, general service electric light lamps.

The selling policies of manufacturers naturally varied therefore with the character of the goods in question. Some manufacturers pursued a limited agency policy and before supplying goods to a retailer made sure that the retailer was fully capable of dealing with the technical problems connected with sales and after-sales service. Others encouraged the distribution of their goods through the widest possible number of outlets. There was a third policy pursued by some manufacturers, that of direct selling to the public by door-to-door canvassing, as for example in the case of some vacuum cleaners. By this method retailers were either not used at all or only used indirectly to fulfil the order once it had been placed. A common feature, however, of the trade irrespective of the type, size or price of the article concerned was the practice of resale price maintenance. This had been common almost from the start of the trade, and in the period of expansion in the inter-war years the growth of trade associations of manufacturers, wholesalers and retailers ensured that the practice became nearly universal.

Another method of distribution of these goods was through the electricity supply undertakings. These undertakings, from the late 'twenties onwards, began to play an important part in the distribution of electrical appliances such as cookers, refrigerators, and fires. Practically all these goods were either hired by the consumer from the supply undertaking or purchased on a hire purchase scheme. The hire or hire-purchase of goods through supply undertakings is, however, excluded from the following discussion, which is concerned only with the distribution of the products through commercial retail shops.

All economic types of retailer played some part in the growth and expansion of the trade after 1920. The department stores opened specialist departments for electrical products and sold a wide range of electrical appliances and radios. The Co-operative Societies similarly entered this field, though their expansion, as in the case of bicycles, was held back by the decision of the manufacturers not to allow the Societies to pay a dividend to members on the purchase of an important group of electrical goods. In 1933 the Societies were stopped from paying dividends on radios. Other electrical fittings subsequently came under the same ban, and in 1937 dividends on many makes of vacuum cleaners were stopped. These events led the Co-operative Wholesale Societies in the 'thirties to develop their own production, and by 1938 radios, general service electric light lamps, vacuum cleaners, electric washers and toasters, and other appliances were being produced by Co-operative factories. The total value of such Co-operative production was, however, extremely small compared to the total output of the industry.

Multiple shop retailers in the radio and electrical goods trade

Multiple shop retailers first appeared in the trade in the middle 'twenties. Some of the multiple shop organizations which later specialized in the sale of electrical goods were in existence before this date, but only one firm, that of John and Max Stone, could be said in 1925 to be a multiple shop specialist retailer in electrical goods. After this date progress was rapid and a number of multiple shop firms either came into the trade from other spheres or developed within the trade itself. By 1935 there were 14 firms in the trade with over 10 branches each specializing in the sale of radio and electrical goods, and these firms had over 350 branches in all. By 1939 the number of firms had risen to 18 and the number of branches to over 600. The leading firms in the trade at this date were J. & F. Stone with over 100 branches, and Loyds Retailers Ltd. and Max Stone Ltd. with 50–100 branches each. These firms were regional rather than national, though the bicycle firm Currys Ltd., which entered the radio field in the 'twenties, had a nearly national coverage. By the 'thirties the turnover in radio merchandise of this firm was approximately equal to that of their cycle department and, as mentioned above, over 200 branches were trading in 1938.

During the Second World War a number of the branches of multiple shop retailers were closed, but in the post-war years, with the great impetus given to the trade by the pent-up demand arising from wartime shortages and the development of television, the lost ground was quickly recovered. New branches were opened, although, as in many other trades, the difficulty of obtaining good sites and the high cost of them in these years proved a limiting factor to expansion.

The distinctive feature of the trading policy of the branches of multiple shop organizations in the radio and electrical goods trade was their effective salesmanship. This took many forms, and the most important examples were the location of the branches in busy shopping streets, the effective use of window space for attractive displays, the stocking of a wide range of articles and types of articles with the advantage of being able to obtain from a neighbouring branch any article not immediately available, the provision of a skilled after-sales service, and, in most cases, the sale of the more expensive types of goods on hire purchase terms.

The multiple shop retailers for the most part offered no advantage to the consumer in regard to price. A wide range of the goods they sold was resale price maintained by the manufacturers, and the integration of production and distribution by multiple shop firms was negligible. In some instances, however, the multiple shop retailers acquired the bulk of the output of a particular manufacturer of certain goods and these lines were sold at low prices. In other instances the retailer, with the agreement of the manufacturer, branded a particular line of goods in his own name and sold them at a price he decided was advantageous. Production conditions, particularly in the radio industry, were far from stable, in part because of innovation and seasonality, and many manufacturers were prepared to come to special terms with multiple shop retailers for the sale of their goods. By and large, however, the buying advantages obtained by the multiple shop firms—and most manufacturers offered quantity rebate terms—and the economies in retail operating costs secured by close stock control, the ability to transfer slow selling goods from branch to branch, and a high rate of stock turn, were passed on to the consumer in the form of the salesmanship and services outlined above, and were used for the expansion of the business rather than to lower retail prices.

Many of the independent electrical specialist retailers could and did offer particular services to the consumer equal to, or better than, those provided by the branch of a multiple shop firm. After-sales service was an example of this. But few small-scale retailers could offer the full range of services provided by the multiple shop firm. The latter had marked advantages in respect of those services requiring large financial resources, that is heavy stockholding, prominent main street sites and extensive hire-purchase trading. That these services were attractive to the consumer is seen from the progress of the multiple shop firms and from the fact that in the late 'thirties some three-quarters of the sales of multiple shop firms are estimated to have been on hire-purchase terms.

In addition to the specialist multiple shop retailers, a number of multiple shop firms in other trades handled some lines of electrical goods. As mentioned above, multiple shop retailers in the furniture and cycle trades sold some of the goods, and in the years following the Second World War the sewing machine multiple shop firms handled a narrow range of such goods. More important, however, was the part played by multiple shop hardware dealers and ironmongers, wallpaper retailers and variety chain stores. While some of the former multiple shop firms handled a fair range of electrical fittings, the latter concentrated on the small low-priced articles such as general service electric light lamps, and in the 'thirties they played a prominent part in the sale of these goods. About one-third of the total retail sales of general service electric light lamps to the public were undertaken by variety chain stores in the late 'thirties. These were goods requiring no skilled retailing whatsoever, and the lamps sold by variety chain stores were lower-priced than those sold by the electrical specialist.

The growth of multiple shop retailing in these trades

The statistical material that exists on the growth of multiple shop retailing in the sewing machine, bicycle and perambulator and electrical goods and radio trades as a whole can now be presented. Table 75 shows the number of multiple shop firms and the total number of branches controlled by them between 1910 and 1950. Included in this table are details of firms which had gone out of existence or had merged with other firms as well as of firms which were still trading in 1950. Altogether data relating to 34 different firms have been included in this table, and of the 13 firms that were no longer trading independently in 1950 6 merged or amalgamated with existing firms and the remainder appear to have gone out of existence or had less than 10 retail branches in 1950.

Table 75. *Estimates of the number of multiple shop firms and branches in the sewing machine, bicycle and perambulator, and radio and electrical goods trades, 1910–50*

Year	10–24 branches Firms	Branches	25–49 branches Firms	Branches	50–99 branches Firms	Branches	100 or more branches Firms	Branches	Totals 10 or more branches Firms	Branches	Totals 25 or more branches Firms	Branches
1910	2	28	4	128	—	—	1	500	7	656	5	628
1915	4	59	4	130	1	96	1	565	10	850	6	791
1920	4	51	3	85	1	70	2	717	10	923	6	872
1925	7	87	2	66	1	80	3	926	13	1,159	6	1,072
1930	8	122	3	92	2	130	3	1,095	16	1,439	8	1,317
1935	9	122	5	175	3	235	3	1,176	20	1,708	11	1,586
1939	11	140	4	144	6	407	4	1,434	25	2,125	14	1,985
1950	9	113	4	153	4	265	4	881	21	1,412	12	1,299

The general picture of growth presented in this table is one of continuous and rapid increase in the number of multiple shop branches operating in these trades, until the Second World War when a sharp decrease takes place. The relative importance of the different trades and the pattern of the increase in the number of multiple shop branches in each, however, varied. Branches of multiple organizations specializing in the sale of sewing machines represented some 80 % of the total number of multiple shop branches in existence in the trade in 1910 and about 56 % in 1930 and 45 % in 1939. By 1950 the proportion had fallen to about 20 %. The actual number of branches of these firms rose steadily and consistently from 1910 to 1939 and then, as discussed above, was drastically reduced during the war years. By 1950 the number operating was less than one-third of the total in existence in 1939.

Throughout the inter-war years the branches of multiple shop firms specializing in the sale of bicycles, cycle accessories and perambulators represented about one-quarter of the total number of branches shown in Table 75 in these years. The growth in the number of branches of multiple shop bicycle dealers was steady until 1939, the period of most rapid growth being 1920–30. After 1939 there was some decrease in number, but in 1950 there were approximately the same number of branches in this trade in existence as in 1939. The branches of multiple shop firms specializing in the sale of radio and electrical goods and musical goods showed the most rapid rise in numbers. In 1930 only some 10–15 % of the total number of branches shown in Table 75 came into this category, by 1939 the proportion was about 30 % and in 1950 it was about 40 %. The number of firms and of branches increased very rapidly between 1930 and 1939. The war years again held back development, but by 1950 the number of branches specializing in these goods was slightly greater than in 1939.

The pattern of growth, then, takes the form of three main waves. First there was the growth of multiple shop sewing machine retailers before 1900, continuing in the inter-war years; secondly there was the growth of bicycle and bicycle accessories multiple shop retailers, particularly between 1920 and 1930; and thirdly there was the growth of radio and electrical goods retailers in the decade before the Second World War. The decrease in total numbers of branches between 1939 and 1950 was due almost entirely to the decrease in the number of branches of firms specializing in the sale of sewing machines.

Shares of the different economic types of retailer in the total trade

Estimates of the shares and the changes in the shares of the total retail trade of these goods that were undertaken by the different economic types of retailer in these years are particularly difficult to make as both the type of goods included and the boundaries of the trade were changing over time. Some tentative estimates of these changes between 1910 and 1950 are presented in Table 76.

Table 76. *Estimated shares of the different economic types of retailer in the total retail sales of sewing machines, bicycles and bicycle accessories, perambulators, musical instruments, radios and electrical goods, 1910–50**

Year	Proportion of total sales undertaken by			
	Co-operative Societies %	Department stores %	Multiple shop retailers %	Other retailers (by difference) %
1910	Under 1	Under 1	10·0–12·0	86·0–88·5
1920	About 1	3·5–4·5	13·0–15·0	79·0–83·0
1925	About 1	4·5–5·5	11·0–14·0	79·0–84·0
1930	About 1	5·0–6·5	11·0–14·0	78·5–83·0
1935	About 1	6·0–7·5	13·0–15·0	75·5–81·0
1939	1·0–2·0	6·0–8·0	18·0–22·0	68·0–75·0
1950	1·5–2·5	7·0–9·0	20·0–24·0	64·5–71·5

* For a discussion of the basis of these estimates see Appendix A. The sales by multiple shop retailers include the sales by all types of multiple shop firms, variety chain stores, furniture multiple shop firms and so on as well as the sales by specialist multiple shop retailers. The 'other retailer' group, a residual group, includes the sales by manufacturers using door-to-door canvassers and the sales by mail order. The sales direct or on hire purchase terms or the hire of these goods by supply authorities have been excluded from the estimates of total sales, as have the purchases of these goods by industrial and commercial users.

In interpreting the trends shown in Table 76 it will be appreciated that considerable shifts took place in these years in the relative importance of the different classes of goods making up this combination of trades and that the fluctuations in the shares of the different types of retailers reflect these shifts. In 1910, for example, bicycles and bicycle accessories was the largest single group and sewing machines the second largest group in terms of retail sales. By 1939, however, some two-thirds of the total retail sales were represented by radio and electrical goods and about one-quarter by the sales of bicycles and bicycle accessories. The sales of sewing machines at this date were a relatively small proportion of the total sales.

The share of the large-scale retailers in the distribution of the different product groups naturally varied. In the case of sewing machines practically the whole of the sales in these years were undertaken by the branches linked with the manufacturers. In the case of bicycles and bicycle accessories the share of the multiple shop retailers of the total trade is estimated at over 10–15 % in 1925 and had risen to 24–28 % by 1939. Multiple shop retailing was never so prominent in the distribution of perambulators and baby carriages. In the case of radios and electrical goods multiple shop retailers, including variety chain stores, played an insignificant role in the trade in 1925 and handled under 10 % in 1930. Between 1930 and 1939, however, there was a rapid increase in their importance, and in 1939 they are estimated to have been responsible for 20-24 % of the total sales. Multiple shop retailers in the electrical goods trade after 1930 played a more important part in the distribution of radios and general service electric light lamps than of electrical appliances and fittings.

The main reasons for these shifts in importance have been touched upon in the discussion above. Apart from the sewing machine trade, where particular factors operate, the general picture of development is one of the sale of a new product being handled first by various types of retailer, of whom practically all were small, independent retailers and many were mechanic/retailers. As familiarity with the products grew and their reliability was improved their sale became more widespread. The sales emphasis shifted from novelty and the need for continual repairs to sales promotion and the stocking of a range of models and types. At this stage, as the products become more homogeneous and technically standardized, the advantages of the centralized buying methods and stock control of the multiple shop retailers began to be apparent. Further, these firms were able to take a lead in sales promotion by way of sites in main streets, emphasis on display, and extensive use of hire-purchase trading methods. To a much smaller extent the department stores were in a position to benefit by this change.

Low pricing policy by multiple shop retailers, except in the case of the sale by variety chain stores of general service electric light lamps, was not important, and the independent specialist retailer, well serviced by wholesalers or factors, could, in an important measure, keep pace in range of goods stocked and in the replacement of parts with the multiple shop specialist. In repair work and after-sales service the independent specialist retailer was often superior to the multiple shop firm. But while the independent retailer may have maintained his position, an increasing share of the expanding market passed to the multiple shop retailers owing to the ability of the latter, in their larger and better-sited shops, to attract and promote sales and to make buying 'easy'.

Suggestions as to future trends in the trade

In the future, a further increase in the share of the trade held by multiple shop retailers in the bicycle and electrical goods trades would seem probable. The radio, television and electrical goods trade would appear certain to continue to expand, and the multiple shop retailers are in a good position to increase the number of their branches and attract trade. There would not, however, appear to be much possibility of further expansion of department store trading in these goods, as the specialist shops can and do offer, in more convenient locations from the point of view of after-sales service, a wider selection of goods than can the stores. The Co-operative Societies, unless the manufacturers change their distribution policy, are under an even greater disadvantage in regard to stocking a wide range of different products and models.

Developments regarding resale price maintenance would not appear to affect these conclusions. If this practice continues in force multiple shop retailers will, as in the past, attract trade by the provision of a greater all-round service to the customers and by more vigorous sales promotion policies. If resale price maintenance is no longer permitted, the multiple shop retailers will probably be able to advance still further by reason of the lower prices on certain lines that they can offer in competition with other types of retailers. These conclusions may, however, be partly invalidated, on the one hand by a decline in the bicycle trade and a corresponding increase in the motor cycle and motor car trade, in which for various reasons multiple shop trading is practically non-existent, and on the other hand by a considerable increase in the importance of retail trading in electrical goods by supply undertakings. These authorities, in respect of central buying, stock holding, display and after-sales service, could, if the most-up-to-date sales promotion methods were employed, equal and perhaps surpass the service provided by the branches of multiple shop organizations. Whether the supply authorities will pursue such a course would appear, however, to depend on political rather than economic considerations.

414

CHAPTER XVII

THE JEWELLERY, TOY, SPORTS GOODS AND FANCY AND LEATHER GOODS TRADES

The sales of jewellery, including fancy jewellery, watches and clocks, of fancy and leather goods and of toys to wide sections of the people of the United Kingdom developed only in the twentieth century. While the real jewellery and watch and clock-making trades are of great antiquity, the sale of the products was confined to a limited group of the population until inexpensive real jewellery began to be produced in the late nineteenth century, and until the silver and electro-plate and the fancy or imitation jewellery industries developed, and, in the inter-war years, large quantities of mass-produced cheap watches and clocks were imported from abroad. The toy-making and fancy and leather goods trades similarly have a long history, particularly on the leather goods side, but the general retail sale of articles such as hand-bags, wallets, leather cases, costume jewellery and toys of all descriptions was developed mainly in the inter-war years. The factors operating here were the spread of fashion consciousness among all sections of the female population and the transition of the leather and toy-making trades from the handicraft and home-made stage to the factory production stage. The retail sale of these goods was also influenced by large imports, particularly of toys, in the inter-war years.

Features of the different trades

The characteristics of retail trading in these goods, and the changes taking place in these characteristics as the output of and demand for the goods increased, varied between the different trades. A detailed history of each separate section is not necessary, but some of the main trends may be suggested. The jewellery and watch and clock trade was largely in the hands of specialists at the turn of the century, and the jewellers and watch and clock dealers, increasing in numbers, continued down to 1950 to be responsible for the bulk of the sales of real jewellery, silver and electro-plate, and watches and clocks. In the inter-war years, however, the position of the specialist retailer was beginning to be challenged by the non-specialist, by department stores, drapers, fancy goods dealers, chemists, variety chain stores and even hardware dealers and ironmongers. Such retailers were particularly prominent in the sale of imitation jewellery and of the cheaper imported watches and clocks. The non-specialist retailer of these goods represented a break in the earlier tradition of exclusive trading by master craftsmen.

Fancy and leather goods throughout these years were handled by a wide variety of retailers. While there was some tradition of specialization on the leather goods side arising from the utilitarian importance of leather in general clothing and other trades, the tradition was weakening in the twentieth century with the changes in the types of leather goods sold. Drapers and department stores sold fancy and leather goods from the turn of the century onwards, and other retailers, ranging from chemists to milliners, also began to handle some of the products. The wide variety of goods in this trade, the uneven demand for them, and the joint demand for fancy goods and accessories and women's clothing, limited the possibility of specialization. Only in some types of leather goods, for example handbags and travel goods, was specialization practicable to any extent. Equally the retailing of toys, once it had been divorced from the toy-maker, was essentially a non-specialist trade. The marked seasonality in the sale of toys limited the number of retailers who could sell only toys and associated goods throughout the year. Therefore as the demand for manufactured toys, home or imported, grew, those retailers, such as department stores, which could give over a whole section of their stores to the display and sale of toys at peak periods, utilizing the space for the sale of other goods during the rest of the year, played a leading part in the sale of these goods. In addition a large number of other non-specialist retailers, ranging from confectioners and newsagents to sports goods dealers and variety chain stores, stocked the cheaper types of toys alongside their other goods and added to their displays at the peak sales periods.

Large-scale retailing in the form of department store trading, multiple shop retailing and, to a very much smaller extent, Co-operative store retailing, developed in the jewellery, fancy and leather goods and toy trades from the first decades of the twentieth century, as the general demand for the goods grew. The department stores played a relatively more important role in the sale of toys than in the sale of fancy and leather goods or jewellery. Multiple shop trading by contrast was insignificant in the toy trade, except for the sales by variety chain stores, was of little importance in the fancy and leather goods trades, and developed mainly in the jewellery trade.

The development of multiple shop retailing

The multiple shop organizations in the jewellery trade were of two types. On the one hand, and most important, there were the specialist jewellers and watch and clock retailers. On the other hand there were the multiple branch pawnbrokers who undertook some sale of jewellery along with that of a variety of other goods. The first multiple shop jeweller, according to existing records, was H. Samuel of Manchester. This firm traced its history back to the establishment of Moses and Lewis Samuel, well-known clock-makers at the beginning of the nineteenth century. This firm was both a manufacturer and a retailer and had more than 10 branches operating at the turn of the century. By 1914 some 50 branches were in existence. The other multiple shop firms in the trade with 10 or more branches each in the pre-1914 years included Sanders & Company and some pawnbroking firms, the most prominent of which were Hill Brothers, Harvey & Thompson, and Owen & Robinson.

The development of multiple shop trading in jewellery in the interwar years was marked by the continued growth of H. Samuel Ltd. and the emergence of a second large firm, James Walker, Goldsmith and Silversmith Ltd., which had taken over some of the shops of Sanders & Company. Both of these firms had close on 100 branches each in 1930, but there were no other multiple jewellers or watch and clock dealers with more than 25 branches each. Between 1930 and 1938 the number of branches operated by these two large firms fluctuated and in 1935 the number was approximately the same as in 1930. During the Second World War the number of branches was reduced drastically owing to shortage of goods and enemy action, but in the post-war years up to 1950 the ground lost had been practically made good. Apart from these two firms, the other multiple shop retailers handling jewellery were practically all multiple branch pawnbroker/jewellers. These firms were local in their activities and the largest at any time possessed some 30 branches. On the watch and clock side, only one important multiple shop specialist firm, Ingersoll Ltd., appeared in the inter-war years, and this firm also had less than 30 branches at the peak of its growth.

In the fancy goods trade only one multiple shop firm of any importance developed. This was A. L. Salisbury Ltd., which, after a slow growth up to 1930, started specializing in the sale of handbags and by 1950 had over 50 branches in different parts of the country. No multiple shop organization emerged that specialized in the sale of sports goods or toys.

A general picture of the development of multiple shop retailing in these trades in the years 1910–50 is presented in Table 77. Included in this table are details of firms that have gone out of existence or had less than 10 branches by 1950. Altogether the information relating to some 20 firms has been included.

A feature of the pattern of growth shown in Table 77 is the relative stability in the number of branches in existence between 1930 and 1950 (though the number had been reduced sharply by 1945). The stability in the number of branches of the leading jewellery multiple shop organizations during these years was, of course, the main factor at work here, and this stability in its turn arose from the depression in the trade in the late 'twenties and early 'thirties, and the growing competition in the cheaper end of the trade from non-specialist retailers such as variety chain stores.

Table 77. *Estimates of the number of multiple shop firms and branches in the jewellery, toy, sports goods, and fancy and leather goods trades, 1910–50*

Year	10–24 branches		25–49 branches		50–99 branches		100 or more branches		Totals 10 or more branches	
	Number of		Number of		Number of		Number of		Number of	
	Firms	Branches	Firms	Branches	Firms	Branches	Firms	Branches	Firms	Branches
1910	8	103	1	45	—	—	—	—	9	148
1920	8	114	1	55	—	—	—	—	9	169
1925	13	165	2	68	1	78	—	—	16	311
1930	14	195	1	25	1	98	1	100	17	418
1935	13	177	2	62	2	159	—	—	17	398
1939	10	146	1	25	3	229	—	—	14	400
1950	11	158	—	—	2	133	1	120	14	411

The wide range of articles that had to be carried by the jewellers and the very slow rate of stock turn in this trade—at least up to 1939—did not present many opportunities for the employment of multiple shop trading techniques. Where there was an important measure of integration of production and distribution it was possible for the retail branches to maintain style and novelty in their displays and often to sell at slightly lower prices. In other cases the multiple shop jeweller had few advantages over the small-scale jeweller except for some small economies arising from large-scale buying and the possession of financial resources to develop hire-purchase trading and main-street siting of the branches. In selling techniques, however, the multiple shop jewellers were far ahead of the small-scale craftsman-jeweller, particularly in the medium and low-price markets. The multiple shop jewellers placed great emphasis on display of their goods; rings, ornaments, plate, cutlery, clocks and watches, practically the whole stock of a branch, were in the windows. To make full use of display space these firms were among the first to develop the arcade shop. Further, and most important, in order to encourage the public to buy, all goods were clearly described and plainly ticketed with the price, a practice the small-scale jeweller adopted only slowly. Both the retail turnover and the retail employment of the multiple branch retailers, averaging some 5–6 persons per branch in the inter-war years, were larger than those of the average independent retailer.

In the case of fancy goods and leather goods the main advantages of the multiple shop specialist retailers lay in the close relationships which the firms could develop with the manufacturers, ensuring the regular supply of up-to-date styles and designs, and in the wide selection of particular lines that could be offered the consumer owing to specialization in a narrow range of goods.

Multiple shop organizations, particularly variety chain stores and chemists, played an important part in the growth of non-specialist retailing of jewellery, fancy and leather goods, and toys. As suggested above, they were concerned primarily with the cheaper end of the trade and never carried a wide range of these goods. The appeal of this type of multiple shop retailing of these goods lay chiefly in open display of the goods and in low prices.

Shares of the different economic types of retailer in the total trade, and suggestions as to future trends

An attempt is made in Table 78 to show the shares of the total retail trade in these goods undertaken by the different economic types of retailers at different dates. These estimates can only be very tentative because the boundaries of the trades discussed are so indistinct. The share of the trade undertaken by Co-operative Societies is not shown separately, as it is estimated to be less than 2 % of total retail sales throughout this period.

The main feature of this table is the rapid rise in the importance of multiple shop trading in the inter-war years. In the 'twenties this increase was due mainly to the increase in the number of specialist multiple shop jewellers. From the late 'twenties onwards, however, the increase in the share of multiple shop retailers was the result almost entirely of extensive trading in these goods by non-specialist multiple shop firms, particularly by variety chain stores. The specialist multiple shop retailers, in fact, from the early 'thirties onwards, did not increase in numbers, and as the trade expanded were undertaking a slightly smaller proportion of the total trade.

Suggestions as to future trends in the retail structure of the trades covered in this discussion are not easy to make, owing to the difficulty of forecasting the character of future consumer demand. Very generally, however, it may be argued that, as neither the goods nor the type of demand for them is likely to change radically in the future, there is unlikely to be any further significant growth of large-scale retailing. Different factors operate in the different trades discussed, but all the trades, jewellery and watches and clocks, toys, sports goods and fancy and leather goods, are characterized by absence of standardization of the goods sold, variations and irregularities in demand, an important fashion element and a relatively slow rate of retail stock turn. These combine to limit the advantages of large-scale retailing.

Table 78. *Estimated shares of the different economic types of retailer in the total retail sales of jewellery, watches and clocks, toys, sports goods and fancy and leather goods, 1910–50**

Year	Proportion of total sales undertaken by		
	Department stores %	Multiple shop retailers %	Other retailers (by difference) %
1910	1·5– 3·0	1·5– 2·5	94·5–97·0
1920	4·0– 6·0	2·0– 3·5	90·5–94·0
1925	6·0– 7·0	5·5– 7·0	86·0–88·5
1930	7·0– 8·0	12·0–14·0	78·0–81·0
1935	8·0– 9·0	16·0–18·0	73·0–76·0
1939	8·0–11·0	20·0–24·0	65·0–72·0
1950	10·0–12·0	21·0–25·0	63·0–69·0

* For a discussion of the basis of these estimates see Appendix A. The sales by multiple shop retailers include the sales of multiple shop organizations in the trades named and also the sales of these goods by multiple shop firms engaged in other trades, for example chemists' goods, stationery, drapery, electrical and radio goods, hardware and ironmongery, as well as the sales by variety chain stores. The 'other retailers' group is a residual group and included the sales of small-scale retailers, mail order sales undertaken by manufacturers, and the very small proportion of total sales undertaken by Co-operative Societies.

In certain sections of the different trades large-scale methods of retailing have been shown to have advantages over the small-scale independent retailer, for example the success of variety chain stores in handling low-priced fancy goods and the success of department stores in selling toys, and in these sections of the trade the importance of large-scale retailing will no doubt be maintained. In other sections, for example medium-priced leather goods, specialist multiple shop retailing will probably increase in importance as the trade expands. But taking the trades as a whole it would appear that, unless and until a more standardized demand develops for particular categories of the goods sold by these trades, the advance of the large-scale retailers relying on the advantages of bulk orders, of good selection within a limited range, and of simplified retailing techniques will be slow.

CHAPTER XVIII

THE FURNITURE AND FURNISHINGS TRADE

In the first half of the nineteenth century the demand for new furniture and new furnishings was almost exclusively a demand of the well-to-do classes, and the production of the goods themselves was largely in the hands of the craftsman/retailer. The working classes of both the towns and the countryside relied on furniture and furnishings made by themselves and on the inheritance or the purchase of second-hand furniture. In the second half of the century, while certain goods such as iron bedsteads began to be mass-produced and found their main sale among the working classes, the market for new wooden and upholstered furniture remained limited. The few goods that were sold to the working classes, such as chests of drawers, tables, chairs and sideboards, were well constructed and meant to last for generations. Not until the turn of the century did less expensive—and less lasting—furniture begin to appear in significant quantities, and with it the market for the goods widened.

The changes in the methods of production

The output of low-priced furniture for the working-class and middle-class markets was made possible by improvements in the methods of production which transformed the industry from one based on handicrafts to one based on factories and machines. These improvements in technique, which were beginning to be introduced in the last decades of the nineteenth century[1] and were continuous throughout the first half of the twentieth century, took many forms. Few changes were made in upholstery, but in cabinet-making widespread replacement of hand methods by machines took place in these years. Examples of these developments were the use of machines in place of hand tools for milling and machining, the use of complex machines such as multi-spindle dovetailing machines, gang mortisers and double tenoning machines, the introduction of new materials such as plywood, and the use of devices for the speeding up of production, such as automatic and power-operated clamps for joints and spray polishing with cellulose lacquers in place of hand polishing.

In the carpet-making industry the outstanding change occurred in the last two decades of the nineteenth century when power looms for

---

[1] *The Furniture Record* was reporting in 1900 that 'woodworking machinery is being more generally adopted in factories' and electricity was being used to drive the machines. (*The Furniture Record*, 24 June 1949, p. 4, quoting the issue of 1900.)

weaving carpets were first introduced in place of the centuries-old hand-loom system. In the twentieth century the developments were mainly in the direction of increasing output per loom and per man-hour, and the production of cheaper carpets and rugs. Linoleum was not widely produced until the end of the nineteenth century, but in the twentieth century the progress of the industry, as reflected in technical methods, the size of factories and the volume of output, has been continuous. After the First World War, felt base was added to the range of floor coverings produced by this industry.

By 1914 new furniture and furnishings, produced by a wide variety of methods and in many different-sized production units, were being bought by the working classes in appreciable quantities. The purchase of second-hand furniture, the use of furniture passed down through generations, and the home making of furniture were still important in these households, but the better-off sections of the working classes were buying suites of matching furniture and furnishings and not just the odd articles, the tables, the chests of drawers, the chairs and the chiffoniers.

The important change in demand, however, occurred in the inter-war years. The growing mechanization of production, though this by no means meant a marked trend towards large-scale production units, increased the volume of output and reduced the price of the goods. Demand was further stimulated by other changes. The rapid rise in the number of houses built, particularly after 1931, was one factor, and the increase in the number of families and households at a rate faster than the increase in the population, owing to the fall in the size of families, was another. Also—of great importance in relation to working-class and middle-class demand—the spread of the hire-purchase method of trading helped to make the potential demand effective.

These developments in the techniques of production and in the character of the demand for furniture and furnishings brought about changes in the retail structure of the trade in the last part of the nine-teenth and first half of the twentieth century. Some of these changes are discussed below. The main emphasis is placed on the development of multiple shop retailing, but as a preliminary to this analysis a brief account is given first of the position of the small-scale, independent furniture dealer and of the role of department stores and Co-operative Societies in the retailing of furniture and furnishings in these years.

The small-scale furniture dealer

There were three main types of small-scale dealer in new furniture and furnishings in the United Kingdom in these years. First there was the craftsman, the cabinet-maker who himself made the furniture that he sold to the public. This type of retailer was important in the nineteenth century, but in the twentieth, with the development of mechanization of production, a fairly clear division in the trade began to appear between the production and the retailing sides. The craftsman producer/retailer lost ground to the second main type of dealer, the specialist furniture retailer. These dealers, buying goods from manufacturers, varied in size from those who sold only a limited range of new and second-hand furniture to complete house furnishers, stocking everything from curtains, carpets and suites to occasional tables. The third group of retailers belonged to many trades and sold certain ranges of furniture and furnishings. For example many drapers handled furnishings, floor covering and bedding, and hardware dealers often sold linoleum, felt base and various kinds of metal and kitchen furniture.

The specialist furniture retailer was the most important type of dealer in the trade in the twentieth century. He usually controlled only one shop, though small groups of 3 or 4 shops in a town were not uncommon. The heavy outlay needed to finance stocks and to acquire premises large enough to display the stocks limited entry to the trade, and the turnover among specialist furniture dealers was small. A factor of importance in this connexion was the personal reputation of the dealer. As manufacturer branding was unusual on the furniture side of the trade the goods sold were linked with the name of the dealer, and a dealer long-established in a particular area had an advantage over new-comers. In the absence of branding and price fixing the trading policies adopted by the specialist dealer were individual.

The department stores

Some details of the development of the department store method of trading as a whole have been given in the chapter dealing with women's and girls' wear. The drapery origins of a large number of the stores led to an early specialization by these stores in the sale of furnishings, and a furniture department was often the next step in growth. In the first decade of the twentieth century department stores were already an important outlet for the higher-priced furnishings and carpets, and their sales of furniture were increasing. The main demand for furniture and furnishings in these years came from the growing middle classes and the well-to-do classes, and the department stores with their wide selection of goods, shopping comfort and extensive services proved attractive to these customers.

In the inter-war years the position of department stores in the furniture and furnishings trade was maintained. While they made little attempt to cater for the growing working-class demand or to compete in the 'easy terms' hire-purchase field, they could and did offer a range, particularly of furnishings and floor coverings, that few independent retailers could match. And to this range of goods the stores added the provision of credit, free delivery, and sometimes free laying and fitting. Department stores did not exclude all hire-purchase trading, but limited their agreements to approved customers only and rarely advertised the service. In furniture the reputation of department stores was not quite so high as in furnishings, though again certain stores were practically without rivals in their stock of special lines, such as kitchen furniture. In the 'thirties and in the years following the Second World War the emergence of department stores which catered for a lower-priced market brought department store shopping of furnishings within the range of the working classes, and a few of the stores began to sell the goods widely under hire-purchase arrangements. By and large, however, the main sales of department stores remained in the medium- and high-price markets.

The Co-operative Societies

The Co-operative Societies, like the department stores, moved into the furnishings and furniture trades from drapery. The Retail Societies were pressed by their members to carry a range of household goods alongside clothing and food, and in the 'seventies and 'eighties curtain material, bedding, a few rugs and carpets, and iron bedsteads and crude wooden furniture were appearing in some of the branches. An impetus was given to retail sales of furniture by the development of manufacturing of these goods by the Wholesale Societies in the late 'eighties and 'nineties. The Scottish Wholesale Society's first cabinet factory was established at Shieldhall in 1888, and the English Co-operative Wholesale Society opened furniture factories at Broughton during the period 1889–1893 and at Pelaw-on-Tyne in 1903. To these were added other units at Bristol and Birmingham in 1919 and 1920. These factories concentrated at first on wooden furniture—tables, chests of drawers and wardrobes, and later, with growing working-class demand, parlour suites, bedroom suites and sideboards became the fashion. These productive activities, while successful from the point of view of showing that furniture could be made under fair working conditions for the employees, were not a great success financially. The Retail Societies were hesitant about carrying a wide range of furniture which involved heavy stock-holding costs and required a large space in the shops, and in few stores were the goods adequately displayed.

In the inter-war years, particularly from 1930 onwards, there was an advance in furniture sales by Co-operative Societies. There were three reasons for this. First, the developing Societies planned their furniture departments with adequate space instead of tacking on a furniture department as an after-thought to their other departments. Secondly, the reorganization of Co-operative production of furniture after 1930 and the building of new furniture factories at Enfield (1930) and Radcliffe, near Manchester (1936) gave the Co-operative Wholesale Societies the largest furniture-making group of factories in the country. Additional units were also opened to produce mattresses and bedding. A measure of specialization in the individual factories was introduced, the latest machinery and mechanical aids were installed, and the Co-operative furniture in quality and price was able to compete directly with the products of both the other large-scale manufacturers and the myriads of small producers still in the trade. The third factor assisting Co-operative sales of furniture was the development of the club system of trading and particularly of hire-purchase. After a hesitant start, most of the Societies in the inter-war years operated a hire-purchase system for members, run in the usual way, and this became a popular method of buying furniture.

The development of multiple shop retailing

Multiple shop retailing in the furniture and furnishings trade can be said to have started round about the turn of the century. At this date, according to existing records, there were some 4 firms in the trade with 10 or more branches each. The best known of these were Jacksons Stores Ltd., furnishers and drapers, of Lancashire and Yorkshire, the Warwickshire Furniture Company Ltd., and Smart Brothers Ltd. of London. With the exception of Jacksons Stores Ltd., which had some 30–40 branches just before the First World War, the growth of multiple shop trading was slow. Neither the production nor the demand conditions yet existed for a rapid development of this type of retailing. In 1914 there were only some 9 multiple shop firms in existence and the total number of branches controlled by these firms was under 150. In addition to those already mentioned, other firms trading were the British and Colonial Furniture Company Ltd. (which had been formed in 1913 to take over the shops of the Clayton Furnishing Company of Newcastle, of James Woodhouse & Company of Scotland, and of Arthur Smith of Sunderland), Godfrey & Company Ltd., the music, piano and furniture dealers of London, and Jay's Furnishing Stores.

The main development of multiple shop retailing in this trade took place in the inter-war years. This is clear from the figures given in Table 79 of the number of firms with 10 or more branches each and the number of branches controlled by them in the years 1910–50. Included in this table are details of firms that have gone out of existence or have amalgamated with existing firms as well as those still trading independently in 1950. Altogether data relating to 35 firms have been included, and of the 18 firms no longer trading separately in 1950 13 amalgamated with other firms and 5 appear to have gone out of existence.

Table 79. *Estimates of the number of multiple shop firms and branches in the furniture and furnishings trade, 1910–50*

Year	10–24 branches		25–49 branches		50–99 branches		100 or more branches		Totals 10 or more branches	
	Number of		Number of		Number of		Number of		Number of	
	Firms	Branches	Firms	Branches	Firms	Branches	Firms	Branches	Firms	Branches
1910	8	101	1	27	—	—	—	—	9	128
1920	10	131	2	65	—	—	—	—	12	196
1925	16	212	1	32	1	55	—	—	18	299
1930	20	254	2	51	2	126	—	—	24	431
1935	23	290	5	173	1	95	—	—	29	558
1939	24	334	3	106	1	73	1	175	29	688
1950	19	285	1	36	1	73	1	442	22	836

The figures in Table 79 suggest that the increase in the number of branches of multiple shop retailers was consistent and rapid throughout the inter-war years. Also evident from the 'thirties onwards is the growth in size and in concentration of multiple shop retailing. A series of amalgamations and mergers began in the 'thirties and, continuing through the war and post-war years, resulted in the emergence of one firm, the Great Universal Stores Ltd., controlling over one-half of the total number of multiple shop branches in existence in the furniture trade in 1950. The main furniture retailing firms acquired by Great Universal Stores in these years were Jays & Campbells, the British and Colonial Furniture Company Ltd. (James Woodhouse), the Cavendish Furnishing Company Ltd., Jacksons Stores Ltd., and Smart Brothers Ltd. The number of shops selling furniture that were controlled by Great Universal Stores in 1950 was larger than the estimates given in Table 79, as this organization also controlled mixed drapery and furniture stores and some department stores.

The trading methods of multiple shop retailers

The multiple shop furnishers of the pre-1914 years took any site that was available and tended to adopt the same display methods as those of retailers in other trades such as clothing and footwear; that is, the branches had almost as much of their stock on the pavement outside the shop as in the shop itself. In the inter-war years changes took place in both respects. The multiple shop furniture firms began to adopt a planned policy of obtaining positions in main shopping streets and, because of the size of the shops required for the adequate interior display of the furniture and furnishings, many of the firms were involved in complicated property mortgage deals. The display of furniture began to be confined to the windows of the shops in these main street sites and the size of the shops themselves tended to increase. In the 'thirties the employment per branch averaged some 8–12 persons. The large shops in main street sites with elaborate window displays were in themselves an advertisement, and in addition the multiple shop firms undertook extensive newspaper advertisement and the liberal distribution of catalogues.

The major factor influencing the rapid growth of multiple shop retailing in the furniture trade in the inter-war years was, however, hire-purchase trading. The goods stocked by the multiple shop retailers were for the most part low-priced and, with the addition of 'easy terms' of purchase, the working classes were able for the first time to make significant purchases of new furniture and furnishings. Once one firm had started hire-purchase trading and advertised widely to this effect, competitors had to follow suit or lose part of their trade. The hire-purchase system was used for most of goods stocked and in some instances over 90 % of the retail sales of multiple shop furniture firms in the inter-war years were on such terms.

The techniques of hire-purchase trading varied between firms. Some firms went as far as stating that there were 'no references required', though in practice checks had to be made on the standing of all potential customers. Others emphaszied that only 'small deposits' were required and others that 'all goods were delivered in plain vans' so that the purchasers need not let their neighbours know that they were buying on the 'never never'. The methods of some of the firms engaged in this form of trading came under heavy fire from competitors, such as department stores, which, although they were also engaged in hire-purchase trading, claimed that their methods were less open to· abuse. Equally vocal in their criticism were sections of the legal profession and the press and some politicians. To these critics the 'snatching back' of hired articles in the event of default of payment seemed unjust and unfair, particularly when perhaps more than three-quarters of the payments for the article had been made. This pressure led to some of the worst evils of the system being removed under the Hire Purchase Act of 1938.

The hire-purchase system of trading of the multiple shop retailers and of other retailers in the inter-war years had however enabled a great many families to furnish their homes in a style hitherto beyond their reach. It could be argued that the full price paid under hire-purchase methods was much higher than the cash value of the goods. 'Hire-purchase—high prices' was a catch phrase frequently used by competing retailers. But without hire-purchase to stimulate demand and to bring dining-room and bedroom suites within the reach of working-class households there would have been few economies in the scale of production. With a smaller demand the cost of goods produced by small-scale production methods may well have been higher than the cost of the mass-produced furniture including the hire-purchase charges.

Hire-purchase trading added considerably to the staff required to conduct a retail business. Contracts had to be drawn up, accurate records of purchases, payments made, and payments due over long periods of time had to be kept, and outside staff was required by most firms to collect the instalments due and if necessary handle the delicate business of recovery of the property in cases of default. Further, the working capital required was considerable. As the method of trading developed, the financial strength and financial ingenuity of the retailing firms became a more important factor in their success than the quality of the goods sold or the particular techniques of buying and selling employed. The multiple shop retailers had advantages over the small-scale furniture dealer in this respect, but the multiple shop firms did not all steer clear of financial difficulties. To secure the capital for their activities many multiple shop furniture retailers became public companies in the 'twenties, but in the 'thirties over-trading on hire-purchase was common. The resulting financial weakness was one of the reasons leading to amalgamations and mergers between firms and to the transfer of the control of multiple shop furnishing firms to finance companies or groups.

Some multiple shop retailers bought the whole of the output of small manufacturers and others owned small furniture factories, but integration of large-scale production and distribution was of little importance in this trade. The large amounts of capital locked up by retailers in hire-purchase agreements was one factor that limited its development. A firm which had to wait three or more years for full payment of the goods sold was unlikely to be tempted to undertake manufacturing in addition. Another factor in this connexion was the unpredictable nature of consumer taste, particularly in relation to furniture. For example, if the consumers decided that a particular design or pattern was not sufficiently 'up-to-date' there was a very real danger, if supplies were limited to the output and designs of one factory, of the retail branches being left with unsaleable goods. In buying, however, while the multiple shop firms usually spread their orders over several producers they were able to secure considerable economies in price by purchasing large quantities, and, equally important, were able to obtain special lines the sale of which was confined to the shops of the particular firm. The rise of the Great Universal Stores group in the years 1940–50 changed the position in the trade slightly in that this company controlled some important manufacturing units as well as retail outlets. By 1950, however, the proportion of the goods sold by the retail branches that had been produced by units controlled by the Company was still very small.

Shares of the different economic types of retailer in the total trade

This discussion of the development of the different types of retailers in the furniture and furnishings trade can be concluded by presenting estimates of the proportion of the total retail sales of these goods that were undertaken by different economic types of retailers between 1910 and 1950. These estimates are given in Table 80.

Table 80. *Estimated shares of the different economic types of retailer in the total retail sales of furniture and furnishings, 1910–50**

Year	Proportion of total sales undertaken by			
	Co-operative Societies %	Department stores %	Multiple shop retailers %	Other retailers (by difference) %
1910	3·5–5·0	6·0– 7·0	1·0– 2·5	85·5–89·5
1920	4·0–5·5	9·0–11·0	3·0– 4·5	79·0–84·0
1925	4·0–5·0	10·5–12·0	5·5– 7·0	76·0–80·0
1930	4·0–5·5	14·5–16·0	9·5–11·0	67·5–72·0
1935	4·0–5·5	15·0–18·0	12·0–15·0	61·5–69·0
1939	4·5–6·0	16·0–19·0	15·0–17·0	58·0–64·5
1950	6·0–7·0	16·0–19·0	19·0–23·0	51·0–59·0

* For a discussion of the basis of these estimates see Appendix A. The sales of multiple shop retailers include the sales of furniture and furnishings by multiple shop drapers, hardware dealers, electrical goods retailers and other multiple shop firms as well as those by multiple shop furnishers. The sales of furniture and furnishings by manufacturers direct to the public and by mail order have been included in the sales of 'other retailers', as have the sales by cabinet-makers making furniture to customers' specifications.

The main trends in the retail structure of the trade as shown in Table 80 are the rapid rise in the share of the multiple shop retailers, particularly in the inter-war years, the importance of department store trading throughout these years, though the rate of increase tended to slow down after 1930, and the relatively small growth of Co-operative trading. Many of the factors influencing these trends have been mentioned in the above discussion of the characteristics of the different types of retailers. Low prices and the appeal made to the working-class market, backed by extensive use of hire-purchase trading methods, were important in the case of multiple shop trading. Further, the multiple shop firms with their greater capital resources were able to finance both hire-purchase trading methods and costly sites in main shopping streets more readily than their competitors. These financial advantages appeared to be of greater importance in the expansion of the large multiple shop firms than the economies associated with centralized buying, delivery and stock control and the employment of experts in the different functions of trading. In the case of the small multiple shop firms, however, the advantages obtained from the control of a small number of branches were more in the nature of economies of transport and stock-holding costs and the wider range of goods that could be offered to the customer.

The department stores played an important role in the middle-class market for both furnishings and furniture throughout these years. The slowing down in the rate of increase of department store trading would appear to have resulted partly from the limited appeal made by the stores to the working-class market and partly from the relatively small use made by these firms of hire-purchase methods of trading. The slow growth in the share of the Co-operative Societies in the trade was due mainly to the absence of specialization on the retailing side, the limited display space in most of the branches, and the rather higher prices charged for the goods compared with those of the multiple shop retailers. In most Societies the stocking and sale of furniture was an additional service provided for members, and the dividend on purchases made this service attractive. Few Societies, however, set out to 'sell' their furniture and furnishings department to members. Some improvements were being made in the late 'thirties in the organization of Co-operative manufacturing, in the style of the goods produced and in their display in the branches, and the growth of hire-purchase and mutuality trading by the Societies was assisting this expansion.

The decline in the relative importance of the small-scale retailer in these years was due mainly to the greater attractiveness and advantages of the multiple shop retailer on the furniture side of the trade and of the department store and Co-operative Society on the furnishings side of the trade. The small-scale furnisher could often compete with the multiple shop retailer in price but not in main-street siting or in generous hire-purchase terms. And again the small-scale retailer had a local reputation that was of importance but he could not compete with department stores in the wide range and selection of furnishings stocked.

Suggestions as to future trends in the trade

The possible developments in the character of the furniture and furnishings trade and in the retail structure of the trade can only be put forward very tentatively. There are a number of unknowns. The products themselves may change through the extensive use of plastics, metals and rubber in the place of wood, springs, upholstery and cloth, and such changes would result in much larger production units. Similarly demand will be influenced by the part that hire-purchase plays in the trade in the future. However, leaving aside guesses as to the long-term future of the trade, some tentative suggestions may be made on the basis of past developments as to possible trends in retail organization.

First it may be suggested that an increase of the share of the trade undertaken by multiple shop retailers is most probable. Any developments by way of larger-scale production units and increased emphasis on colour, shape and design in this trade will probably be to the advantage of the larger-scale retailers in that they possess the best display sites, have the resources to acquire additional sites, and can secure economies in buying and in stockholding. Further advantages to the large-scale retailer may arise from the ability to plan deliveries of orders from several branches in a given area and to arrange for direct delivery from factories, and to some extent from an increase in integration of production and distribution. The demand for furniture alone is not sufficient in many areas to maintain a branch specializing in furniture and furnishings, and there will undoubtedly be a trend towards the stocking by multiple shop branches of a wider range of products such as electrical goods and household appliances. Whether such mixed branches will be able to compete with the more specialist electrical multiple shop branches is, however, rather doubtful. If hire-purchase trading continues to be of major significance, this factor again should increase the advantages of the multiple shop retailers with their greater financial resources and ability to plan and organize this type of trading.

The share of the trade held by Co-operative Societies may be expected to increase to some extent as the benefits of the reorganization of Co-operative production are felt. In these goods, as in the case of most of the 'dry goods' sold by the Societies, a great deal will, however, hinge on the extent to which the individual, autonomous and relatively small-scale buying methods of the separate Societies are replaced by co-ordinated production and selling policies throughout the whole movement. Improved taste and greater variety in furniture and furnishings will also call for an entirely fresh approach by the Societies to the siting of the furniture departments and the display of their goods.

The department store may also increase their share of the furniture and furnishings trade, as they have the advantages both of size of unit to display the goods effectively and of the turnover to enable a wide range of goods to be stocked. Further, there are few signs that either the multiple shop retailers or the Co-operative Societies will enter the same price market as that served by the department stores. In many respects the lead of department stores in the furnishings trade is less likely to be challenged by other forms of retailing than their position in other trades such as women's wear and footwear.

An important factor, however, that may influence the relative rates of progress of the different economic types of retailer in these trades in the future is the extent to which one type rather than another succeeds in winning the confidence of the consumer as to the quality of the products sold. In buying furniture and furnishings the consumer is largely an amateur, often buying and judging products by wrong or irrelevant criteria such as the layout of the shop, the charm of the sales assistant, the bevelling of the mirror or the carving on the legs of the chairs. Too late, having bought the goods, he discovers that the quality and lasting nature of the product leave much to be desired. Few retailers, with the exception of some in the medium and high price ranges, have gained a completely sound reputation for good quality articles. As suggested above, such a reputation is difficult to build, partly because the retailer has little control over the quality of the goods supplied to him by manufacturers, and partly because the purchases by customers are so infrequent.

The large-scale retailers, the department stores, the Co-operative shops and the multiple shop organizations in theory have a better opportunity to control the quality of the goods purchased from the manufacturers than has the independent small-scale retailer. Particularly is this so in the case of integrated firms, for example the Co-operative Societies with their links with the productive units of the Wholesale Societies and, if they emerge in the future, the integrated multiple shop firms. On the whole, however, it would appear that the fulfilment of this consumer need is more likely to be met by the manufacturers by the production of furniture to known and recognized standards and, a part of such a process, the use of branding, than by any particular form or method of retail trading or organization. Such a trend may result in a strengthening of the position of the small-scale retailer in that a branded good is the same wherever it is sold.

CHAPTER XIX

THE HOUSEHOLD GOODS AND HOUSEHOLD STORES TRADES

The household goods trades are defined as covering the somewhat heterogeneous collection of articles purchased for household use that come under the general description of hardware and ironmongery, cutlery, pottery, glass and china, paints, wallpaper and brushes, oils and colours and miscellaneous household stores. Many changes in the character of the articles covered by these trades and in the relative importance in total sales of different types of product took place between the middle of the nineteenth and the middle of the twentieth century. Further, many different trade-types of retailers handled some or all of the goods at different times, their sale at no time being confined to specialists. These two factors make it impossible to give, in a reasonable space, any detailed account of the developments and changes in the methods and in the structure of the retail trade in these goods in these years. All that will be attempted here, therefore, is a very brief outline of the main trends in the trades as a whole, followed by a discussion of the data that are available on the growth of multiple shop retailing and the importance of large-scale retailing in these trades.

Changes in the character of the trade

In the second half of the nineteenth century the most important groups of retailers handling supplies of general household goods were ironmongers, oil and colourmen, chandlers of various types, drysalters, blacksmiths, a small number of china and glass retailers and cutlers, and, prominent in the case of some of the goods, travelling tinkers and pedlars. Many of these retailers combined wholesale and retail businesses and played a part in supplying tools and raw materials to industry, agriculture and the building trades as well as household goods to the domestic consumer. The lines of demarcation between the different types of retailers were never clear, for example ironmongers in many cases sold exactly the same type of goods as, say, oil and colourmen, and there were variations in the names used, the type of trade undertaken, and the goods stocked in different parts of the country.

The main developments in the trade during the closing decades of the nineteenth century and the first half of the twentieth may be suggested as three in number. First the character of the goods sold changed and the scope or range of the goods coming under the general heading of household goods widened considerably. The change in the character of the goods was chiefly in the direction of a decline in the importance of raw materials or semi-finished products and an increase in the importance of manufactured goods. Lamp black, brick-dust, colours and crude chemicals, for example, were replaced by goods prepared and mixed ready for use. Articles in their natural state were replaced by made-up, packaged and branded goods. More important was the tremendous widening in the range of the goods manufactured and offered for sale. The increasing use of ferrous and non-ferrous metals in place of the less adaptable wood led to a transformation in the house and the kitchen. Kettles, buckets, saucepans, hearth furniture, tools and implements, screws, nails, hooks and small metal wares began to be mass-produced at a cost that made them available to all sections of the people. At the same time the number of different types of the same article was greatly increased. The housewife for example had dozens of different types and makes of saucepan to choose from instead of a selection of half a dozen iron pots, dozens of different types and shapes of brooms and brushes instead of a few all-purpose designs. To this improvement in the construction of the products and the great increase in the number of types was added a group of entirely new products and gadgets. Growing urbanization and the building of small suburban houses with gardens in the inter-war years led to a demand for all sorts and types of gardening tools and appliances, and for labour-saving devices in the home and in the smaller kitchens. Shorter hours of work led to the demand for goods for hobbies of various kinds, and certain types of goods such as firelighters that no retailer would have stocked half a century earlier began to be sold in the shops.

The second main development in the trade was an increase in the number of retailers, and in the towns a trend towards specialization in particular sectors of the trade. For example some ironmongers in industrial towns concentrated on tools, while others in suburban districts stocked few tools but displayed a wide range of kitchen utensils and garden equipment. Retailers concentrating almost exclusively on the sale of wallpaper, paints, distemper and brushes appeared, and to some extent specialization in the sale of china, glass and pottery increased. Part of this change was reflected in the gradual disappearance of some of the older trade names such as oil and colourman, chandler and retail drysalter. But alongside this trend towards specialization on the part of some retailers and in some sectors of the trade, the opposite trend could also be observed. The increasing proportion of the goods that were being sold ready-packaged, and the development of branding by manufacturers, led to some decrease in the skill and knowledge demanded of the retailers in buying, mixing, processing and selling. Many firms and sections of the trade that had been relatively specialized and limited in the middle of the nineteenth century began to increase the range of goods handled. The oil and colourman, for example, who at one time was a specialist in paints and oils for mixing them, while in some instances he continued to specialize in paints, wallpaper, distemper and such goods more frequently added lines such as pickles, sauces, soap, tinned goods, jams, brushes, baskets, ironmongery, hardware, lamps and china to his stock. In the inter-war years a further extension of the range of goods sold by most hardware and ironmongery shops occurred when the sale of some electrical fittings and appliances was undertaken.

The third development in the trade, again a reflection of the changes in the type of goods sold, was the sale of a fairly wide group of household goods by retailers engaged in other trades. The grocer and provision dealer had always, in the smaller towns and villages, sold some household goods as well as foodstuffs, but in the twentieth century an increasing number of the grocers in the larger towns, other than the specialist provisions retailers, began to sell branded household goods alongside foodstuffs. The rising bicycle and electrical goods trades also sold some of the articles, and department stores and Co-operative stores by the turn of the century had entered the trade. Both the latter types of retailers were prominent in the sale of kitchen utensils of various sorts and of pottery and glass. But more important still was the growth in the inter-war years of bazaar and variety chain store trading. These firms sold a range of the smaller household goods, including pottery and glass, small hand tools and fittings, and various types of tin and metal wares. The retailers who confined their activities to the trade or specialized in one or other sectors of it remained the core of the trade and alone could offer the consumer the full range of articles available, but the non-specialist retailer had begun to handle in significant quantities those goods which required no skill in selling and which were in constant demand.

The development of multiple shop retailing to 1914

As mentioned above, some of the first multiple shop organizations in existence in the United Kingdom were to be found in the oil and colour trade. According to existing records the first multiple shop firm in this trade was that of George Mence Smith, which was founded in the 'fifties and by 1870 had over 20 branches in the London area. By 1875 there were 3 other firms trading mainly in oil and colours with more than 10 branches each: Joseph Salmon, Davies and Evans, and

Searle and Powell, all of London. In the next twenty-five years, to the turn of the century, the number of multiple shop firms in the trade rose to 14 and the number of branches to over 350. Practically all the firms operated in the London area and nearly one-half of the total number of branches at the end of the century were controlled by the two largest firms, George Mence Smith and Davies and Evans. The largest of the other firms were Joseph Salmon and Albert Simmonds.

These early oil and colour multiple shop firms were not specialists in a few lines. While oils and colours and paraffin or kerosene and appliances for lighting represented a good proportion of their sales, and in the buying of these goods for a number of branches important economies were obtained, the multiple shop firms at an early date started stocking a range of other goods, mainly 'hard' groceries, soap, and general hardware. The turnover in oils and colours alone was often not sufficient to maintain the shop, and with the growing demand for other manufactured household goods the multiple shop oil and colour-men widened the range of goods stocked. The proportion of other goods sold varied between firms and between branches according to their location. Some of the George Mence Smith shops, for example, in the country areas around London were mainly grocery merchants, and Salmon's shops also emphasized this side of the trade. Davies and Evans, on the other hand, stressed the sale of oils and colours, hardware and household goods in their shops.

The early success of multiple shop retailing in this trade was due mainly to the low price policy pursued. The branches were small and were located in the poorer and working-class districts of London, no attempt being made to secure fashionable or high-class sites. But the goods and the prices were vigorously displayed outside and inside the shops; very long opening hours were the rule, and the sales appeal was directed successfully to the working-class housewife. Two-pennyworth, three-pennyworth or six-pennyworth of the various goods, rather than shillingsworth, was the usual cash transaction.

The closing decade of the nineteenth century represented the end of the first phase of the growth of multiple shop organizations in this trade. In the following twenty years there was a second phase when the number of multiple shop firms and the number of branches in existence remained practically static. One firm grew to medium size—Timothy White, which sold hardware and household goods in dual shops with chemists' goods—but on the other hand Davies and Evans declined in importance, and the total number of multiple shop branches in existence hardly changed between 1895 when there were some 360 branches and 1920 when there were some 380 branches. This relative stability was in marked contrast to the rapid growth of multiple shop retailing in the

28-2

grocery and provisions trade during these years; a pertinent comparison in that multiple shop retailing began in both trades at the same time.

The main reasons for the stability in the number of branches would appear to be these. First, the original rapid development of the firms in the 'seventies and 'eighties owed a great deal, probably more than in a number of other trades, to the ability and energy of the founders; and by the turn of the century the founders, who had run the organizations practically single-handed, were retiring. Secondly, many of the firms were reaching the limit of their growth in the London area, and the step to expand to the provinces was not taken for administrative and financial reasons. The third, and probably the most important, reason was that the widening of the range of household goods being manufactured presented the firms with more problems than opportunities. The branches of these firms already carried a wide range of goods, from groceries to ironmongery; in fact they could be called multiple general shops. Competition in the working-class market in the sale of these goods was increasing from the grocery and provisions multiple shop firms on the one hand and to a lesser extent from the specialist paint and wallpaper multiple shop firms on the other. Any increase in the range of goods handled presented the firms with problems of physical space for stockholding and display and of the slowing down of the rate of stock turn. Also, with smaller quantities of each line being required fewer economies from bulk buying could be secured, and the advantage of low prices would not be so marked. The multiple shop firms in this trade were beginning to be faced with alternatives; on the one hand that of specializing in a particular line of household goods; on the other hand, that of developing in better-placed and much larger shops the sale of a very wide range of household goods at low prices. Some of the firms followed the first course and specialized, either by dropping almost entirely their oils and colours and concentrating on groceries, or by dropping their groceries and specializing in the paint trade. None of the existing multiple shop firms followed the second alternative directly, but just before the First World War a few bazaars and variety chain stores had begun to make their appearance. Most of the multiple shop firms between 1895 and 1920 pursued a middle policy of carrying a wide, but not too wide, range of household stores and some groceries, but for the reasons given above their economic advantages over other types of retailer in this field were no longer very great and their progress, as measured by the number of branches opened, was slow.

The development of multiple shop organizations between 1920 and 1939 was in striking contrast to the stability of the previous twenty-five years. This can be seen clearly in Table 81, which shows the number of multiple shop firms in existence and the number of branches controlled by these firms in the household goods trades between 1890 and 1950.

Table 81. *Estimates of the number of multiple shop firms and branches in the household goods and household stores trades, 1890–1950*

Year	10–24 branches		25–49 branches		50–99 branches		100 or more branches		Totals			
									10 or more branches		25 or more branches	
	Number of		Number of		Number of		Number of		Number of		Number of	
	Firms	Branches	Firms	Branches	Firms	Branches	Firms	Branches	Firms	Branches	Firms	Branches
1890	9	120	—	—	2	144	—	—	11	264	2	144
1895	13	177	1	25	2	160	—	—	16	362	3	185
1900	11	169	1	25	2	165	—	—	14	359	3	190
1905	11	147	3	90	2	160	—	—	16	397	5	250
1910	12	156	2	50	3	198	—	—	17	404	5	248
1915	13	177	1	25	2	148	—	—	16	350	3	173
1920	16	217	1	25	2	142	—	—	19	384	3	167
1925	20	286	4	114	1	77	1	127	26	604	6	318
1930	22	304	5	157	4	279	1	132	32	872	10	568
1935	20	286	7	236	2	163	4	517	33	1,202	13	916
1939	20	298	6	190	6	431	3	635	35	1,554	15	1,256
1950	22	330	4	134	1	59	3	721	30	1,244	8	914

All multiple shop organizations with 10 or more branches specializing in the sale of hardware, ironmongery, oils and colours, pottery, glass and china, paint, wallpaper, distemper and brushes and general household stores, and whose records have been traced, have been included in Table 81. Firms such as variety chain stores and general bazaars selling some of these goods but also a range of other products are not included. The table attempts to include details of firms that have gone out of existence or ceased to trade independently, as well as of those existing in 1950. Altogether data relating to 47 firms have been included in this table, and of the 17 firms no longer trading separately in 1950 6 have amalgamated or merged with other firms while the remainder appear to have ceased trading or controlled fewer than 10 branches in 1950. The number of branches of firms that are controlled by multiple shop firms operating in other trades has been included in the table, but the subsidiary firms have not been counted as separate organizations.

The development of multiple shop retailing after 1920

Table 81 brings out clearly the two further phases in the growth of multiple shop organizations in this trade. First, there was a rapid and continuous increase in the number of branches between 1920 and 1938.

This growth was not the result of renewed expansion of the general grocery, oil and colour and hardware multiple shop firms, which had been established but had been somewhat static in the years before the First World War, but of the expansion of newer firms specializing in various types of products. The most important of these was the group of multiple shop firms which specialized in the sale of wallpaper, paints, distemper and brushes, and, to a lesser extent, the group of firms that specialized in the sale of pottery and glass.

In 1920 not more than 10 % of the total number of multiple shop branches in the household goods trade could be said to specialize in these two types of goods. By 1930 the proportion had risen to 30 %, in 1939 to 43 %, and in 1950 to about 48 %. Put in a different way, some two-thirds of the net increase in the number of multiple shop branches between 1920 and 1950 was represented by the increase in the number of branches specializing in the sale of wallpaper, paint and distemper and in the sale of pottery, glass and china. Other types of multiple shop organizations, those dealing in general hardware and kitchen equipment and in general household stores, increased the number of their retail branches in these years, but their growth continued to be relatively slower than, and was overshadowed by, the growth of the more specialist type of firm. Multiple shop organizations in the ironmongery and tool trades proper were very few in numbers and operated on a very small scale.

The reasons for the rapid growth of the multiple shop firms specializing in the sale of wallpaper, paints, distemper and brushes were many. The demand for these goods had increased with the growth of home owner-ship and the greater attention paid to decoration in the home. The variety and the quality of the goods had improved, providing a wider choice of styles of wallpaper and of different colours and qualities of paint. The relatively narrow range of goods stocked by these dealers in contrast to the very wide range of products handled by the general hardware retailers and ironmongers gave considerable scope for the development of multiple shop trading techniques. But probably the most important factor was the integration of production and distri-bution. Practically all the large multiple shop wallpaper and paint firms had close links with wallpaper and paint manufacturers, and in some instances the retail branches were established directly as outlets for the products of the manufacturing firm. In the case of some firms over four-fifths of the goods sold by the retail branches were produced by the parent manufacturing company, and taking this group of specialist retailers as a whole more than one-half of the goods sold was represented by goods produced by the associated manufacturing units. Integration was also important in the case of the leading pottery and glass multiple shop organizations. This integration of production and distribution gave the firms, in most instances, a price advantage over other retailers, and to this were added the economies of multiple shop retailing techniques. Further, the multiple shop retailer specializing in a relatively narrow range of products could offer a better selection of, say, wallpaper and paint, or pottery and glass, than could the general ironmonger or hardware dealer who dealt in a wide range of other goods as well. The branches of these specialist multiple shop retailers, with the exception of the pottery and glass specialists, were usually smaller than the branches of the general hardware and household goods multiple shop retailers, the employment being 2–3 per branch in the inter-war years as against the 4–5 per branch of the general hardware firms. The retail turnover per branch was also lower. The branches of the wallpaper and paint and the pottery and glass multiple shop organizations were located for the most part in busy or main shopping streets, and the window displays of these firms were an important factor in sales.

The second phase of development was the decline in the number of branches of multiple shop firms between 1939 and 1950. This decline was due almost entirely to the severe shortages of goods and the pressure on manpower. A few firms went out of existence altogether in the war years and most organizations were forced to reduce the number of their branches. By 1945 the number of branches in existence had decreased by one-third compared with 1939. In the post-war years branches began to be re-opened and new ones started, so that by 1950 the number of branches trading was only some 15 % below the number in 1939.

During the 1939 to 1950 period a number of amalgamations took place between some of the leading firms. This trend is shown in Table 81 and the general effect was to increase the relative importance of the largest firms. In 1939 the largest multiple shop firm controlled some 14 % of the total number of branches and the two largest firms about 20 %. In 1950 the largest firm (using financial control rather than trading names as the criterion) controlled some 29 % of the total number of branches and the two largest firms about 46 %.

The variety chain store

Side by side with the growth of multiple shop firms dealing mainly or exclusively in household goods, the importance of other types of multiple shop retailers in these trades increased in the inter-war years. Many multiple shop grocers and some multiple shop furniture and electrical goods retailers began to handle a small range of household goods, but more important was their sale by variety chain stores and bazaars. Variety chain stores in the late 'twenties and the 'thirties displayed many of the goods that had hitherto been handled almost exclusively by the general ironmonger and hardware dealer or pottery and glass retailer. Galvanized buckets for sixpence, cups, saucers, plates, and glasses for twopence, threepence and sixpence each, and nails, screws, hammers, screwdrivers, pliers and even saws at comparable prices were displayed for the public to choose and buy. The low prices asked were stressed by the stores, though in some lines the difference between the prices charged by the specialist retailer and the variety chain store was not great. More important was the appeal of the open display of the goods, a practice that the general hardware retailer rarely adopted owing to the wide range of articles that he carried.

The variety chain stores did not, however, compete with the specialist retailer in the higher-priced articles. The success of variety chain store trading in these goods was due mainly to the initiative of these organizations in fulfilling the need that was arising just before the First World War, and grew in the inter-war years, for simple low-priced retailing of the growing range of small household goods. The multiple shop oil and colourman had in the nineteenth century, for the London area at least, fulfilled a part of this need, but in the twentieth century the variety chain stores, with their very much larger shops, very much greater purchasing power and closer links with suppliers, and highly developed merchandising and stock control techniques, fulfilled the need in towns throughout the country.

Shares of the different economic types of retailer in the total trade

This discussion of the developments in the retail structure of these trades may be concluded by presenting estimates of the share of the total trade undertaken by different economic types of retailers at different dates. To give a clearer indication of the trends an attempt has been made to distinguish between what may be called the household goods trades and the household stores trades. The household goods trades relate to the durable and semi-durable household goods coming under the headings of pottery and ironmongery, hollow-ware, hardware, tools, wallpaper, paint, and so on. The household stores trades relate to non-durable household supplies such as soap, paraffin, candles, matches and household cleaners. In retail trading there is, of course, an overlap in that many retailers sell both categories of goods, and this factor necessarily makes the estimates of the share of the different economic types of retailer rather tentative.

The estimates relating to household goods are presented in Table 82 and the estimates relating to household stores in Table 83. No attempt has been made to show the share of department stores in the total trade of household stores, as department stores are estimated to have undertaken less than 2 % of total retail sales.

Table 82. *Estimated shares of the different economic types of retailer in the total retail sales of household goods, 1900–50**

Year	Proportion of total sales undertaken by			
	Co-operative Societies %	Department stores %	Multiple shop retailers %	Other retailers (by difference) %
1900	2·0–3·5	1·5– 2·5	1·0– 2·0	92·0–95·5
1910	3·0–4·5	3·5– 5·0	1·0– 2·0	88·5–92·5
1920	3·5–4·5	5·5– 7·0	2·0– 3·0	85·5–89·0
1925	3·5–4·5	8·0–10·0	4·5– 5·5	81·0–84·0
1930	3·5–4·5	10·0–11·5	10·0–12·0	72·0–76·5
1935	4·0–5·0	10·0–13·0	17·0–20·0	62·0–69·0
1939	4·0–5·5	11·0–14·0	23·0–27·0	53·5–62·0
1950	5·5–6·5	12·0–15·0	24·0–28·0	50·5–58·5

* For a discussion of the basis of these estimates see Appendix A. The goods included in the category of household goods are: hardware, hollow-ware and ironmongery, cutlery, pottery, glass and china, paint, wallpaper and distemper, brushes and brooms, oils and colours, tools, non-electrical domestic appliances, and garden furniture and equipment. The sales of these goods by variety chain stores and by multiple shop organizations in other trades, for example the groceries and provisions, electrical goods, and jewellery trades, are included in the share of multiple shop retailers given in this table, along with the sales of specialist multiple shop retailers. The sales by manufacturers using mail order methods or door-to-door canvassers are included in the sales of 'other retailers', a residual group.

Table 83. *Estimated shares of the different economic types of retailer in the total retail sales of household stores, 1900–50**

Year	Proportion of total sales undertaken by		
	Co-operative Societies %	Multiple shop retailers %	Other retailers (by difference) %
1900	9·0–11·0	2·5– 4·0	85·0–88·5
1910	10·5–12·0	6·0– 7·0	81·0–83·5
1920	12·0–13·5	8·5– 9·5	77·0–79·5
1925	11·0–14·0	10·0–11·0	75·0–79·0
1930	12·5–14·0	11·5–13·5	72·5–76·0
1935	13·0–15·0	13·0–16·0	69·0–74·0
1939	14·0–17·0	15·0–18·0	65·0–71·0
1950	13·5–15·5	16·0–19·0	65·5–70·5

* For a discussion of the basis of these estimates see Appendix A. The goods included in the category of household stores are: soap (other than toilet soap), household cleaners and polishes, kerosene, matches, candles, firewood. The sales of these goods by variety chain stores and by multiple shop grocers and provision dealers and tobacconists are included in the sales by multiple shop retailers given in this table along with the sales by specialist multiple shop retailers.

The main features of Table 82 are the rise in the importance of department store trading in household goods up to 1925 and the subsequent very rapid rise in the importance of multiple shop trading. These two types of retailers catered for somewhat different price markets in these goods, and while department stores offered a wide range and choice of medium- and high-priced household goods to the growing middle classes the multiple shop retailers concentrated on the low-price market. The rapid rise in multiple shop trading from the middle of the inter-war years onwards was due on the one hand to greater specialization of some multiple shop firms, for example in pottery and glass and wallpaper and paint, and on the other hand to the rise of variety store trading in these goods. Some of the specialist multiple shop firms were able to offer a greater range of lines within the given types of goods than could either the department store or the small-scale retailer. The variety chain stores were able to offer a few ranges of household goods at lower prices and in a more effective manner than could other retailers, owing to their large economies of buying and the size of their stores.

Household stores were sold in large part by grocery and provisions dealers, and the shares of the different economic types of retailers in the total trade follow broadly along the same lines as those shown above in the chapter dealing with the grocery and provisions trade.

Suggestions as to future trends in the trade

Future trends in the retail structure of household goods trades are difficult to discuss in detail as the nature of these trades changes with the development of new inventions and materials and with changes in social habits. The plastics and synthetic resins industry, for example, may revolutionize the pottery and glass trade, and new, indestructible wall covering may change the paint and wallpaper trade. Leaving forecasts as to new inventions on one side, however, and following the lines of the trends discussed above, it is possible to make some tentative suggestions as to the future pattern of the trade. The small-scale ironmonger and hardware dealer would appear certain to maintain a prominent position in the trade as the supplier of a wide range of household, industrial and agricultural wants. Shops that can supply the occasional, irregular and out-of-the-way needs of the public for replacement parts, for fixtures, for special tools will remain a necessity both in industrial and in rural areas, and no large-scale retailer, as at present organized, can compete in this field where thousands of lines have to be kept in stock and the demand for each line is small. Against this, when the demand for a particular range of goods stocked by the general ironmonger becomes sufficiently consistent and regular the large-scale retailers, particularly multiple shop retailers, may be expected to stock and sell the goods.

In densely populated areas where the demand for certain types of household stores was consistent and concentrated, multiple shop retailers of both the specialist and variety chain store type entered the field. Wallpaper and pottery are examples of trades when the specialist multiple shop retailer grew in importance. The variety chain stores sold small tools and appliances and pottery. In the future there would appear to be room for further expansion of both types of multiple shop retailer. While the specialist may be reaching a limit in the wallpaper and paint trade, expansion in the pottery trade will probably continue, and some multiple shop organizations may develop the sale of medium- and higher-priced articles such as gardening equipment and home labour-saving devices as the output of the latter increases. The variety chain stores, on the other hand, unless they change radically their pricing and stockholding policies, are likely to keep to the lower-priced and quicker-moving goods. But unless the number of variety chain store branches increases appreciably in the future their share of the total trade in these goods appears unlikely to rise greatly.

Neither the Co-operative Societies nor the department stores would appear likely to make substantial gains in the trade in the future. If the Co-operative share of the grocery and provisions trade increases, the Co-operative share of the household stores trade will undoubtedly rise, but the present trading methods of the Societies in household goods give them no advantage over the multiple shop retailer in this field and little advantage over the small-scale retailer. As regards department stores, their future role in the household goods trade is of course bound up with their importance in the retail structure as a whole. Apart from this, however, if multiple shop retailing organizations do develop a measure of specialization in the medium- and higher-priced household goods this will represent a considerable threat to the position of the department stores in this section of the trade.

APPENDIX A

THE METHODS OF RESEARCH AND SOURCES OF INFORMATION

1. Until the publication of the results of the first Census of Distribution no official or comprehensive information on the structure of retail trade in the United Kingdom existed. Trade associations, government departments, market research firms and other bodies had from time to time published data or estimates relating to certain aspects of the retail organization of particular trades. Much of the material however was incomplete, was sometimes contradictory owing to the use of differing definitions, and was often the by-product of the collection of information for other purposes, for example rationing, rather than the result of a direct and specific investigation of the retail structure at a given point of time. A similar position existed in regard to information on the development of the different economic types of retailer. Some estimates have been made at different dates by various bodies, but with the exception of the data on the retail sales and membership of Co-operative Societies, which exist in a continuous series since 1882, data on the trading activities of other large-scale retailers have been very limited in scope or else non-existent.

2. To obtain information therefore on the development of large-scale retailing, other than Co-operative retailing, since the middle of the nineteenth century considerable research had to be undertaken. The most difficult sector was that of multiple shop retailing, and an account of the methods of research used in this case is given in some detail as a guide to the sources of the information and to the possible margins of error that may be present in the estimates set out in the foregoing chapters. This account is followed by similar but shorter descriptions of the sources of the estimates made in relation to Co-operative and department store trading.

The estimates relating to multiple shop organizations

3. First, as no organization was able to provide a list,[1] an index, as complete as possible, had to be compiled of all firms in 1950 controlling 3 or more retail branches in the United Kingdom.[2] This index was based on a complete search of all the reference books and directories available. Secondly, all firms in this index with more than 20 branches each were approached or interviewed, while a sample of those with over 3 and up to 19 branches received a postal questionnaire. This direct approach to firms provided, in the great majority of instances, a fairly complete record of the

---

[1] A partial, though not always accurate, list is given in *Store Annual Retail Directory of the United Kingdom*, London, 1950 edition.

[2] Throughout the study a branch is defined as a fixed retail shop selling commodities retail to the public. Travelling shops are therefore excluded, as are depots, for example the distributing dairies of milkmen from which the retailing floats operate.

history and development of the individual firms, and the sample gave a useful indication of the accuracy of the original index and of the general pattern of the growth of the smaller firms. The multiple shop organizations were questioned as to their origins, their growth as measured by the number of retail branches existing at different dates, the amalgamations if any with other firms, their retail employment, their retail turnover, their buying and pricing policies, their links if any with manufacturing units, the changes in the character of their business over time, their suggestions as to the advantages secured by their methods of trading, and their views or opinions as to future trends in the trade.

4. These questions yielded an important part of the information required, but there remained the problem of the large number of multiple shop firms that had gone out of existence, or that had amalgamated with existing firms which no longer had details of the earlier history of the amalgamated firm. There were also the problems of the firms which, while in existence, had had their records lost or destroyed or sent to salvage, and of the few firms who felt unable to co-operate in the inquiry. In these instances the methods used to collect data and to trace the existence and histories of the firms were searches in company files, company prospectuses and company reports, a careful study of trade and commercial papers and journals and a practically page-by-page checking of trade and street directories from the eighteen-sixties onwards. Such a procedure was laborious in the extreme, but the results obtained, when tested against details provided by firms whose records were complete, were sufficiently encouraging to warrant the use of and reliance upon this method. Finally the data obtained from these varied sources could be further checked in some instances against the information, mentioned above, published from time to time by government departments, trade associations and other bodies.[1]

5. The material obtained from individual firms and from other sources was then combined to provide a picture of the total number of multiple shop organizations in existence in different trades and of the number of retail branches controlled by them at different points of time. To place all the data regarding individual firms on a comparable time base some interpolation of the number of branches was necessary, but there were a large enough number of five-yearly and yearly series of the development of individual firms available for the different trades to enable this to be done with a measure of confidence. Sufficient data did not exist to permit the construction of a year-by-year series of the number of all multiple shop branches, but the numbers at five-yearly intervals could be estimated with the exception of the period of the Second World War, when unsettled trading conditions led to the use of the years 1939 and 1950.

6. The method of collection of the data on the number of firms and the number of branches made it almost certain that details of some of the smaller

[1] In all, the records of 1,132 firms with 10 or more branches each have been traced and used in the construction of the tables presented in this study. Some 255 of these firms are known to have amalgamated with or been acquired by other firms and 239 appear to have gone out of existence.

organizations, mainly those with under 25 branches each, were omitted. The smaller organizations, for example, were rarely limited companies and would not be mentioned in the trade press. Further, in the searching of directories firms with say 10 branches were more likely to be overlooked than firms with 30. Again, from the index prepared of the number of multiple shop organizations in existence in 1950 it is known that details of a group of the smaller firms have been omitted from the estimates owing to the lack of information on the history of the firms. In the same way information regarding multiple shop firms that related to the number of branches in existence in one year only or in two years close together was excluded from the estimates, as the inclusion of the details of such firms for one year only, without information as to when they started operations or when they ceased to trade, would have distorted the trend. Finally, some omissions may have occurred in the case of firms whose retail branches traded under entirely separate names, in other words giving no outward indication of being a multiple shop organization. The well-known instances of this practice were covered but the less well-known instances may have been omitted.

7. The final series of estimates therefore of the number of multiple shop organizations as a whole and in different trades, and of the number of branches controlled by them in different years is, so far as careful planning could make possible, consistent throughout in its construction in that the same methods and sources were used, and there is no reason to assume that the reliability of the sources varied materially over time. The trend therefore that is shown is probably correct, though the level is almost certainly below the actual level.

8. Two checks, one partial and one full, of the estimates of the number of multiple shop firms and branches could be made. The full check was provided by the results of the Census of Distribution, and this is discussed later. The partial check was provided by the figures relating to the sale of government butter in 1919. These figures, which are discussed above in the chapter on the grocery and provisions trade, have been analysed by S. Bushell to show by size-groups the total number of multiple shop firms and branches holding permits to sell government butter in 1919.[1] These figures provide a check on the estimates made in this inquiry of the number of multiple shop firms and branches in the grocery and provisions trade. To make this comparison some adjustments have to be made to the figures given in Table 25 above. First an alternative size-grouping to fit that of the Ministry of Food grouping has to be used. Secondly the estimates have to be moved back a year from 1920 to 1919. Thirdly trading practice has to be used to determine the number of organizations, rather than financial control as adopted in Table 25. If a subsidiary firm traded under its own name and applied separately for a permit the Ministry of Food classed it as a separate firm. These adjustments having been made, the comparison of the estimates made in this inquiry and the Ministry of Food 1919 figures is set out in Table 84.

---

[1] S. Bushell, 'The Relative Importance of Co-operative, Multiple and other Retail Traders', *Economica*, vol. I, no. I, January 1921.

Table 84. *Number of multiple shop firms and branches holding butter registrations in 1919 compared with National Institute estimates of the number of multiple shop firms and branches in the grocery and provisions trade in 1919*

Size-group Number of branches	National Institute figures		Ministry of Food figures	
	Number of		Number of	
	Organizations	Branches	Organizations	Branches
10– 19	64	864	52	702
20– 29	25	581	22	533
30– 49	17	623	9	363
50– 99	10	622	11	742
100–149	12	1,421	9	1,050
150–249	3	620	3	648
250–900	5	2,820	5	2,790
Totals	136	7,551	111	6,828

9. This table suggests an overstatement rather than an understatement of the number of branches listed in this inquiry. Bushell in her article however gives a number of reasons why the number of multiple shop firms and branches holding permits for the sale of butter is an understatement of the total number engaged in the grocery and provisions trades. The reasons given are as follows. First, not all multiple shop grocery retailers sold imported butter. There were 2 firms with over 100 branches each in this category and perhaps 20–30 in the 10–99 size group. Taking 30 as the number of firms omitted from the Ministry of Food figures for this reason, the number of branches omitted would be some 900–1000. Secondly, Bushell noted 3 other firms, one with over 100 branches and 2 with over 50 branches, of which, while they were technically multiple shop firms, the branches would have applied for permits individually rather than through head office. Such firms were not listed as multiple shop retailers. The branches of such firms usually traded under separate names and not under the name of the controlling firm. According to the data collected in this inquiry there were at least 5 other firms in the 25–50 size-group that adopted the same procedure. These 8 firms would have had approximately 450–500 branches in all. If the multiple shop firms omitted for these reasons are included in the Ministry of Food figures there is a suggested understatement of about 10 % in the National Institute figures.

10. These estimates of the number of organizations and of the number of branches trading in different years form the main basis of the analysis in the foregoing chapters of the growth of multiple shop trading, but in addition it was also possible to make some estimates of the retail sales of multiple shop organizations at different points in time. As mentioned above, existing firms were asked to provide details of their retail employment and retail sales, as well as information regarding the number of branches. Figures of sales were not given in all cases, but in a number of instances very complete records of

turnover and breakdown of sales were made available. There was however no method of obtaining information as to the retail sales of the multiple shop firms that had gone out of existence, though occasionally such details were given in company prospectuses and reports. A similar difficulty was present in the case of firms whose records had been lost or destroyed or who were unwilling to provide data.

11. A sufficient number of firms in different trades had, however, provided information which, used in conjunction with data obtained from other sources, made possible some tentative estimates of the retail sales of all multiple shop firms and branches listed in this inquiry at different points in time and in different trades. In building up such estimates every use was made of information regarding the character, type of trade and size of the organizations for which turnover details were not available. For example, in some instances figures of retail employment per branch were available but not figures of average retail sales per branch. In such cases, unless there was any known difficulty, the branches were assumed to have the same average turnover and breakdown of sales as similar-sized branches of other firms in the same trade. In those instances where the only facts available related to the number of branches in existence at a particular date, the turnover per branch and the breakdown of sales was assumed to be of the same order as the average of all firms of that size in that particular trade and at that particular date for which data were available. Such a procedure cannot and does not claim to yield accurate results, but multiple shop branches in the same trade, at least up to 1914, did not vary greatly in size, employment or turnover. Greater differentiation between the branches of different firms in the same trade occurred after the First World War, but rather more data were available in these years. There must remain however an important error in the estimates, and the error is probably on balance rather greater in the estimates given relating to the earlier years of the period covered than those relating to the later years. Fewer data were available regarding the activities of individual firms in the years before, say, 1914 than for the later years and, further, the relative importance of firms which have since ceased trading was greater in the earlier years.

12. Apart however from the error in the estimates of total sales of multiple shop firms which arose from incomplete information on the turnover of individual firms and on the breakdown of sales into groups of commodities, there was the further problem that the total number of multiple shop firms and branches listed in this inquiry was known to be, as discussed above, an understatement of the total number of multiple shop firms and branches in existence. As it was most important to make the figures relating to multiple shop firms comparable with those of Co-operative Societies and department stores, which related to sales of all Societies and stores and were not knowingly understated, an attempt was made to adjust the estimates of multiple shop sales upwards so that they related to all multiple shop firms and not only those listed in this inquiry. The results of the Census of Distribution were used for this purpose and the method adopted is discussed later.

The estimates relating to Co-operative Societies

13. The estimates of the number of branches of Co-operative Societies and of their retail sales used in this study are all based on the published statistics of the Co-operative movement. A number of adjustments to the figures of sales had however to be made in order to make them comparable with the data relating to other types of organization. The most important of these adjustments were as follows.

14. The first problem was to eliminate from the annual totals the sales of goods such as coal which are not included in this study and the very small proportion of the total represented by the sales of services such as laundering, footwear repairing and funeral furnishing which are similarly excluded. Up to 1935 some transfers from one department to another department within the same Society or between Societies also had to be excluded. Such exclusions could, within limits, be calculated on the basis of the departmental sales analysis published by the Co-operative Union covering the years 1925–50, but before 1925 the exclusions had to be estimated by using the 1925–50 trend figures and other information as to the activities of the Retail Societies. The Co-operative departmental sales analysis made possible a further breakdown of the sales. In attempting however to determine the retail sales of individual commodities and commodity groups further adjustments, mainly of a minor character, had to be made to the published figures. These were necessary as some of the departmental groups had to be regrouped or subdivided for the purposes of this study; for example, an attempt had to be made to distinguish the sales of bread from the sales of groceries and provisions as a whole, and also allowance had to be made for the failure of some Societies, usually the smaller ones, to return an accurate and precise departmental breakdown of their sales.

15. As stated above, the departmental analysis of sales of Co-operative Societies was available only from 1925, and on a consistent basis only from 1930. Estimates therefore had to be made of the departmental sales, or sales by trade groups, of commodities before that date. Some assistance in doing this was provided by the published figures of output of goods manufactured or processed within the Co-operative Movement and also by enquiries made recently of some of the larger Societies as to the pattern of departmental sales in 1914.[1] The general conclusion reached and used in this study was that the broad division of Co-operative retail sales between food and non-food goods did not differ radically in the two decades before 1914 from the division in the inter-war years. Undoubtedly a slightly higher proportion of total Co-operative sales in say 1900 was represented by the sale of food than in say 1925 or 1930, corresponding with the shift in national demand, but the relative shift away from food sales in the Co-operative movement in the latter years was very slight.

16. The probable error in the estimates of total Co-operative sales made in this study is, of course, much smaller than in the case of the estimates

[1] See J. A. Hough, *Co-operative Retailing, 1914–1945*, London, International Co-operative Alliance, 1949, pp. 50–1.

made of multiple shop and department store sales, as far more data has been recorded and published. It will be appreciated, however, from the foregoing discussion that the probable error increases in the case of the estimates made of the sales of individual commodities and commodity groups which are used in the chapters on the different trades; and again the probable error is greater in the estimates made for the years before 1930 than in those relating to the years subsequent to 1930. In the presentation of the estimates of sales by Co-operative Societies, therefore, ranges rather than single figures have been used.

The estimates relating to department stores

17. In making estimates of the number of department stores existing at various dates, and of their retail sales and retail employment, somewhat the same methods were used as in constructing the estimates relating to multiple shop organizations. The main differences in approach arose on the one hand from the fact that far more data which could be adapted for the purposes of this study have been published on the department store form of retailing, and on the other hand from the absence of a generally recognized or easily measurable definition of a department store, which made very difficult the collection of data that were comparable over time. Information on the activities of the largest and the leading department stores was relatively abundant, for example in company reports, publications of trade associations, and histories of individual firms, but little data existed on the history of the smaller stores. Considerable problems were faced, for example, in attempting to determine whether a large draper in a provincial town who called himself a department store did, in fact, come within the definition adopted, and, if not included at one point of time, whether he should be included at another point of time.

18. The estimates therefore of department store trading made in this study are subject both to a margin of error arising from incomplete data on numbers and sales and to a margin of error arising from the difficulty of strict application of the definition adopted. On the whole, as a policy of excluding firms from the classification of department store in any case of doubt was adopted rather than one of inclusion, the estimates made in this study are more likely to underestimate the importance of department store trading than to overestimate it. Further, the estimates made are rather more reliable for the later years than for the years before 1914. Again, the estimates are presented in the form of ranges rather than as single figures.

The estimates of national retail sales

19. The estimates of national retail sales of consumer goods at different dates which are used throughout this study in order to calculate the relative importance of the different economic types of retailer in the total retail trade are based on the estimates made by A. R. Prest and Richard Stone in their volumes on consumers' expenditure in the United Kingdom from

1900 to 1938.[1] The estimates relating to the years 1938–50 are based on the information given in the government White Papers on National Income and Expenditure.[2] No estimates on a comparable basis are available for the years before 1900.

20. The methods used by Prest and Stone and the reliability of the estimates presented are fully discussed in the volumes referred to above. This ground need not be covered here. Some explanation is however necessary of the exclusions and adjustments that have been made to these published series in order to provide estimates of the retail sales of different commodities as distinct from the series relating to consumers' expenditure. The first stage was the exclusion from the estimates of consumers' expenditure of the expenditure on services and on goods, for example coal, not coming within the scope of the present study. The second stage was the exclusion of the element represented by producers' consumption of their own produce as such goods did not pass through retail trade channels. Both these adjustments to the series could be made readily as the consumers' expenditure represented by these different items was given by Prest and Stone.

21. The third adjustment was of a different genre. An attempt was made to exclude from the estimates of consumers' expenditure the purchases by catering establishments. This exclusion could only be made approximately for the years up to 1938, this being the first year for which close estimates were available. The method adopted for the earlier years was to assume that the relative proportion of such non-domestic purchases to total expenditure in the different categories declined only slightly over the whole period from that shown in 1938.

22. In the case of the estimates relating to the years 1900–19 two further types of adjustment to these published series had to be made. First, the individual commodity series in these years were not all presented in the detail required to determine the expenditure by consumers on different main types of consumer good—for example bread and cakes are not distinguished from flour—and an attempt has been made to estimate the expenditure on some of the commodities not listed separately, using the trend of the 1920–38 figures and the calculations given in the Appendix to Prest's volume, which considers the reconciliation of the two series. Secondly, an adjustment had to be made in respect of expenditure by consumers in Southern Ireland. As the estimates of multiple shop, Co-operative and department store trading related to Great Britain and Northern Ireland only, an attempt was made on the basis of the population figures to exclude from the estimates of

---

[1] A. R. Prest, assisted by A. A. Adams, *Consumers' Expenditure in the United Kingdom, 1900–1919*, Cambridge University Press, 1954, and Richard Stone, assisted by D. A. Rowe and by W. J. Corlett, Renée Hurstfield and Muriel Potter, *The Measurement of Consumers' Expenditure and Behaviour in the United Kingdom, 1920–1938*, vol. i, Cambridge University Press, 1953 (nos. 3 and 1 respectively in the Series *Studies in the National Income and Expenditure of the United Kingdom* issued under the joint auspices of the National Institute of Economic and Social Research and the Department of Applied Economics of the University of Cambridge).

[2] *National Income and Expenditure of the United Kingdom, 1946 to 1950*, Cmd. 8203, 1951, and the preceding issues.

consumers' expenditure on the different items the expenditure in Southern Ireland.

23. For the years 1920–38 figures relating to consumers' expenditure on food and tobacco only were available in the source quoted. Estimates therefore had to be made of consumer retail expenditure on non-food goods for these years. The methods adopted to do this followed closely those used by Prest and Stone in their work. Heavy reliance was placed on the results of the Censuses of Production for 1924, 1930 and 1935, and on some estimates at present unpublished.[1]

24. The estimates of consumers' retail expenditure on the different groups of commodities for the years 1938–50 are based, as mentioned above, on the figures published in the government White Papers. In addition, the Ministry of Food and the Board of Trade kindly provided some further estimates which enabled a series to be constructed consistent with those used by Prest and Stone. The subsequent adjustments that had to be made to the figures followed the same procedure as that outlined above.

25. The series of estimates of retail sales of the different commodities were then grouped together in 18 commodity groups or trade categories. The purpose of this grouping was to place together the commodities which were usually sold by the same retail trading group. Table 10 above showed the estimates of retail sales by 4 main commodity groups. Table 85 presents the estimates of the sales of the 18 commodity groups between 1900 and 1950 that make up the 4 main groups.

26. The main commodities making up each of the 18 commodity groups are given below along with the names of the chief trade type of retailer concerned with their sale:

Foodstuffs

Groceries and provisions, sold mainly by Grocers and Provision Dealers:
Flour; Biscuits; Breakfast cereals; Oatmeal; Miscellaneous cereals, i.e. barley, rice, etc.; Bacon and ham; Eggs; Butter; Cheese; Margarine; Lard; Edible oils; Dried and canned vegetables; Dried and canned fruit; Nuts; Condensed milk; Sugar; Tea; Coffee; Cocoa; Jam and marmalade; Honey; Syrup and treacle; Vinegar; Pickles and sauces; Canned meat; Meat essence and extract; Meat and fish paste; Canned fish; Soft drinks (not Table waters); Salt, mustard, pepper; Miscellaneous manufactured foods, i.e. Canned soups, custard powders, blancmange, cornflour, etc.

Meat and Meat Products, sold mainly by Butchers:
Home-killed and imported meat; Sausages; Other meat products such as meat pies; Poultry, game and rabbits.

Fruit and Vegetables, sold mainly by Fruiterers and Greengrocers:
Home-grown and imported fresh fruit and vegetables.

Fish, sold mainly by Fishmongers:
All types of Fish, excluding Fried fish.

---

[1] To appear in *The Measurement of Consumers' Expenditure in the United Kingdom, 1920–1938*, vol. II, by Richard Stone and D. A. Rowe, to be published by Cambridge University Press (no. 2 in the Series *Studies in the National Income and Expenditure of the United Kingdom*).

Table 85. *Estimated total retail sales by individual commodity groups, 1900–50*

Commodity group	1900 £m.	1905 £m.	1910 £m.	1915 £m.	1920 £m.	1925 £m.	1930 £m.	1935 £m.	1938 £m.	1950 £m.
Groceries and provisions	204	217	235	315	629	484	460	403	440	899
Bread and cakes	38	48	56	75	147	113	100	99	110	279
Fruit and vegetables	50	54	53	61	163	137	138	134	144	328
Milk	33	36	39	41	105	85	85	91	99	210
Fish	14	14	15	17	47	32	30	26	26	64
Meat, poultry, etc.	102	108	117	160	360	286	265	228	253	361
Total food	441	477	515	669	1,451	1,137	1,078	981	1,072	2,141
Confectionery and ice cream	13	16	20	43	92	70	72	67	77	141
Tobacco	26	30	35	47	119	117	141	155	177	778
Reading matter and stationery	18	22	23	26	54	55	64	73	78	202
Total tobacco, confectionery, newspapers, stationery, books	57	68	78	116	265	242	277	295	332	1,121
Men's and boys' clothing	37	39	47	53	200	107	119	119	127	290
Women's and girls' clothing	83	84	95	108	400	216	219	209	246	541
Footwear	24	25	26	23	105	72	72	68	73	174
Total clothing	144	148	168	184	705	395	410	396	446	1,005
Chemists' goods	14	18	19	25	53	51	55	66	73	177
Bicycles, radios, sewing machines, electrical goods, musical instruments	7	10	9	11	27	38	46	68	60	158
Jewellery, sports goods, toys, fancy, leather and miscellaneous goods	14	19	25	32	80	63	70	73	76	170
Furniture and furnishings	25	25	28	41	116	101	117	123	128	340
Pottery, glass, hardware, ironmongery	28	28	29	34	83	58	51	51	56	92
Household stores	20	20	21	30	83	62	59	54	59	108
Total other goods	108	120	131	173	442	373	398	435	452	1,045
Total retail sales	750	813	892	1,142	2,863	2,147	2,163	2,107	2,302	5,312

Milk, sold mainly by Dairymen:
All milk sold retail to final consumers, excluding school milk.

Bread and Cakes, sold mainly by Bakers and Pastrycooks:
All types of bread, cakes and flour confectionery.

Confectionery, Reading and Writing Material and Tobacco Goods

Sugar Confectionery, sold by Confectioners:
Chocolates, sweets and ice cream.

Tobacco Goods, sold by Tobacconists:
Tobacco and cigarettes; Snuff and cigars.

Newspapers, Books, Stationery, sold by Newsagents, Booksellers and Stationers:
Newspapers, magazines and periodicals; Books other than those purchased by libraries; Stationery goods, paper and cardboard products; Pens and pencils; Writing inks and accessories.

Clothing and Footwear

Men's and Boys' Clothing, sold mainly by Men's Tailors, Outfitters, Hatters, and Clothiers:
Ready-to-wear and bespoke outer clothing including rainwear; Men's and boys' hosiery and underwear; Shirts, collars, ties; Hats; Accessories.

Women's, Girls' and Children's Clothing, sold mainly by Women's Tailors, Outfitters, Gown Shops, Milliners, and Drapers:
Ready-to-wear and bespoke outer clothing; Women's and girls' hosiery, knit goods and underclothing; Millinery; Babies' clothing; Dress piece goods; Corsets and brassières; Gloves, haberdashery, fancy drapery and hand-knitting yarn.

Footwear, sold mainly by Boot and Shoe Retailers:
Men's, women's, boys' and girls' and children's footwear of all types; excluding footwear repairs.

Other Goods

Chemists' Goods, sold mainly by Chemists and Druggists:
Proprietary and non-proprietary medicines; Beauty preparations and requisites; Perfumes and toilet waters; Dentifrice and toothbrushes; Razors and razor blades; Photographic and optical goods; Surgical sundries; Dispensing.

Speciality Goods, sold mainly by Speciality retailers such as Bicycle dealers, Radio and electrical dealers, Sewing machine retailers, Perambulator dealers, Musical instrument retailers:
Bicycles and bicycle accessories; Radio and radio accessories; Electrical domestic appliances and apparatus; Electric light lamps, lampshades, lighting fittings and other accessories; Sewing machines; Perambulators and baby carriages; Musical instruments; excluding repairs to these goods.

Jewellery, Sports Goods, Toys, Fancy and Leather Goods, sold mainly by
Jewellers, Sports Goods dealers, Toy shops, and Leather Goods dealers:
Real and imitation jewellery; Silver and electro-plate; Clocks and watches;
Cutlery; Sports goods, toys and games of all sorts; Fancy goods; Leather
goods including handbags and travel goods.

Furniture and Furnishings, sold mainly by Furniture dealers:
Furniture and bedding; Soft furnishings and furnishing fabrics; Household textiles; Carpets and rugs; Linoleum and other floor coverings.

Pottery, Glass, Hardware, and Ironmongery, sold mainly by Hardware
dealers, Ironmongers, Pottery and glass dealers:
Pottery, china and glassware; Hardware and hollow-ware; Tools; Paints
and wallpaper; Brushes and brooms; Non-electrical domestic appliances;
Garden furniture and equipment.

Household Stores, sold mainly by Grocers and General Stores:
Matches; Soaps; Polishes; Candles and nightlights; Miscellaneous
cleaning materials; Kerosene.

27. The estimates of the retail sales of the different trade categories of
goods that have been distinguished and of the total retail sales at various
dates have all been expressed in the foregoing chapters as single figures—
that is, no range or indication of the probable error has been given. This
method of presentation is not, of course, meant to convey the impression that
these estimates are not subject to error. It has been adopted because the
figures used for the most part are taken directly from other published sources
and are not the outcome of original research in connexion with this study.
As mentioned above, for a discussion of the probable errors in the original
series the sources referred to must be consulted. It is true that the adjustments made to the original published series in order to present the figures
in retail trade groupings and to exclude non-retail sales are the responsibility
of the author of this study and not that of the authors of the original series.
There was, however, nothing to be gained in the direction of clarity by
showing statistically the probable margins of error in relation to the adjustments by themselves. All that should be noted is that the adjustments and
re-allocation of groups of commodities that had to be made to the series
relating to the years 1900–19 were greater than in the case of the series
relating to 1920–50 and therefore the probable errors may be greater.

The Census of Distribution, 1950

28. The results of the 1950 Census of Distribution[1] were not published
until after the collection of the data used in this study had been completed.
The Census returns, however, afforded some check on the methods used in
this study and, as explained in Chapter IV, the Census returns have been
used to adjust the estimates of the sales by multiple shop organizations.

[1] Board of Trade, *Census of Distribution and other Services 1950: Retail Trade, Short Report*,
H.M. Stationery Office, 1952.

Table 86. *Comparison of the National Institute estimates of the number of multiple shop branches in different trades in 1950 with the Census of Distribution returns*

Trade	Number of branches of firms with 10 or more branches	
	National Institute estimates	Census of Distribution returns
Grocery group	13,663	15,801
Dairymen	1,637	1,399
Butchers	3,775	3,640
Fishmongers and poulterers	507	552
Greengrocers, fruiterers and florists	662	898
Bread and flour confectioners	2,193	2,624
Total food	22,437	24,914
Chocolate and sugar confectioners	1,409	987
Tobacconists	1,856	1,925
Newsagents, booksellers, stationers	1,669	1,345
Mixed trades:		
Confectioner, tobacconist and newsagent	—	1,564
Tobacconist, newsagent	—	575
Total confectioners/tobacconists/news-agents/booksellers/stationers	4,934	6,396
Footwear	5,210	5,428
Men's and boys' wear	3,068	3,393
Women's wear	1,769	3,045
Total clothing	10,047	11,866
Hardware, ironmongery, pottery and builders' materials	1,244	1,455
Radio and electrical goods, sewing machines	899	908
Chemists' and photographic goods	2,508	2,570
Furniture and furnishings	836	1,019
Jewellery, leather goods, sports goods, fancy goods, toys	411	486
Total other goods	5,898	6,438
Variety chain stores and other general	971	1,037
Total	44,287	50,551

Multiple shop retailers listed in the Census returns in the following trades have been excluded from the above table to make for comparability between the two sets of figures:

Off-licences	Department stores
Boots and shoes with repairs	Coal merchants
Radio and electrical goods with repairs	Corn merchants
Electrical goods with contracting	Nurserymen, garden seedsmen
Electricity showrooms	Pets, pet food dealers
Gas showrooms	Pawnbrokers
Antique dealers	Other non-food trades except sewing machines

Total number of branches excluded: 6,131.

Cooked meat and delicatessen shops have been included with the grocery group. Florists have been included with greengrocers and fruiterers. Sewing machine dealers and musical instrument dealers have been included with radio and electrical goods. The 'other general' group in the Census returns has been included with variety chain stores. The National Institute estimates do not cover organizations in this 'other general' category.

Multiple shop retailers selling bicycles and accessories have been excluded from the National Institute estimates as they are not included in the Census returns, and a readjustment between the variety chain store group and the women's clothing group has been made to bring the National Institute figures into line with the definitions used in the Census.

29. The estimate of the number of branches of Retail Co-operative Societies and of the total retail sales of the Societies made in this study corresponds almost exactly with the Census returns when allowance is made in the latter for the exclusion of Northern Ireland and the inclusion of sales of services and of goods such as coal that are not covered in this study. As the Co-operative movement publishes full details of its activities, this correspondence between the National Institute estimates and the Census returns was to be expected.

30. The estimates of the number and of the retail sales of department stores in 1950 made in this study are higher than the figures given in the Census returns. The latter gives 360 department stores, other than Co-operative department stores, with a total turnover of £259 millions (including receipts from catering and other services, but excluding stores in Northern Ireland). The estimates in this study relate to some 500 stores with a total turnover of £275 millions (excluding catering and services and including stores in Northern Ireland). The difference would appear to arise mainly from the definitions used, in that the Census figures relate only to firms with a turnover of over £100,000 in 1950 and, further, the Census has a group described as 'other general' stores in which, no doubt, are included some of the retailers defined as department stores in this study. The difference in the estimates for 1950 was not considered to be sufficiently great to warrant any alteration in the estimates of department store sales made in this study.

31. A comparison of the Census returns of the number of multiple shop branches in existence in 1950 with the estimates made in this study is presented in Table 86. A number of adjustments to the Census materials had to be made to make the figures fully comparable, and these are explained in the note to the table.

32. The table suggests that the estimates of the total number of multiple shop branches in existence in 1950 made in this study were some 87·5 % of the total number returned in the Census of Distribution for the same trades. The Board of Trade suggests that the Census coverage of the total number of establishments was only 91 % of the actual number, but it would appear most unlikely that the retailers (9%) making no return included any multiple shop firms with more than 10 branches each. A small addition to the Census figures—say 400–500 branches—is, however, necessary to allow for the non-inclusion in the Census figures of Northern Ireland.

33. The coverage of this study was lowest—77·5 %—in the confectionery, tobacco, newsagent, bookseller, stationer group, but was approximately 90 % in all the other main groups. In the individual trade groups the coverage varied more widely, but this would appear to be the result of differing definitions of trades. The National Institute estimates of the number of multiple shop dairymen, for example, undoubtedly include firms classified as grocers in the Census returns, for not only are the National Institute estimates higher than the Census returns but the Census returns include distributing depots which have been excluded from the National Institute estimates. A similar difference of interpretation or definition of trade would appear to be present in the estimates relating to the butchery trade and possibly the radio, electrical goods and sewing machine trades. The marked underestimate of the number of branches in the confectionery, tobacco and newspaper trades may have arisen from a difference of practice in regard to the inclusion or exclusion of sub-stalls, but the 'search' methods used in this study were, in general, less effective in tracing the existence of multiple shop retailers in mixed trades than in specialist trades.

34. As expected, the coverage in this study of the larger multiple shop organizations was much more complete than that of the smaller organizations. The comparison by size groups of the two sets of figures is as follows:

Size group	National Institute estimates	Census of Distribution returns
10–24 branches	4,907	9,992
25 or more branches	39,380	40,659

The National Institute coverage of the 10–24 branches size-group is just under 50 %, and of the 25 or more branches size-group about 97 %.

35. The National Institute estimates of the total retail sales by multiple shop organizations of the commodities covered by this inquiry was £885–915 millions. This estimate related to the retail sales of the 44,287 branches given above, and included in addition the sales by multiple shop retailers in the bicycle and perambulator trades and the retail sales of consumer goods by multiple shop organizations engaged in trades other than those covered in this study, for example the retail sales of bread, milk and groceries by multiple shop caterers and the sales of tobacco goods by multiple shop off-licences. The sales figure corresponding to the 50,551 branches in the

Census returns is £1,029 millions. This figure includes some sales of services, for example the revenue from cafés and restaurants attached to variety stores, to bakers, grocers, delicatessen shops and so on, and the sales of other services such as repairs. Some approximate adjustments can be made to both the National Institute estimate and the Census returns to make them of greater comparability, and if this is done the revised National Institute estimate of total multiple shop sales, excluding bicycles and perambulators, is £878–908 millions, and the revised Census figure, including estimated sales by other multiple shop firms and sales of multiple shops in Northern Ireland and excluding sales of services, is £1,040–1,060 millions. These figures suggest that the National Institute estimates of multiple shop sales in 1950 were some 85 % of the actual figure.

36. The National Institute estimates, therefore, of the total number of multiple shop branches and of the total multiple shop turnover consumer goods in 1950, were both 14–15 % below the actual figures as shown by the Census returns after adjustments have been made. The Census report does not give the sales of multiple shop retailers by commodities, for example the sales of tobacco or confectionery by multiple shop grocers, or the division of sales of variety chain stores, but using the information relating to the breakdown of sales of multiple shop retailers collected in the course of this inquiry and obtained from other sources such as rationing statistics it was possible to rearrange and re-group the total Census sales of £1,045–1,060 millions of multiple shop organizations by main groups of commodities.

37. This analysis of the Census sales was then compared with the National Institute estimates of multiple shop sales. By main groups of commodities there was again a close correspondence between the underestimate of the number of multiple shop branches and the underestimate of the total multiple shop turnover in the same commodity group. This correspondence did not extend in all instances to the estimates relating to individual commodity groups, as differences of classification of multiple shop firms distorted the comparison of the number of branches and, less important as easier to isolate, the allocation of the sales of variety chain stores between the various commodity groups influenced the ratio of numbers of branches and turnover.

38. This analysis of the Census returns of multiple shop sales by commodity groups provided a base year by which the National Institute estimates of multiple shop sales could be corrected both for 1950 and for earlier years. As the information on the number of multiple shop branches and turnover had been obtained in the same way in this inquiry throughout the period studied, an assumption was made that the understatement or error shown by the Census data to be present in the 1950 National Institute estimates was of a similar order throughout. The understatement or error in the estimates of the 10–24 branches size-group was however known to be greater than the understatement of the 25 or more branches size-group, and allowance had to be made for this bias. The National Institute estimates showed that the proportion of the total number of branches in, say, 1900 in the 10–24 branches size-group was higher than in 1950, and therefore the error in the estimates

of the number of branches for 1900 was assumed to be greater, i.e. 18·5%, than the 1950 error, 12·5%. The alternative series constructed in this way of the number of multiple shops in existence in different years in each trade was then related to the information available on the average turnover of the branches, to yield a new series of estimated total sales of multiple shop organizations. This method of adjusting the original sales figures of multiple shop organizations was adopted in all instances where there was a close correspondence in 1950 between the understatement of the number of branches and the understatement of the total turnover.

39. In some trades, for example women's clothing, household stores, hardware, confectionery and chemists' goods, a special adjustment had to be introduced to allow for the rapid rise in importance of variety chain store trading. This was done by calculating the sales of specialist shops and of variety chain stores separately. Where, for reasons of definition, there was no correspondence in the understatement of branches and turnover in 1950, the number of multiple shop branches in existence in different years, after making adjustments as above for the proportional understatement of the different size groups, was used as an index linked with the sales of the commodity by multiple shop retailers as shown by the analysis of the Census of Distribution figures for 1950. Total multiple shop sales of the commodity in earlier years were then obtained by using the index of the estimated number of branches in existence in various years, deflating with a price index of the commodity or commodity group and adjusting for changes, if any, in the average size, turnover or employment per branch. Information on these items had been obtained in the ways described above.

40. These methods of 'blowing up' the original estimates to correspond with the Census data were not entirely satisfactory, but it will be appreciated that the original estimates covered over 80% of total turnover and numbers of shops. There is little doubt, however, that the possible error in the adjusted estimates of turnover of multiple shop retailers is greater in the case of the estimates relating to individual commodity groups than in the case of the main commodity groups and the total sales of all multiple shop firms.

41. The Census of Distribution returns of total retail sales in 1950 do not correspond with the estimates of the total retail sales in this year presented above in Table 85, which are based on the government National Income and Expenditure estimates. There is no call to attempt here a full reconciliation of the two sets of figures, but the main adjustments that have to be made can be noted briefly. To the Census figures must be added:

(a) retail sales in Northern Ireland, the Isle of Man and the Channel Isles;

(b) an estimated addition of 5% for the retailers making no return;

(c) retail sales of finished consumer goods by trades excluded from the Census, e.g. on-licences, hairdressers, caterers, the motor and cycle trade, garages and the sale of newspapers by street vendors.

From the Census figures must be deducted the sales of services, for example catering, repairs and contracting.

APPENDIX B

CO-OPERATIVE MEMBERSHIP AND SALES

The number of members of Co-operative Retail Societies and the total Co-operative retail sales of all goods at different dates between 1881 and 1950 are presented in Table 87.

Table 87. *Membership and retail sales of Co-operative Societies, 1881–1950*

Year	Number of members	Total retail sales £
1881	547,212	15,411,185
1885	746,772	19,872,343
1890	961,616	26,887,638
1895	1,274,994	33,900,674
1900	1,707,011	50,053,567
1905	2,153,015	61,086,991
1910	2,541,734	71,861,383
1915	3,264,811	102,557,779
1920	4,504,852	254,158,144
1925	4,910,983	183,584,049
1930	6,402,966	217,318,001
1935	7,483,937	220,429,517
1940	8,716,894	298,880,990
1945	9,404,877	361,075,967
1950	10,691,543	613,765,220

APPENDIX C

ECONOMIC ASPECTS OF MULTIPLE SHOP TRADING

1. The discussion in the foregoing chapters of the economic advantages of multiple shop trading may be summarized here. Following the approach adopted by R. Bellamy,[1] four main factors that influence the Net Profit Rate of distributive organizations can be distinguished. These factors are:

(1) Retail price.
(2) Invoice cost.
(3) Operating expenses.
(4) Money volume of sales in relation to the capital invested. The rate of stock turn is an approximation to this.

The position of multiple shop retailers can be considered in relation to each of these factors in turn.

(1) *Retail price*

There is no evidence of multiple shop retailers charging higher prices than those of competitors: rather the reverse was usual.

(2) *Invoice cost*

Multiple shop retailers can obtain lower invoice costs:

(a) By large-scale purchases on behalf of all their branches.
(b) By payment for goods in cash, thus securing cash discounts.
(c) By special discounts and allowances obtained by negotiation with producers, including the right to sell some lines under 'own brand' marks. In some instances these advantages are obtained by placing forward orders with producers.

(3) *Operating expenses*

Multiple shop retailers can secure lower operating costs—that is costs of administration, occupancy, merchandising, publicity and transport—expressed as a percentage of sales:

(a) By specialization of function and division of labour made possible by the scale of operations combined with standardization of procedure, practice and method in all the branches. Common examples of functions that are specialized and for which experts are employed are: administration; buying; advertising; display, printing and ticketing; stock control; real estate and shop siting; shop layout, fittings and maintenance; transport; and staff recruitment, welfare and training. In some instances multiple shop firms employ outside specialists, for example advertising agencies and transport

[1] R. Bellamy, *Bulletin of the Oxford Institute of Statistics*, vol. 8, 1946: August, 'The Changing Pattern of Retail Distribution'; October, 'Size and Success in Retail Distribution'; November, 'Private and Social Cost in Retail Distribution'.

contractors; in other instances separate departments are set up within the firm, for example a shop-fitting and maintenance department or a small printing works. In each instance, specialization and standardization lead to lower costs in relation to sales and the economies range for example from bulk purchases of paper bags and string to lower managerial costs per shop.

(b) By integration of wholesaling and retailing operations. Control of the goods throughout the journey from producer to consumer enables economies to be introduced in stockholding and transport.

(c) By lower stock holding costs arising from a faster rate of stock turn.

(d) By higher sales per employee.

(4) *Stock turn*

Multiple shop retailers can obtain a faster rate of stock turn:

(a) By having a smaller stock ratio to sales through the use of close stock control systems and of depots and central warehouses to carry the stock coverage for a number of separate branches.

(b) By moving stock between branches in response to varied demand in different areas.

(c) By avoiding slow-moving stocks as a result of knowledge of the character of current demand and of anticipation of future changes in demand. Close links with producers and manufacturers, expert buying and data from all branches on stocks and sales combine to bring about this result.

2. Multiple shop firms have other advantages over the small-scale retailer, as follows:

(i) Risks are spread so that a failure at one branch or particular economic conditions in one area does not affect the position of all branches. In the same way new branches can be 'carried' in the initial stages by existing branches.

(ii) Greater capital resources and higher credit-rating enable the multiple shop firms to obtain better sites, to finance hire-purchase trading and to obtain greater credit when necessary.

(iii) The scale of operations permits more attention to be paid to the interests of the staff, and this factor, combined with the opportunities for promotion within a large organization, attracts a better-quality staff.

(iv) In some instances, in addition to the wholesaling and retailing advantages outlined above, multiple shop firms have the further advantage of integration of production and distribution.

3. The methods of organization of multiple shop firms and the extent to which all or some of these advantages are obtained varies of course between one firm and the next and between the firms engaged in different trades. The position in each trade has been discussed in the above chapters and it has been pointed out that the methods of organization and the incidence of the different advantages have also varied over time. One illustration not given above of the variations in method of organization between trades is shown in the analysis made in 1948 of the buying responsibility of the

branch managers of multiple shop firms in different trades.[1] Branch managers were questioned as to their degree of responsibility for buying for their branch. The answers in individual cases may have been coloured by the formulation of the questions, but the general pattern of the answers set out below shows some important differences in buying practice between multiple shop firms in different trades.

Trade	Proportion of total branch managers stating	
	They had no responsibility for buying	They were solely responsible, or had unlimited responsibility but through Head Office
	%	%
Sugar confectionery	70	20
Tobacco goods	53	33
Grocery and provisions	37	31
Men's wear	37	36
Women's wear	28	40
Electrical goods and radio	22	55
Ironmongery	16	44
Pharmaceutical goods	13	48

The category of buying responsibility omitted from these figures is 'some responsibility but under control by Head Office'.

4. The importance of hire-purchase trading and of integration of production and distribution similarly varies between trades. Details have been given in the above chapters but may be summarized here. Only in the furniture and furnishings trade, the sewing machine, electrical goods, bicycle and radio trades and to some extent the jewellery trade is hire-purchase trading by multiple shop retailers important. The trades in which many of the multiple shop firms undertake some production as well as distribution are:

Footwear   Chemists' goods
Men's outer clothing   Bread and flour confectionery
Sewing machines   Chocolate and sugar confectionery
Wallpaper   Grocery

In the meat trade some of the multiple shop firms, before control by the Ministry of Food, owned overseas meat packing stations, shipping and cold storage plants. In the dairy trade the multiple shop retailers undertake pasteurization and bottling. Integration by multiple shop retailers is at present non-existent or unimportant in the fruit and vegetables and fish trades, the tobacco trade, the newspaper and book trade, the women's wear trade except sections of the underwear trade, the bicycle, perambulator, radio and electrical goods trades, the furniture and furnishings trade and the ironmongery, hardware and household goods trade.

[1] *The Hulton Retailer Readership Studies*, compiled by J. H. Hobson and H. Henry, London, Hulton Press, 1948, nos. 1–10.

APPENDIX D

THE DEFINITIONS OF THE DIFFERENT ECONOMIC TYPES OF RETAILER

The definitions of the different economic types of retailer adopted throughout this study are as follows.

Co-operative Society

A Co-operative Society is defined as a Co-operative retailing organization trading on Co-operative principles, affiliated to the national Co-operative movement and registered under the Industrial and Provident Societies Acts. Many of the Co-operative Retail Societies control a number of separate branch shops and therefore their organizational framework is somewhat similar to that of multiple shop organizations. There are however many differences between the two types of organization in other respects, the chief ones being the Co-operative practice of democratic control by the members and the payment of a dividend on purchases.

The sales of local federations of Retail Societies and of the retail organizations controlled by the Co-operative Wholesale Societies are included as well as the sales of Retail Societies.

Department store

A department store is defined as a large store selling under one roof, but in physically separate departments, four or more different classes of consumer goods one of which is women's and girls' clothing. In some instances a large number of department stores are controlled by one firm but the individual stores making up the group usually trade as autonomous units. These stores therefore have not been classed as the branches of a multiple shop organization.

Multiple shop retailer

A multiple shop organization is defined as a firm, other than a Co-operative Society, possessing 10 or more retail establishments. A firm controlling 10 or more department stores is not, however, classified as a multiple shop retailer but as a department store. The character of the information and the methods of research used determined in part the use of the definition of 10 or more branches rather than 5 or more or 2 or more. The definition adopted, however, also has some economic justification in that in most trades significant economies of scale were not present until a firm operated from at least 10 branches. The number of establishments in 1950 belonging to firms with 2–9 branches each are discussed in Appendix E.

In determining the number of branches of individual multiple shop firms, the main consideration was financial control. In those instances where one multiple shop firm has financial control over one or more other multiple shop retailers, only the parent firm was counted among the number of multiple shop organizations and the total of the branches of the parent firm and of the subsidiary firms has been used to indicate the size of the firm. This principle of financial control has been used in all instances including those where the subsidiary firms trade under entirely different names and the connexion with the parent firm may not be known generally.

Variety chain store

A variety chain store is defined as a multiple shop retailer with 10 or more branches each of which sells a wide variety of low-priced articles under one roof, usually without any clear division between different sections selling different goods. The articles sold are usually displayed on open counters or racks. The number and sales of variety chain stores are included with those of multiple shop retailers.

Other retailers

This is a residual category and therefore includes all retail establishments and organizations not listed above. The majority of the retailers in this group are one-shop, small-scale retailers, but the group also includes retailers controlling 2 to 9 branches, market stalls and barrows, small-scale producer/retailers, mail order houses and so on.

APPENDIX E

THE STRUCTURE OF RETAILING IN GREAT BRITAIN IN 1950

1. The Census of Distribution returns make it possible to provide a fairly definitive picture of the structure of retailing as a whole in Britain in 1950. Table 88 gives a summary of the information relating to numbers of shops and sales by trades and by economic types. The trades covered in this table and the definitions used correspond broadly to those studied and the classifications adopted in this volume. Direct comparisons between the figures in this table and the estimates given in the above chapters are, however, difficult to make, as there remain some differences of scope between the Census and this study. The main differences are as follows:

(a) The Census covers only 91 % of the estimated total number of retail establishments in existence in 1950 and only 95 % of the estimated total sales. The coverage of the activities of the large-scale retailers is however undoubtedly greater than the coverage of the small-scale retailers.

(b) The Census does not cover Northern Ireland.

(c) The Census includes in many trade categories (e.g. bakers, department stores, variety stores) the sales of services, e.g. catering, as well as of finished consumer goods; whereas this study is confined to the sale of goods only.

(d) This study includes the sales of finished consumer goods by retailers outside the scope of the *Short Report* of the Census, e.g. the sale of tobacco goods by on-licences, caterers, hairdressers, garages, cinemas, theatres, etc., the sale of chocolate and sugar confectionery, milk, bread and grocery goods by caterers, and the sales of bicycle and perambulator dealers.

2. The main effect of the failure to make returns by 9 % of retailers and of the exclusion of Northern Ireland is an overstatement of the relative importance of large-scale retailers. If an estimated allowance for these omissions is made the total number of retail establishments in the trades covered by the table would be increased to some 540,000–550,000 and the total sales to £4,900–5,000 millions. The shares in the total trade of the different economic types of retailers would then be of the following order: Co-operative Societies 11·6 %, multiple shop organizations 21·2 %, department stores 5·3 %, and other retailers 61·9 %.

3. With the help of the Census returns a closer examination can be made of the relative importance of the small multiple shop organizations, i.e. the firms with 2–9 branches, and of the one-shop retailers. This further breakdown of establishments and sales by economic type and size is made in Table 89.

4. This table suggests that some 71 % of the total number of establishments in 1950 were those of one-shop retailers and these establishments were

Total food group	20,374	430,962	21·3	24,914	394,707	19·5	205,695	1,197,732	59·2	250,983	2,023,401
Sugar and chocolate con-fectioners	17	118	0·8	987	4,907	33·6	3,268	9,588	65·6	4,272	14,613
Tobacconists	98	2,506	2·1	1,925	32,099	26·8	8,261	85,259	71·1	10,284	119,864
Booksellers, stationers	10	42	0·1	1,283	16,807	24·6	8,235	51,479	75·3	9,528	68,328
Confectioners/tobacconists/newsagents	42	538	0·2	2,201	19,405	6·0	49,513	300,665	93·8	51,756	320,608
Total confectionery, tobacco, newspapers, books and stationery	167	3,204	0·6	6,396	73,218	14·0	69,277	446,991	85·4	75,840	523,413
Boots and shoes	575	8,017	6·3	5,428	76,953	60·3	6,001	42,697	33·4	12,004	127,667
Men's wear	427	9,543	5·0	3,393	75,281	39·3	10,767	106,600	55·7	14,587	191,424
Women's wear and other clothing	1,685	36,558	6·6	3,045	144,172	25·9	52,638	376,532	67·5	57,368	557,262
Total clothing group	2,687	54,118	6·2	11,866	296,406	33·8	69,406	525,829	60·0	83,959	876,353

Trade	All retailers Number of establishments	All retailers Total sales £000's	Co-op Establishments Number	Co-op Sales £000's	Co-op %	Multiple Establishments Number	Multiple Sales £000's	Multiple %	Dept stores Establishments Number	Dept stores Sales £000's	Dept stores %	Other retailers Establishments Number	Other retailers Sales £000's	Other retailers %
Radio, electrical goods, sewing machines, musical instruments	9,651	109,283	62	928	0·8	908	15,193	13·9	—	—	—	8,681	93,161	85·3
Chemists' goods, photographic goods	16,733	158,606	983	9,662	6·1	2,570	54,711	34·5	—	—	—	13,180	94,233	59·4
Furniture and furnishings, pictures	10,985	237,661	481	16,210	6·8	1,019	58,085	24·5	—	—	—	9,475	163,366	68·7
Jewellery, leather, sports, fancy goods, toys	13,944	79,767	47	505	0·6	486	7,423	9·3	—	—	—	13,411	71,839	90·1
Total other goods	74,225	706,715	1,900	30,751	4·4	6,438	146,661	20·8	—	—	—	65,877	529,302	74·8
Variety stores and other general	—	163,003	7	579	—	1,037	118,494	—	—	—	—	1,136	43,930	—
Department stores	—	308,339	169	49,210	—	—	—	—	360	259,129	—	529	—	—

Summary

All retailers		Co-operative Societies				Multiple shops				Department stores other than Co-operative				Other retailers			
Number of establishments	Total sales £000's	Establishments Number	%	Sales £000's	%	Establishments Number	%	Sales £000's	%	Establishments Number	%	Sales £000's	%	Establishments Number	%	Sales £000's	%
486,672	4,601,223	25,313	5·2	568,824	12·4	50,651	10·4	1,029,486	22·4	360	0·1	259,129	5·6	410,348	84·3	2,743,784	59·6

This table is based on Table 5 of the Census of Distribution *Short Report* on Retail Trade. 44,471 retail establishments listed in the Census table are excluded from this table as they were either engaged in trades not included in this study, e.g. coal, off-licences, nurserymen and seedsmen, corn merchants, dealers in pets, second-hand and antique dealers, etc., or were engaged to a significant extent in the provision of services as well as finished goods, e.g. boot and shoe repairs, electrical repairs and contracting, builders' materials and contracting, dispensing opticians, etc. Of the establishments excluded, 1,154 were branches of Co-operative Societies with retail sales of £24,056,000, 3,501 were branches of multiple shop organizations, that is firms with 10 or more branches, with retail sales of £54,585,000, and 39,826 were other retailers, with retail sales of £243,067,000. The variety store and other general group includes some retailing activities excluded from this study, e.g. mail order, but it has not been possible to subdivide this group.

In one or two instances where actual figures are not disclosed in the Census report estimates have had to be made and this may affect some of the individual totals but will not affect the overall total. The branches of gas and electricity authorities have been classed as other retailers and not as multiple shop retailers.

responsible for some 45 % of the total retail sales. The importance of the
one-shop retailer varied of course between trades and the five trades in
which the one-shop retailer played the most significant role and the five
trades in which the one-shop retailer was least significant in 1950 were as
follows:

Trade	Number of establishments and total sales of one-shop retailers as a proportion of	
	Total establishments %	Total sales %
Chocolate, sugar confectioner-tobacconist-newsagent	90·2	83·7
Tobacconist-newsagent	87·7	83·0
Greengrocer-fruiterer and florist	80·3	70·1
Radio, electrical goods, sewing machines, musical instruments	75·7	68·3
Domestic hardware, iron-mongery, china, glassware	73·7	68·0
Bread and flour confectioners	53·2	37·6
Men's wear	54·9	33·6
Dairymen	66·9	25·1
Variety stores and other general	5·9	23·6
Boots and shoes	32·6	19·1

5. In interpreting these figures it will be appreciated that the actual
share of the one-shop retailer in the total trade was in many instances lower
than the proportion of the total sales given above. The proportions of the
establishments and sales relate only to the establishments mainly engaged in
the particular trade and do not include the sales of variety stores, other
general stores and department stores. Using information collected in the
course of this inquiry it is possible to allocate the sales of these general
retailers to particular trades, and if this is done the proportion of the total
sales represented by the one-shop retailer decreases. In footwear for example
the one-shop retailer was responsible for only about 15 % of total sales and
in men's wear for about 24 % of total sales.

6. Table 89 suggests that the multiple shop organizations with 2–24
branches each were responsible for exactly the same proportion, 18·4 %, of
total sales as were the organizations with 25 or more branches each. The
Census figures also throw some light on the size pattern in different trades.
Taking the small multiple shop organizations first, the trades in which the
number of branches and the sales of firms with 2–9 branches each was
greater than the number of branches and sales of firms with 10 or more
branches each were as follows:

Butchers   Tobacconist-newsagents
Fishmongers and poulterers   Hardware, ironmongery, china, glass

Greengrocers, fruiterers and florists

Bread and flour confectioners

Confectioners/tobacconists/ newsagents

Radio, electrical goods, sewing machines, musical instruments[1]

Furniture and furnishings

Jewellery, sports goods, toys, leather and fancy goods

In the case of four of these trades the small multiple shop organizations, i.e. firms with 2–9 branches each, were responsible for more than 20 % of the total sales by all retailers classified in that trade. These four were, fishmongers and poulterers (23·2 %), bread and flour confectioners (25·3 %), furniture and furnishings (25·8 %) and jewellery, sports goods, toys, leather and fancy goods (24·8 %).

Table 89. *Retail establishments in Great Britain in 1950,*
by economic type and by size

Type of organization	Number of establishments	Proportion of total establishments %	Total sales £000's	Proportion of total sales %
Co-operative Societies	25,313	5·2	568,824	12·4
Department stores	360	0·1	259,129	5·6
Organizations with 2–4 branches	53,348	11·0	508,600	11·1
Organizations with 5–9 branches	12,677	2·6	151,087	3·3
Organizations with 10–24 branches	9,992	2·1	181,966	4·0
Organizations with 25 or more branches	40,659	8·3	847,520	18·4
Organizations with only 1 branch	344,323	70·7	2,084,097	45·2
All types of organizations	486,672	100	4,601,223	100

7. These ten trades are, then, trades in which the small, local multiple shop firm is the dominant type of multiple shop organization. The nature of the product handled and the stage of development of the trade would appear to have made uneconomic the emergence of large-scale multiple shop organizations, but to have favoured (with the exception of the confectionery, newsagent, tobacco group) the development of small-scale multiple shop organizations.

8. By contrast the trades in which the number of branches and the sales of firms with 25 or more branches each exceeded the number of branches and sales of firms with 2–24 branches each were as follows:

Grocery

Dairymen

Chocolate and sugar confectioners

Booksellers and stationers

Boots and shoes

Variety stores and other general

[1] If the branches of electricity and gas supply undertakings are classed as multiple shop retailers, the number and sales of firms or organizations with 25 or more branches each would exceed those of firms in the 2–24 branches size-groups.

In the case of the men's wear and chemists' trades the total sales of firms with 25 or more branches each exceed the sales of the firms with 2–24 branches each, but the actual number of branches in the first group is slightly less than the number in the second. In the women's wear and tobacconist's trades the sales and number of branches of firms with 10 or more branches exceed those of firms with 2–9 branches each, but the number of branches and sales of firms in the 25 or more branches group is smaller than the number of branches and sales of firms with 2–24 branches each. Included in these ten trades, in which the typical form of multiple shop organization is the large-scale firm, are the trades in which multiple shop retailing first developed in the second half of the nineteenth century, i.e. books and stationery, grocery and boots and shoes. The scale of production in these ten trades is also, in almost all cases, larger than that of the ten trades where the small multiple shop retailer is prominent.

9. Finally the Census data can be arranged to show the variations between trades in the relative importance of the different size groups of multiple shop organizations, and also the effect of using different definitions of multiple shop organizations, i.e. 2 or more branches, 5 or more branches and so on. This information is set out in Table 90.

10. One further analysis of the structure of multiple shop retailing in Britain in 1950 can be attempted by combining data given in the Census of Distribution with the estimates made in Table 16 above. The Census provides information on the size distribution of multiple shop firms with 2 to 24 branches each, while Table 16 gives information on the size distribution of firms with 25 or more branches each. The combined figures are as follows:

Size-group	Number of organizations	Proportion of total number of establishments and of total sales	
		Establishments %	Sales %
2–4 branches	17,750 (?)	11·0	11·1
5–9 branches	1,800 (?)	2·6	3·3
10–24 branches	700 (?)	2·1	4·0
25–99 branches	305	2·0	3·6
100–199 branches	51	1·5	2·8
200–499 branches	26	1·5	3·5
500–999 branches	9	1·3	4·8
1,000 or more branches	5	2·0	3·7
Total	20,646	24·0	36·8

The number of organizations in the size groups up to 25 or more branches is not known with accuracy, and the above figures given for these groups are estimates.

APPENDIX E 473

Table 90. *Share of multiple shop retailers in total retail sales in different trades in 1950, by size groups*

Trade	Share of total trade of multiple shops defined as organizations controlling			
	2 or more branches %	5 or more branches %	10 or more branches %	25 or more branches %
Grocery group	30·5	23·6	21·6	18·7
Dairymen	40·3	32·7	28·3	21·7
Butchers	34·5	18·8	15·4	11·5
Fishmongers and poulterers	38·9	19·8	15·7	13·4
Greengrocers, fruiterers and florists	24·1	8·2	5·3	3·9
Bread and flour confectioners	42·8	25·4	17·5	8·6
Total food	32·4	22·4	19·5	15·8
Chocolate and sugar confectioners	50·0	37·0	33·5	29·5
Tobacconists	45·0	31·4	26·8	20·5
Booksellers and stationers	41·5	29·6	24·6	21·6
Confectioners-tobacconists-newsagents	16·6	7·2	6·1	5·0
Total confectioners-tobacconists-newsagents-booksellers-stationers	27·3	16·5	14·0	11·4
Boots and shoes	74·6	64·8	60·2	54·4
Men's wear	61·4	46·2	39·3	34·2
Women's wear	46·6	31·2	25·9	18·1
Total clothing	53·9	39·3	33·8	26·9
Hardware, ironmongery, pottery, glass	29·2	11·7	9·3	5·6
Radio, electrical goods, sewing machines, musical instruments	30·9	17·1	13·9	10·4
Chemists' and photographic goods	49·7	37·0	34·5	32·7
Furniture and furnishings	50·3	30·7	24·5	16·9
Jewellery, sports goods, leather goods, fancy goods, toys	34·1	14·6	9·3	6·9
Total other goods	41·7	24·9	20·8	16·4
Variety stores and other retailers	76·2	73·4	72·9	71·4
All trades	36·8	25·7	22·4	18·4

474

APPENDIX F

MULTIPLE SHOP TRADING IN THE DYEING
AND CLEANING TRADE

1. The discussion of the development of large-scale retailing in the above chapters has been confined to the trades selling consumer goods. Some data were, however, also obtained on the growth of multiple shop retailing in the dyeing and cleaning trade, and a very brief summary of the information is presented here.

2. The chemical processes for cleaning garments and furnishings that form the basis of the present-day dyeing and cleaning trade originated in France in the middle of the nineteenth century and were first introduced into Britain in the early eighteen-sixties. Many of the British firms that developed domestic 'dry cleaning' or 'French cleaning' were already well established as dyers, and these older firms were joined in the second half of the nineteenth century by newer firms attracted by the wide possibilities of dry cleaning. Up till the end of the First World War there was a rapid increase in the relative importance of dry cleaning as against dyeing, but between 1920 and 1950, except for the Second World War and the immediate post-war years, the proportions of dyeing and cleaning in the total domestic trade would not appear to have varied greatly. The division of the total domestic trade in these years is suggested as 15–25 % dyeing and 75–85 % dry cleaning, though the turnover of individual firms would depend on the particular bias of their trade.

3. Records of the multiple shop organizations in this trade have been difficult to trace, but it would appear that dyeing and cleaning firms first began to establish a number of retail branches—that is other than agencies—in the eighteen-seventies, and by 1880 existing records show at least three firms with over 10 branches each. The largest of these were P. & P. Campbell of Perth, which had over 30 branches trading in that year. The other firms were Pullars, also of Perth (established in 1824 and with whom Campbell later amalgamated) and Eastmans of London (established 1802). In the following two decades a number of other firms began opening branches, including W. & J. Bowie of Glasgow, Brand and Mollison, and Lush & Cook (established 1847) of London, and the largest firm of them all was Johnson Brothers of Liverpool (established 1817), with over 100 branches.

4. The subsequent development of multiple shop trading in the dyeing and cleaning trade, as shown by the number of organizations in existence and the number of branches controlled by them, is shown in Table 91.

5. This table brings out clearly the steady increase in the number of multiple shop organizations and branches in this trade, and only in the depression years of 1931–34 was there a slowing down in the rate of

expansion. The number of branches in existence between 1920 and 1950 increased more rapidly than the number of separate organizations in the trade, but this arose in part from amalgamations between firms. The largest group to emerge was Johnson Brothers (Dyers) Ltd., which had over 1,300 branches by 1950. The process of amalgamation, however, did not result in any important shift in the size structure, in that the largest firm controlled some 33 % of the total number of branches in both 1920 and 1950.

Table 91. *Estimates of the number of multiple shop firms and branches in the dyeing and cleaning trade, 1880–1950*

Year	10–24 branches		25–49 branches		50–99 branches		100 or more branches		Totals			
									10 or more branches		25 or more branches	
	Number of		Number of		Number of		Number of		Number of		Number of	
	Firms	Branches	Firms	Branches	Firms	Branches	Firms	Branches	Firms	Branches	Firms	Branches
1880	2	26	1	30	—	—	—	—	3	56	1	30
1885	2	33	1	33	—	—	—	—	3	66	1	33
1890	3	50	1	40	—	—	—	—	4	90	1	40
1895	4	58	2	70	1	50	—	—	7	178	2	120
1900	9	127	1	26	1	50	1	101	12	304	3	177
1905	10	138	4	118	1	60	1	170	16	468	6	348
1910	18	262	1	40	4	265	1	275	24	836	6	574
1915	16	215	5	130	2	126	4	697	27	1,168	11	953
1920	24	321	5	148	1	55	3	830	33	1,354	9	1,033
1925	27	391	6	168	3	168	3	1,281	39	2,008	12	1,617
1930	32	459	11	364	3	231	3	1,476	49	2,530	17	2,071
1935	36	520	11	362	6	367	4	1,534	57	2,783	21	2,263
1939	34	502	17	591	6	398	5	1,911	62	3,402	28	2,900
1950	30	462	15	553	7	457	6	2,373	58	3,842	28	3,383

6. The organization of multiple shop dyeing and cleaning is based on a central plant to which all work collected at the branches is brought, treated, then sorted and sent back to the branches. The branch shops are, therefore, essentially receiving departments. The larger multiple shop firms operating over a wide area maintained two or more central plants, but it was most unusual for a multiple shop firm to install small processing plants in each of their branches. The majority of the multiple shop firms preferred to operate through their own branches rather than through agencies, though Pullars of Perth, with over 1,000 agencies in 1950 and at one time as many as 8,000, was a notable exception to this rule.

7. The multiple shop branches were almost always located in prominent positions in main shopping streets, though the branches were physically very small. Employment per branch rarely exceeded 3 persons, and the average was below this. In the inter-war years many firms undertook collection of garments from customers and delivery to the home, but since 1940 this service, owing to the rise in transport costs and the scarcity of juvenile labour, has practically ceased.

8. Taking the domestic dyeing and cleaning trade as a whole, while there are no exact figures available there is little doubt that from 1920 onwards more than half the trade has been in the hands of the multiple shop firms. The proportion in 1950 is probably nearer three-quarters. Several reasons for this preponderance of multiple shop trading may be suggested. In the first place, the multiple shop firm with a large central works is able to offer a much more comprehensive service than the one-shop firm, since only in a large establishment, employing skilled, specialist staff, can some of the facilities be provided. This applies particularly to dyeing, which is only practicable when a fairly large quantity of work is being undertaken. The firm which undertakes all the cleaning on the premises can offer a quicker and more personal service, but a factory plant provides a more economical service, and with lower working costs, including transport, the multiple shop firm offered lower prices. Again, dyeing and cleaning is a seasonal trade and the larger plant is able to cope by overtime with sudden increases in work more easily than can the small trader in one shop; and at the same time the actual fluctuations in the volume of work undertaken by the large firm are less, owing to the wider range of work done, than those in the one-shop firm. The multiple shop firm with the large plants also secures some economies in the bulk purchase of dyes and chemicals and is also, in many cases, able to reclaim them after use. Bulk handling of orders entails a greater risk of loss, but the evidence would not suggest that this is a fundamental drawback to large-scale operation. More important is the danger that the lower unit costs of handling articles centrally may be offset by the costs of transporting the goods from and to the branches.

BIBLIOGRAPHY

The bibliography given below is limited to those books, pamphlets and articles that have been of direct value in this inquiry. A division has been made between general works on different aspects of distribution and consumers' expenditure, and particular studies relating to individual firms or associations. The list of books, pamphlets, articles and reports on separate trades or commodities which appeared in the earlier study, *The Distribution of Consumer Goods*, has not been reproduced here and the reader is referred to that volume. Further, no list has been given of the very large number of Trade, Classified and Street Directories, or books, prospectuses, financial and commercial papers and miscellaneous sources, that we consulted in the course of this inquiry in order to check and to build up estimates of the total number of multiple shop branches in existence in different years. Such a list, since it is not confined to works dealing with the distributive trades, would be of little value to other researches in this field.

I. GENERAL STUDIES

(a) *Books, pamphlets and articles*

Anglo-American Council on Productivity, *Retailing*, Productivity Team Report, London, 1952.

Association for Planning and Regional Reconstruction, *Retail Shops*, Report No. 23, London, 1943. (Typescript.)

Braithwaite, Dorothea and S. P. Dobbs, *The Distribution of Consumable Goods*, London, Routledge, 1932.

British National Committee, International Chamber of Commerce, *Trial Census of Distribution in Six Towns*, London, British National Committee, 1937.

Bushell, Sydney M., 'The Relative Importance of Co-operative, Multiple and other Retail Traders', *Economica*, vol. I, no. 1, January 1921.

Cadbury Brothers Ltd., *Industrial Record, 1919–1939*, Bournville, Cadbury Brothers Ltd. [1945?].

Chapman, Agatha L., assisted by Rose Knight, *Wages and Salaries in the United Kingdom, 1920–1938*, Studies in the National Income and Expenditure of the United Kingdom, 5, published under the joint auspices of the National Institute of Economic and Social Research and the Department of Applied Economics, University of Cambridge by Cambridge University Press, 1953.

Chisholm, Cecil (ed.), *Marketing Survey of the United Kingdom*, London, Business Publications, second edition 1937, third edition 1939, first post-war edition 1948.

Cohen, Leonard, 'Costs of Distribution in Department Stores , *Transactions of the Manchester Statistical Society*, Session 1951–52.

Critchell, J. T. and J. Raymond, *A History of the Frozen Meat Trade*, London, 1912.

The Economist, 27 April 1946, 'Britain's Shops', by a Correspondent.

Eveley, Richard, 'Concentration in U.K. Multiple Shop Trading', *Cartel*, vol. 2, no. 2, October 1951.

Fabian Society, *Distribution: The Case for a National Census*, Research Series No. 108, London, Fabian Publications and Victor Gollancz, 1946.

Ford, P., 'Excessive Competition in the Retail Trades. Changes in the Numbers of Shops, 1901–1931', *Economic Journal*, vol. XLV, no. 179, September 1935, p. 501.

Grether, Ewald T., *Re-sale Price Maintenance in Great Britain with an Application to the Problem in the United States*, Berkeley, University of California Publications in Economics, vol. II, no. 3, 1935.

Hall, Margaret, *Distributive Trading: An Economic Analysis*, London, Hutchinson's University Library, 1949.

Hallsworth, J. and Rhys J. Davies, *The Working Life of Shop Assistants: A Study of Conditions of Labour in the Distributive Trades*, Manchester, 1910.

Hammond, A. E., *Multiple Shop Organisation*, London, Pitman, 1930.

Hoffman, P. C., *Shops and the State and State of the Shops*, London, The Shop Assistant Publishing Company, no date.

Hoffman, P. C., *They also Serve, the Story of the Shop Worker*, London, Porcupine Press, 1949.

The Hulton Retailer Readership Studies, compiled by J. W. Hobson and H. Henry, Numbers 1–10: *The Grocery Trade*; *The Sugar Confectionery Trade*; *The Ironmongery Trade*; *The Women's Wear Trade*; *The Pharmaceutical Trade*; *The Electrical, Radio and Gramophone Trades*; *The Men's Wear Trade*; *The Hairdressing and Beauty Trades*; *The Garage and Car Accessory Trade*; London, Hulton Press, 1948.

Johnson-Davies, K. C., *Control in Retail Industry*, London, Trade and Publishing Company, 1945.

Kaldor, Nicholas and Rodney Silverman, *A Statistical Analysis of Advertising Expenditure and of the Revenue of the Press*, National Institute of Economic and Social Research, Economic and Social Studies VIII, Cambridge University Press, 1948.

Klingender, F. D., *The Little Shop*, Bureau of Current Affairs, *Current Affairs* No. 127, March 1951.

Kuipers, J. D., *Resale Price Maintenance in Great Britain, with special reference to the Grocery Trade*, Wageningen, N. V. Drukkerij Vada, 1950.

Levy, Hermann, *Retail Trade Associations*, London, Kegan Paul, 1942.

Levy, Hermann, *The Shops of Britain*, London, Kegan Paul, 1948.

Lewis, W. Arthur, 'Competition in Retail Trade', *Economica*, New Series, vol. XII, no. 48, November 1945, p. 202.

Madge, Charles, 'War and the Small Retail Shop', Institute of Statistics, Oxford, *Bulletin*, vol. 4, Supplement no. 2, April 1942.

Manchester Guardian Commercial Weekly, series of articles, 1938–39, on the distributive trades.

Mayhew, H. (ed.), *Shops and Companies of London*, 2 vols., 1865.

Moride, Pierre, *Les maisons à succursales multiples en France et à l'étranger*, Paris, 1913.

Neal, Lawrence E., *Retailing and the Public*, London, Allen & Unwin, 1932.

Pasdermadjian, H., *Le grand magasin: son origine—son évolution—son avenir*, Paris, Dunod, 1949.

Pasdermadjian, H., *Management Research in Retailing*, International Association of Department Stores; London, Newman Books, 1950.

Philp, R. K., *Handy Book of Shopkeeping*, London, 1892.

Plant, Arnold (ed.), *Some Modern Business Problems*, London, Longmans, 1937.

Plant, Arnold and R. F. Fowler, 'The Analysis of Costs of Retail Distribution', *Transactions of the Manchester Statistical Society*, Session 1938–39.

Prest, A. R., assisted by A. A. Adams, *Consumers' Expenditure in the United Kingdom, 1900–1919*, Studies in the National Income and Expenditure of the United Kingdom, 3, to be published under the auspices of the National Institute of Economic and Social Research and the Department of Applied Economics, University of Cambridge by Cambridge University Press.

Reddaway, W. B., 'Some Problems of Taking a Census of Distribution', *Transactions of the Manchester Statistical Society*, Session 1946–47.

Rees, J. Aubrey, *The Grocery Trade: Its History and Romance*, 2 vols., London, 1910.

Retail Distributors' Association Incorporated, *Report on Department Store Trading for the Trade Year 1949, Analysis by Departments*, London, 1950. Also for the trade year 1950, published 1951. *Report on Operating Costs and Results of Department Stores for the Trade Year 1949*, London, 1950. Also for the trade year 1950, published 1951.

Robertson, W. B. (ed.), *Encyclopaedia of Retail Trading*, 2 vols., London, 1911.

Rothwell, Tom S., *A Nation of Shopkeepers*, London, Herbert Joseph [1947?].

Silverman, Rodney, *Advertising Expenditure in 1948*, Advertising Association, 1951.

Smith, Henry, *Retail Distribution*, Oxford University Press, 1948 (second edition).

Smith, Henry, *Wholesaling and Retailing*, Fabian Society Tract No. 272, London, Fabian Publications and Victor Gollancz, 1949.

Stone, Richard, assisted by D. A. Rowe and by W. J. Corlett, Renée Hurstfield, Muriel Potter, *The Measurement of Consumers' Expenditure and Behaviour in the United Kingdom, 1920–1938*, vol. I, Studies in the National Income and Expenditure of the United Kingdom, 1, to be published under the auspices of the National Institute of Economic and Social Research and the Department of Applied Economics, University of Cambridge by Cambridge University Press.

United States Department of Commerce, *Trade Information Bulletin* no. 697, 'Chain Store Developments in Great Britain', 1930.

United States Department of Commerce, *Trade Promotion Series* no. 94, 'The United Kingdom', 1929.

Urwick, L. and F. P. Valentine, *Europe—United States of America, Trends in the Organisation and Methods of Distribution in the Two Areas*, Paris, International Chamber of Commerce, 1931.

Vallance, Aylmer, *Hire-Purchase*, London, Nelson, 1939.

Yamey, B. S., 'The Origins of Resale Price Maintenance: A Study of Three Branches of Retail Trade', *Economic Journal*, vol. LXII, no. 247, September 1952.

(b) Books on the Co-operative Movement

Barou, N. (ed.), *The Co-operative Movement in Labour Britain*, London, Gollancz, 1948.

Carr-Saunders, A. M., P. Sargant Florence and Robert Peers, *Consumers' Co-operation in Great Britain*, London, Allen & Unwin, 1942 (third, revised, edition).

Cole, G. D. H., *A Century of Co-operation*, Manchester, Co-operative Union, 1946.

Co-operative Union, *Census of Shops: A Census of Shops and Retail Outlets operated by Co-operative Societies in 1946*, Manchester, Co-operative Union, 1947.

Co-operative Wholesale Society Ltd., *A Consumers' Democracy*, Manchester, C.W.S. Ltd., 1952.

Elliott, Sidney R., *England, Cradle of Co-operation*, London, Faber, 1937.

Hough, J. A., *Co-operative Retailing, 1914–1945: A Statistical Analysis of the Development of Retailing in the British Co-operative Movement*, London, International Co-operative Alliance, 1949.

Hough, J. A., *Dividend on Co-operative Purchases*, Manchester, Co-operative Union, 1936.

Hough, J. A., *Report of the Economic Survey of the Services Provided by Retail Co-operative Societies*, Manchester, Co-operative Union, 1938.

The People's Year Book, prepared by the Publicity Department, Co-operative Wholesale Society, Manchester, C.W.S. Ltd. (annual).

Redfern, P., *The New History of the C.W.S.*, London, Dent, 1938.
Redfern, P., *The Story of the C.W.S.*, *1863–1913*, Manchester, C.W.S. Ltd., 1913.
Report of the Co-operative Congress, Manchester, Co-operative Union (annual).
Twigg, H. J., *Economic Advance of British Co-operation, 1913–1934*, Manchester, Co-operative Union, 1934.
Webb, Sidney and Beatrice, *The Consumers' Co-operative Movement*, London, 1921.

(c) *Official Reports*

Report from the Select Committee on the Shop Hours Regulation Bill, 1886.
Report and Special Report from the Select Committee on the Shop Hours Bill, 1892.
Report from the Select Committee on Shops (Early Closing) Bill, 1895.
Report of the Departmental Committee appointed to inquire into Combinations in the Meat Trade, Cd. 4643, 1909.
Report of the Sub-Committee on Fixed Retail Prices appointed by the Standing Committee on Trusts, Cmd. 662, 1920.
Ministry of Labour, *Reports of investigations into the rates of wages, the hours of employment and the degree of industrial organisation* in the following trades:
Drapery and Allied Trades, 1926.
Wholesale and Retail Grocery and Provisions Trade in England and Wales, 1926.
Wholesale and Retail Meat Distribution Trade, 1926.
Report of the Departmental Committee on the Shops (Early Closing) Acts, 1920 and 1921, Cmd. 3000, 1927.
Special Report from the Select Committee on Shop Assistants, 1930.
Report from the Select Committee on Shop Assistants, 1931.
Board of Trade, *Report of the Committee appointed by the Lord Chancellor and the President of the Board of Trade to consider certain Trade Practices (Restraint of Trade)*, 1931.
Board of Trade, *Second Interim Report of the Retail Trade Committee: The Impact of the War on the Retail Trades in Goods other than Food*, 1942.
Board of Trade, *Third Report of the Retail Trade Committee: Concentration in the Retail Non-Food Trades*, 1942.
Report of the Census of Distribution Committee, Cmd. 6764, 1946.
Report of the Committee on Resale Price Maintenance, Cmd. 7696, 1949.
A Statement on Resale Price Maintenance, Cmd. 8274, 1951.
Board of Trade, *Britain's Shops: A Statistical Summary of Shops and Service Establishments*, 1952.
Board of Trade, *Census of Distribution and Other Services, 1950, Retail Trade, Short Report*, 1952.

II. HISTORIES OF FIRMS

Barratts, *The Romance of Barratts*, Northampton [1946?].
Benefit Footwear Ltd., *A Brief History, 1897–1947*, Leeds, 1947.
Burton, Montague, Ltd., *Ideals in Industry, being the story of Montague Burton Ltd., 1900–1950*, Leeds, 1951.
Chemist and Druggist, 16 March 1946, vol. CXLV, no. 3449, 'Fifty Years of Price Protection, Jubilee of the P.A.T.A., 1896–1946'.
Dick, R. & J., Ltd., *100 Years of Guttapercha*, Glasgow, 1946.
Flatau, A. & W., & Co. Ltd., Henry Playfair Ltd., Metropolitan Boot Co. Ltd., *Foundation and History, 120 years*, London, 1948.
Greig, H. S., *My Life and Times*, privately printed, London, 1940.
Harrods Limited, *A Story of British Achievement, 1849–1949*, London, 1949.
Irwin, John, Sons & Co. Ltd., *The Story of Irwin's*, Liverpool, 1950.

Lambert, Richard S., *The Universal Provider, A Study of William Whiteley and the Rise of the London Department Store*, London, Harrap, 1938.

Lipton Ltd., *The Golden Jubilee of a Great Business*, Lipton Ltd., London, 1948.

Oliver (George) Footwear Ltd., *Oliver's, 1860–1950*, Leicester, 1950.

Platt's Stores Ltd., *A Family Album, 1877 to 1948*, London, 1948.

Proprietary Articles Trade Association, *The Story of a Crusade, 1896–1946*, London, 1947.

Roberts, Cecil, *Achievement: A Record of Fifty Years' Progress of Boots Pure Drug Company Ltd.*, privately printed, 1938.

Stead & Simpson Ltd., *A Hundred Years in the Boot and Shoe Trade*, Leicester, 1934.

Timpson, W. H. F., *Seventy Years Agrowing, or An Early History of Timpsons*, Gloucester, 1947.

Timpson, W. H. F., *My Father: Stages in the Life of William Timpson*, Gloucester, 1947.

Waugh, A. R., *The Lipton Story*, London, Cassell, 1951.

Winkler, J. K., *Five and Ten: The Fabulous Life of F. W. Woolworth*, London, Robert Hale, 1941.

482

INDEX

(n. = Note; t. = Table; tn. = Table Note.)

Adams, A. A., 124 *and* n. 1, 183 tn., 227 tn., 253 n. 1, 268 tn., 451 n. 1
Advertising
  as an aid to the consumer, 111, 133–4; to the small-scale retailer, 174
  by Co-operative Societies, 34 n., 160
  by department stores, 59 *and* n. 1
  effect on cost of distribution, 99
  as a feature of multiple shop retailing, 27–8, 146, 151
  by manufacturers, 49, 54, 93
  and proprietary medicines, 381–2
  as a selling technique, 4, 6, 12, 37, 38, 54, 131
  See also Branding, Window display
Agriculture, 1, 5
  decline after Industrial Revolution, 7, 8
Amalgamations and mergers
  of department stores, 345–6
  a feature of the development of multiple shop retailing, 63–6, 107
  in specific trades
    chemists' and druggists', 64, 385, 387–8
    dyeing and cleaning, 474, 475
    footwear, 359 *and* n. 1
    furniture, 424–5, 427
    grocery and provisions, 137, 140, 150
    household goods, 437, 439
    meat, 191–3
    men's and boys' clothing, 300
    milk, 64, 228–9, 232
Anglo-American Council on Productivity, 118 n. 1
Apprenticeship in retail trading, 2, 36 n. 1, 52
Arnold, E., 230 n. 1
Astor, Viscount, 226 n. 2
Auctioneering of perishable goods, 37, 190, 198

Bacon and ham consumption (statistics), 9, 129 t., 182 t.
Bakery trade, *see* Bread and flour confectionery trade
Bankruptcies in wholesale and retail trades, 103 *and* n. 3, 309
Bargaining as a characteristic of retail trading, 5–6, 37 *and* n. 2, 297, 328
Bazaars, 53
Bellamy, R., 30 n. 1, 462 *and* n. 1

Bicycle and perambulator trade, 28, 44, 68, 72, 77, 86 n., 93, 400, 434
  comparison of different economic types of retailer, 410–12
  Co-operative and department store retailing, 403, 404
  future trends, 412–13
  growth of the trade, 402–3
  multiple shop retailing, 403–5; statistics, 409–10
  resale price maintenance, 404, 405, 413
  total retail sales, 453 t.
Book trade, *see under* Newspaper, etc.
Booksellers' Association, 283 n. 1
Boot, Jesse, 25, 385, 388, 389
Booth, Charles, 325 n. 1
Branding of goods, 38, 41, 54, 69
  as an aid to the consumer, 111; to the small-scale retailer, 93, 174
  by Co-operative Societies, 160
  effect on cost of distribution, 99
  by manufacturers, 38, 41, 113
    of chocolate and sugar confectionery, 254, 259–60
    of footwear, 374
    of hosiery goods, 333–4
    of proprietary medicines, 381–2, 383, 389, 394
    of tobacco, 270–1, 274
  by multiple shop bakers, 218, 220; grocers, 152
Bread and flour confectionery trade
  comparison of different economic types of retailer, 223–5
  consumption, 217 t.
  Co-operative retailing, 57, 58, 83, 84 n., 210–11, 219–20
  delivery by retail round, 213, 214–15, 217, 219
  historical survey
    in the nineteenth century, 210–11
    development of new production techniques, 211–13
  multiple shop retailing
    general development, 66, 68–9, 72, 212–16; statistics, 23 t., 62 t.
    flour confectionery, growing importance of, 217, 254
    move to main shopping streets, 216–17, 224

494

INDEX OF COMPANIES AND FIRMS

Waterworth Brothers, 244
West End Clothiers Company Ltd., 296
West Kensington Stores, 327
Whiteley, William, Ltd., 20, 325 n. 2, 326, 328, 330, 343
Whites, Timothy, 25, 64, 385, 435
Whites, Timothy, & Taylors Ltd., 387
Williams, John, 148
Willsons (London & Provinces), Ltd., 66, 340

Willsons of Newcastle, 148
Wilson, Walter, 327
Wilts United Dairies Ltd., 227, 228; *see also* United Dairies Ltd.
Woodhouse, James, & Company, 424
Woolworth, F. W., & Company, 69–70
Wylie & Lochhead, 327
Wyman & Sons Ltd., 286

Zeeta Company Ltd., 214

PUBLICATIONS OF THE
NATIONAL INSTITUTE OF ECONOMIC
AND SOCIAL RESEARCH
published by
THE CAMBRIDGE UNIVERSITY PRESS

None of the Institute's publications is sold direct by the Institute. They are available through the ordinary booksellers who can supply the latest details of prices and availability. Enquiry can also be made of the Cambridge University Press.

ECONOMIC & SOCIAL STUDIES

STUDIES IN THE NATIONAL INCOME AND EXPENDITURE OF THE UNITED KINGDOM. General Editor: RICHARD STONE

Published under the joint auspices of the National Institute of Economic and Social Research and the Department of Applied Economics, Cambridge.

Published jointly for the Institute of Chartered Accountants and the National Institute of Economic and Social Research.

Printed in the United States
By Bookmasters